REPORT INTO THE LOSS OF THE
SS TITANIC
A CENTENNIAL REAPPRAISAL

Samuel Halpern

Cathy Akers-Jordan, George Behe, Bruce Beveridge,
Mark Chirnside, Tad Fitch, Dave Gittins, Steve Hall,
Lester J. Mitcham, Captain Charles Weeks, Bill Wormstedt

Foreword by J. Kent Layton

The
History
Press

First published 2011

The History Press
The Mill, Brimscombe Port
Stroud, Gloucestershire, GL5 2QG
www.thehistorypress.co.uk

British Library Cataloguing in Publication Data.
A catalogue record for this book is available from the British Library.

ISBN 978 0 7524 6210 3

Typesetting and origination by The History Press
Cover design Steve Hall
Printed in Great Britain
Manufacturing managed by Jellyfish Print Solutions Ltd

CONTENTS

FOREWORD

by J. Kent Layton

One hundred years later, she lives on . . . a century after her sinking, the story of *Titanic* fascinates, enthralls, tantalises and perplexes us as much as she ever has. She has been researched, investigated and probed, been the subject of countless books, documentaries and films. One would think that after ten decades of such intense scrutiny, we would know everything that there is to know about her life and demise – that it would all have been said already.

Unfortunately, despite the formal investigations into the loss of *Titanic* conducted following her sinking, despite all of the books and specials, and despite the recent advent of the internet with all its ability to disseminate information, the history of *Titanic* is still shrouded in myth, legend and inaccuracy. Many details of the ship's generally accepted history are not accurate. With each new generation of books or websites on the subject, many errors from the previous generations of books – and now websites – have been perpetuated.

In the quest to break fresh ground on the subject, to carve out a niche in the 'great saga of the *Titanic*', some researchers and authors have made outlandish claims about certain details of the ship's history. To make their theories look plausible, they 'zoom in' on certain details and, in so doing, lose all perspective on what the larger historical record shows. At the same time revisionist historians, eager to cut down long-held beliefs and identify them as 'legend', have actually further muddied the waters by identifying as inaccurate things which the historical record clearly shows transpired.

Thus, arriving at the truth of what happened that April is difficult enough. Getting the correct information to the public, and in one single place, adds a further layer to the challenge. All of the inaccuracies, half-truths, distortions and mistakes are spread out over a world that is literally awash – in print, the media and cyberspace – with works on *Titanic*. Helping to set the historical record straight is more difficult than ever before, for how is the average reader to sort the fact from the fiction?

With all of those who stepped aboard *Titanic* now deceased, the story of the events that they experienced – events which affected them, their families, their friends, and people throughout the world during the last century – have passed into the hands of historians and researchers. We now must serve as custodians of the historical record and do our best to preserve it as accurately as possible. The responsibility is ours, and ours alone. There is no room for ego, self-interest, or the sacrifice of facts for the telling of a 'good story'. The time has come for a complete reappraisal of the historical record. Original source material – fortunately available in abundance as it never has been before – must be consulted. Perspective must be regained. Emotional attachment to ideas and theories must be dispassionately cast aside and conclusions drawn from cold, hard facts.

Walter Lord, author of the legendary 1955 book *A Night to Remember*, also wrote a sequel to that volume in 1986, entitled *The Night Lives On*. In that latter book, he wrote – as only a writer of his calibre could – that it would be 'a rash man indeed who would set himself up as the final arbiter on all that happened the incredible night the *Titanic* went down.' In the last twenty-six years, those words have proved nearly prophetic. One person working alone can fall into the trap of their own pet ideas or preconceptions. It becomes difficult to think beyond his or her own experiences, to make up for gaps in their own knowledge, and to view things from more than a single perspective. Additionally, an expert in one particular aspect of the history can carefully craft a solid case in his own field, yet can easily become entangled in a minefield of the erroneous when he writes on a subject that falls outside his immediate specialty.

On the other hand, a team of experts, all united in working toward the common goal of laying bare historical accuracy, can more easily steer clear of such pitfalls. This is especially the case where some members of the team have built up a broad general knowledge on many aspects of the history, while others have very specific areas of proficiency. Like a highly specialised military team united in pursuing a common goal, each member brings his own skills and knowledge to the group. Soon the separate individuals come together to form a single, unstoppable entity. The objective case that they can then build begins to come together, forming an interlocking, broad-spectrum picture which then slices – like *Titanic*'s own prow through the chill waters of the North Atlantic on that maiden voyage – through a record filled with inaccuracies and misconceptions.

I have had the privilege of personally working, behind the scenes, with just such a team. It is the team which has compiled the work you now read. I have watched as members of the group bring in a piece of evidence or broach a controversial point, offering it to the team in the hopes of finding an answer among the team's shared knowledge. I have then watched in awe as each time, that information has been 'plugged-in' to the larger picture. I have seen members of the group passionately debate conflicting evidence, and just when there seems no hope of arriving at the truth, someone produces the key which unlocks the answer. I can tell you that this team is interested in arriving at the facts; nothing else will satisfy them. In this reappraisal, you will find a fully referenced, authoritative and resoundingly comprehensive work which presents the historical picture more clearly than it has ever heretofore been made available.

Despite their proficiency, this team humbly acknowledges that there are still many areas where the historical record on *Titanic*'s maiden voyage is incomplete and at times irreconcilable. In such cases, the authors do not set themselves up as Walter Lord's rash but ultimately foolhardy 'final arbiter'. Instead they point the reader to the facts and then take a step back.

The loss of *Titanic* was not just some fantasy concocted in the imagination of a brilliant writer. It was a real-life tragedy that took the lives of nearly 1,500 people. It left genuine scars on the survivors – either physically, emotionally or financially. This volume's authors do their best to discharge their responsibility as custodians of that history. You owe it to yourself to turn the pages which follow with an open mind, for therein you will find the history of *Titanic* presented as you have never, *ever* known it before.

PREFACE

by Samuel Halpern

In August 2010 I found myself scanning through a hard copy of the 1912 British Wreck Commission report on the loss of *Titanic* while doing some research for an article I was writing. What struck me was how much we have learned about *Titanic* after all these years compared to what was known then. The thought then occurred to me: What would this report look like if they knew then what we now know almost 100 years after that fateful voyage? What if a group of responsible and dedicated researchers issued a modern report on the loss of the SS *Titanic*? And so began a project that has pulled together the resources, knowledge and expertise of eleven unique individuals from all parts of the world to produce an updated report on the ship, the circumstances leading up to and including her foundering, the rescue of her survivors, and the role played by other nearby vessels.

This project would never have taken place without the unselfish contributions of all who worked so hard to make this happen. Not only have my fellow co-authors provided their own individual writings and images, but we all took part in a collective effort to review each other's work, offering many constructive suggestions, recommendations and at times criticisms to enhance the overall work that is presented. For that I am most grateful.

Cathy Akers-Jordan (Davison, Michigan, USA) was introduced to me in April 2004 at a *Titanic* seminar arranged by Capt. Charles B. Weeks at the Maine Maritime Academy in Castine, Maine. Cathy has a Master's degree in Liberal Studies and teaches research and writing at the University of Michigan's Flint campus. She has taught Titanic Science to middle school students at U of M's Super Science Friday, and was a volunteer guide at '*Titanic*: the Artifact Exhibit' at the Detroit Science Center, February – September 2003. She is a member of the Titanic Historical Society, and with Capt. Charles Weeks wrote the article 'True Course' which was published online at *Encyclopedia Titanica*. Cathy's primary interests in *Titanic* research are the treatment of third class passengers and the existence of passenger segregation gates on *Titanic*.

George M. Behe (Mount Clemens, Michigan, USA) has been a good friend to me ever since we started corresponding many, many years ago. His advice and encouragement are most highly valued. George is an accomplished researcher and prolific author. His knowledge about the people and events that took place over that period of time 100 years ago is second to none. He has written numerous articles for the Titanic Historical Society's journal *The Titanic Commutator* and for the British Titanic Society's journal *Atlantic Daily Bulletin*. He is also a past vice-president of the Titanic Historical Society. His website, *Titanic Tidbits*, contains a number of interesting articles. Particularly revealing are the verbatim transcripts of his correspondence with Leslie Harrison, probably the best-known supporter of *Californian*'s Captain Stanley Lord. Among George's most recent books are:

'Archie': The Life of Major Archibald Butt from Georgia to the Titanic [3 vols.] (Lulu.com Press, 2010)
On Board RMS Titanic: Memories of the Maiden Voyage (Lulu.com Press, 2011)
The Carpathia and the Titanic: Rescue at Sea (Lulu.com Press, 2011)
A Death of the Titanic: The Loss of Major Archibald Butt (Lulu.com Press, 2011)

Bruce Beveridge (Chicago, Illinois, USA), a fellow Chicagoan, is one of the world's foremost authorities on *Titanic*'s exterior and general working arrangements. He is a recognised authority on the technical aspects of *Titanic*'s construction. He has written numerous articles and columns for many publications based on the *Olympic* class liners. Bruce is an honorary lifetime member of the British Titanic Society, and is a founding member and trustee of the Titanic Research and Modeling Association. His general arrangement plans of *Titanic* are considered to be the most detailed and complete ever produced. In 2008 Bruce, along with Scott Andrews, Art Braunschweiger, Steve Hall and Daniel Klistorner, published *Titanic: The Ship Magnificent* (The History Press, 2008), the most comprehensive work about the ship to date. Since 2003, both he and Steve Hall have co-authored four *Titanic* titles, their latest being: *Titanic in Photographs* (The History Press, 2011).

Mark Chirnside (West Midlands, United Kingdom) and I have teamed up on a number of occasions, beginning in summer 2006 when we uncovered a 100-minute error in *Olympic*'s maiden voyage crossing time that was never before realised. Together, Mark and I co-authored three articles dealing with *Titanic* and her sister ship *Olympic*. We have consulted with each other on many other occasions, and I highly value his knowledge, opinion and insight.

Mark is an accomplished researcher and historian when it comes to *Olympic*, *Titanic* and *Britannic*. He has written numerous articles for various journals, such as the British Titanic Society's *Atlantic Daily Bulletin*, Titanic Historical Society's *The Titanic Commutator*, Irish Titanic Historical Society's *White Star Journal* and the Titanic International Society's *Voyage*. He has authored a number of books about these historic vessels and, in recent years, he has expanded his research to include other ships such as *Aquitania*, *Majestic* and others. His latest book, *The 'Olympic' Class Ships* (The History Press, 2011), is a revised and expanded edition of a detailed and original history of *Olympic* and her two sisters. When it first came out, it won *Ships Monthly*'s Book of the Month, the first of three such awards for Mark's books. His website, *Mark Chirnside's Reception Room*, contains a wealth of information with links to many of his articles and papers. It is a must for the serious researcher.

Tad Fitch (Brook Park, Ohio, USA) and I met for the first time at the 2006 *Titanic* Technical Symposium in Toledo, Ohio. He is a member of the Titanic Historical Society and a participant on a number of *Titanic* message boards. Tad has written a number of articles related to *Titanic* that were published in the Titanic Historical Society's journal *The Titanic Commutator*, and online at *Bill Wormstedt's Titanic* and *Encyclopedia Titanica*. He, along with Bill Wormstedt and George Behe, co-authored 'The Lifeboat Launching Sequence Re-Examined', a landmark article written to correct the errors in a table that first appeared in the 1912 final report of the British Wreck Commission. Tad also co-authored a book with J. Kent Layton and Bill Wormstedt, *On a Sea of Glass: The Life & Loss of the R.M.S. Titanic* (Amberley Publishing, 2012).

Dave Gittins (Adelaide, South Australia) has been a *Titanic* researcher since 1985, and has participated on several *Titanic* message boards. He is a retired public servant and a yachtsman whose favourite activity is cruising the South Australian coast in his small yacht, *Chloe II*. Dave has written a number of online articles related to *Titanic* which are available on his website, *All at Sea With Dave Gittins*. Dave is also the author of an ebook, *Titanic: Monument and Warning*, which remains one of the most extensive accounts of the disaster and its aftermath following its publication in 2005. It is a book that lays to rest many of the rumours, exaggerations and falsehoods that have surrounded the disaster.

Steve Hall (Angels Beach, New South Wales, Australia) is a renowned *Titanic* visual historian; having collected, studied and researched the ship's photographic record for over three decades. He holds membership in several *Titanic* societies worldwide, and in 1997 became a foundation member of the Titanic & Steamship Historical Society of Australia. His first book, *Olympic & Titanic: The Truth Behind the Conspiracy* (Infinity, 2004), co-authored with Bruce Beveridge, conclusively lays to rest one of the most outrageous conspiracy theories ever concocted. He also co-authored *Titanic: The Ship Magnificent* (The History Press, 2008) and *Titanic in Photographs* (The History Press, 2011) with Bruce Beveridge, Art Braunschweiger, Scott Andrews and Daniel Klistorner.

Besides co-authoring the section dealing with the description of the ship, Steve is the person responsible for collecting and organising the two photographic inserts that appear in this book, and for the book cover art. For that, and more, I am greatly indebted.

Lester J. Mitcham (Auckland, New Zealand) has had a lifetime interest in *Titanic*. He is a former member of several *Titanic* societies, and is active on several *Titanic* message boards. In 2000 he completed a study of the Passenger Statistics of the Disaster and subsequently undertook a study with regard to the Crew Relief Fund Case Numbers, both of which were published online at *Encyclopedia Titanica*. His painstaking efforts have enabled us to provide the reader with the name of every single passenger and crewmember (including those with aliases) who sailed on *Titanic's* maiden voyage.

Captain Charles B. Weeks (Hampden, Maine, USA) has become a good friend of mine ever since we first met in 2004 at a *Titanic* seminar he arranged at the Maine Maritime Academy (MMA) in Castine, Maine. He is a holder of an Unlimited Master's License from the United States Coast Guard for steam or motor vessels upon oceans. He sailed for eight years with American Export Isbrandtsen Lines in various officer positions, including Second Officer on the liner SS *Constitution*.

Charlie has been researching and analysing various technical aspects about *Titanic* for many years, and has written six articles that were published online at *Encyclopedia Titanica*. Today he is Professor Emeritus in Marine Transportation at the Maine Maritime Academy where he still teaches an elective class on *Titanic*. Charlie is the person I turn to for critical review and advice on all technical matters regarding ships, navigation and shipboard procedures and operations. He has been kind enough to introduce my work to several of his colleagues at MMA, including experts on celestial navigation and casualty analysis. Because of him, I was kindly invited to present a forensic analysis of the *Andrea Doria/Stockholm* collision before a class on casualty analysis at MMA in November 2008.

Bill Wormstedt (Shoreline, Washington, USA) and I first met in 2004 at the *Titanic* seminar arranged by Capt. Charles Weeks at the Maine Maritime Academy in Castine, Maine, and again in 2006 at the *Titanic* Technical Symposium held in Toledo, Ohio. Over the years, I have looked to him for consultation and advice on numerous issues. His ability to find the smallest of oversights in a written manuscript has saved me from embarrassment on many occasions. Bill and I, along with Tad Fitch and George Behe, have collaborated on a number of occasions to address certain issues and inaccuracies that have been raised by others over the years.

Bill has been a member of the Titanic Historical Society since 1988. He has written a number of articles that he published on his website at *Bill Wormstedt's Titanic* and also at *Encyclopedia Titanica* and in Titanic Historical Society's journal *The Titanic Commutator*. Bill is probably most noted for his expansive work on *Titanic's* lifeboats, including his landmark work with Tad Fitch and George Behe on re-examining the lifeboat launch sequence, and most recently, his work with Tad Fitch on lifeboat occupancies. Bill is also a co-author of *On a Sea of Glass: The Life & Loss of the R.M.S. Titanic* (Amberley Publishing, 2012) along with J. Kent Layton and Tad Fitch.

I would also like to take this opportunity to express my sincere thanks to J. Kent Layton for writing the foreword to this report. Kent is a well-known and accomplished author who has spent more than two decades studying the history of the liners that sailed the Atlantic. He is also an active member of the *Titanic Research and Modeling Association*, and has his own website, *Atlantic Liners*, which provides an interactive and informative supplement to his books on the great ships of the Cunard, White Star, and Hamburg-Amerika lines.

In addition to my co-authors named above, I would like to acknowledge and thank R. Terrell-Wright, Daniel Klistorner, Günter Bäbler, Ray Lepien, Ioannis Georgiou, Charles Haas and Charles Milner for use of some of their images in this report.

Samuel Halpern As for myself, I am a systems engineer and technologist by profession, with a longstanding interest in steamships and sailing vessels, the study of naval architecture and the practice of celestial and coastal navigation. I have been involved with the study of *Titanic* for many years, and have written numerous research articles for the Titanic Historical Society's *The Titanic Commutator*, the British Titanic Society's *Atlantic Daily Bulletin*, the Irish Titanic Historical Society's *White Star Journal* and the Titanic International Society's *Voyage*. I have also published a number of online articles at *Encyclopedia Titanica*, the *Great Lakes Titanic Society*, the *Titanic Research and Modeling Association*, *Mark Chirnside's Reception Room* and on my own *Titanicology* website. I also hold a private pilot's certificate for single-engine land aircraft, and I was a yachtsman's mate on a Catalina 25 where I spent many a happy summer in the 1980s with my neighbour cruising the waters off Staten Island, Sandy Hook and Lower New York Bay.

1

INTRODUCTION

Samuel Halpern

Background and Purpose

On the night of 14 April 1912, the SS *Titanic*, on her maiden voyage from Southampton to New York, collided with an iceberg in the North Atlantic and sank in just 2 hours and 40 minutes. Less than a third of the people on board were saved.

On 17 April 1912 the United States Senate Committee on Commerce issued a resolution calling for a formal investigation into the causes leading to the loss of *Titanic* and its attendant loss of life. The formal American inquiry began on 19 April 1912, and ended on 25 May 1912. A report on the findings was presented before the United States Senate on 28 May 1912.

On 30 April 1912 the British Board of Trade (BOT) requested that a formal investigation be held into the circumstances attending to the loss of *Titanic*. Twenty-six questions were formulated to which they sought answers. Those questions dealt with such items as:

- The ship (her design, construction, size, speed, equipment, lifesaving appliances and wireless installation);
- Orders received and course taken;
- The passengers and crew;
- An account of the casualty (its cause and effect);
- Means taken for saving those on board;
- A report on the Rules and Regulations of the BOT and its administration;
- And recommendations to obviate a similar disaster from happening again.

The formal British inquiry began on 2 May 1912 and ended on 3 July 1912. The findings were presented in a 'Report of the Court' that was issued on 30 July 1912. After almost 100 years since the loss of *Titanic*, much new evidence has come to light including new forensic discoveries and analysis. In addition to the full transcripts and reports from both the American and British inquiries that were held in 1912, we have available to us evidence given at the Limitation of Liability Hearings in New York (1913–15), the Ryan Vs Oceanic Steam Navigation Company trial of 1913 and affidavits of some key participants that were withheld from the original inquiries, as well as letters, books and affidavits written by survivors and other participants in the aftermath of the disaster.

In 1985 the wreck of *Titanic* was discovered by a team led by Dr Robert Ballard and Jean-Louis Michel. Since then there were many expeditions to the wreck that produced a wealth of new information about the ship and what happened to her as a result of colliding with an iceberg. Technical papers have been written dealing with all imaginable aspects, from the ship's design and construction to detailed analyses of the sinking process itself. In addition, many articles and books have appeared dealing with the circumstances leading up to the collision, what transpired on board the ship prior to and immediately after the collision, the ensuing rescue by SS *Carpathia* and the aftermath that followed. In addition, many articles and books have also appeared that deal with the actions and inactions of several nearby vessels, in particular the steamships *Californian* and *Mount Temple*.

Unfortunately, much of what has been presented in some recent books, movies, documentaries and on websites is a regurgitation of the same old stuff that has been out there for years. In many cases, references are nowhere to be found, and the reader or viewer is supposed to accept what is presented as undisputed fact. In some cases, demonstrably false information or findings are presented as new by those who have their own unique perception of reality. The usual technique is the selective use of available evidence to support their particular view while totally dismissing evidence that may prove to be unfavourable to their view. Far too often, unproven theories, speculations and other forms of misinformation are accepted as fact by the general public.

This report is a collective effort that was put together by a team of dedicated individuals and authors of various backgrounds and expertise that have spent years researching, studying and analysing the wealth of information now available to us today. In support of this effort, every attempt was made to identify where our information came from. In many cases we reference the primary source material directly. In other cases, we provide reference to a particular article or book that delves into much more detail than space here will allow. Where answers are not so clear cut, we make that known to the reader and provide reference to where additional information may be found.

Questions to be Addressed

This report attempts to address as best we can the following set of questions:

About the Ship

1. How well was *Titanic* designed and how did she compare to other vessels of the period?
2. Could *Titanic* stand up to the most exacting conditions of the North Atlantic service?
3. What provisions did *Titanic* have in her design for the safety of the vessel and those on board in the event of collisions and other casualties?
4. What lifesaving appliances were carried on board, and how did that compare to the requirements of the BOT and other ships of the time?
5. What means besides wireless telegraphy was provided to communicate with other vessels, and were those means utilised?
6. What type of wireless installation was on board *Titanic* and what was its expected range?
7 What accommodation did the ship have for her passengers and crew, and how would they gain access to the boats in case of emergency?
8. Did *Titanic* comply with the requirements of the rules and regulations in effect at the time with regard to passenger steamers and emigrant ships when she departed on her maiden voyage?

About Passengers and Crew on Board

1. How many crewmembers were on board *Titanic* when she left Queenstown (distinguishing by department and positions held)?
2. How many passengers were on board *Titanic* when she left Queenstown (distinguishing by class, men, women and children)?
3. How many (and who) were lost and saved?

About the Route Followed and Warnings Received

1   What instructions were given or known prior to the sailing as to the route to be followed and precautions taken for any dangers likely to be encountered during the voyage?
2.   How far did the ship advance each day along the route she took? What were her noontime positions for each day, and what was her average speed of advance along the route for each day?
3.   What was the weather like along the route of travel?
4.   Did *Titanic* have an adequate supply of coal on board? Was this a factor in limiting the speed of the vessel? Was *Titanic* out to break any records?
5.   What warnings reached *Titanic* concerning the existence of ice along the route, when were they received, and what were the reported locations?
6.   Was *Titanic*'s course altered as a consequence of receiving such information, and if so, in what way?
7.   Were any directions given as to the speed of the vessel as a consequence of ice information received, and were they carried out?
8.   What precautions were taken by *Titanic* in anticipation of meeting ice? How did that compare to what was done on other vessels being navigated in waters where ice was expected?
9.   Was a good and proper lookout for ice kept on board? Were binoculars provided for and used by the lookout men? Is the use of binoculars necessary or desirable in such circumstances?
10.   Were searchlights provided for and used on *Titanic*? If not, should searchlights have been provided and used?

About the Collision and Flooding

1.   What time was carried on *Titanic* the day of the accident, and how did it compare to time in New York?
2.   What was the time and location of *Titanic* when she collided with an iceberg?
3.   How far ahead of the ship was the iceberg when it was first seen?
4.   How fast was *Titanic* going before the moment of impact?
5.   What actions were taken to avoid collision or mitigate damage to the vessel once the ship came in contact with the iceberg? Was the collision unavoidable?
6.   What was the extent of the damage caused by the collision?
7.   What steps were taken, if any, to prevent the vessel from sinking?
8.   How quickly was water entering the ship, and how did that affect the vessel's longitudinal and transverse stability?
9.   Did a fire in one of the coal bunkers contribute to the loss of the ship?
10   When was it determined that the ship would not survive?
11   What was the affect of flooding on the stresses imposed on the hull of the vessel?
12.   At what angle did the ship break in two? When did the break occur, and how long after did the ship sink?
13.   What was the time and location when *Titanic* foundered?
14.   How deep is the wreck and what does the wreck site show?

About Taking to the Boats and Calling for Assistance

1.   What was the number, type and carrying capacity of the boats carried on board *Titanic*? Were there prior arrangements for manning and launching the boats should an emergency arise, and were any boat drills held?
2.   How soon after the collision was the crew called out to uncover the boats?
3.   How and when were passengers appraised of the situation?

4. When was the order given to actually load the boats with women and children and send them away?
5. Were passengers treated differently by class?
6. In what order and at what times were the lifeboats launched? Who supervised the individual launchings? Who was put or took charge of each boat when it was sent away?
7. How many people were in each boat as they arrived at *Carpathia*?
8. In what sequence did the boats arrive at *Carpathia*?
9. When did *Titanic* first call for help? When was the last call sent out?
10. How many ships responded to *Titanic's* call for assistance and how far away were they from *Titanic's* reported position?
11. When did *Titanic* first fire distress rockets (socket signals)? When was the last one fired? Were they seen or heard by any other vessel, and did they respond?

About the Rescue and Actions of Other Vessels

1. What actions were taken by *Carpathia* when they first learned about *Titanic*? How long did it take for *Carpathia* to arrive on the scene, and what did they find?
2. When did *Carpathia* leave the scene? When was the decision made to return to New York, and what path did *Carpathia* take when she departed the area of the wreckage?
3. Were *Titanic's* distress rockets seen from *Californian*? How well do events seen from *Californian* correlate with events that took place on *Titanic*? Where was *Californian* relative to *Titanic* when *Titanic* foundered?
4. What actions were taken by *Mount Temple* when they first learned about *Titanic*? When did *Mount Temple* arrive on the scene and where was she relative to the location of *Carpathia* and *Californian*? What was reportedly seen by those on *Mount Temple*, and what actions were taken if any?

A Note About References

Throughout this report many references to sources will be identified by abbreviations. For example, the reference notation BI 11163–5 refers to question numbers 11163 through to 11165 transcribed at the proceedings of the 1912 British inquiry into the loss of *Titanic*. Similarly, AI pp.971–2 refers to evidence transcribed on pages 971 through to 972 at the proceedings of the 1912 American inquiry into the loss of *Titanic*. Other abbreviations used can be found in the references listed in the appendices. They are given in brackets.

TWO NATIONS, TWO INQUIRIES

Dave Gittins

After *Titanic* sank, two extensive inquiries into the disaster were held in Britain and the United States. In this introductory chapter we consider the origins of the inquiries and examine their conclusions. We also explain the nature of the British Board of Trade, whose Marine Department was responsible for all aspects of British merchant shipping.

The American Inquiry

The American inquiry was instigated by Senator William Alden Smith (R – MI), a member of the Senate Committee on Commerce. Smith reasoned that *Titanic* was bound for America and was American owned. Her passengers were largely Americans, or potential Americans. Her loss and any faults in her design or equipment were thus proper subjects for an American inquiry.[1] On hearing of the sinking, Smith moved swiftly, after ascertaining that President William Howard Taft was unlikely to act on the matter.[2] On 17 April he moved in the Senate that a sub-committee of the Senate Committee on Commerce be formed, with authority to investigate the disaster, administer oaths and issue subpoenas. The Senate passed the necessary resolutions.[3]

Resolved, That the Committee on Commerce, or a subcommittee thereof, is hereby authorised and directed to investigate the causes leading to the wreck of the White Star liner *Titanic*, with its attendant loss of life so shocking to the civilised world.

Resolved further, That said committee or a subcommittee thereof is hereby empowered to summon witnesses, send for persons and papers, to administer oaths, and to take such testimony as may be necessary to determine the responsibility therefore, with a view to such legislation as may be necessary to prevent, as far as possible, any repetition of such a disaster.

Resolved further, That the committee shall inquire particularly into the number of lifeboats, rafts, and life preservers, and other equipment for the protection of the passengers and crew; the number of persons aboard the *Titanic*, whether passenger or crew, and whether adequate inspections were made of such vessel, in view of the large number of American passengers travelling over a route commonly regarded as dangerous from icebergs; and whether it is feasible for Congress to take steps looking to an international agreement to secure the protection of sea traffic, including regulation of the size of ships and designation of routes.

Resolved further, That in the report of said committee it shall recommend such legislation as it shall deem expedient; and the expenses incurred by this investigation shall be paid from the contingent fund of the Senate upon vouchers to be approved by the chairman of said committee.

Senator Smith was appointed chairman of the committee. Its six other members were chosen for their wide range of political opinions, rather than for their nautical expertise. As it chanced, three members did possess a general knowledge of ships and the shipping industry. These were Senators Theodore Burton (R – OH), George Perkins (R – CA) and Jonathan Bourne (R – OR). Burton was chairman of the Senate Committee on Rivers and Harbours. Perkins, a former sailor, operated several coastal steamships. Jonathan Bourne, a lawyer and businessman, had a little practical experience at sea, his father being a ship owner. The other members were Senators Francis Newlands (D – NV), Duncan Fletcher (D – FL) and Furnifold Simmons (D – NC). The racist Senator Simmons, a fierce political foe of Senator Smith, attended only one committee meeting and took no part in proceedings. The committee naturally had access to the resources of the government of the United States, most notably those of the United States Navy.

Titanic was a British-registered ship and the accident had occurred on the high seas. Some Britons questioned America's right to inquire into the case. James Bryce, the British ambassador to the United States, personally detested Senator Smith, describing him as 'most unsuitable' and possessed of 'singular incompetence'. He sought legal advice on the possibility of preventing the inquiry but was disappointed. The United States Senate had the right to investigate any subject on which it had power to legislate. It could undoubtedly legislate on the safety of foreign ships entering American waters, though its right to 'investigate the causes leading to the wreck of the White Star liner *Titanic*, with its attendant loss of life' was more dubious. The British Government and its foreign secretary, Sir Edward Grey, decided not to antagonise a friendly nation and raised no formal objection.[4]

The American inquiry began on 19 April 1912 and ended on 25 May. The first two days of hearings took place in the Waldorf-Astoria Hotel in New York. Most of the remainder were held in the Senate in Washington, with the exception of several further days in the Waldorf-Astoria and a visit to *Olympic* on 25 May. Senator Smith presented its findings to the Senate on 28 May. He supplemented the findings with a speech that revealed his personal opinions, which were often more stridently critical than the report. Copies of the transcript of Smith's inquiry and his speech were sent to Britain as quickly as possible and were available to Lord Mersey's court.

The Board of Trade

In 1912, the Board of Trade was one of the most powerful organisations in Britain. It had existed in various incarnations since 1621, when King James I established a committee to relieve his Privy Council of mundane duties related to trade and commerce. It was repeatedly dissolved and recreated by successive governments. The 1912 version was constituted by an Order in Council of King George III, dated 1786. Its numerous members included all of the principal secretaries of state, the Chancellor of the Exchequer, the Speaker of the House of Commons and, because it was involved in appointing colonial bishops, the Archbishop of Canterbury. From its earliest days it was concerned with British shipping and mercantile law. Later, its powers extended to such diverse matters as the operation of railways, industrial relations, employment statistics, weights and measures, patents and meteorology.[5]

The rules governing the Board of Trade were rather loose. No quorum was prescribed and great discretion was given to its president, who was a Member of Parliament. Early presidents were often members of the House of Lords, but by the early twentieth century presidents were generally drawn from the governing party in the House of Commons.

During the nineteenth century, the clerical staff assisting the Board evolved into a large government department under a Minister of the Crown, who retained the traditional title of president. By 1912, more than 7,000 Board of Trade officers were employed throughout Great Britain. The actual Board had not held a meeting since 23 December 1850 and would not meet again until 21 March 1986, when it marked its bicentenary.[6] In 1912, its president was Sydney C. Buxton, who succeeded Winston Churchill in February 1910. Acts of Parliament dating from 1850, 1854 and 1894 had formalised the Board's power to control all aspects of merchant shipping. Its Mercantile Marine Department was responsible for ship design and safety, seamen's welfare, aids to navigation and the training and certification of ships' officers. Its interest in a ship began in its builder's yard and ended with its scrapping. If a ship was damaged or wrecked, the Board held an inquiry. Officers or owners considered to be at fault were prosecuted in a court of summary jurisdiction. In exceptional cases, the government of the day appointed an eminent judge to be a Wreck Commissioner, who conducted a thorough investigation, rather in the manner of a royal commission, though with only the powers of a court of summary jurisdiction.

In 1912, the civil servant in charge of the Board of Trade was Sir Hubert Llewellyn Smith. The Marine Department was headed by Sir Walter Howell, a career civil servant. He was provided with technical expertise by his nautical advisor, Captain Alfred Young, who succeeded Sir Alfred Chalmers in 1911. Chalmers had been in an influential position during the years before the creation of the *Olympic* class ships and, as will be shown elsewhere, his views on safety are important in the *Titanic* story.

In modern times, the Board of Trade's duties were devolved to various government departments, but the Board still exists as a legal entity, in order to validate the many regulations originally made in its name.

The Origins of the British Inquiry

Following the disaster, four possible means of inquiry were available to the British authorities:

1. A royal commission, which is an inquiry headed by a senior judge, with the power to compel witnesses to testify, under pain of imprisonment. There is no record of this being proposed.
2. A multi-party parliamentary committee of inquiry. This was proposed in the House of Commons by members of the opposition, but the government refused to consider such a course.[7]
3. An inquiry by officers of the Marine Department of the Board of Trade, followed by the prosecution of persons thought have to broken maritime law.
4. A Wreck Commissioner's Court. This is a court specifically constituted to inquire into a major shipwreck. It is presided over by a senior judge, who is given technical assistance by experts known as assessors.

Because of the seriousness of the *Titanic* case, the government decided to establish a Wreck Commissioner's Court. On 23 April 1912, the Lord High Chancellor, Earl Loreburn, head of the British judiciary, appointed the veteran judge, Lord Mersey (formerly John Charles Bigham), to preside. Five expert assessors were appointed by the Home Secretary, Sir Reginald McKenna. They were Rear Admiral the Hon. S.A. Gough-Calthorpe, CVO, RN; Captain A.W. Clarke, an Elder Brother of Trinity House;[8] Commander F.C.A. Lyon, RNR, a former P&O Line captain; Professor J.H. Biles, LLD, DSc, Professor of Naval Architecture at Glasgow University and Mr E.C. Chaston, RNR, a marine engineer from Newcastle-on-Tyne.

Questions prepared by the Board of Trade were placed before the court. These could be added to, if lawyers representing the Board saw fit:

1. When the *Titanic* left Queenstown on or about 11th April last: –
a. What was the total number of persons employed in any capacity on board her, and what were their respective ratings?
b. What was the total number of her passengers, distinguishing sexes and classes, and discriminating between adults and children?

2. Before leaving Queenstown on or about 11th April last did the *Titanic* comply with the requirements of the Merchant Shipping Acts, 1894–1906, and the Rules and Regulations made thereunder with regard to the safety and otherwise of passenger steamers and emigrant ships?

3. In the actual design and construction of the *Titanic* what special provisions were made for the safety of the vessel and the lives of those on board in the event of collisions and other casualties?

4. Was the *Titanic* sufficiently and efficiently officered and manned? Were the watches of the officers usual and proper? Was the *Titanic* supplied with proper charts?

5. What was the number of boats of any kind on board the *Titanic*? Were the arrangements for manning and launching the boats on board the *Titanic* in case of emergency proper and sufficient? Had a boat drill been held on board, and, if so, when? What was the carrying capacity of the respective boats?

6. What installations for receiving and transmitting messages by wireless telegraphy were on board the *Titanic*? How many operators were employed on working such installations? Were the installations in good and effective working order, and were the number of operators sufficient to enable messages to be received and transmitted continuously by day and night?

7. At or prior to the sailing of the *Titanic* what, if any, instructions as to navigation were given to the Master or known by him to apply to her voyage? Were such instructions, if any, safe, proper and adequate, having regard to the time of year and dangers likely to be encountered during the voyage?

8. What was in fact the track taken by the *Titanic* in crossing the Atlantic Ocean? Did she keep to the track usually followed by liners on voyages from the United Kingdom to New York in the month of April? Are such tracks safe tracks at that time of year? Had the Master any, and, if so, what discretion as regards the track to be taken?

9. After leaving Queenstown on or about the 11th April last, did information reach the *Titanic* by wireless messages or otherwise by signals, of the existence of ice in certain latitudes? If so, what were such messages or signals and when were they received, and in what position or positions was the ice reported to be, and was the ice reported in or near the track actually being followed by the *Titanic*? Was her course altered in consequence of receiving such information, and, if so, in what way? What replies to such messages or signals did the *Titanic* send and at what times?

10. If at the times referred to in the last preceding question or later the *Titanic* was warned of or had reason to suppose she would encounter ice, at what time might she have reasonably expected to encounter it? Was a good and proper look-out for ice kept on board? Were any, and, if so, what directions given to vary the speed – if so, were they carried out?

11. Were binoculars provided for and used by the look-out men? Is the use of them necessary or usual in such circumstances? Had the *Titanic* the means of throwing searchlights around her? If so, did she make use of them to discover ice? Should searchlights have been provided and used?

12. What other precautions were taken by the *Titanic* in anticipation of meeting ice? Were they such as are usually adopted by vessels being navigated in waters where ice may be expected to be encountered?

13. Was ice seen and reported by anybody on board the *Titanic* before the casualty occurred? If so, what measures were taken by the officer on watch to avoid it? Were they proper measures and were they promptly taken?

14. What was the speed of the *Titanic* shortly before and at the moment of the casualty? Was such speed excessive under the circumstances?

15. What was the nature of the casualty which happened to the *Titanic* at or about 11.45pm on the 14th April last? In what latitude and longitude did the casualty occur?

16. What steps were taken immediately on the happening of the casualty? How long after the casualty was its seriousness realised by those in charge of the vessel? What steps were then

taken? What endeavours were made to save the lives of those on board and to prevent the vessel from sinking?

17. Was proper discipline maintained on board after the casualty occurred?

18. What messages for assistance were sent by the *Titanic* after the casualty and at what times respectively? What messages were received by her in response and at what times respectively? By what vessels were the messages that were sent by the *Titanic* received, and from what vessels did she receive answers? What vessels other than the *Titanic* sent or received the messages at or shortly after the casualty in connection with such casualty? What were the vessels that sent or received such messages? Were any vessels prevented from going to the assistance of the *Titanic* or her boats owing to messages received from the *Titanic* or owing to any erroneous messages being sent or received? In regard to such erroneous messages, from what vessels were they sent and by what vessels were they received and at what times respectively?

19. Was the apparatus for lowering the boats on the *Titanic* at the time of the casualty in good working order? Were the boats swung out, filled, lowered, or otherwise put into the water and got away under proper superintendence? Were the boats sent away in seaworthy condition and properly manned, equipped and provisioned? Did the boats, whether those under davits or otherwise, prove to be efficient and serviceable for the purpose of saving life?

20. What was the number of (a) passengers, (b) crew taken away in each boat on leaving the vessel? How was this number made up having regard to:
    a. Sex.
    b. Class.
    c. Rating.

21. How many were children and how many adults? Did each boat carry its full load and, if not, why not?

22. How many persons on board the *Titanic* at the time of the casualty were ultimately rescued, and by what means? How many lost their lives? Of those rescued how many have since died? What was the number of passengers, distinguishing between men and women and adults and children of the 1st, 2nd, and 3rd classes respectively who were saved? What was the number of the crew, discriminating their ratings and sex, that were saved? What is the proportion which each of these numbers bears to the corresponding total number on board immediately before the casualty? What reason is there for the disproportion, if any?

23. What happened to the vessel from the happening of the casualty until she foundered?

24. Where and at what time did the *Titanic* founder?

25. What was the cause of the loss of the *Titanic*, and of the loss of life which thereby ensued or occurred? Was the construction of the vessel and its arrangements such as to make it difficult for any class of passenger or any portion of the crew to take full advantage of any of the existing provisions for safety?

26. When the *Titanic* left Queenstown on or about 11th April last was she properly constructed and adequately equipped as a passenger steamer and emigrant ship for the Atlantic service?

The Court is invited to report upon the Rules and Regulations made under the Merchant Shipping Acts, 1894–1906, and the administration of those Acts, and of such Rules and Regulations, so far as the consideration thereof is material to this casualty, and to make any recommendations or suggestions that it may think fit, having regard to the circumstances of the casualty with a view to promoting the safety of vessels and persons at sea.

Following evidence from members of the crew of *Californian*, question 24 was amended to read:

24. (a) What was the cause of the loss of the *Titanic*, and of the loss of life which thereby ensued or occurred? (b) *What vessels had the opportunity of rendering assistance to the* Titanic *and, if any, how was it that assistance did not reach the* Titanic *before the SS* Carpathia *arrived?* [Author's emphasis] Was the construction of the vessel and its arrangements such as to make it difficult for any class of passenger or any portion of the crew to take full advantage of any of the existing provisions for safety?

The court's hearings were conducted almost entirely within the Scottish Drill Hall, a large London building normally used for military exercises. Hearings commenced on 1 May 1912 and concluded on 3 July. Lord Mersey handed down his report on 30 July.[9]

The Conduct of the Inquiries[10]

The conduct of the inquiries differed considerably. The American inquiry was very informal. Senator Smith asked the great majority of the questions, although at one point witnesses were questioned privately by single senators, in order to speed up proceedings. Affidavits from several witnesses were accepted, a practice not followed in Britain.[11] Lawyers representing *Titanic*'s owners were present, but played almost no part.

Smith's inquiry suffered from a lack of witnesses from Britain, including the designers of *Titanic*, White Star officials and Board of Trade officers. It is thus lacking in technical details of *Titanic*'s construction and the steps taken to ensure her safety. Nobody was on hand to explain the dearth of lifeboats, or the lack of lifeboat drills. It may be said that Smith's inquiry largely established *what* had happened. The British inquiry would show *why*.

The American inquiry spent a great deal of time on matters scarcely relevant to the Senate resolution that established it. These included the conduct of Bruce Ismay and his escape from *Titanic*, possible conspiracies to withhold information after the sinking and the personal adventures of various survivors. The transcript of the inquiry is a treasured source for modern *Titanic* enthusiasts, but Smith is open to the charge of madly riding off in all directions.[12]

The British inquiry was far more formal. Various parties, including White Star and the Board of Trade, were represented by barristers, who played major roles in proceedings. Politics played a silent role, with many of the inquiry's participants being past or present Members of Parliament. Harland & Wolff staff and Board of Trade officers provided technical advice. The inquiry generally avoided going into personal stories, except for the special cases of Bruce Ismay and the Duff Gordons. Its report was formal, sober and dry by comparison with Senator Smith's findings and his accompanying speech.

Findings of the Inquiries

In broad terms, the two inquiries agreed on the main events of the disaster and its causes. *Titanic*, in the face of repeated wireless ice warnings, had steamed at close to her top speed into an iceberg. Lord Mersey spelled it out:

> The Court, having carefully inquired into the circumstances of the above mentioned shipping casualty, finds, for the reasons appearing in the annex hereto, that the loss of the said ship was due to collision with an iceberg, brought about by the excessive speed at which the ship was being navigated.[13]

Senator Smith's report was less succinct, but it amounts to the same thing. One passage reads:

> This enables the committee to say that the said ice positions definitely reported to the *Titanic* just preceding the accident located ice on both sides of the track or lane which the *Titanic* was

following, and in her immediate vicinity. No general discussion took place among the officers; no conference was called to consider these warnings; no heed was given to them. The speed was not relaxed, the lookout was not increased, and the only vigilance displayed by the officer of the watch was by instructions to the lookout to keep 'a sharp lookout for ice.'[14]

Both inquiries pointed to the lack of lifeboat accommodation and criticised the loading of the boats. Lord Mersey was restrained:

> These explanations are perhaps sufficient to account for so many of the lifeboats leaving without a full boat load; but I think, nevertheless, that if the boats had been kept a little longer before being lowered, or if the after gangway doors had been opened, more passengers might have been induced to enter the boats. And if women could not be induced to enter the boats, the boats ought to then to have been filled up with men. It is difficult to account for so many of the lifeboats being sent from the sinking ship, in a smooth sea, far from full. These boats left behind them many hundreds of lives to perish. I do not, however, desire these observations to be read as casting any reflection on the officers of the ship or on the crew who were working on the boat deck. They all worked admirably, but I think that if there had been better organisation the results would have been more satisfactory.[15]

Senator Smith, in a speech made after the presentation of his report, was more strident:

> No general alarm was given, no ship's officers formally assembled, no orderly routine was attempted or organised system of safety begun. Haphazard, they rushed by one another on staircase and in hallway, while men of self-control gathered here and there about the decks, helplessly staring at one another or giving encouragement to those less courageous than themselves.[16]
>   There were 1,324 passengers on the ship. The lifeboats would have easily cared for 1,176 and only contained 704, 12 of whom were taken into the boats from the water, while the weather conditions were favorable and the sea perfectly calm. And yet it is said by some well-meaning persons that the best of discipline prevailed. If this is discipline, what would have been disorder?[17]
>   Some of the men, to whom had been intrusted [*sic*] the care of passengers, never reported to their official stations, and quickly deserted the ship with a recklessness and indifference to the responsibilities of their positions as culpable and amazing as it is impossible to believe.[18]

Since 1912, the main findings of both inquiries have stood the test of time. *Titanic* had steamed at close to her top speed towards known ice, trusting in her lookouts to sight danger in time to take evasive action. Her inadequate lifeboats were not fully utilised and the evacuation of the ship was imperfectly carried out. As with Senator Smith and Lord Mersey, opinions on the conduct of the crew vary, but basic facts are agreed on.

Lord Mersey reported that *Titanic* had complied with all Board of Trade regulations regarding her design, equipment and manning. On paper, she was everything expected of a British passenger liner.

When we turn to other topics, the picture is less clear and is open to reassessment in the light of modern research. On 1 September 1985, a joint French/American expedition, led by oceanographer Jean-Louis Michel and Dr Robert Ballard, discovered the wreck of *Titanic*, lying at a depth of just under 4,000 metres. Her position is far from the distress position reported in 1912. In later years, many items were recovered from the wreck site, including parts of *Titanic's* hull. Many images of the wreck were obtained, in the form of movies, photographs and sonar images. Attempts were made to detect the damage done by the iceberg, using ultrasound.

As well as studying new data revealed by examination of the wreck, modern researchers have investigated other matters inadequately covered by the 1912 inquiries and have provided more accurate information than has been hitherto available. Much of the new research has been published only on the internet and remains little known to the general public. The purpose of this book is to consider the shortcomings of the 1912 inquiries and present the best modern findings in a convenient form for *Titanic* enthusiasts.

The material covered falls into three broad categories: the navigation of *Titanic* and other ships, the sinking of the ship with possible structural failures, and information on the ship's company and the casualty figures.

Navigational Matters

Both inquiries agreed *Titanic* sank at 41° 46'N, 50° 14'W, as given in her distress signals.[19] This was in spite of evidence to the contrary from *Mount Temple*'s Captain James Moore and *Californian*'s Captain Stanley Lord.

The inquiries differed a little on *Titanic*'s speed before the collision. Lord Mersey found it was 22 knots while Senator Smith put it at 'not less than 21 knots'.[20]

Lord Mersey found that at the time of the collision *Titanic* was on a course only a few miles south of the normal track but 'this change of course was so insignificant that in [his] opinion it cannot have been made in consequence of information as to ice.'[21] Senator Smith's report does not mention the matter.

Both inquiries accepted Captain Rostron's account of *Carpathia*'s rescue mission, according to which he had steamed 58 miles at up to 17½ knots and reached the distress position reported by *Titanic*.[22]

Both inquiries also agreed that *Titanic* followed the normal track for westward-bound steamers for the time of year. Accepting evidence from Third Officer Herbert Pitman, Senator Smith gave her first three days' runs as 464, 519 and 546 miles.[23]

It was agreed that the freighter *Californian* had been sighted from the sinking *Titanic* and vice versa, that she was closer to *Titanic* than claimed by her master, and could have rescued all or most of *Titanic*'s company had her crew acted upon sighting distress signals fired by *Titanic*.[24] Senator Smith made a point of dismissing the possibility of a third ship being between *Titanic* and *Californian*, thus confusing observers.[25] Lord Mersey agreed. Senator Smith censured Captain Lord of *Californian* directly, but Lord Mersey made a point of criticising only *Californian* in general, possibly because he thought Captain Lord was liable to prosecution in another court.[26]

Neither inquiry took a great interest in *Mount Temple* and the reports mention her only in passing, mainly in connection with her wireless records.

Titanic's Structure and Sinking

With limited information on hand, Senator Smith had little to say on *Titanic*'s structure, other than to criticise the watertight compartments.[27] Lord Mersey, using copious testimony from Board of Trade officers and Edward Wilding, gave a detailed description of the ship and established that *Titanic*'s design complied with all relevant regulations.[28] Both agreed that *Titanic* sank intact, though some witnesses stated that she broke in two before sinking.[29]

Passengers, Crew and Casualties

The inquiries attempted to determine how many persons had been aboard *Titanic* at the time of the sinking and establish casualty figures. Senator Smith, with limited data, produced lists of passengers and crew that are of little worth. His overall numbers are little better. He gave the total on board as 2,233, the dead as 1,517 and the survivors as 706.[30] Lord Mersey did not attempt to produce passenger and crew lists, this being the province of White Star and the Board of Trade. Question 20, parts a, b and c, was given up as insoluble.[31] Mersey's figures for the total ship's company, the dead and the survivors were 2,201, 1,490 and 711.[32] Both inquiries noted that witnesses exaggerated the number of persons loaded into the lifeboats.[33]

Lord Mersey tried to establish when individual lifeboats left the ship and produced the following table.[34]

No.	Starboard side	No.	Port Side
7	At 12.45a.m.	6	At 12.55a.m.
5	" 12.55	8	" 1.10
3	" 1.00	10	" 1.20
1	" 1.10	12	" 1.25
9	" 1.20	14	" 1.30
11	" 1.25	16	" 1.35
13	" 1.35	2	" 1.45
15	" 1.35	4	" 1.55
C	" 1.40	D	" 2.05
A	Floated off when ship sank and was utilised as a raft	B	Floated off when ship sank and was utilised as a raft

We now proceed to examine the findings of the two inquiries in the light of modern research.

Notes

1. The United States allowed British ships to enter its waters on condition that they complied with British safety standards and vice versa.
2. Taft was grieving for the loss of his aide, Major Archibald Butt, in the sinking and was involved in increasingly bitter arguments over the coming 1912 presidential election.
3. See *The Titanic: End of a Dream*, Wyn Craig Wade, Rawson Associates, US, 1979.
4. James Bryce's messages to the Foreign Office are in PRO FO 115/1710.
5. *The Board of Trade*. Sir Hubert Llewellyn Smith. London: G.P. Putnam's Sons Ltd, 1928.
6. *The Times*, 22 March 1986.
7. *The Times*, 2 May and 10 May 1912.
8. Trinity House is the organisation responsible for British lighthouses.
9. The most complete account of the British hearings, short of the full transcript, is in *Titanic: Monument and Warning*, an e-book by Dave Gittins (2005).
10. The easiest (and cheapest!) way to obtain the transcripts of both inquiries is via http://www.titanicinquiry.org/. The transcripts have been thoroughly checked and are the most accurate versions available.
11. In Britain, statements were taken from potential witnesses before the hearings began, but only testimony given in person in court was admitted to the record.
12. *The Titanic: The End of a Dream*, by Wyn Craig Wade, covers the US Inquiry in great detail. An alternative, more cynical, view is in *Titanic: Monument and Warning*.
13. Lord Mersey's report, p.1.
14. Senator Smith's report, p.7.
15. Lord Mersey's report, p.40.
16. Senator Smith's speech, p.9.
17. Senator Smith's speech, p.75.
18. Senator Smith's speech, p.75.
19. Lord Mersey's report, p.41. Senator Smith's report, pp.10–17.

20 Lord Mersey's report, p.64. Senator Smith's report, p.7.
21 Lord Mersey's report, p.27
22 Senator Smith's report, p.15. Lord Mersey's report, p.41.
23 Lord Mersey's report, p.26. Senator Smith's report, p.7.
24 Senator Smith's report, p.11. Lord Mersey's report, pp.43–6.
25 Senator Smith's speech, p.79.
26 Senator Smith's speech, p.78. Lord Mersey's report, pp.45–6.
27 Senator Smith's report, p.9.
28 Lord Mersey's report, pp.7–22, p.61.
29 Senator Smith's report, p.14. Lord Mersey's report, p.34.
30 Senator Smith's report, p.5.
31 Lord Mersey's report, p.69.
32 Lord Mersey's report, p.70.
33 Senator Smith's report, p.13. Lord Mersey's report, p.39.
34 Lord Mersey's report, p.38.

3

DESCRIPTION OF THE SHIP

Bruce Beveridge and Steve Hall

Titanic was one of a fleet of thirteen ships employed in the transport of passengers, mails and cargo between Great Britain and the United States. The usual ports of call for the service in which she was engaged were Southampton, Cherbourg, Queenstown, Plymouth and New York.[1] This section deals with the ship itself, including her construction, specifications, safety appliances, and means for passengers and crew to gain access to the lifeboats.[2]

The White Star Line

The owner of *Titanic* was the Oceanic Steam Navigation Company Ltd, usually known as the White Star Line (WSL). It was a British-registered company with a capital of £750,000 and the directors of the company were Mr J. Bruce Ismay (chairman), the Right Hon. Lord Pirrie and Mr H.A. Sanderson.[3]

In 1912, the White Star Line owned twenty-nine steamers and tenders, had a large interest in thirteen other steamers, and also owned a sailing ship for training officers. All of the shares of the company, with the exception of eight,[4] were held by the International Navigation Company Ltd of Liverpool. This was a British-registered company with a capital of £700,000. The directors of the International Navigation Company were Mr J. Bruce Ismay (chairman), and Messrs H.A. Sanderson, Charles F. Torrey and H. Concanon.

The International Navigation Company also owned almost the entire capital of the British & North Atlantic Steam Navigation Company Ltd, and the Mississippi & Dominion Steamship Company Ltd (the Dominion Line). It also owned the entire capital of the Atlantic Transport Company Ltd (the Atlantic Transport Line), and most of the ordinary share capital and about one-half of the preference share capital of Frederick Leyland and Company Ltd (the Leyland Line).

As against the above-mentioned shares and other property, the International Navigation Company Ltd had issued share lien certificates for £25 million. Both the shares and share lien certificates of the International Navigation Company were held by the International Mercantile Marine (IMM) Company of New Jersey, or by trustees for the holders of its debenture bonds.

Overall Specifications of the Vessel

Titanic was the second of three *Olympic* class ships built by Messrs Harland & Wolff for the White Star Line service between Southampton and New York. She was registered as a British steamship at the port of Liverpool. The following is a list of the main particulars for *Titanic*, submitted by Harland & Wolff for approval by the Board of Trade:[5]

Hull number	401
Registration number	131,428
Length overall	882ft 9in
Length between perpendiculars	850ft 0in
Breadth extreme	92ft 6in
Depth moulded to shelter deck	64ft 3in
Depth moulded to bridge deck	73ft 3in
Total height from keel to navigation bridge	104ft 0in
Sheer forward	About 12ft 0in
Sheer aft	About 4ft 0in
Camber	3in (full width each deck)
Load draft	34ft 6in (34ft 7in completed)
Displacement at load draft	52,310 tons
Gross tonnage	46,328 tons
Net register tons	21,831 tons
Indicated horsepower of reciprocating engines	30,000 IHP
Shaft horsepower of turbine engine	16,000 SHP

Titanic's keel was laid on 31 March 1909, in slip No.3 at Harland & Wolff 's Queen's Island Shipyard in Belfast.[6] Construction of *Titanic* commenced a few months after that of her sister ship *Olympic* which lay beside her in slip No.2. On 31 May 1911 at 12.13p.m., *Titanic* was launched into the River Lagan. *Titanic*'s fitting out occurred over the next year when finally, on Monday 1 April 1912, she was ready for her sea trials which were designed to ensure that she handled as intended, and that all her systems worked as they were supposed to.

Titanic's sea trials got underway early on 2 April 1912. She returned to Belfast at 6.30 that evening, and a Board of Trade certificate of seaworthiness, valid for one year, was signed by Francis Carruthers. This certificate attested that he had been satisfied with the ship's performance throughout the trials.

At about 8:00p.m. *Titanic* weighed anchor, bound for Southampton. It was just after midnight, 4 April 1912, when she was finally secured alongside Berth 44.

Titanic was designed with a 'schooner' rig, straight stem and a graceful, elliptical counter stern. She had four funnels and two masts. She was classed by the Board of Trade as a 'shelter deck vessel' and was built to adhere to the regulations for both passenger and emigrant ships.

Titanic's decks consisted of the boat deck, promenade deck (A), bridge deck (B), shelter deck (C), saloon deck (D), upper deck (E), middle deck (F) and lower deck (G). At each end of the ship there was a partial deck known as the orlop deck.

The after end of the orlop deck aft of watertight bulkhead (WTB) 'O', and immediately above the after shaft tunnels, was also referred to on the main structural drawings as the 'tunnel deck'. This portion of the deck was designed to create a watertight flat above the after shaft tunnel in order to prevent flooding of the hold above in the event of a complete failure of any of the shafts or stern tubes. There was also an additional deck located forward within the No.1 hold, called the lower orlop deck. At the very lowest level within the ship, the top plating of the double bottom was called the 'tank top'. These last three levels were not considered decks in the formal sense of the term, and in many publications dealing with the *Olympic* class ships are often omitted when the various decks are described. This meant that although *Titanic* had eight 'passenger' decks, there were actually eleven deck levels in total.

Watertight Subdivision and Floodable Lengths

The watertight subdivision of *Titanic* was considered very comprehensive at the time of her building. *Titanic* and her sister ship *Olympic* were built with a cellular double bottom and divided into sixteen major watertight compartments with fifteen transverse watertight bulkheads that ran clear across the ship. These watertight bulkheads were labelled 'A' through 'H' and 'J' through 'O' (the letter 'I' was not used). The first two and last six of these bulkheads ran as high as D deck while the middle seven ran as high as E deck. *Titanic* and *Olympic* were labelled as 'two compartment vessels' because they could remain afloat with any two adjacent watertight compartments completely open to the sea without in any way involving the safety of the ship. Since no one could imagine anything worse than a collision near the juncture of two of these compartments, the ships were often referred to as being 'practically unsinkable'.

In reality, the design of these vessels almost met a three-compartment standard except for three conditions: flooding in hold 3 and adjacent boiler rooms 5 and 6, flooding in adjacent boiler rooms 4, 5 and 6, and flooding in both engine rooms and the electric dynamo room aft. Other than these three conditions, the ship would remain afloat with any three adjacent compartments open to the sea.[7] In fact, she would remain afloat with all of the first four compartments flooded, all of the last four compartments flooded, flooding in adjacent boiler rooms 1 through 4, or flooding in the reciprocating engine room and boiler rooms 1 through 3. Unfortunately, on the night of 14 April 1912, *Titanic* suffered uncontrollable flooding in her first five major watertight compartments, and so the eventual loss of the vessel was inevitable.

The location of *Titanic*'s sixteen major watertight compartments and fifteen watertight bulkheads are shown below.

The compartmentalisation of *Titanic* in 1912 was equivalent to that of passenger liners of the 1920s and 1930s. The length of damage suffered by *Titanic* (in absolute length or percentage of length between perpendiculars) would have sunk every post-First World War ship that had their floodable length curves published, including such vessels as *Europa*, *Rex*, *Normandie* and *America*. The fact that the Safety of Life at Sea (SOLAS) 1929 conference ships were compartmented no better than *Titanic* reflects a consensus that *Titanic*'s damage was both statistically unlikely and unaffordable to implement. Current Safety of Life at Sea rules use the ship's length, number of passengers carried, passenger space below the margin line, whole ship volume below the margin line, and machinery space volume to determine a factor of subdivision. *Titanic*'s compartmentalisation would have met current SOLAS floodable length standards despite bulkheads that only extended as high as E and D decks forward. Calculations conducted by Hackett and Bedford found that *Titanic*'s design would also have met additional modern SOLAS rules on residual righting arm (lessons from the *Stockholm/Andrea Doria* accident of 1956) except for one damage case that would have had nothing to do with the actual damage *Titanic* suffered from the iceberg. In fact, over much of her length, including the

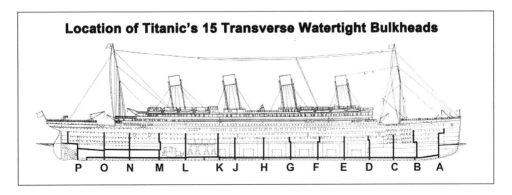

Fig. 3-1 *Titanic*'s watertight compartments.

region in the bow, *Titanic* greatly exceeds current SOLAS requirements which still view the ship-to-ship collision threat as the most probable.[8]

Decks and Accommodation

The following describes the various decks and accommodation on *Titanic* (a complete set of deck plans are included at the end of this section for reference).

The Boat Deck was the uppermost deck of the ship. Much of it was open to passengers for promenading and leisure. Dividing the deck along much of its length were deckhouses constructed around the boiler and machinery casings, as well as raised roofs over the several first class public rooms located on the deck below. The majority of the ship's ventilators were located here as well, but owing to the use of Sirocco fans to assist with moving air, *Titanic's* boat deck was not obstructed with the typical unsightly forest of ventilation heads prominent on so many other ships of the period.

   The majority of the boat deck space was reserved for first class passengers, while a smaller area aft was reserved exclusively for second class passengers. In addition, the engineers and officers each had their own areas reserved exclusively for them; the latter space also served as a natural barrier which prevented uninvited 'visitors' from wandering forward onto the bridge.

   The navigation bridge and wheelhouse were located at the very forward end of the deck, adjoining the forward end of the deckhouse that also housed the chart room and other related spaces, the officers' quarters, the Marconi rooms, six first class staterooms, the first class gymnasium and the forward first class entrance. Other deckhouses, some of which surrounded the bases of the funnels themselves, held the officers' mess, tank rooms, engineers' smoke room and forward second class entrance. The skylights enclosing the domes above both first class staircases were also situated here – the aft one at deck level, and the forward one located on top of the deckhouse roof over the first class entrance hall.

   The light and air shafts above the reciprocating and turbine engine rooms terminated here as well as at the roof level of the deckhouses surrounding them; the former was capped by a skylight while the latter opened into the base of the No.4 funnel. Flanking both sides of the boat deck were the ship's fourteen 30ft-long main lifeboats and two 25ft-long emergency cutters.

A Deck (the Promenade Deck) extended over a length of 546ft, running the entire length of the superstructure. It was exclusively the province of first class passengers, who could enjoy a turn about the deck in the open air without having to ascend to the boat deck above. The promenade deck was open at the sides along its length, with the outer bulwarks capped with a teak rail, except along the forward half where it was enclosed by windows. It was sheltered overhead along its entire length, except at the after end where it extended out into the open air. Inside, in addition to a number of first class staterooms forward, were located some of the principle first class public rooms. These rooms had large, broad windows facing the outside promenade and admitting abundant amounts of light to the spaces within; these windows were arranged in a series of bays.

   The interior spaces of A deck were all contained within a single long deckhouse extending nearly the entire length of the deck. It was of irregular width due to alcoves and window bays. To identify the entranceways, lighted signs were mounted to the deck head indicating the compartments inside. Storm railings of teak were fitted to the bulkheads with brass brackets in sections around the exterior of the deckhouse.

B Deck (the Bridge Deck) was the topmost strength deck of the vessel and extended continuously for 555ft amidships. Though the forecastle and poop decks were at the B deck level, they were separated by well decks approximately 52ft in length each, and hence

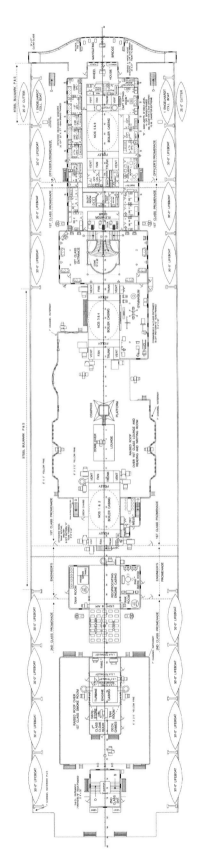

Fig. 3-2 *Titanic's* boat deck.

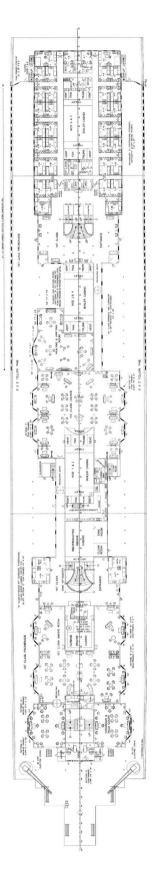

Fig. 3-3 *Titanic's* promenade deck (A).

were not considered part of the deckhouse proper. For the forward two-thirds of its length, except for the space taken up by the first class entrance hall and staircase, B deck was almost entirely given over to first class accommodation, including the palatial parlour suites. In total there were ninety-nine first class bedrooms having berths for 183 passengers. Abaft the first class staterooms was the reception room for the *à la carte* restaurant, with the restaurant itself located further aft at the end of a short passageway that led past the restaurant galley and pantry. Adjoining the restaurant on the starboard side was the novel Café Parisien, intended to resemble a French sidewalk café. Further aft, beyond the restaurant and the Café Parisien, was the second class entrance foyer and second class smoke room, both of which were flanked on either side by a covered second class promenade. This promenade extended aft out into the open air, with another entrance and staircase for second class passengers at its after end inside a separate deckhouse. From here, two teak deck ladders gave access to the after well deck. At the forward end of B deck, outside the deckhouse, was a small open deck area overlooking the forward end of the ship. This deck area led to the forward well deck by way of a portable teak deck ladder on the port side (a vertical iron ladder was permanently mounted to the bulkhead behind it), and was used as a means for the crew to access the forward decks from the bridge via the port and starboard crew stairwells. Two service doors 4ft 6in wide were fitted within the outboard port and starboard bulwarks of this forward open deck area.

C Deck (the Shelter Deck) was the highest deck that extended continuously from bow to stern. The forward area under the forecastle deck held the steam engines and gear for working the ship's anchor-handling and forward mooring and warping equipment, as well as the carpenter's shop, lamp store, and other rooms associated with the workings of the ship. In this area were also the crew hospital and galley and the messes for the seamen, firemen and freasers. Amidships, between the two well decks, was a deck structure 555ft long and extending across the full breadth of the ship. The general arrangement of this area of the deck was similar to that of B deck above, in that the forward two-thirds was largely given over to first class accommodation, with two parlour suites and the larger, more luxurious rooms amidships.

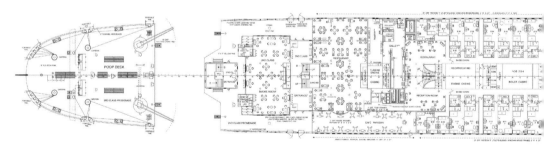

Fig. 3-4 *Titanic's* bridge deck (B).

Fig. 3-5 *Titanic's* shelter deck (C).

In addition to 135 staterooms for first class passengers, there was a dining saloon for the passengers' maids and valets, a separate dining saloon for postal clerks and Marconi operators, and various service rooms. Abaft the first class accommodation was the second class library and second class enclosed promenade. The area at the after end of the ship – under the poop deck – held the massive steering engines for working the rudder, as well as the third class general room and the third class smoke room. The forward and after well decks were used for mooring and cargo handling in port, and served as promenade spaces at sea for third class passengers.

D Deck (the Saloon Deck) was a continuous deck that ran the full length of the ship. At its forward end was accommodation for firemen, and further aft, a large third class open space. Aft of this were first class accommodation extending as far aft as the forward first class entrance. This entrance was one of the principle boarding locations for first class passengers, and opened into the large reception room which served not only to welcome the passengers boarding the ship, but also as a gathering place prior to taking seats in the dining saloon just aft.

The first class dining saloon, extending the full width of the ship, was the largest afloat at the time *Titanic* was built. Some distance further aft was the second class dining saloon, and between the two saloons, the combined first and second class galley, flanked fore and aft by the first and second class pantries, respectively. This arrangement permitted a large, single galley to serve both dining saloons. Abaft the second class dining saloon were second and third class accommodation, the ones for third class being located furthest aft. This was also the highest deck on which second and third class berths were located.

Recessed within the after bulkhead of the second class pantry and located against the forward bulkhead of the forward second class staircase was a narrow athwartship companionway containing a set of stairs leading up into the pantry from E deck. These stairs were provided as an emergency escape route for both passengers and crew berthed on E and F decks in between WTBs L and M, as these areas were cut off from the regular passenger and crew stairs when the watertight doors within the passageways were closed.

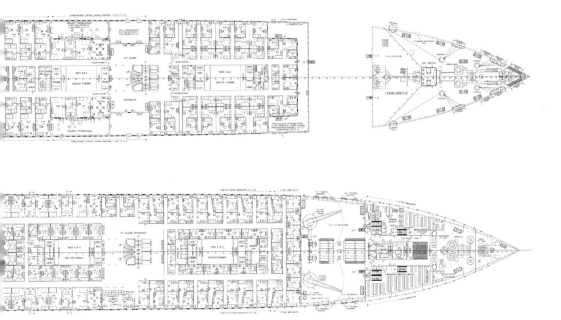

E Deck (the Upper Deck) extended the full length of the ship. Structurally, E deck was called the 'freeboard deck', as it was the highest continuous deck to which all the watertight bulkheads rose. The first two (A and B) and last six (K, L, M, N, O and P) watertight bulkheads extended further to D deck, but the middle seven (C, D, E, F, G, H and J) only went as high as E deck. Except for the spaces occupied by the engine and boiler casings, crew messes and various service rooms, the entire deck was given over to accommodation for passengers and crew. Forward were quarters for seamen and trimmers, along with the forward third class latrines and a limited number of third class cabins. On the port side amidships was the working crew passageway, nicknamed 'Scotland Road' by the crew and also used by third class passengers to access the companionway leading to their dining saloon on F deck below. A large number of the crew had their accommodation along Scotland Road; the majority of the stewards were berthed here.

The quarters for the restaurant staff were also located on the port side, as was the engineers' mess. On the starboard side amidships was first class accommodation, with second class further aft and third class occupying the remaining area at the stern. These areas were physically separated from one another, but with doors that could be used for crew access or for passengers in an emergency. This was the lowest level to which the first class elevators ran, although the forward staircase continued down one deck further to give first class passengers access to the Turkish, electric and swimming baths. The entrances for passengers boarding by tender were also located at this level. This deck, perhaps more than any other, illustrates the complex arrangement of an ocean liner below decks, where accommodation for the crew had to share spaces with accommodation for no less than three classes of passenger, keeping all three separate from one another while at the same time providing them ready access to and from their respective areas here and on other decks.

The starboard side of Scotland Road was largely formed by the steel bulkheads enclosing the boiler casings, reciprocating engine casing and turbine engine casing. The bulkhead along

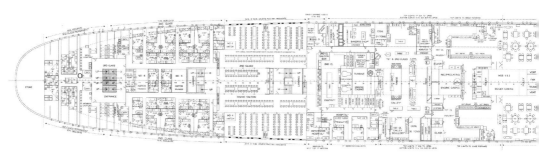

Fig. 3-6 *Titanic's* saloon deck (D).

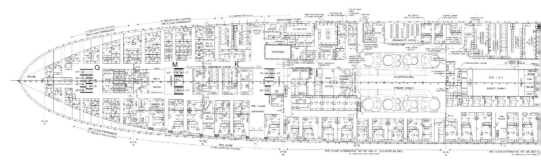

Fig. 3-7 *Titanic's* upper deck (E).

this side was fitted with doors at intervals to access these casings. These doors provided the engineers with access to the various ladders and platforms leading down into the boiler and machinery spaces, and to a similar network of ladders which provided passage up through the fidley trunks. The latter network served to facilitate maintenance of the equipment and piping located within these trunks, and also provided a direct emergency escape route to the boat deck for crewmen in the compartments below.

F Deck (the Middle Deck) consisted of four large areas for third class accommodation, with more third class cabins than on any other deck. Second class passengers were also berthed here, the lowest deck on which their permanent staterooms were located. The large third class dining saloon was located amidships, along with the relatively small third class galley and pantries. Additional crew accommodation was located forward, and amidships were the engineers' quarters as well as accommodation for those crewmembers of the victualling department who were not based on E deck above. The swimming bath, Turkish baths and electric bath were all located on F deck, as was access to the squash racquet court. All areas between watertight bulkheads on F deck had direct stairway communication with the deck above, so that if it became necessary to close the watertight doors an escape route would be available. Also on this deck were the rooms for the Sirocco fans used to ventilate the stokeholds. The inclined pipes of the boiler rooms' ash ejectors terminated here, discharging through the side of the ship, and the coaling doors through the shell plating were located at this level as well. Various service rooms also occupied this deck. Due to the fact that the watertight bulkheads amidships ran to the underside of E deck, the boiler casings at this level and below were divided and were no longer referred to in combined fashion; instead, each carried only the number of the boiler room immediately below.

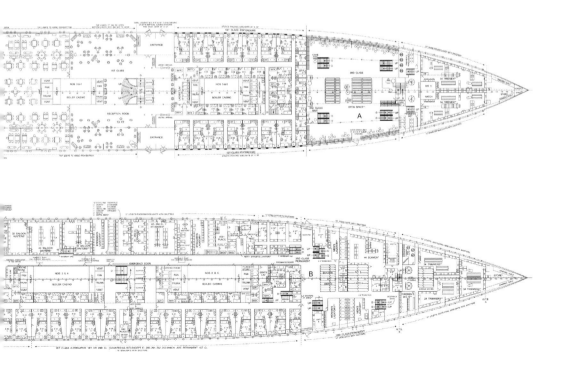

Fig. 3-8 *Titanic's* middle deck (F).

Fig. 3-9 *Titanic's* lower deck (G).

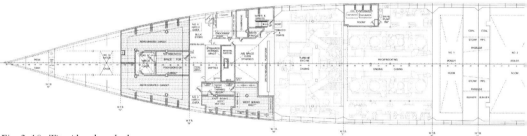

Fig. 3-10 *Titanic's* orlop deck.

G Deck (the Lower Deck) was the lowest deck on which any passengers were carried, and the lowest deck to have sidelights in the hull. G deck was not a continuous deck fore to aft, occupying 187ft 9in forward of the boiler rooms and 209ft abaft the turbine engine room casing. The intervening space, except for two flats on either side of the turbine engine room casing, was taken up by the boilers, boiler uptakes, steam pipe passages and cross bunkers, as well as the engines and auxiliaries. In the forward deck space as far aft as WTB D, crew accommodation was provided along with third class accommodation; space was also given over to the post office and squash racquet court. In the deck space aft of WTB N were located storerooms for the ship's provisions, and abaft those, additional third class accommodation.

The Orlop Deck, like G deck above, was a partial deck in that it was in two separate sections rather than one continuous deck throughout the length of the ship. The forward section extended from the forepeak aft to WTB D, with the after section extending from WTB M to the afterpeak tank at WTB P. The area in between was occupied by the boiler spaces, cross bunkers and machinery spaces.

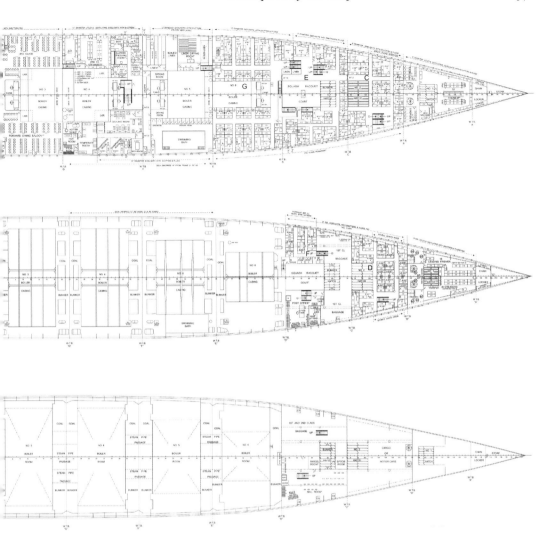

The Lower Orlop Deck extended only as far aft as WTB B, the space forward of WTB A being occupied by the forepeak tank. At the after end of the deck was the No.1 hatch to the cargo hold on the tank top below. The lower orlop deck was used only for cargo storage.

The Tank Top was the lowest level of the ship, and was not a deck in the true sense of the term. It was actually the plating forming the inner bottom of the ship, and by definition was the plating forming the top of the double bottom. The tank top plating was fitted to the tops of the floor plates, longitudinals and centre keelson, and made a nearly complete inner skin along the bottom and was carried out to the sides of the hull throughout much of the ship's length.

Being the top plates of the double bottom tanks, the plating of the tank top was watertight. This was also the plating that the boiler stools, engines and other machinery seatings sat on. The strakes were riveted in the in-and-out fashion with the landings being joggled. The edges of the landings and butts were not planed, and the bulkhead foundation bars were joggled over the landings. The plates were increased in thickness in the engine and boiler rooms, and heavy sole plates were fitted under the reciprocating engines. The wells for drainage were fitted at half depth of the double bottom in the turbine and reciprocating engine rooms and the boiler rooms.

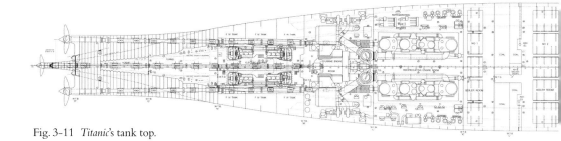

Fig. 3-11 *Titanic's* tank top.

Access of Passengers and Crew to the Boat Deck

Passengers

The following routes led directly from the various parts of the first class passenger accommodation to the boat deck: from the forward ends of A, B, C, D and E decks by the staircase in the forward first class entrance direct to the boat deck. The elevators led from the same decks as far as A deck, where further access was obtained by going up the top flight of the main staircase. The same route was available for first class passengers forward of midships on B, C and E decks.

First class passengers abaft amidships on B and C decks could use the staircase in the after main entrance to A deck, and then could go out onto the deck, and then by midships stairs along the house sides aft of the first class lounge, ascend to the boat deck. They could also use the stewards' working staircase between the reciprocating engine casing and No.3 boiler casing, which led directly to the boat deck. This last route was also available for passengers on E deck in the same divisions who could use the forward first class main stairway and elevators.

Second class passengers on D deck could use their own after stairway to B deck, and could then pass up their forward stairway to the boat deck, or else could cross their saloon and use the forward stairway throughout.

Of the second class passengers on E deck, those abreast of the reciprocating engine casing, unless the watertight door immediately abaft them was closed, went aft and joined the other second class passengers. If, however, the watertight door at the end of their compartment was closed, they passed through an emergency door into the engine room, and directly up to the boat deck by the ladders and gratings in the engine room casing.

The second class passengers on E deck in the compartment abreast the turbine casing on the starboard side, and also those on F deck on both sides below, could pass through M watertight bulkhead to the forward second class main stairway. If this door were closed, they could pass by the stairway up to the serving space at the forward end of the second class saloon, and go into the saloon and from there up the forward second class stairway.

Passengers between M and N bulkheads on both E and F decks could pass directly up to the forward second class stairway to the boat deck.

Passengers between N and O bulkheads on D, E, F and G decks could pass by the after second class stairway to B deck, and then cross to the forward second class stairway and go up to the boat deck.

Third class passengers at the fore end of the vessel could pass along the working passage on E deck and through an emergency door at the forward first class main stairway, the crew staircase that runs through the first class pantry and up to the boat deck, the stewards' staircase to the second class pantry on D deck, and a set of doors at both the fore and aft second class staircases. Alternatively, they could go through the door at the forward end of the first class alleyway on the starboard side and then to the first class stairway and directly to the boat deck. They might also pass by the staircases to C deck, then cross the forward well deck and go

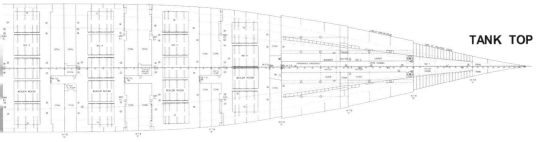

up stairs to B deck, and then take stairs on the port and starboard sides directly to the boat deck outside the officers' accommodation.

The third class passengers at the after end of the ship could take their stairway there to E deck, and then into the working passage. Or, alternatively, they could continue up their own stairs and entrance to C deck, from there go across the aft well deck to a set of ladders, one on each side of the ship, accessing B deck where direct access was obtained to the second class staircase and directly to the boat deck.

Crew

From each boiler room an escape or emergency ladder was provided direct to the boat deck by the fidleys, in the boiler casings, and also into the working passage on E deck, and from there, by the stairs immediately forward of the reciprocating engine casing, go direct to the boat deck.

From both the engine rooms ladders and gratings gave direct access to the boat deck. From the electric dynamo room, the after tunnels, and the forward pipe tunnels, escapes were provided directly to the working passage on E deck, and from there by one of the several routes already detailed from that space to the boat deck.

From the crew's quarters they could go by their own staircases up to the forward well deck, and from there, like the third class passengers, to the boat deck. The stewards' accommodation being all connected to the working passage or the forward main first class stairway, they could use one of those routes from there to the boat deck. The engineers' accommodation also communicated with the working passage, but as it was possible for them to be shut between two watertight bulkheads if the doors were closed, they had the option of taking a direct route by the gratings in the engine room casing to the boat deck.

On all the principal accommodation decks, the alleyways and stairways provided a ready means of access to the boat deck, and there were clear deck spaces in way of all main entrances and stairways on the boat deck and all decks below. However, even though all available deck plans and other documents suggest that steerage passengers had unimpeded access to *Titanic's* boat deck, a considerable body of anecdotal evidence exists which suggests that locked or guarded barriers were encountered by some steerage passengers blocking them from gaining easy access to the upper decks during the evacuation. The evidence for the existence of these barriers will be discussed in detail in Appendix J.

Structure of the Vessel

The structural design and arrangement of *Titanic* included a multitude of parts chosen for strength, watertightness and/or safety. Generally speaking, the ship as a whole can be regarded as a huge box girder, three sides of which are composed of the shell plating and the fourth by the main strength deck – in *Titanic's* case, the bridge deck. These four sides of the box girder are, in turn, strengthened by support structures such as the keel, frames, beams, keelsons, stringers, girders and pillars, each of which has its own function within the whole.

The keel was the backbone upon which the ship was built and consisted of a rigid fabrication of plates and structural shapes running fore and aft along the centreline of the ship. At the forward end, the keel was connected to the stem; at the after end, the keel was connected to the stern frame which supported both the rudder and propellers. The frames, acting as the ribs of the ship, determined the ship's form. Their lower ends were attached to 'floor plates' – essentially transverse, vertical, deep web frames – which were attached to the keel at intervals, while their upper ends were attached through brackets to beams which supported the decks. Internal bracing was provided by keelsons and stringers running fore and aft. The frames also supported and stiffened the shell plating. The shell plating, in addition to being necessary for watertightness, was one of the principal strength members of the ship. The shell plating ran continuously from the stem to the stern frame and from the keel to the main strength deck and, as noted, formed three sides of the box girder. The plating, aided by the frames, had to withstand the pressure of the water outside and the stresses which arise from outside forces such as the buffeting of the waves or from rubbing against a dock. The main strength deck, forming the fourth side of the girder, had to be of strong construction. The deck plating was connected to beams which extend from side to side across the ship. Additional strength was provided by doubling plates in regions weakened by openings such as hatchways and companionways as well as beneath all deck machinery, chocks and bitts. The decks were supported from below by girders and pillars as required.

The average shell plate on *Titanic's* midship section was 6ft wide and, on average, 30ft long, with the largest plates ranging up to a length of 36ft and weighing 4¼ tons each. The thickness of the shell plates was generally 1in for approximately one half the ship's length about the area amidships, especially in those areas requiring extra strength. The thickness of the plating was gradually reduced within most strakes to $^{12}\!/_{20}$in at the fore and aft ends, with the ending thickness of some strakes being either thinner or thicker as design considerations dictated.

Some parts of the shell plating required more strength than others. In this case *Titanic's* strakes were doubled. The term 'doubled' means that plating was thickened by the addition of another layer of plating added in proportion to the amount of load to be carried or in proportion to the calculated loss in strength resulting from an opening cut in the plate. In very large vessels such as *Titanic*, with her extreme length in proportion to her depth, doublers were fitted to the sheer strake amidships and to the strake immediately above at B deck. Doubling of the shell plating was also carried out for ⅗ the length of the vessel in the plating of the 'J' strake located midway through the turn of the bilge. The bilge plating formed the lower extremity of the ship girder, just as the sheer strake formed the upper.

Watertight Bulkheads, Doors and Double Bottom

The ship was divided in sixteen major watertight compartments by fifteen transverse bulkheads. Although these were watertight, the deck that they extended up to, called the bulkhead deck, was not watertight with the exception of the orlop deck abaft of the turbine engine room, and the one forward of the collision bulkhead A over the peak tank, both of which were watertight flats. In all instances, the tops of the watertight bulkheads were well above the load waterline and exceeded the regulations of the time.

Watertight Bulkhead A (WTB A) – The first watertight bulkhead, also called the collision bulkhead. It extended up from the bottom of the hull at frame 134F to the underside of E deck. The lower portion of this bulkhead formed the forward end of the foremost double bottom tank, and the after bulkheads of both the forepeak tank and the chain locker. At E deck, the bulkhead was stepped forward to frame 140F and then continued up to the underside of C deck as a structural element, but was made watertight to the underside of D deck only.

Watertight Bulkhead B (WTB B) – The second watertight bulkhead aft of the bow, located at frame 114F, where it extended up to the underside of G deck. At G deck the bulkhead was stepped aft horizontally to frame 111F, at which point it was extended to the underside of D deck. The compartment space measured 46ft 4in forward to WTB A at the bottom. WTB B formed the aft side of the No.1 hold from the tank top to the bottom of G deck. This bulkhead was also the point at which the watertight firemen's tunnel started. This tunnel allowed access from the firemen's quarters to the stokeholds. It passed through WTB C and ended at a watertight door at WTB D. The tunnel was accessed by a pair of spiral staircases that led down from the firemen's quarters on the forward side of WTB B above G deck to the aft side of WTB B down at the tank top. The tunnel itself was considered part of the second compartment.

Watertight Bulkhead C (WTB C) – The third watertight bulkhead aft, located at frame 95F. In addition to its primary purpose, this bulkhead was one of a pair of bulkheads which enclosed a fresh-water tank. The corresponding shorter bulkhead was located two frames aft at 93F. WTB C extended up to the under side of E deck. The corresponding bulkhead, which formed the after end of the fresh-water tank, extended to the underside of the orlop deck. The compartment area of WTB C measured 50ft 6in forward to WTB B at the bottom and formed part of the after side of the No.2 hold.

Watertight Bulkhead D (WTB D) – The fourth watertight bulkhead aft of the bow, located at frame 78F and extended up to the underside of E deck. The compartment space measured 51ft to WTB C, inclusive of the fresh-water tank at the forward end. This bulkhead was located at the after end of the watertight firemen's tunnel, where it formed the forward side of a cofferdam which took the form of a small watertight vestibule. This small compartment was constructed in such a way as to incorporate a capped watertight vertical shaft, or 'trunk', within its roof to accommodate the tunnel's vertical-sliding watertight door and closing mechanism. The vestibule extended aft to frame 75F where it was fitted with a second vertical-sliding watertight door providing access into No.6 boiler room. Within the forward bulkhead of the vestibule was a pair of vertically hinged watertight doors, one located to either side of the watertight door leading into the firemen's tunnel. These doors gave access to No.3 hold which could also be used as a reserve coal bunker.

Watertight Bulkhead E (WTB E) – The fifth watertight bulkhead aft of the bow, located at frame 60F and extending up to the underside of E deck. The compartment space measured 54ft to WTB D. WTB E formed the after end of the compartment containing No.6 boiler room and the forward end of the compartment containing No.5 boiler room. It divided the coal bunkers that were on the underside of F deck and the boiler casing on the underside of E deck, and provided structural support for the boiler uptakes of these two boiler rooms going up to No.1 funnel. At F deck, it formed the forward wall of the swimming bath compartment on the starboard side, and the forward wall of the linen drying room on the port side.

Watertight Bulkhead F (WTB F) – The sixth watertight bulkhead aft of the bow, located at frame 41F and extending up to the underside of E deck. The compartment space measured 57ft to WTB D. WTB F formed the after end of the compartment containing No.5 boiler room and the forward end of the compartment containing No.4 boiler room. It divided the coal bunkers that were on the underside of F deck and the boiler casing on the underside of E deck. At F deck, it formed the forward wall of the Turkish bath suite on the starboard side, and the after wall of the linen store on the port side.

Watertight Bulkhead G (WTB G) – The seventh watertight bulkhead aft of the bow, located at frame 22F and extending up to the underside of E deck. The compartment space measured 57ft forward to WTB F. WTB G formed the after end of the compartment containing No.4

boiler room and forward end of the compartment containing No.3 boiler room. It divided the coal bunkers that were on the underside of F deck and the boiler casing on the underside of E deck, and provided structural support for the boiler uptakes of these two boiler rooms going up to No.2 funnel. At F deck it formed the after walls of the Turkish bath suite on the starboard side and stewards' and cooks' accommodation on the port side.

Watertight Bulkhead H (WTB H) – The eighth watertight bulkhead aft of the bow, located at frame 3F and extending up to the underside of E deck. The compartment space measured 57ft forward to WTB G. WTB H formed the after end of the compartment containing No.3 boiler room and forward end of the compartment containing No.2 boiler room. It divided the coal bunkers that were on the underside of F deck and the boiler casing on the underside of E deck. It also divided the third class dining saloon on F deck into two rooms.

Watertight Bulkhead J (WTB J) – The ninth watertight bulkhead aft of the bow, located at frame 18A and extending up to the underside of E deck. The compartment space measured 60ft to WTB H. WTB J formed the after end of the compartment containing No.2 boiler room and forward end of the compartment containing No.1 boiler room. It divided the coal bunkers that were on the underside of F deck and the boiler casing on the underside of E deck, and provided structural support for the boiler uptakes of these two boiler rooms going up to No.3 funnel. It also formed the after wall of the port and starboard third class pantries, and the forward walls of the third class galley on the starboard side and bakers' accommodation on the port side.

Watertight Bulkhead K (WTB K) – The tenth watertight bulkhead aft of the bow, located at frame 30A and extending up to the underside of D deck. The compartment space measured 36ft to WTB J. WTB K formed the after bulkhead of No.1 boiler room and forward bulkhead of the reciprocating engine room. It also separated the third class galley complex on the starboard side and the third class stewards' accommodation on the port side from the engineers' accommodation on F deck.

Watertight Bulkhead L (WTB L) – The eleventh watertight bulkhead aft of the bow, located at frame 58A. It extended up to the underside of D deck and measured 69ft to WTB K. WTB L formed the after bulkhead of the reciprocating engine room to the underside of D deck, and the forward bulkhead of the turbine engine room. On G deck, WTB L separated the engineers' workshop on the starboard side and the oil tank flat and brine tank room on the port side from the condenser discharge recesses. On F deck it separated the engineers' accommodation on either side of the reciprocating engine casing from the second class passenger accommodation immediately aft; and on E deck it bisected the aftermost first class passenger accommodation while on the port side it separated the engineers' accommodation from that of the *à la carte* restaurant staff. This was the first bulkhead through which the wing propeller shafts passed.

Watertight Bulkhead M (WTB M) – The twelfth watertight bulkhead aft of the bow, located at frame 71A. It extended up to the underside of D deck and measured 54ft to WTB K, excluding the recess let into the bulkhead for the after rotor bearing seats and centre shaft bulkhead gland of the turbine engine. WTB M formed the after bulkhead of the turbine engine room and forward bulkhead of the electric dynamo room. On G deck, WTB M was stepped forward parallel to the keel on both sides and formed much of the port and starboard casings of the turbine engine room as well as the after bulkheads of both condenser discharge recesses. The decks between the casing and shell were caulked watertight to form 'flats' which contained both uninsulated and insulated (refrigerated) store rooms for the galleys. WTB M separated the refrigerated stores area on the orlop and G decks from the turbine engine room. On F deck, it was the forward one of two bulkheads dividing the second class passenger accommodation into three separate areas. On E deck, WTB M separated the first and second class passenger accommodation on the starboard side, while on the port side it separated the accommodation of the *à la carte* restaurant staff from those of third class passengers.

Watertight Bulkhead N (WTB N) – The thirteenth watertight bulkhead aft of the bow, located at frame 93A. It extended up to the underside of D deck and measured 63ft to WTB M. WTB N formed the after bulkhead of the electric engine room and the forward bulkhead of the forward shaft tunnel. It separated the ship's stores area from the refrigerated cargo hold on the aft side of the bulkhead, and on G deck, it separated the refrigerated stores from the third class passenger accommodation. On F deck, WTB N was the after one of two bulkheads dividing the second class passenger accommodation into three separate areas. On E deck this bulkhead bisected the second class passenger accommodation on the starboard side, while on the port side it was the forward bulkhead of two dividing the third class passenger accommodation into three separate areas.

Watertight Bulkhead O (WTB O) – The fourteenth watertight bulkhead aft of the bow, located at frame 111A, and extending up to the underside of D deck. The compartment measured 54ft to WTB N. WTB O subdivided the shaft tunnel into two compartments. It divided the refrigerated cargo hold from the general cargo hold beneath the No.6 hatch on the orlop deck. On G deck, WTB O bisected the third class accommodation, while on F deck it separated the aftermost second class accommodation from those of third class. On E deck it separated the second class accommodation on the starboard side from those of third class aft, while on the port side it was the after bulkhead of two dividing the third class passenger accommodation into three separate areas.

Watertight Bulkhead P (WTB P) – The fifteenth watertight bulkhead aft of the bow. The compartment space measured 57ft 6in to WTB O at the bottom levels. WTB P formed the after bulkhead of the shaft tunnels, and was also the forward bulkhead of the afterpeak tank. WTB P was located at frame 133A, where it extended up from the tank top to the underside of G deck. At G deck, WTB P was stepped aft horizontally to frame 139A, forming part of the watertight flat above the forepeak tank. At frame 139A, WTB P was extended vertically to the underside of D deck. The space between WTB P and the sternpost was taken up by the afterpeak tank up to the underside of G deck, and a store space up to the underside of D deck. This area was the sixteenth watertight compartment.

Watertight Doors – Watertight Bulkheads E through O inclusive each had a vertical-sliding watertight door fitted at the level of the deck plates of the boiler and machinery spaces for the use of the engineers, firemen, trimmers and greasers. At WTB D there were, in effect, two vertical-sliding doors, with one located at the forward end and one at the aft end of the vestibule by the forward entrance to No.6 boiler room. All of these twelve doors on the tank top level were remotely operable from the navigation bridge by a single electrical switch. On the orlop deck, there was one door of the lateral-sliding type located on the forward side of WTB N for access to the refrigerated hold. There were no watertight doors in the bulkheads on G deck. All watertight doors on F and E decks were of the manually operated, lateral-sliding type.

The twelve automatic doors on the tank top were arranged on the drop system. Each door was held up in the open position by a multiple-disc friction clutch that was kept engaged by a weighted bell crank. Lifting the weighted bell crank lever caused the release of the clutch, which then allowed the door to drop by its own weight in closing. The bell crank lever could be instantly raised by a powerful electromagnet or solenoid. The switch for activating all of them was located on the navigation bridge. All one had to do was to move the switch to its 'on' position to energise these solenoids thereby releasing all of the doors simultaneously. There was no centrally located device to close the doors independently of one another, nor was there an indicator panel to show the status or positions of any of the doors. An electric bell push, located close to the watertight door switch on the navigation bridge, was pushed immediately before the switch was thrown to activate a warning bell at each door location so as to give warning to anyone nearby that the door was closing. A notice near the switch on the bridge read:

> In case of emergency, to close watertight doors on tank top, press bell; push for 10 seconds to give alarm; then move switch to 'on' position and keep it there. Note: Doors cannot, however, be operated mechanically whilst switch is on.

In addition to being remotely operable, each of these doors could also be individually closed by lifting a hand lever fitted in connection with the friction clutch on the fore side of the door. A hand gear for each door was also fitted at the bulkhead deck above which allowed the door to be lowered or raised by manual means.

As a further precaution against a compartment flooding accidentally, hollow cylindrical floats were provided beneath the stokehold deck plates that lifted the clutch lever of the door thereby automatically closing the door to a compartment that was flooding. The only way to raise a door after it had closed was by turning a hand crank located alongside each door that was geared to the gear shaft of the door. This could only be done if the clutch remained engaged. Therefore, the electrical switch on the bridge had to be in the 'off' position for the doors to be raised.

The manually operated horizontal-sliding watertight doors above the level of the tank top operated on the 'rack and pinion' system. They were designed to be cranked open or shut both locally and from the bulkhead deck above. There were nine of these horizontal-sliding watertight doors located on E deck, ten on F deck and one on the orlop deck aft.

Cellular Double Bottom – *Titanic*'s cellular double bottom was divided transversely into four longitudinal sections. The two sections immediately adjacent to the keel ran nearly the full length of the hull. The inner sections contained fifteen tanks arranged symmetrically about the vertical keel, with all but the two end tanks subdivided by the vertical keel into thirteen port and starboard tanks. The two outer sections, which only ran under the machinery spaces, were subdivided into eight wing tanks per side, occupying the space between the margin plates and the intersection of the inner bottom plating with the side shell plating. In total there were forty-four separate tanks in the double bottom. Some were used as ballast tanks, others to carry fresh water for the boilers. The total capacity of these double bottom tanks was 5,449 tons.[9]

The subdivision of the double bottom into separate tanks added to the stability of the ship, as it would prevent the shifting of large volumes of water that might otherwise occur. The double bottom protected the ship from flooding in case of a grounding accident that ripped the outer plates open to the sea.

Side Doors and Accommodation Ladder

The various openings required in the shell plating for sidelights, shell doors and coaling ports, sea chests and other through-hull openings were made after the shell plates were installed and the openings doubled for strength. Portholes were cut in with a pneumatically powered cutting device. Doors provided for the loading of coal were secured by means of strongbacks and turnbuckles in order to make a watertight fit. The outsides of the doors were made flush with the shell plating by means of doublings.

C Deck Doors – Two gangway doors, one port and the other starboard, accessing the second class entrance by way of the second class enclosed promenade.

D Deck Doors – One door starboard (between frames 95F and 97F) for unloading baggage at New York from third class open space. Two gangway doors port and two starboard (between frames 40F and 46F) into the first class entrance foyer. One door port (between frames 51A and 52A) to coal space port side of first and second class galley. One door starboard (between frames 43A and 44A) to coal space starboard side of first and second class galley.

E Deck Doors – One port (between frames 84F and 86F) by third class section B, one starboard (between frames 84F and 86F – 4ft 11in x 6ft 0in, third class section B, one port between frames 63F and 64F) to the Ash Place, one starboard (between frames 36F and 37F) to the Ash Place, one port (between frames 6F and 7F) to the Ash Place, one starboard (between frames 14A and 15A) to the Ash Place, one port (between frames 51A and 53A) to the working crew passageway, one port (between frames 78A and 80A) to the third class entrance, one starboard (between frames 78A and 80A) to the second class entrance, one port (between frames 91A and 93A) to the stores entrance, one starboard (between frames 91A and 93A) to the stores entrance.

Titanic was also fitted with a teak accommodation ladder, 21ft long by 2ft 1in wide, that could be positioned on either side of the ship in the gangway doors opposite the second class entrance on E deck. It had a folding platform and portable stanchions, rope rail, etc. The ladder extended to within 3ft 6in of the vessel's light draft, and was stowed overhead in the entrance abreast the forward second class main staircase. Its lower end was arranged so as to be raised and lowered from a block and tackle rigged from an eye affixed to the A deck overhang above.

Masts and Rigging

Titanic was rigged with two pole masts spaced about 600ft apart. These masts were made of steel, except for a 15ft teak section at the top of each mast. The tops of the masts stood approximately 205ft above the maximum load line, a height necessary to accommodate the Marconi aerial wires. This ensured that at its lowest point, the aerial would be at least 35ft above the top of the funnels and away from constant contact with the corrosive funnel gases. Unlike the masts in sailing vessels whose primary purpose was to carry sail, the primary purpose of *Titanic*'s masts was to provide support for derricks and rigging for cargo handling, and secondarily, to carry the Marconi aerial aloft.

The foremast was stepped at D deck. It had a diameter of 36in at the bottom and terminated in a 15ft teak pole mounted at the top. The foremast was about 157ft 6in in length from the forecastle deck to the teak top head. An iron ladder was mounted to the starboard side of the mast just above the bottom hound to provide access to the masthead navigational light located 102ft 6in up the mast from the forecastle deck. The crow's nest, which was attached to the masthead, consisted of a thin, sheet-steel cage provided with a portable telephone and a 15in-diameter alarm bell mounted overhead. Stanchions were fitted around the bulwarks of the cage to support a canvas weather shield. The crow's nest was accessed through an opening in the forward face of the mast on C deck; inside was a ladder mounted internally to the mast. On the aft side of the foremast on the forecastle, about 8ft above the deck, was mounted a 25in-diameter bell used when handling cargo.

The after mast, correctly termed the 'mainmast', was stepped on C deck. Like the foremast, it had a diameter of 36in at the bottom and terminated in a 15ft teak pole mounted at the top. The mainmast was 154ft 6in in length from A deck to the teak top head. *Titanic* was *not* equipped with a masthead light on her mainmast.

Titanic's rigging was divided into two categories, 'standing rigging' and 'running rigging'. Standing rigging includes lines that are fixed (attached) at both ends. The majority of this category included lines that were used to support the masts and funnels. On land these would be termed 'guy wires'; on a ship they are termed 'stays' and 'shrouds'. The term 'stay' normally refers to a supporting line of rigging that is in line with the centreline of the ship. Stays can be divided further into forestays and backstays, depending on whether they run fore or aft, respectively, from the mast or funnel. (The term 'backstay' also applied to rigging that ran both aft and outward from the mast.) The term 'shroud' traditionally refers to any supporting line rigged athwartships, or out toward the sides of the ship, although all the lines supporting the funnels were considered shrouds.

'Running rigging' includes all lines that are hauled on: that is, used to hoist or lower cargo, men, flags or anything else. By the time of *Titanic*, the running rigging on a mast was comparatively simple and consisted chiefly, but not limited to, halyards for hoisting flags, gantlines, lines for hoisting and lowering cargo and the rigging required for working the mast derricks.

The No.1 funnel was fitted with special links within the inner two shrouds on each side. These were designed for attaching falls to handle the Engelhardt collapsible lifeboats mounted on the roof of the officers' quarters deckhouse. The links were installed at different elevations on their shrouds to compensate for the sheer of the deck and the angle of the shroud to the funnel.

Lifesaving Appliances

Lifebuoys – There were forty-eight solid white lifebuoys on *Titanic*, fitted with beckets. These were of the type approved by the Board of Trade, and were placed at various locations about the weather decks. However, the ship's name was not painted on them. Per regulations, at least one lifebuoy was intended for each lifeboat.

The outside diameter of an approved lifebuoy was not less than 30in and its inside diameter not less than 17in. All lifebuoys were fitted with lines becketted and securely seized to the lifebuoy. At least two lifebuoys, one on each side of the ship, were fitted with lifelines 15 fathoms in length.

Titanic was provided with six 'Holmes Lights' for lifebuoys. These were devices attached to the lanyard that would go over with a lifebuoy in the instance of a person overboard. When the lifebuoy was thrown in the water, its weight removed a plug within a copper cylinder, igniting a light within 1 minute of reaching the water. This form of light was widely used in the English merchant service, although objection was sometimes made to the use of lights like the 'Holmes' on the grounds that the fumes given off were offensive and, in some cases, asphyxiating. Due to these objections, they were not connected rigidly to the buoy but attached to it by a short line which would let them float some distance from the person in the water. The lights were usually stowed in the area of the bridge and individually sealed until needed.

Lifebelts – 3,560 lifebelts of the latest improved overhead pattern approved by the Board of Trade were placed on board the vessel by Fosbery & Co. of London and distributed throughout the sleeping accommodation. In some third class areas the belts could also be found in metal lockers located in the alleyways. All lifebelts were to be placed so as to be readily accessible to all persons on board. (An approved lifebelt was a device which did not require inflation before use and which was capable of floating in the water for 24 hours with 15lb of iron suspended from it.)

Lifeboats – *Titanic's* lifeboats were the 'double ender' type, and were supplied with the equipment required by the Board of Trade at the time. In 1912, *Titanic's* lifeboat accommodation complied with current regulations, which specified that vessels over 10,000 tons with approved watertight subdivisions need only have sixteen lifeboats. There were twenty lifeboats carried aboard *Titanic*, divided among three types of boat. The majority were the main 30ft open boats of which there were fourteen, classified under Section A of the Board of Trade regulations. These lifeboats each hung in their own pair of Welin davits.

There were two 25ft cutters classified under Section D of the regulations. These were similar to the main lifeboats, but smaller. They also hung in their own pair of Welin davits. The two cutters, also called emergency boats, were carried near the navigation bridge, one on each side of the vessel, swung outboard of the ship's rail while at sea and ready for immediate use. In emergencies, such as persons falling overboard, these boats could be rapidly manned, gripes slipped, and lowered into the water fairly rapidly. Special men, usually two quartermasters, were selected for manning these particular boats, this number being sufficient for proper handling and navigation. As the necessity for lowering these boats usually occurred when the vessel was under way with considerable speed, it was necessary that the men managing these boats be well trained and proficient.

Lifeboats stored on the starboard side were given odd numbers, while those on the port side were given even numbers. The numbering ran from forward to aft. To provide additional lifeboat capacity, *Titanic* was equipped with four Engelhardt collapsible lifeboats which fell under Section E of the regulations. These were similar to a wooden lifeboat with small depth. When needed, canvas sides were raised to increase the boat's freeboard before it was connected to the lifeboat falls. They were intended to use the same sets of davits used by the two emergency cutters after they were sent away. With the four collapsibles added, *Titanic* actually exceeded the lifeboat capacity required of her under the antiquated regulations that were in effect at that time.

The dimensions of *Titanic*'s lifeboats and their rated capacities are listed below:

Description	Measurements	Rated Capacity
14 wood lifeboats	30ft 0in x 9ft 1in x 4ft 0in	65
1 wood cutter	25ft 2in x 7ft 2in x 3ft 0in	40
1 wood cutter	25ft 2in x 7ft 1in x 3ft 0in	40
4 Engelhardt collapsibles	27ft 5in x 8ft 0in x 3ft 0in	47
Total indicated capacity for all boats was 1,178 persons		

The wood lifeboats and cutters were all clinker design equipped with copper buoyancy tanks to meet the Board of Trade requirements. They were fitted with Murray's disengaging gear with arrangements for simultaneously freeing both ends if required. Lifelines were fitted round the gunwales of the lifeboats. The davit blocks were treble for the lifeboats and double for the cutters.

The fourteen lifeboats were stowed on hinged wood chocks on the boat deck. They were in groups of three at the forward end on both sides of the deck, and four at the after end on both sides of the deck. On each side of the boat deck forward, a cutter was arranged forward of each group of three lifeboats and fitted to lash outboard as emergency boats. They were immediately abaft the navigation bridge.

An Engelhardt collapsible lifeboat was stowed abreast each one of the cutters, one on each side of the ship. The two remaining Engelhardt collapsible lifeboats were stored on top of the officers' quarters, one on each side of No.1 funnel, abaft the navigation bridge. That location proved to be highly problematic during the evacuation.

The type of equipment stowed within a lifeboat was determined by the class of vessel. Kept within the boats were some of the gear and provisions required such as oars, sails and masts, water, etc. Oil lamps, biscuits and compasses were stored on the ship 'in some convenient place' ready for use as required. However, due to the circumstances of confusion and excitement at the time of sinking, many of the lifeboats were launched without these provisions.[10]

Titanic was fitted with sixteen sets of double-acting quadrant davits manufactured by the Welin Davit and Engineering Co., London. These Welin davits had long cast-steel arms intended to carry a boat well over the side of the ship; these could also accommodate the stowing of lifeboats one on top the other, and/or inboard of each other. Thus, the lifeboat capacity could easily have been doubled or trebled without the need for structural alterations.[11] This extra capacity was not used on *Titanic* or her sister ship *Olympic* despite existing plans for carrying thirty-two lifeboats this way.[12]

The Welin davits allowed the lowering of boats from many different athwartship positions, whether the boats were positioned directly between the davits or inboard of them. The spacing between the davit arms equalled the distance between the forward and after ends of each boat. The bases of the davit arms were cast in the shape of a quadrant and fitted with teeth which engaged with a corresponding toothed casting at the base of the davit frame. The davits were doubled up in that one frame held the forward arm of one boat and the after arm of the boat next to it; the end davit frames held a single arm. The shared-arm arrangement meant that only one boat adjacent to another could be swung out over the rail at one time.

To facilitate lowering the boats from the boat deck, there was a bitt and sheave at the heel of each davit. In each case, the falls could be taken across the deck; this allowed a number of men to speedily lift and easily control the boat and davits.

Distress Signals – *Titanic* was issued Passenger Certificate No.1415 for a foreign-going steam ship by the Board of Trade on 4 April 1912. In it they list the following items under the heading 'Equipments, Distress Signals, &c.'

> A fire hose capable of being connected with the engine, and a sufficient length to be used in any part of the ship.
> A safety valve on each boiler, out of the control of any person on board, except the master, when the steam is up.
> Compasses properly adjusted.
> Twelve blue lights, two storm signals, six small signal lights for attachment to life-buoys.
> One cannon and twenty-four cartridges or other approved means of making signs of distress.
> Twelve rockets or other approved signals for distress.

The use of a cannon 'or other approved means' for making signs of distress, as well as twelve rockets 'or other approved signals' for distress, had to do with meeting the requirements of Article 31 of the Rules of the Road under Section 434 of the Merchant Shipping Act of 1894, then in effect, which said:[13]

BY DAY —
1. A gun or other explosive signal fired at intervals of about a minute;
2. The International Code Signal of Distress indicated by NC;
3. The distant signal, consisting of a square flag, having either above or below it a ball or anything resembling a ball;
4. A continuous sounding with any fog-signal apparatus.

BY NIGHT —
1. A gun or other explosive signal fired at intervals of about a minute;
2. Flames (i.e., signal fires) on the vessel (as from a burning tar-barrel, oil-barrel, etc.);
3. Rockets or shells, throwing stars of any colour or description, fired one at a time, at short intervals;
4. A continuous sounding with any fog-signal apparatus.

For purposes of distress, *Titanic* was equipped with thirty-six socket distress signals in lieu of guns or rockets. They were manufactured by the Cotton Powder Co. Ltd, London. As described by the manufacturer, they were 'a substitute for both guns and rockets in passenger and other vessels', and Lloyd's Calendar yearly remarked, 'Socket distress signals are fired from a socket, ascend to a height of 600 to 800 feet, and then burst with the report of a gun and the stars of a rocket.' The Board of Trade had authorised these types of distress signals as far back as 1876 under Section 18 of the Merchant Shipping Act for use on board foreign-going steamships and emigrant ships in lieu of carrying guns and rockets. There were to be two sockets fitted to a vessel, one forward and one aft, on opposite sides of the ship. On *Titanic*, the forward gunmetal socket was located on the starboard side of the navigation bridge in the rail of the bulwark forward of where emergency boat No.1 was located. The aft socket was mounted to the rail of the docking bridge on the port side.

The distress signal consisted of a cylindrical shell that contained the explosive signal, a timed fuse, and a firing charge. When needed, this shell was dropped into the gunmetal socket with its wooden conical side facing up. A friction tube was then inserted as far as it would go through a hole in the centre of the shell. A lanyard was then hooked to the loop of the friction tube when in place, and the shell was fired by pulling on the lanyard horizontally, which upon tearing away the loop of the tube, fired the charge in the base of the shell projecting it upward and igniting the timed fuse. After about 6 or 7 seconds, the timed fuse would ignite the detonator in the shell causing the shell to burst with a loud report and throw out white stars.

Other signals carried on *Titanic*, though not specifically for signalling distress, included twelve blue lights (Roman Candles), two deck flares, and six lifebuoy lights. The twelve blue lights, known as 'flare-up' lights, were 'Roman Candles' which ejected a ball of fire in blue. They were used for specific signalling purposes as outlined in the regulations, for instance, signalling the need for a pilot at night. It is important to note that these blue lights were not the same as the distress rockets, which emitted stars at high altitude. The Roman Candles did not have the height of a distress rocket, and consequently were not visible at long range. They were utilised mainly for shore or harbour purposes.

The Board of Trade also required passenger ships to carry two deck flares, not for distress signals *per se*, but for use at anchor in case another ship came too close, especially in fog. *Titanic* carried Manwell-Holmes deck flares to fulfill these requirements. Deck flares were designed to burn in an open receptacle filled with water, thereby permitting their use on deck. While ships at anchor in limited visibility were required to sound a gong at regular intervals in addition to displaying riding lights as at night, fog could obscure sound as well as the light signals. Deck flares, then, could be used as emergency signals for any unaware vessel that was close aboard. They were to be capable of burning strongly for at least forty minutes, and were self-igniting in water.

Titanic also carried a quantity of green pyrotechnic lights for use as company signals. White Star Line regulations specified that two of these green pyrotechnic lights were to be burned simultaneously when it was necessary at night to identify its ships as being of the White Star Line. Being waterproof and hand-held, they were similar to the modern road flare. A number of these were burned by Fourth Officer Joseph Boxhall from Boat No.2 on the morning of 15 April.

Working Arrangement of the Ship

Compasses – *Titanic* was fitted with four main compasses. One steering compass was located in the wheelhouse and another on the navigation bridge, a third on the elevated compass platform on the raised roof over the first class lounge and a fourth located on the docking bridge aft.

Order Telegraphs – Five telegraphs were located on the navigation bridge, three on the port side and two on the starboard side. Three of the telegraphs were called 'engine order telegraphs' and were linked to indicator telegraphs down in the engine room. They all were fitted so that the starboard handle sent orders for the starboard reciprocating engine, and the port handle sent orders for the port engine. The outermost (outboard) telegraphs on each side were the main engine order telegraphs, and were mechanically linked to each other so they both showed the same commands. The third engine order telegraph, known as the emergency engine telegraph, served as a back-up in case the linkage for the main telegraphs failed. It was located immediately to port of the wheel.

The two remaining telegraphs, one immediately to starboard of the wheel and the central one to port of the wheel, were for communicating with the docking bridge on the poop deck. One was the docking/steering telegraph, the other was the docking bridge engine order relay telegraph.

Motorised Sounding Machines – *Titanic* was fitted with the latest Lord Kelvin motorised sounding machines. They were mounted on the boat deck on both sides of the officers' quarters deckhouse forward just inboard of the collapsible lifeboats mounted on the deck. They were covered with wooden cabinets when not in use. Wooden spars were mounted on pivots attached to the outboard bulwarks port and starboard just aft of the emergency cutters; these spars held the lines from the sounding machines well clear of the side of the ship when soundings were being taken.

Patent Log – *Titanic* was provided with a Walker's Patent Neptune taffrail log used for vessels of high speed. This device consisted of a rotator which was towed through the water and thus made to rotate with a velocity varying directly with the speed of the ship. The motion of the rotator was transmitted by a cord to a series of gears and dials mounted on the docking bridge at the after end of the ship. The dials registered the distance the ship travelled through the water. *Titanic's* log was deployed continuously while at sea and checked every 2 hours by the quartermaster stationed on the poop deck. The log was reset at noon every day when solar observations were taken for the ship's position.

Steering Arrangements – *Titanic* had three steering wheels. The main steering wheel was located in the wheelhouse, and this is where the ship was normally steered from while at sea. A secondary wheel was located on the navigation bridge just forward of the wheelhouse, and a third wheel was located on the docking bridge on the poop deck aft. *Titanic's* main steering wheel was manipulated just as on modern vessels in that it was turned in the direction one wanted the bow to move. However, the helm commands on all British vessels of the era were a relic of the days of tall ships. The steering commands indicated the direction the ship's tiller (or helm) was to be moved and not the direction the top of the wheel was to be turned. To 'starboard the helm', the top of the wheel was turned to port and the ship's head went to port. To 'port the helm', the top of the wheel was turned to starboard. When *Titanic's* wheel was put 'hard over', the rudder was turned a maximum of 40°.

The steering gear was situated at the after end of the shelter deck (C) under the poop. Providing power to move the steering gear was a pair of steam engines. *Titanic's* steering gear was of the well-known Wilson Pirrie type, made by Harland & Wolff, and consisted of a spring quadrant and tiller on the rudder-head worked through wheel-and-pinion and bevel gearing by either of two steam engines. Either engine sufficed for the working of the gear, the other being a standby.

The steering gear was controlled from the wheelhouse by a Brown Telemotor and from the docking bridge aft by mechanical means. The number of turns of each wheel was generally limited to four between amidships and 'hard over' in either direction. An indicator on top showed the amount of helm that was put in.

The navigation bridge wheel was typically used when the ship was under direction of a pilot or in any other situations where frequent helm orders were necessary. The navigation bridge wheel stand was connected to the telemotor by a horizontal overhead brass drive shaft that ran vertically up the forward bulkhead to a gearbox, aft along the ceiling through a plummer block, and into the Brown's Patent Telemotor located in the wheelhouse. To allow the ship to be steered directly from the wheelhouse, the shafting from the navigation bridge wheel stand was disengaged from the telemotor while simultaneously engaging the wheel in the wheelhouse by moving a clutch lever located on the change-over gearbox incorporated into the telemotor pedestal. The ship could also be manoeuvred from the docking bridge through the use of the wheel at that location; however, this wheel was considered an auxiliary wheel and for use only during docking or emergencies. The docking bridge wheel was not part of the Brown Telemotor system and was mechanically coupled to the valve linkage controlling the steering engines on the shelter deck (C) below.

Navigation Lights

Titanic carried four electric navigation lights; a masthead light mounted on the foremast, red and green sidelights under the wing cabs on the outside of the forebridge, and a stern light on the outside of the rail out on the poop. They all were equipped with dual filament bulbs and more than met the minimum requirements concerning navigation lights that were in effect at the time. Those requirements specified:[14]

Art. 2. A steam vessel when under way shall carry –

(a) On or in front of the foremast . . . a bright white light, so constructed as to show an unbroken light over an arc of the horizon of 20 points of the compass, so fixed as to throw the light 10 points [112.5°] on each side of the vessel . . . from right ahead to 2 points [22.5°] abaft the beam on either side, and of such a character as to be visible at a distance of at least 5 miles.

(b) On the starboard side a green light so constructed as to show an unbroken light over an arc of the horizon of 10 points [112.5°] of the compass, so fixed as to throw the light from right ahead to 2 points [22.5°] abaft the beam on the starboard side, and of such a character as to be visible at a distance of at least 2 miles.

(c) On the port side a red light so constructed as to show an unbroken light over an arc of the horizon of 10 points [112.5°] of the compass, so fixed as to throw the light from right ahead to 2 points [22.5°] abaft the beam on the port side, and of such a character as to be visible at a distance of at least 2 miles.

(d) The said green and red side lights shall be fitted with inboard screens projecting at least 3 feet forward from the light, so as to prevent these lights from being seen across the bow.

(e) A steam vessel when under way *may carry* [our emphasis] an additional white light similar in construction to the light mentioned in subdivision (a). These two lights shall be so placed in line with the keel that one shall be at least 15 feet higher than the other, and in such a position with reference to each other that the lower light shall be forward of the upper one. The vertical distance between these two lights shall be less than the horizontal distance.

Art. 10. A vessel which is being overtaken by another shall show from her stern to such last-mentioned vessel a white light or a flare-up light. The white light required to be shown by this Article may be fixed and carried in a lantern, but in such case the lantern shall be so constructed, fitted, and screened that it shall throw an unbroken light over an arc of the horizon of 12 points [135°] of the compass, viz., for 6 points [67.5°] from right aft on each side of the vessel, so as to be visible at a distance of at least 1 mile. Such light shall be carried as nearly as practicable on the same level as the side lights.

Titanic did not carry a mast light on her mainmast. There was nothing in *Titanic's* rigging plan that included provision for an electric mast light there, nor was there provision in the rigging plan for the hoisting of an oil masthead light on that mast,[15] something which would have been a requirement under the IMM company rules that were still in effect at the time.[16] If an oil masthead light were somehow put up there it would likely have been in violation of the rules

Coverage Arcs of Navigation Lights

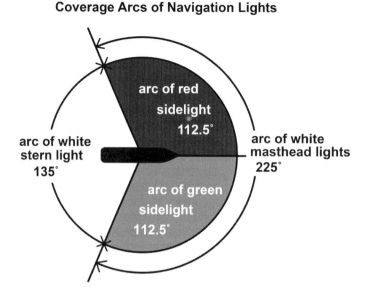

Fig. 3-12 Required arcs of coverage for masthead lights, sidelights and
stern light.

of the road which required that *if* a ship carried two masthead lights, they were to be 'similar in construction' to each other. In an answer to a question in a 1910 exam for second mate it stated that 'a second [mast light] *may be carried exactly similar to the first* [our emphasis]. They must be placed in a line with the keel, the forward light at least 15 feet lower than the after one, and the horizontal distance must be greater than the vertical.'[17]

Titanic's electric masthead light developed a total of 32 candlepower (CP) from its dual filament bulb. One candlepower is equivalent to 12.57 lumens. Therefore the filaments produced a total of 402 lumens of light intensity, about as much as a typical 40W incandescent bulb of today. Without any lens amplification, a 32 CP light would appear as a 1st magnitude star when seen at a distance of 3.4 nautical miles.[18] However, the dioptric lens in *Titanic's* masthead light amplified the brightness of the light by about twenty-five times.[19] It would appear as a 1st magnitude star at a distance of about 17 miles away on clear dark night. Since *Titanic's* masthead light was about 142ft above the waterline, it would be seen coming up over the horizon from a distance of about 22 nautical miles away by someone standing on the bridge of a vessel with a height of eye of about 45ft above the water. At that distance, it would appear as bright as a star of magnitude 1.56 coming up over the horizon, about as bright as the star Castor in the constellation Gemini.

Electrical Installation

Titanic's central generating station was situated between the wing propeller shafts in a separate watertight compartment immediately abaft the turbine engine room at the tank top level. The main generating plant consisted of four 400-kW dynamos. In total, these produced 16,000 amps at 100 volts DC – greater than the output of many large municipal stations of the era. The four sets of dynamos and their steam engines were arranged in pairs; one pair on the port side and the other pair on the starboard side, with a gangway running fore-and-aft between the two pairs.

Emergency generating sets, also steam-driven, consisted of two 30-kW dynamos and were available for use in any situation which might disrupt the supply of electricity from the main generating sets. These were situated in a recess or 'flat' in the turbine engine casing on D deck, well above the waterline. The emergency dynamos were engaged every night after sunset.[20]

Emergency lighting deriving current from the emergency dynamos was on circuits separate from those of the main lighting, placed at intervals in the passages, public rooms and compartments throughout the vessel. There were enough of these lights to provide limited illumination throughout the ship even if the main dynamos became completely inoperative.

In addition to supplying electrical power for the emergency lighting circuit, the emergency sets were of sufficient capacity to supply the Marconi apparatus, the running lights, all lights on the bridge including the navigating and chart rooms, wheelhouse, telegraphs and compasses, Morse lamps and boat winches. Additionally, the ship's gangway lamps, cargo lamps and arc lamps had alternate connections to the emergency circuit.

About 10,000 incandescent light bulbs were installed on board *Titanic*, ranging from 16 CP to 100 CP. The majority were of the Tantalum-filament type because of their reduced power consumption and ranged from 16 or 25 CP. Carbon lamps were fitted in the cargo spaces and for the portable fittings.

Communications and Signalling

Telephones – *Titanic* was fitted with numerous telephones for communicating between certain areas of the ship, some on a central exchange system and others with direct connections that did not require the services of a switchboard. Of the latter type, the following telephone connections were provided on what was termed the 'navigating group': from the wheelhouse to the reciprocating engine room, from the wheelhouse to the forecastle deck, from the wheelhouse to the crow's nest, from the wheelhouse to the docking bridge, from the chief engineer's quarters to the reciprocating engine room, from the reciprocating engine room to boiler room nos 1, 2, 3, 4, 5 and 6.

The telephones on the navigating group were supplied by Alfred Graham & Co. and were of the 'Patent Loud-Speaking Navy' design. An exception to the Navy-type telephone was in the chief engineer's quarters, where his was of the universal 'cabin' type in which calls were given by means of an interrupter as well as by voice.

The main telephone switchboard was located in a room just forward of the first class elevators on C deck, and was capable of handling fifty lines. These included the rooms of senior officers and various service rooms. A light activated on the switchboard when a call was incoming. The user on the other end was only required to talk into the mouthpiece and state the room with which he desired to be connected. The user's voice would activate a speaker in the switchboard room, where the operator would simply connect the cable from the user's line to the appropriate jack after hearing the request.

The central exchange was capable of handling calls between the following telephone stations: captain's quarters, chief engineer's quarters, chief engineer's office, purser's office, assistant purser's office, chief steward, first class smoke room bar, first class dining saloon bar, chief second class steward, chief third class steward, grocery room, chef's office, baker's shop, butcher's shop, third class galley, surgeon, first and second class surgery, second class smoke room bar, *à la carte* restaurant pantry, steward's office, Marconi operating room, enquiry office and the third class surgery.

Besides the telephones on the exchange system and those on the navigating group, there was also a separate group of circuits provided to communicate directly between the following stations without the necessity of being connected by an operator at the central switchboard: first class pantry (port side) to first and second class galley, first class pantry (port side) to baker's shop, first class pantry (port side) to butcher's shop, first class pantry (starboard side) to first and second class galley, second class pantry to baker's shop, second class pantry to first and second class galley.

Wireless Telegraphy – The wireless transmitting equipment on *Titanic* consisted of a 5-kW rotary spark-gap generating set. The guaranteed working range of the equipment was 250 miles, but usually it would work to about 400 miles or more. At night the range was often increased considerably. The aerial was supported by the two masts, 200ft high, stepped 600ft apart and had a mean height of 170ft. It was of the twin T type and was used for the dual purpose of transmitting and receiving.

There was also an emergency backup transmitter available that was powered from a set of batteries. This apparatus was one of Marconi's early 1½-kW sets and would only be needed after a failure of the complete main and emergency generators. It was not used on *Titanic*.

The receiver was the Marconi standard magnetic detector used in conjunction with their multiple tuner, providing for reception of wavelengths between 100 and 2,500 metres. The multiple tuner was calibrated to permit the instrument being set to any pre-arranged wavelength, and was provided with a change switch to permit of instantaneous change of circuit from a highly tuned condition to an 'untuned' condition (for stand-by), especially devised for picking up incoming signals of widely different wavelengths.

Morse Lamps – *Titanic* was fitted with Morse signalling lamps fitted on the roofs of the wing cabs on each side of the navigation bridge, designed to meet Board of Trade requirements for signalling to other ships at night by means of Morse code. The control switches were located on the forward bulkhead inside the wing cab enclosures. The lamp assembly was fitted to a short pole that raised it above the wing cab roof. Inside the lens was an electric lightbulb of 25 to 50 CP. Such a light source could never have been seen at any distance except for the special character of the dioptric lens which concentrated and focused the light from the small electric bulb into a much brighter and more powerful beam that radiated straight out over 360° in the horizontal plane.

Signal Flags – *Titanic* carried a full complement of flags as required for company identification, signalling, dressing ship and displaying the colours of Great Britain and the countries at which the ship would call. This included White Star house flags, Blue Ensigns, American and French ensigns, Pilot Jacks, US Mail flags and Royal Mail pennants. A full set of the flags and pennants of the 1897 version of the International Code of Signals was also carried.

Submarine Signalling – *Titanic* was fitted with a Submarine Signal Company's apparatus for receiving submarine bell signals. With this system the sound of submarine bells was received through the hull of the vessel. Submarine bells, used as fog signals, were located on lightships, at lighthouses and even a limited number of specially equipped buoys. The bells were established by Trinity House in Great Britain and the Lighthouse Service in the United States. Typically a submarine bell could be heard from a distance of 12 to 15 miles or more. By locating the direction of the sounds, the position of the vessel, when in the vicinity of the coast, could be accurately ascertained.

Arrangement of Machinery and Pumps

Nearly the entire space beneath the upper deck (E) was occupied by the steam-generating plant, coal bunkers and propelling machinery. The boiler installation and bunkers occupied six watertight compartments throughout the mid-body of the vessel over a total length of 320ft. *Titanic* was a triple-screw steamer, each wing propeller being driven by a reciprocating engine, and the centre propeller being driven by a low-pressure turbine engine. Because of the massive size of these engines, it was necessary to place the turbine in a separate compartment abaft the reciprocating engine room and separated from it by a watertight bulkhead.

Reciprocating Engines – *Titanic*'s two sets of reciprocating engines were of the four-cylinder, triple-expansion, direct-acting inverted type, balanced on the Yarrow, Schlick and Tweedy system. Steam from the boilers arrived at the high-pressure cylinder of each engine at 210lb per square inch gauge (PSIG). Steam exhausted from the high-pressure cylinder was then directed to the intermediate-pressure cylinder, where it was received at a pressure of 78 PSIG. After doing its work in the intermediate-pressure cylinders, the steam was then exhausted to the respective low-pressure cylinders, where it was received at 24 PSIG for further expansion.

After having been expanded as far as practical within the reciprocating engines' low-pressure cylinders, the steam was exhausted at a pressure of about 9lb per square inch absolute (PSIA), and then directed towards either the low-pressure turbine or directly to the main condensers.

Each reciprocating engine was designed to indicate about 15,000hp at 75 revolutions per minute (rpm), though in service the designed output was exceeded by a fairly comfortable margin.

Turbine Engine – The turbine driving the centre propeller shaft was of the Parsons low-pressure exhaust type and was designed to take steam from the two reciprocating engines at a pressure of about 9 PSIA. This steam was then expanded down to a pressure of about 1 PSIA, this expansion being accomplished in approximately six stages, with the condensing plant operating at about 28 to 28½in vacuum. The turbine was designed to develop approximately 16,000 shaft horsepower when running at 165rpm.

The turbine engine was used only when the ship was moving ahead and typically when the reciprocating engines were revolving at 50rpm or greater. It was disconnected when the ship was manoeuvring or going astern. The revolutions of the turbine engine depended entirely on the steam supplied from the reciprocating engines. The greater the revolutions of the reciprocating engines, the greater the revolutions of the turbine.

Shafting and Propellers – *Titanic's* engines were directly coupled to their respective propellers through the propeller shafts. When an engine was turning ahead or astern, the revolutions of the propeller created a thrust acting on the ship. This thrust occurred as a result of the propeller exerting a force along the shaft in the respective direction. The crankshafts of the reciprocating engines, however, revolving in simple bearings, were not designed to absorb this thrust. To take up this thrust and convey it to the hull, thrust blocks were introduced just abaft the reciprocating engines. These served to transmit the fore-and-aft thrust generated by the propeller to the ship's structure. The thrust blocks were situated in the turbine engine room, just aft of the watertight bulkhead dividing this compartment from the reciprocating engine room.

The line of shafting driving *Titanic's* central propeller from the turbine engine was directly coupled to the turbine at the end of the aft spindle of the turbine rotor. There was no reduction gearing.

Each tailshaft exited the ship through an assembly known as a 'stern tube'. The stern tube served as a bearing to support the weight of the propeller and tailshaft and as a gland around the shaft to prevent water from entering the hull.

Titanic's wing propellers each had three manganese-bronze blades fastened onto a cast-steel boss by special high-strength studs and nuts. The centre propeller was cast of manganese bronze and was of solid construction. An engineering notebook recently uncovered from Harland & Wolff indicates that *Titanic's* massive wing propellers had a diameter of 23ft 6in, a pitch of 35ft 0in, and a surface area of 160sq.ft. *Titanic's* centre propeller shows up in the engineering notebook as having three blades with a diameter of 17ft, a pitch of 14ft 6in, and a surface area of 120sq.ft.[21] *Titanic's* centre propeller does not appear in any known photograph, and is hidden from view under the mud at the wreck site. It should be noted that *Olympic's* four-bladed centre propeller was replaced with a three-bladed one of 17ft diameter and pitch of 14ft 6in in March 1913. It wasn't until 1919 that they went back to a four-bladed centre propeller for *Olympic*.

Boilers – Steam was generated by a plant comprised of twenty-four double-ended and five single-ended boilers, designed for a working pressure of 215lb PSIG, maintained under natural-draft conditions. The aftermost, or No.1, boiler room contained the five single-ended boilers, while boiler rooms 2, 3, 4 and 5 each contained five double-ended boilers, and the foremost, No.6 boiler room, contained four double-ended boilers. The five single-ended boilers in No.1 boiler room were arranged for running the auxiliary machinery when in port, including the main generator sets, as well as being provided with connections to the main steam supply lines.

Each double-ended boiler was 15ft 9in in diameter, 20ft long, and contained six furnaces, three to a face. The single-ended boilers were of the same diameter as the double-ended but only 11ft 9in long and contained three furnaces. This resulted in a total of 159 furnaces.

The upper portions of the coal bunkers consisted of 'tween deck space on each side of the ship between the middle (F) and lower (G) decks. Coal was first shipped into these spaces through coal chutes accessed from the bunker doors located along the hull at the middle deck level. From there, the coal was distributed by wheelbarrows and shovels into cross-bunkers which extended the full width of the vessel in each boiler room. Rectangular openings with counterbalanced vertically-sliding doors were let into the cross-bunker end bulkheads at the stokehold level immediately opposite each trio of furnaces. From these doors, the trimmers working as coal passers loaded wheelbarrows of coal, which they then deposited within easy reach of the firemen tending the furnaces. This arrangement reduced the amount of handling of the fuel for each boiler to a minimum. A further advantage of this bunker arrangement was that no watertight doors were required in the bunker ends.

Total capacity within the bunkers surrounding the boiler rooms was 6,611 tons.[22] A further supply of 1,092 tons could be stowed in the No.3 hold, just forward of No.6 boiler room if needed. Access into this compartment from the boiler rooms was gained through two manually operated, vertically hinged watertight doors in the forward bulkhead within the vestibule between the firemen's tunnel and the door through the watertight bulkhead into No.6 boiler room.

The steam supply was carried from the boilers to the reciprocating engines by two main steam pipes. Branch lines were carried out from the various boilers to these pipes. Each main steam line gradually increased in diameter as it approached the forward bulkhead of the reciprocating engine room. On the forward side of the bulkhead separating the reciprocating engine room and No.1 boiler room, on each main pipeline, was a Cockburn quick-acting balanced emergency stop valve, which could be closed in a few seconds in case of rupture of the line. Cross-connections were fitted between the mains in each boiler room, with stop valves so arranged that any section of the main, with the boilers connected to it, could be cut out. This allowed for shutting down any of the boilers without affecting the remainder of the steam supply to the main. Additionally, portions of each main steam line could be isolated from the remainder by shut-off valves fitted into each line at three of the watertight bulkheads. On the after side of the reciprocating engine room bulkhead were the main bulkhead stop valves, 24in in diameter. Each of these valves was provided with a large separator which was automatically drained by steam traps. A cross-connection was provided at this stage as well, which allowed either range of piping to be used for either or both engines.

Lastly, located at the inboard side of the high-pressure valve chest of each reciprocating engine were the main stop valves, which were operated by hand wheels and screws from the starting and manoeuvring platform situated in the centre of the reciprocating engine room at deck level.

A separate range of piping was fitted to supply steam for working the engines of the main electric generating sets, and to supply steam to the ship's auxiliary machinery. This range was connected to the five single-ended boilers in boiler room No.1 as well as to two boilers each in boiler room No.2 and No.4. Further redundancy was added in the form of a cross-connection between the main and auxiliary pipes in the reciprocating engine room so that the auxiliaries could be worked from any boiler in the ship. Steam pipes also were led separately from boiler room nos 2, 3 and 5 above the watertight bulkheads and overhead along the working passage on the upper deck (E) to the emergency electric generating sets located on saloon deck (D) in the turbine engine room casing. Pipes were also led from this steam supply to the pumps which were connected to the bilges throughout the ship.

Funnels – *Titanic* had four funnels. The first three funnels were utilised to vent combustion gases from the boilers. The fourth funnel, a 'dummy funnel', was designed to function primarily as a ventilator.

Each funnel had an elliptical cross-section that measured 24ft 6in x 19ft externally, with an aft rake of 2in per ft, or about 80°. Their average height above the level of the furnace bars (firebars) was 150ft and they reached approximately 70–74ft above the boat deck.

Each funnel was fitted with a ladder and platform on the forward side to provide access to the whistles. Also fitted to the exteriors of the funnels were the boiler steam escape pipes both fore and aft. The steam escape pipes were not led to the top of the funnel. The steam supply pipes for the whistles were mounted separately on the forward side of the funnels, running parallel and forward of the steam escape pipes. The whistles on the No.3 and No.4 funnels were non-operational, although visual continuity was upheld by fitting these funnels with access ladders, platforms and non-functional steam supply pipes.

Condensing Plant and Pumps – The condensing plant was designed to operate at about 28 to 28½in vacuum at a barometric pressure of 30in Hg and a circulating water temperature of 55° to 60°F. The two main condensers were fitted on opposite sides of the turbine. There were two main circulating pumps located on each side of the turbine engine room for each main condenser. There was also an auxiliary condenser and circulating pump located on the starboard side of the reciprocating engine room for dealing with the exhaust steam from all of the auxiliary engines, including those of the main generating sets, while the vessel was in port.

There were also four main air pumps that discharged the condensate removed from the condensers into two feed tanks, one placed on each side of the ship just abaft the bulkhead dividing the engine rooms. From the feed tanks, the water drained into two Weir control tanks, one on each side of the reciprocating engine room. The water was drawn from the control tanks by four Weir single cylinder, vertical direct-acting hotwell pumps located in pairs on each side of the ship immediately adjacent to the control tanks. From the hotwell pumps, the feedwater was discharged through the main feed filters located against the forward bulkhead of the reciprocating engine room, two on each side of the ship.

From the feed filters, the water flowed to a Weir 'Uniflux' horizontal-surface feedwater heater located on the forward transverse bulkhead on the starboard side of the reciprocating engine room. Here the feedwater, still under the pressure from the hotwell pumps, flowed through the tubes of the heater which received exhaust steam at 5 PSIA from the four steam engines that ran the ship's electric dynamos. This heat exchange process raised the feedwater temperature from about 70° F to 140° F.

Still under the pressure from the hotwell pumps, the feedwater leaving the surface heater flowed upward to a Weir's direct contact heater located high up at the level of D deck at the ship's centreline on the forward bulkhead of the reciprocating engine room. Here the feedwater fell in droplets through a cloud of exhaust steam that was admitted from the ship's many auxiliary engines that ran various pumps and the refrigeration equipment. This simultaneously raised the temperature of the feedwater from 140° F to 230° F while condensing the incoming exhaust steam from the auxiliary engines which added to the feed supply.

From the direct contact heater, the feedwater flowed down by gravity to four pairs of Weir's main feed pumps, two pairs being located at floor level on both sides of the forward end of the reciprocating engine room. The feed pumps supplied boiler feedwater through a set of feed mains to the various boiler rooms at a pressure greater than the working pressure of the boilers. These pumps were connected to the feed mains through valve chests which allowed any pump to feed any feedwater main. From there, the water was manually admitted to the boilers, the level being carefully maintained to keep the boiler tubes and furnaces submerged while maintaining the correct volume of space above the surface of the water for the production of steam.

Bilge Suctions and Pumping Arrangement – The general arrangement of piping was designed so that it was possible to pump from any flooded compartment by two independent systems of 10in mains having cross-connections between them. These were controlled from above by rods and wheels led to the level of the bulkhead deck. By these it was possible to isolate any flooded space, together with any suctions in it.

The following bilge suctions were provided for dealing with water above the double bottom:

No.1 hold – two 3½in suctions
No.2 hold – two 3½in and two 3in suctions
No.3 hold – two 3½in and two 3in suctions
No.6 boiler room: three 3½in, one 4½in and two 3in suctions
No.5 boiler room: three 3½in, one 5in and two 3in suctions
No.4 boiler room: three 3½in, one 4½in and two 3in suctions
No.3 boiler room: three 3½in, one 5in and two 3in suctions
No.2 boiler room: three 3½in, one 5in and two 3in suctions
No.1 boiler room: two 3½in, one 5in and two 3in suctions
Reciprocating engine room: two 3½in, six 3in, two 18in and two 5in suctions
Turbine engine room: two 3½in, three 3in, two 18in, two 5in and one 4in suctions
Electric engine room: four 3½in suctions
In the store rooms above the electric engine room there was one 3in suction
In the forward tunnel compartment there were two 3½in suctions
In the watertight flat over the tunnel compartment there were two 3in suctions
In the tunnel after compartment there were two 3½in suctions
In the watertight flat over the tunnel after compartment there were two 3in suctions

The valves in connection with the forward bilge and ballast suctions were placed in the firemen's tunnel, the watertight pipe tunnel extending from No.6 boiler room to the after end of No.1 hold. In this tunnel, in addition to two 3in bilge suctions, one at each end, there was a special 3½in suction with valve rod that led up to G deck above the load line, so as always to be accessible should the tunnel be flooded accidentally.

The ship was also fitted with five ballast and bilge pumps, each capable of discharging 250 tons of water per hour, and three bilge pumps, each of 150 tons per hour capacity. One ash ejector pump was placed in each of the large boiler compartments to work the ash ejectors, and to circulate or feed the boilers as required. This pump was also connected to the bilges except in the case of the three boiler rooms where three of the ballast and bilge pumps were placed. The pumps in each case had direct bilge suctions as well as a connection to the main bilge pipe, so that each boiler room might be independent.

The remainder of the auxiliary pumps were placed in the reciprocating and turbine engine rooms. Two ballast pumps were placed in the reciprocating engine room, with large suctions from the bilges direct and from the bilge main. Two bilge pumps were also arranged to draw from bilges. One bilge pump was placed in the turbine room and one of the hot salt-water pumps had a connection from the bilge main pipe for use in an emergency. A 10in main ballast pipe was carried fore and aft through the ship with separate connections to each tank, and with filling pipes from the sea connected at intervals for trimming purposes. The five ballast pumps were arranged to draw from this pipe. A double line of bilge main piping was fitted forward of No.5 boiler room and aft of No.1 boiler room.

Notes

1 Sanderson, BI 19589–19597.

2 A more comprehensive description of the ship can be found in the two-volume book by Bruce Beveridge, Scott Andrews, Steve Hall and Daniel Klistorner, *Titanic: The Ship Magnificent*, History Press, 2008. [*TTSM*]

3 British Wreck Commission Report on the Loss of the SS *Titanic*, 30 July 1912.

4 These eight shares were held by Messrs E.C. Grenfell, Vivian H. Smith, W.S.M. Burns, James Gray, J. Bruce Ismay, H.A. Sanderson, A. Kerr and the Right Hon. Lord Pirrie.

5 *TTSM*, Ch.1.

6 The date commonly referred to in most publications and in Harland & Wolff's own 'List of Particulars' is 31 March 1909; however, 22 March 1909 is the date recorded in the Harland & Wolff records held by the Public Records Office of Northern Ireland, document number D2805/Ship/3.

7 From a series of floodable-length curves derived by Hackett and Bedford and published in their landmark article, 'The Sinking of S.S. TITANIC - Investigated by Modern Techniques', 1997 RINA Transactions.

8 Philip Sims, 'Comparative Naval Architecture of Passenger Ships', *Transactions of the Society of Naval Architects and Marine Engineers (SNAME)*, Vol.111, 2003.

9 The ship also had two peak ballast tanks, one fore the other aft, that were used for trimming the ship. The capacity of the forepeak tank was 190 tons, and the aft peak tank was 115 tons. They were not considered part of the double bottom.

10 Oil lamps for the fourteen main boats were brought out by the ship's lamp trimmer after a number of them had already been launched. The lamps intended for the emergency cutters were lit every night at 6:00p.m. and were stowed in the wheelhouse. It must also be remembered that there were no ship-wide lifeboat drills for the crew, nor was there any means by which the bridge could easily communicate with the crews at the individual boats short of detailing someone to go to each boat to relay instructions.

11 AI p.958.

12 Carlisle, BI 21279.

13 A footnote to the Rules of the Road remarked, 'The master of a vessel who displays, or allows anybody under his authority to display, the signals when his vessel is not in distress, will be liable to pay compensation for any labour undertaken, risk incurred, or loss sustained in consequence of the signals having been taken for signals of distress.'

14 From 'The Regulations For Preventing Collisions At Sea', as printed in *Nicholls's Seamanship and Viva Voce Guide*, 4th Edition, London, August 1910.

15 Some people have tried to argue that an oil mast light was carried on *Titanic*'s mainmast based on a very popular account written by passenger Elizabeth Shutes. In it she wrote: 'A sea, calm as a pond, kept our boat steady, and now that mammoth ship is fast, fast disappearing. Only one tiny light is left – a powerless little spark, a lantern fastened to the mast. Fascinated, I watched that black outline until the end.' This description does not come close to describing a masthead light, nor does it say how high up the mast it was, or for that matter, which mast it was mounted on. It could very well have been a small oil lantern that was hoisted up on one of the halyards used for hoisting arc lamps to the back stay. We just don't know. There is also a pencil sketch in the collection of Walter Lord that was drawn by *Titanic*'s Steward Leo James Hyland showing *Titanic* trimmed down by the head, lifeboats being launched and in the water, the firing of one of her socket signals, and steam blowing off from the three forward funnels. In that sketch, drawn well after the event took place, Hyland also drew what looks like a glare of light on both the foremast and mainmast of equal intensity where mast lights would be. And this too has been used to argue that *Titanic* carried two mast lights.

16 IMM Company, 'Ships' Rules and Uniform Regulations', issued 1 July 1907, **Rule 20**. Navigation Lights: ' … At all times one of the two mast-head lights carried must be oil; where only one is carried, it may be electric light, except under the foregoing circumstances.' Those foregoing circumstances included navigating channel crossings and when in conditions of fog or haze. Under those circumstances, only oil navigation lights were to be used. Clearly, there was a distrust in the reliability of electric lights. By the time of *Olympic* and *Titanic*, and the use of dual filament electric lights, this IMM rule was obsolete. The reason that an electric mast light was not installed on the mainmasts of *Olympic* and *Titanic* at that time seems to be that they were not allowed to do so

because of an antiquated set of company rules that were still in effect. It also makes little sense to put up a relatively dim oil light on the mainmast because it would defeat the purpose of using two lights for ranging if only one of them could be seen from far off. An oil lamp may typically produce about 12 CP with a ¾in wick compared to the 32 CP of a dual-filament electric light. At 40 per cent the light intensity, the range of an oil lamp would be reduced to 60 per cent of that of an electric lamp, a loss of 1 stellar magnitude in brightness. This IMM rule was obviously changed by the time the *Britannic* was built since an electric masthead light for the mainmast was included in her rigging plans even before she was converted to a hospital ship. (See Simon Mills, *Hostage to Fortune*, Wordsmith Publishing, 2002.)

[17] From the *Requirements for Second Mate*, London, August 1910, *Seamanship for Ordinary Certificate*, 'The Regulations for Preventing Collisions at Sea'. The term 'exactly similar' does not mean identical but it does imply that the lights would appear as if they were the same. For example, a light with 32 CP filaments and an 8in-high lens, and another with 64 CP filaments and a 4in-high lens, would both appear the same when viewed from far off.

[18] A single candle has the same brightness as a star of magnitude 1 when seen at a distance of 1,098 metres, or 3,602ft. (See, http://mysite.verizon.net/michaelcapobianco/PhotometryStarlight.htm.) Since brightness falls off as the square of the distance, something that is thirty-two times as bright as a single candle should be seen at a distance of 5.66 (the square-root of 32) times further away and appear just as bright. Therefore, without any lens amplification, a 32 CP light would appear as a 1st magnitude star when seen at a distance of about 20,400ft (3.4 nautical miles) on a clear dark night.

[19] Samuel Halpern, 'Titanic's Masthead Light', GLTS, www.glts.org/articles/halpern/masthead_light.html, 2008.

[20] Wilding, BI 19827.

[21] Mark Chirnside, 'Mystery of Titanic's Central Propeller', Titanic International Society's journal *Voyage 63*, spring 2008.

[22] Based on 44 cu.ft per ton of coal.

A view of the partially plated tank top and wing tank floors of *Olympic*, looking aft, taken on 2 July 1909. *Titanic* is in the background. Note the large hydraulic riveting machine suspended from overhead. (*The Engineer*/Beveridge & Hall)

Olympic and *Titanic*, August 1910. As clearly seen, work on both hulls is well advanced. *Olympic's* hull would soon be painted white for her launch; not so for *Titanic* though, she remained in her black primer paint for launch. (*The Engineer*/Beveridge & Hall)

Launch day, 31 May 1911. Crowds start gathering around the side of the slip and any other vantage point to watch the launch. For the privileged and invited dignitaries, a spectators' platform was available from which to observe *Titanic*'s launch. (Period Picture Card/R. Terrell–Wright)

The ship's stern seen here sliding down the ways in the Lagan River. The hull reached a speed of 12½ knots before being brought to a halt via wire hawser cables connected to anchors embedded in the river and drag chains. (Period Picture Card/Beveridge & Hall)

From her first movement on the slip until she was brought to a standstill, only 62 seconds had passed. Workmen, on station around the river in small craft, would soon move in and release the river anchor cables and drags from the now afloat hull. (Period Picture Card/R. Terrell-Wright)

Titanic, as seen from the West Twin Wharf; with all launch cables and hawsers detached. *Titanic* is taken in tow by the yard tug *Hercules* and other tugs provided by the Liverpool firm, Alexandra Towing Company. (Period Picture Card/Beveridge & Hall)

Titanic berthed alongside the Fitting-Out Wharf, June 1911. In the weeks following, all the ship's heavy machinery will be lifted and lowered into the hull by the yard's floating crane. These would include her engine components and boilers. (Period Picture Card/Ray Lepien)

By early September 1911, both masts have been fitted; work is now progressing on the alteration of the ship's B deck. This deck, once an open promenade, is now turned over for provision of additional staterooms and later inclusion of the Café Parisien. (Period Picture Card/R. Terrell-Wright)

Titanic at the Fitting-Out Wharf in January 1912. Now, with all her funnels fitted, work continues apace with the internal fitting out of the ship. Work on painting the funnels is proceeding. Note the cable-suspended platforms on the third and fourth funnels. (Period Picture Card/Daniel Klistorner)

Titanic in dry-dock, mid-February 1912. She entered the dock on Saturday 3 February 1912 where the painting of her hull started in earnest. The recently fitted lifeboats can be seen hanging beneath the Welin davits. (Period Picture Card/Beveridge & Hall)

Forced to return back to Belfast for repairs, *Olympic* is seen entering dry-dock on 2 March 1912. *Titanic* can be seen alongside the Fitting-Out Wharf. This would be the last time the sisters would be together. (R. Terrell-Wright/Period Picture Card)

Titanic departing Belfast Lough on her sea trials, 2 April 1912. On successful completion of her trials, the Board of Trade's representative, Francis Carruthers, issued a passenger service certificate, 'good for one year'. (Period Picture Card/Ioannis Georgiou)

4

PASSENGERS AND CREW/ LOST AND SAVED

Lester J. Mitcham

When *Titanic* left Queenstown, there were 1,317 passengers and 891 crew on board. The breakdown of passenger and crew numbers is shown in the following tables. Included in the passenger numbers are the nine members of the Guarantee Group from Harland & Wolff and the eight members of the ship's orchestra. Included in the Victualling Department crew numbers are the two Marconi operators, sixty-nine restaurant staff, and the five mail clerks.

Passengers							
	Men		Women		Children		Total
First Class	176		143		5		324
Second Class	167		95		22		284
Third Class	452		181		76		709
Total Number of Passengers	795		419		103		1,317
	Lost	Saved	Lost	Saved	Lost	Saved	Lost	Saved
First Class	118	58	4	139	1	4	123	201
Second Class	154	13	12	83	0	22	166	118
Third Class	392	60	90	91	46	30	528	181
Number Lost/Saved	664	131	106	313	47	56	817	500

Crew					
	Men		Women		Total
Deck Department	66		---		66
Engine Department	325		---		325
Victualling Department	477		23		500
Total Number of Crew	868		23		891
	Lost	Saved	Lost	Saved	Lost	Saved
Deck Department	23	43	---	---	23	43
Engine Department	253	72	---	---	253	72
Victualling Department	400	77	3	20	403	97
Number Lost/Saved	676	192	3	20	679	212

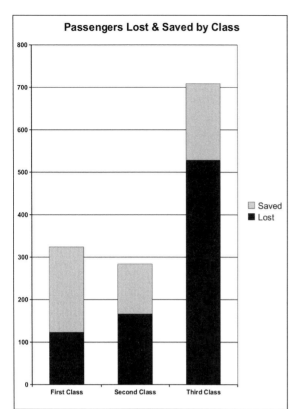

Fig. 4-1 Passengers lost and saved.

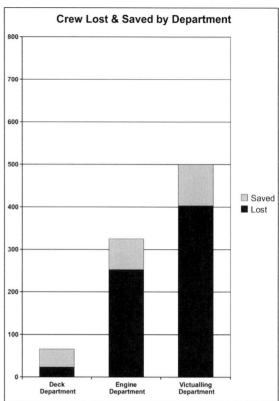

Fig. 4-2 Crew lost and saved.

Passengers and Crew							
	Men		Women		Children		Total
Total Number of Passengers and Crew	1,663		442		103		2,208
	Lost	Saved	Lost	Saved	Lost	Saved	Lost	Saved
Number Lost/Saved	1,340	323	109	333	47	56	1,496	712

These numbers are derived from a study of copies of original *Titanic* documentation. The main source documents are those held by the National Archives (formally known as the Public Record Office (PRO)) at Kew in England.

Passenger numbers are established by counting the names, which can then be broken down into lost and saved. While the numbers vary both between what was concluded by the 1912 inquiries and what some modern researchers conclude, the number of names is not in doubt. This means that because the inquiries have related lists their numbers can be name count corrected.

The best-known Passenger List is the list of May 1912 published by Walter Lord in: *A Night to Remember.*[1] The two main lists of deceased passengers are the British National Archive documents BT 100/260 and MT 9/920/201. For saved passengers most of the names are contained in the surviving pages of the *Titanic-Carpathia* lists which are online under *Carpathia*

Fig. 4-3 Total passengers and crew lost and saved.

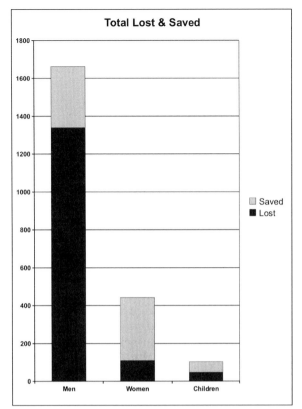

at www.ellisisland.org. Most of these pages can also be viewed online at: www.archives.gov/research/immigration/titanic-survivors-to-ny.html. The Contract Passenger Ticket List which is held by the US National Archives and Records Administration in New York is useful for confirming the number of passengers.

Crew numbers come from the Particulars of Engagement, which can be viewed online at: www.encyclopedia-titanica.org. Under Crew List look at: Southampton, Crew: Agreement and Account of Crew (PRO Ref: BT100/259):

1. Deck Department
2. Engine Department – Engineers / Misc
3. Engine Department – Book 1
4. Engine Department – Book 2
5. Engine Department – Book 3
6. Victualling Department – First Class
7. Victualling Department – Second Class
8. Victualling Department – Third Class / Galley
9. Victualling Department – *à la carte* Restaurant (Supplement: Address List)
Supplement (Part I.): 'Seamen who have failed to join or otherwise left the ship'
Supplement (Part III): 'Substitutes Engaged'

The five mail clerks need to be added as they did not sign the Particulars of Engagement.

Crew lost and saved numbers are confirmed by National Archive documents BT 100/259, BT 100/260 and MT 9/920C. The deceased crew were also assigned numbers by the *Titanic* Relief Fund. As with the passengers the crew inquiry numbers can be name count corrected.

The Passenger and Crew lists, Appendices A to F, have been compiled using the lists and biographies at: www.encyclopedia-titanica.org, Craig Stringer's *Titanic People*, Hermann Söldner's *Passenger and Crew List*, a number of other published lists and sundry other information. If compared to names that are published elsewhere, readers will notice a difference in the spelling of some of the names in the appended lists. In a few cases this is due to how names have been Anglicised. For example, the spelling of some of the Syrian passengers' names in Appendix C are based on relatively recent publications that address some name discrepancies and inaccuracies that have occurred because of the way those names have been transliterated (and translated).[2] Other cases, such as the correct spelling of the name of Saloon Watchman James Johnstone, who testified before the British inquiry, was discovered after studying his signature as it appears in a number of documents. (The British inquiry has him listed as Johnson, but his signature clearly shows that his name was Johnstone.)

In all cases, I have tried to be as accurate as possible. Any errors in a person's name, or in the capacity in which a crewmember was engaged, are the result of an inability to resolve conflicting information.

Notes

[1]   That list has four passengers [one first class and three third class] each listed by two names. It does not list the six members of the nine-man Harland & Wolff Guarantee Group who travelled on second class tickets, nor does it list the eight bandsmen who travelled on a second class ticket. One third class lady passenger is missing from the list, while a man who was not on board remains on the list as a third class passenger. (Those using the illustrated edition need to re-add the name of first class passenger Frank Carlson.) Many on the list are incorrectly shown as lost when they were saved, or as saved when they were lost.

[2]   Leila Salloum Elias, 'The impact of the sinking of the *Titanic* on the New York Syrian community of 1912: the Syrians respond.' http://findarticles.com/p/articles/mi_m2501/isv1-2_27/ai_ n15694707/?tag=content;col1.

ACCOUNT OF THE SHIP'S JOURNEY ACROSS THE ATLANTIC

Samuel Halpern

Sailing Orders

Commanders of White Star Line vessels were not given any special 'sailing orders' before the commencement of a voyage.[1] However, there was the following requirement written in the International Mercantile Marine's (IMM) book of *Ship's Rules and Uniform Regulations* (Issue 1 July 1907) that was in effect at the time:

> **113. Transatlantic Tracks**. – Commanders are required to navigate their vessels as closely as possible on the Transatlantic routes adopted by the principal Atlantic Passenger Lines.

Deviating from these routes was permitted if they were done in the interests of safety. Rule 101 specifically instructed commanders that they must 'run no risk which might by any possibility result in accident to their ships.' Furthermore, all White Star Line commanders were sent a letter from the company when they were appointed to command ships which told them:[2]

> You are to dismiss all ideas of competitive passages with other vessels and to concentrate your attention upon a cautious, prudent and ever watchful system of navigation, which shall lose time or suffer any other temporary inconvenience rather than incur the slightest risk which can be avoided.

The Route Followed and Speed of the Ship

Titanic began her maiden voyage to New York on Wednesday 10 April 1912. She departed the pier at Southampton at about 12.15p.m. and proceeded across the English Channel to Cherbourg carrying 68rpm on her reciprocating engines.[3] She arrived at Cherbourg that same evening to take on additional passengers and mails. She then departed Cherbourg for Queenstown, arriving there before noon the following morning to take on additional passengers and mails.

Titanic raised anchor and departed Queenstown harbour early Thursday afternoon, 11 April 1912, to begin her maiden voyage crossing of the Atlantic Ocean. After taking departure off the Daunt's Rock light vessel at 2.20p.m. GMT, *Titanic* proceeded at 70rpm along a path that hugged the southern coast of Ireland toward Fastnet Light.[4] From there, she would follow the Great Circle track westbound to a location in the middle of the North Atlantic referred to as 'the corner' at 42° N, 47° W,[5] the turning point for westbound steamers heading for the east coast of North America for that time of the year. She would then follow a rhumb line track taking her just south of the Nantucket Shoals light vessel,[6] and from there to the Ambrose Channel light vessel marking the arrival point and entrance to New York harbour.[7]

The key points along the planned route of travel are listed below:

> Departure off Daunt's Rock light vessel – 51° 43' N, 08° 16' W.
> Turning point off the Old Head of Kinsale[8] – 51° 33' N, 08° 32' W.
> Turning point off Fastnet Light – 51° 23' N, 09° 36' W.
> Turning point at the corner – 42° N, 47° W.
> Turning point south of the Nantucket Shoals light vessel[9] – 40° 35' N, 69° 36.5' W.
> Arrival off Ambrose Channel light vessel[10] – 40° 28' N, 73° 50' W.

As we all know, *Titanic* never completed her maiden voyage. On the night of 14 April 1912, *Titanic* struck an iceberg at 11.40p.m. Apparent Time Ship (ATS) and sank just 2 hours and 40 minutes later. By making use of the daily reported mileage runs for the first three days out, as well as the planned route of travel, we are able to retrace the route of *Titanic* from the time she left Queenstown to the time of collision and foundering.

What we know about the distances covered for the first three days of *Titanic*'s Atlantic crossing comes from a memorandum offered in evidence at the American inquiry by *Titanic*'s Third Officer Herbert Pitman and confirmed by other sources.[11] These distances are shown in the table below:

Day	Time Interval	Distance Run
1	From 2.20p.m. GMT 11 April to local apparent noon 12 April	484 nautical miles
2	From noon 12 April to local apparent noon 13 April	519 nautical miles
3	From noon 13 April to local apparent noon 14 April	546 nautical miles

The total distance run from departure from the Daunt's Rock light vessel at 2.20p.m. GMT 11 April to local apparent noon 14 April was 1,549 nautical miles. By using the distance travelled per day along the known route of travel we can derive an estimate of the position of the ship at local apparent noon for 12, 13 and 14 April.

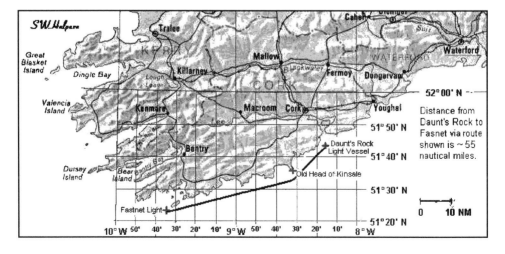

Fig. 5-1 Track of *Titanic* from Daunt's Rock to Fastnet Light.

For the first day we considered the route taken from the Daunt's Rock light vessel to Fastnet Light, and from there along the great circle route to local apparent noon on 12 April. The route from Daunt's Rock to Fastnet consisted of two segments. The first was from the Daunt's Rock light vessel to a turning point about 3 miles off of the Old Head of Kinsale Lighthouse, a distance of about 14 nautical miles. The second segment was from that turning point to a point off Fastnet Light which was located on a rock off the south-west coast of Ireland, a distance of about 41 nautical miles. The total distance taken along this part of the route is about 55 nautical miles.[12] This is shown in Fig. 5-1.

From Fastnet Light to *Titanic*'s noontime position for 12 April is a remaining distance of 429 nautical miles along the great circle route.[13] To get to the noontime position for 13 April we continue along the route to a reported position at 49° 45'N, 23° 38'W for 7 00p.m. GMT that was sent in a wireless message from *Titanic* to *La Touraine* at 7.45p.m. GMT on 12 April, a distance of 114 nautical miles from her noontime position. From that reported position, we continue a distance of about 405 nautical miles to a point on the great circle track to reach the position for noon 13 April. The total distance travelled from noon 12 April to noon 13 April is 519 nautical miles as reported.

To get to the noontime position for 14 April, we travel a distance of 546 miles from the 13 April noontime position to a point on a line of bearing extending 060.6° True and 126 nautical miles from the corner point.[14]

A plot of the intended overall transatlantic route of *Titanic* from the Daunt's Rock light vessel to the Ambrose Channel light vessel is shown in Fig. 5-2 along with her estimated noontime positions for 12, 13 and 14 April. For completeness, the location of the wreck site is also indicated as well as the 7p.m. GMT position reported to *La Touraine* on 12 April.[15]

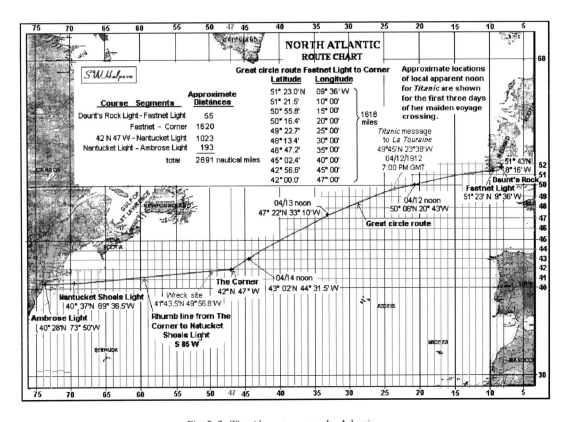

Fig. 5-2 *Titanic*'s route across the Atlantic.

The table below shows times and the approximate coordinates of *Titanic* for each day's run starting from departure off Daunt's Rock light vessel on 11 April, to local apparent noon on 14 April.

Location	Coordinates	GMT at location
Departure Daunt's Rock 11 April	51° 43' N, 08° 16' W	2.20p.m.
Local Apparent Noon 12 April	50° 06' N, 20° 43' W	1.24p.m.
Local Apparent Noon 13 April	47° 22' N, 33° 10' W	2.13p.m.
Local Apparent Noon 14 April	43° 02' N, 44° 31' W	2.58p.m.

The interval of time between each day's run is simply the difference between the time at one location on one day to the time at the next location the following day taken from the table above. These intervals are shown in the table below:[16]

Day's Run	Time Interval
Daunt's Rock to Noon 12 April	23 hours 04 minutes (23.07 hours)
Noon 12 April to Noon 13 April	24 hours 49 minutes (24.82 hours)
Noon 13 April to Noon 14 April	24 hours 45 minutes (24.75 hours)

The average speed made good for each day's run was derived by dividing the distance run by the time interval of the run. The results are shown in the following table:

Day's Run	Average Speed Made Good[17]
Daunt's Rock to Noon 12 April	484/23.07 = 20.98 knots
Noon April 12 to Noon 13 April	519/24.82 = 20.91 knots
Noon April 13 to Noon 14 April	546/24.75 = 22.06 knots

It should be noted that the ship's speed made good is not necessarily the same as the ship's speed through the water. Despite an increase in engine revolutions from 70rpm on Thursday to 72rpm on Friday, and then to 75rpm on Saturday,[18] the speed made good did not necessarily increase by the same proportion because the ship was affected by the North Atlantic Drift which varied in intensity along the route of travel. This can be seen in modern-day satellite data that measures the drift of oceanic currents. Despite the reported increase in revolutions on her second day out from Queenstown from 70rpm to 72rpm, the ship averaged about the same speed made good for the second day as she did on the first day. An increase of a little more than 1 knot in her speed made good can be seen for the third day out when the revolutions were raised from 72rpm to 75rpm. It should also be noted that a further increase in revolutions was carried out Sunday evening about 7p.m. ship's time when additional boilers were put on line.[19] It was also reported that the ship was averaging about 22½ knots through the water less than 2 hours before the accident happened.[20]

   With a remaining distance of 126 nautical miles from noon to the corner on 14 April, *Titanic* would have travelled a total distance of 1,675 miles from Daunt's Rock when she passed close to the corner point that same evening. This compares well to the 1,677, 1,674 and 1,676 nautical miles to the corner travelled by *Titanic's* sister ship *Olympic* during her first three westward crossings, respectively, over the same route the year before. *Titanic* was indeed following the agreed upon route just as her sister ship had done the year before in accordance with IMM Rule No.113.

At 5.50p.m. ATS, *Titanic's* course was changed from S 85° W (265°) to N 71° W (289°) as seen on the steering compass in the wheelhouse.[21] The change in compass heading was a change of 24° to starboard. From this information it seems that the intended change in the ship's heading at 5.50p.m. was to put the ship on a rhumb line course close to 265° True taking it to a point south of the Nantucket Shoals lightship, the proper course from the corner to New York for westbound steamers for that time of year.[22]

At the British inquiry, *Titanic's* Second Officer Charles Lightoller was asked about the course that the ship was making when it was handed over to him at 6.00p.m. He answered, 'I cannot remember the compass course. I know from calculations made afterwards that we were making S. 86 [W.] True.'[23] The calculations that he was referring to were made by *Titanic's* Fourth Officer Joseph Boxhall after working up a set of celestial star sights that were taken by Lightoller and Third Officer Herbert Pitman about 7.30p.m. As Boxhall explained to Senator Burton at the American inquiry, 'After I had worked these [stellar] observations of Mr Lightoller's I was taking star bearings for compass error for myself, and was working those out.'[24]

At the British inquiry Boxhall had this to say while being questioned:

15315.   Between 4 and 6, while you were on watch do you remember the course being altered?
Boxhall: The course was altered at 5.50.
15316.   Do you remember what it was altered to?
Boxhall: I do not remember the compass course, but I remember the true course was S. 86 W [266° true.]
15317.   I think you worked that out yourself?
Boxhall: Yes, I had stellar observations afterwards.

It is very clear from both Lightoller and Boxhall that the ship's true heading after the ship's course was changed at 5.50p.m. was 266° True. However, it is also very clear that the heading of 266° True was determined much later on when Boxhall was able to ascertain the compass error after first working up the ship's position from those 7.30p.m. star sights. When the ship's course was altered at 5.50p.m., the intent was to have her make 265° True for the Nantucket Shoals light vessel, the charted course to New York from the corner.[25]

In setting a time of 5.50p.m. to alter the ship's course, it appears that Captain Smith may have allowed for a speed of 21.6 knots to cover the 126 nautical miles from noon to the corner. That would be about a ½ knot less than what the ship's average speed made good was from noon Saturday to noon Sunday. He may have allowed for some effect of the Gulf Stream that usually was encountered in that area at that time of the year. However, if the ship maintained the same average speed as she did from noon Saturday to noon Sunday, she would have gone about 3 miles past the corner point when her course was actually altered.

Considering the course from her noontime position for 14 April to a turning point taken about 2 to 3 miles to the south-west of the corner, and then to a collision point close to the location of the wreck site,[26] we find a total distance made good of about 258 nautical miles. It is interesting to note that the reported distance travelled through the water since noon as recorded on the taffrail log at the time of the accident was 260 nautical miles.[27]

Titanic had 5,892 tons of coal on board when leaving Southampton,[28] a number which represents 89 per cent of her total bunker capacity of 6,611 tons, excluding the capacity of her reserve coalbunker which was empty. But was this enough to run her at high speed across the Atlantic? The answer is yes. Despite a coal strike that affected other White Star Line ships at that time, there was no shortage of coal on board *Titanic* during her maiden voyage despite what some people may have tried to imply at the 1912 inquiries.

Mr Ismay: She had about 6,000 tons of coal leaving Southampton.
Senator Perkins: Sufficient to make the voyage to New York and return to Southampton?

| **Mr Ismay:** | No, but sufficient coal to enable her to reach New York, with about two days' spare consumption. |

In spite of this testimony given in America, J. Bruce Ismay, then Managing Director of White Star Line and *Titanic* survivor, seemed to imply that there was a shortage of coal on board when he was later questioned before the British inquiry. Although he knew that there was plenty of coal on board, he implied in his testimony before Lord Mersey that they wanted to economise on coal and stated that it would not have been possible for *Titanic* to arrive in New York before Wednesday morning, and by that he meant arrival at the Ambrose Channel light vessel.[29] However, this was not the case – *Titanic* was perfectly capable of arriving late Tuesday night at Ambrose, and was well on her way to doing that except for the unfortunate accident.[30]

With all of the comparative data available from *Olympic* and other sources, we have a very good knowledge of *Titanic*'s coal supply and the amount of coal that she was likely to consume over the course of the maiden voyage.[31] There was indeed plenty of coal available to increase speed as she was doing and still have two days of spare consumption remaining. The amount of coal on board was never really an issue, and played no part in the increase in speed that took place during *Titanic*'s ill-fated maiden voyage.

Time Changes that Took Place

There has been much confusion over the years concerning the time kept on *Titanic* and other vessels, and how it compared to time kept elsewhere.[32] In 1912, the American inquiry decided in their report that there was a 1 hour 33 minute time difference between *Titanic* time and New York time on the night of 14 April 1912. The British inquiry decided on a 1 hour and 50 minute time difference, and during the 1915 Limitation of Liability Hearings in New York, the White Star Line suggested that the time difference between *Titanic* and New York was 1 hour and 39 minutes. All three were wrong because they failed to look into the navigational evidence that determined exactly what that difference was, and to pursue evidence of how clocks were adjusted on board *Titanic*. How these three erroneous conclusions most likely came about is discussed in Appendix G.

On *Titanic*, as on other White Star Line vessels heading westward, ships' clocks were set back each night so that at local apparent noon the following day the clocks would read 12.00. The time carried on board while at sea was known as Apparent Time Ship, or ATS. From the IMM book of Rules and Uniform Regulations:

> **259. Ship's Time.** – The Officer of the Watch [OOW] will see that the ship's time is changed between the hours of 10p.m. and 6a.m., the clocks to be set for Noon before 6a.m. The boiler room Clock must at all times agree with the Clock in the wheelhouse, and must be corrected accordingly.

The operative words in this rule is that the clocks were 'to be set for Noon'. On White Star Line vessels this clock adjustment was done about midnight. As further explained in a 1924 White Star Line brochure given to passengers on westbound voyages:

> It is necessary to put the clock back every 24 hours. The alteration in time is made at about midnight, and the clock is usually put back from 35 to 45 minutes on each occasion, the exact amount of time depending upon the distance the ship is estimated to make by noon the next day. During the first 24 hours, however, owing to the change from Mean time to Apparent time, the alteration is likely to be considerably more than 45 minutes. . . .

Once again we find that time carried on board these ships was adjusted to keep 'Apparent Time'. Direct evidence that this was done on *Titanic* comes from Second Officer Charles Lightoller and Third Officer Herbert Pitman:[33]

Lightoller: The clocks are set at midnight, but that is for the approximate noon position of the following day.

Pitman: They are corrected in the forenoon, perhaps half a minute or a minute; that is all.[34]

In addition to this, there is direct historical evidence that proves that Apparent Time was carried on board ship during *Olympic's* maiden voyage that comes from noontime positional data printed on her log card, and from an intercepted wireless message sent by Captain Smith to White Star Line's New York office on 19 June 1911.[35] There is no reason to believe that it would have been any different with *Titanic* in 1912.

The following table shows the adjustments that would have been made each night to a master clock in the chart room that controlled slave clocks in public places from the time *Titanic* left Southampton on 10 April to an expected arrival at the entrance to New York harbour late on 16 April.[36] The adjustment on the night of 10 April would have been to change clocks from GMT to Dublin Mean Time (DMT) so they would show the local mean time when they arrived at Queenstown the next day. The change on the night of 11 April would be from DMT to ATS based on the expected longitude that would be reached at local apparent noon on 12 April. Thereafter, the nightly change and forenoon correction would be to adjust the clocks so that they would accurately keep ATS until the night of arrival off the Ambrose Channel light vessel. The last clock change that would have taken place would be from ATS to New York Time (NYT)[37] on the night of 16 April.

Date	Amount of Clock Setback
Night of 10 April	25 minutes from GMT to DMT
Night of 11 April	59 minutes from DMT to ATS
Night of 12 April	49 minutes
Night of 13 April	45 minutes
Night of 14 April	*47 minutes*
Night of 15 April	*48 minutes*
Night of 16 April	*27 minutes from ATS to NYT*

The table below shows the difference in time between *Titanic* ATS and GMT or *Titanic* ATS and NYT as a function of date:[38]

Date	*Titanic* ATS	
Wednesday, 10 April	GMT − 00:00	NYT + 05:00
Thursday, 11 April	GMT − 00:25	NYT + 04:35
Friday, 12 April	GMT − 01:24	NYT + 03:36
Saturday, 13 April	GMT − 02:13	NYT + 02:47
Sunday, 14 April	GMT − 02:58	NYT + 02:02
Monday, 15 April	*GMT − 03:45*	*NYT + 01:15*
Tuesday, 16 April	*GMT − 04:33*	*NYT + 00:27*
Wednesday, 17 April	*GMT − 05:00*	*NYT + 00:00*

It should be noted (as shown above) that on the night of 14 April there was a planned clock setback of 47 minutes that was to occur about midnight.[39] Because of the accident, that change was not carried out.[40] However, we also know that local apparent noon for 15 April would have come 13 hours and 7 minutes after the 11.40p.m. collision time if not for the accident. At an average maintained speed of 22 knots over that interval, the ship would have travelled a distance of 289 nautical miles westward beyond the location of the wreck site. What we find is that *Titanic* would have reached a projected longitude of 56° 22'W at noon on 15 April. For that longitude and date, local apparent noon came at 3.45p.m. GMT. For *Titanic's* 14 April noontime longitude of 44° 31'W, local apparent noon came at 2.58p.m. GMT. The difference in those times is exactly 47 minutes; exactly equal to the amount of time that *Titanic's* clocks were to have been put back the night of the accident. This is clear navigational proof that *Titanic's* clocks were adjusted to carry Apparent Time as required by IMM rules and procedures.

On Sunday 14 April 1912, *Titanic's* clocks were 2 hours 58 minutes behind GMT, or 2 hours 2 minutes ahead of New York Mean Time. This is not a new discovery. In the early 1960s, Leslie Harrison, a friend and supporter of Capt. Stanley Lord of the SS *Californian*, had argued that *Titanic* was keeping Apparent Time for a longitude of 44½° west thereby putting her clocks 2 hours and 2 minutes ahead of New York Time. He was absolutely correct, but few people were willing to accept that fact because of his support for Captain Lord in what was called 'the *Californian* affair'.

A time difference of 2 hours and 2 minutes between *Titanic* ATS and New York Mean Time was directly observed by *Titanic's* junior wireless operator Harold Bride on the two clocks that were kept in *Titanic's* wireless cabin:[41]

Senator Smith:	Did you have a watch or clock in your room?
Mr Bride:	We had two clocks, sir.
Senator Smith:	Were they both running?
Mr Bride:	Yes, sir; one was keeping New York time and the other was keeping ship's time.
Senator Fletcher:	The difference was about 1 hour and 55 minutes?
Mr Bride:	There was about 2 hours difference between the two.

Notice that Bride immediately corrected the erroneous impression put forth by Senator Fletcher that there was a 1 hour 55 minute difference between the clocks. Obviously, if the time difference were anything like 1 hour 33 minutes, 1 hour 39 minutes, or even 1 hour 50 minutes, Bride would not have answered the way he did.[42]

Up to now we have been talking about clock adjustments made around midnight to clocks carried throughout public places on the ship. It is well known that some people purposely stayed up late waiting for the midnight clock change to take place so they could set their personal timepieces to the new time.[43] However, for the deck and engineering departments of the crew, the 47-minute time adjustment for the night of 14 April was to be equally split between two watch sections so that no one section would have to work more than half the total extra time created by putting the clocks back. On the night of 14 April, those working the 8 to 12 watch (the first watch) were to get 23 minutes of extra time added, while those working the 12 to 4 watch (the middle watch) were to get 24 minutes of extra time added.[44] This was to be done by putting the wheelhouse and engine room clocks back 23 minutes a little before midnight, the same time that clocks in public places were to be put back the full 47 minutes. This partial adjustment would delay the striking of eight bells, the signal that the watch on deck had ended, by 23 minutes at that time. The second change to the wheelhouse and engine room clocks was to come when it showed close to 4a.m. at which point it was to be put back the remaining 24 minutes thereby delaying the striking of eight bells by that amount at that time.[45]

It has been suggested that the first of these two partial adjustments to what the IMM rule book called 'bridge time' was made before the collision had taken place, even as early as 10p.m. in unadjusted 14 April hours. However, it is easily shown that this was not the case. The navigational evidence shows *Titanic* ran about 260 nautical miles from her noontime location to the location where she came to a stop following the collision averaging about 22.11 knots in 11 hours and 40 minutes; a performance consistent with what she did the previous day. Her distance by taffrail log over the same period was 260 nautical miles, giving an average of 22.28 knots through the water; a performance consistent with an increase in engine revolutions noted by many late Sunday night, and consistent with a 2-hour taffrail log reading that was taken at 10p.m. that showed that the ship was making about 22.5 knots through the water at that time.

However, the most overwhelming evidence that there was no prior clock adjustment comes from passengers and crew alike who looked at some timepiece when the accident happened. Most put the time of the accident between 11.40 and 11.45p.m.[46] There was no dichotomy between what most passengers said or what most crewmembers said as to the time of collision, or the time of foundering. This would *not* have been the case if a partial clock adjustment was actually carried out beforehand. As boatswain's mate Albert Haines testified,[47] 'The right time, without putting the clock back, was 20 minutes to 12.'

Weather Encountered Along the Route – *George Behe*

The following is a summary of the weather conditions that *Titanic* encountered during her voyage.

10 April – Wednesday

Titanic departed Southampton in a 'high wind'[48] at noon on 10 April to begin her 6-hour run toward Cherbourg, France. The weather was very fine but cold,[49] and the sky was overcast.[50] The sea was 'calm and beautiful' in the harbour at Cherbourg that evening.[51]

From Cherbourg *Titanic* headed toward Queenstown, Ireland; it was windy and cold on that run,[52] and the ship passed a 'windy night' on the Irish Sea.[53]

11 April – Thursday

It was partly cloudy and relatively warm as *Titanic* steamed towards Ireland, and the sea was mostly calm.[54] A high-pressure ridge was approaching Ireland, and a brisk 15 to 20-knot north-westerly wind was sweeping over the cloudy, 50° [Fahrenheit] city of Queenstown when *Titanic* arrived there at noon.[55]

That afternoon *Titanic* sailed westward toward the high-pressure ridge that was moving toward Ireland.[56] The clouds became scattered and the wind gradually died away as darkness approached, and that night the vessel faced light winds as she passed into the high-pressure ridge under generally clear skies.[57] During the night *Titanic* continued to steam WSW and left the high pressure ridge behind her, after which she encountered a 15-knot headwind that was destined to stick with her for most of her voyage.[58]

12 April – Friday

On 12 April the sky was clear, and by noon the temperature rose to around 60°.[59] That afternoon the skies over *Titanic* gradually clouded over as a weakening cold front approached from the west. Scattered showers were reported north-west of *Titanic's* position, and that night the ship found herself steaming into a 20-knot headwind under generally cloudy skies.[60]

13 April – Saturday

Morning dawned with broken cloud cover, but by noon the temperature had again risen to near 60°. The ship was now approaching a second cold front that lay west and north of her present course.[61]

It might have been on 13 April that *Titanic* encountered a small bank of fog for about 10 minutes during the day.[62] That night the sky was cloudy, and temperatures remained at around 55 to 60° with a 15 to 20-knot headwind coming out of the south-west.[63]

14 April – Sunday

It was apparently during the wee hours of the morning of 14 April that *Titanic* crossed the cold front that had been lying ahead of her to the west. Scattered showers were associated with the front,[64] and *Titanic* was steaming through rainy weather after daylight arrived.[65]

After passing through the cold front, *Titanic* experienced a change in the weather that included brisk north-west winds of 20 knots,[66] and these 'strong winds'[67] and 'moderate seas'[68] with 6 to 8ft waves[69] continued throughout the day.[70] Temperatures began to drop and probably reached 50° at around noon.[71] The wind continued,[72] and it turned even colder that afternoon as the sky began clearing and a large Arctic high-pressure system located over Sable Island moved slowly south-eastwards towards *Titanic*.[73] The air was described as 'icy' despite the sunshine,[74] but that evening the brisk north wind gradually died away as the sun neared the western horizon.[75]

Between 7p.m. and 9p.m. the temperature dropped from 43° to 33°,[76] and by 10.00p.m. the air temperature around *Titanic* had dropped to 31°[77] with the weather being clear and calm.[78] *Titanic* was steaming through an Arctic high-pressure system,[79] and at 11.40p.m. the moonless skies over the vessel were crystal clear and the stars cast their brilliance down on the sea, which was like glass.

Ice Messages Received

The following, in chronological order, is a list of wireless messages sent to *Titanic* that contained ice warnings as well as any reply messages received back from *Titanic*.[80] Times for these messages are shown in *Titanic* ATS along with the time (in brackets) that was logged on company service forms.[81] Also shown (in brackets) are the three-letter call signs of the various wireless stations involved and the message prefixes that were used.

Date and Time	From/To	Text of Message
12 April 5.46p.m. *Titanic* [7.10p.m. GMT]	*La Touraine* [MLT] to *Titanic* [MGY]	[MSG] (De) *Touraine* (a) Captain *Titanic*. My position 7p.m. GMT lat. 49.28 long. 26.28 W. Dense fog since this night. Crossed thick icefield lat. 44.58, long. 50.40 Paris. Saw another icefield and two icebergs lat. 45.20 long. 45.09 Paris. Saw a derelict lat. 40.56 long. 68.38 Paris. Please give me your position. Best regards and *Bon Voyage*. Caussin.
12 April 6.21p.m. *Titanic* [7.45p.m. GMT]	*Titanic* [MGY] to *La Touraine* [MLT]	[MSG] (De) *Titanic* (a) Captain *La Touraine*. Thanks for your message and information. My position 7p.m. GMT, lat. 49.5 long. 23.38W Greenwich. Had fine weather. Compliments. Smith.

14 April 9.12a.m. *Titanic* [7.10a.m. NYT]	*Caronia* [MRA] to *Titanic* [MGY]	[MSG] Captain *Titanic*. West bound steamers report bergs, growlers, and field-ice in 42N from 49 to 51 West April 12. Compts. Barr.
14 April 10.28a.m. *Titanic* [1.26p.m. GMT]	*Titanic* [MGY] to *Caronia* [MRA]	[MSG] Captain *Caronia*. Thanks for message and information. Have had variable weather throughout. Smith.
14 April 11.47a.m. *Titanic* [2.45p.m. GMT]	*Noordam* [MHA] to *Titanic* [MGY] via *Caronia* [MRA]	[Message forwarded by MRA to MGY at 2.45p.m. GMT. Sent from MHA to MRA at 2.30p.m. GMT.] [MSG] Captain SS *Titanic*. Congratulations on new command. Had moderate westerly winds, fair weather, no fog. Much ice reported in lat. 42.24 to 42.45 [N] and long. 49.50 to 50.20 [W]. Compliments. Krol.
14 April 12.31p.m. *Titanic* [3.29p.m. GMT]	*Titanic* [MGY] to *Noordam* [MHA] via *Caronia* [MRA]	[Message sent at 3.29p.m. GMT from MGY to MRA and then forwarded by MRA to MHA at 3.50p.m. GMT.] [MSG] Captain *Noordam*. Many thanks. Had moderate variable weather throughout. Compliments. Smith.
14 April 1.49p.m. *Titanic* [11.47a.m. NYT]	*Amerika* [DDR] to *Titanic* [MGY] for forwarding to Hydrographic Office, Washington, DC via Cape Race [MCE]	[MXG] Hydrographic Office, Washington, DC. *Amerika* passed two large icebergs in 41° 27' N., 50° 8'W. on the 14th of April. Knuth. [There is no evidence that this message was delivered to *Titanic*'s bridge, but it was forwarded from *Titanic* to Cape Race at 7.30p.m. NYT.]
14 April 1.54p.m. *Titanic* [11.52a.m. NYT]	*Baltic* [MBC] to *Titanic* [MGY]	[MSG] Capt. Smith, *Titanic*. Have had mod. var. winds and clear fine weather since leaving. Greek steamer *Athenai* [MTI] reports passing icebergs and large quantities of field ice today in lat. 41.51 N, long. 49.52 W. Last night we spoke German oil-tank steamer *Deutschland* [GZD], Stettin to Philadelphia, not under control, short of coal, lat. 40.42 N, long. 55.11 W. Wishes to be reported to New York and other steamers. Wish you and *Titanic* all success. Commander [Ranson]. [This message showed ice in the direct path of *Titanic*.]
14 April 2.57p.m. *Titanic* [12.55p.m. NYT]	*Titanic* [MGY] to *Baltic* [MBC]	[MSG] Commander *Baltic*. Thanks for your message and good wishes. Had fine weather since leaving. Smith.

14 April 7.37p.m. *Titanic* [5.35p.m. NYT]	*Californian* [MWL] to *Antillian* [MJL] intercepted by *Titanic* [MGY]	[MSG] Capt. *Antillian*. 6.30p.m. ATS lat. 42.3 N, long. 49.9 W. Three large bergs five miles to southward of us. Regards. Lord. [This would put the position of the icebergs at 41° 58'N, 49° 09'W. This message was acknowledged by *Antillian's* Capt. Japha at 6.00p.m. NYT.]
14 April 9.32p.m. *Titanic* [7.30p.m. NYT]	*Titanic* [MGY] to Cape Race [MCE] from *Amerika* [DDR]	[MXG] Hydrographic Office, Washington. *Amerika* passed two large icebergs in 41.27N, 50.8W on the 14th of April. Knuth. [This message, received from *Titanic*, was forwarded by Cape Race to office 29Z at 8.34p.m. NYT.]
14 April 9.52p.m. *Titanic* [7.50p.m. NYT]	*Mesaba* [MMV] to *Titanic* [MGY]	[SG] In lat. 42 N to 41.25 [N], long. 49 W to long. 50.30 W saw much heavy pack ice and great number large icebergs, also field ice. Weather good, clear.

Messages connected with or affecting the navigation of a vessel took precedence over ordinary messages. In the Marconi *Handbook for Wireless Telegraph Operators* that was in effect at the time:[82]

49. Priority of Messages. – In the transmission of radiotelegrams priority must be assigned, first of all, to messages of distress (see Section 73); then to messages of the British Admiralty and other British Government Departments and to the messages of other Governments (see Section 74). As between the two communicating stations themselves, the following order should be maintained:

(1) Messages relating to navigation.
(2) Service messages relating to the conduct of the Radiotelegraphic Service, or to previous radiotelegrams transmitted by the station concerned.
(3) Ordinary correspondence.

Messages affecting the navigation of a ship, sent from the commander of one vessel to the commander of another vessel, were known as Master Service Messages (or Masters' Service Grams) and were prefixed with the letters MSG.[83] They were written on proper forms supplied for the purpose, were signed by the captain and then hand delivered to the wireless operator.

The ice warning message from *Mesaba* was acknowledged as received by *Titanic* according to *Mesaba's* Service Form, but there is no evidence that this message was ever delivered to the bridge. It was not prefixed with an MSG. *Mesaba* had sent the same ice report (with prefix SG) to other eastbound ships that afternoon and evening, including *Campanello* [MGU] at 2.32p.m. NYT, *Menominee* [MNE] at 2.40p.m. NYT, *Columbia* [MOI] at 6.04p.m. NYT, and *Pennsylvania* [DDN] at 9.25p.m. NYT.

At 9.05p.m. NYT [11.07p.m. *Titanic* ATS], *Californian's* wireless operator Cyril Evans interrupted a lengthy communication between *Titanic* [MGY] and the land station at Cape Race [MCE] with a seemingly casual message from one wireless operator to another:

MGY [*Titanic*] this is MWL [*Californian*]. Say, old man, we are stopped and surrounded by ice.

No position was given, and it was not prefixed with an MSG. When *Californian's* signal came blasting into his headset, *Titanic's* senior wireless operator Jack Phillips transmitted a reprimand to Evans, 'Shut up, shut up, I am busy; I am working Cape Race.'[84] Phillips then sent Cape Race

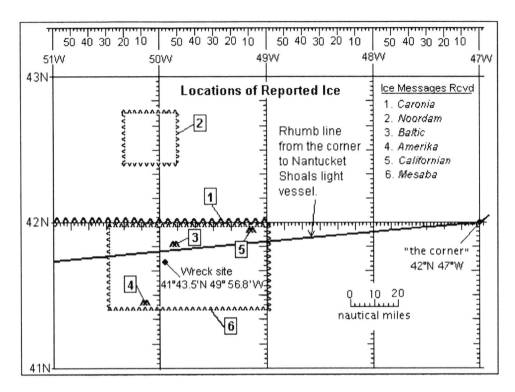

Fig. 5-3 Locations of reported ice received 14 April 1912.

an apology, 'Sorry, please repeat, jammed,' and then continued to take down a batch of private messages for *Titanic's* passengers. Phillips would continue to communicate with Cape Race for another 40 to 45 minutes even after *Titanic* came to stop following the accident. He was trying to clear a batch of messages that had accumulated on his desk. When the accident happened, Phillips assumed that the ship had been damaged some way and thought that it might have to return to Belfast for repairs. It was only after Captain Smith came by later on that Jack Phillips and junior operator Harold Bride were told that the ship had collided with an iceberg and may need assistance.[85]

The locations of ice reported in the messages received by *Titanic* on 14 April 1912 are shown in Fig. 5-3. Also shown is the planned route of *Titanic* from the corner to the Nantucket Shoals light vessel as well as the now known location of the wreck site.

Actions Taken or Not Taken to Avoid Ice

With all these ice messages received, there were two courses of action that Captain Smith could have taken. One was to significantly reduce speed before nightfall. The other was to take the vessel well to the southwards before turning for New York. Captain Smith did neither.

The evidence available shows that the speed of the ship was continually increased up to the time of the accident. The last increase took place when additional double-ended boilers that were first lit about 8a.m. Sunday morning were put on line about 7p.m. that Sunday evening. Increased vibration from the engines was noted by a number of passengers, and over a 2–hour period from 8p.m. to 10p.m., the ship ran a distance of 45 nautical miles by taffrail log.[86]

There is no evidence to suggest that Captain Smith was unduly influenced in pushing *Titanic* by having Bruce Ismay, the Managing Director of the White Star Line, on board for the maiden voyage crossing. There is nothing to suggest he would have acted any differently. Yes, there is evidence that the two discussed the progress that the ship was making on more than one occasion, but Captain Smith also knew what his ship was capable of doing, having taken *Olympic* across many times before.[87] By Saturday afternoon they both knew that they could be well on their way to setting a maiden voyage record for a White Star Line vessel.[88] At the average speed *Titanic* was making between noon Saturday and noon Sunday, she was well on her way to bettering *Olympic*'s maiden voyage crossing time by about 2 hours. However, as a seasoned commander, Smith also knew that things don't always work out the way you want them to. Fog may develop. A storm may come out of nowhere. Machinery may unexpectedly break down. There were just too many things that could go wrong that nobody has control over.

Captain Smith put his trust in maintaining a lookout to avoid any ice that they may encounter. From testimony taken, it is very clear that *Titanic*'s senior officers fully expected to be up to the ice that night. They also believed that they would be able to see it in enough time to prevent a dangerous situation from developing. They were following the practice of the time that steaming at night in perfectly clear weather, they would keep to the course and maintain speed until the ice was sighted. The subsequent events of that night were to prove that practice unsound.

Captain Smith could also have taken his ship well to the south before turning for New York. During the British inquiry both Third Officer Herbert Pitman and Fourth Officer Joseph Boxhall testified that they believed *Titanic* was taken well past the corner before her course was changed at 5.50p.m. on 14 April. The navigational evidence, however, does not bear this out.

Based on the total distance the ship travelled since taking departure off Daunt's Rock light vessel to noon on 14 April, and also from data independently supplied by Fifth Officer Harold Lowe, we found that *Titanic* was about 126 miles from the corner at noon, 14 April. The time from noon to when the ship's course was subsequently altered was 5 hours and 50 minutes. However, the distress coordinates worked out by Fourth Officer Boxhall following the collision, 41° 46'N, 50° 14'W, was a distance of 146 miles beyond the corner. Boxhall used a speed of 22 knots in working up his position. At that speed it would take *Titanic* 6 hours and 37 minutes from the corner point to reach the vicinity of the distress coordinates. However, *Titanic* collided with the iceberg at 11.40p.m., and her course was altered at 5.50p.m. The time interval from the alter-course point to the collision was 5 hours and 50 minutes, or a distance of 128 nautical miles at 22 knots. If one worked back 128 nautical miles from the distress coordinates on the reciprocal of the course heading that *Titanic* was on, one will end up at a location that is about 18 nautical miles west and a little south of the corner.[89] And since all of *Titanic*'s surviving officers believed that Boxhall's position was absolutely correct, it can only mean to them that the ship had to have turned the corner late for it to have travelled as far as it did when it collided with the iceberg. The problem, of course, is that we now know that Boxhall's calculated position was about 13 miles to the west of the wreck site. In short, there was no delayed turn of the corner. *Titanic* was reasonably close to the corner when her course was altered at 5.50p.m.

We believe Captain E.J. Smith did not consider that he was taking any greater risk than he, or many other crack steamship captains, had not taken before. Being in the largest, most modern and well-equipped vessel the White Star Line had to offer, he may well have felt he was taking less of a risk than in some other ships he commanded earlier in his career.[90] If his actions or inactions that night were the result of having Ismay on board, at a minimum one would think that he would have taken some extra precautions such as increasing the lookout, sending word down below to the engine room to be on the standby, or for him to personally have stood watch on the bridge along with the Officer of the Watch until they were well past the known region of reported ice. He did none of these, probably because he felt they were unnecessary.

The only precautions attributed to Captain Smith was his making sure that his senior officers understood the indications of ice, and ordering them to watch out for the slightest change in the weather. There was no talk of changing the ship's course or increasing the number on lookout. The only talk about slowing down was a comment made by Smith to Second Officer Charles Lightoller, 'If it does come on in the slightest degree hazy we shall have to go very slow.' The last words that Smith said to Lightoller before leaving the bridge about 9.25p.m. were, 'If it becomes at all doubtful let me know at once; I will be just inside.'[91]

We also know that shortly after Smith left Lightoller out on the bridge the lookouts were told 'to keep a sharp lookout for ice, particularly small ice and growlers', and also to pass the word along to the lookouts who were to relieve them at 10p.m.[92] Before that, at about 9p.m., word had been sent to the carpenter and to the engine room to take the necessary precautions to prevent fresh water pipes from freezing as the temperature was then close to the freezing mark.[93] According to Lightoller, he expected that *Titanic* might be up to the ice close to 9.30p.m., and that Sixth Officer James Moody thought they may reach the ice by 11p.m. When First Officer William Murdoch took over the watch at 10p.m., Lightoller briefed him about the ship's course, the temperature, that he sent word to the carpenter and engine room about the possibility of freezing, and about the conversation he had with Captain Smith earlier. He also mentioned to Murdoch that 'we might be up around the ice any time now', or words to that effect.[94]

Visibility Conditions Encountered Sunday Night

Visibility conditions on the night of 14 April were described as perfectly clear with not a cloud in the sky. The sea was absolutely flat in the region where the accident happened. There was not even a swell or any form of wave motion, something now known to be indicative of approaching an area of pack ice.[95] There was no moon, just a multitude of stars in the sky. But it was also very cold, with the temperature having dropped below the freezing point between 9 and 10p.m. as previously noted.

Despite the clarity of the night, it was not easy to spot icebergs. The distance at which an iceberg can be seen visually depends upon the meteorological visibility, the height of the iceberg, the source and condition of lighting, and the location of the observer. It was generally believed that on a dark, clear night icebergs could be seen at distances from 1 to 3 miles,[96] appearing either as white or dark objects with occasional light spots where waves broke against them. Under such conditions of visibility, growlers (small icebergs less than 14ft in height and 46ft in length) are considered an even greater menace to vessels, and we have noted that the lookouts were warned to keep a sharp lookout for them. But on the night of 14 April 1912, the only light coming off a berg was reflected starlight. And with the total absence of wind or swell, there were no breaking of waves at the base of a berg to help spot them earlier.[97]

Data on iceberg visibility distances was collected in 1925 by Lieutenant Commander Fred Zeusler of the United States Coast Guard who was the Ice Observation Officer for International Ice Patrol that season. That data showed that an average-sized iceberg could be expected to be spotted at a distance of about a ½ nautical mile on clear, dark, moonless nights.[98] Sir James Bisset, former Commodore of the Cunard Line and second officer of the rescue ship *Carpathia* at the time of the *Titanic* disaster, also stated that on dark, moonless nights with clear visibility, icebergs were visible by starlight at a distance of about ½ mile.[99] It should also be pointed out that *Carpathia* had come to within a ¼ mile of a 30ft-high iceberg before it was spotted on the way to picking up the first lifeboat from *Titanic*.[100]

With a low-lying haze around the horizon, the distance that an iceberg can be spotted is further reduced.[101] And here we have some conflicting reports. Lookout George Symons was on duty up in the crow's nest between 8 and 10p.m. during the last half of Charles Lightoller's watch. Symons testified that it was 'a fine night, rather hazy; if anything a little hazy on the horizon, but nothing to speak of.'[102] Lookout Reginald Lee, who was on duty up in the Nest from 10p.m. to midnight along with Frederick Fleet, testified that it was 'a clear, starry night overhead, but at the time of the accident there was a haze right ahead … in fact it was extending more or less round the horizon.'[103] Lee also said that he did not notice it when he and Fleet first came on watch:

It was not so distinct then . . . not on going on watch, but we had all our work cut out to pierce through it just after we started. My mate happened to pass the remark to me. He said, 'Well; if we can see through that we will be lucky.' That was when we began to notice there was a haze on the water. There was nothing in sight.

Unfortunately for Lee, Frederick Fleet did not quite back up his story when he took the stand to testify. Fleet also said that he saw a slight haze on the horizon, and that 'it was nothing to talk about.' He also said that when he saw it, 'it was only about 2 points on each side [of the bow],' and that 'it was somewhere near seven bells [11.30],' just about 10 minutes before the ship struck the iceberg. Fleet said that it was then that he told his mate, Lee, that 'there was a slight haze coming,' but it did not affect their ability to see the iceberg. When confronted with what Lee had said about 'if we can see through that we will be lucky,' Fleet's immediate response was, 'Well, I never said that.'[104]

According to Second Officer Charles Lightoller, there never was any haze during his watch, from 8 to 10p.m., or afterwards when he came back on deck following the collision.[105] He was also confronted with what Symons, Fleet and Lee had to say about haze, and strongly disagreed. He did not believe it was possible for them to see haze on the horizon from the crow's nest while he did not see any haze at all from the bridge.[106] *Titanic*'s bridge was about 65ft above the waterline, and her crow's nest was about 20ft higher.[107]

If haze was visible on the horizon from the crow's nest, it should have been just as visible from the bridge. And if haze was seen on the horizon by Symons during Lightoller's watch, it should have also been seen from the bridge by Lightoller and by Captain Smith when he was out on the bridge wing between 8.55 and 9.25p.m. talking to Lightoller about the seeing conditions, the weather, and their ability to spot icebergs in time to avoid them.[108]

Haze was not reported by any other ship that came into or was in the vicinity where *Titanic* struck ice. So why would *Titanic*'s lookouts claim they saw what appeared to be haze on the horizon? To try and answer this question we must dig deeper into the issue of what we have been calling 'haze'.

When the words haze or hazy is used it refers to a condition where there is a lack of distinctness or clarity, or something indefinite or obscured such as the horizon. When Antarctic explorer Sir Ernest Shackleton talked about haze at the British inquiry he actually was talking about mist as we know it today. True haze, meteorologically speaking, is caused by suspended microscopic pollutants, while mist is suspended microscopic water droplets that form usually when a cold air mass is carried over warmer water, or a warm air mass is carried over colder water. We also must keep in mind that the only light available that night was starlight. A hazy horizon can only mean that there was some lack of clarity where the sky and sea met. Maybe someone like Symons attributed the lack of a clearly defined horizon as due to haze? You cannot see haze or mist or fog on a starlit night out on the horizon unless there is starlight that is obscured from passing through it, or starlight that is reflected off of it.

Some idea of what the visual conditions were like may be gleaned from the testimony before the British inquiry of *Californian*'s Captain Stanley Lord whose vessel was stopped several miles north-west of where *Titanic* eventually came to a stop:

7193. You have said that there was no haze that night?
Lord: Yes.
7194. Did you tell the American Court of Enquiry that the light that night was very extraordinary; the conditions were very deceiving?
Lord: I told them it was a very strange night; it was hard to define where the sky ended and the water commenced. There was what you call a soft horizon. I was sometimes mistaking the stars low down on the horizon for steamer's lights.
7195. What is that condition of things due to, if it is not due to a haze?
Lord: I do not know; just a flash, that is all.

7196. What do you suggest as a characteristic of the atmosphere on a night of that sort?

Lord: I really could not say. We could see a light the full limit of my vessel.

Lord mentioned a soft horizon with no clearly defined line that can be seen that would separate the sky from the sea. The black of the sky blended with the black of the sea. There was nothing to indicate exactly where the horizon was except that stars could be seen above it and only blackness below it. Only a star rising or setting, by its sudden appearance or disappearance, would indicate exactly where the horizon was.

Lawrence Beesley, a second class passenger on *Titanic*, wrote about the clarity of the night as seen from lifeboat No.13 while waiting to be rescued:[109]

> The complete absence of haze produced a phenomenon I had never seen before: where the sky met the sea the line was as clear and definite as the edge of a knife, so that the water and the air never merged gradually into each other and blended to a softened rounded horizon, but each element was so exclusively separate that where a star came low down in the sky near the clear-cut edge of the waterline, it still lost none of its brilliance. As the earth revolved and the water edge came up and covered partially the star, as it were, it simply cut the star in two, the upper half continuing to sparkle as long as it was not entirely hidden, and throwing a long beam of light along the sea to us…All night long we had watched the horizon with eager eyes for signs of a steamer's lights…But what a night to see that first light on the horizon! We saw it many times as the earth revolved, and some stars rose on the clear horizon and others sank down to it: there were 'lights' on every quarter.

Both described a complete absence of haze. Both described making mistakes with stars low down on the horizon for steamer's lights. Captain Lord spoke of a 'soft horizon', while Beesley, a young science master from a British public school, spoke of a line 'as clear and definite as the edge of a knife'. As Sir Ernest Shackleton explained to the British Wreck Commission, 'if the temperature of the air is approximately the temperature of the sea there is practically no haze; it is only when the water is warmer or the air is warmer that the haze occurs.'[110] The air and surface water temperatures were never more than 2°F apart in the region where the accident happened.[111]

Could Fleet have seen a phenomenon called ice blink? The answer is no. Ice blink is caused by the reflection of light from a distant wide body of ice onto the underside of low-lying clouds. On that Sunday night the sky was dark and cloudless.

According to Frederick Fleet, it was close to seven bells when he first noticed a haze on the horizon in the direction that the ship was headed. We know there was a vast field of pack ice about 5 to 6 miles wide that was located 2 to 3 miles beyond where *Titanic* went down. At 11.30p.m. *Titanic* was about 4 miles from the collision point, or 6 to 7 miles from the eastern edge of that pack ice. Where the sea and sky met as seen from the crow's nest would have been about 11 miles distant. Theoretically, most of the width of the pack ice would have been inside the visible horizon if it were bright enough to be seen at that distance.

According to *Californian*'s Captain Lord, he noticed a brightening along the western horizon about 5 to 6 minutes before he rang his engine room telegraph to full-speed astern and ordered hard-a-port on the helm just as his lookout men reported sighting ice ahead.[112] *Californian* then swung around and came to a stop within ¼ to ½ mile from the edge of a low-lying field of pack ice, the same vast field of pack ice that lay ahead of *Titanic*. Travelling at 11 knots, *Californian* was no more than a little over 1 mile from the edge of the pack ice when the first indication of something ahead was noticed. *Titanic* would have been about 6 times further away when Fleet thought he noticed a haze ahead.

Whatever one wants to believe, the overall visibility was such that those responsible for the safety and lives of those on board *Titanic* did not deem it necessary to reduce speed as the ship approached a known region of ice. Even according to lookout Reginald Lee, who gave the impression that haze had some affect on their ability to see the iceberg in time, the berg appeared about ½ mile away, more or less, when it was first spotted up in the Nest.[113] At the speed *Titanic* was making, it would take 1 minute and 20 seconds to close that distance. More than enough time to avoid if evasive actions were taken immediately.

The Row About Missing Binoculars[114]

The lookouts had no binoculars. They had been provided with a pair between Belfast and Southampton and these were returned to the then second officer, David Blair, at the end of the passage. Blair entrusted lookout George Hogg with the task of locking them in his cabin and Hogg in turn had asked a seaman called Weller to return the key. After leaving Southampton, Hogg was asked by his fellow lookouts to obtain the binoculars from Lightoller, the new second officer, who fobbed him off, saying he would get them later. An attempt by Lookout George Symons met with an even worse result. Lightoller bluntly told him there were no glasses for the lookouts. According to Lightoller, he had asked Chief Officer Wilde to look into the matter and was not sure if glasses for the lookouts existed. It is very possible that this was in fact the case. Both Hogg and Fleet were sure that the glasses used between Belfast and Southampton had been marked 'Second Officer'. David Blair had seen fit to lend them to the lookouts, perhaps because of the amount of shipping likely to be met with on the passage, and the need to sight navigational marks along the way. Apparently Lightoller was not so obliging and kept them for his own use.

Charles Lightoller was a key witness at the 1912 inquiries. He played up the visibility of icebergs, stating his belief that a growler could be seen at a distance of 1 mile. He added a detail to his well-known conversation with Captain Smith, claiming that the master had agreed that an iceberg would be visible 3 or 4 miles off. He sought to show that the lack of binoculars for the lookouts was unimportant, declaring that he would 'most utterly condemn glasses' if he thought that they would use them to identify an object before reporting to the bridge that something was sighted. The duty of the men was to look out, and the use of glasses limited the field of the lookout's vision, and hence their ability to quickly spot an object.[115]

To Fredrick Fleet, who was in the crow's nest at the time the iceberg was sighted, not having glasses in the nest was a disappointment. He believed that if he had a pair of glasses, he would have spotted the berg sooner, 'In time for the ship to get out of the way.' He had been a lookout on *Oceanic* for four years where he had been provided with binoculars, albeit of 'very poor' quality.[116] On *Titanic* he had none. However, in all four years on *Oceanic*, Fleet had never sighted a single iceberg.[117] And he was not alone in having limited or no experience crossing a region of pack ice and icebergs.[118]

It is evident that neither Lightoller, nor any other officer, thought it worthwhile to give the lookouts one of the several pairs of binoculars kept on the bridge for the use of the officers. To this day, most mariners are of the opinion that it is best to search for dangers with the naked eye and to use glasses only to identify anything seen. Binoculars are of more use when searching for an object whose bearing is known, as when approaching a light or a landmark.

If an object is to be seen at sea it must be illuminated in some way, even a white object. There must be some ambient light to reflect off an object. The light produced at sea on a typical moonless night has been estimated at being equal to the light of a single candle at a height of 180ft. The big majority of this is produced by the phenomenon of airglow, which is the general dim light produced in the upper atmosphere by the action of solar radiation. In 1912, even the airglow was limited, the sunspot cycle then being at a minimum. With twilight long gone, *Titanic* was steaming into darkness with only the light of the stars, plus a little airglow that was available.[119]

The Collision

Titanic collided with an iceberg on Sunday night, 14 April 1912, at about 11.40p.m. ATS. It is estimated that the ship came to a stop near 41° 46' N, 49° 56'W, and then drifted with the local current toward the south-south-west at a little over 1 knot until she foundered 2 hours and 40 minutes later at 41° 43.5' N, 49° 56.8'W.[120]

From eyewitness reports, the iceberg was of medium size with a peak height that reached slightly higher than *Titanic*'s boat deck.[121] It was described as being high at one point with another point that came up at the other end, similar in shape to the Rock of Gibraltar.[122] It was described as 'a dark mass', as 'dark blue', and as 'ordinary ice' by various eyewitnesses.

The classical story of how *Titanic* encountered the iceberg was summarised in the final report of the British Wreck Commission back in 1912:

> At a little before 11.40, one of the look-outs in the crow's nest struck three blows on the gong, (Hichens, 969) which was the accepted warning for something ahead, following this immediately afterwards by a telephone message to the bridge 'Iceberg right ahead.' Almost simultaneously with the three gong signal Mr. Murdoch, the officer of the watch, gave the order 'Hard-a-starboard,' and immediately telegraphed down to the engine room 'Stop. Full speed astern.' (Boxhall, 15346) The helm was already 'hard over,' and the ship's head had fallen off about two points to port, when she collided with an iceberg well forward on her starboard side.
>
> Mr. Murdoch at the same time pulled the lever over which closed the water-tight doors in the engine and boiler rooms. (15352) The Master 'rushed out' on to the bridge and asked Mr. Murdoch what the ship had struck. (Hichens, 1027) (Boxhall,15353) Mr. Murdoch replied: 'An iceberg, Sir. I hard-a-starboarded and reversed the engines, and I was going to hard-a-port round it but she was too close. I could not do any more. I have closed the watertight doors.' (15355).

The report then went on to state the following conclusion:

> From the evidence given it appears that the 'Titanic' had turned about two points [22.5°] to port before the collision occurred. From various experiments subsequently made with the SS 'Olympic,' a sister ship to the 'Titanic,' it was found that travelling at the same rate as the 'Titanic,' about 37 seconds would be required for the ship to change her course to this extent after the helm had been put hard-a-starboard.[123] In this time the ship would travel about 466 yards [1,398ft], and allowing for the few seconds that would be necessary for the order to be given, it may be assumed that 500 yards [1,500ft] was about the distance at which the iceberg was sighted either from the bridge or crow's nest.

During the British inquiry into the loss of the SS *Titanic*, Edward Wilding, naval architect from the shipbuilding firm of Harland & Wolff, the builders of *Olympic* and *Titanic*, presented data on the turning characteristics of these vessels. In addition to the aforementioned fact that it took *Olympic* 37 seconds to turn two points (22.5°) from the time the order was first given, Wilding also stated that with the ship running at about 74rpm on her reciprocating engines (corresponding to about 21½ knots) the distance run from the time the order was given to when the ship turned 2 points was 1,200 to 1,300ft.

Wilding also gave evidence at the Ryan vs. Oceanic Steam Navigation Company trial in June 1913 and at the Limitation of Liability Hearings in New York in May 1915. From all the evidence presented, as well as knowing how a ship handles in a turn,[124] we were able to reproduce the turning circle for *Olympic* and *Titanic* for a turn with the helm put 'hard-a-starboard' (left full rudder) and an approach speed of 22.5 knots. This is shown in Fig. 5-4 along with some of the key turning parameters that were derived.[125]

Claims that *Titanic* did not respond well to her rudder are entirely without foundation. The size of a ship's rudder in square feet of immersed surface is usually expressed as a percentage of the product of the ship's length between perpendiculars and the ship's draft. For *Titanic*, this works out to be about 1.37 per cent. In comparison, *Lusitania* had a value of about 1.67 per cent. However, a relatively narrow, deep rudder like *Titanic*'s will tend to produce a greater pressure force than a rudder of broad, shallow shape with the same area. But more importantly, having the rudder placed directly behind one of a ship's propellers increases it's efficiency due to the greater speed of the slipstream of water that runs past it, an advantage that *Titanic*'s rudder had being positioned directly aft of her central propeller. The issue of turning responsiveness lies more with the abilities of the ship handler and his knowledge of the turning capabilities of the vessel under his command.

According to the conclusion of the 1912 British Wreck Commission, the iceberg was first sighted about 1,500ft ahead of the ship, which is only about 40 seconds of travel time for a ship moving at 22.5 knots. Yet they also stated that the lookouts gave the warning to the bridge that an object was seen ahead by striking the lookout bell three times when first sighted, then called down by telephone to inform the bridge that it was an iceberg that was sighted 'right ahead'. In looking at the testimony of Quartermaster Robert Hichens,[126] who was at the wheel at the time, the helm order was given *after* the phone call was received by Sixth Officer James Moody, who was standing right behind him. Moody then repeated to First Officer William Murdoch what the lookout had just told him and it was then that Murdoch first took evasive action. Hichens also said that Murdoch's order came about a half-a-minute following the three-bell warning, a time interval that is also supported by the testimony of Lookout Frederick Fleet who struck the lookout bell and called down on the phone to reported an iceberg ahead.[127] Despite this evidence, the Wreck Commission concluded that Murdoch's order came 'almost simultaneously with the three gong signal,' not allowing any time for the phone call and the relaying of information that took place immediately after.

A good estimate of the time interval between the three-bell warning from the lookouts to when the ship struck the iceberg can be derived from the testimony of Quartermaster Alfred Olliver who was out on the standard compass platform amidships trimming the lights in the compass when those three bells were struck up in the Nest.[128] Olliver left the standard compass platform right after hearing the three-bell warning and was just entering the bridge as the ship struck. Knowing the distance that it takes to get down from the platform and walk to the bridge, and using a typical walking speed for pedestrians crossing a busy intersection, plus allowing for some reaction time as well, it is estimated that it would have taken Olliver about 50 to 55 seconds to come onto the bridge after hearing those warning bells.

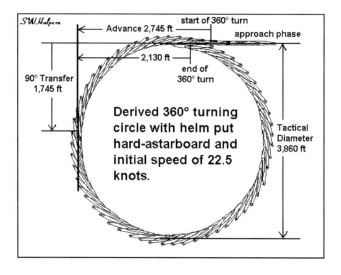

Fig. 5-4 *Titanic*'s turning circle.

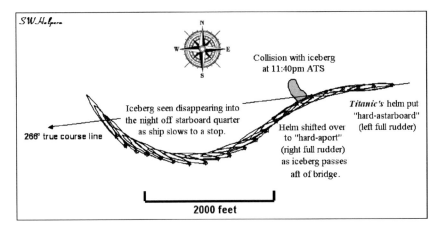

Fig. 5-5 Collision sequence manoeuvres.

We also know from Olliver that an order of 'hard-a-port' was given by Murdoch after the peak of the iceberg was seen to pass aft of the bridge, after most of the damage to the ship had been done.[129] It seems that *Titanic's* first officer was trying to swing the aft end of the ship away from the iceberg after it had passed aft of the ship's pivot point in an attempt to minimise any further damage to the vessel's starboard side. According to Quartermaster George Rowe, who was stationed out on the poop when the collision took place, it looked like the iceberg was going to hit the docking bridge there, passing within less than 10ft of the ship's rail.[130] But Rowe also thought that the ship was not under hard-a-starboard helm as the iceberg passed astern, because if it were, then the iceberg would have been up against the ship's stern scraping along the side which it was not. In addition there were several others who saw the iceberg shortly after the collision disappearing into the night off the ship's starboard quarter which would not have been possible if the ship had continued to turn under starboarded helm. One crewmember, Able-Bodied Seaman Joseph Scarrott, said he saw the stern slewing away from the iceberg as if the ship was going to circle around it with the ship's head turning to starboard.[131]

In addition to issuing helm orders, First Officer Murdoch also rang down engine orders on the engine order telegraphs. Here, however, we have some conflicting accounts. Fourth Officer Joseph Boxhall told the inquiries that Murdoch had ordered the engines be put 'full speed astern' about the same time that he ordered the helm be put hard-a-starboard.[132] According to Boxhall's story, he was just coming out of the officers' quarters on the starboard side when he heard three bells from the lookouts. He then heard the first officer give the order 'hard-a-starboard' and also heard the engine telegraph bells ring. Then, before he reached the bridge while still abreast of the captain's quarters, the ship struck the iceberg at 'the bluff of the bow'. As soon as he arrived on the bridge, he saw Murdoch closing the watertight doors, and turned around to find Captain Smith standing alongside of him who then asked Murdoch what it was they had struck. Of the three surviving eyewitnesses who were on the bridge at the time of the accident (Boxhall, Hichens and Olliver), only Boxhall talked about Murdoch telling Smith that he rang full speed astern on the engines. Hichens and Olliver only spoke of Murdoch telling Smith that they struck an iceberg, and that he had already closed the watertight doors.[133]

Boxhall presented all these events as taking place in a very short time frame. We know the distance from the door leading out of the officers' quarters to the bridge was only about 60ft. We find that it should have taken no more than about 15 seconds, including what is called startup time, for Boxhall to walk that distance. During that time, all of the following had to have happened: three bells struck by the lookout, a phone call report that came down from the crow's nest, the lookout report given to the first officer, an order then given to put the helm over hard, engine orders rang down on the engine telegraphs, and then enough time for the ship to turn off her course line so as to strike the berg at the bluff of the bow on the starboard side before Boxhall even reaches the bridge.

In contrast to this, we saw before that standby Quartermaster Olliver was at the compass platform amidships when those three bells were struck up in the nest. Olliver had to go down the platform ladder and then down from the roof over the first class lounge to get to the boat deck in order to get to the bridge. He had to cover a walking distance of about 250ft in all. That we estimated would take him about 50 to 55 seconds.

So did Boxhall really witness all that he said he did, or was he just trying to give the impression before the inquiries that there simply was not enough time for Murdoch to take any possible action that could have prevented the ship from striking the berg?

We cannot find any confirmation that Murdoch had given an order to reverse the engines full speed astern, as Boxhall claimed, by any surviving eyewitness who was working either below in the engine rooms or on the bridge when the accident happened. Even Second Officer Charles Lightoller said that he did not believe the engines were ever put full speed astern. And he should know because he took part in *Titanic's* sea trials off Belfast Lough where they actually did that.[134] If Murdoch was trying to swing the ship clear of the iceberg, the last thing he would want to do is reduce the ability of the ship to turn rapidly. On *Titanic*, the turbine engine that ran the central propeller must be stopped when going astern. This would reduce the rudder's response somewhat because of the loss of the added slipstream that comes from the ship's central propeller. But even if Murdoch gave an order to reverse, there just was not enough time to get the reciprocating engine propellers reversing before the collision took place. It was about 2 minutes after the collision that the valves that fed exhaust steam from the reciprocating engines to the turbine engine were seen to have lifted thereby bypassing the turbine engine,[135] and it was about then that people first noticed that the engines had come to a stop.[136] What we do know about the engines going in reverse comes from eyewitnesses who said that the engines were seen to reverse slowly for a very short time soon after they had first come to a stop. This was a minute or two after the collision, and apparently was enough to take the way off the ship and bring her close to a complete stop. The bottom line in all of this is that the engines played little or no part in any collision avoidance manoeuvre even if the order to reverse was given.

So what really did happen in those moments just prior to and after the collision? What we can state after considering all the evidence available to us,[137] as well as considering the turning characteristics of the ship, is the following:

- An iceberg was sighted ahead by the lookouts about a minute before impact, possibly very fine off the ship's starboard bow,[138] and at a distance of about 2,000ft.

- Within moments of sighting, Frederick Fleet struck three bells indicating an object ahead.

- Within moments of giving this bell signal, Fleet turned to go from his station on the port side of the crow's nest to the back of the starboard side to get to the loud-speaking telephone. He then called down to the wheelhouse to tell them that an iceberg was sighted 'right ahead'.

- The phone in the wheelhouse was answered by Sixth Officer James Moody who acknowledged Fleet with a polite 'Thank you,' and then immediately relayed the information reported by Fleet to First Officer Murdoch.

- Murdoch then called out for the helm to be put 'hard-a-starboard' and ran to the engine telegraphs to ring down engine orders. The helm order was carried out by Quartermaster Hichens and acknowledged by Sixth Officer Moody.

- After Fleet left the phone and started to go back to his station on the port side of the nest, his lookout mate, Reginald Lee, told him it appeared that the ship was starting to veer to port.

• A few moments before the ship struck, a 'stop' signal was seen on the illuminated boiler room telegraphs in the stokeholds telling the men to shut the dampers on the boilers.

• After the ship's head turned between 1 to 2 points to port, the iceberg appeared to strike the ship just ahead of the foremast on the starboard side, and the sound of rending metal could be heard for several seconds after.

• At the time of impact Murdoch was seen at the switch that closed the watertight doors that were down in the machinery spaces. The doors began to drop within seconds following the collision as the warning bell by the doors was being sounded.

• In the wheelhouse, the ship's head was seen to swing south of west on the steering compass, having turned about 2 points to port from a compass heading of N 72° W.

• After the berg passed aft of the starboard bridge wing Murdoch was heard to call out for the helm to be put hard-a-port. That action was carried out and acknowledged.

• A few moments after the collision, Captain Smith was seen rushing onto the bridge after passing through the wheelhouse from his quarters to ask Murdoch, 'What have we struck?'

We can only speculate as to why it took First Officer Murdoch possibly close to half-a-minute from the time the lookout bells were rung to the time he took decisive action. It is most likely that Murdoch saw the berg as soon as the lookout bell was struck if not before. In such a situation it is important for any ship handler to immediately judge the relative bearing and distance to the object, as well as knowing how your ship responds to a turn for the speed she is making. If the object appears to be close at hand but somewhat off to the side, trying to turn the ship away may very well cause a collision since the initial movement of a ship entering a turn is for the stern to swing to the outside of the turn while the ship continues to go straight ahead. In that situation, the best action might be to hold her steady if it appears that the object may actually clear along the side. As all ship handlers know well, if the bearing to an object is opening up, you are *not* on a collision course. If it remains the same, you are on a collision course.

All of this must have raced through Murdoch's mind before he ordered the helm over hard to starboard (left full rudder). In 1903, when he was second officer on board the *Arabic*, Murdoch allegedly was able to avoid a collision at night with a sailing vessel by countermanding an order to port the helm that was given by Chief Officer Fox, the man Murdoch was about to relieve as Officer of the Watch. According to the story, Murdoch brushed aside the quartermaster and held the wheel steady thereby preventing a collision that otherwise would have taken place.[139] What we find from this is that William Murdoch did not merely react out of pure instinct, but took the time to access a situation before acting. By the time Sixth Officer Moody repeated to Murdoch what Fleet had just told him on the phone, Murdoch had decided that some evasive action must be taken, and so he ordered the helm be put hard-a-starboard to swing his ship's head over to port away from the iceberg that was looming ever so larger in his direct field of view, fine on the starboard bow. The bearing line to the object was not opening as much as he would have hoped it would.

As it turned out, the ship was just too close to completely avoid contact with the iceberg by the time the order was given. It struck an underwater spur of ice on the starboard side in the vicinity of the peak tank. Within seconds, the visible part of the berg above the waterline appeared to strike the ship's side just ahead of the foremast where the crow's nest was located. Large chunks of ice then fell off the berg and onto the forecastle head and into the forward well deck immediately aft of the foremast. For about 200–250ft, damage was rendered just above the level of the ship's tank top, opening up five major watertight compartments to the sea. Soon after the peak of the iceberg passed aft of the bridge, Murdoch ordered the helm put hard-a-port to swing the stern clear in the apparent hope of preventing further damage to the ship. But as the berg passed aft, some small amounts of ice fell through a few open portholes on E deck, and onto the windows of the Café Parisien high up on B deck.[140] To Quartermaster George Rowe stationed out on the poop, it looked like the berg was going to hit the docking bridge there, passing within 10ft of the ship's rail. Finally, with her swing over to port completely checked, the ship started to swing the other way, and the iceberg was seen fading away into the night off the ship's starboard quarter by several crewmembers who came topside to see what had happened.

When *Titanic* finally came to a stop several minutes later, she was facing northwards. Later, it was noticed that she was swinging very slowly in a clockwise direction as she drifted with the local current. As witnessed by Quartermaster George Rowe during the time that he was on the bridge firing off distress socket signals and trying to signal a stopped vessel off their port bow by Morse lamp,[141] 'Her head [*Titanic's*] was facing north. She was coming round [very slowly] to starboard.'

Notes

[1] Ismay, BI 18625.

[2] BI Report, p.24.

[3] Pitman, AI p.261; Ismay, AI p.3.

[4] In 1880 the legal time for Great Britain was made Greenwich Mean Time (GMT) by Act of Parliament. In the same Act the legal time for all of Ireland was made Dublin Mean Time (DMT) and was not changed until 1916 to be the same as GMT. Dublin is at longitude 6° 15'W, which meant that DMT was 25 minutes behind GMT. [For a more detailed history of events up to this point, see Derek Howse, *Greenwich Time and the Longitude* (National Maritime Museum / Philip Wilson Publishers, 1997).] However, according to International Mercantile Marine Company (owners of the White Star Line) Rule 116 that was in effect in 1912, departure and arrival times when entering or leaving English or Irish waters were always to be recorded in GMT. Once out to sea, time was kept according to where the ship would be at local apparent noon, the instant of time when the true sun would reach its highest point in the sky. Time being kept this way was known as Apparent Time Ship or ATS. When arriving or departing points in the United States or Canada, ship's time would be changed to the mean time for the 75th meridian of longitude which was exactly 5 hours behind GMT.

[5] A great circle track is the path you would get if you took a tightly stretched string and used it to connect any two points on a globe. It is the shortest distance that connects those two points.

[6] A rhumb line track is the path that you would get by following a fixed compass direction without change. If the compass direction you followed was due north or due south, you would also be following a great circle track on one of the earth's meridians. You would also be on a great circle track if you happened to be on the earth's equator and went due east or due west. Any other fixed direction to the north or south of due east or due west will eventually spiral in toward one of the earth's poles.

[7] This route was known as the *southern track* taken by steamers heading westbound across the Atlantic leaving Queenstown. It was in effect from 15 January through 23 August. The point called 'the corner' marked the end of the great circle part of the westbound voyage. Eastbound steamers on the *southern track* would reach a corner point 60 nautical miles to the south of the westbound corner point before they would take to the great circle part of their eastbound voyage. From 24 August through 14 January these routes were shifted northwards by about 120 nautical miles, and were know as the *northern track*. A voyage taken on the *northern track* made the passage across the Atlantic about 110 nautical miles shorter. After the *Titanic* disaster the southern tracks were shifted further southward.

[8] We take the turning point to be about 3.3 miles south of the Old Head of Kinsale lighthouse. The lighthouse itself is located on the coast at 51°36.3' N, 8°31.9'W (Ref: The Commissioners of Irish Lights at www.cil.ie).

[9] Following *Olympic's* second voyage of 1911, we will take this point to be about 2 miles south of the Nantucket Shoals light vessel. The light vessel itself was listed in the US Coast Pilot Part III for 1912 at 40° 37' 05" N, 69° 36' 33" W.

[10] The Ambrose Channel light vessel was listed in the US Coast Pilot Part IV for 1909 at 40° 28' 02" N, 73° 50' 01" W. Before passing Ambrose the ship would also pass the Fire Island light vessel located at

40° 28' 40" N, 73° 11' 26" W. But it was the Ambrose Channel light vessel that marked the end of the Atlantic crossing and entrance to lower New York harbour.

[11] Although there were several noted errors in the memorandum submitted by Pitman (AI p.420–421), the distances provided for each day's run can be confirmed from other testimonies and sources. Confirmation of the 484-mile run for day one comes from the testimony of J. Bruce Ismay. Confirmation of the 519-mile run for day two comes from Ismay and second class passenger Lawrence Beesely. (In his book, *The Loss of the SS Titanic*, Beesley wrote that the purser had mentioned to him that the 519-mile run for day two was a disappointment.) Confirmation of the 546-mile run for day three comes from Ismay, and passengers Lawrence Beesley, Henry Stengel and Archibald Gracie.

[12] Commander J.G.P. Bisset, *Ship Ahoy!! Nautical Notes for Ocean Travellers, with Charts and Diary*, Charles Birchall Ltd, Liverpool, Alphabetical List of Distances, p.110.

[13] This noontime position for 12 April falls on a line from Fastnet Light to an apparent alter course position for 7.00p.m. GMT that was sent in a wireless message from *Titanic* to *La Touraine* that very day. The distance between the position at noon and the position sent in that message is about 114 nautical miles. This 7.00p.m. GMT position, which was transmitted from *Titanic* to *La Touraine* at 7.45p.m. GMT, is about 6 miles north of the great circle track at the reported longitude. It is interesting to note that in the log of *Olympic*'s second voyage to New York (in July 1911), the last two out of three noontime positions along the great circle part of her route were 10 and 8 miles north of the great circle track line, respectively. Additionally, the first noontime position for the part of *Olympic*'s route from the corner to the Nantucket Shoals light vessel was 6 miles north of the rhumb line track that she was expected to be on.

[14] From testimony given by *Titanic*'s Fifth Officer Harold Lowe (AI p.381), the course from noon to the corner was 240.6° True, and the distance was 126 nautical miles (after correcting what appears to be a transposition error of two digits in the transcript of his testimony). Working back from the corner at 42° N, 47° W, and going 126 nautical miles along the reciprocal heading (060.6° True) gets us to a noon position of 43° 02' N, 44° 31' W. This position is a total distance run of 1,549 miles from the Daunt's Rock light vessel over the course that was travelled.

[15] Samuel Halpern, 'A Minute of Time', *THS Commutator*, Vol.29, No.171 and 172, 2005.

[16] The time interval from local apparent noon (LAN) one day to LAN the next day is just 24 hours plus the amount of time the clocks were set back. This holds for all days except the first day out. Because they took departure in the afternoon at 2.20p.m. GMT off the Daunt's Rock light vessel, the time of the first day's run is 24 hours *minus* the difference between their departure time in GMT on 11 April and the time of LAN in GMT on 12 April. That difference was 2.20 − 1.24 = 0:56. Therefore 56 minutes from 24 hours leaves 23 hours and 4 minutes, the time interval from departure at the Daunt's Rock light vessel on 11 April to local apparent noon on 12 April.

[17] Speed made good is not the same as speed through the water. Speed made good is the vector addition of speed through the water plus the net affect of current and wind.

[18] Ismay, AI p.3.

[19] Samuel Halpern, 'They Were Gradually Working Her Up', http://www.titanicology.com/WorkingThenUp.htm.

[20] Hichens, BI 965.

[21] Rowe, BI 17590. At the British inquiry Second Officer Charles Lightoller said, 'The [steering] compass course is not the compass we go by. I believe by standard [compass] we were steering N. 73 ... I think that works out as 73 by [standard] compass, and 71 was the steering compass.' If Lightoller was correct, it would indicate a 2° difference in deviation error between the standard compass located amidships and the steering compass in the wheelhouse when the ship was on that particular heading (see BI 13501).

[22] Boxhall, BI 15661. Adding 24° to Lowe's 240.6° gives a course of 264.6° True which is very close to Boxhall's course of S 84 ¾ W (264.75° True) when asked about the rhumb line course to Nantucket that was marked on a chart at the British inquiry (see BI 15670).

[23] Lightoller, BI 13498.

[24] Boxhall, AI p.932. Boxhall also told the British inquiry (on day thirteen) that, 'I had the 7.30 position in my work book ... I had used that same position two or three times after giving it to the Captain, and that same course I used two or three times after giving it to the Captain as well, between 10

o'clock and the time of the collision, for the purpose of working up stellar deviations . . . checking the compass error.'

25 On page 27 of the Wreck Commission Report they wrote: 'At 5.50p.m. the *Titanic's* course (which had been S 62° W) was changed to bring her on a westerly course for New York . . . altering course at 5.50p.m. about four or five miles south of the customary route on a course S 86° W True.' The course S 62° W is 242° True. They got that result by simply subtracting 24°, which was the change in magnetic heading that the ship took at 5.50p.m., from the 266° True heading that Boxhall gave them. However, Fifth Officer Harold Lowe gave evidence that the course to the corner from noon was 240.6° True. Some researchers have used 242° as the true course of the ship prior to the turn at 5.50p.m. for the same reason the Wreck Commission did. However, this is not necessarily correct even if the true heading after the turn was later seen to be 266° True. The reason is that a change of 24° in compass heading may not correspond to a 24° change in true course heading because the compass deviation error is a function of the ship's magnetic heading, something that depends on the ship's true heading and the earth's magnetic variation. Compass deviation is simply *not* a constant. This can easily be seen in compass data taken from *Olympic* for both her standard compass and her steering compass. In one example, at 4.40p.m. on 29 March 1931, *Olympic* turned from a heading of 243.25° True to a heading of 260.75° True, a change of 17.5° in her true heading. However, on the steering compass the course went from 269° to 284°, a change of 15°. It was noted that the steering compass deviation was 1¼° east when heading 269°, and changed to 3° east when heading 284°; almost a 2° increase in compass deviation for a 17.5° change in her true course.

26 Samuel Halpern, 'Collision Point', *Great Lakes Titanic Society (GLTS)* website, http://www.glts.org/articles/halpern/collision_point.html.

27 Rowe, BI 17608.

28 From a report filed with the BOT Surveyor's Office in Dublin.

29 'I [Ismay] told him [Chief Engineer Bell] I thought we should arrive at the Ambrose lightship about 5 o'clock on Wednesday morning' (BI 18653).

30 Mark Chirnside and Samuel Halpern, '*Olympic* and *Titanic*: Maiden Voyage Mysteries', journal of the Titanic International Society, *Voyage*, spring 2007, p.123.

31 Mark Chirnside and Samuel Halpern, 'Speed and More Speed', *The Titanic Commutator*, journal of the Titanic Historical Society, Vol.32, Nos 182 and 183.

32 An in-depth examination of the issue of time is given in a two-part article by Samuel Halpern called 'The Mystery of Time', published in the journal of the Titanic Historical Society, *The Titanic Commutator*, Vol.31, Nos 178 and 180. The article also deals with how clocks were changed on board *Titanic* and the impact it had on the watch schedules of the crew, the time difference between Ship's Time and New York Time, the times logged in several wireless messages, the times of collision and sinking as observed by passengers and crew, and a few time enigmas and paradoxes.

33 AI p.294.

34 The adjustment of ½ to 1 minute of time that Pitman mentioned would take place, if needed, after a sun line was taken in the forenoon to determine the ship's longitude more precisely. The same procedure in setting Apparent Time was also done on ships of the Cunard Line and explained in great detail by Commander James Bisset in his book, *Ship Ahoy!! Nautical Notes for Ocean Travellers, With Charts and Diary*, Third Edition, Charles Birchall Ltd, Liverpool, 1924.

35 Samuel Halpern, 'Time and Time Again', *White Star Journal*, the official newsletter of *The Irish Titanic Historical Society*, Vol.19, Issues 1 and 2, 2011. This article is also available online at: http://www.titanicology.com/Californian/TimeandTimeAgain.pdf.

36 The clock adjustments shown in the table for the nights of 15 and 16 April are projected estimates only. They are based on the assumption that there was no accident or a need to divert from her planned course, and that the ship would maintain an average speed of 22 knots from midnight 14 April until arrival off Ambrose. At that speed, consistent with what *Titanic* was averaging all day Sunday, we get an estimated time of arrival off Ambrose at 10.54p.m. NYT on 16 April 1912, after crossing the Atlantic in five days, 13 hours and 34 minutes.

37 IMM Co. Rule 116 stated that when arriving or departing points in the United States or Canada, Ship's Time would be changed to the mean time for the 75th meridian of longitude which was exactly 5 hours 0 minutes behind GMT. Standard time zones were already in use in most places in the United States and Canada, including New York, ever since the railroads adopted it on 18 November 1883. They were later established officially into law across the entire United States

with the Standard Time Act of 1918, enacted on 19 March.

38   Time differences for 15, 16 and 17 April are projected based on an average sustained speed of 22 knots for the last three days of *Titanic*'s ill-fated voyage.

39   Hichens, AI p.451.

40   Pitman, AI p.294.

41   Bride, AI p.906.

42   See also Samuel Halpern. 'Rockets, Lifeboats, and Time Changes', published in the journal of the Titanic International Society, *Voyage*, winter 2009, and in the journal of the British Titanic Society, *Atlantic Daily Bulletin*, December 2009.

43   For example, A.H. Barkworth's account published in the *New York Sun*, 25 April 1912.

44   Hichens, AI p.451.

45   Samuel Halpern, 'Changing Watch Schedules', http://www.titanicology.com/WatchSchedules.html.

46   Samuel Halpern, 'The Mystery of Time', No.180.

47   Haines, AI p.656.

48   George Behe, *On Board RMS Titanic: Memories of the Maiden Voyage*, p.98.

49   Behe, p.80.

50   Behe, p.84.

51   Behe, p.337.

52   Behe, p.79.

53   Behe, p.110.

54   Behe, p.99, p.103.

55   Robert Paola, 'Weather and the *Titanic*', *Weatherwise*, April/May 1992, p.18.

56   Paola, p.18.

57   Paola, p.18.

58   Paola, p.18.

59   Paola, p.18.

60   Paola, p.19.

61   Paola, p.19.

62   In his testimony at the Limitation of Liability Hearings on 8 April 1914, Bruce Ismay said that *Titanic* encountered 'a few minutes of fog one day'. He thought it might have been on 13 or 14 April.

63   Paola, p.19.

64   Paola, p.19.

65   Behe, p.124.

66   Paola, p.19.

67   Jewell, BI 233, BI 277.

68   Lord, AI p.720.

69   Lord, AI p.720. The quantification of 'fresh wind' to 17–21 knots and 'moderate sea' to 4–8ft comes off the Beaufort Scale that defines Force 5 conditions which are 'fresh winds and moderate seas', as Captain Lord described. Ref: 'Estimating Wind Speed and Sea State', National Oceanic & Atmospheric Administration (NOAA), National Weather Service, http://www.wrh.noaa.gov/pqr/info/beaufort.php.

70   Jewel, BI 233 & BI 277.

71   Paola, p.19.

72   Paola, p.19; Jewell, BI 233.

73   Paola, p.19.

74   Behe, p.337.

75   Paola, p.19; Jewel, BI 280.

76   Lightoller, BI 13595, BI 13601–4.

77   Lightoller, AI p.68.

78   Lightoller, AI p.67.

79   Kilian Harford & Gerry Murphy, 'Titanic's Weather', *White Star Journal*, Irish Titanic Historical Society, Vol.14, No.3, December 2006.

80   Compiled from evidence presented at the 1912 British inquiry and from the book by John Booth and Sean Coughlan, *Titanic – Signals of Disaster*, White Star Publications, 1993.

81   Wireless message times were logged by Marconi shipboard operators in GMT when east of 40° W longitude, and in New York Time (NYT) when west of 40° W longitude. GMT = NYT + 5 hours.

On 12 April, *Titanic* ATS was 1 hour 24 minutes behind GMT. By 14 April, *Titanic* ATS was 2 hours 58 minutes behind GMT.

[82] BI 24919-24943.

[83] Turnbull, BI 16059.

[84] Cyril Evans, BI 9148-9150, 9165-9166. The words 'shut up' were communicated by sending the letters 'DDD'. This was known as the 'silent signal', meaning that all other stations must cease transmitting. (See AI p.147.)

[85] Halpern, 'Time and Time Again'.

[86] Chirnside and Halpern, 'Speed and More Speed'.

[87] Chirnside and Halpern, 'Speed and More Speed'.

[88] This does not mean that they were out to capture the Blue Riband from Cunard's *Mauretania*. If *Titanic* would have arrived off Ambrose light vessel at anytime before midnight on Tuesday 16 April, she would easily have logged the best maiden voyage crossing time of any previous White Star Line vessel, something that would not go unnoticed by the press.

[89] Third Officer Pitman told the British inquiry that he thought the ship should have turned the corner at 5p.m. (BI 15183). It is easy to see how he really got that. At 22 knots it would take the ship 49 minutes to cover 18 nautical miles. So if the ship was 18 miles from the corner at 5.50p.m. it would have been close to the corner about 5p.m. Thirty-six days earlier at the American inquiry, Pitman testified that 'we were supposed to be at the corner at 5.50' (AI p.303).

[90] When commanding *Adriatic*, Captain Smith was reported to have said, 'I cannot imagine any condition which would cause a ship to founder. I cannot conceive of any vital disaster happening to this vessel. Modern shipbuilding has gone beyond that.'

[91] Lightoller, BI 13635.

[92] Lightoller, AI p.439.

[93] Lightoller, BI 13595.

[94] Lightoller, BI 13707.

[95] National Imagery and Mapping Agency, *The American Practical Navigator [Bowditch]*, Pub. 9, US Government Printing Office, 2002 Bicentennial issue, Ch.33.

[96] Lightoller, BI 13560–9, BI 13648–52.

[97] Lightoller, BI 13615–22.

[98] Leo Shubow, *Iceberg Dead Ahead!*, Bruce Humphries, Inc., 1959.

[99] James Bisset and R. Stephensen, *Tramps & Ladies*, Angus & Robertson, 1988.

[100] Rostron, BI 25405–13, BI 25425–32.

[101] Bowditch, Ch.33.

[102] Symons, BI 11983.

[103] Lee, BI 2401–2.

[104] Fleet, BI 17245–72.

[105] Lightoller, BI 13679–81, BI 14196, BI 14280.

[106] Lightoller, BI 14281–86.

[107] The distance to the visible horizon as seen from *Titanic's* bridge would be about 9.8 nautical miles, and from the crow's nest it would be about 11 nautical miles.

[108] At the Ryan trial in 1913, Fourth Officer Joseph Boxhall testified that there was no haze at the time of collision, and Fifth Officer Harold Lowe testified there was no haze when he went off duty at 8p.m., and conditions were the same when he came back on deck after the collision.

[109] Lawrence Beesley, *The Loss of the SS Titanic*, Houghton Mifflin Co., 1912.

[110] Shackleton, BI 25060.

[111] AI p.1142.

[112] Affidavit of Stanley Lord, June 1959.

[113] Lee, BI 2447-2448.

[114] Adapted from Gittins, *Titanic: Monument and Warning*.

[115] In 1912 two main types of binoculars were in use at sea. Prismatic binoculars, of the pattern commonly seen today, generally had object lenses of around 30mm and magnified six or seven times. So-called 'night glasses' sacrificed magnification for light-gathering. They were in effect pairs of Galilean telescopes, having object lenses of around 50mm and magnifying about four times. Zoom designs were also in use. George Hogg recalled that the glasses use by *Titanic's* lookouts between

Belfast and Southampton were marked 'Theatre, Marine and Field'. This indicates a zoom design, with a variable field of view. All types had uncoated lenses and were subject to light losses at the lens surfaces and internal reflections.

116 Fleet, AI p.323.

117 Fleet, BI 17439.

118 *Titanic*'s surviving officers seemed to have had limited experience of ice; Lightoller, BI 13685, Pitman, AI p.308, Boxhall, AI, p.252. Lowe had never sailed the North Atlantic before.

119 The English textbook author and seamanship instructor Graham Danton is a little more optimistic and states that, 'On a clear night without moonlight it is unlikely that a sharp lookout will detect a berg at distances beyond about 500 metres'. He goes on to say that, with the aid of binoculars, breakers on a berg may be seen at a distance of up to 1 mile, *if the bearing of the berg is known* [our emphasis]. Danton is assuming the use of modern binoculars, which are markedly superior to those of 1912. Such evidence reduces the credibility of Lightoller's theory that all would have been well had a sea been running to create white water.

120 Samuel Halpern, 'Collision Point'.

121 Olliver, AI p.528; Scarrott, BI 359. A medium-sized iceberg is characterised by the International Ice Patrol as being between 51 and 150ft in height, and from 201 to 400ft in length.

122 This comes from several eyewitnesses including AB Joseph Scarrott (BI 361–2), and passengers Henry Stengel (AI p.974) and Esther Hart (*The Ilford Graphic*, 10 May 1912).

123 The evidence presented by Edward Wilding was that *Olympic* turned 2 points from the time the order was first given, not after the wheel was put hard over. The order 'hard-a-starboard' was in reference to the position of the tiller on the rudder post, a throwback to the days of early sailing ships. To starboard the helm, the wheel would be turned to the *left* which would cause the tiller to be put over to the right, to starboard. The rudder, which faced aft of the rudder post, would go to the left, and the action of the water on the rudder would cause the stern of the ship to swing out to starboard while the ship's head turned to port. In 1912, the term 'starboarded' was used to indicate that the ship's stern swung out to starboard causing the ship to turn to port. Similarly, the term 'ported' meant the ship's stern swung out to port causing the ship to turn to starboard.

124 Professor Fotis A. Papoulias, 'Ship Dynamics', TS4001 Lecture Series, Department of Mechanical Engineering, Naval Postgraduate School, Monterey, CA.

125 Samuel Halpern, 'She Turned Two Points in 37 Seconds', *Titanic Research & Modeling Association (TRMA)* website, http://titanic-model.com/articles/Two_Points_in_Thirty_Seven_Seconds/Two%20Points%20in%20Thirty-Seven%20Seconds.pdf.

126 Hichens, BI 973 and BI 993.

127 Fleet, AI p.361.

128 Olliver, AI p.526-537.

129 Olliver: 'I know the orders I heard when I was on the bridge was after we had struck the iceberg. I heard hard aport, and there was the man at the wheel [Hichens] and the officer [Moody]. The officer was seeing it was carried out right.'

130 Rowe, AI p.522-523.

131 Scarrott, BI 354–6.

132 Boxhall, BI 15343–57.

133 Hichens, BI 1026–36; Olliver, AI p.533.

134 Lightoller, BI 13759; AI p.50.

135 Ranger, BI 3995–4003.

136 Dillon, BI 3719–29; Lightoller, 13743; Stengel, AI p.975.

137 From the combined testimonies of Frederick Fleet, Reginald Lee, Robert Hichens, Alfred Olliver and Frederick Barrett.

138 When Frederick Fleet was asked to sketch what he saw when the iceberg was first sighted before he rang the lookout bell, he placed the berg fine off the ship's starboard bow, not directly ahead. See: Samuel Halpern, 'She Turned Two Points in 37 Seconds', p.22.

139 See the account, 'The Life of William McMaster Murdoch', http://www.dalbeattie.com/titanic/wmmlifea.htm.

140 Affidavit submitted by Alfred Fernand Omont to the British Wreck Commission.

141 Rowe, BI 17671.

6

DESCRIPTION OF THE DAMAGE TO THE SHIP

Captain Charles Weeks and Samuel Halpern

Extent and Nature of the Damage Caused by the Allision

The allision with the iceberg took place along *Titanic's* starboard side. Due to the speed of the ship, contact with the iceberg lasted less than 7 seconds. During this time the iceberg caused damage to the ship's hull about 10ft above the keel. The damage started in the vicinity of the forepeak tank and extended intermittently for about 250ft aft. Damage was done to the forepeak tank, No.1 hold, No.2 hold, No.3 hold, No.6 boiler room, and to the forward starboard coal bunker in No.5 boiler room.[1] Using the work and equations of naval architect Shengming Zhang,[2] we were able to calculate that the initial impact impulse was just under 3,900 ton-seconds.[3] *Titanic's* speed at the moment of impact is estimated to be about 20.7 knots, reduced from 22.5 knots due to hydrodynamic drag as the ship was entering a hard turn to port. The loss of kinetic energy caused by the initial impact was calculated to be only about 14,100 foot-tons, or a mere 1½ per cent of the ship's total kinetic energy before contact.[4] As *Titanic's* Quartermaster Alfred Olliver put it, the contact was just 'a glancing blow'.

The damage incurred to the vessel was *not* one continuous gash along the side. As stated before the British Wreck Commission in 1912 by Harland & Wolff naval architect Edward Wilding:

> I cannot believe that the wound was absolutely continuous the whole way. I believe that it was in a series of steps . . . [a] series of wounds which flooded the different spaces.

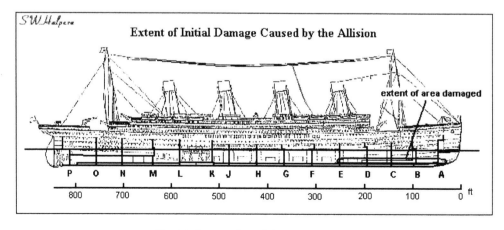

Fig. 6-1 Extent of initial damage to *Titanic*.

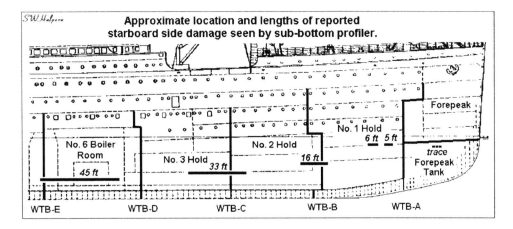

Fig. 6-2 Regions of starboard-side damage seen by sub-bottom profiler.

During the week of 29 July through 3 August 1996, Paul Matthias of Polaris Imaging used a sub-bottom profiler to image the bottom part of the bow section of the wreck below the sediments. Matthias was able to identify separations in the hull along both starboard and port sides of the bow. Unfortunately, a report by the Marine Forensics Panel (SD-7) written in 1997 by William Garzke and others,[5] attributed the cause of the observed damage along the starboard side to the collision with the iceberg, but failed to mention that similar damage was also found on the port side.[6] However, location information (including a graphic attributed to Polaris Imaging) of the starboard side damage was given in a Society of Naval Architects and Marine Engineers (SNAME) report and in other subsequent articles.[7] In the 1997 SNAME report, it was admitted that 'the damage seen from the sub-bottom profiler through 16.75 metres of sediment may have been exacerbated by the bow's encounter with the seabed.' Nonetheless, the reported locations of the imaged starboard side damage were shown, and the lengths of the open seams were documented. From the information given, trace damage was seen in the area of the forepeak, two slits of 5 and 6ft in length in No.1 hold, one slit of 16ft in length across watertight bulkhead B extending into No.2 hold, one slit of 33ft in length across watertight bulkhead C extending well into No.3 hold, and one slit of 45ft in length in No.6 boiler room extending just a few feet across watertight bulkhead E into No.5 boiler room. There was no reported damage across watertight bulkhead D separating No.3 hold from No.6 boiler room. The approximate areas of starboard side damage observed by the sub-bottom profiler are shown in Fig. 6-2.

It should be pointed out that the only viable data derived from the imaging were the lengths of the reported damage, not their widths. As was written in footnote No.10 of the 1997 SNAME report, 'The imaging provided the horizontal extent of the six openings. The width of these openings was below the resolving power of the sub-bottom profiler.' Even if the extent of these openings were exacerbated when the bow made contact with the seabed, the results do confirm that there is no continuous gash along the starboard side.

In 1912, Edward Wilding presented evidence that the cumulative amount of openings in *Titanic*'s side amounted to something on the order of 12sq.ft. As he was quick to clarify, the individual punctures along the side 'can only have been a comparatively short length'. It was the aggregate area of all the openings that amounted to 12sq.ft. In a deposition taken at the Limitation of Liability Hearings in New York on 13 and 14 May 1915, Wilding explained how he arrived at this:

It was known that certain spaces were filled up in a certain number of minutes, approximately. You couldn't say to a stop watch, but in about 40 minutes certain compartments forward were filled up to a certain level. The capacity of those compartments was known, and therefore the

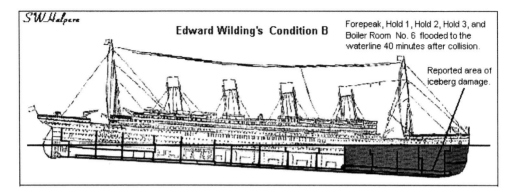

Fig. 6-3 Wilding's 'condition B' taken for 40 minutes after impact.

amount of water which got in, in the 40 minutes was known. The approximate depth of the position of the damage was known and it was then possible to calculate the rate of inflow per square foot of opening. I have the total inflow and I can divide that by the number of minutes and get the total inflow per minute. I can get the inflow per square foot per minute, and by dividing the one by the other I can get the square feet . . . My memory is 12 square feet;…For your information, the accuracy of that is probably one quarter either way; that is, it is more than 9 and less than 15, and 12 is the most probable.

From the evidence presented at the British inquiry by various eyewitnesses, Wilding concluded that water flooding the forward compartments had come up to the waterline in about 40 minutes' time, with some compartments having filled faster than others. Knowing the volumes of those compartments, and allowing for how much space was taken up by various obstructions in them, he estimated that 16,000 long tons of seawater had entered the ship over that period of time. He also heard evidence that openings in hull plates were seen 2ft above the level of the stokehold plates in No.6 boiler room and the forward bunker of No.5 boiler room. That would be about 25ft below the outside waterline. Thus Wilding assumed a 25ft pressure head for the initial water inflow. With that information he could use a form of Bernoulli's equation to solve for the inflow rate of water as a function of time, and from that derive the equivalent area of openings in the hull. Using the same assumed information that Wilding had available to him, we find that the equivalent aggregate area of openings amounts to 11.7sq.ft, which is in excellent agreement with what Wilding estimated back in 1912.[8]

Flooding in the Early, Middle and Latter Stages

With regard to analysing the flooding of the ship, Edward Wilding presented a series of plans to the Wreck Commission that were worked from evidence given at the inquiry as it came out day to day. The set of plans he presented are listed below:

Plan A – Showing flooding in No.1 and No.3 holds, and No.6 boiler room.
Plan B – Showing flooding in the forepeak, in nos 1, 2 and 3 holds, and No.6 boiler room.
Plan C – Showing flooding in nos 1, 2 and 3 holds, and No.6 boiler room, but a dry forepeak.
Plan D – Showing flooding in the forepeak, nos 1, 2 and 3 holds, and No.6 boiler room, plus some considerable amount of water in No.5 boiler room, and a trace of water in No.4 boiler room.
Plan E – Presented but not discussed.

Flooding-by-Compartment – A sequential flooding of compartments beginning with the forepeak tank all the way to, and including, part of No.4 boiler room.

Plan A was presented by Wilding to show that *Titanic* could float with any three of the first five compartments flooded. He showed that the ship would float with No.6 boiler room flooded plus nos 1 and 3 holds flooded, or with No.6 boiler room flooded plus nos 2 and 3 holds flooded. The bending moment (weight multiplied by distance) of flooding No.2 hold had about the same effect as flooding No.1 hold because of the greater weight of water that would have entered No.2 hold despite it having a shorter moment arm (as measured from amidships).

Wilding's plan B (Fig. 6-3) showed that *Titanic* could not be saved with the first five compartments open to the sea as reported by several eyewitnesses. It was this condition that he used to derive the 12sq.ft of aggregate damage as discussed above.

Wilding's plan C was the same as his plan B but without the forepeak flooded. Although it was not discussed much, it would have shown that water would still have overtopped watertight bulkhead E between nos 5 and 6 boiler rooms causing the progressive flooding of the ship.

Wilding's plan D was presented to show that water would have overtopped watertight bulkhead F between nos 4 and 5 boiler rooms even if that bulkhead had been extended as high as D deck with the first six compartments flooded.

Wilding's flooding-by-compartment presentation (Figs 6-4 through 6-11) was most illustrative and very useful to later analysts. This plan was developed to show how *Titanic* would trim down by the head as individual compartments are flooded one at a time beginning with the first and working aft. It was used solely to show how the waterline of the ship would

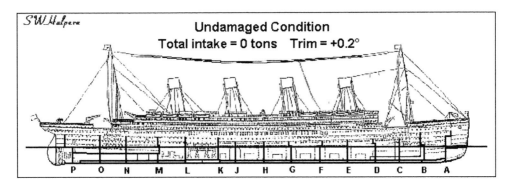

Fig. 6-4 *Titanic's* intact condition before collision.

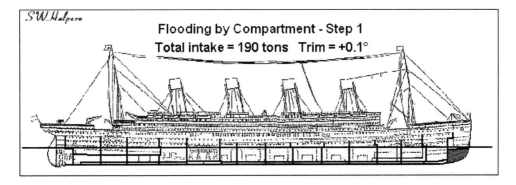

Fig. 6-5 Step 1 of Wilding's 'flooding-by-compartment' sequence.

change as subsequent compartments are allowed to flood completely, and it was used to show when water would have overtopped the transverse watertight bulkheads if carried to various heights. It was never intended to demonstrate how the ship actually flooded as some people mistakenly believe. In all, seven flooding-by-compartment steps were presented. This sequence is reproduced below in the set of diagrams beginning with the ship in the undamaged condition. Listed on these diagrams is the amount of water that would have entered the ship in long tons as well as the angle of trim derived from the landmark analytical work of Hackett and Bedford.[9]

Step 1 – 'The first thing was to flood the forepeak tank, that was the foremost compartment of the ship ...'

Step 2 – 'I then flooded No.1 hold ... That is No.1 hold plus the forepeak.'

Step 3 – 'I then, in addition to having the forepeak flooded and No.1 hold flooded, flooded No.2 hold ... When No.2 was flooded it would flood the firemen's tunnel, because, the waterline has then got above the step in the bulkhead and can go down the stairs. Of course, as you will see, the water is still at that time below the level of the top of the bulkheads which run to the E deck ...'

Step 4 – 'Then, having flooded the forepeak and No.1 and No.2 holds, I also flooded No.3 hold...'

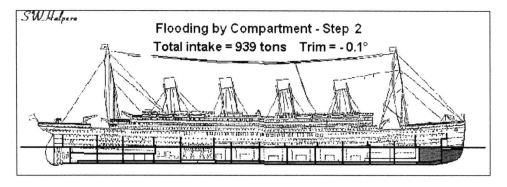

Fig. 6-6 Step 2 of Wilding's 'flooding-by-compartment' sequence.

Fig. 6-7 Step 3 of Wilding's 'flooding-by-compartment' sequence.

Step 5 – 'I then flooded No.6 boiler room, in addition to the others . . . You will now see that the water had got up above the top of 'A' bulkhead, and would get down into the rest of the forepeak. It means the eventual foundering of the ship.'

Step 6 – 'I then flooded No.5 boiler room in identically the same way as I had previously flooded No.6, adding its flooding effect to the forward spaces . . . which, as you will notice, puts the forecastle entirely under water, and also the forward end of forward deck, B deck.'

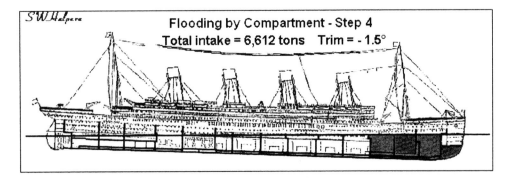

Fig. 6-8 Step 4 of Wilding's 'flooding-by-compartment' sequence.

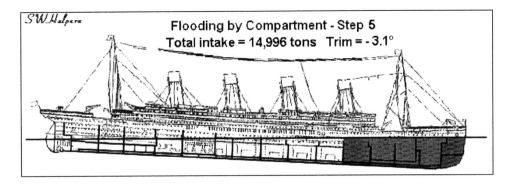

Fig. 6-9 Step 5 of Wilding's 'flooding-by-compartment' sequence.

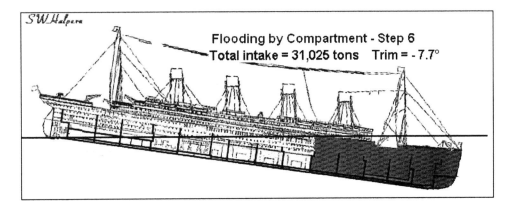

Fig. 6-10 Step 6 of Wilding's 'flooding-by-compartment' sequence.

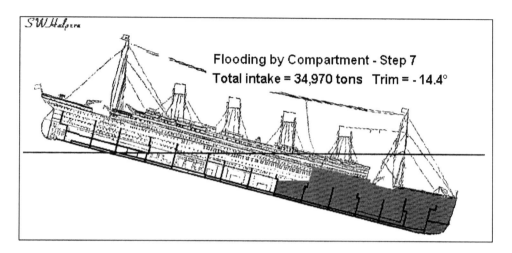

Fig. 6-11 Step 7 of Wilding's 'flooding-by-compartment' sequence.

Step 7 – The next condition was the partial flooding of No.4 boiler room 'and it shows that the stern is out of the water as far about as the base of the mainmast [located aft of the fourth funnel], or a little further forward.'

When No.2 hold was flooded in step 3, the ship had trimmed down to a level that water in No.1 hold would have also flooded the firemen's tunnel, but the waterline would still be below the level of the top of the bulkheads which run up to E deck. However, when No.6 boiler room was also flooded in step 5, the ship had trimmed down enough so water from No.1 hold got above the top of bulkhead A and would flood the rest of the forepeak space. Also, the water would reach over the height of bulkhead E between boiler rooms 5 and 6 which meant the eventual loss of the ship due to progressive flooding of compartments.

The following table lists the total water intake for each step of the flooding-by-compartment sequence as well as the total displacement, the mean draught, and the trim angle that is produced:[10]

Condition	Water Intake (tons)	Displacement (tons)	Mean Draft (ft)	Trim Angle
Undamaged	0	48,300	32.25	0.2°
Step 1	190	48,490	32.42	0.1°
Step 2	939	49,239	32.83	–0.1°
Step 3	3,135	51,435	34.17	–0.7°
Step 4	6,612	54,912	36.20	–1.5°
Step 5	14,996	63,296	40.95	–3.1°
Step 6	31,025	79,325	53.87	–7.7°
Step 7	34,970	83,270	74.38	–14.4°

Wilding's starting point was the undamaged condition of the ship on the night of 14 April 1912. Having completed about two-thirds of her maiden voyage, the particulars were:

Mean draught	32ft 3in
Trim by stern	3ft 0in
Draught aft	33ft 9in
Draught forward	30ft 9in
Displacement	48,300 tons

To determine the flooded state of the ship from eyewitness accounts we were able to map localised observations to an angle of trim for the ship. This is where we can make use of a set of waterline curves which show the progressive flooding of the ship from the work of Hackett and Bedford. As the ship trimmed down by the head, the draught forward and aft changed over time.[11] For any given flooded condition, the draught forward and aft defines the waterline in that flooded condition. We can draw a set of these waterlines against detailed profile plans of the ship such as the ones shown in Fig. 6-12 and 6-13. Then, if we have an eyewitness report that water was seen at the level of a certain deck in a certain compartment, we know that the external waterline had to be at, or somewhat above, that particular level at that particular time. Then using a relation between trim angle for that waterline and the amount of water intake that would produce that trim angle, we can find the approximate amount of water that had flooded into the ship when that particular observation was made.

The trim of the vessel as a function of time can thus be derived from a list of key eyewitness accounts which are detailed in Appendix H. In each case the appropriate waterline was determined based on their specific observation. In doing so, the reported list of the vessel at that time was also factored in if the observation was anywhere away from the ship's centreline. The estimated times of these observations, in minutes past the collision time, is taken either directly from the testimony, or implied from some immediate action taken in relation to time taken from the testimony.

In the early stages of flooding in the vicinity of the mail room we have a number of eyewitness accounts which allow us to plot the rise of water in No.3 hold as a function of time. This is shown in Fig. 6-14 along with the names of the witnesses involved.

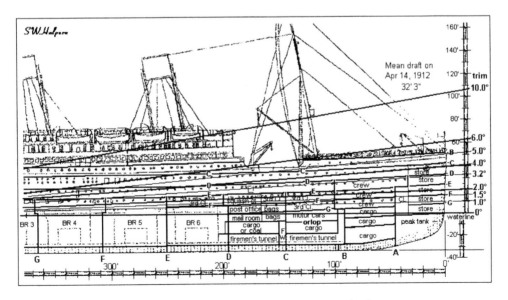

Fig. 6-12 Trim angles shown on bow section detail.

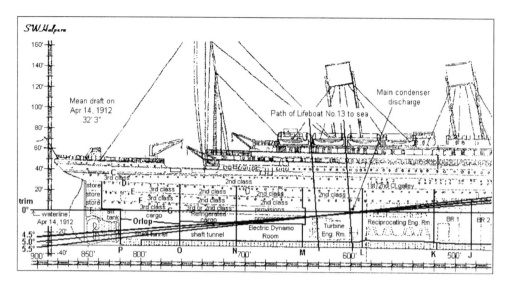

Fig. 6-13 Trim angles shown on stern section detail.

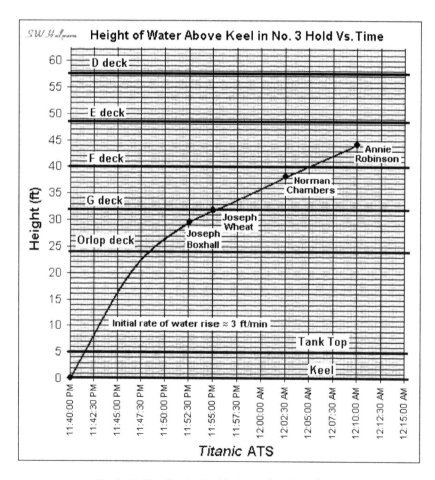

Fig. 6-14 Flooding in No.3 hold as a function of time.

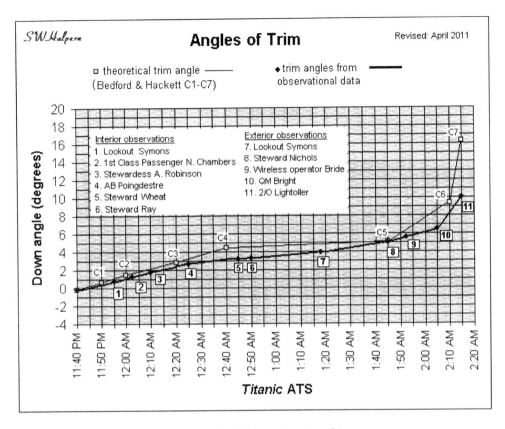

Fig. 6-15 Angle of trim as a function of time.

From other quantifiable observations we were able to establish how far the ship had trimmed down by the head over time. This result is shown in Fig. 6-15 with the specific observations identified. For comparison, we show a theoretical curve marked by conditions C1 through C7 that came from the work of Hackett and Bedford.

Also from the work of Hackett and Bedford, we were able to plot the amount of water that would enter the ship as a function of angle of trim of the ship for various flooded conditions. This is shown in Fig. 6-16 for trim conditions C1 through C7. Notice that the relationship between trim angle and total water intake is approximately linear up to and including condition C5. The reason for this is that the moment arm to the centre of volume of the floodwater did not change very much as the water was initially confined to the first six compartments. In that situation, the trim angle would change in approximate proportion to the weight of the floodwater for the relatively small angles of trim as shown.

Armed with this relationship between trim angle and approximate water intake, we were then able to plot the approximate amount of water intake as a function of time using the trim versus time curve previously derived. This result is shown in Fig. 6-17.

If the flooding were confined to only the first four major watertight compartments ahead of watertight bulkhead D, the ship would have settled down by the head to a trim angle of 1.5° and taken in about 6,600 tons of seawater. We know this from step 4 of Wilding's flooding-by-compartment submission that was reproduced in the work of Hackett and Bedford. But the actual curve of trim versus time continues well beyond this, passing a 1.8° down angle within 30 minutes after the collision, and a 2.7° down angle by 45 minutes after the collision. The reason for this was that there was a significant amount of flooding taking place in No.6 boiler room as well as the flooding in the forepeak tank, nos 1, 2 and 3 holds, and a small amount of

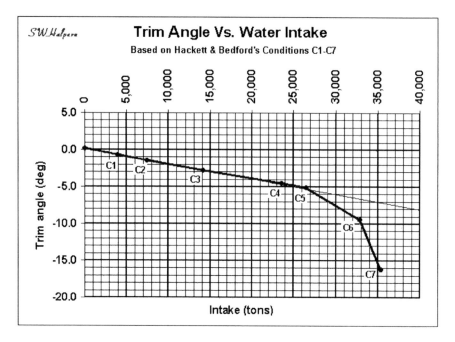

Fig. 6–16 Angle of trim as a function of water intake.

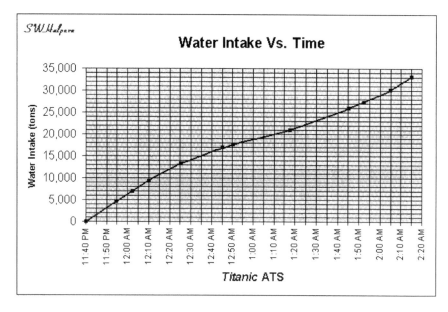

Fig. 6–17 Water intake as a function of time.

flooding in the forward bunker of No.5 boiler room. There is also evidence that a very small amount of damage may have taken place between the level of the tank top and the stokehold plates in No.4 boiler room amounting to at most 11sq.in of opening in a split seam just above the turn of the bilge in that section.[12]

We also know that there was no initial damage to the store room above the forepeak tank,[13] which would remain dry until the bow trimmed down to about 3.2° at which point water

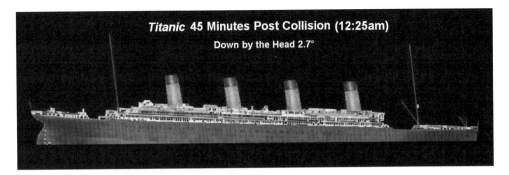

Fig. 6-18 *Titanic* at 45 minutes after the collision.

from No.1 hold would get above watertight bulkhead A and flow forward to flood the rest of the forepeak space. In No.5 boiler room, the observed flooding in the empty forward starboard-side coal bunker was described as resembling the output of an ordinary fire hose.[14] It was seen to come in at a level 2ft above the stokehold plates (corresponding to a depth of about 25ft below the surface), and about 2ft abaft the watertight bulkhead there. Assuming an equivalent 3¼in-diameter opening with a pressure head of 25ft, the initial intake rate at that point would be about 4 tons per minute.[15]

In No.4 boiler room, water was first seen to come over the stokehold plates at the forward end of that section about 1 hour 40 minutes after the collision. It has been estimated that the maximum inflow rate to this compartment was about 6.4 tons per minute, but that 100 tons of water would have been pumped out between 12.10 and 12.25 after the lights in the stokeholds came back on leaving about 187 tons of unchecked water under the stokehold plates in No.4 boiler room at 12.25a.m. Only in No.6 boiler room, the most forward boiler section of the ship just aft of No.3 hold, would there be enough flooded volume to cause the ship to trim down by 2.7° within 45 minutes as previously noted. At that time, the flooding in nos 1, 2 and 3 holds appeared to have reached close to the level of the outside waterline. From the total intake versus trim angle curve, we know that the total water intake into the ship had to be close to 13,500 tons to produce that angle of trim 45 minutes after the collision (Fig. 6-18).

Using the flooding-by-compartment sequence in the work of Hackett and Bedford, we were able to calculate the amount of water that would flood various compartments to the outside waterline for a number of trim angles.[16] Using a trim angle of 2.7° that was observed within the first 45 minutes, we get the results listed below for flooding in holds 1, 2 and 3, plus the flooded peak tank and the estimates for the small amount of flooding in nos 5 and 4 boiler rooms as noted above:

Water Intake Per Compartment 45 Minutes After Collision	
Forepeak tank	190 tons
No.1 hold	1,730 tons
No.2 hold	3,040 tons
No.3 hold	3,515 tons
No.5 boiler room	180 tons
No.4 boiler room	187 tons
Total excluding No.6 boiler room	8,842 tons

To produce a total of about 13,500 tons of water intake in 45 minutes, No.6 boiler room had to have taken in the remaining 4,658 tons of water, which means that it only reached to about 90 per cent of what it would have flooded to if the water inside had reached as high as the outside waterline at that time.[17] Notice also that 13,500 tons is quite a bit less than the 16,000 tons that Edward Wilding assumed when he worked up his famous 12sq.ft of aggregate hull openings. In coming up with his number, Wilding made it very clear that he assumed that the ship had taken in 16,000 tons of water in the first 40 minutes.[18] Part of this assumption was that water had reached the outside waterline in *all* of the first five forward compartments including the entire forepeak and No.6 boiler room. However, this does not appear to be the case. What we find at 45 minutes with the ship trimmed down by about 2.7° is that only the forepeak tank was flooded in the first compartment, and water had only reached to about 90 per cent of the outside waterline in No.6 boiler room. What all this means is that Wilding may have overestimated the total damage to the ship based on the limited information available to him at the time. Using 13,500 tons of water intake in the first 45 minutes, the aggregate size of the openings in the hull would have added up to almost 10sq.ft of total damage, not 12sq.ft. In the Limitation of Liability Hearings in 1915, Wilding admitted that his estimate had an accuracy that was 'probably one quarter either way'. The initial inflow flooding rate would be about 11.2 tons of seawater entering the ship per second, or 672 tons per minute. Of course this inflow rate would decrease as the water level in the various compartments approached the level of the outside waterline. It should also be noted that the total pumping capacity of all the ballast and bilge pumps in the ship (see Chapter 3) was 1,700 tons per hour, or 28 tons per minute.

The volume of water to enter a particular compartment is just the average area of that compartment, multiplied by the height of water in that compartment, multiplied by the compartment's permeability (the percentage of space that can be filled by water flooding into that compartment).[19] By knowing the average flooding rate in cubic feet of seawater per minute for a compartment, we can find the rate at which the water was rising in that compartment. For No.6 boiler room, the average inflow rate appears to be about 3,625 cubic ft of seawater entering the compartment per minute.[20] The average rate that water would be rising in No.6 boiler room calculates out to about 11.5in per minute.[21] In the first 10 minutes water would have risen to about 9.6ft above the tank top in that section. Since the stokehold plates were 2ft 7.5in (2.6ft) above the tank top, the water would have reached a level of about 7ft above the plates in the first 10 minutes of time, or close to halfway up the height of the double-ended boilers which were 15ft 9in in diameter. This condition is shown in Fig. 6-19 which also takes into account that the ship had taken on a list of 5° to starboard within the first 10 minutes following the collision.[22] The view is looking aft near stokehold No.10.

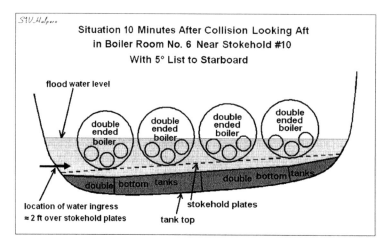

Fig. 6-19 No.6 boiler room, 10 minutes after collision.

Leading Fireman Frederick Barrett was standing on the starboard side at the aft end of No.6 boiler room talking to Second Engineer John Hesketh when the collision happened. A few seconds before the collision, a bell rang and the illuminated boiler room telegraph went to 'STOP'. Barrett and Hesketh immediately called out for the men to shut the dampers, but before all of them could be shut, the crash came. As Barrett explained later to second class passenger Lawrence Beesley in lifeboat No.13, the incoming water had 'rushed him off his feet'. He then picked himself up and, along with Hesketh, sprang for the compartment doorway that separated No.6 boiler room from No.5 aft. They both made it through the aperture just as the watertight door dropped down behind them 'like a knife'.

When Frederick Barrett came into the No.5 boiler room, he went over to an open bunker door on the starboard side where he saw water coming in 'the very same as an ordinary fire hose'. He then shut the bunker door and informed Assistant Second Engineer Jonathan Shepherd who then informed Hesketh. Soon the engineers got the pumps started and Hesketh, who was in charge of the watch below at that time, ordered 'all hands stand by your stations', which was an order for the men in that section to stand by their fires. Although they knew that No.6 boiler room was taking in water, Barrett and Shepherd decided to go up the escape from No.5 boiler room to E deck, and then down the escape to No.6 to see how bad the situation had become in there. But they soon discovered that they could not get down to the bottom as there was 'eight feet [of water] above the plates'. According to Barrett, 'it was not a quarter of an hour, just on ten minutes' following the collision. From what we have independently calculated, the rise of water in No.6 boiler room would reach about 7ft above the stokehold plates in about 10 minutes, which is in good agreement with Barrett's visual estimate.

We also estimate that the amount of damage in No.6 boiler room was equivalent to about 212sq.in (1.47sq.ft) of composite hull opening to produce the rate of flooding observed in that compartment.

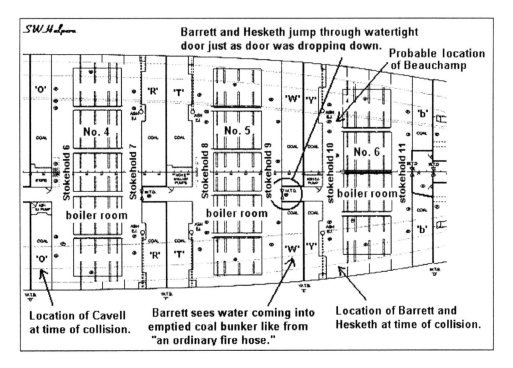

Fig. 6-20 Frederick Barrett's escape from No.6 boiler room into No.5 at the time of collision.

Effect of Flooding on the Ship's Stability

There are few vessels that stay on an even keel under damaged conditions. *Titanic* was no exception. Floating vessels have two types of stability; transverse stability and longitudinal stability. Transverse stability is associated with list and roll. Longitudinal stability deals with trim and pitching motion. Trim is the difference between the vessel's draught forward and draught aft, and is a function of how weights are distributed fore and aft. A vessel's draught is how deep the bottom of the ship is below the surface of the water. A ship with the same draught at bow and stern has zero trim and floats level in the transverse plane. *Titanic* started the night of 14 April with a very slight but unnoticeable trim by the stern before the accident took place. After the accident happened, water flooded into the hull forward and caused her trim to change dramatically over time as we have seen.

When a ship is floating at rest in calm water, it is acted upon by two sets of forces, the downward force of gravity, and the upward force of buoyancy. The force of gravity is the result of a combination of all downward forces including the weight of the ship's structure plus all the equipment, cargo, fuel and personnel on board. The combined weight of the ship, which equals the ship's displacement in tons, may be considered as a single force which acts vertically downward through a single point in the hull called the centre of gravity (G). For a ship with no list and zero trim, G lies on the ship's centreline and not too far from the ship's midship section under normal conditions.

The force of buoyancy is also a combined force which results from the pressure of seawater acting on all parts of the ship's hull that is below the waterline. This force also equals the ship's displacement in tons and may be regarded as acting vertically upward through a single point in the hull called the centre of buoyancy (B). This is the geometric centre of the ship's underwater body and lies directly under the centre of gravity on the ship's centreline, not far from the ship's midship section when the ship is on an even keel carrying no list. Its vertical height above the keel (K) is usually a little more than half the vessel's draught.

When a ship is at rest in calm water, the forces of buoyancy and gravity must be equal and opposite, and lie on the same vertical line as shown in Fig. 6-21 for a ship on an even keel in the transverse plane.

A ship may be disturbed from rest in the transverse direction by conditions which tend to make it heel over to an angle. These include such things as wave and wind action, forces during a turn, shifting of weights or location of weights off-centre such as the uneven usage of coal or fuel oil. When a disturbing force exerts an inclining moment to the vessel, the ship's underwater body changes shape. The centre of the underwater volume is shifted in the direction of the heel which causes the centre of buoyancy to relocate off of the vessel's centreline (originally at B) and move to the geometric centre of the new underwater body (at B). As a result, the lines

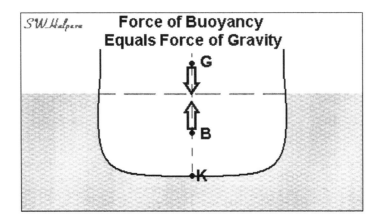

Fig. 6-21 Forces of buoyancy and gravity for ship on an even keel.

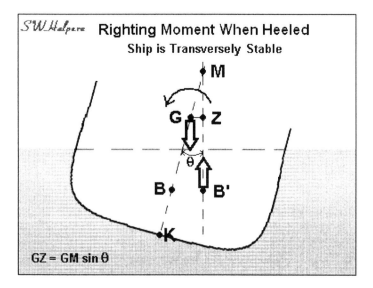

Fig. 6-22 Righting moment for stable ship in a heeled condition.

of action of the forces of buoyancy and gravity are no longer acting in the same vertical line, but are separated, thereby creating what is called a 'righting moment' that wants to restore the ship back to an even keel as shown in Fig. 6-22.

The righting moment is usually taken about the centre of gravity point G. It is the product of the force of buoyancy times the distance GZ that separates the line of action of the buoyancy force from the centre of gravity as shown above. The distance GZ is called the 'righting arm'. Since the force of buoyancy must equal the weight of the ship, the restoring moment is simply equal to the ship's displacement in tons times the length of the righting arm GZ in feet. The righting arm is a true indicator of the amount of stability a vessel has at any angle of inclination. The greater the righting arm the more tendency the vessel has to return to the upright.

A ship's metacentre (M) is the intersection of two successive lines of action of the force of buoyancy as the ship heels through a small angle. When the ship is on an even keel and not carrying a list, the buoyant force is directed upward along the line from B through G. When the ship is heeling, the buoyant force is directed upward from B passing through Z to a point where it intersects the original buoyant force line. For small angles of heel, about 10° or less, that intersection point will remain essentially stationary. It is called the initial position of the transverse metacentre. The initial position of the metacentre is most useful in the study of transverse stability because the greater the height of the metacentre above G (the distance GM) the greater the righting arm will be for a given small angle of heel thereby producing greater initial transverse stability.

If the distance GM is too large, the righting arm that develops at small angles of heel will also be large. Such a ship is very 'stiff' and will roll with a short period and large amplitude as it tries to follow the slope of the waves coming broadside. It can become very uncomfortable for passengers and crew, especially in a moderate to heavy seaway. On the other hand, if GM is too small, the righting arms that develop will also be small. Such a ship is considered 'tender' and will have a long rolling period. In that case, the risk of capsizing in rough weather increases, and it also puts the vessel at risk of developing large angles of heel if cargo or ballast should shift. A ship with a very small GM is also less safe if the ship is damaged because it leaves less of a safety margin against capsizing.

For a passenger ship a GM equal to about 2 per cent of her beam is considered a good compromise.[23] For *Titanic* in the intact condition just before the accident on the night of 14 April 1912, her GM was estimated to be at 2ft 7½in,[24] or about 2.8 per cent of her beam.

Fig. 6-23 shows the location and values of these points on *Titanic* prior to the accident.

The stability of a ship in a damaged condition will change as she takes in more and more water. At first, the value of GM may increase somewhat, but it will eventually move in the other direction and decrease dramatically as more and more water enters the ship. This can be seen in the pioneering work of Hackett and Bedford where they calculated the value of GM for various flooding conditions as shown in Fig. 6-24.

In addition to changes in GM, the peak value of the righting arm, GZ, will decrease as more and more water enters the hull. Fig. 6-25 shows how the size of the righting arm changes as function of angle of heel for two different flooded conditions, C2 and C6, corresponding the early and late stages of flooding, respectively.

Also from the work of Hackett and Bedford, we can find the maximum angle of heel beyond which the ship is likely to capsize as the righting arm goes negative. This is shown in Fig. 6-26.

In *Titanic*'s case transverse stability was never really a major issue until the very late stages of the sinking process. We know she took on a measured list of about 5° to starboard within 5 to 10 minutes after colliding with the iceberg.[25] This was due to asymmetrical flooding on her starboard side primarily in nos 2 and 3 holds due to the location of the firemen's tunnel that ran under these holds on the ship's centreline at the tank top level. Once the water began to overtop the tunnel in these holds, it would start to fill space on the port side, and the ship would slowly start to right herself again. Later in the flooding process the ship took on a list to port, apparently due to greater flooding on the port side of E deck and a possible reduction

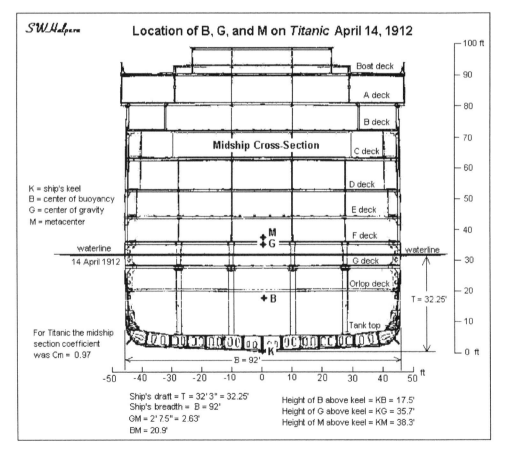

Fig. 6-23 Location of centres of buoyancy, gravity and metacentre on *Titanic* before collision.

Fig. 6-24 Value of GM
for different amounts of
flooding.

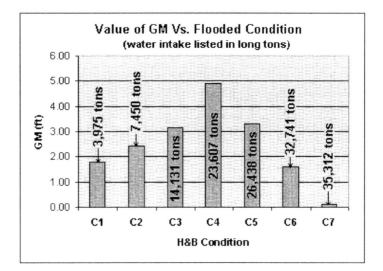

Fig. 6-25 Righting arm
as a function of angle of
heel for two different
amounts of flooding.

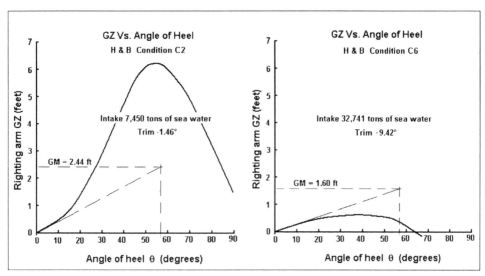

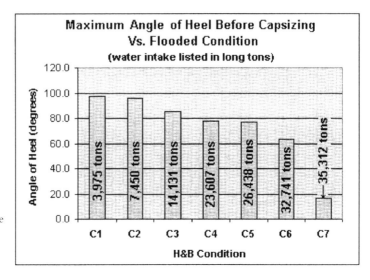

Fig. 6-26 Maximum angle
of heel before capsizing
for different amounts of
flooding.

Fig. 6-27 *Titanic* at 2.15a.m.

of GM due to free surface effect and the weight of added water. The port side of E deck had a major passageway referred to as Scotland Road which was 9ft wide and completely open at the forward end. Water spreading along this passage would tend to penetrate downward more on the port side of the ship. On the starboard side there was a much narrower passageway serving a number of small cabins with a door at the forward end, all of which would tend to inhibit flooding on the starboard side. The list to port that developed measured about 10° at about 1.50a.m., just 30 minutes before the ship sank, when the last of the 30ft lifeboats were being launched. At the time there was a reported gap of about 2½ft that separated the lifeboat's gunwale from the rail of the ship on the port side of the boat deck as they were passing people across.[26] At 1.50a.m. the ship would have taken in about 27,000 tons of seawater. Yet despite carrying that 10° list, the vessel was not in any danger of capsizing.

The bulk of *Titanic's* stability issues that night were longitudinal. As the flooding progressed her forward draught increased and her after draught decreased as we have seen in the graph of trim angle versus time in Fig. 6-15. Initially, the rate seemed to slowly increase until the ship was down by the head about 2.7° by 12.25a.m. as water was coming up to the outside waterline in the forward flooding compartments. Thereafter, the rate of increase in trim angle tended to slow down giving a false sense of hope to those who were on board. This very slow increase in trim continued until about 1.45p.m. when the ship had reached an angle of trim of about 5°, at which time her propellers were half out of the water. Then the rate of trim increase started to slowly accelerate until about 2.15a.m. the ship had reached a down angle of about 10° when the crow's nest was level with the sea and water was seen coming over the top of the wheelhouse (Fig. 6-27).[27] It was a minute or two after this that the ship became longitudinally unstable and started to tip over.

Stresses Imposed on the Hull and the Observed Breakup

Titanic not only sank, but she broke apart in the process of doing so. Lookout George Symons was in lifeboat No.1 about a ¼ mile away from the ship when she sank. This is what he had to say before the British Wreck Commission:[28]

> Her foremost lights had disappeared [under the water], and her starboard sidelight left burning was the only light, barring the masthead light, on that side of the bridge that I could see . . . You could not see her keel . . . You could just see the propellers . . . A little while after that we pulled a little way and lay on the oars again. The other boats were around us by that time, and some were pulling further away from us. I stood and watched it till I heard two sharp explosions in the ship. What they were I could not say. Then she suddenly took a top cant,

her stern came well out of the water then ... She took a heavy cant and her bow went down clear ... Head down, and that is the time when I saw her lights go out, all her lights. The next thing I saw was her poop. As she went down like that so her poop righted itself and I thought to myself, 'The poop is going to float.' It could not have been more than two or three minutes after that that her poop went up as straight as anything; there was a sound like steady thunder as you hear on an ordinary night at a distance, and soon she disappeared from view.

Asked to explain some of this further, Symons went on to say:

Her head was going well down ... her stern was well out of the water ... It righted itself without the bow; in my estimation she must have broken in half ... I should think myself it was abaft the after expansion plate ... I should say it would be about abeam of the after funnel, or a little forward ... I saw the poop right itself ... then it went up and disappeared from view.

Just before the ship lost longitudinal stability the bow of the ship forward of the bridge was under water while the stern was high enough so that the ship's propellers were clearly visible to those in the boats. Suddenly two sharp cracks that sounded like explosions to some were heard, and the ship dipped further down by the bow as the stern started to come well out of the water. Then all the lights on the ship went out as the stern settled back to a point where it almost righted itself. The part of the ship ahead of the vicinity of the fourth funnel was now completely gone. To Symons, and to a few others in the boats, it looked like the remaining stern section of the ship was going to stay afloat. However, within two or three minutes, the forward end of the remaining stern dipped downward as its after end came almost straight up in the air. Then, with a steady rumbling sound that was heard across the water, the stern slid down and sank below the surface.

We feel that as the ship became longitudinally unstable the water-laden bow section pulled the stern further up out of the water until the stress on the hull far exceeded its design strength and a fracture occurred. Theoretically, the maximum stress on the hull would have occurred in the neighbourhood of about 10 to 15° of trim as shown in Fig. 6-28.

It is likely that peak stresses occurred when those two sharp cracks were heard as the bow started to take that sudden cant forward. The remaining connections between the bow and stern would have pulled the stern further upward before it started to settle back as the last connections between bow and stern finally parted. From several eyewitness accounts, the stern may have been pulled up as much as 30° before it started to settle back.[29] After returning to a near horizontal position, the broken forward part of the remaining stern section would start to flood very rapidly. With the furthest aft compartments still intact, and rapid flooding in its

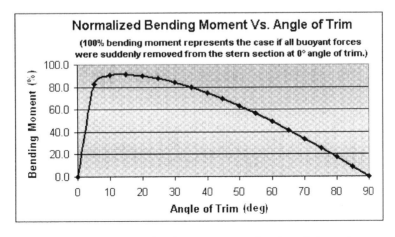

Fig. 6-28 Approximate bending moment as a function of trim angle.

foremost part, the remaining stern section would trim down to a relatively steep angle before going under.

In the summer of 2005, the History Channel sponsored an expedition to the wreck site. During that expedition, two large previously undocumented sections of *Titanic's* double bottom structure were found. After examining these sections, and analysing results of the computer modelling, it was concluded that the tank top plating failed in tension while the bottom plating failed in compression. Roger Long, a naval architect hired to consult on the project, came up with the theory that the hull started to break at a relatively shallow angle of trim under the aft expansion joint. He theorised that as the crack propagated down the sides of the ship, seawater would flood into the stern part of the hull causing stress to be reduced to the point where a sagging moment was created leading to a failure of the keel, and separation of the double bottom sections from the hull.[30]

Alternate theories on how the hull broke have been put forward by others. Parks Stephenson suggested a break that started when the ship reached an angle of trim of about 30° on the starboard side near the aft expansion joint. This then propagated downward and then across the bottom.[31] Roy Mengot and Richard Woytowich suggest that a break occurred at an angle of trim of 15 to 17°, and started in the double bottom and propagated up both sides.[32] This last theory would have the doubled-up plating of the sheer strake at the level of the bridge deck act as a hinge about which the bow and stern sections bent before it separated.

By the end of the nineteenth century, naval architects had a good understanding for predicting loads on vessels and the structural strength that would be needed in the design of the hull girder. Complete curves of buoyancy, load, shearing forces, and bending moments could all be calculated for a variety of conditions for any particular ship. However, it was a very laborious process, taking up to several months in some cases to get a complete set of curves.[33] One design standard at the time was that a ship built with mild steel, such as *Olympic* and *Titanic*, should be able to sustain hogging and sagging stresses of up to 10 tons per square inch when meeting waves of her own length with a crest-to-trough height of 5 per cent of her length (an L/20 wave) under conditions of minimum draught near the end of a voyage.[34] For *Olympic* and *Titanic*, this works out to a hypothetical trochoidal wave 850ft long with a height of 42½ft as shown in Fig. 6-29.

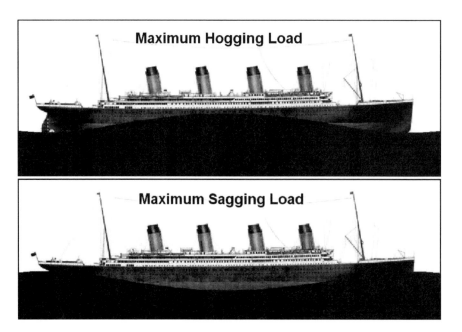

Fig. 6-29 Maximum hogging and sagging loads imposed by 850ft trochoidal waves.

They also had other well-established procedures that could be followed in the design process. One was to treat the ship as a beam or girder and form an estimate of what the stress on the vessel's sheer strake (the upper strake of shell plating) would be in tons per square inch to determine the thickness of plate needed. The 'rule of thumb' that was used was to subject the design to a bending moment equal to its displacement in long tons multiplied by 1/30th her length between perpendiculars in feet. In the case of *Titanic*, that works out to be 1,473,333ft-tons using a displacement of 52,000 tons. This produced a stress value of 9.9 tons per square inch on the bridge deck sheer strake.[35]

As a point of comparison, the table below shows the calculated stress in tons per square inch on the sheer strake of three contemporary vessels also built with mild steel.[36]

Contemporary Vessel	Length [p-p] (ft)	Displacement (tons)	Draught	Bending Moment (ft–tons)	Stress on Sheer Strake (tons/sq.in.)
Titanic	850	52,000	34ft 6in	1,473,333	9.9
Aquitania	866	51,700	35ft 4in	1,492,407	8.5
Imperator	882.5	60,610	37ft 9in	1,782,944	10.2

For *Lusitania*, another contemporary vessel, the maximum imposed bending moment when subjected to an L/20 wave of her own length in the hogging condition was calculated at 1,020,000 foot-tons. This produced a stress in tension of 10.6 tons per square inch on her uppermost structural deck (her shelter deck), while the compressive stress on the keel was calculated at 7.8 tons per square inch. Although the maximum stress in tension on the shelter deck exceeded the 10 tons per square inch design goal for mild steel, *Lusitania* used high-tensile steel which would theoretically allow a 20 per cent higher loading.[37]

Assertions have been made that the materials used on *Titanic* were neither of the quality nor mass required by a ship of her size. These are totally unfounded. The thicknesses of hull plating for large liners of *Titanic's* era are well documented. Leaving aside the fact that the thicknesses of hull plating varied somewhat throughout the vessel, or that plating was doubled in areas like the sheer strake, we find that the typical thickness of shell plating amidships on *Titanic* and *Olympic* were similar to other large vessels of the time as shown in the table below.[38]

Contemporary Vessel	Launched	Gross Tonnage	Plate Thickness (inches)
Lusitania	1906	31,550	1.1
Olympic/Titanic	1910/1911	45,324	1.0
Aquitania	1913	45,647	1.1
Homeric (ex *Columbus*)	1913	34,351	0.94
Majestic (ex *Bismarck*)	1914	56,551	1.02

As with other vessels, *Titanic* and *Olympic* were strengthened at the upper flange of the equivalent hull girder by making the bridge and shelter deck plating thicker and doubling the sheer strake plating at these points. The ship was also strengthened at the lower flange of the hull girder by doubling the bilge plating. In many places, treble and quadruple riveting was used.

Was *Titanic* built well enough to withstand the worst service conditions on the North Atlantic? That question was asked of the marine engineering firm of Jamestown Marine Services (JMS) of Groton, Connecticut, as part of the History Channel's *Titanic's Achilles Heel* programme in early 2007.[39]

JMS determined that the maximum 'design' bending moment, the maximum bending moment calculated from a set of thirteen different intact condition cases, was 661,768 foot-tons in hog and 151,840ft-tons in sag. Harland & Wolff designed *Olympic* and *Titanic* to handle a bending moment of 1,473,333ft-tons, or more than a factor of two times greater than the maximum bending moment in the JMS theoretical 'design' case.

JMS also calculated the bending moment and peak stress on the vessel in several flooding conditions. In their case 22, they had *Titanic* down by the bow by 10° after flooding the first seven compartments. Their calculated bending moment was then determined to be 1,538,892ft-tons in hog, which was slightly greater than the Harland & Wolff design point. Their analysis also showed that the bending moment that resulted from their assumed flooding scenario exceeded their 'design' case bending moment by a factor of 2.33. They also determined that the peak shear stress calculated from their 'design' case was 4,285 tons located 216ft aft of amidships (frame 72 aft). The calculated flooded peak shear stress with enough flooding to create 10° of trim was determined to be 7,847 tons located 63ft forward of amidships (frame 22 forward). As we have seen, *Titanic* was still in one piece when she assumed a trim of 10° down by the head, the time Second Officer Lightoller left the ship.

The JMS engineering team concluded, as do we, that if damage to the hull girder occurred as a result of the flooding condition of the ship and its associated bending moment, then that does *not* mean that the vessel was insufficiently designed. They disproved the supposition that *Titanic* and her sister *Olympic* were weakly designed ships. Their analysis does confirm that relatively high bending moments could be expected at about a 10° angle of trim, supporting the notion of a fracture starting at a relatively low angle rather than at a high angle as some people were led to believe. As we have seen, the highest bending moments would tend to happen at an angle near 15°. JMS also found that the ship's longitudinal stability would be lost at a much shallower angle than what was widely believed to be *Titanic's* final intact attitude.

To summarise, *Titanic* was not a weak ship. The ship did not sink because she broke up. She broke up in the very last stages of sinking which imposed excessive stresses and bending moments on the hull as the stern was pulled further out of the water as the ship lost longitudinal stability. She had only a few minutes remaining at best when the fracture occurred.

Fire Down Below

It was known that a small fire was smouldering in one of *Titanic's* coal bunkers at the time she departed Southampton on 10 April.[40] It was caused by spontaneous combustion. According to leading firemen Frederick Barrett and Charles Hendrickson, work to dig out the coal to get to the fire did not start until the first watch began after the ship left Southampton.[41] It was not until sometime on Saturday 13 April, the day before the accident, that the fire was finally put out.[42] According to Barrett, in addition to digging all the coal out, the firemen and trimmers also played a hose on it.[43]

The most effective way to fight a bunker fire is to dig out as much coal as possible to get to where the fire is. The application of water would be to prevent it from spreading further and to extinguish the fire once it could be reached. Even today, 'water alone is the most common extinguishing agent for a silo or bunker fire' in coal-fired electric power generating stations.[44] However, water would never be used to wet down coal in a non-burning bunker because wet coal is much more prone to oxidize quickly, generating heat in the process, and eventually igniting spontaneously.

Spontaneous combustion fires in coal bunkers were not unusual occurrences on board steamships of that day. In fact, according to Rule No.248 of the IMM Company's 'Ship Rules and Uniform Regulations' that was in effect at the time:

248. *Examination of Coal Bunkers.* – The respective senior engineers of each watch, before going off duty, must go through the coal bunkers, and note their condition on the log-slate, and should there be any signs of spontaneous combustion taking place, they are at once to report same to the Chief Engineer, who is immediately to notify the Commander. All coal should, as often as possible, be worked out of the bunkers.

We also know that the 56/100in steel watertight bulkhead that formed part of the bunker wall was slightly distorted from the fire. According to Barrett, 'The bottom of the watertight compartment was dinged aft and the other part was dinged forward.' And according to Hendrickson, 'You could see where it had been red hot; all the paint and everything was off. It was dented a bit … yes, warped … I just brushed it off and got some black oil and rubbed over it.' Although Hendrickson talks about the bulkhead being 'red hot', he did not actually say that he ever saw it in that condition. But even if the fire never got hot enough for the bulkhead to glow red, it had to have been above the 750°F ignition point of coal for it to smoulder, and it had to be close enough to the bulkhead to cause it to expand and distort. Any coal on the other side could easily have been ignited by heat conduction across the bulkhead in the vicinity.

Barrett made it very clear that the bunker space on the starboard side of the ship aft of watertight bulkhead E that separated No.5 boiler room from No.6 (the starboard-side bunker space marked 'W' in the diagrams) was emptied out because of the fire.[45] It was in that space that he saw water entering the ship immediately after the collision at the rate of an ordinary fire hose. When he was asked if there were any other bunkers empty forward, he said 'No.'[46] But, what exactly did he mean by that?

When he was being questioned at the British inquiry about the cause of this rush of water that he saw come through the pass between the boilers moments before he escaped from No.5 boiler room, Barrett told them that it may have come from the bunker that was at the forward end of the room; the one that had been emptied out. When it was suggested that it may have been a bunker bulkhead that gave way, Barrett said, 'It would be possible, because there are watertight compartments inside the bunker. There is a watertight compartment going through the centre of the bunker.'[47] And that answer generated some confusion over *Titanic*'s transverse bunker arrangement.

Consider the follow series of questions that were asked of him concerning these coal bunkers:

2066.	The Solicitor-General: I think there are the elements of a little confusion over this. The [watertight] bulkhead runs across the ship from the starboard side to the port side, does it not?
Barrett:	Yes.
2067.	Is there a coal bunker on either side of the bulkhead on the starboard side?
Barrett:	There is a watertight compartment running right through the centre of the bunker.
2068.	There is the watertight bulkhead?
Barrett:	Yes.
2069.	The Commissioner: But the bunker is partly on one side of the watertight bulkhead and partly on the other?
Barrett:	Yes.
2070.	And the watertight bulkhead goes through the middle of the bunker?
Barrett:	Yes.
2071.	And then across the ship?
Barrett:	Yes.
2072.	The Solicitor-General: If you imagine this box is the bunker and that is the starboard skin of the ship, the watertight bulkhead runs through it like that does it not, down the middle?
Barrett:	Yes.
2073.	And you were on the after-side of this No.5?
Barrett:	I was in No.6 when we shipped it; I was on the after-side of the bulkhead later.

Notice that in his answer to the question as to whether there is a bunker on either side of the watertight bulkhead on the starboard side (2067) he could have simply said, 'yes'. But instead he tried to explain that the bunker was divided in the centre into two compartments by a watertight bulkhead, and agreed that 'the bunker is partly on one side of the watertight bulkhead and partly on the other' side. He was not describing it as two separate bunkers that happen to be on opposite sides of a watertight bulkhead, which they were.

The significance of how Barrett viewed things has to do with identifying the bunker space where coal was taken out of when they fought the fire. It seems probable that coal was taken out of the bunker space on both sides of watertight bulkhead E, from the bunker space on the forward side of No.5 boiler room, and from the bunker space on the aft side of No.6 boiler room (bunker spaces marked 'W' and 'Y' in the diagrams).

Further evidence that coal may have been removed from the bunker space on both sides of the watertight bulkhead is suggested by Fireman George Beauchamp who was also in No.6 boiler room when the collision happened. His station was Stokehold No.10, at the aft end of the room. Beauchamp heard Barrett and Second Engineer John Hesketh call for the dampers to be shut. He said that when the crash came it was 'just like thunder, the roar of thunder'. Then the watertight doors dropped and soon someone called out for them to draw the fires. As he explained it:[48]

> After the order was given to shut up, an order was given to draw fires. I could not say how many minutes, but the order was given to draw fires . . . Water was coming in on the plates when we were drawing the fires . . . coming through the bunker door and over the plates . . . coming through the bunker like.

This picture from Beauchamp suggests that water was flowing out from the bunker onto the plates that the firemen stood on. We know from Barrett that water was also coming in from the starboard side of the hull in that compartment when he ran to escape into No.5 boiler room just as the doors were closing. But this observation of Beauchamp confirms that the hull was also pierced in the aft bunker space of No.6 boiler room, ahead of the watertight bulkhead, and may suggest that the bunker space was empty enough for water to quickly fill the bunker space and rise to the level of the bunker doors and spill out onto the stokehold plates that the firemen and trimmers stood on.[49]

Fires were also drawn from the furnaces in No.5 boiler room that night. When that task was completed, the men working there were sent up except for Barrett. As a leading fireman, he was asked to remain below to open a manhole plate on the starboard side so the engineers could get at some valves in the piping system. The air being thick with steam from all the water that was thrown onto the fires in the furnaces, Assistant Second Engineer Jonathan Shepherd did not see the open manhole and fell in and broke his leg. Barrett and another engineer, Herbert

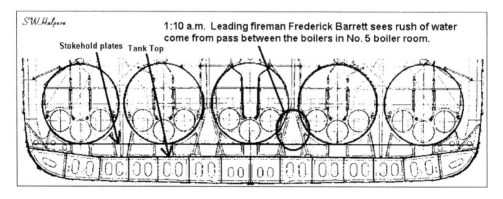

Fig. 6-30 Frederick Barrett sees water coming from pass between boilers.

Harvey, lifted Shepherd out and carried him aft to the pump room where they attended to him as best they could for a while. About 15 minutes later, according to Barrett, 'a rush of water came through the pass – the forward end, a space between the boilers where we walk through . . . I never stopped to look [where the water came from]. I went up the [escape] ladder. Mr Harvey told me to go up.' When Barrett was asked if it could have been a bunker bulkhead at the head of the compartment that gave way, he replied. 'I have no idea on that, but that is the bunker that was holding the water back.'

According to his best recollection, Barrett went up the escape from No.5 boiler room at about 1.10a.m. When he came out onto E deck there was water there, 'coming down the alleyway from forward.'[50] Prior to that, while they were drawing the fires out of the furnaces, he felt the ship was down by the head and getting noticeably worse.[51]

There are some people who believed that it was watertight bulkhead E, weakened by the fire in the coal bunker, that gave way which caused that rush of water that Barrett saw. They also believed that this was 'the first falling domino in an escalating and ultimately catastrophic chain reaction.'[52] However, forensic science does not support such a catastrophic event.

Coal burns at a fixed temperature with a given supply of oxygen. Lacking a good draft of air to feed the fire, the coal would only smoulder at some relatively low temperature. There would have to had been a good draft of air feeding the fire if it became so hot as to make the steel

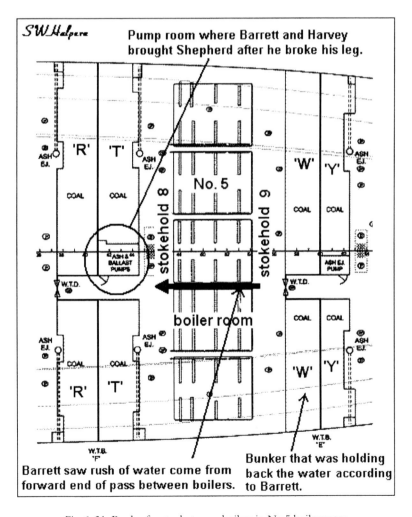

Fig. 6–31 Rush of water between boilers in No.5 boiler room.

bulkhead actually glow red. In that case, a lot of coal would have been burnt and a lot of fumes would have been produced. But this apparently was not the case.

Spontaneous ignition of coal in a bunker usually begins deep down where the coal absorbs oxygen and gives off hydrogen, carbon monoxide, carbon dioxide and some aerosols under rising temperatures. With no real draft of air in the bunker, coal will ignite and smoulder at about 750°F. Since the bulkhead was riveted tight around its edges to angle iron which was riveted to the hull and decks, thermal expansion caused by heat from the fire would cause the bulkhead plate to bulge outward to relieve the stress. After cooling back to room temperatures, it would remain somewhat dented as observed. But to get that bulkhead, which was made of mild steel, to glow red hot, would take a temperature of about 900°F or more from a fire being fed with a good draft of air. Despite the drama that some subsequent newspaper accounts wanted people to believe, it certainly was *not* a raging blaze that was completely out of control.[53]

In a metallurgical analysis, bulkhead plate similar to that used on *Titanic* was heated to about 1,200°F so that it became red hot. The plate was attached to other pieces modelling the shell and floor plates by riveting it to angle iron pieces which in turn were riveted to the other pieces. The results showed the bulkhead plate had distorted by about 6in, and the rivets holding the plate would only have been stressed to only 10–20 per cent of their failure load. Even if the bulkhead was first heated red hot and then cooled down by seawater or water from a fire hose, it would not affect the low temperature properties of the bulkhead. The conclusion of modern-day forensics is that the bunker fire would *not* have weakened the watertight bulkhead sufficiently to cause it to collapse.[54]

The most likely cause of that rush of water seen by Barrett was the collapse of a bunker door on the bunker bulkhead at the forward starboard side of No.5 boiler room. As noted before, water was seen entering that empty bunker space from the time the collision took place. Taking into account the capacity of the transverse bunker space and allowing for some remaining coal, a build up of about 440 tons of seawater could easily have filled that space between the tank top and F deck if gone unchecked. We know that water was seen falling down the first class staircase from E deck onto F deck as early as 12.50a.m. by Steward Joseph Wheat; a location that was a good 60ft aft of where watertight bulkhead E, between nos 5 and 6 boiler rooms, was located. There very well could have been sufficient down-flooding into that forward cross bunker to create a sufficient pressure head even with water draining out of four very small drain holes at the bottom of the bunker bulkhead, especially if any coal or debris still remained in the bunker to impede the flow through those holes onto the plates of the tank top. The bunker doors on the bulkhead were not designed to be watertight, nor designed to hold back a large force pushing against them. If water had reached a height of just 10ft over the stokehold plate level in the bunker by that time, it would have created a total force against each bunker door of about 3 tons. These bunker doors slid in thin channels that were only ½in wide. If a bunker door gave way as a result of a pressure head of about only 10ft, the velocity of water that would come bursting out of the bunker would be close to 25ft per second, easily creating 'a wave of green foam come tearing through' the walk space between the boilers. If it were the main watertight bulkhead between the two boiler rooms that failed, Barrett would not have had time to reach the escape, let alone hear Engineer Harvey order him up.

Location and Time of Foundering

Titanic disappeared from sight at 2.20a.m. Apparent Time Ship (ATS) on 15 April 1912. She was not seen again by human eyes until 1 September 1985 when a team led by Dr Robert Ballard found the wreckage sitting on a gently sloping plain on the Newfoundland Ridge at a depth of 12,460ft, about 2½ miles down. The discovery of the wreck confirmed the testimony of fourteen individuals back in 1912 who said that they saw the ship break in two before she sank. The testimony of these individuals, however, was discounted in favour of four individuals, including two of *Titanic's* surviving officers, who testified that the ship sank intact.[55]

The centre of the bow section is located on the ocean floor at 41° 43' 57" N, 49° 56' 49" W; the centre of the stern section is located at 41° 43' 35" N, 49° 56' 54" W; and the location of the centre of the boiler field, the point above which the ship broke in two, is at 41° 43' 32" N, 49° 56' 49" W.[56] When you compare these positions to the distress positions sent out by *Titanic*'s wireless operators, it becomes obvious that the distress positions were significantly in error. The initial CQD position, 41° 44' N, 50° 24' W, was 20.8 miles W by N of the wreckage, while the so-called 'corrected' CQD position, 41° 46' N, 50° 14' W, was 13.2 miles W by N of the wreckage.

The Wreck Site

The 450ft-long bow section is dug into the ocean bottom about 60ft at its forward end by the anchors. The rear of the bow section sits almost on top of the mud and is fully exposed. It broke free of the stern section at the surface and could have taken as little as 6 minutes to reach the bottom based on observing other ships that have been scuttled. *Titanic* was pointing to the northward just before she broke in two.[57] After the bow broke free, it planed slightly forward moving a little more than 1ft forward for each 6ft of drop. It ended up about 830 yards to the north of the centre of the boiler field and pointing to the east of north.

It is thought that the bow descended at close to a 45° angle and hit the bottom moving at about 20 knots or more. When the tip of the bow impacted with the bottom, it dug itself into the mud. The impact also caused two bends in the hull. The forward bend under the well deck cranes was estimated by Dr Robert Ballard at about 6°. More recent views indicate that it may be more like a 10° bend. The second bend under the forward expansion joint is about 4°. Both bends represent a portion of the keel that has been compressed, and the decks above them are correspondingly deformed.[58]

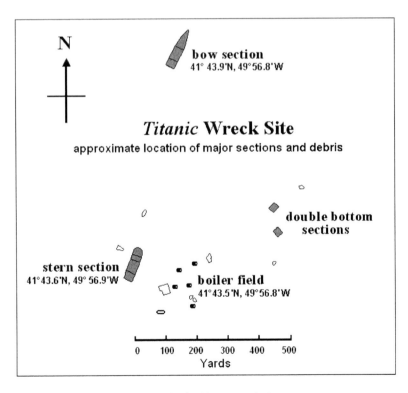

Fig. 6-32 The *Titanic* wreck site.

The 350ft stern section underwent a series of forces far different than the bow. Unlike the bow section, which still shows the general appearance of the ship, the stern section is completely devastated. The starboard shell plate is missing for some 160ft aft of the forward tear. The debris alongside the wreck is a mixture of deck and shell plate sections that comprise only a fraction of the original mass. It is thought that a huge section of plating fell off sometime well before the stern section impacted with the ocean floor. The port side shell plate is still present, but is separated from the keel for about 120ft aft of the tear. The bow section shows no evidence of the shell plate separating from the keel despite the impact with the ocean floor. The poop deck is peeled up as far as the aft end of the third class public rooms and folded back on itself. The docking bridge juts out from under the folded poop deck in the broken starboard aft corner. The centre propeller is totally buried. The outboard wing propellers and shafts were sheered upward from the ship when it hit the bottom, and are bent at nearly a 20° angle leaving the wing propellers visible almost at the level of the portholes on G deck. Number '401', *Titanic's* hull number, can be seen on the starboard wing propeller blade.

Fig. 6-32 shows the approximate locations of the major parts of the wreck on the bottom of the Atlantic.

Notes

1 Wilding, BI 20317.
2 S. Zhang, 'The Mechanics of Ship Collisions', Dept. of Naval Architecture and Offshore Engineering, Tech. University of Denmark, 1999. The thesis presents mathematical models for ship collisions showing collision energy losses, collision forces and structural damages. A number of examples for full-scale ship collisions are analysed, and a method relating the absorbed energy and the destroyed material volume is developed and verified.
3 This is only about 28 per cent of the impact impulse that took place during the 1956 collision between *Andrea Doria* and *Stockholm*. Reference: Samuel Halpern, 'Lights to Port - Lights to Starboard – An Objective Forensic Analysis of the Collision Between *Stockholm* and *Andrea Doria*', Presented before a class on casualty analysis at the Maine Maritime Academy, Castine, Maine, November, 2008. Available for download at: http://www.titanicology.com/AndreaDoria/Stockholm-Andrea_Doria_Collision_Analysis.pdf.
4 For a complete summary of the finding and calculation assumptions, see: Samuel Halpern, 'The Energy of Collision', http://www.titanicology.com/EnergyOfCollision.html.
5 William Garzke *et al.*, '*Titanic*, The Anatomy of a Disaster, A Report from the MFP (SD-7), Proceedings of the 1997 Annual Meeting of the Society of Naval Architects and Marine Engineers (SNAME)'.
6 Jennifer McCarty and Tim Foecke, *What Really Sank The Titanic*, Citadel Press, 2008, p.113.
7 Garzke *et al.*, 'A Marine Forensics Analysis of the RMS *Titanic*', presented to the Chesapeake Section of SNAME, Norfolk, VA, June, 2002.
8 Samuel Halpern, 'Somewhere About 12 Square Feet', *TRMA* Website Research Article, http://titanic-model.com/articles/Somewhere_About_12_Square_Feet2/Somewhere_About_12_Square_Feet2.pdf.
9 Hackett and Bedford, 'The Sinking of S.S. *Titanic* - Investigated by Modern Techniques', 1996 RINA Transactions.
10 The data roughly corresponds to Hackett's and Bedford's conditions B1-B4, A2, B6-B7. The main difference being in limiting the flooding in step 1 to the capacity of the forepeak tank which was 190 tons.
11 For a ship down by the head, the trim angle is given by the arctangent of the draught forward minus the draught aft divided by the ship's length between perpendiculars.
12 Samuel Halpern, 'Where Did That Water Come From?' http://www.titanicology.com/FloodingInBR4.html.
13 BI 17716.
14 BI 2105.
15 This comes about by multiplying the area of the assumed opening (0.06sq.ft) by the velocity of water intake from a pressure head of 25ft (40ft/sec), and converting to tons per minute. The 250 ton/hour

ballast and bilge pump located in the pump room of No 5 boiler room should have been enough to keep this inflow in check once the drain rate out of the bunker equalised with the inflow rate coming into it.

[16] It should be noted that these particular results have nothing to do with any assumptions made regarding how fast any compartment would take to flood or the size of the area of damage. It only assumes that the water level inside a compartment had reached the outside waterline for the given angle of trim.

[17] For a trim angle of 2.7°, No.6 boiler room would have taken in about 5,095 tons of water if the level of water inside had reached the level of water outside.

[18] BI 20422.

[19] No.6 boiler room has an average width of about 82ft and a length of 54ft at the tank top. This gives an area of 4,428sq.ft. The permeability factor for the space is taken at 0.85.

[20] There are 35 cubic ft of seawater per long ton.

[21] $h = 3,625/(4,428 \times 0.85) = 0.96$ft per minute.

[22] AI pp.450–451.

[23] La Dage, John & Lee Van Gemert, *Stability and Trim for the Ship's Officer*, 3rd Ed., Cornell Maritime Press, page 49.

[24] Hackett & Bedford.

[25] AI p.451.

[26] AI p.676.

[27] See Appendix H.

[28] BI 11501–25.

[29] Elmer Taylor and Mildred Brown both provided accounts that gave quantified estimates for the angle reached by the ship before seeing the ship break apart. They both had the stern point up at about 30° before settling back. Major Arthur Peuchen thought that she had achieved 'a considerable angle . . . an angle of not as much as 45°' while still intact.' (AI p.339.)

[30] Ship Structure Committee Project SR-1451, 'RMS *TITANIC*: ALTERNATIVE THEORY: Complete Hull Failure Following Collision with Iceberg,' Ship Structure Committee, US Coast Guard (CG-5212/SSC). Article submitted by JMS Naval Architects and Salvage Engineers.

[31] Parks Stephenson, 'More Questions Than Answers – Another Point of View Re: Titanic's Final Moments – Missing Pieces', *THS Commutator*, Vol.30, No.173, 2006.

[32] Roy Mengot & Richard Woytowich, 'The Breakup of *Titanic*', A Progress Report from the Marine Forensics Panel (SD-7), 16 April 2009.

[33] BI 25319.

[34] W.J. Luke, 'On Some Points of Interest in Connection With the Design, Building, and Launching of the *Lusitania*', 48th Session of the Institute of Naval Architects, 21 March 1907.

[35] BI 24355–6.

[36] Research finds of Mark Chirnside.

[37] Mild steel was expected to have an ultimate tensile strength of 28 to 32 long tons per square inch, while high-tensile steel was expected to have an ultimate tensile strength of 34 to 38 long tons per square inch. (W. J. Luke, 'On Some Points of Interest in Connection With the Design, Building, and Launching of the *Lusitania*')

[38] Research finds of Mark Chirnside.

[39] Ship Structure Committee project SR-1451.

[40] BI 19630. It was rumoured that the fire had started while the ship was in Belfast (BI 5239), but that may not be true. *Titanic* had brought over 1,880 tons of coal from Belfast when she arrived in Southampton. She was loaded with 4,427 additional tons while in Southampton, and burned 415 tons while in port after the loading. It is highly unlikely that they would have added extra coal to a bunker if a fire was known to be smouldering in it. It is more likely that the fire started while the ship was in Southampton after the bunkering, and was discovered on sailing day. It was not a big enough problem to keep the ship from starting her maiden voyage.

[41] BI 5240 and 2297.

[42] BI 5243 and 2301.

[43] BI 2340.

[44] The danger of using water alone is that the surface tension of the water and the heat from the fire

may prevent the applied water from penetrating deep into the coal pile. If that happens, gases such as hydrogen sulfide and carbon monoxide, which become explosive at high enough concentrations, may start bubbling out. That is why chemical agents are sometimes added to reduce the surface tension and allow the water to further penetrate the pile. See: Diana Merritt and Randy Rahm, 'Managing Silo, Bunker, and Dust Collector Fires', Special Section: Asset Management, *POWER* magazine, November/December, 2000.

45   BI 2087–91.

46   BI 2292–9.

47   BI 2064.

48   BI 671–4. When gathering information for his book, *A Night to Remember*, Walter Lord contacted sixty-three survivors, including George Beauchamp, who may have been a bit more candid than when he testified at the British inquiry. In his book, Lord wrote: 'Fireman George Beauchamp worked at a fever pitch as the sea flooded in from the bunker door and up through the floor plates. In five minutes it was waist deep – black and slick with grease from the machinery. The air was heavy with steam. Fireman Beauchamp never did see who shouted the welcome words "That will do!" He was too relieved to care as he scurried up the ladder for the last time.' Water being waist deep in five minutes fits rather well with our estimate of water rising at a rate of nearly 1ft per minute, because in 5 minutes the water would have reached 5ft above the tank top, or about 2½ft above the stakehold plates.

49   There is also some indirect evidence that coal had been removed from the bunker on the opposite side of watertight bulkhead E, between nos 5 and 6 boiler rooms. A story was told to the newspapers by an unnamed fireman that a fire had started in one of the coal bunkers of the vessel shortly after she left her dock at Southampton, which was not extinguished until Saturday afternoon. According to the fireman, 'It had been necessary to take the coal out of sections 2 and 3 on the starboard side, forward, and when the water came rushing in after the collision with the ice the bulkheads would not hold because they did not have the supporting weight of the coal.' (Marshall Everett, ed., *The Wreck and Sinking of the Titanic*, L.H. Walter, 1912, p.102.) Despite the obvious exaggerations, what we find consistent with Barrett's and Hendrickson's testimonies about the bunker fire is that it was being fought since the ship left Southampton, and was extinguished on Saturday, the day before the collision. It is likely that the reporter who wrote the article may have misunderstood the location of where that coal was taken out of when he wrote 'sections 2 and 3'. If the fireman actually spoke of 'the second and third stokeholds on the starboard side, forward,' that would actually point to the bunkers marked 'Y' and 'W' in stokeholds nos 10 and 9, respectively, as seen when going aft coming from the firemen's quarters. Although it should be obvious that the presence or absence of coal in a bunker has nothing to do with the strength of a watertight bulkhead, it is easy to see how such a misconception on the part of a fireman could come about. The important thing here is that this fireman mentioned that coal was taken out of two apparently adjacent bunker spaces, one on each side of the same watertight bulkhead when fighting the fire. As we have seen, Barrett referred to a bunker as having 'a watertight compartment going through the centre of the bunker,' one bunker separated by a watertight bulkhead into two spaces. The other witnesses who testified about fighting the bunker fire, Charles Hendrickson and Thomas Dillon, did not give any location information, and the fire was not considered important enough to have it reported to the Assistant Emigration Officer of the Board of Trade when the ship was docked in Southampton (BI 24118–21).

50   BI 2349–53.

51   BI 2047–9, 2054–5. From our own analysis, the ship would have trimmed down about 3.5° by that time.

52   Charles Pellegrino, 'Time Line of the *Titanic* Descent', http://www.charlespellegrino.com/time_line.htm.

53   Marshall Everett, ed., *Wreck and Sinking of the Titanic*, Castle Books, first published in 1912, pp.100–2.

54   Dr Tim Foecke, *Encyclopedia Titanica Message Board*, 18 July 2003, http://www.encyclopedia-titanica.org/cgi-bin/discus/show.cgi?tpc=5919&post=96005#POST96005; and Jennifer McCarty & Tim Foecke, *What Really Sank The Titanic*, Citadel Press, 2008, pp.175–180.

55   Bill Wormstedt, 'The Facts – What Did the Survivors See of the Breakup of the *Titanic*?' http://wormstedt.com/titanic/The_Facts.html, 2011.

56   Dr Robert Ballard, *The Discovery of the Titanic*, Madison Publishing Inc., 1987.

57   BI 17669–74.

58   Roy Mengot, 'The Wreck of RMS *Titanic*', http://home.flash.net/~rfm/.

7

AN ACCOUNT OF THE SAVING OF THOSE ON BOARD

Bill Wormstedt and Tad Fitch

Order Given to Clear the Boats

Within a very few minutes after *Titanic* collided with the iceberg at 11.40p.m., Fourth Officer Joseph Boxhall made the first of two trips down into the bow section to check for damage. Just after Boxhall headed below, Captain Smith ordered Quartermaster Olliver below to find the carpenter, and instruct him to 'take the draft of the water'.[1]

Having gone below as far as the steerage quarters on F deck and finding nothing unusual, Boxhall returned to the bridge, probably by 11.50a.m., and reported to Captain Smith that he saw no damage. Apparently Olliver had not returned yet, and Boxhall was asked by Smith to find the carpenter and have him sound the ship forward. As Boxhall headed off the bridge, he ran into the carpenter coming up the ladder from A deck who told him that *Titanic* was taking on water. Sending the carpenter up to report directly to the captain, Boxhall headed farther down, and met a mail clerk (John Richard Smith) coming up, who said that 'the mail hold is full' or 'filling rapidly'. Boxhall sent the clerk up to the bridge to report to the captain, and then headed down to the mail room to see for himself. He found the other mail clerks in the process of moving the mail, and the water within 2ft of the deck he was on (G deck). He then headed back up to report to the captain himself.[2]

Olliver must have returned to the bridge very shortly after Boxhall headed below on his second trip, just after 11.50p.m. He was given a written note, and sent back below to give it to Chief Engineer Bell. Olliver found Bell below, delivered the message, and then headed back up with the reply that Bell would get it done as soon as possible.[3] Since Olliver did not know what the message said, he also did not know what the 'it' was that Bell was going to do.

Alarmed by what he had been told by the carpenter, Smith headed below and was seen by Steward Charles Mackay and Saloon Watchman James Johnstone heading toward the engine room about 10 to 15 minutes after the collision.[4] Moments before Smith was seen going toward the engine room, Harland & Wolff shipbuilder Thomas Andrews was seen by Johnstone going in the same direction. Minutes later, Andrews was seen coming back and going forward toward the mail room, while Smith was seen heading back up the same working staircase that he came down from minutes before.[5] Smith apparently arrived back on the bridge very shortly before Boxhall got back from inspecting the mail room. At that time, knowing that the ship was seriously damaged, Smith proactively ordered the lifeboats to be uncovered.

The off-duty officers were in their cabins on the boat deck trying to get some sleep. Second Officer Charles Lightoller felt the collision and went on deck for a quick look around, but found nothing out of the ordinary except that the ship was slowing down. He went back to his room, expecting that he would be called if he was needed. Third Officer Herbert Pitman, who was awakened by the sound of the accident (he thought the ship was coming to anchor), got up a few minutes after and took a quick look out on deck and soon went back to his room. On his way back he met Lightoller, and they both agreed that the ship had struck something.[6] Due back on duty at the next change of watch, Pitman decided that it was no use trying to sleep anymore, so he lit his pipe, and after a few minutes, started to dress. Fifth Officer Harold Lowe slept through the accident and did not recall being awakened by anyone.

Below decks, the collision woke up many of the passengers, and some appeared in the passageways to ask the stewards what was going on. They were told that all was well, and that there was no cause for alarm. Others dressed, and went up on deck. Those who came onto the forward well deck discovered that ice had toppled onto the deck from an iceberg that slid past.

Fourth Officer Boxhall testified that it was approximately 20 to 30 minutes after the impact when he returned from his second trip below and called upon the off-duty officers Lightoller, Pitman and Lowe.[7] Lightoller and Pitman estimated that Boxhall called them out about 20 minutes after the accident, which supports the timing given by Boxhall.[8] A 'few minutes' after this, Boxhall heard an order given to unlace the covers and clear the boats.[9]

According to Lightoller, steam was venting from the escape pipes on the funnels due to excessive boiler pressure being blown off when he came out on deck.[10] The noise of the steam made it difficult for people to hear each other, which just added to the confusion. Almost 'immediately after' Lightoller came on deck, Chief Officer Wilde told him to start taking the covers off the boats, and informed him that all hands had been called.[11]

Consequently, the order to uncover and clear the boats appears to have been proactively given by Captain Smith at around 12.00a.m. Apparent Time Ship (ATS), even before the full extent of the damage to the ship was known.

Order Given to Get Passengers on Deck and Wearing Lifebelts

Soon after ordering the boats uncovered, Smith made another trip below. Stewardess Annie Robinson saw the captain heading toward the mail room with a mail clerk and Chief Purser Hugh McElroy down on E deck.[12] Andrews must have met Smith in the mail room, because after they left that location together, Andrews was overheard telling Smith that 'three have gone already', a reference to three watertight compartments.[13] This was about 12.10a.m., just before the two men separated, with Andrews continuing his inspection while Smith went back up to the bridge. Just minutes later, Quartermaster Robert Hichens heard Smith give the order to 'get all the boats out and serve out the belts',[14] an order for stewards to awaken the passengers and get them up to the boat deck, and for the boats to be swung out in preparation for loading. Assistant Second Steward Joseph Wheat testified that Purser McElroy gave an order to get lifebelts on the passengers and get them on deck at 'a quarter-past twelve, or round about that time.'[15] Second class passenger Imanita Shelley, and Stewards John Hart and Charles Mackay all testified that the order to get the women and children up to the boat deck came down to them around 45 minutes following the collision.[16]

It is apparent that the order to get the passengers up on deck was given at some time between 12.10 and 12.20a.m. ATS, and shortly afterwards passengers began appearing on deck.

Order Given to Load the Boats with Women and Children

After separating from Smith following their joint inspection of the flooding mail room, Andrews must have soon learned that boiler room No.6 was flooding uncontrollably as well as the three compartments forward. With the second, third, fourth and fifth watertight compartments flooding, as well as the forepeak tank, the ship was doomed. The shipbuilder was seen rushing up the grand staircase on D deck by Mrs Frank Warren with a 'look of terror' on his face at a time she estimated as approximately 45 minutes after the collision. Mr William Sloper saw him running up the grand staircase on A deck taking 'three steps at a time' and hurrying towards the bridge. He did not respond to passenger inquiries about what was wrong.[17]

There is significant evidence that Captain Smith and other crewmembers did not actually realise that the ship would sink prior to 12.25a.m. Although he already knew that the ship was badly damaged, he had no reason to order the evacuation of the ship prior to that time. It was known that the ship would remain afloat even with the first four watertight compartments completely open to the sea. But once Andrews had returned to the bridge from below decks and delivered the bad news, there was no longer any question. *Titanic* was sinking. It was time to start loading the boats and to call for assistance. According to Andrews, the ship had 'from an hour to an hour and a half.'[18]

Second Officer Lightoller thought it took 45 minutes from the time of the collision until the time the orders to fill the boats came down, or 12.25a.m.[19] First class passenger Colonel Gracie concluded from his own observations 'and those of others', that it was 45 minutes after the collision when Captain Smith gave the order to begin loading the women and children into the boats, in agreement with the 12.25a.m. time estimate.[20] Seaman John Poingdestre's testimony agrees with this estimate. After first spending some time uncovering a few boats, Poingdestre went below to the forecastle to get his boots. After witnessing the collapse of a wooden bulkhead due to seawater on the other side of it, he quickly returned to the upper decks where he overheard Captain Smith give the order to 'start putting the women and children into the boats'. He estimated the time was about three-quarters of an hour after the ship had struck when that bulkhead collapsed, and got out within half a minute.[21]

An order to load the boats coming down at 12.25a.m. is also consistent with the evidence of survivors such as Mr Albert Dick, who stated that it was 'fully an hour after the vessel struck that the lifeboats were launched,'[22] and Mr Dickinson H. Bishop who said the time that the first boat was launched 'was about a quarter to 1'.[23] This is particularly true considering that even though many of the covers had been stripped off by this point, falls would have to be coiled, plugs put in, rudders shipped, boats swung out and lowered level to the deck, and then first loaded with passengers before being launched.[24]

Access to the Lifeboats

All the lifeboats, except for two collapsible boats located on top of the officers' quarters, were stored on the boat deck. The boat deck itself was divided into several areas marked off by low railings. As shown in Fig. 7-1, the most forward part of the deck was reserved for use by the ship's officers, and included the area around lifeboats 1 and 3 on the starboard side, and 2 and 4 on the port side. The next area aft, with lifeboat 5 on the starboard side and 6 on the port side, was first class promenade space. It went as far back as aft of the third funnel. Second class promenade space included the area where all the aft lifeboats, 9 through 15 on the starboard

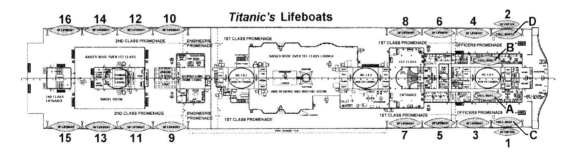

Fig. 7-1 Location of *Titanic's* lifeboats.

side and 10 through 16 on the port side, were kept. There were no lifeboats stored in deck areas assigned to third class passengers. Those spaces were the forward well deck, the aft well deck, and the poop deck at the very stern of the ship.

Collapsibles A and B (starboard and port, respectively) were stored on the roof of the officers' quarters alongside the first funnel. Collapsibles C and D (starboard and port, respectively) were stored on the boat deck just inboard of lifeboats 1 and 2.

Passengers who were forced to leave their quarters because of flooding in the early stages of the sinking, mainly third class men sleeping in the areas under the forward well deck, ascended to the well deck, some with their luggage, where a group of approximately fifty to a hundred gathered. There is no evidence that the gate at the top of the stairway leading up to B deck was locked or obstructed. However, third class stewards were seen conversing with the men who had gathered at that location, and it seems likely that they relayed to them that only women and children were allowed to go to the boats at that time, and that they had to stay were they were for the time being. However, no accounts of passengers actually being forcibly detained at the fore well deck have been uncovered.[25]

First and most second class passengers reported no difficulty gaining access to the boat deck or to A deck where the lifeboats were loaded.

Third class passengers in the aft end of the ship, including both men and women, congregated on the stern well deck, up on the poop deck, and also in the third class general room, under the poop deck. They found they were also blocked from going up to the boat deck by closed gates on the stairways leading up, and in some cases, crewmen stationed at the gates.[26] In the later stages of the sinking, the gates were unlocked, but the ascending passengers then found that many of the lifeboats had already left the ship. Two parties of third class passengers were escorted from the steerage quarters up through the second and first class areas to the lifeboats by Steward John Hart.[27]

It does not appear that there were any organised efforts to help get them up on deck and to the boats, Steward Hart being a notable exception. As third class passenger Berk Pickard testified,[28] many of the stewards and passengers, himself included, did not know the ship was sinking. The stewards tried to keep the third class passengers quiet, saying that nothing was seriously wrong, and reassuring them in general.[29] This lack of situational awareness on the part of some of the crew, and the false sense of security it created in the steerage passengers, may have led to many staying below deck until it was too late for them to be rescued.

Lifeboat Launch Sequence

In the final report of the British inquiry, the Assessors included a chart of the times they estimated each lifeboat left *Titanic*. Subsequent research has shown that their times and sequence of events do not entirely agree with the testimony at both inquiries, or with eyewitness accounts given outside the inquiries. The table presented below, and its supporting article, clarifies and corrects these errors.[30] The most significant differences between this revised timeline and the British inquiry timeline are:

Lifeboat No.8 being lowered before No.6.

The three most aft port side lifeboats being lowered before the aft starboard side lifeboats.

Lifeboat No.10 being lowered after all the other aft port side lifeboats were lowered.

The aft port side boats leaving in the opposite order from what the British inquiry had.

Collapsible C being lowered after boats No.2 and No.4 were lowered, as the forward well deck began to submerge.

Once the order was given to start loading the lifeboats, the officers in general started loading and lowering the lifeboats from forward to aft. First Officer Murdoch, Third Officer Pitman and Fifth Officer Lowe worked on the forward starboard lifeboats, while Second Officer Lightoller started trying to load passengers in the forward portside boats. In the meantime, Captain Smith and Chief Officer Wilde were busy generally superintending the evacuation and sending for aid for the ship. Despite popular belief, there is substantial evidence that Captain Smith was heavily involved in all aspects of the evacuation and the boat loading and lowering process, and that Chief Officer Wilde was heavily involved in the loading of the boats as well. Fourth Officer Boxhall was put in charge of sending up distress signals, and Sixth Officer Moody was busy uncovering the lifeboats on the port side aft. As the evacuation progressed, the officers moved aft to load boats and control the crowds gathering there, in some cases leaving the remaining fore boats to be set up and used later on. The four collapsible boats could not be used until the forward davits were clear of lifeboat nos 1 and 2, and were not utilised until the rest of the lifeboats were away from the ship.

The table below shows the launch times for *Titanic*'s lifeboats. The launch time is taken as the time that a boat first began to be lowered, or in the case of collapsibles A and B, the time they floated off the ship.

	Port Lifeboats		Starboard Lifeboats	
Overview of Lifeboat Launch Times				
All times shown are approximate, and refer to the beginning of lowering from the deck. From '*Titanic*: The Lifeboat Launch Sequence Re-Examined' by Bill Wormstedt, Tad Fitch and George Behe at: http://wormstedt.com/Titanic/lifeboats/lifeboats.htm				
Time	Boat	Launched by:	Boat	Launched by:
12.40			7	Murdoch, Lowe
12.43			5	Murdoch, Lowe, Pitman
12.55			3	Murdoch, Lowe
1.00	8	Lightoller, Wilde, Smith		
1.05			1	Murdoch, Lowe
1.10	6	Lightoller		
1.20	16	Moody		
1.25	14	Lowe, Wilde, Lightoller		
1.30	12	Wilde, Lightoller	9	Murdoch (Moody?)
1.35			11	Murdoch
1.40			13	Murdoch, Moody on A deck
1.41			15	Murdoch, Moody on A deck
1.45	2	Wilde, Smith		
1.50	10	Murdoch		
	4	Lightoller		
2.00			C	Murdoch, Wilde
2.05	D	Lightoller, Wilde		
2.10				
2.15	B	Lightoller (floated off)	A	Murdoch, Moody (floated off)
2.20	*Titanic* sinks			

Lifeboat Occupancy Estimates

One of the few published analyses of lifeboat occupancy rates was completed by Colonel Archibald Gracie, a first class passenger and survivor rescued from collapsible B, who published his results in his 1913 book *The Truth About the Titanic*. Gracie was able to correspond with a number of other survivors, and was able to obtain additional accounts and information not available at the inquiries. However, his data is heavily slanted towards first class passengers and crewmembers, with not a lot of detail regarding the second and third class passengers.

The British inquiry did not attempt to determine the specific identities of each lifeboat's occupants. However, as part of their final report, they did give their estimated totals of the survivors per each individual lifeboat. In some instances, these totals agree with Gracie's totals, but not in all cases. The following table shows their published totals:

Various Estimates of the Number of Survivors by Lifeboat, as Picked up by *Carpathia*		
Boat Number	**British Inquiry**	**Gracie**
1	12	12
2	26	25
3	50	40
4	40	40
5	41	41
6	28	28 (from BI)
7	27	28
8	39	28
9	56	56
10	55	55
11	70	70
12	42	43
13	64	64
14	63	60
15	70	70 (from BI)
16	56	56
A	picked up by D	picked up by D
B	picked up by 12	picked up by 12
C	71	39
D	44	40
Totals	**854**	**795**

In the table above, Gracie and the Assessors of the British inquiry included the survivors from collapsibles A and B in the totals for D and No.12, respectively. As can be seen, when the estimated number of occupants in each boat are added up, they far surpass the actual number of survivors. The exact number of people rescued by *Carpathia* as we show in this report was 712, the same number as listed in the final British inquiry report, a figure that is nearly universally accepted in the field of *Titanic* research at the current time.

A recent analysis of lifeboat occupancy by the current authors examined various estimates of the number of people in each boat given by survivors, along with forensic evidence such as presented in photographs of the lifeboats as they approached *Carpathia*. This analysis produced results that are far more in keeping with the known total number of survivors that were picked up.[31] The following is a summary of our findings presented in chronological order of lifeboat launching times:

Boat 7 – Launched at about 12.40a.m. ATS under the supervision of First Officer Murdoch, supported by Fifth Officer Lowe. Lookout George Hogg was put in charge. Third Officer Pitman also helped load and lower the boat.

The crew, with the exception of Lookout Hogg, gave rough estimates of the number aboard, some fairly high. The passengers were consistent in giving lower and more specific estimates, and one passenger, Mrs Bishop, mentioned that they counted off just after they reached the water. The actual number of occupants was probably close to twenty-eight. With an additional six transferred in from No.5 once the boats were afloat, thirty-four is the best estimate of the number of people when picked up by *Carpathia*.

Boat 5 – Launched about 2 to 3 minutes after boat No.7, No.5 was also under the supervision of First Officer Murdoch, with the assistance of Third Officer Pitman and Fifth Officer Lowe. Third Officer Pitman was put in charge of this boat by Murdoch.

The occupancy numbers given are all in the thirty-five to forty-two range, and based on the bulk of evidence, an estimate of thirty-six is probably close to the actual total. The passengers were reluctant to board the boats earlier in the sinking, and the earlier boats were significantly under capacity when lowered away. Since about six people were transferred to boat No.7, boat No.5 reached *Carpathia* with around thirty occupants.

Boat 3 – Launched at about 12.55a.m. ATS under the supervision of First Officer Murdoch, supported by Fifth Officer Lowe. Able-Bodied Seaman George Moore was put in charge.

An occupancy of around thirty-two on board this boat appears to be an accurate estimate since this specific number was mentioned by both a crewmember and a passenger, and is consistent with the earlier lifeboats being lowered far from full.

Boat 8 – Launched at about 1.00a.m. ATS under the supervision of Captain Smith, Chief Officer Wilde and Second Officer Lightoller. Able-Bodied Seaman Thomas Jones was put in charge.

Crewmembers gave higher occupancy estimates than passengers, but that is a common thread for most crew estimates. The authors feel that the passenger estimates were closer to the correct count, and based on the available evidence, around twenty-five on board appears to be the correct amount.

Boat 1 – Launched at about 1.05a.m. ATS under the supervision of First Officer Murdoch and supported by Fifth Officer Lowe. Lookout George Symons was put in charge.

Unlike the other lifeboats, there is no question about the exact number of people in this boat. It was exactly twelve; eleven occupants testified at the inquiries, and by cross-referencing their testimonies, all the occupants can be identified. *Carpathia* passenger Dr Frank Blackmarr took group photographs of all the occupants of this boat. The photographs confirm the small number of occupants that were saved in No.1.

Boat 6 – Launched at about 1.10a.m. ATS under the supervision of Second Officer Lightoller. Quartermaster Robert Hichens was put in charge.

Using a photograph of No.6 as it approached *Carpathia* allows a visual count of twenty-four people on board, very close to the estimate given by Major Arthur Peuchen. This count of twenty-four includes a crewman who was transferred to No.6 from No.16.[32]

Fig. 7-2 The survivors of boat No.1 posed for this group photograph aboard *Carpathia*.
(Authors' Collection)

Fig. 7-3 Lifeboat No.6 approaching *Carpathia*. (National Archives and Records Administration,
Northeast Region)

Boat 16 – Launched at about 1.20a.m. ATS under the supervision of Sixth Officer Moody. Master-at-Arms Bailey took command of the lifeboat after being ordered down the falls by Moody.[33]

Taking into account the tendency of the crewmembers to overestimate the number of occupants in the boats, and taking into account the one crewman transferred to boat No.6, it appears that around fifty-two people were aboard this lifeboat when it reached *Carpathia*.

Boat 14 – Launched at about 1.25a.m. ATS under the supervision at various times of Chief Officer Wilde, Second Officer Lightoller and Fifth Officer Lowe. Lowe superintended the final loading and lowering, and assumed command of the lifeboat when it reached the water.

The current authors believe No.14 was lowered with around forty people aboard as Able-Bodied Seaman John Poingdestre said. Fifth Officer Lowe transferred about thirty-three people out of No.14, leaving him with eight to nine people, himself included, to go back into the wreckage to look for survivors, as he also brought over seamen Buley and Evans from No.10. These thirty-three had to be split up among boats 4, 10, 12 and collapsible D which were all tied together. Since around twelve were transferred to collapsible D,[34] that leaves twenty-one for the rest of the boats. There is no evidence that any of these passengers were transferred to No.10, since it was more heavily loaded than boats 4 and 12. The authors believe that No.4 received around ten of these people, and that No.12 picked up the remaining eleven. When combined with the occupants already in boats 4 and 12, this made about fifty people in each, before they both picked up more survivors from overturned collapsible B.

Taking all these movements into account, we believe No.14 reached *Carpathia* with twenty-five people aboard – the eight to nine that Lowe had in the lifeboat when they went back to the wreckage, three picked up alive from the sea, and thirteen picked up from collapsible A. A photograph of boat No.14 as it approached *Carpathia* is too dark to count the individual passengers, however, it plainly shows that the boat was far from full.

Fig. 7-4 Lifeboat No.14 approaching *Carpathia*. (National Archives and Records Administration, Northeast Region)

Boat 12 – Launched at about 1.30a.m. ATS under the supervision of Chief Officer Wilde, with Second Officer Lightoller assisting. Able-Bodied Seaman John Poingdestre was put in charge.

Lowered away with around forty-two aboard, boat No.12 picked up around eleven people from No.14 when Fifth Officer Lowe was moving his people out of his boat in preparation for going back to the site of the sinking. It also picked up around sixteen of the approximately twenty-eight surviving men on collapsible B, and reached *Carpathia* with around sixty-nine or more.

Boat 9 – Launched at about 1.30a.m. ATS under the supervision of First Officer Murdoch on the boat deck, possibly assisted by Sixth Officer Moody. Boatswain's Mate Albert Haines was put in charge, although multiple survivor accounts indicate the belief that Able-Bodied Seaman George McGough was in charge of this boat, probably due to the fact that he sat at the tiller.

All of the crewmembers gave counts substantially higher than the passengers, and some of their numbers are simply not believable, particularly considering that the capacity of this type of lifeboat was rated at sixty-five. The current authors believe the passenger counts to be closer to the truth, and that No.9 was lowered with around forty people on board.

Boat 11 – Launched at about 1.35a.m. ATS under the supervision of First Officer Murdoch. Able-Bodied Seaman Sidney Humphreys was put in charge.

Boat No.11 was one of the more heavily loaded boats when lowered. An estimate of around fifty aboard is probably close to being accurate.

Boat 13 – Launched at about 1.40a.m. ATS under the supervision of First Officer Murdoch on the boat deck, with Sixth Officer Moody assisting on A deck. Leading Fireman Frederick Barrett assumed command of the lifeboat when it reached the water.

Boat No.13 was another heavily loaded boat, with about fifty-five people in it.

Boat 15 – Launched less than 1 minute after No.13, No.15 was also under the supervision of First Officer Murdoch on the boat deck, with Sixth Officer Moody assisting on A deck. Fireman Frank Dymond assumed command of the lifeboat when it reached the water, however Bathroom Steward Samuel Rule claimed Steward Jack Stewart was in charge.[35] This was obviously a mistake, though it is possible that Stewart was put in charge before Dymond boarded the boat, and then relinquished control.

Boat No.15 was the most heavily loaded boat when launched. Rule claimed that the gunwales of the boat were far down in the water,[36] a detail that is supported by the private accounts of Bertha Mulvihill, a third class passenger rescued in No.15, who stated that when she leaned against the gunwale, it was so low that her hair dangled in the water. With no evidence to the contrary, we believe a total of around sixty-eight aboard appears likely.

Boat 2 – Launched at about 1.45a.m. ATS under the supervision of both Chief Officer Wilde and Captain Smith. Fourth Officer Boxhall was put in charge.

The authors believe seventeen is the correct occupancy, that specific number having been independently mentioned by two passengers. Additionally, there are seventeen survivors who can be firmly established as having been aboard this boat.[37]

Boat 10 – Launched at about 1.50a.m. ATS under the supervision of First Officer Murdoch. Able-Bodied Seaman Edward Buley was put in charge. However, once afloat, Buley was transferred to No.14 by Fifth Officer Lowe, to go back into the wreckage to look for survivors.

Since No.10 was more heavily loaded than boats 4, 12 and collapsible D, it appears that nobody was transferred into No.10 from No.14. Nobody in No.10 testified to picking up any people at that time. The last of the aft port side boats lowered had around fifty-seven people on board. However, by the time she reached *Carpathia*, both seamen Buley and Evans had transferred to No.14, leaving No.10 with fifty-five people.

Boat 4 – Launched at about 1.50a.m. ATS under the supervision of Second Officer Lightoller. Quartermaster Walter Perkis was put in charge.

Examination of the available evidence and the process of elimination supports that No.4 picked up around ten people from No.14, as Fifth Officer Lowe transferred people out of his lifeboat before returning to the wreckage to look for survivors in the water. It appears likely that about thirty were aboard when the boat was lowered, plus eight pulled from the water, plus the ten transferred in from No.14, and twelve more picked up from the overturned collapsible B. This all suggests that No.4 reached *Carpathia* with around sixty people aboard.

Collapsible C – Launched at about 2.00a.m. ATS under the supervision of Chief Officer Wilde and First Officer Murdoch. Quartermaster George Rowe was ordered to assume command of the lifeboat.

Rowe's estimate of forty-three aboard was very specific, close to the estimates given by Bruce Ismay and William Carter. His estimate was probably close to being correct.

Collapsible D – Launched at about 2.05a.m. ATS under the supervision of Chief Officer Wilde and Second Officer Lightoller. Quartermaster Arthur Bright was put in command.

It appears that D must have left *Titanic* with around twenty people aboard, picked up three male passengers between A deck and the water, plus twelve transferred from No.14 later on, giving a total occupancy of about thirty-five. A visual count of the number of occupants in collapsible D in a photograph of it approaching *Carpathia* shows a count of around thirty-five on board.

Fig. 7-5 Collapsible D approaching *Carpathia*. (National Archives and Records Administration, Northeast Region)

Collapsible A – This boat was washed off the boat deck around 2.15a.m. ATS. First Officer Murdoch and Sixth Officer Moody were trying to attach the collapsible to the forward falls when the boat deck dipped under and the boat washed off. Consequently, nobody was in charge of this boat.

Most of the occupants of collapsible A climbed in from the water. Over the course of the night, many died and fell back into the sea. The number left alive when picked up by collapsible D was probably twelve to thirteen, including just one woman.

Fig. 7-6 Collapsible A was found adrift and was recovered by the crew of the White Star Line's *Oceanic* one month after the disaster, with three bodies still aboard. (*Daily Sketch / Southampton* and *District Pictorial*)

Collapsible B – This boat was washed off the boat deck upside down at about 2.15a.m. ATS. Second Officer Lightoller and a number of others pushed the boat from the roof of the officers' quarters where it landed upside down on the boat deck below, just as the boat deck dipped under washing it off. Once he climbed on top of the lifeboat, Lightoller assumed command.

Approximately twenty-eight occupants were left alive on collapsible B in the morning, and were taken off into other boats. Both John Thayer Jr and Archibald Gracie said that the men were taken off of collapsible B into two lifeboats, and Gracie said he had learned that they were boats No.4 and No.12.[38]

Fig. 7-7 Collapsible B was found adrift and photographed by the crew of the cable ship *Mackay-Bennett* out of Halifax on a victims recovery mission. (*The Truth About the Titanic*, Archibald Gracie, 1913)

During the early morning hours, lifeboats nos 4, 10, 12, 14 and collapsible D tied up together after leaving the ship, and many undocumented transfers of passengers were made between these boats. No.14 must have lowered with around forty occupants, but Lowe transferred almost all of these to other lifeboats before he took a very empty lifeboat back into the debris to look for survivors. None of these transfers were detailed, and we are forced to estimate the number of occupants, and which boats they were moved to, in order to determine the counts of people in each boat as they reached *Carpathia*.

The following table provides our best estimate for the number of survivors in each lifeboat when it arrived at *Carpathia*. In the analysis presented in the table, the total of the estimated numbers comes out to 726 or fourteen more than the 712 actual survivors that were picked up. It must be emphasised that the number of occupants listed for each boat as being saved are, for

Estimated Lifeboat Occupancy when Picked Up by *Carpathia*	
Boat Number	Estimated Survivors
1	12
2	17
3	32
4	60
5	30
6	24
7	34
8	25
9	40
10	55
11	50
12	69
13	55
14	25
15	68
16	52
C	43
D	35
Estimated Total	726
Actual Total	712

the most part, estimates based on an analysis of eyewitness statements regarding the number in each boat. While future research may allow for more accurate estimates of the number saved in each boat, it is unlikely that precise numbers will ever be arrived at with the exception of boat No.1 where the names of all those who were on board can be established by multiple lines of evidence. Survivors generally gave a range of estimates of the number saved in each boat. Photographic evidence is limited to just a few of the lifeboats as they approached *Carpathia*, and even then, only a few of the pictures are clear enough to rely upon. Most survivors were otherwise occupied during the sinking, and did not count each person in their boat individually. This means that researchers are forced to rely on subjective survivor estimates and circumstantial evidence to get an idea of the number rescued in many of the boats.

Part of the issue is that crewmembers tended to give higher estimates than did the passengers. This discrepancy was noted by the Assessors at the British inquiry, who attributed it to 'a natural desire to make the best case for themselves and their ship.' A clear example of this is Lookout George Hogg and Third Officer Pitman testifying that there were forty, or thirty to forty aboard boat No.7, while first class passengers Mr J. McGough and Mrs D. Bishop both agreed there were only twenty-eight on board. Another example is how Fifth Officer Lowe's estimates were almost always higher than those given in other accounts. The best example of this is his estimate of twenty-seven in lifeboat No.1, while we know for certain there were only twelve in this boat.

While it may not be possible to state the exact number on board each individual lifeboat as it approached *Carpathia* with certainty, cross-checking sources and lines of evidence, as has been done in this analysis, does allow for a more accurate picture of the occupancy of each boat than what was presented at the two inquiries or in Gracie's book. In general terms, it appears that survivors likely overestimated the numbers present in the aft boats, which were generally heavily loaded and lowered later in the sinking. The earlier boats left far from full, which would have made at least some of the counts easier and more accurate.

It is difficult for many to comprehend why so many lifeboats were sent away with relatively few persons in them compared to their rated capacities. After all, the sea was smooth as glass and there was no wind. If we look at the totals, we find that the average lifeboat reaching *Carpathia* had just under forty people in it. Some of the explanations put forth as to why this happened, include:

• many passengers were reluctant to leave the ship early on as it was not clear that *Titanic* was actually sinking

• some women did not want to leave their husbands

• some considered the ship 'unsinkable' and safer than being lowered 65ft to the water

• the belief that additional passengers could be lowered from gangway doors after the boat reached the water

• and the unfounded apprehension that a fully loaded boat might buckle if they were filled and lowered from the boat deck

However, it seems that better results could have been obtained if there was better organisation and communication. For example, Captain Smith made no special effort to inform many of his officers that *Carpathia* was on the way, or how long *Titanic* actually had left. Key officers, including Lightoller and Pitman, were never told, and the urgency of the situation was not recognised until much later on.

The Recovery of *Titanic's* Lifeboats – *George Behe*

The following table lists our best attempt to estimate the arrival times of *Titanic's* lifeboats at *Carpathia*. The supporting details and sources are given in Appendix I. However, the reader is cautioned that these, and indeed all times derived from eyewitness statements and other post-disaster documentation, are necessarily only rough approximations, since they are based on a number of often-contradictory accounts.

Lifeboat Arrival Sequence	
Boat	**Time**
No.2	4.10a.m.
No.1	4.45a.m.
Collapsible C★	5.45a.m.
No.5	6.00a.m.
No.7	6.15a.m.
No.9	6.15a.m.
No.13	6.30a.m.
No.16	6.45a.m.
No.11	7.00a.m.
No.14★	7.15a.m.
Collapsible D★	7.15a.m.
No.3	7.30a.m.
No.8	7.30a.m.
No.15★	7.30a.m.
No.4★	8.00a.m.
No.6	8.00a.m.
No.10	8.00a.m.
No.12	8.15a.m.
★ boat set adrift and not taken aboard *Carpathia*	

Of the eighteen lifeboats that arrived at *Carpathia*, only thirteen of them were taken back to New York. They were stored at White Star Line's Pier 59 and their contents inventoried in a four-page report by C.M. Lane Lifeboat Co. of Brooklyn, NY. The recovered lifeboats brought back by *Carpathia* were nos 1, 2, 3, 5, 6, 7, 8, 9, 10, 11, 12, 13 and 16.[39]

Means Taken to Procure Assistance

There were three means available on *Titanic* to procure assistance from other vessels that had an opportunity to render such assistance. These were the use of:

1. wireless telegraphy
2. standard distress socket signals (distress rockets), and
3. electric Morse signalling lamps

Wireless

It seems that Captain Smith had taken some time to work up the ship's position in case it was needed while damage to the ship was still being assessed. It appears that soon after giving the order to have passengers come up on deck with lifebelts on, he went to the wireless cabin and told the two operators to prepare to send a call for assistance. According to Junior Marconi Operator Harold Bride, Smith told them:[40]

> We've struck an iceberg, and I'm having an inspection made to tell what it has done for us. You better get ready to send out a call for assistance. But don't send it until I tell you.

It was about 10 minutes later that Captain Smith came by again and told them to send out the call.

The first wireless distress message from *Titanic* was sent out at 10.25p.m. New York Time (NYT) 14 April 1912 (12.27a.m. *Titanic* ATS 15 April 1912). It was received by the steamships *La Provence*, *Mount Temple* and *Frankfurt*, and the land station at Cape Race. This message, with distress call sign 'CQD', was sent with coordinates 41° 44'N, 50° 24'W. The timing of this first distress call indicates that it was sent out soon after Thomas Andrews reported to Captain Smith that the ship was sinking, in juxtaposition with the order to begin loading the lifeboats with women and children.

According to Harold Bride, the steamer *Frankfurt* was the first to respond.[41] When the *Frankfurt* responded, *Titanic's* Senior Marconi Operator Jack Phillips sent Bride out to inform Captain Smith. Bride found the captain out on the starboard boat deck 'superintending the loading of the lifeboats',[42] just a few minutes after the order was given to load the lifeboats with women and children. Smith told Bride to go back and ask *Frankfurt* to send her position.

At 10.35p.m. NYT (12.37a.m. *Titanic* ATS) Phillips sent out a wireless distress message with 'corrected' coordinates of 41° 46'N, 50° 14'W. These were the coordinates that were picked up by the rescue ship *Carpathia*. As we now know, both locations given in these wireless distress messages were wrong. The initial distress coordinates, transmitted at 10.25p.m. NYT, are about 20 nautical miles west of the now known position of the wreck site. The so-called 'corrected' distress position, transmitted at 10.35p.m. NYT, is about 13 miles west of the wreck site. The first set of coordinates has been attributed to having been worked up by Captain Smith, while the second set of coordinates was worked up by Fourth Officer Joseph Boxhall.

One possibility as to why these coordinates were wrong is that there was a simple error made when Third Officer Herbert Pitman was reading the time difference between a hack watch used for taking star sights, and the time in GMT shown on the chronometer in the chartroom. A simple error of 1 minute of time would result in all star sights being shifted by 15 minutes–of–arc in longitude. This type of systematic error would tend to go unnoticed since all sights would be affected exactly the same way with all lines-of-position from all sights crossing at the same place. Such an error would then affect all dead reckoning positions derived off of that one celestial fix, including the two distress positions that were transmitted by wireless from *Titanic* that night. As noted before, it is likely that it was this undiscovered error in the distress coordinates that led Third Officer Pitman and Fourth Officer Boxhall to conclude that the ship must have turned the corner much later than what was originally thought.

It is also possible that an oversight in simple addition by Captain Smith may have led to the initial CQD coordinates being even further westward from the wreck site than those worked up by Joseph Boxhall. If simple errors such as these were not made, it is likely that the CQD position would have come out very close to where *Titanic* actually foundered. Unfortunately, there is no direct proof that a misreading of a clock took place, or that a simple error in addition was made in the haste to work up the initial distress coordinates. But what we do know is that both distress positions transmitted from *Titanic* were well to the west of where *Titanic* actually foundered. The explanations presented here are entirely consistent with what we do know about how ship positions were calculated back in 1912, and make use of evidence presented in the historical record, including that presented by *Titanic's* surviving officers and several others.[43]

The following table lists in chronological order those ships that received *Titanic's* distress calls, the approximate time (in NYT and *Titanic* ATS) that the call was first received (either directly or indirectly), the ship's approximate distance from the distress coordinates, and the immediate actions that were taken:

Ship [call sign]	Approximate Time First Distress Call Received		Approximate Position of Ship Relative to Distress Position and Immediate Actions Taken
	NYT	*Titanic* ATS	
Frankfurt [DFT]	10.25p.m. 14 April	12.27a.m. 15 April	Bound east for Bremerhaven from Galveston.[44] At 10.40p.m. NYT she was asked to render assistance and told by *Titanic*, 'We are on ice.'[45] At 10.46p.m. NYT, *Frankfurt* reported that her ship's midnight position was 39.47N, 52.10W, a location that put her about 140 miles to the south-west of the initial CQD position.[46] She was told in a clarifying statement at that time that *Titanic* was sinking and to come at once. She soon turned around and headed for *Titanic*. She arrived near the scene too late to render any assistance.
La Provence [MLP]	10.25p.m. 14 April	12.27a.m. 15 April	Bound east for Le Havre from New York. She was reported to be about 600 miles away at the time, and did not attempt to go to *Titanic's* assistance as other ships were reported closer.[47]
Mount Temple [MLQ]	10.25p.m. 14 April	12.27a.m. 15 April	Bound west for St John, New Brunswick, from Antwerp. She was turned around at 10.40p.m. NYT heading for the 'corrected' CQD position that she received at 10.35p.m. NYT. At the time, she was about 49 miles away to the SW.[48] She came to a stop on the western side of a vast field of pack ice about 2.45a.m. NYT, and later in the morning saw *Carpathia* picking up lifeboats on the eastern side of the field which was reported to be 5–6 miles wide. She did not attempt to cross the ice field.

Ypiranga [DYA]	10.28p.m. 14 April	12.30a.m. 15 April	Bound east but diverted southward on 13 April to help the German–Australian Line steamer *Augsburg* who was reported drifting. At 10.36p.m. NYT, she received the 'corrected' CQD position from *Titanic*, and was reported to have proceeded toward that position but never getting closer than 50 miles.[49]
Caronia [MRA]	10.31p.m. 14 April	12.33a.m. 15 April	Bound east for Liverpool via Queenstown from New York. She was reported 728 miles eastward of the CQD position when the message was received, and did not attempt to go to *Titanic's* assistance as other ships were reported closer.[50]
Asian [MKL]	10.34p.m. 14 April	12.36a.m. 15 April	Bound west and in the process of towing the German oil tanker *Deutschland* to Halifax. She was located about 325 miles south-west of the CQD position at 37.36 N 54.44 W. In a message received from *Titanic* at 11.12p.m. NYT, the wrong distress latitude was recorded due to the faintness of the signal. This was corrected in a message received at 11.17p.m. NYT. She did not attempt to render assistance since other ships were much closer, and she had the oil tanker in tow.[51]
Carpathia [MPA]	10.35p.m. 14 April	12.37a.m. 15 April	Bound east for the Mediterranean from New York. Ship turned around 3 minutes later and headed for 'corrected' CQD position which was 58 miles away to the NW.[52] On her way to the erroneous CQD location, green flares were sighted from boat No.2 in the early morning hours. She reached that lifeboat at 4.10a.m. 15 April *Carpathia* ATS. All survivors were picked up by 8.30a.m. ATS, and *Carpathia* brought them back to New York departing the area about 8.50a.m. ATS.[53]
Baltic [MBC]	10.35p.m. 14 April	12.37a.m. 15 April	Bound east for Liverpool. About 243 miles east of CQD position when she received a relayed message from *Caronia*. She tried to contact *Titanic* at 10.45p.m. NYT but failed to get through. She received further information from *Caronia* at 10.58p.m. NYT. After about 10 minutes, she turned around and headed for the CQD position. At 7.15a.m. NYT 15 April, she resumed her course to Liverpool having come westward 134 miles after *Carpathia* told her that she was not needed.[54]
Birma [SBA]	10.35p.m. 14 April	12.37a.m. 15 April	Bound east for Rotterdam and Libau from New York. She was about 107 miles south-west of the 'corrected' CQD position which was sent out at 10.35p.m. NYT. She was turned around at 10.45p.m. NYT and headed toward *Titanic* expecting to arrive at the site about 7½ hours later.[55] She arrived near the scene too late to render any assistance.
Olympic [MKC]	10.50p.m. 14 April	12.52a.m. 15 April	Bound east for Southampton via Plymouth and Cherbourg from New York. At 11.10p.m. NYT she was about 505 miles west of the CQD position. All boilers were reported lit up by 11.50p.m. NYT as she rushed eastward. At 2.00p.m. NYT 15 April she was told by *Carpathia* that *Titanic* had sunk and that all survivors were picked up.[56]

Celtic [MLC]	10.55p.m. 14 April	12.57a.m. 15 April	Bound west for New York. She was about 798 miles away to the east of the CQD position,[57] and too far away to render assistance.[58]
Cincinnati [DDC]	11.05p.m. 14 April	1.07a.m. 15 April	Location reported at 37.36 N, 54.44 W, about 325 miles SW of CQD position at this time.[59] Assistance not thought necessary because other ships were reported closer to the scene.
Virginian [MGN]	11.10p.m. 14 April	1.12a.m. 15 April	Bound east for Liverpool from St John via Halifax. 178 miles bearing N55°W from CQD. Tried to contact *Titanic* at 11.12p.m. NYT but did not get through. At 11.30p.m. NYT she informed Cape Race to tell *Titanic* that she was 170 miles north, and going to her assistance.[60] At 9a.m. NYT 15 April, she was told by *Carpathia* to resume their course after coming to within 25 miles of the scene.[61]

At about 11.18p.m. NYT (1.20a.m. *Titanic* ATS), all firemen, trimmers and greasers were released from below and told to go up on deck by the engineers as it became clear that the ship would not last much longer.[62] Soon after, the steam supply to the electric dynamos started to run down slowly which started to affect the power generated by *Titanic*'s 5-kW Marconi transmitter as well as the general lighting circuits causing the lights to start to get somewhat dimmer near the end.[63] By about 11.35p.m. NYT (1.37a.m. *Titanic* ATS), the land station at Cape Race could no longer hear *Titanic*.[64]

The last wireless message sent from *Titanic* may have been transmitted at about 12.10a.m. NYT (2.12a.m. *Titanic* ATS). It was a general 'CQD MGY' call according to Harold Bride. *Virginian*'s wireless operator put it down in his wireless log as, 'Hear MGY calling very faintly, his power greatly reduced.'[65] According to Harold Bride, he and Phillips abandoned the wireless cabin about 10 minutes before the ship sank, and 10 to 15 minutes after Captain Smith released them just as *Carpathia* and *Frankfurt* had called. We know that these two ships called *Titanic* at 11.55p.m. NYT (1.57a.m. *Titanic* ATS).[66]

There were two wireless signals picked up by *Virginian* after the one logged at 12.10a.m. NYT; one at 12.20a.m. NYT (2.22a.m. *Titanic* ATS) and another at 12.27a.m. NYT (2.29 *Titanic* ATS). *Virginian*'s operator attributed both of these to *Titanic*. However, these very faint signals, the first consisting of the transmission of the letter 'V' twice, and 7 minutes later, the transmission of a very 'ragged' sounding CQ call up signal, were most likely from some far-off station equipped with a rotary spark gap generator that was first coming on and trying to establish communications with other stations that might be listening.[67] None of the more nearby ships to *Titanic* reported hearing what *Virginian*'s operator heard. This exact issue came up during the questioning of *Carpathia*'s operator Harold Cottam at the British inquiry. Cottam said he had his headphones on the entire time waiting to hear back from *Titanic*, and should have heard anything sent out after his last contact with the ship. He thought the final signals recorded by *Virginian*'s operator were false.[68]

According to Harold Bride, the last message transmitted by Phillips, a general distress call of CQD MGY, was not answered. Believing that they were not generating a spark anymore, both he and Phillips then abandoned the cabin '10 minutes before the ship went down'.[69] It was just enough time for Bride to get up on the roof of the officers' quarters to help Second Officer Lightoller and others push collapsible B down to the boat deck before the bow took a sudden plunge causing an induced wave to wash both him and the overturned lifeboat off the deck.

The following table lists in chronological order the approximate time that a vessel or land station last heard from *Titanic* or was in communication with *Titanic*:

Ship or Land Station	Last Known Contact		Source
	NYT	*Titanic ATS*	
Cape Race [MCE]	11.35p.m. 14 April	1.37a.m. 15 April	PV *Virginian*
Mount Temple [MLQ]	11.47p.m. 14 April	1.49a.m. 15 April	PV *Mount Temple*
Baltic [MBC]	11.47p.m. 14 April	1.49a.m. 15 April	PV *Ypiranga*; PV *Baltic*[70]
Ypiranga [DYA]	11.50p.m. 14 April	1.52a.m. 15 April	PV *Ypiranga*
Birma [SBA]	11.53p.m. 14 April	1.55a.m. 15 April	Telegraphic office form[71]
Frankfurt [DFT]	11.55p.m. 14 April	1.57a.m. 15 April	PV *Caronia*
Carpathia [MPA]	11.55p.m. 14 April	1.57a.m. 15 April	*Carpathia's* Harold Cottam[72]
Caronia [MRA]	11.55p.m. 14 April	1.57a.m. 15 April	PV *Caronia*
Olympic [MKC]	11.55p.m. 14 April	1.57a.m. 15 April	PV *Olympic*
Asian [MKL]	11.58a.m. 14 April	2.00a.m. 15 April	PV *Olympic*
Virginian [MGN]	12.10a.m. 15 April	2.12a.m. 15 April	PV *Virginian*

A complete list of wireless messages involving *Titanic* is included in the detailed chronology of events listed in Chapter 13.

Distress Socket Signals

Titanic carried thirty-six socket distress signals on board. They were fired from a socket in a rail, and ascended to a height of 600 to 800ft where they then burst with a loud report and threw out stars. As explained by Second Officer Charles Lightoller:

> In the rail is a gunmetal socket. In the base of this cartridge [shell], you may call it, is a black powder charge. The hole down through the centre of the remainder is blocked up with a peg. You insert the cartridge in this socket; a brass detonator, which reaches from the top of the signal into the charge at the base, is then inserted in this hole. There is a wire running through this detonator, and the pulling of this wire fires that, and that in turn, fires the charge at the base of the cartridge. That, exploding, throws the shell to a height of several hundred feet, which is nothing more or less than a time shell and explodes by time in the air.[73]

Distress socket signals were sent up from *Titanic* in an attempt to attract the attention of a vessel that was first sighted off *Titanic's* port bow to the north while crewmembers were first clearing the boats.[74] As noted by Fifth Officer Lowe, the first distress socket signal was sent up as lifeboat No.3 was being filled with passengers.[75] This observation was supported by Third Officer Pitman who said that no rockets were fired until shortly after he left in lifeboat No.5, an observation further supported by first class passenger Norman Chambers who also left in that boat.[76]

Boxhall testified that he was returning the firing lanyard to the wheelhouse after firing a rocket when he got a phone call from someone out on the poop deck to inform the bridge that a boat was seen in the water off the starboard side.[77] That call came from Quartermaster George Rowe who was stationed out there at the time. Rowe was accompanied at the time by Quartermaster Arthur Bright who admittedly was late in coming out to the poop to relieve Rowe. During that phone call, Rowe was asked to bring additional boxes of distress signals that were stored under the poop to the bridge with him. Both he and Bright found two boxes in the quartermaster's locker under the poop deck, and carried them to the bridge.[78] Considering that Fourth Officer Boxhall was putting the firing lanyard away when he received the call from

Rowe, and considering Rowe's timing as to when he called the bridge, we have assigned a time of 12.47a.m. *Titanic* ATS for when the first rocket was fired.

Both Rowe and Bright claimed to have assisted Boxhall in sending these distress rockets up at intervals. Nobody actually counted the exact number that were sent up.

First class passenger Mrs Mahala Douglas stated that rockets were still going up while boat No.2 was being lowered away with Joseph Boxhall in command at 1.45a.m.[79] Quartermaster Rowe testified that he asked Captain Smith whether he should fire another rocket before being ordered to take command of collapsible C.[80] Chief Second Steward John Hardy testified that he saw Captain Smith 'superintending the rockets, calling out to the quartermaster about the rockets' a little before he left the ship in collapsible D, the boat that lowered at 2.05a.m. using the same davits previously used by lifeboat No.2 with Joseph Boxhall in it.[81]

The available evidence supports that Fourth Officer Boxhall was in charge of firing the rockets until he was ordered to take command of boat No.2 just before it was lowered at 1.45a.m. At that point, Captain Smith personally began supervising the firing of the distress rockets, and Quartermaster Rowe was the one who sent up the last rocket under Smith's direction before being ordered to help out at collapsible C. Rowe was ordered to collapsible C just after firing the last rocket at around 1.50a.m. ATS, which would have given him about 10 minutes to help get the last few passengers on board before they started lowering the boat at 2.00a.m., just 20 minutes before *Titanic* sank.

Titanic's distress socket signals were seen from the bridge of the SS *Californian* that was stopped at the eastern edge of a field of pack ice to the northward of where *Titanic* was. The first of eight white rockets seen was noticed about 12.45p.m. *Californian* time, while the last was seen about 1.40a.m. *Californian* time.[82] Despite knowing that rockets or shells throwing stars sent up one at a time at short intervals at night meant signals of distress, the second officer on *Californian*, who was in charge of the deck at the time, failed to grasp the meaning of what was being witnessed.

The circumstances regarding the SS *Californian* and her relation to *Titanic* will be more fully addressed in Chapter 10.

Morse Signalling Lamps

Both Joseph Boxhall and George Rowe said that attempts to use the ship's Morse signalling lamps to contact the vessel seen off *Titanic's* port bow took place concurrently with the firing of distress rockets.[83] Since Boxhall also said he was firing off rockets and Morsing up until the time he left *Titanic*, the times for Morsing can only be specified as taking place during the same period of time that Boxhall was overseeing the firing of the distress rockets. According to Boxhall:[84]

> There were a lot of stewards and men standing around the bridge and around the boat deck. Of course, there were quite a lot of them quite interested in this ship, looking from the bridge, and some said she had shown a light in reply, but I never saw it. I even got the quartermaster who was working around with me – I do not know who he was – to fire off the distress signal, and I got him to also signal with the Morse lamp – that is just a series of dots with short intervals of light – whilst I watched with a pair of glasses to see whether this man did answer, as some people said he had replied.

Apparently, the distance between the two ships was at, or beyond, the limit where Morse signalling could be reliably used.

Reported Incidents and Conduct of Those in the Boats

Boat 1 – Emergency lifeboat No.1, one of two emergency boats that were swung out and kept at the ready while *Titanic* was at sea, was lowered with only twelve people aboard. This was probably due to a lack of passengers in the forward starboard area that were willing to leave the ship when the boat was loaded. Fourth Officer Boxhall reported that for safety purposes, he had to keep people clear of No.1 when firing distress rockets. This was because the socket for firing the detonator was located on the bridge railing aft of the starboard bridge wing just ahead of where the davits for boat No.1 were located.[85] First Officer Murdoch and Fifth Officer Lowe were both involved in the loading of this boat.

The passengers who did board consisted of first class passengers Sir and Lady Cosmo Duff Gordon, Lady Duff Gordon's maid Laura Francatelli, Abraham Saloman and Charles Stengel. A number of crew also boarded No.1: Lookout George Symons (in charge), Seaman Albert Horswill, Firemen Samuel Collins, Robert Pusey, Charles Hendrickson and James Taylor, and Trimmer Frederick Sheath. This is one of the few boats where the identities of all on board have been firmly established.

As the boat lowered past B deck, it got caught up on what was alternately described as a 'wire guy' and a 'painter', and could not be freed.[86] A crewmember was sent below to chop away this wire before the lowering continued. The lowering of a lifeboat normally took around 5 minutes, but this slowed the lowering process. Once the boat touched down in the water, the crewmembers were told to 'stand off a little way and come back when called', which indicates that the crew had intentions of loading more men into it later once it was afloat.[87]

After No.1 went away from the ship, and *Titanic* was sinking, it was suggested by several in the lifeboat that they go back to pick up survivors, as they had a lot of space left in the boat. However, the passengers convinced the crewmen not to go back toward *Titanic*, and Lookout Symons, in charge of the lifeboat, did not dispute this.

At some point after *Titanic* sank, Sir Cosmo Duff Gordon heard the crewmembers remark that they had lost everything on the ship. Additionally, their pay stopped the moment the ship sank. Upon hearing this, Sir Cosmo Duff Gordon offered to pay each of them £5 for a new kit. This led to rumours that Duff Gordon had used his wealth to bribe the crewmembers not to return to pick up more survivors, but there does not appear to be any real evidence to support this claim – the subject was even brought up at the British inquiry, but after hearing the evidence, the Assessors felt the rumours were groundless.

Boat 2 – Emergency lifeboat No.2 was the second of *Titanic's* two emergency boats that were kept at the ready in case it was needed to be manned and lowered quickly. While No.2 was being loaded with women and children, a whole group of males climbed aboard while Chief Officer Wilde was trying to round up more women and children. Captain Smith ordered the men out, and the women and children were taken aboard.[88] He then ordered Fourth Officer Boxhall, who had been sending up distress rockets for about an hour, into the boat. Once Boxhall entered the boat, Chief Officer Wilde gave the order to lower away.

Remarkably, even though this boat was lowered just 35 minutes prior to the ship sinking, there were just seventeen occupants on board: Miss Elisabeth Allen, Mrs Charlotte Appleton, Mrs Malvina Cornell, Mrs Mary Coutts, Master William Coutts, Master Neville Coutts, Mrs Mahala Douglas, Miss Emilie Kreuchen, Mr Anton Kink, Mrs Luise Kink, Miss Luise Kink, Miss Berthe Leroy, Miss Georgette Madill, Mrs Elisabeth Robert, Fourth Officer Joseph Boxhall, Saloon Watchman James Johnstone and Able-Bodied Seaman Frank Osman.[89] Boxhall and Osman both mention a 'cook' in their evidence, however no one else does, so it is unknown as to whether such a person was saved in this boat.

Once No.2 was afloat, Boxhall heard a whistle, and Captain Smith sang out to him to come around to the starboard gangway doors to take on additional passengers there.[90] Boxhall testified that he wasn't sure who it was that ordered him to return to the ship. However, in his 1962 BBC radio broadcast, Boxhall clarified that it was Captain Smith.

Boxhall obeyed orders, and had the lifeboat rowed toward the stern of *Titanic*, where he rounded the ship and came back along the starboard side. This was done with much difficulty, since the fourth officer only had one sailor aboard, Able-Bodied Seaman Frank Osman. Boxhall had intended to come along side the liner, however, when he got close in, he claimed that he detected a small amount of suction, and was forced to pull away. In an interview years after the sinking, Boxhall claimed that the gangway doors were open when he rowed around the stern, but that there was a crowd standing in them, and he was hesitant to come alongside fearing that they would be swamped.[91]

Boxhall had a supply of green flares put in the lifeboat, and with these he was able to signal the rescue ship *Carpathia* as she came up from the south-east. Boat No.2 was the first lifeboat picked up by *Carpathia*, and once Boxhall was aboard, he was brought to Captain Rostron where he reported that *Titanic* had sunk.

Boat 3 – First Officer Murdoch had difficulty finding enough women and children willing to leave the ship at that early stage to fill boat No.3. Successfully lowered to the sea, it was moved away from *Titanic* to stay away from any suction that might possibly happen when *Titanic* went down. They later rowed toward the light of the ship seen off *Titanic's* bow, but never reached it.[92]

Boat 4 – Lifeboat No.4 was one of the first lifeboats readied for loading. Second Officer Lightoller intended to load it from the promenade, and ordered the passengers on the scene down to A deck. However, he found the screens over the A deck windows were closed, and the passengers, having traipsed below, had to return to the boat deck. After sending two stewards below to find the window cranks to open the windows, Lightoller abandoned No.4, and moved aft to work at boats No.6 and No.8.[93] Boat No.4 then sat idle until relatively late in the launching sequence, when the screens on the A deck windows were finally opened, and Lightoller returned and proceeded to load women and children through them into the lifeboat by using deckchairs as a sort of makeshift stairs for them to step up to the windows. However, by this time late in the disaster, *Titanic* was listing heavily to port. Earlier in the sinking, Lightoller had anticipated that a list might develop at some point, and realised that he might be able to tie No.4 to the wire hawser line running along the outside of A deck to prevent it from swinging away from the ship's side.[94] It appears that his plan was carried out, as this boat was not reported as having swung away from the ship's side to as large a degree as boats No.10 and collapsible D did. This kept the passengers from having to cross a large gap between the window sill and the lifeboat,[95] as happened at No.10, which was loading around the same time. Despite this, some hesitant passengers had to be flung across the gap that did exist.

After No.4 was in the water, a seaman in the boat shouted up to the boat deck that they needed another hand to help work the boat. Quartermaster Perkis, followed by a sailor, slid down the falls into No.4 and took charge.

No.4 was close to *Titanic* when it went under, and was one of the few boats to return to the wreck site to pick up people struggling in the water. They recovered around eight people. Two of the crewmen who were recovered died in the boat before she arrived at *Carpathia*. At least one other crewmember lost consciousness from hypothermia after being pulled into the boat, and woke up later with dead bodies on top of him.

Boat No.4 tied up to lifeboats 10, 12, 14 and collapsible D. It took on around ten more people from No.14, as people were moved out of that boat prior to Fifth Officer Lowe taking it along with nine crewmen back into the wreckage. Boat No.4 also picked up around twelve of the people rescued from the overturned collapsible B.

Boat 5 – After Third Officer Pitman removed No.5 from its chocks and lowered it even with the deck, Bruce Ismay, chairman of the White Star Line, suggested to Pitman that they start loading the lifeboat immediately. Pitman did not recognise Ismay initially, and replied that he was awaiting the commander's orders to start loading. Pitman then went to the bridge, found the captain, and got the order to load the boat. First Officer Murdoch, Pitman, and Fifth Officer Lowe loaded the boat with passengers and crew, and Ismay lent his assistance as well. Before the boat lowered, Murdoch told Pitman to take charge of the boat, and to stay nearby and come to the aft gangway when hailed in order to take on more passengers.

As the boat was lowering away, Ismay became overanxious, and yelled out repeatedly to Fifth Officer Lowe to lower away. Like Pitman, Lowe did not recognise Ismay, and felt he was interfering with his duties. Lowe exploded, saying, 'If you will get to hell out of that I shall be able to do something!' When Ismay did not reply to this, Lowe said, 'Do you want me to lower away quickly? You will have me drown the whole lot of them!' Ismay then moved along to help at boat No.3.[96] As No.5 lowered, the falls on one end of the boat were played out faster then the other end, causing it to tip precariously. It was quickly straightened out, and reached the water safely.[97]

No.5 rowed away from the ship, and the occupants sat idle until *Titanic* sank. Pitman wanted to go back to the wreck site to pick up survivors, but the passengers protested so strongly that Pitman was dissuaded from the idea. They did not go any closer.

Lifeboat No.7 was floating near No.5, so Pitman had the two lifeboats lashed together to make them easier to find when a rescuing ship came along. Two men, a woman and child, along with one or two others, were transferred from No.5 to No.7 to even up the numbers in each boat.[98]

Boat 6 – The crewmembers had trouble finding women willing to board this boat as it was being filled. Second Officer Lightoller also had difficulty finding enough crewmembers to man the boat and also man both sets of davits as the boat was being lowered. Despite having been ordered into the boat by Lightoller previously, Lamp Trimmer Samuel Hemming leapt back aboard when he realised there were no crewmembers to man the aft set of falls. As the boat lowered, it hung up against the ship's side because there was a slight starboard list at the time.[99]

As lifeboat No.6 was halfway down the falls to the sea, the boat began to lower unevenly as had No.5. After it was straightened out, a passenger in the boat called out to Second Officer Lightoller on the deck above that there weren't any seamen to help row.[100] There being no seamen handy beyond the men at the falls, first class passenger Major Arthur Peuchen offered to go. Lightoller told him if he was seaman enough to go down the falls, he could go, and Peuchen climbed down.

Once down, No.6 pulled away from the ship quickly. The boat was under the command of Quartermaster Robert Hichens, who was worried that the ship was about to founder. Some time later, a whistle was heard, and Captain Smith hailed the boat, commanding No.6 to come back to *Titanic* to take on more passengers. Many of the women on board wanted to go back, but Hichens, who was at the tiller, refused to go because he feared that the lifeboat would be swamped by people trying to get in.[101] Boat No.6 did not go back to *Titanic*. Passengers in the boat later complained about Hichens' conduct, saying that he was belligerent, threatening, disrespectful to the women, and refused to assist in the rowing of the boat.

Toward morning, No.6 tied up with lifeboat No.16, and one crewman was transferred from No.16 to No.6 to help row.

Boat 7 – Lifeboat No.7 was the first lifeboat launched from *Titanic*. As such, and as *Titanic* was not exhibiting obvious signs of distress at the time (no rockets had been fired, and the ship itself only had a slight starboard list), passengers were very reluctant to come out on deck in the cold, much less climb into the small lifeboat. Since there were so few women and children nearby, First Officer Murdoch let several men board the boat.

When No.7 was lowered, it was ordered to stand by close to the ship, so that a gangway could be opened and passengers loaded into the lifeboat from there. This plan did not come to fruition, and No.7 was eventually rowed away from the sinking ship to escape the feared suction.

Boat No.7 eventually tied up with No.5, and five or six people were transferred from No.5 to No.7 to even up the number of people in each lifeboat.[102]

Boat 8 – Captain Smith and Chief Officer Wilde both helped load and lower boat No.8, though not necessarily at the same time. Captain Smith appears to have been at No.8 when the order was given to lower, and Able-Bodied Seaman Thomas Jones was ordered in and put in charge.

The crewmembers had great difficulty in finding enough women and children willing to board the boat. It was at this boat that Ida Straus saw her maid safely off the ship before famously refusing to leave her husband Isidor.[103]

Jones was ordered to pull for the light in sight off the port bow, land the passengers on the ship there, and come back for more people.[104] Jones took an oar, put the Countess of Rothes at the tiller, and headed toward the light. The countess did quite well at handling the tiller. However, boat No.8 was never able to reach the light or make any tangible progress towards it despite rowing 3 to 4 miles away from *Titanic*.[105] Eventually, the occupants of this boat saw a light come up from behind them, and turned around and rowed for what turned out to be the rescue ship *Carpathia* coming up from the south-east.

Boat 9 – In addition to First Officer Murdoch, Sixth Officer Moody and Purser McElroy helped load boat No.9 with passengers from the boat deck. Boat No.9 had been swung out earlier in the evening, but was not loaded right away. A rumour that men were going to be taken off on the aft port side had been spread, resulting in the aft starboard side being left 'almost deserted', as noted by second class passenger Lawrence Beesley.[106] Many of the officers and crew subsequently headed to the aft port side of the boat deck to calm the disorder which culminated with warning shots being fired at No.14. Once the situation at No.14 was under control, several crewmembers headed to the aft starboard boats to assist there, at which point the efforts at No.9 were resumed. Among these crewmembers were Sixth Officer Moody and Able-Bodied Seaman George McGough, who had been at boat No.16 and boat No.14 on the port side respectively. First Officer Murdoch and a number of stewards and other members of the victualling department had to pass women and children over from the port side to fill up boat No.9.[107] Bruce Ismay assisted in the loading of this boat.

No disorder was recorded as No.9 was lowered to the sea. Once there, the passengers of the lifeboat noted that *Titanic* was noticeably down by the head, so they pulled farther away to escape any suction.

Boatswain's Mate Albert Haines, who was put in charge, consulted with the other sailors in the lifeboat about going back to rescue people in the water when they heard cries in the dark when *Titanic* sank. They decided, however, that it was unsafe to go back with so many people, around forty, already in their boat.[108]

Boat 10 – For some unknown reason, lifeboat No.10 was not swung out at the same time as other boats in the area, and was left sitting in its chocks. First Officer Murdoch oversaw the preparation and loading of this boat after he finished up on the aft starboard side. After most of the port lifeboats had been lowered to the sea, boat No.10 was finally unhooked from its chocks on the deck and swung out by Seaman Evans.[109]

By this time, *Titanic* was listing heavily to port, about 10°, and No.10 was hanging about 2½ft from the edge of the boat deck. This large list to port was not reported at any of the other aft starboard or port boats, all of which were lowered earlier (either no list or a slight list to port was reported at those boats and it didn't significantly interfere with the loading and lowering process at that point). As No.10 was being loaded, passengers had to jump the large gap to get into the boat, and Chief Baker Charles Joughin chucked small children across after their parents. One woman slipped and fell between the ship and the lifeboat, but luckily, someone below on A deck caught her and pulled her in.[110] She then proceeded back up to the boat deck to No.10, and successfully made the jump to the lifeboat. As the boat was lowering past A deck, an unknown passenger jumped down into the lifeboat, landing on and injuring second class passenger Lucinda Parrish.[111]

Boat No.10 pulled away from *Titanic*, and soon joined up with a number of other lifeboats, nos 12, 14, 4 and collapsible D. Under the command of Fifth Officer Lowe in No.14, passengers were successfully transferred from No.14 to the other boats, and Seamen Buley and Evans climbed into No.14, which went back into the wreckage to look for any survivors. Two men were found hiding in the bottom of the boat, but neither appeared to be able to speak English.[112]

Boat 11 – Unlike most of the earlier boats lowered from the starboard side, lifeboat No.11 was loaded from A deck. First Officer Murdoch, in charge up on the boat deck, had several crew climb down the falls to start loading it. The first officer saw a group of men who looked poised to climb into the boat, and reminded them that the women and children were to be loaded into the boat first.

On its way down the side of the ship, boat No.11 avoided a stream of water coming from the side of *Titanic*, a pump discharge from inside the ship. Other than some minor difficulty in hoisting the block to disconnect the after falls, No.11 was successfully launched.[113]

Boat 12 – The loading of boat No.12 was primarily handled by Second Officer Lightoller, although Chief Officer Wilde assisted at this boat at one point. It was the last of the three aft port boats (No.16, No.14 and No.12) that were all loaded at around the same time. No.10 was still in its chocks at this time.

Boat No.12 had no problems being lowered to the sea. After pulling about 100 yards from *Titanic*, it tied up with nos 10, 12, 14, 4 and collapsible D. Fourth Officer Lowe, now in command of this small flotilla of boats, moved passengers and crew from one boat to another, and No.12 ended up with about eleven more women passengers than it had when it left the ship. Around daylight, No.12 heard Charles Lightoller's officer's whistle coming from collapsible B. Boat 12 then came alongside to pick up approximately sixteen of the twenty-eight people left alive on top of the overturned collapsible boat.[114]

Boat 13 – First Officer Murdoch ordered both No.13 and No.15 loaded from A deck, the deck immediately under the boat deck. Sixth Officer Moody took charge on the lower deck, and loaded both boats with passengers that were already there, and other passengers that had been sent down from the boat deck. It appears that most of the passengers loaded into No.13 boarded from A deck.

As No.13 was being prepared to be lowered to the water, second class passenger Lawrence Beesley, on the deck above, was asked if there were any ladies there. When he replied no, he was told, 'Then you had better jump.' Beesley dropped into the stern of the lifeboat, to be followed by two more ladies from A deck, followed by a man, his wife and a baby. Before departing for the port side to assist there, Murdoch ordered the men manning the falls to lower away, and told Leading Fireman Frederick Barrett, who had taken charge of the boat, to row around.[115]

Boat No.13 then ran afoul of the same pump discharge that had almost caused problems for lifeboat No.11 minutes earlier. Using oars, the passengers and crewmembers prevented No.13 from being swamped by the circulating pump discharge, but unfortunately, they had pushed it astern, right under boat No.15, which was lowering down directly on top of them. People in No.13 shouted up to the boat deck to stop lowering, and gained enough time for Leading Fireman Frederick Barrett to cut the after fall, and move No.13 way from the hull of *Titanic*. Barrett, now in charge of No.13, directed the lifeboat to pull away from the sinking ship.

Boat 14 – One of the aft portside lifeboats, No.14 was one of the three boats (nos 12, 14 and 16) that were loaded and lowered at nearly the same time. It was the second of the three to reach the water. Chief Officer Wilde was involved in the early stages of the loading of this boat, and Second Officer Lightoller was briefly involved in the loading at some point during the process. Fifth Officer Lowe oversaw and completed the final stages of loading. Before Lowe had come along, a large group of unruly passengers, spurred on by the rumour that men were being taken off on the port side aft, began to congregate at that location. Some men tried rushing the boat, and Able-Bodied Seaman Joseph Scarrott had to use the boat's tiller to hold them back.[116]

As the boat was lowering, Fifth Officer Lowe was afraid that some among the growing crowds of passengers on A and B decks would leap into the boat. Lowe believed that he had overloaded No.14, and that the sudden jerk could cause the boat or davits to buckle. He fired two shots between the hull of *Titanic* and the lifeboat to scare the potential jumpers off.[117]

As No.14 got near to the water, the after fall got twisted and hung up, and the crew were forced to release the tackle to allow the stern of the lifeboat to fall to the surface of the water, shaking up the passengers.

Boat No.14 joined up with nos 10, 12, 4 and collapsible D, and Lowe transferred passengers and crew between the lifeboats. During this process of transferring people, Lowe discovered a passenger who 'had a shawl over his head, and I suppose he had skirts.' Lowe pulled the shawl off, discovered he was a man, and Lowe 'pitched him' into one of the other boats.[118] At least two passengers have been identified as possibly 'the man who got off dressed as a woman'.[119]

When all the transferring was done, Lowe asked for volunteers to go back and search the wreckage for survivors. Able-Bodied Seamen Buley and Evans (both transferred from No.10), Able-Bodied Seaman Joseph Scarrott, Saloon Steward George Crowe, Bathroom Steward Frank Morris, Steward Alfred Pugh, Leading Fireman Thomas Threlfall and second class passenger Charles Williams all volunteered.[120] About an hour after *Titanic* sank, once the cries of those in the water died down, they headed back into the debris.

Three to four people were recovered alive.[121] One of them, first class passenger William F. Hoyt, was bleeding from his mouth and nose when pulled aboard, and died in the lifeboat. His body was taken on board *Carpathia* and buried at sea. Another of the recovered people was an oriental passenger, who had tied himself to a floating door, often identified as a Chinese third class passenger, Fang Lang. Once aboard the lifeboat, this man took an oar from a tired sailor, and proceeded to row like his life depended on it, after being in the freezing water. Saloon Steward Harold Phillimore was also pulled into No.14. The identity of the fourth survivor, if there was one, has not been established.

Unable to find any more people alive, Lowe pulled away from the wreckage, and set up the mast and sail that No.14 contained. He was the only officer to do so, a testament to his skills as a boatman and sailor. As it was now turning daylight and a breeze and chop on the surface were beginning to pick up, Lowe spotted collapsible D, and took her in tow. Then, seeing a group of people who looked like they were standing in the water, Lowe pulled alongside the swamped collapsible A, and rescued about twelve people still standing in the lifeboat. Three bodies were left in collapsible A. As Lowe testified, he was not there to worry about bodies.[122]

In regards to his behaviour while loading lifeboats, Lowe told first class passenger Margaret Brown that 'they saw to it that, among those who were saved would not be any of the rich nabobs,' and that 'they would take their chances with good men.' He also admitted chasing a male passenger out of the lifeboat, who several times tried to get into the boat with his wife.[123]

There were some other complaints about Lowe's behaviour in No.14. The account of Daisy Minihan claims Lowe was shouting and cursing at the passengers trying to crowd into his lifeboat.[124] Once in the water, he snapped and swore at people to jump from one boat to another, and it was even suggested he was under the influence of liquor (there is evidence that he was a teetotaler). Contrary to this, the account of first class passenger Sara Compton to Colonel Gracie shows that despite Lowe being rough in his language, he performed his duties admirably.[125] Compton's opinion was that Lowe's 'manly bearing gave us all confidence.'

Boat 15 – Lifeboat No.15, like No.13, was primarily loaded from A deck, although a few passengers and crew boarded from the boat deck. Murdoch had been in charge of the loading on the boat deck, while Sixth Officer Moody was in charge of the loading from A deck. By the time No.15 lowered away, a very slight list to port had developed, although it doesn't appear to have affected the lowering process. As the boat was lowered to A deck to be filled there, a group of men tried to force their way into the boat. First Officer Murdoch yelled out 'Stand back! Women first!' The rush abated, and the loading continued.[126] Murdoch ordered nos 13 and 15 lowered away, and then crossed over to the port side to help at No.10.[127] Moody supervised the remainder of the loading process from A deck.

No.15 was loaded at the same time as No.13, and started lowering just about 30 seconds after the latter headed down. As happened at boat No.10, a passenger jumped down into the boat as it lowered, injuring third class passenger Bertha Mulvihill. With First Officer Murdoch already headed over to port, and no officer present to supervise those working the falls on the boat deck, a near catastrophe almost took pace. Because of the tilt of the ship forward, and No.13 being moved aft to avoid the circulating pump discharge, boat No.15 was coming down on top of No.13. It was only when shouts to stop lowering were heard by those up on deck that boat No.15 was then held up long enough to allow No.13 to get clear.

Fireman Frank Dymond took charge of boat No.15. When it reached the water, it was pulled away from the ship to await rescue. Assistant Steward Walter Nichols claimed that some passengers were pulled from the water into No.15 after it was lowered down. Though no one else reported this, if this is accurate, then these passengers likely jumped or fell into the water during the loading process.[128]

Boat 16 – Located on the aft port quarter, No.16 had been loaded at the same time as its neighbouring lifeboats nos 12 and 14, but was the first of the three to be lowered. A large crowd of passengers had collected in this area, and officers Wilde, Lightoller, Lowe and Moody were all involved in controlling the crowd and successfully loading and lowering the lifeboats. No.16 was lowered by Sixth Officer James Moody. Both Lowe and Moody talked about going away in one of the aft port boats since they had seen several boats lowered without an officer. Moody decided to stay on the ship, telling Lowe he should go. Lowe went away in No.14.[129]

As boat No.16 lowered away, it was realised that there was only one seaman aboard. Master-at-Arms Joseph Bailey climbed down the falls and took charge of the boat. Toward morning, No.16 tied up with lifeboat No.6, and one crewman was transferred from No.16 to No.6 to help with the rowing.[130]

Collapsible A – Collapsible lifeboat A had been lowered from the roof of the officers' quarters and was being attached to the falls by First Officer Murdoch and Sixth Officer Moody when the boat deck submerged. There was a group of women standing by to board the boat at the time, and there was a 'scramble' on the part of passengers to get in the boat once water reached their location. Crewmembers cut the falls, and collapsible A washed away from the sinking ship, becoming a refuge for people in the water. Because the boat was not properly launched, her collapsible sides had never been raised, and survivors who did make it to this lifeboat were forced to stand in knee-deep freezing water that came inside the lifeboat. Many people did make it to collapsible A, but did not survive the freezing water, and died of hypothermia. When they did, many either fell overboard, or were pushed overboard by the others in the lifeboat to lighten the load to keep the boat afloat.

By the time the remaining survivors were picked up by Fourth Officer Lowe in boat No.14, only about twelve to thirteen people remained alive in the swamped boat. Three dead bodies were left inside the flooded collapsible, and were eventually discovered by the White Star Liner *Oceanic* a month later adrift on the Atlantic. The three bodies, first class passenger Thomson Beattie, an unidentified sailor and a fireman, were buried at sea.[131]

Several surviving passengers reported shots being fired during the attempt to attach collapsible A to the falls. Both first class passenger George Rheims and third class passenger Eugene Daly, in personal letters to family members, reported being nearby the forward collapsibles in the final stages of the sinking, and seeing or hearing an officer shoot a passenger or passengers before turning the gun on himself in the final stages of loading the lifeboats. First class passenger Richard Norris Williams heard a gunshot from this location as water reached the boat deck, but he did not see what had happened. Talk among the passengers while still on board *Carpathia*, and supposition in the press, speculated that this officer may have been either First Officer Murdoch, or Captain Smith, but there is no definite proof. If the incident described by Rheims, Daly and others did indeed occur, the identity of the officer in question is far from certain. Second Officer Lightoller specifically wrote to Murdoch's widow, denying the rumours.[132]

Collapsible B – When Second Officer Charles Lightoller and Marconi Operator Harold Bride and other crewmen attempted to lower collapsible B from the roof of the officers' quarters, the boat landed upside down on the boat deck, falling into the water which had by then just reached above the level of the boat deck. As the water continued to come onto the deck, it washed the collapsible boat free of *Titanic*, with Bride finding himself trapped under the boat. He then struggled to get out from under the overturned boat, and was able to board it after a short time.

Collapsible B somehow came to the starboard side of the ship, ending up near the forward funnel there. When the funnel collapsed into the water, it just missed the collapsible, and pushed it farther away from the sinking ship.[133] Like collapsible A, collapsible B also became a refuge for people struggling in the water, and Bride and Lightoller were among those who managed to climb aboard and stand on the bottom of the overturned boat. Many other swimmers in the water attempted to grab onto B, but given the small amount of space available, and the instability of the boat itself, many were turned away, and in some cases, beaten off with oars.[134]

During the course of the next several hours, some of the survivors standing on B either collapsed or died, and had to be lowered into the water. As it grew light the next morning, Lightoller used a whistle he still had in an attempt to attract attention. Lifeboat nos 12 and 4 heard it, spotted the people standing on B, and came over and took the approximately twenty-eight people remaining on B aboard, with about sixteen going into No.12, and twelve into No.4.[135]

Collapsible C – Collapsible C was stored on the boat deck, just inboard of emergency lifeboat No.1. The boat could not be readied or loaded until emergency boat No.1 was launched, over an hour after *Titanic* hit the iceberg. Chief Officer Wilde appears to have been in charge when collapsible C was first being loaded, but he then crossed over to collapsible D on the port side, to oversee the loading there. First Officer Murdoch then took over the loading of C. After firing the final distress rocket at about 1.50a.m., Quartermaster George Rowe was ordered to take charge of the boat by Captain Smith. The boat was lowered about 10 minutes later.

Two first class passengers, White Star chairman Bruce Ismay, and William Carter (who had previously seen his family into lifeboat No.4) entered C in the last moments before it was lowered from the deck. It is not known whether Ismay entered the lifeboat on his own initiative, or if he was asked to enter by either Wilde or Murdoch. There are accounts supporting both versions of events.[136]

As collapsible C was lowered down the side of the ship with about thirty-nine people, the boat's rubbing strake caught on the rivets of the hull due to the 10° list to port.[137] The boat's occupants had to push off the ship's side as it was going down. It took a good 5 minutes for the collapsible to reach the water because of this.[138]

Quartermaster Rowe reported that as C left the ship, the fore well deck was awash, but that it was submerged by the time they reached the water. The forecastle head and well deck were submerging when collapsible D began lowering away at 2.05a.m., thus proving that collapsible C left *Titanic* quite late in the launch sequence, about 2.00a.m.[139]

Once in the water, collapsible C pulled for the light previously seen off the bow of *Titanic* until they saw *Carpathia* coming up from the south-east. According to Rowe, sometime in the morning, four Chinese or Filipino men came up from between the seats.[140] These four were in addition to the thirty-nine he said were lowered from the ship.

Although Quartermaster Rowe and Bruce Ismay denied that there was any commotion during the loading of collapsible C, several people reported warning shots being fired at that boat. First class passenger Jack Thayer claimed that he saw Purser McElroy fire two shots in the air as two stewards climbed into collapsible C.[141] First class passenger Hugh Woolner told a similar version, testifying that he saw First Officer Murdoch fire two warning shots in the air as the first collapsible was being loaded on the starboard side because men were swarming the boat.[142] Mauritz Björnström-Steffansson, who was with Woolner, gave an account confirming his friend's story.[143] Fireman Henry Senior said that he saw First Officer Murdoch fire warning shots over the heads of two or three men trying to rush the boat.[144] Third class passengers Emily and Frankie Goldsmith each individually claimed that as collapsible C was about to lower away, men rushed the boat, and an officer fired warning shots to keep them back.[145]

Collapsible D – Although collapsible D had been partly readied at about 12.30a.m. by Quartermaster Robert Hichens, it had to be left alone until emergency lifeboat No.2 could be launched. Once No.2 was gone, about 1.45a.m., collapsible D was connected up to the same set of davits and lowered to the deck.

Since collapsible D was the last lifeboat left on the ship, other than the two collapsibles on top of the officers' quarters, passengers and crewmen started crowding around it. In response, the officers in charge, Chief Officer Wilde and Second Officer Lightoller, had the crew nearby link arms to stop any rush on the lifeboat and allow only women and children through.[146] According to Colonel Archibald Gracie's testimony, Lightoller later told him that he (Lightoller) had been forced to fire a pistol to stop men trying to rush the boat.[147] By the time his book came out in 1913, Gracie changed his story saying only that Lightoller had brandished a revolver. Lightoller later denied having fired shots at this time admitting only to warning passengers back with an 'unloaded' revolver. Besides Lightoller's alleged comments to Gracie, there is some circumstantial evidence that suggest that shots may have been fired near this boat, or that men on the scene were warned away with revolvers.

Like collapsible C, the lowering of D was also complicated by the strong list to port of *Titanic*. However, in this case, the list made it more difficult to load, but much easier to lower as it kept the boat away from the ship's hull.

In the final stages of loading the lifeboat, Lightoller was ordered to go away with the lifeboat by Wilde, his superior, but Lightoller refused, and jumped back aboard the ship. By the time D was being lowered, the distance from the deck to the sea on the port side was only 10ft, and the water was already reaching the deck below the bridge.

First class passengers Hugh Woolner and Mauritz Björnström-Steffansson, after witnessing the scramble at collapsible C on the starboard side, had gone down to A deck below and found it deserted. They crossed around the front of A deck and reached the railing below collapsible D just as the collapsible was being lowered past them at a distance of about 9ft out. Water was starting to pour onto the deck. Realising this was their very last chance, both men climbed on top of the railing and jumped into the bow of the lifeboat. One more man was plucked from the water into D just after Woolner and Steffansson got in, first class passenger Frederick Hoyt.

Quartermaster Arthur Bright had been put in charge of collapsible D. He had been told to pull away from the ship to escape any possible suction. The lifeboat was about 50 to 100 yards away when *Titanic* sank about 15 minutes later.

Collapsible D became part of the flotilla of boats gathered around lifeboat No.14, and Fifth Officer Lowe transferred about a dozen men into the collapsible as it was not completely full. After Lowe had later rescued a few people from the wreckage, he brought No.14 over to the collapsible and towed it to *Carpathia* once it was daylight.[148]

Notes

[1] AI 533–4.
[2] AI pp.231–2.
[3] AI 534.
[4] BI 10696, BI 3367. Mackay's estimate of 20 minutes appears to be too long, in light of other related events.
[5] BI 10697
[6] AI p.60; BI 14930–43.
[7] BI 15378–9. However, Lowe must have fallen back asleep, as he testified that the first he knew of the accident was when he was awakened by voices around his cabin and found there were passengers with lifebelts on.
[8] BI 13781–5; BI 14949. Lightoller gave estimates of between 15 to 30 minutes.
[9] BI 15379–80.
[10] BI 13795–6.
[11] BI 13800.

12 BI 13282

13 Shan Bullock, *Thomas Andrews, Shipbuilder*, 1912.

14 BI 1037–44. Hichens said this was after 12.00a.m., and since he stated that he was at the wheel until 12.23a.m., we know that Smith's order had to have been given between 20 and 40 minutes after the collision.

15 BI 13229.

16 AI p.1147, BI 9926–9, BI 10693–701.

17 *The Oregonian*, 1912, Mrs Warren refers to Andrews as 'Mr Perry, one of the designers of the vessel'; William Sloper, *The Life and Times of Andrew Jackson Sloper*, 1949.

18 Fourth Officer Boxhall testified that he had asked Captain Smith in the early part of the evening, 'Is it really serious?' and Smith replied, 'Mr Andrews tells me he gives her from an hour to an hour and a half.' (BI 15610).

19 AI p.431.

20 Colonel Archibald Gracie, *The Truth About the Titanic*, Ch.2, 1913.

21 BI 2843–6; BI 2870–4.

22 *The Waterloo Times Tribune*, 19 April 1912.

23 AI p.1003.

24 Quartermaster George Rowe testified that he saw a boat in the water at 12.25a.m. (AI p.519), but it appears that he was using adjusted time knowing that the wheelhouse clock was to be put back by some 23 minutes at midnight, thereby extending his watch on deck by that amount of time. In unadjusted hours, his '12.25' would have been 12.48a.m. Pitman's estimate that lifeboat No.5 was in the water at 12.30 does not seem to be realistic given all the things he said he did between the time he first came on deck and the boat being lowered (BI 15036). His estimates are at variance with the testimony of other surviving officers regarding how long it would take to prepare a lifeboat for loading, and how long it would then take to load a boat and lower it to the sea. The estimates given by Rowe and Pitman do not agree with numerous accounts from passengers such as the aforementioned Albert Dick and others. If the times given by these two crewmembers for lifeboats in the water were in true unadjusted hours, then the order to first load the lifeboats would have had to be given about 5 to 10 minutes after midnight, before the full extent of damage to the ship was known, and in sharp disagreement with the evidence of so many others. For further details relating to Rowe and Pitman's testimony, and for a more in-depth look at the evidence supporting that the first lifeboat was lowered at 12.40a.m., see 'Titanic: The Lifeboat Launch Sequence Re-examined' at http://wormstedt.com/Titanic/lifeboats/lifeboats.htm.

25 BI 2875–904.

26 Many detailed accounts of passengers being blocked from going up to the boat deck, either by closed or locked gates, or by crewmen stationed in certain areas of the ship, are contained in Appendix J.

27 BI 9931–72.

28 Berk Pickard's legal name was 'Berk Trembisky' which is what he used when he booked passage on *Titanic*. However, he assumed the name 'Pickard' while in France, and used that name with regard to private business. His testimony at the American inquiry is under 'Pickard' (AI p.1054).

29 AI p.1055.

30 'Titanic: The Lifeboat Launch Sequence Re-examined' at http://wormstedt.com/Titanic/lifeboats/lifeboats.htm.

31 'Titanic Lifeboat Occupancy Totals' by Bill Wormstedt and Tad Fitch, at http://wormstedt.com/Titanic/lifeboats/occupancy.pdf.

32 AI p.365.

33 AI p.645.

34 AI pp.833–4.

35 BI 6596.

36 BI 6618, BI 6621.

37 Researcher Don Lynch has compiled a list of survivors for Lifeboat No.2, see 'Titanic Lifeboat Occupancy Totals' by Bill Wormstedt and Tad Fitch, at http://wormstedt.com/Titanic/lifeboats/occupancy.pdf for details.

38 Colonel Archibald Gracie, *The Truth About the Titanic*, Ch.5, 1913.

39 National Archives.

40 Exclusive statement by Harold Bride to the *NY Times*, 19 April 1912.

41 According to the wireless log of *Mount Temple*, *Titanic*'s operator (Jack Phillips) was having difficulty hearing the ships that responded to his distress calls at that time. We know that this was due to the noise of steam blowing off from *Titanic*'s boilers.

42 AI p.147; BI 16526–7.

43 For further details, see 'It's a CQD Old Man' by Samuel Halpern. This two-part article had appeared in the journal of the Titanic International Society, *Voyage*, Issues 64 and 65, and also in the journal of the British Titanic Society, *Atlantic Daily Bulletin*, September and December 2008.

44 AI p.1117.

45 Wireless log SS *Frankfurt*.

46 Wireless log SS *Ypiranga*.

47 *The New York Times*, 19 April 1912.

48 PV *Mount Temple*; AI p.760.

49 *The New York Times*, 25 April 1912.

50 Marconi Office Report submitted to British Wreck Commission on 1 May 1912; 03.31 GMT in wireless log of SS *Caronia*.

51 Initial contact time from wireless log of SS *Ypiranga*. In his report to the Marconi International Marine Corporation, *Asian*'s Marconi operator Howard wrote, 'At 10.30p.m. ... *Titanic* again called Cape Race but to my knowledge there was no response as I did not hear the *Titanic* again till he called me at 11.12p.m.' (Ref: Paul Lee, '"*Titanic*: A Desperate Dialog,' http://www.paullee.com/titanic/pv.html.)

52 Samuel Halpern, '12.35a.m. Apparent Time *Carpathia*', http://www.glts.org/articles/halpern/1235_ats_carpathia.html.

53 Capt. Arthur H. Rostron's report to the general manager of Cunard Steamship Co., 19 April 1912.

54 AI pp.1057–8, 1062; Marconi Office Report submitted to British Wreck Commission 1 May 1912.

55 Samuel Halpern, 'The Enigmatic Excursion of the SS *Birma*', http://www.titanicology.com/Titanica/Inigmatic_Excursion_of_SS_Birma.pdf.

56 Wireless log SS *Olympic*.

57 Marconi Office Report submitted to British Wreck Commission 1 May 1912.

58 '*Celtic* Passengers in Panic', *Chicago Tribune*, 21 April 1912, available at: http://www.encyclopedia-titanica.org/celtic-passengers-in-panic.html.

59 Wireless log SS *Ypiranga*.

60 Wireless log SS *Virginian*; Statement by Capt. Gambell to Press Association Special Telegram, Liverpool, 21 April 1912.

61 PV SS *Olympic*.

62 BI 5707–27.

63 In a letter from Harold Bride to W.R. Cross (traffic manager of the Marconi Co.) 27 April 1912, Bride wrote, 'We had nearly the whole time been in possession of full power from the ship's dynamo, though toward the end the lights sank and we were ready to stand by, with emergency apparatus and candles, but there was no necessity to use them.' Some people reported that the ship's lights started to take on a reddish glow near the end.

64 Noted in a 12.05a.m. NYT communication between Cape Race and *Virginian*. (Ref: PV SS *Virginian*)

65 Samuel Halpern, 'Rockets, Lifeboats, and Time Changes', at http://www.encyclopedia-titanica.org/rockets-lifeboats-and-time-changes.html.

66 PV SS *Mount Temple*.

67 Samuel Halpern, 'Rockets, Lifeboats, and Time Changes'.

68 BI 17146–7, 17177–9, 17210–15.

69 AI p.158.

70 PV *Baltic* shows a message sent to *Titanic* at 11.50p.m. NYT stating she was 243 miles east and coming, but all her entries were in 5-minute increments. PV *Ypiranga* has *Baltic* message saying she is rushing to *Titanic* at 11.47p.m. NYT.

71 Samuel Halpern, 'The Enigmatic Excursion of the SS *Birma*'.

72 BI 17145–6.

73 BI 14155.

74 Joseph Boxhall, BI 15385; Deposition of Harold Godfrey Lowe, Fifth Officer *Titanic*, taken May 1912 before the British Consulate General in New York.

75 AI p.401.

76 AI p.293; Lawrenceville Alumni Bulletin of October 1912, printed in *On Board the RMS Titanic*, George Behe, 2011.

77 BI 15593.

78 In a Cotton Powder Company patent description document, mention is made that these socket distress signals come in boxes of twenty-four for immediate use, and they also were available in boxes of six and twelve.

79 *The New York Herald*, 20 April 1912.

80 AI p.519.

81 AI p.601.

82 Samuel Halpern, 'Rockets, Lifeboats, and Time Changes'.

83 AI p.237, AI p.525.

84 AI p.934.

85 AI p.239.

86 BI 11454; *Newark Star*, 19 April 1912.

87 BI 5011, BI 6453.

88 AI p.1101.

89 List provided by researcher Don Lynch. See 'Titanic Lifeboat Occupancy Totals' by Bill Wormstedt and Tad Fitch, at http://wormstedt.com/Titanic/lifeboats/occupancy.pdf for details.

90 BI 15450–3.

91 Boxhall's 1962 BBC radio broadcast.

92 AI pp 564–6.

93 BI 13834.

94 BI 13834, AI 81–2.

95 AI p.81.

96 AI p.389–90.

97 AI p.1030–1.

98 AI p.578, AI p.1031.

99 BI 1375–7.

100 Actually, No.6 had Quartermaster Hichens at the tiller and Lookout Fleet at one of the oars.

101 AI p.337.

102 AI p.578, AI p.1031.

103 AI p.112; AI p.827; Jay Henry Mowbray, *The Sinking of the Titanic*, Ch.17, 1912.

104 AI p.570.

105 AI p.831.

106 Lawrence Beesley, *The Loss of the SS Titanic*, 1912, Chapter 3.

107 BI 13187-13189.

108 AI p.657.

109 AI p.604, AI p.675.

110 AI p.676.

111 AI p.1147.

112 AI p.823.

113 AI p.544.

114 Memo from the office of the first vice-president, Pennsylvania Lines of West of Pittsburgh, printed in *On Board the RMS Titanic*, George Behe, 2011.

115 Lawrence Beesley, *The Loss of the SS Titanic*, Ch.3, 1912.

116 BI 383–6.

117 AI pp.417–19.

118 AI p.407-408.

119 George Behe, 'The Man Who Dressed as a Woman', at http://home.comcast.net/~georgebehe/titanic/page4.htm.

120 AB Evans, AI p.677; AB Buley, AI p.605 and AI p.677; AB Scarrott, BI 439; Steward Crowe, AI p.616; Steward Morris, BI 5341; Steward Pugh, letter from Edward Phillimore to Ed Kamuda, 12 June 1964 (courtesy of Don Lynch); Fireman Threlfall, *The Bridgewater Mercury*, April 1912 and *The Herts Advertiser & St. Albans Times*, 4 May 1912; Passenger Williams, AI p.406 and AI p.621.

121 AI pp.408; 605; 612; 677–8.

122 AI p.412.

123 Account from Margaret Brown, printed in the *Newport Herald*, 28 & 29 May 1912, also printed in *On Board the RMS Titanic*, George Behe, 2011.

124 AI p.1109.

125 Gracie, *The Truth About the Titanic*, 1913.

126 BI 6537; 6587–90; 6648–58.

127 Lawrence Beesley, *The Loss of the SS Titanic*, Ch.3, 1912.

128 *The New York Times*, 22 April 1912.

129 BI 15832–7.

130 AI p.451, BI 1342.

131 *Cork Examiner*, 16 May 1912.

132 For more details and analysis of the multitude of accounts of shots being fired in the final stages of the sinking of *Titanic*, see 'Shots in the Dark' by Bill Wormstedt and Tad Fitch at http://wormstedt.com/ Titanic/shots/shots.htm.

133 AI p.72.

134 Letter from George Rheims to Mary Rheims, 19 April 1912, printed in *On Board the RMS Titanic*, George Behe, 2011; *The New York Times*, 19 April 1912; *The Washington Post*, 20 April 1912.

135 Memo from the office of the first vice-president, Pennsylvania Lines of West of Pittsburgh, printed in *On Board the RMS Titanic*, George Behe, 2011.

136 See Paul Lee's article: 'Ismay's Escape' at http://www.paullee.com/titanic/ismaysescape.html for more details.

137 AI p.523.

138 AI p.524.

139 For a detailed analysis of when collapsible C was lowered, see the sections 'The Distress Rockets and Quartermaster Rowe' and 'Combined Launch Sequence and Timings' at http://wormstedt.com/ Titanic/lifeboats/lifeboats.htm.

140 AI p.520.

141 *The Sinking of the S.S. Titanic*, Jack Thayer, 1940. Thayer claimed this decades after the disaster, and his account is of questionable reliability. He says that this incident happened 'on "A" deck, just under the boat deck.' On the face of it, this seems problematic. Collapsible C did not load from A deck. However, earlier in his account, Thayer describes seeing the boats uncovered on '"A" deck', then later going to the deck below, i.e. the 'lounge on "B" deck'. The first class lounge was on A deck, not B deck. It appears that Thayer was mistakenly referring to the boat deck as A deck, and was referring to A deck as B deck. What he refers to as the 'boat deck' must have been the roof of the officers' quarters.

142 AI p.886.

143 See the articles 'Setting the Record Straight' at http://www.encyclopedia-titanica.org/setting-record-straight.html, and 'The Record Speaks' at http://www.encyclopedia-titanica.org/ the-record-speaks.html.

144 *Daily Sketch*, 29 April 1912.

145 *Detroit News*, 24 April 1912; *Echoes in the Night*, Frank Goldsmith, 1991; Audio recording of a talk given by Frank Goldsmith. Frank Goldsmith claimed to have been rescued in collapsible D. However, details in accounts given by his mother and he prove they were rescued in collapsible C. Both mention their boat getting caught on rivets as it was being lowered, and that the occupants had to keep pushing it away from the ship's side. Collapsible D swung away from the ship's side as it lowered, while collapsible C hung up against it. Mrs Goldsmith mentioned four Chinese stowaways in her boat. These four stowaways were also mentioned as having been in collapsible C by Quartermaster Rowe and Bruce Ismay.

146 AI p.992.

147 AI p.991.

148 AI p.409.

8

TOO FEW BOATS, TOO MANY HINDRANCES

Dave Gittins, Cathy Akers-Jordan and George Behe

The Origin of the Lifeboat Rules – *Dave Gittins*

Titanic operated under Board of Trade regulations last revised in 1894. The number of boats required on ocean-going passenger ships and their prescribed volume varied according to a ship's Gross Registered Tonnage. The scale drawn up extended to a GRT of 10,000 tons. Even in 1894, the scale was of questionable value on two grounds. Although in theory GRT measured a ship's carrying capacity, in practice it bore no relation to the number of passengers carried. It was common for a vessel of 10,000 GRT or less to carry more than 2,000 emigrants in open dormitories. Furthermore, at the time the scale was published, ships of more than 10,000 GRT were already in service, or under construction. By the end of the nineteenth century, reality exceeded theory by more than 10,000 tons. Thus it was that *Titanic*, of 46,328 GRT, was compelled to carry only the lifeboats laid down for ships of 10,000 GRT. The number and volume of the boats was arrived at by logic that is not readily apparent, to put it kindly.[1]

The Board of Trade divided lifeboats into five classes, according to the nature of their buoyancy arrangements. Only classes A, D and E need concern us. Class A boats were wooden boats provided with internal buoyancy tanks of a prescribed design and volume. Class D boats normally had no buoyancy tanks and class E boats were collapsibles. A 10,000 GRT ship was required to carry under davits at least sixteen lifeboats, none of which were permitted to be class E boats, though two could belong to class D. The class D boats were normally kept ready for immediate use, in case an emergency arose, such as somebody falling overboard. The volume of these boats had to total at least 5,500 cubic ft, as calculated by the Board's formulas.

The volume of the boats in cubic feet was calculated by the formula L x B x D x 0.6, where L is overall length, B is the beam and D is the depth of the hull. The passenger capacity was arrived at by dividing the number of cubic feet by ten, in the case of class A, and by eight for classes D and E. The area available was calculated to be L x B x 0.8, or about 3 sq.ft per person.[2]

Under current SOLAS rules, *Titanic's* 30ft lifeboats would have a capacity of twenty-four persons. With a minor breach of the rules, thirty-four could be carried.[3] To carry the official Board of Trade capacity, passengers would have to be crammed into all available space, with some standing up. In practice, this occurred as *Titanic* sank, notably in the case of boat No.13.[4]

Even in 1912, some realised that the capacities so calculated were very nominal. *Titanic's* Second Officer Charles Lightoller told Lord Mersey that the capacities only applied 'in absolutely smooth water, under the most favourable conditions.'[5] Harold Sanderson, a vice-president of IMM, said that in a typical Atlantic seaway a capacity of about forty would be appropriate.[6]

If the boats provided were insufficient to carry all persons on board, the volume provided had to be increased to 175 per cent of the minimum (9,625 cubic ft). The additional 75 per cent could be supplied by boats or life rafts of any approved type, not necessarily under davits. However, the additional 75 per cent capacity was not required if the ship's subdivision was exceptionally good, in accordance with a regulation known as Rule 12. *Titanic* was unable to comply with Rule 12, and therefore had to provide 9,625 cubic ft. Any boat capacity in excess of that prescribed could be provided by boats of any class.[7]

Titanic met the Board's requirements by carrying fourteen class A boats and two of class D. Because her class A boats were relatively large, the required capacity of 9,625 cubic ft was exceeded by her conventional wooden boats alone, without resort to collapsibles or rafts. In addition, four collapsible boats, having a calculated volume of 1,504 cubic ft, were carried. The total volume provided was 11,325 cubic ft and the capacity of the boats, as calculated by the Board's rules, was 1,178 adults.[8] This was less than one third of the 3,547 *Titanic* was authorised to carry.[9] How had this position been reached?

Successive presidents of the Board of Trade had depended on the assistant secretary in charge of its Marine Department for advice on marine safety. Since 1899, this post had been held by Sir Walter Howell, a career civil servant. During the time when the *Olympic* class ships were being designed, Sir Walter was advised on technical matters by Sir Alfred Chalmers, a very experienced master mariner, who was the Marine Department's professional advisor from 1877 to 1911. Sir Alfred summarised his views on lifeboats in Lord Mersey's court:

> I considered the matter very closely from time to time. I first of all considered the record of the trade – that is to say, the record of the casualties – and to see what immunity from loss there was. I found it was the safest mode of travel in the world, and I thought it was neither right nor the duty of a State Department to impose regulations upon that mode of travel as long as the record was a clean one. Secondly, I found that, as ships grew bigger, there were such improvements made in their construction that they were stronger and better ships, both from the point of view of watertight compartments and also absolute strength, and I considered that that was the road along which the shipowners were going to travel, and that they should not be interfered with. I then went to the maximum that is down in the Table – 16 boats and upwards, together with the supplementary boats, and I considered from my experience that that was the maximum number that could be rapidly dealt with at sea and that could be safely housed without encumbering the vessel's decks unduly. In the next place, I considered that the traffic was very safe on account of the routes – the definite routes being agreed upon by the different companies, which tended to lessen the risk of collision, and to avoid ice and fog. Then, again, there was the question of wireless telegraphy which had already come into force on board of these passenger ships. I was seized of the fact that in July, 1901, the *Lucania* had been fitted with wireless telegraphy, and the Cunard Line, generally, fitted it during that year to all their ships. The Allan Line fitted it in 1902, and I am not sure that in 1904 it had not become quite general on the trans-Atlantic ships. That, of course, entered into my consideration as well. Then another point was the manning. It was quite evident to me that if you went on crowding the ship with boats you would require a crew which were not required otherwise for the safe navigation of the ship, or for the proper upkeep of the ship, but you are providing a crew which would be carried uselessly across the ocean, that never would be required to man the boats. Then the last point, and not the least, was this, that the voluntary action of the owners was carrying them beyond the requirements of our scale, and when voluntary action on the part of shipowners is doing that, I think that any State Department should hold its hand before it steps in to make a hard-and-fast scale for that particular type of shipping. I considered that that scale fitted all sizes of ships that were then afloat, and I did not consider it necessary to increase it, and that was my advice to Sir Walter Howell.[10]

Outside the Board of Trade, similar views were held. Seamen were aware that in many cases lifeboats were of little use in a crisis. It was more important to make the ships as close to unsinkable as possible. This point of view was summed up by the former Commander-in-Chief of the British Channel Fleet, Lord Charles Beresford, in a speech in Parliament on 21 May 1912:

Try to keep the ship afloat as long as you can and then you will be able to use what lifesaving appliances you have. Put what boats you like on a ship, but remember that on not more than one day in twelve all the year round can you lower a boat. With the roll of the ship the boats swing and will be smashed into smithereens against the side of the ship. The boats then should not be overdone…It might be fairly supposed that had the *Titanic* floated for twelve hours all might have been saved.[11]

What Might Have Been – *Dave Gittins*

It was the duty of Sir Walter Howell and his staff to enforce the law on lifeboats as it stood. His department was permitted to propose amended regulations that might be enforced after being tabled in Parliament. That is, the proposals would be placed before the House of Commons and would come into force if no objection were raised.[12] In the absence of such action, any amendments to the regulations would have to come from the politicians, but it was not until 1911 that any serious consideration was given to making changes.[13]

The impetus for this came from Horatio Bottomley, a maverick member of Prime Minister Herbert Asquith's Liberal Party, via questions in the House of Commons.[14] On 22 November 1910 he asked whether the president of the Board of Trade was aware *Olympic* was to carry only fourteen lifeboats. Bottomley claimed this was far less boat accommodation than was provided on other large liners. He was informed that *Olympic* was to carry sixteen boats, with a capacity of 9,752 cubic ft. This was slightly more than was required by the existing regulations.

On 18 February 1911, Bottomley asked whether the Board of Trade was considering revising the lifeboat regulations, given the increasing size of ships. He was told the matter was under consideration and would be referred to the Board of Trade's Merchant Shipping Advisory Committee. On the same day, Sir Walter Howell requested Captain Alfred Young, the new professional adviser to the Marine Department of the Board of Trade, to give his opinion on possible new lifeboat regulations. Three other officials received similar requests. The resulting reports varied considerably, but none recommended sufficient boats for all on board a ship of *Titanic*'s size.

The matter was now passed to a sub-committee of the Merchant Shipping Advisory Committee. The sub-committee included representatives from shipowners, shipbuilders, pilots, officers, crew and the insurance industry. Its task was to make recommendations on the provision of lifeboats with a view to amending the regulations of 1894. It did not have the benefit of the opinions of Captain Alfred Young and his colleagues, who had kept their reports from the committee 'in order to give the Advisory Committee a free hand and get an unbiased opinion.'[15]

On 26 May 1911, the committee signed a report that recommended only small changes to the regulations. It proposed that a ship of *Titanic*'s size should carry lifeboats with a capacity of 14,525 cubic ft. This could be reduced to 8,300 cubic ft if the builders could convince the Board of Trade that the ship's hull was exceptionally well subdivided. The proposals followed the lead of Sir Alfred Chalmers and other advocates of 'every ship her own lifeboat'. Had they been put into effect, it is possible *Titanic* could have carried fewer boats than she in fact did.[16]

We will never know what would have happened had the committee's recommendations been enforced. The Board of Trade deferred action on them because its officials were reporting cases of unsafe lifeboats being constructed by unscrupulous builders. For the sake of a few feet of timber, boats were being made excessively fine in the bow and stern, or being given an exaggerated capacity by excessive freeboard. It was decided to put lifeboat designs right before looking at their numbers. The Board's immediate action was to require a Belfast ship surveyor, William Chantler, to supervise the building of lifeboats for *Titanic*, paying special attention to their stability.[17]

The work of the committee ended in embarrassment. In Lord Mersey's court, it fell to Sir Walter Howell to explain a document in the Board of Trade's files. As explained, the recommendations of the Advisory Committee, made in May 1911, were not acted upon, pending an investigation into lifeboat design. This had occupied the last half of 1911 and the results were in Sir Walter's hands by early 1912. By 4 April he had made up his mind to instruct the Advisory Committee to reconsider its recommendations in the light of lifeboat tests conducted by his officials, who had discovered grave design failings. On that day, he gave instructions for a letter to that effect to be sent to the committee. The letter was not sent until 16 April, the day after *Titanic* sank.

The delay was probably due merely to the Easter holidays and clerical inertia, but it gave an impression of a slumbering bureaucracy stung into wakefulness by the disaster. The letter was promptly countermanded on 20 April. The committee was now asked to have 'full regard to this new situation, and the facts of the disaster so far as ascertained.' *Titanic* had changed maritime safety forever.[18]

Separation of Classes – *Samuel Halpern*

As is well known, *Titanic* accommodated three classes of passengers: first class, second class and third class. On the Certificate for Clearance for an immigrant ship that was issued to her, first and second class passengers were grouped under the heading of Cabin Passengers, while third class passengers were grouped under the heading of Steerage Passengers.[19] Immigration laws required barriers on immigrant ships in order to prevent the spread of disease. Ships not in compliance with these regulations could be held in quarantine for up to forty days until all passengers were medically examined, so passenger segregation was taken seriously by the shipping lines.[20] Is it possible that such barriers as well as other causes were responsible for the great loss of life suffered by *Titanic*'s steerage passengers when compared to those in first and second class?

Consider the following statistics taken from Chapter 4. Of the 1,317 passengers on board *Titanic* the night of 14 April, 500 were saved, or 38 per cent of the total. But if we look at this from a class perspective, we find that 319 of 608 first and second class passengers were saved, or 52 per cent; while only 181 out of 709 third class passengers were saved, a mere 26 per cent.

What is more striking is the number of women and children saved by class. Of the 265 women and children in first and second class on board, 248 of them were saved, or almost 94 per cent. However, of the 257 women and children in third class on board, only 121 were saved, or just 47 per cent.

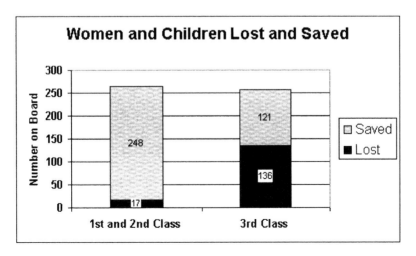

Fig. 8-1 Women and children lost and saved.

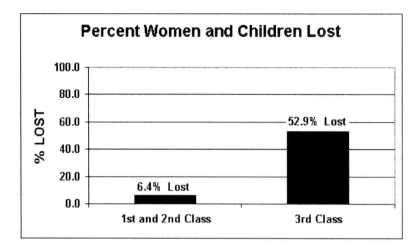

Fig. 8-2 Percentage of women and children lost.

Considering that the BOT-rated capacity of the boats carried on *Titanic* was 1,178 persons, it should be obvious that if priority and a concerted effort were truly given to save all 522 women and children passengers in the almost 2 hours that were available to them, almost all of them should have been saved. Yet, 52.9 per cent of the women and children in steerage were lost, while only 6.4 per cent of all the women and children in first and second class were lost.

There is no evidence that any woman or child of any class was kept from entering any of the boats. So why was it that so many in steerage never even found their way to the few boats that were there?

A Question of Locked Gates – *Cathy Akers-Jordan and George Behe*

It is often claimed that, during the sinking, *Titanic's* steerage passengers were detained behind locked gates, but specific evidence to that effect has been sparse and poorly documented in the past. A detailed discussion of this topic can be found in Appendix J; the conclusions are summarised here.

Most films about the *Titanic* disaster depict the restriction of third class passengers behind locked floor-to-ceiling gates on the lower decks as having been a universal experience. While the detention of at least some steerage passengers behind locked gates apparently did happen, these experiences seem to have been the exception rather than the rule.

Before third class passengers could encounter physical barriers, though, they first had to overcome their own language and cultural barriers as well as the absence of printed notifications about how to get around the ship or how to ascend from the steerage areas to the upper decks.[21] Approximately half the third class survivors were native English-speakers from the US, England, Canada or Ireland,[22] but – even if not all of these people were literate – the absence of printed signs probably wasn't as much of a hindrance to them as were the obstacles faced by non-English-speaking passengers. These foreigners were forced to rely on stewards to help them find their way around the ship, but their inability to understand the stewards' instructions meant that – to a certain extent – these passengers would have been on their own during the sinking.

While language barriers could explain the loss of many third class passengers, especially whole families of non-English speakers like the Anderssons and Paulsons (from Sweden), they do not explain the loss of so many English-speaking families like the Goodwins and the

Sages (from England). These families must have been either trapped below decks, were late in arriving on the upper decks, or else chose to stay together rather than be parted at the lifeboats.

It is clear that some third class passengers waited patiently for someone in authority to tell them what to do. When that didn't happen, some passengers took the initiative to save themselves, while others waited in vain or simply gave up. According to Wyn Craig Wade, author of *The Titanic: End of a Dream*, survivor August Wennerström wrote in a detailed account that he was appalled by those third class passengers who made no effort to help themselves, but instead prayed with Father Byles:[23]

> Hundreds were in a circle with a preacher in the middle, praying, crying, asking God and Mary to help them. They lay there and yelled, never lifting a hand to help themselves. They had lost their own will power and expected God to do all the work for them.

Gus Cohen had almost the same experience.[24] Despite the inertia exhibited by these passengers, however, survivor testimony makes it clear that many other third class passengers succeeded in saving themselves by their own initiative.

With a few notable exceptions, most passengers who encountered physical barriers barring access to *Titanic's* upper decks seem to have been detained at gates located at the tops of the stairways leading from the aft well deck up to B deck. These low, waist-high gates were guarded by crewmen whose duty was to prevent steerage passengers from leaving their own deck until they were granted permission to do so. Even so, several passengers succeeded in pushing their way past these crewmen or finding other ways to gain access to the boat deck.

As for the steerage areas located below decks, it appears that several exits from these lower decks were open and gave steerage passengers unrestricted access to the second class decks after the collision. The door through which Steward Hart led passengers from steerage into first class seems to have been unlocked and freely accessible to all passengers, but it is possible that unescorted passengers were deterred from using it and similar doors because of signs warning steerage passengers that they (ordinarily) were not permitted to open or pass through the doors in question.

Despite the fact that a number of exits from the lower steerage decks were open and were manned by stewards who directed passengers toward the upper decks, some steerage passengers reported walking through gated barriers that were then closed and locked behind them, which might explain why other passengers told of encountering closed gates that they were forced to climb over. (Perhaps a passenger's chance of survival depended on *when* he or she attempted to pass through those barriers.) Other hindrances below decks consisted of crewmen (some of whom were armed) who were assigned to prevent passengers from passing through specific barriers and ascending to the boat deck. Indeed, these guarded barriers seem to have prevented quite a few passengers from leaving *Titanic's* lower decks even though a number of people did succeed in forcing their way past the guards.

Although there is not yet any concrete physical evidence of floor-to-ceiling gates inside *Titanic's* wreck, there is too much circumstantial evidence (passenger accounts, existing gates on her two sister ships, etc.) for us to conclude that *Titanic* had no physical barriers that prevented at least some third class passengers from reaching the boat deck.

For more details and evidence pertaining to locked gates and guarded barriers, refer to Appendix J.

Notes

[1]   The complex story of the lifeboat regulations is found in the testimony of Sir Walter Howell on days 21 and 22 of Lord Mersey's inquiry.
[2]   Regulations and Suggestions as to the Survey of the Hull, Equipments, and Machinery of Steam Ships Carrying Passengers (1905). (Board of Trade handbook.)
[3]   See *Titanic: Monument and Warning*, Chapter 'From Shell to Ship'.

4   Lawrence Beesley, *The Loss of the SS Titanic*.
5   Charles Lightoller, AI p.431.
6   Harold Sanderso, BI 19172–4.
7   See long discussion after question 22207 in the British inquiry. It was agreed that Rule 12 was virtually obsolete by 1912.
8   There are small discrepancies in the dimensions seen for the lifeboats. The British inquiry gave their beam as 9ft 1in and their capacity as sixty-five persons. Some sources give 9.1ft. The capacity plates carried on *Titanic's* large lifeboats showed dimensions of 30ft x 9ft x 4ft and a capacity of sixty-four persons.
9   See *Titanic's* Passenger Certificate.
10 Sir Alfred Chalmers, BI 22875.
11 *The Times*, 22 May 1912.
12 Sir Walter Howell, BI 22391.
13 See discussion beginning on page 949 of the transcript of the British inquiry.
14 Bottomley liked to pose as the protector of the 'little man' and act as a gadfly to his own party. He had the distinction of being twice expelled from Parliament, first for being bankrupt and later for being convicted of embezzlement.
15 Captain Alfred Young, BI 23378.
16 The report of the committee is in MT9/920F, British Archives.
17 Alfred Young, BI 2398 etc. William Chantler, BI 24031 etc.
18 Sir Walter Howell. BI 22479–95.
19 PRO reference – MT 9/920 F [No 356].
20 Act of the Congress of the United States, 'To Regulate the Carriage of Passengers by Sea', 2 August 1882.
21 John Poingdestre, BI 3288. Poingdestre testified that there were no posted signs directing passengers from the steerage areas to the upper decks.
22 Lee Merideth, *Titanic Names: A Complete List of the Passengers and Crew*. Sunnyvale, CA: Historical Indexes Publishing Company, 2002, p.5.
23 Wyn Craig Wade, *The Titanic: End of a Dream*. Rawson, Wade Publishers, p.256.
24 Walter Lord, *A Night to Remember*, New York: Bantam, 1955, p.68.

9

THE RESCUE BY THE SS *CARPATHIA*

Dave Gittins

The Cunard liner *Carpathia* sailed from New York on 11 April, bound for Gibraltar and other Mediterranean ports. Approximately 760 passengers were on board, mostly in third class.[1] Luckily for *Titanic's* survivors, most of *Carpathia's* accommodation was vacant, as she was approved to carry up to 2,550 passengers.[2]

Carpathia is sometimes described as a small ship. Newspapers called her 'the gallant little Cunarder', and Walter Lord later unkindly called her 'a pokey 12,000-tonner'.[3] She was actually of 13,603 GRT and 558ft LOA, making her a substantial ship and one of the larger participants in the *Titanic* drama.[4] Her two quadruple-expansion engines propelled her eastward at a very consistent 14 knots.[5]

Carpathia was commanded by Captain Arthur Rostron, an extra master with twenty-seven years of seagoing experience.[6] He had a reputation for energy and enthusiasm and ended his career as Cunard's Commodore.[7] Acting on ice warnings from Cunard's New York office, he was steering a course well south of the shortest route to Gibraltar.[8]

Carpathia was equipped with a Marconi wireless installation of obsolescent design, with a plain spark transmitter. Under good conditions, its range was about 250 miles, but damp weather reduced this to as little as 100 miles.[9] The wireless set was housed in a small wireless shack above the second class smoking room. Its lone operator slept next to the equipment.[10]

The operator, Harold Cottam, was experienced by the standard of the time, having been a wireless telegraphist for three years, afloat and ashore. He was employed by the Marconi Company, but was answerable to Captain Rostron. He generally worked from morning to midnight. His duties were not very demanding, as *Carpathia* carried few wealthy passengers, the main source of Marconi revenue.[11]

Rescue by *Carpathia*

On the night of 14 April, at the time of *Titanic's* first CQD, Cottam, who had earlier been briefly in touch with *Titanic*, was listening to broadcast messages from the high-powered wireless station at Cape Cod (MCC) after first failing to receive a reply to a message he tried to send to *Parisian*. After picking up four messages in 7 or 8 minutes transmitted by Cape Cod that were intended for *Titanic*, Cottam seized the opportunity to call *Titanic* and advise them that Cape Cod was sending them a batch of messages.[12] Jack Phillips immediately replied, 'Come at once. We have struck a berg. 41.46 N, 50.14 W. It's a CQD OM.'[13] Cottam noted the time was 10.35p.m. New York Time (NYT) and hurried to the bridge, where he reported *Titanic's* signal to First Officer Horace Dean.[14]

Dean and Cottam hurried to Captain Rostron's cabin, where they found him in his bunk, but awake, and gave him the news. Rostron roughly estimated the direction of *Titanic* and ordered Dean to steer north-west at top speed, pending more precise orders. He then closely questioned Cottam, to rule out the possibility of an error or a hoax.

Satisfied the emergency was real, Rostron used dead reckoning to estimate *Carpathia*'s position. He doubtless had the benefit of starting from a fix by star sights taken in the evening. He found his dead reckoning position was 41° 10' N, 49° 12' W, about 58 miles from the CQD position, on a course of 308° True.[15] As will be shown, this position was somewhat in error, perhaps because of the influence of the North Atlantic Drift.

After hastily dressing, Rostron ordered Dean to steer the new course. He then ordered his chief engineer to call out an extra watch of firemen and trimmers and drive *Carpathia* as hard as possible. The lookout was increased, with two men being placed in the ship's bow and one in the crow's nest. Three officers and a quartermaster kept watch from *Carpathia*'s bridge.[16]

At some unknown time, Rostron recorded his orders, with a view to reporting his actions to the Cunard Line:

English doctor, with assistants, to remain in first-class dining room.

Italian doctor, with assistants, to remain in second-class dining room.

Hungarian doctor, with assistants, to remain in third-class dining room.

Each doctor to have supplies of restoratives, stimulants, and everything to hand for immediate needs of probable wounded or sick.

Purser, with assistant purser and chief steward, to receive the passengers, etc., at different gangways, controlling our own stewards in assisting *Titanic* passengers to the dining rooms, etc.; also to get Christian and surnames of all survivors as soon as possible to send by wireless.

Inspector, steerage stewards, and master-at-arms to control our own steerage passengers and keep them out of the third-class dining hall, and also to keep them out of the way and off the deck to prevent confusion.

Chief steward: That all hands would be called and to have coffee, etc., ready to serve out to all our crew.

Have coffee, tea, soup, etc., in each saloon, blankets in saloons, at the gangways, and some for the boats.

To see all rescued cared for and immediate wants attended to.

My cabin and all officials' cabins to be given up. Smoke rooms, library, etc., dining rooms, would be utilised to accommodate the survivors.

All spare berths in steerage to be utilised for *Titanic*'s passengers, and get all our own steerage passengers grouped together.

Stewards to be placed in each alleyway to reassure our own passengers, should they inquire about noise in getting our boats out, etc., or the working of engines. To all I strictly enjoined the necessity for order, discipline and quietness and to avoid all confusion.

Chief and first officers: All the hands to be called; get coffee, etc. Prepare and swing out all boats.

All gangway doors to be opened.

Electric sprays in each gangway and over side.

A block with line rove hooked in each gangway.

A chair sling at each gangway, for getting up sick or wounded.

Boatswains' chairs. Pilot ladders and canvas ash bags to be at each gangway, the canvas ash bags for children.

Cargo falls with both ends clear; bowlines in the ends, and bights secured along ship's sides, for boat ropes or to help the people up.

Heaving lines distributed along the ship's side, and gaskets handy near gangways for lashing people in chairs, etc.

Forward derricks, topped and rigged, and steam on winches; also told off officers for different stations and for certain eventualities.

Ordered company's rockets to be fired at 2.45a.m. and every quarter of an hour after to reassure *Titanic*.[17]

Mustering all possible speed, *Carpathia* hurried at first through open water, but later met isolated icebergs. Changes of course were made as required. Throughout the passage, Harold Cottam attempted to assist *Titanic* by relaying messages and suggesting contact with other ships. He last heard *Titanic* at 11.55p.m. NYT, when Jack Phillips sent 'Come quick; our engine room is filling up to the boilers.'[18]

At about 4.00a.m. ship's time, *Carpathia* reached the vicinity of *Titanic*'s wreck site, having been guided in the final miles by green flares fired periodically by Joseph Boxhall in emergency boat No.2.[19]

We will later examine *Carpathia*'s navigation in the light of the discovery of the position of *Titanic*'s remains, far from the CQD position. It will be shown that Captain Rostron's account of his rescue mission is inaccurate and his discovery of *Titanic*'s boats was fortuitous. We will also consider the curious matter of an unidentified ship sighted from *Carpathia* during the passage.

By 4.10a.m., Boxhall's boat was alongside *Carpathia*. Passengers and crew were taken on board, using a combination of rope ladders, slings and bags. Boxhall informed Captain Rostron that *Titanic* had sunk, leaving her lifeboats in the general area.[20]

Carpathia proceeded to pick up the survivors in the remaining boats, completing the task by about 8.30a.m. About that time *Californian* arrived on the scene, and at Captain Lord's suggestion, she began an unsuccessful search for survivors soon after *Carpathia* departed.[21] Thirteen *Titanic* lifeboats were taken on board *Carpathia*, including the two emergency boats. The remaining lifeboats and all the collapsible boats were abandoned.[22] By 9.00a.m. *Carpathia* was underway, steering roughly southward to get around the vast icefield that lay directly west of the wreck site.[23]

Meanwhile, Episcopalian minister, the Revd Father Roger Anderson, conducted a memorial service in *Carpathia*'s first class lounge, as requested by Captain Rostron.[24]

Captain Rostron now considered his next move. He toyed with the idea of taking *Titanic*'s survivors to the Azores, which lay relatively close to his planned course to Gibraltar. He dismissed the idea as most inconvenient for the survivors.[25] Halifax was fairly close, but the course to it was likely to be cluttered with ice, and the survivors would be faced with a long rail journey to New York, their intended destination. Rostron decided that the best plan was to steam back to New York, which offered the facilities needed to care for the survivors.[26]

At 4.00p.m. *Carpathia* briefly hove to and buried four members of *Titanic*'s company at sea. These were Sidney Siebert, William Lyons, William Hoyt and Abraham Harmer (aka David Livshin).[27]

According to Captain Rostron, he gave clear orders on the use of *Carpathia*'s wireless. He told Senator Smith's inquiry:[28]

> I controlled the whole thing, through my orders. I said I placed official messages first. After they had gone, and the first press message, then the names of the passengers. After the names of the passengers and crew had been sent my orders were to send all private messages from the *Titanic*'s passengers first in the order in which they were given in to the purser; no preference to any message.

The reality was rather more chaotic. In New York, rumours and misinformation about *Titanic* had been spreading since the early hours of 15 April. The only certain facts known were that *Titanic* had collided with an iceberg and called for assistance. It fell to *Carpathia* to make the facts public, but it was well into the afternoon before action was taken. The delay seems to have been caused by the limitations of *Carpathia*'s wireless and Cottam's reluctance to relay information to shore via other ships. The facts emerged at 2.00p.m. NYT when *Olympic*'s wireless operator, Ernest Moore, established contact with *Carpathia*. Harold Cottam replied with a detailed account of the disaster, evidently prepared on his own initiative. Further messages were exchanged and it was decided that *Carpathia* would not meet *Olympic*, as this would distress the survivors. It was 4.00p.m. NYT before Captain Rostron sent a formal message to *Olympic*, confirming Cottam's earlier information and requesting him to relay the story to White Star, Cunard, Liverpool and New York. At 4.35p.m. NYT this was done.[29] The message reached Phillip Franklin, a vice-president of IMM, in New York at about 6.30p.m.. He immediately announced the sinking to waiting reporters.[30]

Cottam had now been awake since around dawn on the previous day, but at about 5.45p.m. NYT he began to transmit the names of the first and second class survivors to *Olympic*. This occupied him until 7.35p.m. NYT. Ernest Moore relayed the messages to the land stations at Cape Sable and Cape Race.[31] Throughout the rest of the night and the following day, Cottam battled with the task of sending a list of surviving crewmembers to *Minnewaska* and attending to various messages. He was much hampered by transmission difficulties caused by fog and the limitations of his wireless set. At some time during the night of Tuesday 16 April, he fell asleep at his Morse key.[32]

It was later claimed that Cottam failed to attend to two important messages. One was sent on behalf of President Taft, inquiring after Major Archibald Butt. According to Captain Rostron, his purser advised him that the message was answered with the words, 'Not on board'. Cottam did not recall the message. Phillip Franklin testified that his office had received telegrams from the president and had advised him that Butt was not saved. Much was made of this incident at Senator Smith's inquiry, but it seems little real harm was done.[33]

The other message was important and its story is better documented. On the morning of 15 April, Bruce Ismay conferred with Captain Rostron and decided to inform White Star's New York office of the sinking. He wrote, 'Deeply regret advise you *Titanic* sank this morning after collision iceberg, resulting serious loss life. Full particulars later.' Had it been sent promptly, this would have been the first formal notice of the disaster, but for some unknown reason it was delayed and did not reach Phillip Franklin until 9.00a.m. on Wednesday 17 April. Marconi inspector Gilbert Balfour suggested that Cottam had been reluctant to send such an important message to shore via other ships.[34]

During Wednesday 17 April a somewhat revived Cottam sent as many survivors' messages as possible, but incoming demands for information delayed his work. Following Captain Rostron's orders, he did not reply to inquiries from the American press. At about 5.00p.m., *Carpathia* time, the injured Harold Bride was carried to the wireless shack, where he assisted Cottam for the remainder of the passage to New York.[35] During Wednesday evening Bride sent the list of third class survivors to USS *Chester*, for relay to shore stations.[36]

By this time, the American press was becoming irate at the lack of detailed news from *Carpathia*. It was even rumoured that Cottam and Bride were wasting time listening to the American baseball scores.[37] During Thursday 18 April dramatic stories about notable passengers were demanded, preferably written by prominent people, such as Francis Millet and Major Archibald Butt.[38] To this day, some suspect Cottam and Bride had at least a vague idea of profiting from their experiences.[39] Wireless operators were well aware that in 1909 *Republic's* wireless operator, John (Jack) Binns, had been handsomely paid for his account of that liner's sinking.[40]

There is no proof that any financial deal was struck in advance. Such a thing would have been impossible to do, as *Carpathia's* wireless transmissions could be widely heard. However, the Marconi Company worked in cooperation with *The New York Times* and something was afoot. At 8.12p.m., as *Carpathia* approached New York, a message was received from Frederick Sammis, of the Marconi Company.[41]

Say, old man, Marconi Co. taking good care of you. Keep your mouth shut, and hold your story. It is fixed for you so you will get big money. Now, please do your best to clear.

At 8.30p.m. a further message defined 'big money'.

To Marconi officer, Carpathia and Titanic: Arranged for your exclusive story for dollars in four figures, Mr. Marconi agreeing. Say nothing until you see me. Where are you now?

On Friday 19 April Bride's extensive account of the disaster occupied most of the front page of *The New York Times*. Cottam's briefer story appeared on page 2. Bride received $1,000 and Cottam $750. Not all the money came from *The New York Times*, as other parties were impressed by the efforts of the wireless operators.[42]

Carpathia arrived in New York harbour on the night of 18 April, having coped with variable weather, including fog, rain, wind and thunderstorms.[43] Reaching the area of the ocean steamers' docks she paused while several of *Titanic's* lifeboats were lowered and towed away. At about 9.30p.m. she was secured at Pier 54, the normal berth for Cunard liners.[44]

For his services, Captain Rostron was awarded a Congressional Gold Medal, a most prestigious honour that he shares with such diverse people as the Wright brothers, Thomas Edison, Frank Sinatra, the Little Rock Nine, Joe Louis and the Navajo Code Talkers. President Taft presented him with the medal on 1 March 1913, during the last days of his presidency.[45]

Fig. 9-1 Captain Rostron and his wife, Ethel Minnie, in Washington to receive his Congressional Gold Medal. (Library of Congress Archive)

Carpathia's Navigation

For many years, the navigational details provided to the two inquiries by Captain Rostron were generally accepted as accurate. During her rescue mission, *Carpathia* had steamed 58 miles on a course of 308° True and had arrived at 41°46'N, 50°14'W, the distress position transmitted by *Titanic*.[46] During the passage, her speed peaked at 17½ knots.[47]

Throughout the twentieth century, these particulars were repeated from book to book, as typified by Walter Lord's *A Night to Remember*:

Faster and faster the old ship knifed ahead – 14...14.5...15...16.5...17 knots. No one dreamed the *Carpathia* could drive so hard.[48]

The accuracy of the CQD position was so widely accepted that until recently the International Ice Patrol conducted an annual memorial ceremony at the spot. On Joseph Boxhall's demise in 1967, his ashes were scattered there, at his request.[49]

In the 1912 testimony, there was evidence that suggested the CQD position was considerably in error. The most important came from Captain Moore of *Mount Temple*. On the morning of 15 April 1912, he had arrived in the general area of the CQD position. As the morning light improved, he saw *Carpathia* to the east, in the process of rescuing *Titanic*'s survivors. Between *Carpathia* and his ship lay an icefield, which *Titanic* obviously had not traversed. Moore ordered his fourth officer to take a sun sight for longitude, which he did. Two sights were taken and his longitude was found to be almost 50° 10'W, which was to the east of the CQD position. *Carpathia* was even further east.[50]

Further evidence came from Captain Stanley Lord of *Californian*, who had also reached the region of the CQD position and found nothing. He testified that he had left the floating debris from *Titanic* in 50° 01'W.[51]

Probably the first to publicly cast serious doubt on the accepted story was Peter Padfield, a notable British seaman and maritime author. In *The Titanic and the Californian*, published in 1965, he strongly suggested the CQD position was incorrect and *Carpathia*'s speed was exaggerated. However, a vital piece of evidence was missing.[52]

The key to the puzzle arrived in September 1985, when the remains of *Titanic* were discovered scattered in about 41° 44'N, 49° 47'W, about 13 miles from the CQD position. How then had *Carpathia* reached *Titanic*'s lifeboats with such apparently unerring precision?

The evidence for the traditional story came mainly from Captain Rostron, but he was not entirely consistent. At Senator Smith's inquiry, he merely said, 'I went full speed, all we could.'[53] In Lord Mersey's court he testified to the famous 17½ knots.[54] During the rescue mission, Harold Cottam, on Rostron's orders, told Jack Phillips *Carpathia* was 'making a good 15 and perhaps 16 knots'. Writing many years later, *Carpathia*'s Second Officer James Bisset mentioned a 'forced speed of sixteen knots'.[55] Bisset also mentions *Carpathia* slowing at times, thus reducing the average speed of the passage.[56]

Rostron's unlikely final estimate of his speed is due to his genuine belief that between 12.35a.m. and 4.00a.m. he covered 58 miles in 3 hours, 25 minutes.[57] This is an average speed of 17 knots. Allowing for slowing down at the end and for the fact that the top speed attained on a passage is generally a little more than the average, a maximum of 17½ would have seemed possible. Not only the speed, but Rostron's times, were worked out to fit the 58-mile run. As will be shown, his calculation was based on incorrect assumptions and his times and speed are therefore incorrect.

Now that the position of the wreck is known, it is evident that Rostron's navigation was in error. From his assumed starting point, the wreck lies only 47 miles away, on a bearing of 315° True. Moreover, his course of 308° True misses the wreck site by about 7 miles.

The clue to Rostron's real course lies in the position of emergency boat No.2, commanded by Joseph Boxhall. Boxhall testified that when *Titanic* sank he was close to the ship. He saw no point in rowing aimlessly away and in any case his boat was inadequately manned and hard to handle.[58] When *Carpathia* arrived on the scene, he must have been within a mile or two of the wreck, having drifted roughly south on the Labrador Current.

Our next clue comes from Captain Rostron, who sighted a green flare fired by Boxhall about ½ a point off his port bow.[59] This was his first indication that he was nearing the wreck. From the Extreme Range Table in *Norie's Nautical Tables*, we see that at this point *Carpathia* must have been not more than about 10 miles from Boxhall's boat. (Perfect precision in this matter is unattainable. We do not know exactly how high Boxhall held his flares and there is no reason to assume that he fired one just as the extreme range was reached). Rostron turned 1 point to port, bringing him to 302° True. He effectively maintained this course thereafter, while occasionally dodging icebergs.

From the direction in which Rostron sighted the flare, it is evident that his course to that point had been almost exactly toward the wreck site. *Carpathia* had evidently started her rescue mission from a point somewhat further east than Rostron had calculated.

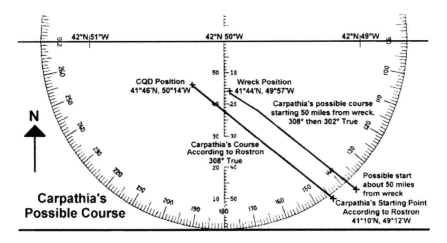

Fig. 9-2 Chart of Rostron's rescue mission, made on a universal plotting chart.

Captain Rostron gave the time at which he sighted the flare as 2.40a.m. ATS.[60] This time must be in error. We know he was now within 10 miles of Boxhall's boat, yet by Rostron's reckoning it took him 1 hour and 20 minutes to cover those final miles. That equates to an average of 7½ knots. Even allowing for the slowing reported by James Bisset, this speed is obviously not correct.[61] Rostron himself reported that *Carpathia* was making 13 to 15 knots in the final miles.[62]

From other sources, we find evidence that Rostron was mistaken in his timing. *Carpathia* passenger, Howard Chapin, in his privately published little book, *The Titanic Disaster,* wrote, 'It was after three when we sighted a faint green light off our port bow which we took for the starboard light of the *Titanic*.' In an affidavit supplied to Senator Smith's inquiry, *Titanic* survivor Mahala Douglas said Captain Rostron told her he had sighted Boxhall's flares from 10 miles away.[63] *Mount Temple*'s wireless operator, John Durrant, provided more evidence. After sighting the flare, Captain Rostron ordered socket signals to be fired at 15-minute intervals, to encourage *Titanic*'s survivors. At 1.16a.m. NYT, *Caronia* heard some ship transmitting 'we are firing rockets . . . look out for rockets.'[64] At 1.25a.m. NYT, *Mount Temple* heard *Carpathia* transmit, 'If you are there we are firing rockets.'[65] These times correspond roughly to 3.13 and 3.22a.m. *Carpathia* ATS, respectively.

In 1998, this author proposed online that Captain Rostron made a simple and understandable error in his timing. He sighted Boxhall's flare, not at 2.40a.m., but 2 hours 40 minutes into his passage toward the wreck. Rostron would have been acutely aware of the passing of time as he hurried to the rescue, as he watched his estimated 4 hours for the passage slipping away.

Accepting this proposal, everything slips into place. Beginning at 12.35a.m. ATS, *Carpathia* steams on a course of 308° True until about 3.15a.m., covering about 40 miles at a feasible 15 knots. She then takes about 45 minutes to cover the final 10 miles, slowing at times to avoid icebergs and averaging about 13 knots. Her total distance run is about 50 miles.

As we do not know *Carpathia*'s precise course before the receipt of *Titanic*'s distress signal, it is impossible to be dogmatic about her starting point. It can only be said that she was some distance further east than Captain Rostron calculated, perhaps having been set eastward by the North Atlantic Drift.

Carpathia's Mystery Ship

One of the genuine mysteries of the *Titanic* story is the ship sighted by Captain Rostron and his officers during his passage to the scene of the disaster. Only Rostron seems to have given an account of this event. It appears only in his testimony in Lord Mersey's court. It is not mentioned in Rostron's memoirs, or in Sir James Bisset's *Tramps and Ladies*. Here is Rostron's testimony:

25552.	(The Attorney-General): Does that state all the vessels that you saw? I think it stated two steamers?
Rostron:	No; I saw one more, but it was during the night previous to getting out of [sic] the *Titanic's* position. We saw masthead lights quite distinctly of another steamer between us and the *Titanic*. That was about quarter-past three.
25553:	The masthead lights?
Rostron:	Yes, of another steamer, and one of the Officers swore he also saw one of the sidelights.
25554.	Which one?
Rostron:	The port sidelight.
25555.	Do you know of any identification of that steamer at all?
Rostron:	No; we saw nothing but the lights. I did not see the sidelights; I merely saw the masthead lights.
Mr Bucknill:	May we have the distance and bearing of these lights that he saw, as far as he can remember?
25556.	(The Commissioner): You did not see the additional lights yourself, the sidelight?
Rostron:	I saw the masthead lights.
25557:	Did you see the lights your Officer spoke of?
Rostron:	I saw the masthead lights myself, but not the sidelight.
25558:	What time was it?
Rostron:	About a quarter-past three.
25559:	And how was the light bearing?
Rostron:	About 2 points on the starboard bow.
25560:	On your starboard bow?
Rostron:	On my starboard bow; that would be about N. 30 W. true. [330° True]

Rostron's testimony is vague. He gave no estimate of how far away the ship was. He did not say whether the ship was underway, though her lights suggest she was. The following chart shows that only a vague idea of her course may be obtained. The key is the bearing of the ship from *Carpathia*. Had she been steering 150° True, directly at *Carpathia*, both her sidelights would have been visible, assuming they were within range, and her steaming lights would have been seen, one above the other. Her sidelights were each visible over an arc of 112.5°, and her steaming lights over an arc of 225°, as required by regulations. This leads to two possibilities.

The mystery ship could have been steering a course between 037.5° True and 150° True. On this course, she would show two steaming lights and a green sidelight, if sufficiently close. Alternatively, she could have steered between 150° True and 262.5° True. She would then show two steaming lights and a red sidelight. If Rostron's officer really saw a red sidelight, the second alternative is the more likely.

Unless we assume the mystery ship was steaming a circuitous course for some unknown reason, the officer's observation shows she must have been somewhere to the east of the longitude of the disaster when sighted. She may even have been far to the east and steering almost westward. Certainly there seems to be no reason to place her near *Titanic* or *Californian* between 11.40p.m. on 14 April and 2.20a.m. on 15 April, nor for an arrival anywhere near the scene later on Monday morning.

The great mystery of *Carpathia's* mystery ship is that none of her crew later appeared to tell of sighting the Cunarder rushing through the night, firing a mixture of socket signals and Roman candles. Given the propensity of seamen to tell good yarns, this silence is remarkable.

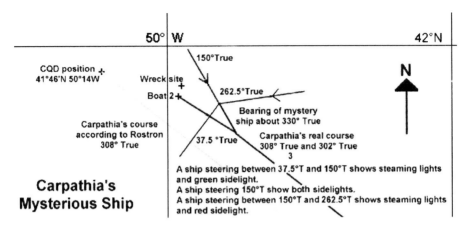

Fig. 9-3 Diagram showing the range of possible courses steered by the mystery ship.

Notes

1   Captain Rostron, AI p.19.
2   Cunard Heritage website.
3   *A Night to Remember*, p.154 of illustrated edition. *Carpathia* was hardly an old ship, having been commissioned in 1903.
4   Tonnage from *Lloyd's Register*. Overall length from website.
5   Sir James Bisset, *Tramps and Ladies*, p.273. Neither Bisset nor Rostron give us *Carpathia's* precise course.
6   Extra master was the highest formal qualification available to British merchant mariners. It was awarded after a candidate passed a 26-hour written and oral examination on all aspects of seamanship, marine law and advanced navigation.
7   Sir James Bisset, *Tramps and Ladies*, p.261.
8   Captain Rostron, BI 25378–81.
9   Harold Cottam, AI p.96. Captain Rostron, AI p.34.
10 Harold Cottam, AI p.96, etc.
11 Part of *Carpathia's* wireless log, known as a *procès-verbal*, can be seen at http://www.marconicalling. co.uk/html/index.html It shows how few messages were normally sent and received and that Cottam ceased to keep a record after hearing *Titanic's* CQD.
12 Harold Cottam, AI pp.101–3.
13 Marconi operators were used to using CQD as a distress signal, though it had been officially replaced by SOS. Operators jocularly addressed each other as OM, meaning 'old man'.
14 Cottam recorded the time of the CQD on a piece of paper, but he didn't publicly produce it until he testified in Britain. BI 17068–70. His timing is confirmed by the *procès-verbal* of *Mount Temple*.
15 Captain Rostron, AI pp.19–20. Position obtained by use of Norie's Nautical Tables, given the CQD position and Rostron's course to it.
16 Captain Rostron, AI p.27.
17 Captain Rostron, AI p.20–21.
18 Harold Cottam, AI p.107, 132; BI 17145–6, 17193–201.
19 Captain Rostron, BI 25394.
20 Captain Rostron, *Home From the Sea*, p.287.
21 Captain Rostron, AI p.22.
22 US court document prepared for the valuation of the lifeboats in connection with civil claims.
23 Captain Rostron, 'The Rescue of the "Titanic" Survivors', *Scribner's Magazine*, 1913, p.359.
24 Captain Rostron, AI p.22.
25 Captain Rostron. Letter to Cunard, made public in Marshall, Logan. *Sinking of the Titanic and Great Sea Disasters*. Philadelphia: John C. Winston Co., 1912.

26   Captain Rostron, AI p.29.
27   *Carpathia* passenger Fred Beachler in *The New York Herald*, 19 April 1912. According to Captain Rostron, one of these persons had been alive when taken on board *Carpathia*, but had later died. The matter remains doubtful.
28   Captain Rostron, AI p.33.
29   Ernest Moore, AI p.1137 etc.
30   Phillip Franklin, AI p.179.
31   Ernest Moore, AI p.1138.
32   Harold Cottam, AI pp.108–9.
33   Captain Rostron, AI p.32. Harold Cottam, AI p.110. Phillip Franklin, AI p.190.
34   Bruce Ismay, AI p.951. Phillip Franklin, AI p.194. Gilbert Balfour, AI p.1061.
35   Harold Cottam, AI p.126.
36   Harold Cottam, AI p.127.
37   Harold Bride, AI p.906.
38   See examples in *Signals of Disaster*. John Booth and Sean Couglan. Neither Millet nor Butt had survived.
39   See supplement to *The New York Times* reprint of *Titanic* items from April 1912.
40   John Binns, AI p.1033.
41   Harold Cottam, AI p.923. Frederick Sammis, AI pp.863–73.
42   Harold Bride, AI p.896. Harold Cottam, AI 918.
43   Lawrence Beesley, *The Loss of the SS Titanic*.
44   Captain Rostron, AI p.24.
45   See pages 81 and 82 of the report of the American inquiry. *The Washington Post*, 1 and 2 March 1913. It is often stated that Captain Rostron received a Congressional Medal of Honor, which is never awarded for non-combat gallantry. The mistake probably stems from Captain Rostron's own misunderstanding of the name of his award. See *Home From the Sea*.
46   Joseph Boxhall, AI p.931.
47   Captain Rostron, BI 25390.
48   Walter Lord, *A Night to Remember*, pp.158–160 of illustrated edition.
49   *Southern Evening Echo*, 27 April 1967.
50   Captain James Moore, AI p.777–8.
51   Captain Lord, BI 7039. Lord's longitude was obtained by dead reckoning from his noon position of 15 April, and would not have been especially accurate.
52   Peter Padfield, *The Titanic and the Californian*, p.270–1.
53   Captain Rostron, AI p.27.
54   Captain Rostron, BI 25390.
55   James Bisset, *Tramps and Ladies*, p.282.
56   James Bisset, *Tramps and Ladies*, p.282–4.
57   According to Captain Rostron's timing, 10 minutes elapsed between Cottam's receipt of the distress signal and him being informed. This seems excessive, but given the general vagueness of many times given in testimony the point is inconsequential. See Captain Rostron, AI p.19 and BI 25385.
58   Captain Rostron, AI p.22. Joseph Boxhall, AI pp.242–3.
59   Captain Rostron, AI p.21. Half a point is 11½°.
60   Captain Rostron, AI p.21.
61   James Bisset, *Tramps and Ladies*, p.283.
62   Captain Rostron, BI 25472.
63   Mahala Douglas, AI p.1101.
64   Wireless log of *Caronia*. *Caronia* logged the time at 6.16a.m. GMT.
65   Wireless log of *Mount Temple*, AI p.929.

10

THE CIRCUMSTANCES IN CONNECTION WITH THE SS *CALIFORNIAN*

Samuel Halpern

The *Californian* affair is one of the most contentious issues when it comes to the subject of *Titanic*. As to be expected, there were contradictions and inconsistencies in the story told by different eyewitnesses. But there is one overwhelming reality that is inescapable: *Titanic*'s distress rockets were seen from the bridge of *Californian* that night, but because of human fallibilities, those in charge failed to respond.

Californian's Route of Travel

The Leyland Liner SS *Californian* was a tramp steamer with an overall length of 464ft, maximum breadth of 54ft, depth from the shelter deck of 42ft 6in, and maximum draft when fully loaded of 27ft. She was built by the Caledon Shipbuilding & Engineering Co., Dundee, Scotland, in 1902. She had a gross tonnage of 6,223 tons, and her propulsion plant consisted of two double-ended Scotch boilers with a working pressure of 200psi supplying steam to a triple-expansion engine linked to one propeller. Her rated full ahead speed was 13.5 knots. She carried a single pink-coloured funnel and four masts, and was equipped with a complete electrical plant that generated 60 volts DC that powered about 260 lamps,[1] including her two electric masthead lights, red and green sidelights, and a stern light. She also was equipped with a standard 1½-kW Marconi wireless set that was designed to work off 100-volt dynamos, but because of the 60-volt system that was installed on *Californian*, her transmitted power was only a little more than half of that.[2] (In comparison, *Titanic* at over 46,300 gross tons, was 90 per cent longer, 71 per cent wider and 51 per cent deeper from the shelter deck. *Titanic* carried four funnels and two masts and was equipped with a single electric masthead light on her foremast.)

The SS *Californian* began her sixth voyage under the command of Captain Stanley Lord on 5 April 1912, bound from London to Boston. Her planned route of travel would first take her from her berth at No.24 Shed in the Royal Albert Dock in London to a point just off Bishop Rock (49° 52'N, 6° 27'W) at the westernmost tip of the Isles of Scilly, a distance of about 400 nautical miles. After taking departure off Bishop Rock, the official starting point of her transatlantic crossing, she would travel 1,734 nautical miles along the great circle route to the corner point (42° 00'N, 47° 00'W) for westbound steamers going to America for that time of year. From there she would travel another 1,067 nautical miles on a fixed course heading of 271° True to the Boston Light Vessel located at a distance of about 15 miles from Boston's famed Customs House. Arrival at the light vessel would mark the official end point of her transatlantic crossing. From the light vessel she would then go on to the Clyde Street pier of the Boston and Albany docks in East Boston.

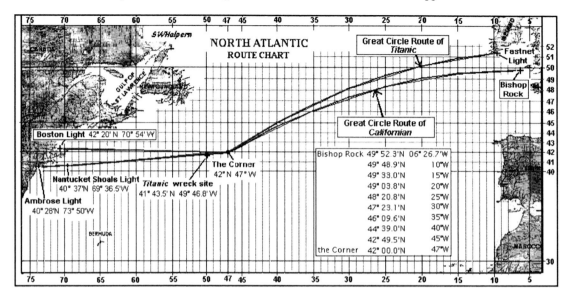

Fig. 10-1 *Californian's* route of travel across the Atlantic.

The planned route of *Californian* as well as the planned route of *Titanic* are shown in Fig. 10-1.

According to data recorded in her logbook, *Californian's* course was changed when she reached the vicinity of the corner to N60°W (300°) by compass at 9.40a.m. ship's time on Sunday 14 April 1912.[3] The magnetic variation, the difference between true north and magnetic north, in the vicinity of the corner on 14 April 1912 was 25° 33' west according to the National Geophysical Data Centre (NGDC).[4] Chief Officer Stewart testified that the compass deviation error, the uncorrected error affecting the magnetic compass caused by the distribution of steel and iron in the ship's hull, was about 5 to 5½° west when the ship was heading westward.[5] Captain Lord also thought the deviation error was about 5° west when heading westward.[6] After adjusting for both deviation error and magnetic variation, we find that *Californian's* true course at 9.40a.m. was 269.5° True, almost exactly due west. According to Captain Lord, his logbook showed that he was at '42 north and 47 west', the westbound corner point, at 9.40a.m. on 14 April 1912.[7]

At 9.55a.m., just 15 minutes later, a 1° course correction was made to N 59° W by compass.[8] This would correspond to a heading of 270.5° True, keeping the ship almost on the same parallel of latitude heading almost due west.

At 12.00p.m., local apparent noon, a measurement was taken of the angular height of the sun which showed that *Californian* was actually at a latitude of 42° 05' N, 5 nautical miles north of the latitude of the corner. So as it turned out, *Californian* never quite made it down to the corner when she turned almost due west at 9.40a.m. It was not until noon that *Californian's* real latitude became known.

At noon another course change was made to N 61° W by compass.[9] This put *Californian* on a heading of 268.5° True. In an affidavit signed in 1959, Captain Stanley Lord wrote, 'I steered this course [North 61° West (magnetic)] to make longitude 51° West in latitude 42° North on account of ice reports which had been received.' He also testified in 1912 that he was heading 'S89W [269°] True' before being forced to stop on account of ice that was encountered.[10] That his intent was to steer back down to the latitude of the corner at 42° 00'N by the time they reached longitude 51°W is easily verified by an ice report that Captain Lord sent to Captain Japha of the steamship *Antillian*, bound east from New Orleans to Liverpool, at 5.35p.m. NYT:[11]

Captain *Antillian*. 6.30pm ATS lat. 42.3 N, long. 49.9 W. Three large bergs five miles to southward of us. Regards. Lord.

This message, which also happened to be picked up by *Titanic*, was acknowledged 25 minutes later at 6p.m. NYT by *Antillian's* Captain Japha:[12]

Captain Lord. 7pm ATS 40.56N 50.22W. Thanks for information. Seen no ice. Bon voyage. Japha.

Californian was making close to 11 knots all that afternoon.[13] At noon, *Californian* should have been about 25 miles west of the corner longitude assuming she 'turned the corner' at 9.40a.m. as recorded in her logbook. For the parallel of latitude that she was on, the change in longitude should have been 34 minutes-of-arc placing her noontime longitude at 47° 34'W. However, the noontime coordinates that were put down in her logbook reported that she was at 42° 05'N, 47° 25'W. It is entirely possible that the 'departure' distance of 25 miles was accidently entered for the minutes-of-arc in the noontime position when the logbook was written up. The longitude given to *Antillian* for 6.30p.m., 49° 09'W, is consistent with *Californian* making just about 11 knots heading west from the corner longitude at 9.40a.m., and consistent with *Californian* making that reported speed if she was at 47° 25'W longitude at noon.[14] To reach 49° 09'W longitude by 6.30p.m. starting from a noontime longitude of 47° 25'W, would require a speed of almost 12 knots.

Californian's Stopped Dead Reckoning Position

At 10.21p.m., *Californian* was forced to stop when she unexpectedly came up to a vast field of pack ice directly ahead of her. We are told that her stopped position was worked out by Captain Lord and later entered into the ship's official logbook the next morning by Chief

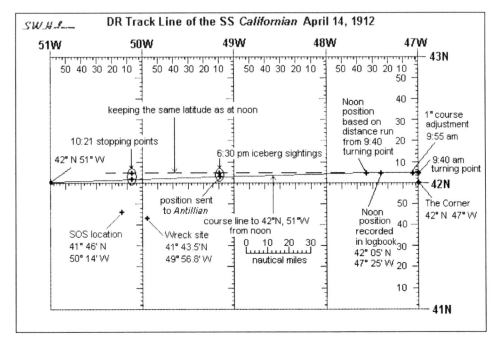

Fig. 10-2 *Californian's* dead reckoning track for 14 April 1912.

Officer George Stewart. If Captain Lord simply took 11 knots as his speed made good, then the distance that *Californian* would travel from noon to 10.21p.m. is just under 114 nautical miles. Starting at a corrected noontime position of 42° 05'N, 47° 34'W on a course 268.5° True toward 42°N, 51°W for 114 miles, we end up at a dead reckoning stopping point at 42° 02'N, 50° 07'W; exactly the same longitude that was entered in *Californian's* official logbook, but 3 miles further to the south.

The chart in Fig. 10-2 shows the track (solid line) and locations for *Californian* at 9.40a.m., 9.55a.m., 12.00p.m., 6.30p.m. and 10.21p.m. based on the navigational evidence that was presented. Also shown are the positions and track (dashed line) that were later recorded in *Californian's* logbook keeping her at the same noontime latitude during all that time.

The positions entered in *Californian's* logbook would have people believe that she kept to the same line of latitude, 42° 05'N, since altering course to the west at 9.40a.m. on 14 April. However, the navigational evidence based on the reported course changes made, the speed of the ship, a wireless message sent to *Antillian*, and the stated true course heading of the ship show that *Californian* was intentionally headed slightly south of due west from noon until the time she came to a stop. What we find is that *Californian's* true stopped dead reckoning position, a position based on speed and true course heading from a known position, would place her 17 nautical miles from the SOS position that was sent out from *Titanic*, not the 19½ to 20 miles that was later claimed by Captain Lord at the 1912 inquiries.[15]

Shortly before 6a.m. on 15 April, *Californian's* overnight position was sent in a wireless message from Captain Lord to Captain Gambell of the SS *Virginian*. This was before Captain Gambell sent back a message to Captain Lord stating that *Titanic* was reported sinking along with *Titanic's* SOS coordinates. Captain Gambell later said that *Californian* was 17 miles north of the SOS coordinates when he was contacted,[16] a distance that Captain Lord himself confirmed in a letter he wrote to the Board of Trade on 10 August 1912, where he admitted that he sent his position to *Virginian* before getting back the official word about *Titanic*.[17]

Fig. 10-3 shows *Californian's* stopped overnight position derived by dead reckoning based on the navigational evidence that was presented and the one given by Captain Lord and put down in *Californian's* official logbook later on.

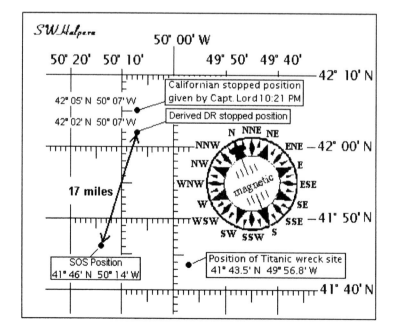

Fig. 10-3 *Californian's* stopped dead reckoning position for 14 April 1912.

So how was it, that despite the evidence presented, the positions put down for 14 April in *Californian's* official logbook, including her position for 6.30p.m. when those three icebergs were sighted, kept *Californian* at the same line of latitude that was observed at noon? We are told that the reason for this was that Chief Officer George Stewart took a Pole star sight about 7.30p.m. that night, which he somehow verified the next day, that showed that *Californian's* latitude had not changed since noon Sunday.[18] However, the information sent to Captain Gambell on Monday morning, 15 April, as well as a message that was sent later that same evening from *Californian* to *Olympic*,[19] cast some doubt on the validity of that alleged Pole star sight.

Summary of Events Seen During the Night

At 10.21p.m. *Californian* ATS, Captain Lord ordered his helm be put hard-a-port (right full rudder) and called down full speed astern on the engine order telegraph because of this large field of pack ice that came up and blocked his way. From then until about 5.15a.m. the next morning, *Californian* lay stopped about ¼ to ½ mile from the eastern edge of that field of pack ice. There she lay surrounded by loose ice while she drifted southward with the local current while slowly swinging around to starboard.

Shortly before 11p.m., the light of a steamer came into view on the eastern horizon. Upon seeing this light, Captain Lord went to Cyril Evans, *Californian's* only wireless operator, to ask what ships did he have nearby. Evans told him that *Titanic* was the only one, and Captain Lord instructed him to call *Titanic* up and tell them that they were stopped because of ice. Jack Phillips, *Titanic's* senior wireless operator, was busy at that time receiving passenger-related messages from the powerful wireless land station at Cape Race, Newfoundland, about 800 miles away. When Evans sent Phillips an informal message that *Californian* was stopped and surrounded by ice, the relative proximity of *Californian* to *Titanic* interfered with the signals coming in from Cape Race. After receiving a reprimand from Phillips, 'Shut up, Shut up, I'm working Cape Race',[20] Evans continued to listen to Phillips work Cape Race for about a half hour more before turning his set off to go to bed. He made no further effort to contact *Titanic*.

To Captain Lord, the steamer that he casually observed approach from the east appeared to have stopped nearby at about 11.30p.m., *Californian* time [11.42p.m. *Titanic* ATS]. On *Californian's* upper bridge, Third Officer Charles Groves, who first noticed the mast light of this steamer come up about 11.10p.m., thought that this steamer was approaching his stopped vessel from abaft his starboard beam close to 11.30p.m., and in accordance with standing orders, decided to go down and inform Captain Lord that a steamer was approaching them. At that time, *Californian* was facing toward the north-east by compass because of the action that Captain Lord was forced to take in stopping his ship about an hour earlier. When Groves went down to the chart room (one deck below) to report to Captain Lord, Lord instructed him to go back up and try to signal the steamer with their Morse lamp, which Groves then did. The unidentified vessel, which was by now stopped, did not respond to his signalling attempts.

When Charles Groves first saw this steamer come up from abaft his starboard beam, his impression was that it was a passenger vessel since it appeared to have a lot of light. At 11.40p.m. *Californian* time [11.52p.m. *Titanic* ATS], one bell was struck to inform the watch below that they were due on deck in 20 minutes. At that time, Groves was certain that the steamer had stopped for the night, and it also looked to him that she may have turned out many of her deck lights, a practice in some lines to encourage passengers to turn in. About 5 minutes later, about 11.45p.m. on *Californian*, Captain Lord came up to the upper bridge to take a closer look at the steamer for himself and to talk to his third officer. Groves told him that he thought it was a passenger steamer who had shut many of her lights out for the night. Lord disagreed, and thought it looked to him like a tramp steamer similar in size to *Californian*. He passed the remark to Grove, 'The only steamer near us is the *Titanic*.' Both thought the vessel that had stopped was only about 5 miles away and slightly abaft their starboard beam at that time.

Shortly after midnight Second Officer Herbert Stone came up to take over the watch from Charles Groves. On his way up, Stone stopped to talk with Captain Lord who pointed out that his own ship was stopped for the night because of the ice, and that there was this steamer that was stopped off their starboard beam. Stone then went up to the upper bridge to relieve Groves. It was now about 12.10a.m. on *Californian*.

Groves also briefed Stone about this mysterious steamer off their starboard beam. He informed him that it had been stopped when 'one-bell' was struck, and that their own ship was swinging around slowly to starboard in a clockwise direction. At the time Stone arrived on deck, *Californian* was pointing ENE by standard compass, and the stranger was bearing dead on her starboard beam to the SSE by compass.[21]

Like Groves did earlier, Herbert Stone also tried to signal this mysterious steamer by Morse lamp. He was joined by Apprentice James Gibson who came on deck about 12.15 with some coffee. They were both unsuccessful in making contact with the steamer. They both thought that she looked like a tramp vessel showing one masthead light, a red sidelight, and according to Gibson, 'a faint glare of lights on her afterdeck.'[22]

However, sometime around 12.45a.m., Herbert Stone saw what appeared to be a white flash come from over the stopped steamer. At first he thought it was just a shooting star until he saw another one which he recognised as a white rocket. Stone would later claim that he first informed Captain Lord after he saw five of these white rockets go up at short intervals. According to Gibson, who meanwhile was sent below to look for a new log line to stream, Stone told him upon coming back on deck that he saw five white rockets go up from the steamer, and that he called down on the speaking tube to report to Lord after seeing the *second* one go up, as he was not too sure about the first one. Captain Lord would later claim that he was told of only one rocket and had asked Stone if it was a company signal that he saw. Stone then told Lord that he didn't know if it was a company signal, and Lord then instructed his second officer to let him know if anything changed by way of sending Gibson down to report to him, and to keep signalling the vessel by way of the Morse lamp. It never occurred to anyone after seeing these rockets to wake up Cyril Evans and try to contact the vessel by wireless.

At the British inquiry following the *Titanic* disaster, Stone and Gibson both admitted to having conversations during their watch about this mysterious stranger. It was reported that Stone remarked to Gibson that 'a ship is not going to fire rockets at sea for nothing.' He also told Gibson at one point, 'Look at her now; she looks very queer out of the water; her lights look queer.' Gibson also told Stone that, 'she looks rather to have a big side out of the water,' and that Stone gave him the impression 'that everything was not all right with her.'

At 2.05a.m. by *Californian's* wheelhouse clock [2.17a.m. *Titanic* ATS], the mysterious stranger was no longer in sight. James Gibson was then sent down to inform Captain Lord that the ship had disappeared and altogether eight white rockets were seen. Lord, who had been asleep on his settee when Gibson arrived, asked whether they were sure there were no colours in the rockets, and Gibson said they were all white and gave him the time. Later, Captain Lord would have no recollection of Gibson's visit.

At about 3.20a.m., according to both Stone and Gibson, more rockets were seen low on the horizon toward the south. The lights of the ship firing them were not visible, but at this exact time, the rescue ship *Carpathia* was coming up fast from the south-east and firing rockets to reassure *Titanic* that help was on the way. *Carpathia* was still a good 10 miles away and to the SE of where *Titanic's* lifeboats were. These rockets, three of which were seen from *Californian*, were not reported to Captain Lord at that time.

At about 4a.m., Chief Officer George Stewart came up to relieve Herbert Stone as watch officer. Stone told Stewart about the steamer that had fired rockets during his watch and that it had steamed away toward the south-west before it disappeared. Stewart then asked if he saw anything else, and Stone told him that he thought he saw a light to the southward at 3.40. Steward then looked around in that direction and pointed out a stopped steamer with two masthead lights to Stone. Stone then insisted that this steamer to the southward was a different steamer than the rocket-firing vessel with one masthead light that he and Gibson saw earlier. But Stewart was not convinced about that. About 4.30a.m. Stewart went down and awoke Captain Lord to tell him that day was breaking, that Second Officer Stone told him about a steamer firing rockets during his watch, and that he believed that the steamer that fired those rockets was still to the southward. He did not tell Lord that the second officer believed it was a different steamer than the one that fired those rockets. Lord admitted to Stewart that he was informed that there was a ship that had fired a rocket, and then went up to the bridge with his chief officer to see this mysterious steamer for himself, and to discuss going through the ice to resume their voyage to Boston.

Summary of Actions Taken at Dawn

At about 5a.m. it was light enough to see clear water on the western side of the pack ice, and Captain Lord told his chief officer to ring down 'stand-by' on the engine order telegraph. According to Lord, they could also see a 'yellow-funnel steamer on the south-west of us, beyond where this man had left, about 8 miles away.'[23] Stewart then asked Lord if he intended to go down to have a look at her because she may have lost her rudder. Lord told him, 'No, I do not think so; she is not making any signals now.' Stewart then agreed, but told him that the second officer had said that she had fired several rockets during his watch. Lord then told Stewart to go and call the wireless operator to find out what ship it was.

George Stewart went off the bridge to the Marconi cabin to awake Cyril Evans. He told Evans, 'There is a ship that has been firing rockets in the night. Please see if there is anything the matter.'[24] At 5.15a.m. *Californian* ATS, about the time that Captain Lord rang down for full speed ahead on the engine telegraph that morning,[25] Evans sent out a general CQ call up signal to communicate with any ship that might answer. Almost immediately his call was answered by *Mount Temple*'s wireless operator John Durrant who informed him that *Titanic* had struck an iceberg and was last reported sinking.[26] The information was given to Stewart who took it to Captain Lord who then told him to go back and find out more. Meanwhile, Captain Lord stopped his ship, waiting to hear more news.

At 5.30a.m. *Californian* ATS, *Frankfurt* got in touch with *Californian* and delivered a similar message. The information was given to Stewart who once again went to Captain Lord and said, 'We have a position here, but it seems a bit doubtful.' Lord then told him, 'You must get me a better position. We do not want to go on a wild goose chase'. Lord then went to mark down a course to the SOS position given to him by *Frankfurt*.

At 5.50a.m. *Californian* ATS, *Virginian* and *Californian* established wireless communications. Fifteen minutes later, at 6.05a.m.,[27] Captain Gambell of *Virginian* replied with an MSG message to Captain Lord:

> *Titanic* struck berg, wants assistance urgent, ship sinking, passengers in boats, his position lat. 41.46, long. 50.14, Gambell, Commander.

It was then that Captain Lord started to put things in motion to go to the rescue of *Titanic*.

A summary of *Californian*'s movements according to what Captain Lord presented at the inquiries in 1912 is listed below:

> 6.00a.m. – Proceeded slowly south-westward across pack ice for 2 to 3 miles.[28]
> 6.30a.m. – Cleared thick pack ice on western side and headed southward at full speed.[29]
> 7.30a.m. – Passed *Mount Temple* who was believed stopped near the SOS position.[30]
> 8.00a.m. – Starboarded [turning her head to port] to cut across the pack ice at full speed toward *Carpathia*.[31]
> 8.30a.m. – Reached *Carpathia* as she was picking up the last passengers and boats.[32]

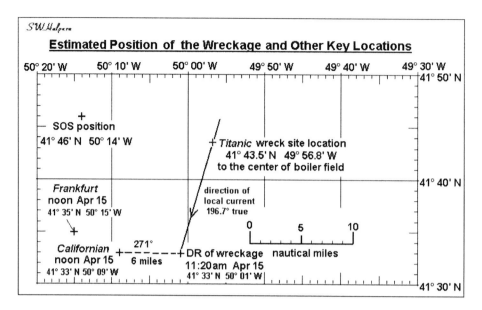

Fig. 10-4 Drift of *Titanic*'s wreckage on the morning of 15 April 1912.

It is interesting to note how all these times came out so neatly to the nearest hour or half hour. That prompted Senator Smith at the American inquiry to ask Captain Lord, 'Then from 6 o'clock in the morning you were under steam in the direction of the *Titanic* for two and one-half hours?' to which Lord replied, 'Yes, sir.'

    After reaching *Carpathia*, *Californian* was told to look around for any more survivors while *Carpathia* pulled up the last lifeboat and headed away from the area at about 9a.m. *Californian* then made a few circular passes to leeward and left the area of the wreckage heading west at 11.20a.m.[33] At noon her officers took a sight of the sun which led to a noontime position at 41° 33'N, 50° 09'W. As *Californian* came out on the western side of the pack ice she met the eastbound *Frankfurt* coming down to take the same passage she came out of to get to the eastern side of the ice. From her noontime position 15 April, Captain Lord determined that the position of the wreckage when he left it at 11.20a.m. was 41° 33'N, 50° 01'W. This is some 11 nautical miles to the south and west of the now known wreck site location as shown in Fig. 10-4.

A Closer Look at Stone's Mysterious Tramp

Second Officer Stone was questioned extensively at the British inquiry back in 1912 about what he saw during his watch on deck.

    7841:   What were they, rockets?

Stone: They had the appearance of white rockets bursting in the sky.

    7842:   Did they come in quick succession?

Stone: At intervals of about three or four minutes.

    7843:   Now what did you think they were?

Stone: White rockets.

    7844:   What do you think they meant?

Stone: I thought that perhaps the ship was in communication with some other ship, or possibly she was signalling to us to tell us she had big icebergs around her.

    7847:   Is that the way in which steamers communicate with each other?

Stone: No, not usually.
7853:   What did you think these rockets were going up at intervals of three or four minutes for?
Stone: I just took them as white rockets, and informed the master and left him to judge.

Stone admitted that those rockets were not being sent up for fun. He knew there was danger about because of the ice. He even admitted that the vessel he was watching might at first be in some sort of trouble:

> Naturally, the first thought that crossed my mind was that the ship might be in trouble, but subsequent events showed that the ship steamed away from us; there was nothing to confirm that; there was nothing to confirm that the rockets came from that ship, in the direction of that ship. That is all I observed.

Unfortunately for Stone, he was about to give concrete evidence that those rockets did indeed come from the ship he was observing. He also was well aware that 'Rockets or shells throwing stars of any colour or description, fired one at a time at short intervals' coming from a ship at night meant signals of distress.[34] But his argument was that the ship he was watching could not have been in distress because she steamed away. And furthermore, those rockets looked to him like they came from beyond where this vessel was:

> I have remarked at different times that these rockets did not appear to go very high; they were very low lying; they were only about half the height of the steamer's masthead light and I thought rockets would go higher than that.

Unfortunately that still posed a slight problem. If those rockets came from some other vessel beyond where this one was, then that could only mean that there was some other vessel that needed assistance, and that *Californian* and this nearby unidentified vessel both failed to respond.
    Stone was also confused about one other little detail that absolutely proved that the rockets could not have come from some other vessel that was beyond where this steamer was. As he said:

> But that I could not understand why if the rockets came from a steamer beyond this one, when the steamer altered her bearing the rockets should also alter their bearings.

When the lights of the steamer that he had under observation changed their bearing, the rockets altered their bearings in a corresponding manner. Though he tried to cast doubt that the rockets came from the steamer he was watching by saying that they were low-lying and appeared to come from beyond, he was easily convinced that they had to come from this apparently nearby vessel because the rockets followed directly over it as it was allegedly steaming away.
    Stone also remarked that the steamer shut out her red sidelight when she steamed away. At first, when he came topside to relieve Third Officer Groves, Stone saw the steamer showing a single masthead light, some deck lights, and a red sidelight, indicating that her port side was facing *Californian* at that time. But afterward, 'I did not see her green light at all. She ported [turning her head to starboard]. She shut in her red sidelight and showed her stern light . . . I did not see any sidelight at all after she started to steam away.'[35] Asked when did he notice the vessel steaming away, Stone replied, 'The second [rocket] – excepting the first flash, which I was not sure about . . . She bore first SSE [by compass] and she was altering her bearing towards the south towards west.'[36]
    According to Stone, the last of the eight white rockets that he saw was fired at about 1.40a.m. *Californian* ATS.[37] About 20 minutes later he sent Gibson down to wake Captain Lord to tell him, 'we had seen altogether eight white rockets and that the steamer had gone out of sight to the SW. Also that we were heading WSW.'[38] Gibson went below to the chart room and told Captain Lord what Stone told him, and Lord asked if there were any colours in the rockets.

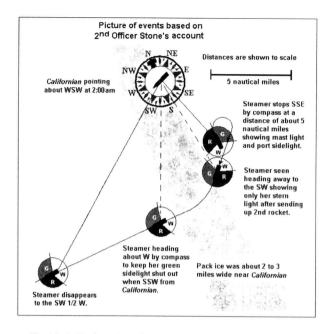

Fig. 10-5 Herbert Stone's account of events seen during the middle watch.

Gibson then told him that they were all white and Lord then asked what the time was. Gibson said it was 2.05a.m. by the wheelhouse clock.[39]

If we put the story together as told by Second Officer Stone we get the picture of events as shown in Fig. 10-5.

Do the events as described by Second Officer Stone hold up to close examination? What we do have to compare his story to comes from Groves, Gibson, Stewart and Lord.

Third Officer Charles Groves said that when Stone came topside to take over as Officer of the Watch, *Californian* was pointing ENE by compass and that she was swinging slowly around to starboard.[40] He certainly would have noticed that because earlier he noticed her head was pointing to the NE by compass, and at 12.10, when Stone arrived, it was pointing ENE, a 2-point change in heading.[41] James Gibson confirmed that the stopped steamer was dead abeam on the starboard side when he came topside at about 12.15 bringing up some hot coffee for Stone and himself.[42] At about 12.25a.m., Gibson was sent below to look for a new log line to stream leaving Stone on the bridge by himself.[43] Between 12.35 and 12.40a.m., Captain Lord called up the speaking tube to inquire about the stopped steamer on their starboard beam. Stone told him that she was on the same bearing as before and that he had called her up on the Morse lamp and received no reply.[44]

Then we learn from Stone that between 12.45 and 1.15 he saw five white rockets go up at intervals and that he called down on the speaking tube to inform Captain Lord about them. As he described it in his signed statement that he wrote to Captain Lord on 18 April while still at sea:

> At about 12.45, I observed a flash of light in the sky just above that steamer. I thought nothing of it as there were several shooting stars about, the night being fine and clear with light airs and calms. Shortly after I observed another distinctly over the steamer which I made out to be a white rocket though I observed no flash on the deck or any indication that it had come from that steamer, in fact, it appeared to come from a good distance beyond her. Between then and about 1.15 I observed three more the same as before, and all white in colour. I, at once, whistled down the speaking tube and you came from the chartroom into your own room and answered. I reported seeing these lights in the sky in the direction of the other steamer which

appeared to me to be white rockets. You then gave me orders to call her up with the Morse lamp and try and get some information from her. You also asked me if they were private signals and I replied, 'I do not know but they were all white.' You then said: 'When you get an answer let me know by Gibson.' Gibson and I observed three more at intervals and kept calling them up on our Morse lamps but got no reply whatsoever. The other steamer meanwhile had shut in her red sidelight and showed us her stern light and her masthead's glow was just visible. I observed the steamer to be steaming away to the SW and altering her bearing fast. We were also swinging slowly all the time through S and at 1.50 were heading about WSW and the other steamer bearing SW by W. At 2.00a.m. the vessel was steaming away fast and only just her stern light was visible and bearing SW ½ W.

We have already seen that Gibson was told by Stone that five rockets were sighted before Gibson arrived back on deck, and that Stone called down to Lord on the speaking tube after seeing the *second* rocket. Gibson himself saw three rockets fired from the steamer while he was on the upper bridge sharing the watch with Stone. He also gave very specific relative bearings to the mysterious steamer during the time he was on the bridge. But the time he said he came back up differed from what Stone said as well as the time that the last rocket was seen. Gibson said he came up at 12.55a.m. and saw three rockets go up between then and about 1.20a.m.[45] Stone had Gibson arriving at about 1.15a.m. and said that the last rocket seen was about 1.40a.m. as previously noted. There was a 20-minute time difference between them, possibly due to Gibson referring to a clock seen below that had been put back by 20 minutes by those who went below at midnight. But the real difference between their respective observations was that Gibson wrote that the steamer's red sidelight had disappeared shortly after he saw the next to last rocket go up leaving only her masthead light remaining visible. It was then that Stone first remarked to him that the steamer was slowly steering away towards the SW after allegedly taking another bearing on it.[46]

What this means is that when Gibson first arrived, the steamer was still showing her red sidelight. Five rockets had already gone up and were seen by Stone. The steamer had *not* turned around after the second rocket was fired as Stone claimed she did. Furthermore, Gibson was directly asked if he ever saw the steamer turn around. His reply was, 'No.'[47] He was also asked if he ever saw what appeared to be a stern light. His reply was, 'No.'[48] Whatever Gibson knew about compass bearings to the steamer came directly from Stone. Gibson observed only relative bearings to the steamer; i.e., angles with respect to his ship's own bow, and that his own ship was slowly swinging round.

Stone was to later testify that he last saw what he took to be the steamer's stern light for another 20 minutes after he sent Gibson down to report to Lord that the steamer was 'disappearing' in the SW,[49] despite writing in his report to Captain Lord on 18 April that he sent Gibson down at 2a.m. to report 'that the steamer had gone out of sight.' In his own report to Captain Lord, Gibson wrote: 'Just after two o'clock, she [the steamer] was then about two points on the port bow, she disappeared from sight and nothing was seen of her again.' For some reason known only to Herbert Stone, the second officer felt a strong need to call down to Captain Lord by speaking tube at 2.45a.m. to report the same information that Gibson reported to Lord in person just 40 minutes earlier. When asked why he did that, Stone's response was:

Simply because I had had the steamer under observation all the watch, and that I had made reports to the Captain concerning her, and I thought it my duty when the ship went away from us altogether to tell him.

When asked why he needed to 'wake up the poor man?', Stone replied, 'Because it was my duty to do so, and it was his duty to listen to it . . . He told me to try and get all the information I could from the steamer. I got none and I thought it my duty to give him all the information I could about the steamer.' Keep in mind that this came 40 minutes after Lord was told everything that was known by Gibson, and 25 minutes after that stern light seen only by Stone had disappeared. Yet, when more rockets were seen later at 3.20a.m., Stone apparently did not feel the same compulsive need to inform his captain about it.

Where was *Californian* Relative to *Titanic*?

Today, especially since the discovery of the wreck site, there is little doubt that *Titanic's* distress rockets were seen from the bridge of *Californian* that night. These signals, actually distress socket signals, reached heights from 600 to 800ft before they exploded into white stars.[50] Even if *Californian* had been as far away as the position later given by Captain Lord, these signals went high enough and were bright enough to be seen from *Californian*. Not only were *Titanic's* signals seen that night, but those of *Carpathia* as well when she was still a good 10 miles beyond where *Titanic* had been. What is still being argued, is whether observers on *Californian* saw the lights of *Titanic*, and vice versa.

In March 1992, almost eighty years after the incidents, the Marine Accident Investigation Branch (MAIB) of the Department of Transport in Britain issued a report regarding the role *Californian* played at the time *Titanic* was lost.[51] The purpose of the report was to address four items:

1. What were the positions of *Titanic* and *Californian* when *Titanic* struck the iceberg on 14 April, and when she foundered on April 15, and to deduce the distance that they were apart from each other?
2. Was *Titanic* seen by *Californian* during this period, and if so, by whom?
3. Were *Titanic's* distress signals seen by *Californian*, and if so were proper actions taken?
4. To assess the action taken by *Californian's* Captain Stanley Lord from when he stopped his ship on 14 April until the time he resumed his voyage on 15 April.

The appointed inspector was Master Mariner Thomas Barnett who reported his findings to Captain P.B. Marriott, Chief Inspector of Marine Accidents. Marriott did not fully agree with Barnett's findings, and subsequently asked Deputy Chief Inspector Captain James De Coverly to examine the issues further and issue a report.

Both Barnett and De Coverly agreed as to the approximate location of *Titanic* when she struck the iceberg, and that both *Titanic* and *Californian* had been under the influence of a strong south setting current of more than 1 knot in the local vicinity. However, Barnett believed that *Californian* had been under the influence of a south setting current since about noon and was between 5 to 7 miles from *Titanic*, while De Coverly believed the south setting current affected *Californian* much later on, and the two ships were between 17 and 20 miles apart. Barnett believed that *Titanic* was seen from *Californian*, while De Coverly believed that if she was seen, it was caused by abnormal refraction. They both agreed that the two ships remained in the same relative position with respect to each other, drifting southward with the current, from the time *Titanic* collided with the iceberg until the time she foundered. They also both agreed that *Titanic's* distress signals were indeed seen from *Californian*, and that proper actions were *not* taken.

In the areas where De Coverly disagreed with Barnett, De Coverly cited five opinionated reasons:

1. The strong southerly current set was unusual to begin with and more unusual if it extended so far east.
2. The Pole star sighting at 7.30p.m. by Chief Officer Stewart showed *Californian* at the same latitude as at noon.
3. The latitude in the ice message to *Antillian* showed *Californian* heading close to due west.
4. The effect of current on *Carpathia* appeared to set her to the north of her track to the SOS position, not to the south.
5. There was no reported ice east of longitude 49°W, suggesting that the axis of the southerly drift probably did not extend east of there.

As far as a mystery ship coming between *Titanic* and *Californian*, the two inspectors also had differing views as summarised in the table below:

Thomas Barnett	James De Coverly
Titanic was seen by *Californian* and was kept under observation from about 11p.m. 14 April until she sank.	A ship was seen by *Californian* and kept under observation from about 11p.m. 14 April until she disappeared.
There is an extent of coincidence between what was seen from *Californian* and what is known of *Titanic*'s movements.	Either a third ship came in between the two vessels, or *Titanic* was seen but at a far greater range due to super refraction.

De Coverly's objections as to why *Californian* would probably not have seen *Titanic* were also listed in the report. They were:

1. At 11p.m. 14 April, *Titanic* would have been 20 miles away which a very long way off to be seen.
2. *Titanic* was turned to port at time of collision, and her red sidelight would not be seen.
3. No ship was seen by *Titanic* until well past midnight.
4. *Californian*'s Second Officer Stone noticed a change of bearings before the other ship disappeared.

It is unfortunate that more time was not spent by the MAIB in researching all the evidence that was available, or that they were not given more time to do a more thorough analysis. When we look closely at De Coverly's objections to Barnett's findings, we find that he came to his conclusions based on a number of assumptions, something that can be dangerous when asked to perform a critical analysis.

Let us first look at each one of De Coverly's five points that he cited alleging that *Californian* was not under the influence of a south setting current for a long period of time.

De Coverly's Point 1: It is unusual for a south setting current to extend so far east.
– This statement needs to be quantified. Sir Ernest Shackleton testified that 'these currents sometimes come far out of their usual route.'[52] We also know that pack ice and icebergs had drifted much further to the south than usual for that time of the year. So was it possible for *Californian* to be under the influence of a cold Labrador Current far to the east of the wreck site area? Rather than relying on a belief, let us look at specific measured air and sea temperature data recorded for the region on the dates in question. This data was provided in a letter from Captain Stanley Lord, dated 11 May 1912, and forwarded by P.A.S. Franklin, vice-president of the IMM Co., to Senator William Alden Smith on 25 May 1912. The measured data is shown graphically in the chart below:[53]

What we see in this data taken by *Californian* every 4 hours is a very significant drop in both air and water temperatures between noon and 4p.m. on 14 April 1912. Of particular interest is the 20°F drop in water temperature between noon and 4p.m. This is a clear indication that *Californian* came under the influence of the cold Labrador Current from at least 4p.m. onward; an effect that could easily set her well to the southward of the dead reckoning track line that she was on. By 4p.m., *Californian* was only 70 nautical miles east of her reported stopped longitude position. She was under the influence of the south setting Labrador Current early enough to certainly have a significant impact on the ship's track made good over ground during the next 6 hours and 20 minutes until she came to a stop.

De Coverly's Point 2: A Pole star sight showed *Californian*'s latitude remained the same.
– This would be an important factor if such an observation actually took place and was accurate.

Air and Water Temperatures from SS *Californian*

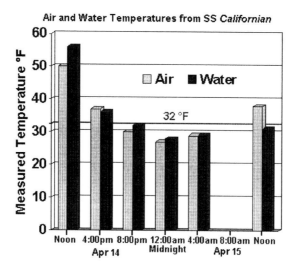

Fig. 10-6 24-hour air and sea temperatures taken by SS
Californian.

First, it is almost inconceivable that *Californian* could have remained on the same line of latitude as she was at noon while heading on an admitted course line of about 269° True and being in the cold waters of the Labrador Current for over 6 hours. Furthermore, as previously noted, the problem with this alleged Pole star sight is that it is not accounted for in the position they sent to *Virginian* early Monday morning that indicated that they were only 17 miles from the SOS position, not the '19½ to 19¾ miles' that Captain Lord said they were when he testified before the inquiries.[54] And, as previously noted, *Californian's* dead reckoning coordinates for the sighting of those three icebergs that were reported to *Antillian* Sunday evening were sent unchanged in an ice report sent to *Olympic* the following day.[55] Yet, in *Californian's* logbook, we find that those coordinates were changed to show a latitude that remained invariant since noon 14 April.

What is interesting about *Californian's* logbook is that we were told by Chief Officer Stewart that the pages from the scrap log, where events of 14 and 15 April were first written up at the end of each watch, were destroyed by 'company's instructions'.[56] We were also told by Third Officer Groves that a new scrap log was started at the beginning of their outbound voyage to Boston on 5 April Good Friday. The book used for the scrap log was large enough to hold about twenty-five days of data, and was also used as a source of paper if some positional calculations needed to be worked out. On their return trip to Liverpool, however, Groves had to start a new scrap log. He said he did not know what happened to the scrap log for the outbound voyage, and suspected it was thrown overboard. When asked if he saw anything in that scrap log concerning events in the middle watch during the early morning hours of 15 April, he said he did not look back to see what entries were made.[57]

What was written up in the ship's official logbook was put there by Chief Officer Stewart. It was a logbook that was devoid of any mention of events that took place during the middle watch between midnight and 4a.m. on the morning of 15 April, the time during which rockets were seen by those in charge, and no actions were taken.

De Coverly's Point 3: The ice message to *Antillian* shows *Californian* heading about due west. – The message sent to *Antillian* only confirms that *Californian's* dead reckoning course set by Captain Lord at noon was intended to make 42°N at 51°W as Lord wrote in his 1959 affidavit. It certainly does not mean that the course made good over ground was nearly due west especially if they were affected by a southerly current set, something that De Coverly, as a master mariner, had to know.

De Coverly's Point 4: *Carpathia* **appeared to be set to the north of her track.** – This conclusion was based on a fallacious assumption. *Carpathia* was heading eastward on a great circle route to Gibraltar at the time she picked up *Titanic's* distress call. She would have been down in latitude 41° 10'N and under the influence of the North Atlantic Drift setting her further eastward all along. Her course was altered to 308° True, and to get to where she sighted and picked up the first boat, her track over ground would have been about 6 miles further east of the track line to the SOS position.

De Coverly's Point 5: There was no ice reported east of 49° W. – This point is completely irrelevant. It is the temperature of the water, not the presence or absence of ice, that is the important indicator of being in a south setting Labrador Current. Even Captain Stanley Lord had stated: 'But in the Arctic current you always get cold water, even if there is not any ice.'[58]

Being under the influence of a strong Labrador Current does not require the presence of ice. As Sir Ernest Shackleton testified at the British inquiry, a fall in temperature does not indicate that ice is about. The bottom line is that you can be in the cold waters of the Labrador without any ice being present.

We will address the issue of a mystery ship coming between *Californian* and *Titanic* after we first look at and analyse the available evidence that can help answer the question of how far apart these two vessels were from the time *Titanic* came to a stop to the time she foundered. We do agree with the MAIB inspectors that the two ships remained in the same relative position with respect to each other, drifting southward with the current. They were not, however, totally stationary throughout that time. The evidence shows that both vessels tended to swing around in the 'light airs and calms' that prevailed; *Californian* much more so than *Titanic*. But the relative distance between them would not likely have changed.

In trying to establish the distance between the two vessels, we cannot, and should not, rely on subjective estimates of distances based on night-time observations. The only thing that people saw that night were the lights of another ship. From *Titanic* they saw the lights of a steamer that seemed to approach them and then turn away. From *Californian* they saw the lights of a steamer that seemed to have stopped for the night on account of the ice just as they had. Just lights were seen. There was no hull form or silhouette that could be seen. Most estimates of distances were based on the brightness of the lights seen, something very subjective and very unreliable. As Dave Gittins wrote in his e-book, *Titanic – Monument and Warning*:

> It is thus not surprising that when we examine the nocturnal observations of the witnesses from *Titanic* and *Californian*, we find that it is possible to prove almost anything. Lights seen from *Titanic* were white. There were coloured sidelights as well as white lights. There was only one light. There were two. They were lights on a steamer. There was only the single stern light of a sailing ship. They moved. They did not move. They advanced. They retreated. The light may have been a star. The other ship was two miles off. It was ten miles off. It was every distance between.
>
> The witnesses on *Californian* are just as unhelpful. They saw a big liner. They saw a small ship like their own. It showed two masthead lights. It showed one. The ship moved off. It simply disappeared. It sent up rockets. The rockets came from beyond the ship.

On that very clear, dark and moonless night that prevailed at the time, lights tended to appear brighter than expected, a condition which led many trained seamen to generally underestimate distances. So what we will do is take a completely different approach that does not depend on subjective estimates.

The key to unlocking this puzzle comes from the mutually supporting observations of Second Office Herbert Stone, Third Offer Charles Groves and Apprentice James Gibson that took place about a quarter past midnight on the upper bridge of *Californian*. When Stone came up to relieve Groves at 12.08a.m., the lights of the stopped steamer off their starboard beam were bearing SSE by compass. Groves pointed out to Stone that their own ship was then pointing ENE by compass, and was swinging slowly to starboard. Stone went to the standard compass and confirmed what Groves just told him. At the time, the steamer was then 'dead abeam' on *Californian's* starboard side. This situation was confirmed by Gibson when he came up with the coffee at about 12.15a.m. We also know that at about 12.35a.m., Captain Lord called up the speaking tube and asked Stone if the position of this stopped steamer on their starboard beam had changed. Stone replied 'that she was on the same bearing.' Then about 10 minutes later, the first of eight white rockets was seen exploding silently over the steamer.[59]

The total compass correction for variation and deviation from true north in that location was about 22° west, or almost exactly 2 points on the compass.[60] This makes the bearing from *Californian* to the steamer and exploding rockets about 135° True, or to the SE from *Californian*. From *Titanic, Californian* had to be on the reciprocal line of bearing of 315° True. And since we know that neither ship had moved relative to each other soon after *Titanic* came to a stop following the collision with the iceberg, *Californian* had to be on that same line of bearing from *Titanic* until she foundered. And thanks to Dr Robert Ballard, we now know precisely where that was.

Fig. 10-7 shows the situation at 2.20a.m. *Titanic* ATS, the time she foundered, along with Capt. Lord's claimed overnight stopped position for *Californian*, the stopped dead reckoning position for *Californian* derived from the dead reckoning course line that she was steaming on, and the SOS position worked out by *Titanic's* Fourth Officer Joseph Boxhall. Also shown is the 315° True line of bearing extending from *Titanic* for the time shown. *Californian* had to be located somewhere on that line at that time.

Only two questions remain:

1. Where on that line of bearing from *Titanic* was *Californian*?
2. How did she get there?

To answer the first question, there are two things that can help us put limits on the distance between the two ships that night. The first has to do with the fact that nobody on *Californian*

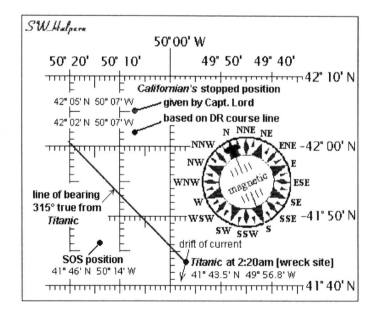

Fig. 10-7 Line of bearing 315° True from where *Titanic* foundered.

saw any of the green flares that were fired by *Titanic's* Fourth Officer Joseph Boxhall from lifeboat No.2 before *Carpathia* arrived on the scene. And the second has to do with a very revealing observation from *Californian's* Apprentice James Gibson when he observed the firing of the sixth of those eight white rockets from the vessel that he and Second Officer Stone had under observation.

Joseph Boxhall said, 'I had been showing green lights most of the time. I had been showing pyrotechnic lights on the boat.' It was these green flares that attracted the attention of *Carpathia* as she came up to the spot where she picked up the boat. Yet nothing of the sort was sighted from *Californian*.

Taking the height of a flare held by someone standing in one of *Titanic's* emergency lifeboats to be about 6½ft above the water, and the height of eye of someone standing on the upper bridge of *Californian* at about 45ft above the water, we find that the maximum range between the light and observer would be about 11 nautical miles. And since Boxhall's boat was at most ½ to ¾ miles southward from where *Titanic* sank, we find that *Titanic* had to be greater than 10 nautical miles from *Californian* for those green flares not to have been seen. This establishes a hard minimum distance apart.

To derive the maximum distance between the two ships we have the following written observation from James Gibson:[61]

> I then watched her for some time and then went over to the keyboard and called her up continuously for about three minutes. I then got the binoculars and had just got them focused on the vessel when I observed a white flash apparently on her deck, followed by a faint streak towards the sky which then burst into white stars.

On *Titanic* to the south-east, Fourth Officer Joseph Boxhall was put in charge of firing off distress socket signals trying to get the attention of what looked to him to be a four-masted steamer that was seen just off *Titanic's* port bow. According to Boxhall, the distress signals were fired from *Titanic's* boat deck out of a 'socket in the rail just close to the bows of the emergency boat on the starboard side.' He said that when they are sent up, 'you see a luminous tail behind them and then they explode in the air and burst into stars.' He also said that they fired off 'between half a dozen and a dozen' as far as he could recall. We know from Stone and Gibson, eight of them were seen.

Fig. 10-8 What hand-held flares would look like from close range.

These socket signals, made by the Cotton Powder Company in Faversham, were explosive shells sent up by a detonator charge fired from a socket similar to today's fireworks. The faint luminous tail alluded to by both Boxhall and Gibson was the burning fuse of the shell as it was sent aloft to a height of 600 to 800ft.

To see the flash of the detonator through binoculars from the bridge of *Californian*, a height of eye of about 45ft above the waterline, means that the two vessels had to be close enough to each other that at least the uppermost deck of the ship firing those rockets was at or above the visible horizon as seen from *Californian*. Gibson saw the flash of a detonator more than half an hour after the first rocket was seen by Stone. By that time, *Titanic* is estimated to have been down by the head about 4° and carrying little or no list. With that trim angle, the height of the rail on *Titanic's* bridge calculates out to be about 40ft above the waterline. Using these parameters, the maximum range between the flash on deck and the observer is about 15.5 nautical miles.

We therefore see that *Californian* had to be on that 315° line of bearing more than 10 but less than 15½ miles from *Titanic*.

As a check on this range we can use the following observation of James Gibson regarding the disappearance of the vessel's red sidelight:[62]

> Nothing then happened until the other ship was about two points on the Starboard bow when she fired another rocket [the seventh one seen from *Californian*]. Shortly after that, I observed that her [red] sidelight had disappeared, but her masthead light was just visible.

The last distress rocket fired from *Titanic* took place about 1.50a.m. *Titanic* ATS. About 10 minutes earlier, at 1.40a.m., *Titanic* was down by the head about 5° and carrying about a 10° list to port while lifeboat No.10 was being loaded. At that time Fourth Officer Boxhall was still involved with firing distress rockets before he was sent away to take charge of boat No.2 about 5 minutes later, at 1.45a.m. Taking both trim and list into account, the height of *Titanic's* red sidelight at 1.40a.m. works out to be about 20ft above the water. With a height of eye on the bridge of *Californian* taken at 45ft, the distance between the two vessels when this sidelight

Fig. 10-9 Launch, ascension and burst of an aerial shell.

would seem to disappear works out to be about 13 nautical miles.[63] At that distance, the sound from an exploding distress rocket would take well over a minute to travel that distance, and be severely attenuated as to go unnoticed above the ambient sounds of a ship at rest in a field of loose ice.[64] And at that distance signalling by use of Morse lamps would be highly problematic. These lights had no resemblance to the later highly directional Aldiss signalling lamps. Morse signalling lamps back then were typically used when a ship came within 5 to 6 miles.[65] Captain Lord thought that *Californian's* could be seen as far as about 10 miles.[66] As noted by Boxhall, he did not see any response to his attempts at signalling by Morse lamp when he was trying to get the attention of this steamer seen off his port bow, but there were others nearby who thought that they may have seen some signalling.[67]

To answer the second question, as to how *Californian* got to that position on the line of bearing, we will use a technique that is well known to mariners when plotting positions. It is known as advancing a line of position. In this case, what we will do is take the line of position that *Californian* had to be on at the time *Titanic* foundered, the 315° line of bearing from the wreck site, and advance it backward in time at a rate of 1.1 knots on the reciprocal heading of the local area current to the time that *Californian* came to stop at 10.21p.m., *Californian* ATS.[68] We will then draw two current vectors from *Californian's* previously derived stopped dead reckoning coordinates to this retarded line of position (shown as a dashed line in the diagram below); one vector pointing directly south at 180° True, and the other vector pointing 197° True matching the set of the local current in the vicinity of the wreck site. What we then get are two estimated positions on that line for where *Californian* most likely was when she came to a stop at 10.21p.m.

The estimated positions derived by this navigational technique place *Californian* at a distance between about 12.5 to 14.5 nautical miles from *Titanic* that night, fully consistent with what we found when we considered the disappearance of *Titanic's* sidelight, and within the range limits we derived before that. The cause of *Californian* ending up where she did was the south setting effect of that cold Labrador Current, the same current that brought all that ice so far south that year; much further than some mariners had ever seen before.[69]

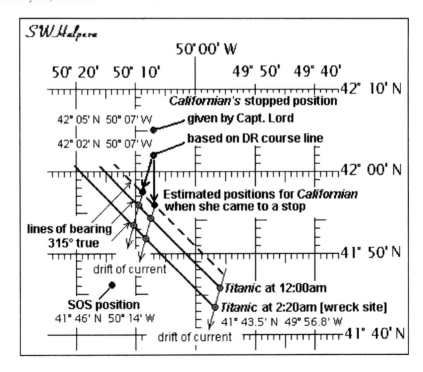

Fig. 10-10 Derived estimated positions of SS *Californian.*

We have seen that *Californian* had come under the influence of the Labrador Current by 4p.m. after recording a drop in water temperature of 20°F since noon. At that time she would have been close to longitude 48° 30'W. The Labrador runs south to south-south-west before converging with the east setting North Atlantic Drift. In this situation, we find that *Californian* was likely set between 4.5 to 6 miles off her dead reckoning course line by a current that averaged between 0.7 to 0.95 knots over a period of about 6⅓ hours. After *Californian* came to a stop at 10.21p.m., she would have continued drifting southward with the local current until her engines were moved ahead again at 5.15a.m. the next morning.

Now one may ask, was *Titanic* similarly affected by a south setting current before she struck the iceberg at 11.40p.m.? The answer is yes. We know *Titanic* altered course close to the corner (42°N, 47°W) onto a true heading of 266° at 5.50p.m. *Titanic* ATS on 14 April. We also know that she came to a stop close to 41° 46'N, 49° 56'W a few minutes after striking the iceberg.[70] Even allowing for an overrun of the corner by about 2 or 3 miles, we find that *Titanic should* have been about 3.5 to 4 miles further north of where she actually was when she came to a stop. We also know that *Titanic*, averaging about 22.3 knots, would have crossed a longitude of 48° 30'W about 8.50p.m., *Titanic* ATS, just 2 hours 50 minutes before striking the iceberg. If *Titanic* was being set southward after crossing that longitude, then *Titanic* would have been under the same influence of that south setting current for only 45 per cent of the time that *Californian* was before stopping. This is shown in Fig. 10-11.

The effect of passing through a south setting current on each vessel's track over ground is shown in Fig. 10-12. Prior to passing west of 48° 30'W longitude, *Californian* was heading close to 289° True toward 42° N, 51° W. *Titanic*, having altered course onto a heading of 266° True at 5.50p.m. near the corner, was heading to make the Nantucket Shoals light vessel. However, both their courses made good would have been set more southward as shown in the diagram below, with *Californian's* track affected much more so than *Titanic's* because she was going only half as fast. The likely positions of where each vessel would have been when they came to a stop, *Californian* at 10.21p.m. her time, and *Titanic* a little after 11.40p.m. her time, are indicated in Fig. 10-12 along with the location of the wreck site. Both vessels, as well as all the pack ice and icebergs in their neighbourhood, would have remained in the same relative position with respect to each other after that, all drifting together southward with the local current.

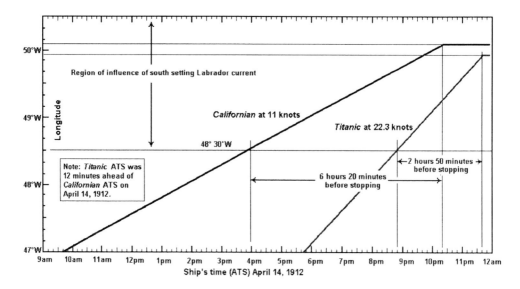

Fig. 10-11 Time spent by *Californian* and *Titanic* under the influence of the Labrador Current before each came to a stop.

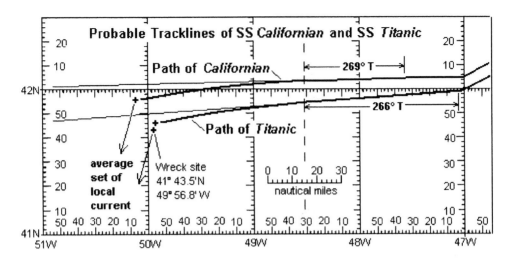

Fig. 10-12 Courses made good of SS *Californian* and SS *Titanic*.

Answers to Objections Raised

Whenever the issue of *Californian* comes up for debate, a host of objections are raised by those who believe that the vessel seen from *Californian* was not *Titanic*, and the vessel seen from *Titanic* was not *Californian*. We have already seen Captain De Coverly's arguments for why he believed that *Titanic* was not likely the ship seen from *Californian*. To that we can add a number of other issues that have been raised. So let us look at some of these, starting with those four objections of Captain James De Coverly:

De Coverly's Objection 1: *Titanic* **would have been 20 miles away from** *Californian* **and therefore too far to be seen.** – This would be true if *Californian* had stopped where Captain Lord claimed he did and was unaffected by a south setting current. But we have seen how *Californian* was set much further southward by coming under the influence of the cold Labrador Current as early as 4p.m. The line of bearing to the rockets, and the now known location of the wreck site, proves that *Californian* could not have stopped where Captain Lord claimed he did.

De Coverly's Objection 2: *Titanic* **turned to port at the time of collision, and her red sidelight would not be seen.** – This is a mistaken conclusion based on incomplete research. *Titanic* was turned to port just before contact was made with the iceberg, but turned to starboard following the impact to avoid further damage along her starboard side. The order to do so (hard-a-port) was overheard by Quartermaster Alfred Olliver who came onto the bridge just as the ship struck the ice. *Titanic* was also seen turning to starboard immediately after the collision,[71] and the iceberg was seen disappearing off her starboard quarter as the ship was slowing soon afterward.[72] When *Titanic* came to a stop, her head was pointing northward as later witnessed from *Titanic's* bridge by Quartermaster George Rowe and by *Titanic's* Fifth Officer Harold Godfrey Lowe.[73] In addition, the wreck on the bottom of the Atlantic shows *Titanic's* bow section buried in the mud about ½ nautical mile due north of the centre of the boiler field, with the bow itself pointing northward in the direction that it planed forward as it sank after breaking free from the stern section while on the surface. *Californian* was north-westward of *Titanic*, and *Titanic* was pointing northward before she sank keeping her red sidelight open to *Californian* until it disappeared below the horizon as *Titanic* trimmed down by the head more and more before she sank.

De Coverly's Objection 3: No ship was seen by *Titanic* until well past midnight. – According to Fourth Officer Joseph Boxhall, he was busy uncovering lifeboats when someone reported 'a light ahead'. He said some of the aft portside boats were then being swung out,[74] which places the time about a quarter past midnight. On *Californian* it would be about the time that Second Officer Stone came up to relieve Third Officer Groves. Earlier, at about 11.30 *Californian* ATS, Groves had noticed that *Californian* was pointing NE by compass, and this vessel that came on the scene showing 'a lot of light', was then approaching his ship from about 3 points abaft the beam.[75] That means that *Californian*'s masthead lights and sidelights were shut out from *Titanic* at that time.[76] When Stone came up to relieve Groves about 40 minutes later, *Californian* had already swung 2 points to starboard and was then pointing ENE by compass, something that Stone himself confirmed. This would have opened up *Californian*'s masthead lights and green sidelight to *Titanic*. *Californian* would have become noticeable. The unfolding situation is depicted in Fig. 10-13.

De Coverly's Objection 4: *Californian*'s Second Officer Stone noticed a change of bearings before the other ship disappeared out of sight. – Everyone agrees that the compass bearing to *Titanic*'s distress rockets could not have changed, and therefore the bearing to the steamer that was seen could not have changed while those rockets were going up. But Herbert Stone said that they did change:[77]

> I could not understand why if the rockets came from a steamer beyond this one, when the steamer altered her bearing the rockets should also alter their bearings.

When Chief Officer George Stewart came up to relieve Stone at 4a.m., Stone told him about the events that happened during his watch. In Stewart's own words:[78]

> He told me he had seen a ship four or five miles off when he went on deck at 12 o'clock, and at 1 o'clock he had seen some rockets . . . I asked him [what sort of rockets]; he said they were white rockets. . . I asked him what he did. He said the moment she started firing the rockets she started to steam away . . . he told me he had called him up repeatedly by the Morse lamp and the ship did not answer . . . He told me he had reported to the captain.

Notice that according to Stewart, Stone told him that the steamer started steaming away as soon as she started firing rockets, not after she stopped firing them. Stone himself testified before the British inquiry that the steamer started to steam away after the second of eight white

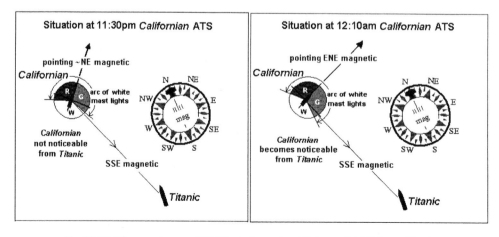

Fig. 10-13 The opening up of *Californian*'s masthead lights and sidelight to *Titanic*.

rockets was seen, the first of which he was not sure about.[79] But we know from Gibson that the steamer was showing a red sidelight from the time he came onto the bridge, a half hour before any rockets were ever seen, until shortly after the seventh of those eight white rockets was seen. If that steamer started to steam away and alter her bearings as early as Stone said she did, then she must have been steaming across the pack ice in reverse in the dead of night still showing her red sidelight to *Californian* while continuing to fire rockets at intervals. That just did not happen.

Gibson wrote that Stone first told him that the steamer 'was slowly steering away towards the SW' shortly after her red sidelight had disappeared, which was just after the seventh rocket went up.[80] If that were true, then the bearing to the steamer and the eight rockets that were seen bursting into stars over her had to have changed by about 6 compass points.[81] Clearly, if a steamer had come between a stopped *Titanic* and a stopped *Californian*, the compass bearing to that steamer could not have changed while rockets were going up above her. Any ship in between had to remain on that fixed line of bearing between *Californian* and *Titanic* at least until the last rocket was fired which was about 25 to 30 minutes before *Titanic* sank. According to Stone, the time the last rocket was seen on *Californian* was about 1.40a.m., *Californian* time, and the time he sent Gibson down to report that the steamer was 'steaming away fast' was about 2a.m., *Californian* time.[82] During those 20 minutes, this alleged steamer in between would have had to have changed compass bearings from SSE to SW by ½ W, a full 6½ points or 73°, keeping her sidelights shut out from *Californian* all the time. To cover the distance that such a tramp steamer would have to travel (shown to scale in Fig. 10-5) would require a speed greater than any vessel afloat at the time.

According to Gibson, the steamer they were watching disappeared at 2.05a.m. by *Californian's* wheelhouse clock, never to be seen again. On *Titanic* it would have been 2.17a.m., *Titanic* time; just about the time when all of *Titanic's* lights went out as her hull was seen to literally split apart.[83]

More insight into the problem with compass bearings reported by Herbert Stone comes from his signed report to Captain Lord on 18 April while *Californian* was still at sea; one of two such documents that were withheld from the 1912 inquiries:

> We saw nothing further until about 3.20 when we thought we observed two faint lights in the sky about S.S.W. and a little distance apart.

As mentioned before, these were rockets that were being sent up from *Carpathia*.[84] They were sent up to 'reassure *Titanic*'.[85] But we know from Captain Rostron that *Carpathia* was coming up from the south-east on a course heading of 308° True. If anything, they should have been seen on a compass bearing close to SSE, not SSW that Stone put in his report.

Something was very wrong about the bearings reported by Herbert Stone during his watch, other than the one taken when he first came on deck at 12.08a.m. which showed the stopped steamer off their starboard beam was bearing SSE by standard compass. For that we have independent confirmation from both Charles Groves and James Gibson. So what could have gone wrong with those other bearings that Stone reported?

One possible explanation has to do with the fact that both vessels, *Californian* and *Titanic*, were slowly swinging around to starboard while drifting with the local current. *Californian* was swinging around much more so than *Titanic*, averaging about 50° per hour, while *Titanic* only averaged about 10° per hour. But the swinging may not have been uniform, but somewhat erratic in those 'light airs and calms' that prevailed. It is entirely possible that *Californian* may have swung unnoticed in the opposite direction for short periods of time, enough to cause confusion about the movements of the vessel under observation. Such a swing would cause the other vessel to appear to be changing her bearing toward the south-west if you did not notice that it was your own vessel's heading that had changed.

Some evidence to this effect comes from when *Carpathia's* rockets were sighted at 3.20a.m. In his report to Captain Lord, James Gibson wrote:

At about 3.20 looking over the weather cloth, I observed a rocket about two points before the beam (Port), which I reported to the Second Officer. About three minutes later I saw another rocket right abeam which was followed later by another one about two points before the beam. I saw nothing else and when one bell went [3.40a.m.], I went below to get the log gear ready for the Second Officer at eight bells [4.00a.m.].

Given the great distance that *Carpathia* would have been from *Californian*, the compass bearing to all three rockets should not have changed. But if *Californian* swung briefly to starboard between the first and second rocket seen, and then swung back to her previous heading by the time the third one went up, then that would explain Gibson's observations. That the second and third rockets were seen on slightly different relative bearings was also noted by Stone who, as we have seen, wrote that they were 'a little distance apart'.[86]

The bottom line is that changes in relative bearings to rockets sent up from *Titanic*, as well as from *Carpathia*, were seen from the bridge of *Californian* that night. Since we know that compass bearings to the rockets could not change, the only valid explanation for the change in relative bearings to those rockets is the swinging of the vessel from which these observations were made. The swinging of *Californian* may have been somewhat erratic at times, possibly even retrograde, causing a misinterpretation of what was being seen. It also seems that careful correlations in time between relative bearings and ship headings may not have been taken, leading to false conclusions about the movements of the vessel from which those rockets came.

Titanic's Mystery Steamer

In addition to *Californian* swinging round to starboard, so too did *Titanic*. This was noted by *Titanic's* Quartermaster George Rowe who was on *Titanic's* bridge working with Fourth Officer Boxhall firing distress rockets, and trying to communicate by Morse lamp with this mysterious steamer seen off their port bow. Rowe noticed that *Titanic's* head was swinging through north.[87] *Titanic's* very slow swing to starboard may also explain why the strange steamer seen off *Titanic's* port bow did not appear to be completely stationary to some observers such as Boxhall.[88]

Titanic was swinging at the very slow rate of about 10° per hour causing the lights of the steamer seen by Boxhall to go from ½ point off the port bow when he first saw her, to about 2 points off the port bow when he was sent away to take charge of boat No.2 leaving Rowe on the bridge to send up the last distress rocket. That small change in relative bearings, plus the swinging of the other vessel, which first showed *Titanic* a green sidelight, then both sidelights, then her red sidelight, gave Boxhall the impression that 'she turned round – she was turning very, very slowly – until at last I only saw her stern light, and that was just before I went away in the boat.'

When Boxhall's boat was lowered to the water, he was ordered to pull around the ship's stern to the starboard side of *Titanic*. He came to about 200ft of the ship a little abaft the starboard beam and decided it was not wise to go back to the ship. As Able-Bodied Seaman Frank Osman described, 'We pulled astern that way again, and after we got astern we lay on our oars and saw the ship go down.'[89] Boxhall never saw the lights of the mystery steamer again:

I saw this single light, which I took to be her stern light, just before I went away in the boat, as near as I can say . . . I saw it until I pulled around the ship's stern. I had laid off a little while on the port side, on which side I was lowered, and then I afterwards pulled around the ship's stern, and, of course, then I lost the light, and I never saw it anymore . . . I do not know whether she stayed there all night, or what she did. I lost the light. I did not see her after we pulled around to the starboard side of the *Titanic*.

Although Boxhall didn't see the lights again, even after *Titanic* sank, other people in the lifeboats not only continued to see the lights of the steamer well after *Titanic* was gone, but some rowed toward them until the lights of *Carpathia* came up from the south-east.[90]

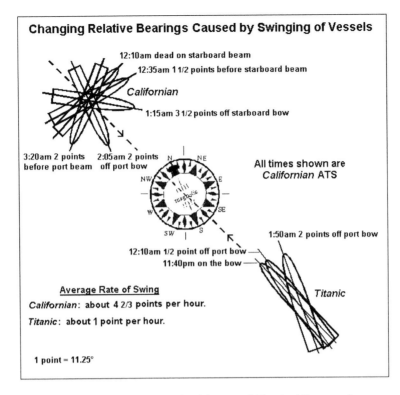

Fig. 10-14 The swinging of *Californian* and *Titanic* while stopped.

Regarding Boxhall's last observation of seeing the steamer's stern light, if a vessel is really far off and pointing toward you with a very narrow angle on the bow, the separation of its mast lights may not be enough to be easily resolved with the naked eye. As Boxhall noted, they 'were fairly close together – the masthead lights.' But many people, including officers Lightoller and Pitman as we shall soon see, saw but one white light with their unaided eyes. Boxhall admitted that he had to use glasses while on the bridge to see both masthead lights of the steamer. It was not until much later on that he was able to resolve them into two lights with the naked eye.[91]

> I could see the light with the naked eye, but I could not define what it was, but by the aid of a pair of glasses I found it was the two masthead lights of a vessel . . . I saw her green light and the red. She was end-on to us. Later I saw her red light. This is all with the aid of a pair of glasses up to now. Afterwards I saw the ship's red light with my naked eye, and the two masthead lights. The only description of the ship that I could give is that she was, or I judged her to be, a four-masted steamer.

For how long he was able to see both mast lights and the red sidelight without the aid of glasses, he does not say.

From the relative bearings provided in Gibson's written report to Captain Lord on 18 April, *Californian* would have been pointing directly at *Titanic* sometime after the seventh rocket was seen, but before the eighth. When the last rocket was seen, *Californian* was showing *Titanic* her port (red) sidelight, and the rocket was seen 1 point off *Californian*'s port bow.

Could the vessel seen from *Titanic* have been the same vessel seen from *Californian* if a mystery ship truly existed on the scene? For one thing, the vessel from *Titanic* had two masthead lights; the vessel seen from *Californian* had but one. Secondly, the vessel seen from *Californian* disappeared at the time when all *Titanic*'s lights went out, just minutes before she sank; the vessel seen from *Titanic* was still seen by those in the boats almost until dawn broke. Thirdly, the vessel seen from *Californian* appeared to be firing white rockets that burst into stars during the same time that *Titanic* was firing distress rockets; while the vessel seen from *Titanic* did not. So if there were mystery ships seen by both *Californian* and *Titanic*, they had to be different vessels.

But now we must also ask, how probable is it that two mystery vessels, one seen only by *Californian* and another seen only by *Titanic*, would happen to shut out their red sidelight and show a stern light to observers on both *Californian* and *Titanic* about the same time?

As we described before, the last distress rocket fired from *Titanic* took place about 1.50a.m. *Titanic* ATS. Gibson said they lost sight of the vessel's red sidelight sometime after the seventh rocket went up. Though Gibson did not, Stone took the white light that remained for the vessel's stern light. Boxhall was involved with firing rockets until he was sent away in the boat. When he went to the boat, he saw only a white light which he took to be a stern light. All this shortly before the last rocket was sent up from *Titanic*.

Is it a coincidence that two separate mystery ships would turn away and show their respective stern lights to their respective neighbours about the same time?

We have already shown how the disappearance of the red sidelight seen by those on *Californian* would have been caused by the angle of trim and the list to port that *Titanic* had taken on about 10 minutes before the last rocket went up. We also know that boat No.2, the one Boxhall got into, was located just aft of where that sidelight was housed. We said the port sidelight, at the level of *Titanic*'s boat deck, was then about 20ft above the water.[92] And to someone standing with a height of eye on *Californian*'s upper bridge at 45ft above the water, they would see that light disappear if the two ships were about 13 miles apart. The height of eye of someone on *Titanic* standing near boat No.2 at that time would be about 26ft above water. *Californian*'s sidelights were about 38ft above the water. To that observer on *Titanic*, *Californian*'s sidelights would be seen to disappear if the two ships were about 13 miles apart. So we see, there is no coincidence. It was the combined angles of trim and list created by the flooding within *Titanic*'s damaged hull that caused the disappearance of sidelights seen from both *Californian* and *Titanic*; a disappearance that happened about the same point in time.

A Few Remaining Issues

A very legitimate question comes up if we accept the likelihood that *Titanic* and *Californian* were within 12 to 14 miles of each other as indicated by this analysis. Simply stated, how can a ship as large as *Titanic* at a distance of 12 to 14 miles be mistaken for a tramp steamer about 5 miles away?

A ship 850ft long would present the same angular width at a distance of 12 miles as one 425ft long would present at a distance of 6 miles. And if the vessel presented a sharp angle on the bow to the observer, as *Titanic* did, the angular width of the vessel would also be foreshortened significantly. For *Titanic*, this amounted to presenting an angular width of only 10 to 38 per cent of her full broadside view to *Californian*.[93] Furthermore, at a distance of 12 to 14 miles, only the lights from her upper decks would be visible because the vessel would be hull down beyond the horizon as seen from the bridge of *Californian*. On that dark, clear, moonless night of 14 April, the horizon itself was invisible. As Captain Lord said, 'We could not distinguish where the sky ended and where the water commenced.'

In the absence of some solid frame of reference, distances at night can only be judged by the relative brightness of lights and their relation to each other. However, given the darkness and clarity of the night, the lights of a far-off vessel could easily have been perceived brighter than normal, thereby giving the appearance of being closer than they actually were. Thus a large vessel far away could easily be perceived as a smaller vessel closer by.

To appreciate how deceiving things were that night, *Titanic*'s Second Officer Charles Lightoller believed the light seen off *Titanic*'s port bow may have been that of a stopped sailing vessel:[94]

A white light about two points on the port bow; whether it was one or two lights I could not say. As to whether it was a masthead light or a stern light, I could not say. I was perfectly sure it was a light attached to a vessel, whether a steamship or a sailing ship I could not say. I could not distinguish any other coloured lights, but merely it was a white light, distinct and plain . . . certainly not over 5 miles away . . . [It was] perfectly stationary as far as I can recollect.

Third Officer Pitman also saw this light after he was sent away in lifeboat No.5. He thought it may be a white light that was on one of *Titanic*'s other lifeboats:[95]

I just saw a white light, and that is all. I said, 'There is no use in pulling toward it until we know what it is.' We saw the light, but I said, 'What is the use of pulling to it?' . . . It might have been one of our own boats with a white light on it . . . but I am not certain what it was attached to. It may have been one of our own boats . . . one of the lifeboats . . . there was no motion in it, no movement . . . It may have been 1 o'clock or half past 1 [when I first saw it]. One of my men called my attention to the white light over there . . . It may have been 3 miles [away].

We know, however, that what these two seasoned officers saw was definitely the light of a steamer, not a light on a sailing ship or a lifeboat. And that steamer was carrying two masthead lights as well as showing red and green sidelights as witnessed by Fourth Officer Boxhall when looking through a pair of glasses.[96]

We do not believe that two experienced White Star Line officers could so easily mistake what they took as lights from a sailing ship or a lifeboat if in fact that vessel off *Titanic*'s port bow was only 3 to 5 miles away as they judged it to be. Like the ship seen from the bridge of *Californian*, appearances can be very deceiving even to the most experienced of seamen, especially when there were no other visual references to compare things to.

But the elusive vessel seen from the sloping decks of *Titanic* was also seen by a number of eyewitnesses who took to the boats. In some cases, they managed to row for hours toward the vessel on the north-western horizon before turning around to get to the rescue ship *Carpathia* when she came up from the south-east. In fact, some were given instructions by Captain Smith himself to row to the mysterious vessel, drop passengers off, and then row back to *Titanic* to pick up more.[97] A lightly loaded 30ft lifeboat, such as boat No.8, being pulled by four men on a calm sea could make about 2½ to 3 knots.[98] In the case of No.8, which was launched about 1.00a.m., they rowed toward the vessel until someone noticed the lights of *Carpathia* coming up, at which point they turned around. Steward Alfred Crawford was one of those pulling at an oar along with seaman Thomas Jones and two other men. The tiller was handled at first by Lucy-Noël Martha, the Countess of Rothes, and later by her cousin Gladys Cherry. Crawford estimated that they had to row about 3 to 4 miles to get back to *Carpathia*. *Carpathia*'s Captain Rostron said that the boats were scattered over a range of 4 to 5 miles from what he could tell after it got light enough to see. Boat No.8, with only about twenty-five people in it, was one of those far-off boats. She got close enough to the steamer that not only were her two masthead lights plainly visible, but so too were both of her sidelights. She was pointing straight at them:[99]

We were pulling the whole night, the four of us . . . There was a lady at the tiller [the Countess of Rothes]; she reported the sidelights in view . . . There was the red and the green light . . . we were right bow on to it; I could see both the lights . . . It seemed to be coming this way, towards the *Titanic*.

Crawford saw the masthead lights of the vessel from the time he left *Titanic*. It was 'just after one, when the Captain pointed it out' to him as boat No.8 was being launched. To see both sidelights from a lifeboat, they had to have come less than 10 nautical miles from the steamer,[100] consistent with the steamer being about 12 to 14 miles from where *Titanic* had been when they first started out. Although they rowed about 3 to 4 miles toward the steamer, the steamer never seemed get any closer. Despite the steamer pointing toward them, it seemed to Crawford that they 'could not seem to make any headway.' By time the lights of *Carpathia* came into view, the bright mast lights of the steamer had disappeared, and boat No.8 was turned around and headed back to where the lights of *Carpathia* were seen.

The same swinging of *Californian* that was noted by her officers easily explains why the lights of this steamer that several of *Titanic's* boats were heading for during the night seemed to vanish before daylight broke. At about 4a.m., when Chief Officer Stewart came up to take over the watch from Second Officer Stone, *Californian* was reported to be heading about WNW by compass as shown in Fig. 10-15. *Californian's* masthead lights and sidelights would be shut out to any vessel or boat that was coming up from where *Titanic* had been. To those in the boats, the stern light would be too low to be seen over the horizon even if they came within 9 miles of the steamer. To *Carpathia* coming up to where Boxhall's boat was, *Californian's* stern light, even if bright enough to be seen, would barely be on the horizon, inconspicuous among the background stars.

When George Stewart came up to relieve Stone at 4a.m., Stone briefed him about the events that took place during his watch, including that he had seen a ship that fired white rockets and steamed away.[101] Stewart then picked up a pair of binoculars and scanned the horizon to the southward. What happened next comes from his deposition submitted to the Wreck Commission:[102]

> I looked to the southward and saw a light. On looking through the glass I saw two masthead lights and a lot of lights amidships, apparently a four-masted steamer. This was 4a.m. I asked Stone if he thought this was the ship he had seen, and he said he did not think it was.

Not until Stewart pointed out a steamer with two mast lights and 'a lot of lights amidships' to the southward did Stone realise that another ship had even come onto the scene.[103]

The ship that had showed up was the rescue ship *Carpathia*, a four-masted passenger steamer that carried two masthead lights. At the time, *Carpathia* was manoeuvring to pick up *Titanic's* lifeboat No.2, the one with Fourth Officer Joseph Boxhall in it.

But *Carpathia* was not the only ship to arrive nearby. At about 4.30, or thereabouts, a four-masted steamer with a single yellow funnel coming up from south-west on her way to the

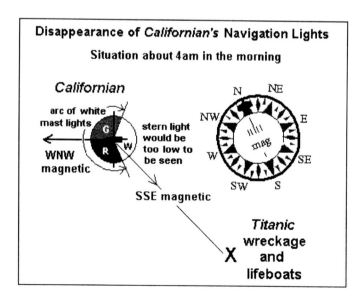

Fig. 10-15 The shutting out of *Californian's* masthead lights and sidelight before dawn.

rescue of *Titanic* came to a stop on the western side of the ice field. It was the Canadian Pacific steamer *Mount Temple* carrying about 1,600 passengers and crew. Later, at about 5a.m., near the beginning of Civil Twilight, we believe that she was sighted to the 'south-west' of *Californian* by Captain Lord,[104] and to the 'northward' of *Carpathia* by Captain Rostron.[105] Though neither of them could identify her at that time, they both judged her to be about 8 miles away in the morning twilight. (We will cover the circumstances regarding *Mount Temple* more thoroughly in Chapter 11.)

When *Californian*'s Captain Lord received official word about *Titanic* sinking from *Virginian*'s Captain Gambell about an hour later, he started out heading westward across 2 to 3 miles of pack ice toward the distress position that was given to him.[106] The time that this message was sent was 6.05a.m. *Californian* time.[107] *Californian* was seen by *Mount Temple* crossing the pack ice going from east to west.[108] By 6.40a.m., *Californian* had cleared the pack and all hands were called up.[109] A half hour later, at 7.10a.m., *Californian* was reported by *Mount Temple* to be very close.[110] *Californian* was then heading about SSE true down along the western edge of the pack ice at 13 knots.[111] Passing *Mount Temple* about a mile off, *Californian* reached a point where *Carpathia* was seen directly off her port beam on the eastern side of the pack ice picking up *Titanic*'s survivors and boats. *Carpathia* was then near the wreckage about 2 to 3 miles off the eastern edge of the ice.[112] The ice field itself was about 5 to 6 miles wide in that region.[113] At about 8a.m., Captain Rostron noticed that *Californian* was 'about five to six miles distant, bearing WSW true, and steaming towards *Carpathia*.'[114] A half hour later, about 8.30a.m., *Californian* finally arrived as the last survivors were being picked up.[115]

Closing a distance of about 5 miles in half an hour to get to *Carpathia* shows that *Californian* was averaging about 10 knots while cutting across the ice. Since *Carpathia* herself was 2 to 3 miles from the edge of the field, and the field itself was reported to be 5 to 6 miles wide, *Californian* had to travel about 7 to 9 miles from the time she turned directly toward *Carpathia* that morning. With this information, and the fact that she arrived about 8.30a.m., we find that *Californian* would have turned directly for *Carpathia* about 7.40a.m. that morning, or about an hour after she had previously cleared the ice and all hands were called out.

The path that *Californian* followed that morning is illustrated in the following diagram.[116] It should be noted that the entire picture of ships, ice and wreckage would be drifting southward together with the local current.

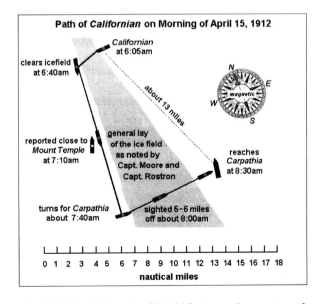

Fig. 10-16 Probable path of SS *Californian* on the morning of
15 April 1912.

Assessment of Actions Taken by Captain Lord

There is no disagreement that *Californian* encountered field ice late Sunday night which forced her to stop for the night, and remain stopped until after it became light enough to move on the next morning. There is no disagreement that another ship was seen to approach *Californian* and stop some miles off. There is no argument that an attempt was made to call her up by Morse lamp, and there is no reason to suggest that any further attempt to communicate with that vessel was required at that point in time after that vessel failed to respond.

There is little argument today, after the discovery of the wreck, that *Titanic's* distress rockets were seen from *Californian* during the middle watch on the same line of bearing as this vessel. Nor is there any argument that Captain Lord was informed that rockets were seen on several occasions, and that no action was taken except to continue to try to communicate with the vessel by Morse lamp. It was only after Chief Officer Stewart and Captain Lord had talked about the events reported during the middle watch while preparing to resume their voyage to Boston that Captain Lord finally decided to take further action by having Stewart call upon Cyril Evans, their wireless operator, to find out what he could.

In discussing the actions or inactions of Captain Lord, several questions come up:

1. What exactly did Lord know?
2. When did he know it?
3. Did he take appropriate actions?

Captain Lord had testified that when he was called on the speaking tube at 1.15a.m. by Second Officer Stone, he was told about only one rocket being seen.[117] According to Herbert Stone, he informed Captain Lord about seeing rockets after he saw the first five of them.[118] According to Apprentice James Gibson, Stone told him that he (Stone) had called down to Lord after seeing the second rocket because the first one he was not too sure about.[119] If Gibson's account is accurate, namely that Stone called Lord after the second rocket was seen, then it is entirely possible that what Stone told Captain Lord is that he had seen, 'lights in the sky in the direction of the other steamer,' and one of them appeared to be a white rocket. If this is the way it really happened, then we have Captain Lord being told by Stone that he saw what looked like a white rocket coming from the direction of the steamer that had stopped for the night over an hour before. Lord's reaction to Stone's report was to ask if they were private signals, which Stone did not know. Lord also told Stone to continue to call up the steamer by Morse lamp and to send Gibson down if he got any reply. If this is the way it happened, then the thought of anything seriously wrong with that steamer probably never even crossed Captain Lord's mind.

Now with hindsight we can say that Captain Lord should have assumed the worst immediately and taken a more active role, including going topside to see for himself what was really going on, or ordering Cyril Evans, the Marconi operator, be woken up to try and contact the steamer by wireless. But if Gibson's account was accurate, and if Lord was told about lights in the sky of which only one looked like a white rocket, then it is easy to understand why Lord reacted initially the way he did.

Here is a steamer that stops for the night. An hour later, after failed attempts at trying to communicate by Morse lamp, signals are sent up from the steamer, one of which appeared to be a white rocket. Was she trying to respond to *Californian's* attempt at signalling her? Was it a white rocket that his second officer saw, or was it a company signal? So Lord asked Stone if what he saw was a company signal, to which Stone replied that he did not know, but that they were white.

As a master mariner, Stanley Lord knew that rockets or shells throwing stars of any colour fired one at a time at night at intervals meant distress. But, if he was told of one rocket, then that by itself did not indicate distress. So he then instructed his second officer to continue to call the steamer up on the Morse lamp and to send Gibson down when they got a reply. So far, there was no apparent need to get alarmed, because what was reported to him by Stone so far was not very alarming.

If, however, he was told by Stone that several rockets were seen at intervals, then that would be a very different story, and his reaction totally inexcusable.

Based on Captain Lord's reaction as soon as he got word later in the morning about *Titanic*, including his willingness to risk his ship twice in cutting across a field of pack ice to go and render aid, it is inconceivable that he would have stood by and done nothing if he was properly informed as to what was really going on that night while it was happening. Lord admitted that Stone's report at 1.15a.m. did not entirely satisfy him.[120] He knew that the only signals used at sea were distress signals, that company signals usually do not go very high or explode into stars, and that what was sent up from that steamer may indeed have been a distress rocket.[121] Yet, he made a mistake in judgement and remained below in his chart room fully dressed instead of coming topside to see for himself what was going on. Lord left subsequent decisions to his second officer, and his second officer was leaving all decisions to him. Not a very good situation in bridge team management.[122]

Later, when Gibson was sent down to wake and inform Lord that altogether eight white rockets were seen, and that the ship that fired them had disappeared in the SW, it was too late to do anything. We could only imagine that he would have wondered why a steamer that appeared to have stopped for the night on account of ice would suddenly start to send up rockets over an hour after stopping? And why would that same steamer, after sending up rockets, then steam away to the SW across an ice field in the dark of night? Steamers in distress do not steam away. So again he asked if there were any colours in the signals, still thinking they may have been company signals, even though he knew that company signals were usually never used at sea.

Although the ultimate responsibility for *Californian*'s actions rests with her commander, Captain Stanley Lord, the actions, or rather inactions, of Second Officer Stone must come into question. As soon as the second officer, who was the responsible Officer of the Watch, was sure that he was seeing rockets being sent up at short intervals, he should have:

1. Called his commander and insisted he come up to the bridge.
2. Rung down 'Standby' to the engine room to place them at the ready.
3. Awakened the wireless operator and get him to see if he could find anything out.

Stone did none of these. Instead he watched a display of distress rockets go on for about an hour, and then waited for the ship to disappear before sending Gibson down to report.

Captain Lord has been accused of many things, including being intoxicated that night, extremely callous, or frightened of manoeuvring his ship at night with ice about. None of these accusations are true. We believe that there was a breakdown in what today is called bridge team management between Captain Lord and Second Officer Stone. The basic cause was human fallibility.

We believe that at some point Captain Lord must have realised that what his second officer and apprentice may have seen that night were distress signals sent up from *Titanic*. The mistake he made was to try to cover up what had taken place. There was nothing written about any of the events that took place in their logbook, and there is some question about some of the positional entries that were put into the official logbook afterward. However, once the story came out that rockets were seen during the middle watch, Stanley Lord found himself having to defend not only his actions and inactions, but those under his command as well. It did not help his cause when he and some of his officers tried at first to cover up the fact that rockets were seen during the middle watch when they were in Boston.[123] At that point the world found someone who was alive that they could point to for the great loss of life that resulted from someone else's failure.

We believe that Captain Lord was unjustly blamed for being asleep while *Titanic* was calling for aid from whoever was able to see her signals and hear her wireless. He lost his job for failing to act when rockets were first reported to him. Yet, if what he said was true about being told of only one rocket initially, his reaction was not entirely inappropriate for the limited information he was given. And when he did receive more information later on that night, it was both confusing and too late. In any case, even if he had acted immediately, the unfortunate truth is that the total number of casualties from *Titanic* would still have been staggering.

Consider the following hypothetical scenario:[124]

Californian ATS	Event/Actions Taken
12.45a.m.	First rocket is seen by Second Officer Stone, but he is not too sure what it is.
12.50a.m.	Second rocket seen by Stone. Stone goes to the speaking tube and informs Captain Lord. He insists that Lord come on deck as he thinks it may be distress signals. He goes over and puts the engine order telegraph on 'Stand-by' and waits for Lord to arrive.
12.55a.m.	Captain Lord comes on deck and sees a rocket go up himself. He decides to take decisive action and orders half-ahead on the engine telegraph and has *Californian* turned toward the direction of the steamer and rockets. He also tells Stone to go and wake Evans to see if he can find out anything on the wireless, and has Chief Officer Stewart called out.
1.00a.m.	*Californian* is now cutting through loose ice at about 6 knots in the direction of the steamer that continues to fire distress rockets. Evans picks up one of *Titanic's* distress messages and reports the SOS coordinates to the bridge. Lord asks Evans to confirm the position, as the position given is about 17 miles to the SSW (True) from his stopped dead reckoning, while the rockets he sees are to the SE (True). Lord is concerned because the steamer firing those rockets to the SE looks like a tramp vessel perhaps 5 miles away, not a large passenger liner like *Titanic*. Meanwhile, Stewart is ordered to get all hands called out and prepare for a rescue. Extra lookouts are posted on forecastle head and bridge.
1.05a.m.	On *Titanic*, Captain Smith is called to the wireless cabin and informed about *Californian* seeing rockets to their SE. He tells Phillips to send an MSG to *Californian* telling them that *Titanic* is firing rockets, to ignore the position given, and to come at once to what they see.
1.10a.m.	Despite a continued concern over the position given and what he sees, Lord instructs Evans to tell *Titanic* that they will fire a couple of rockets to confirm that they have each other in sight. Lord is still reluctant to go at full speed in these ice-infested waters paralleling the edge of the pack ice until he gets some sort of confirmation that they are heading toward *Titanic*.
1.15a.m.	Evans reports that *Titanic* saw their rockets. Captain Lord decides to risk full speed ahead despite having to push through the loose ice as Evans reports that *Titanic* says she is 'going down fast at the head'.[125] *Californian* revolutions quickly increase from 35 to 70rpm as she works up to 13 knots.[126]
1.45a.m.	Evans reports that *Titanic* says, 'women and children in boats, cannot last much longer.'[127] *Californian* is still about 4 to 5 miles away, but the reality of what is seen ahead is now becoming very clear. She continues to close the distance by 1 mile every 5 minutes. Tensions grow high on the small steamer as she continues to approach the sinking vessel.

2.00a.m.	*Californian* is now about a mile off. Lord rings down 'Stop' on his engines to take the way off his ship. He knows he cannot get his ship too close to the stricken liner, and orders Stewart to get ready to lower the boats to take people off *Titanic. Titanic's* forecastle is completely submerged, as men are working desperately on collapsible boats A and B. After sending a last message, Phillips and Bride abandon *Titanic's* wireless cabin. On *Titanic*, it is 2.12a.m. ATS.[128]
2.05a.m.	*Californian* now closes to within ½ mile of *Titanic* as she continues to slow. Suddenly, all of *Titanic's* lights go out as the ship appears to have split apart. Captain Lord immediately rings down 'Full astern' to bring his ship to a complete stop. Within 2 to 3 minutes, what is left of *Titanic* upends and sinks. On *Titanic*, it was 2.20a.m. On *Californian*, it was noted at 2.08a.m.
2.10a.m.	*Californian* comes to a stop and the first of six available boats starts to lower. It is manned by a crew of five, four to row and one to steer. Suddenly a bright green flare is seen from beyond where *Titanic* had been. It is from *Titanic's* boat No.2.
2.15a.m.	The terrible screams of those in the freezing water are heard as the first of *Californian's* boats reaches the water and starts to pull away.
2.25a.m.	The first boat now reaches close to the area of the wreckage and struggling survivors. It has already been about 15 minutes for those in the water, and most are now at the point of near exhaustion and unconsciousness. Most will not survive unless they can be pulled out within the next 15 to 30 minutes.[129]

Is the above scenario realistic? The timing and such of this scenario is probably optimistic considering the confusion that would be caused by first receiving wireless reports that had *Titanic* far off in a different direction from where rockets were coming from. If anything, this probably represents a best-case scenario. Furthermore, it assumes that *Californian* would not have run into an iceberg as she headed for the stricken liner, or forced to slow down because of meeting up with growlers or heavier field ice along the way. *Carpathia* herself was very fortunate in not suffering the same fate as *Titanic* when they had to port around a previously unseen low-lying iceberg that was directly ahead of them just before reaching s boat.[130]

Most people cannot even imagine the difficulty of conducting a rescue operation on a dark, moonless night out on the open sea. Even as *Carpathia* arrived, as day was just starting to break in the east, she managed to find but one of *Titanic's* lifeboats only because of the green flares that Boxhall was lighting. As Rostron said, 'It must have been a quarter of an hour after I got them [the survivors from Boxhall's boat] all on board that I saw the other boats. It was not sufficiently light to see the other boats.'

At best, assuming *Californian's* own boats would not be swamped in the effort, and assuming everyone worked quickly and efficiently in pulling people out of the water, including the help of some of the stronger survivors that made it to the boats, perhaps 100 may have been pulled to safety under the scenario outlined above.[131] But we will never really know. No matter what could have been, we believe a proactive attempt should have been made once that second rocket was seen. Instead, we find that those on *Californian* watched as rocket after rocket went up while their ship stood still.

Notes

[1]   From the Dundee City Archives.

[2]   Evans, AI p.741.

[3]   BI 8793.

[4]   A useful online calculator is available from the NGDC to get magnetic variation for any location on a specified date. It can be accessed at: http://www.ngdc.noaa.gov/geomagmodels/struts/calcDeclination.

[5]   Stewart, BI 8713.

[6]   Lord, BI 7269.

[7]   Lord, AI p.715.

[8]   Stewart, BI 8793.

[9]   Stewart, BI 8709.

[10] Lord, BI 6710.

[11] John Booth and Sean Coughlan, *Titanic – Signals of Disaster*, Msg. 89, p.47.

[12] John Booth and Sean Coughlan, *Titanic – Signals of Disaster*, Msg. 90, p.47.

[13] Lord, AI p.716; BI 7115, 7141–2.

[14] The distance travelled from a corrected noontime position at 42° 05'N, 47° 34'W to when those three icebergs were sighted at 6.30p.m. ATS would be about 71 nautical miles, placing the ship at a longitude of 49° 09'W at 6.30p.m. ATS, as given to *Antillian*. This slight correction in noontime longitude from 47° 25'W to 47° 34'W would not have changed the Apparent Time that she was keeping. Her clocks would still be 1 hour 50 minutes ahead of clocks in New York. (Ref.: Samuel Halpern, 'Navigational Inconsistencies of the SS *Californian*', available online at http://www.titanicology.com/Californian/Navigational_Incosistencies.pdf.)

[15] Lord, AI p.718.

[16] Press Association Special Telegram, 'The *Virginian's* Efforts at Rescue', April 1912.

[17] Stanley Lord, letter to the Assistant Secretary, Marine Department, Board of Trade, 10 August 1912.

[18] Stewart, BI 8706, BI 8804–16.

[19] It was an ice report from *Californian* to *Olympic* sent at 5.20p.m. NYT on 15 April. The information about field ice and icebergs in that message listed the same coordinates that were reported to *Antillian* for 6.30p.m. the previous day, not the coordinates that were later put into *Californian's* logbook adjusted as a result of an alleged Pole star sight taken an hour later. (Ref.: the wireless log of SS *Olympic*, AI p.1139.)

[20] The words 'shut up' were communicated by sending the letters 'DDD'. This was known as the 'silent signal', meaning that all other stations must cease transmitting. (See AI p.147.)

[21] True bearings would be about 2 compass points to port, making *Californian* point NE True, and the mystery vessel bearing SE True from *Californian*. The difference between compass bearings and true bearings is due to magnetic variation and compass deviation.

[22] Groves was to later claim that he eventually saw two masthead lights on this steamer, but Captain Lord, Second Officer Stone and Apprentice Gibson, who also saw this steamer, all said they only saw one. Groves mentioned that to Lord when the two were talking the following morning after they learned about *Titanic*. *Titanic* had but one masthead light.

[23] Lord, AI p.733.

[24] Evans, AI p.736.

[25] Lord, AI p.717.

[26] PV SS *Mount Temple*. The entry recorded at 3.25a.m. NYT read: 'MWL calls CQ. I answer him and advise him of MGY [*Titanic*] and send him MGY's position.'

[27] Captain Gambell said the message was sent at 5.45a.m. *Virginian* ATS. *Virginian* ATS was 1 hour 30 minutes ahead of NY mean time, while Californian ATS was 1 hour 50 minutes ahead of NY mean time. (Press Association Special Telegram, 'The *Virginian's* Efforts at Rescue', April 1912.)

[28] Lord, AI p.718.

[29] Lord, AI p.718.

[30] Lord, BI 7399.

[31] Lord, BI 7402.

[32] Lord, AI p.723.

33 *Californian* saw only a small amount of floating wreckage, as did *Carpathia*. *Carpathia*'s Captain Rostron was mostly concerned about conducting a rescue operation, not a recovery operation. As he said, 'For one reason, the *Titanic*'s passengers then were knocking about the deck and I did not want to cause any unnecessary excitement or any more hysteria among them, so I steamed past [the one floating body], trying to get them not to see it.' (AI p.22–3.) His second officer, James Bisset, later wrote, 'The dead bodies were there, totally or partially submerged, but, in the choppy seas, it was now almost impossible to sight them, as white lifejackets would have an appearance similar to that of the thousands of small pieces of floating ice or white-painted wreckage. A dead body floats almost submerged.' (Bisset, *Tramps & Ladies*.) If James Bisset was right, a floating body would have less surface area on which the wind could act, and therefore would not have been blown to leeward after the wind came up in the morning as much as some of the other wreckage that was more buoyant. It seems that this was a case of *Californian* searching the wrong area after *Carpathia* departed. (See also Samuel Halpern, 'We Could Not See One Body', the Titanic Historical Society's journal, *The Titanic Commutator*, Vol.32, No.181.)

34 Stone, BI 8028.

35 Stone, BI 8085–7.

36 Stone, BI 7938–41.

37 Stone, BI 7935.

38 Signed statement from Herbert Stone to Captain Lord, 18 April 1912, while at sea.

39 Gibson, BI 7565.

40 Groves, BI 8475.

41 Groves, BI 8150–1.

42 Gibson BI 7438–9.

43 Signed statement from James Gibson to Captain Lord, 18 April 1912, while at sea.

44 Signed statement from Stone to Lord, 18 April 1912; Lord, BI 6785–6.

45 Gibson, BI 7466, BI 7505–11.

46 Signed statement from Gibson to Lord, 18 April 1912.

47 Gibson, 7786.

48 Gibson, 7630.

49 Stone, BI 7972.

50 As explained by the manufacturer, the Cotton Powder Company Ltd, 'Socket distress signals are fired from a socket, ascend to a height of 600 to 800ft, and then burst with the report of a gun and the stars of a rocket.' (Leslie Reade, *The Ship That Stood Still*, Patrick Stephens Limited, 1993, Ch.4.)

51 1992 Marine Accident Investigation Branch (MAIB) Report, 'RMS *Titanic*: Reappraisal of Evidence Relating to the SS *Californian*,' 12 March 1992.

52 BI 25111.

53 AI p.1142.

54 American inquiry, p.716.

55 From the *Procès-Verbal* (PV) log prepared by *Olympic*'s wireless operator E.J. Moore. Copy submitted to Senator William Alden Smith for the American inquiry, 25 May 1912.

56 British inquiry, 8658 – 8692.

57 British inquiry, 8503 – 8564.

58 Lord, AI p.721.

59 Signed statement from Herbert Stone to Captain Lord, 18 April 1912.

60 British inquiry, 6782.

61 Signed statement from James Gibson to Captain Lord, 18 April 1912.

62 Signed statement from James Gibson to Captain Lord, 18 April 1912.

63 Other independent analytical methods used to estimate the distance between *Californian* and *Titanic* produce similar results. These methods include using the 'Law of Sines' from geometry and the distance *Titanic* would travel from when her masthead light would first come over the horizon to when she appeared to stop; the geometry of the ice field as reported by Captains Rostron, Lord and Moore who were on the scene; and by the equilateral triangle formed by the independent sightings of what appeared to be *Mount Temple* on the western side of the pack ice about 5a.m. on the morning of 15 April by Captains Rostron and Lord. These techniques are explained in detail in: Samuel

Halpern, 'Light on the Horizon – Part 2,' *The Titanic Commutator* (journal of the Titanic Historical Society),Vol.31, Issue 178, 2007.

64 At 0°C (32°F) sound travels at a speed of 644 knots. It would take 56 seconds to travel 10 miles, and 1 minute 13 seconds to travel 13 miles. At those distances, any sounds that managed to reach *Californian* would not be associated with the rocket bursts that were seen, and would be severely attenuated and lost in the background sounds of the ship. (Ref: Paul Wilkinson, '*Titanic's* Silent Distress Signals – A New Look at a Minor Mystery', 2004, http://www.encyclopedia-titanica.org/ articles/rockets_wilkinson.pdf.)

65 BI 15409.

66 Lord, AI p.729.

67 Boxhall, AI p.934; BI 15406–8.

68 *Californian's* clocks were 12 minutes behind *Titanic's*. The time interval from when *Californian* stopped to when *Titanic* foundered was 3 hours 47 minutes. The local current in the area of the wreck site had a drift of about 1.1 knots, and a set of 197° True. (Ref: Samuel Halpern, 'Collision Point', *Great Lakes Titanic Society (GLTS) website*, http://www.glts.org/articles/halpern/collision_ point.html.)

69 BI 9388. Captain J. Henry Moore: 'I never knew it to be so far south before. Not in my whole experience of twenty-seven years, I never knew it so far south.'

70 Samuel Halpern, 'Collision Point', GLTS website, http://www.glts.org/articles/halpern/collision_ point.html.

71 Scarrott, BI 355–6.

72 Shiers, BI 4543, 4546.

73 Rowe, BI 17671; Deposition of H.G. Lowe before the British Consulate General in New York, May 1912.

74 Boxhall, BI 15385.

75 Groves, BI 8150–1, 8157.

76 The requirements concerning navigation lights carried on steamers that were in effect at the time can be accessed at: Samuel Halpern, '*Titanic's* Masthead Light', GLTS website, 2007, http://www.glts. org/articles/halpern/masthead_light.html.

77 Stone, BI 7922–8.

78 Stewart, BI 8576–94.

79 Stone, BI 7938–9.

80 Signed statement from James Gibson to Captain Lord, 18 April 1912.

81 We know from Gibson that the relative bearing to the steamer between the seventh and eighth rocket had changed from 2 points before the starboard bow to 1 point before the port bow, a change of 3 points. This was due to his own ship swinging round to starboard.

82 Stone, BI 7936.

83 Samuel Halpern, 'Rockets, Lifeboats, and Time Changes', TIS's *Voyage* 70, winter 2009 issue, and in BTS's *Atlantic Daily Bulletin*, December 2009 issue.

84 From the wireless log of *Mount Temple*, '1.25 [NYT] MPA [*Carpathia*] sends: "If you are there, we are firing rockets."' 1.25 NYT corresponded to 3.15a.m. *Californian* time.

85 Rostron, AI p.21.

86 At the British inquiry, Stone described them as 'merely a faint flash', while Gibson, as in his written statement to Captain Lord, described them as rockets. They appeared just above the horizon.

87 Rowe, BI 17671.

88 To Lightoller and Pitman it seemed never to move.

89 Osman, AI p.541.

90 In particular, boat nos 3, 5, 8 and C.

91 Taken from the testimony of Joseph Boxhall before the British Wreck Commission.

92 Because of a 10° list to port at that time, the port side of *Titanic's* bridge would have been about 20ft above the water, while the starboard side would have been about 36ft above the water.

93 When *Californian* was a ½ point off the port bow, *Titanic* would have presented only 10 per cent of her full length to *Californian*. When 2 points off the port bow, she would have presented just 38 per cent of her full length.

94 Lightoller, BI 13894, 14138–49. If the white light was coming from a sailing vessel, it would have to be a stern light because sailing vessels on the high seas do not carry mast lights.

95   Pitman, AI p.292–3, 295–6.
96   Boxhall, BI 15401–2. Fifth Officer Harold Lowe also said he saw a steamer's lights after he got boat
     No.1 away. In his deposition before the British Consulate in May 1912, Lowe wrote that he saw the
     steamer's two masthead lights and a red sidelight off *Titanic's* port bow to the northward. He also
     said that later on the vessel 'seemed to alter her position and open her green.' The sequence of first
     showing red then green is opposite to what Boxhall described seeing. The complete deposition of
     Lowe can be found in: George M. Behe, *On Board RMS Titanic – Memories of the Maiden Voyage*, Lulu.
     com Press, 2011, p.351–4.
97   There are numerous accounts of Captain Smith giving these instructions to boats as they were
     launched. (J. Johnstone, BI 3507–8; T. Jones, AI p.570; A. Crawford, BI 17960–7, 18066–9.)
98   This estimate was given by Lord Mersey's assessors at the British inquiry (BI 18065).
99   Crawford, BI 17856–993.
100 We have estimated that the height of eye for someone seated amidships in one of *Titanic's* 30ft
     lifeboats when lightly loaded would be about 4ft 3in above the water, and *Californian's* sidelights were
     about 38ft above the water. They would come into view if the lifeboat came within about 9.6 miles
     under normal conditions. For someone standing on a thwart, they would be seen within 10.3 miles
     under normal conditions.
101 Stewart, BI 8577–94.
102 Stewart, BI 8612.
103 Taking into account both magnetic variation and compass deviation from evidence given, the
     compass bearing to *Carpathia* at 4a.m. was probably close to S by E with *Californian* heading about
     WNW by compass.
104 Lord, AI p.733.
105 Rostron, BI 25551.
106 Lord, BI 7388.
107 The time reported by Captain Gambel was 5.45a.m. *Virginian* ATS. *Virginian* was 1 hour 30 minutes
     ahead of NY, and *Californian* was 1 hour 50 minutes ahead of NY. This puts the official MSG
     received at 6.05a.m. *Californian* time. Captain Lord said he had it written in his logbook as 'Six
     o'clock'.
108 AI p.778–9.
109 BI 8290–320; AI p.711.
110 An entry in the wireless log of *Mount Temple* read: '5.20 [NYT]. Signals *Californian*. Wants my
     position. Send it. We are very close.' 5.20a.m. NYT corresponded to 7.10a.m. *Californian* ATS.
111 According to Captain Lord, the top speed of *Californian* was between 12½ and 13 knots. (BI 6675.)
112 Rostron, BI 25498, 25502.
113 Moore, AI p.778.
114 Rostron, BI 25551.
115 Lord, AI p.723. Also noted in Captain Rostron's report to the General Manager of the Cunard
     Steamship Company, 19 April 1912.
116 The western side of the ice field trended from NNW to SSE True. This comes from Captain Moore
     and Captain Lord. (Ref: Moore, AI p.767; Lord, AI p.730.) The eastern side trended from NW to SE
     as noted by Captain Rostron. (Ref: Rostron, BI 25501.)
117 Lord, BI 6898–900.
118 Stone's written report to Captain Lord on 18 April 1912.
119 Gibson's written report to Captain Lord on 18 April 1912.
120 Lord, BI 6911.
121 Lord, BI 6936, 6937, 6944.
122 Stone, BI 7853.
123 *The New York Herald*, 23 April 1912; *The Boston Post*, 24 April 1912; *The Boston Globe*, 25 April 1912;
     The Boston Herald, 25 April 1912; *The Boston Journal*, 25 April 1912. (See: http://home.earthlink.
     net/~dnitzer/Frameset.html.)
124 Adapted and modified from Dave Gittins' e-book, *Titanic: Monument and Warning*, chapter: 'The
     Californian Affair'.
125 Words in quotes actually overheard by *Mount Temple* at 11.20p.m. NYT [1.10a.m. *Californian* ATS]
     (Ref: PV *Mount Temple*.)

126 From Captain Lord's 1959 affidavit, full ahead at 13 knots corresponded to 70rpm.

127 Words in quotes actually overheard by *Birma* at about 11.53p.m. NYT [1.43a.m. *Californian* ATS]. (Ref: Samuel Halpern, 'The Enigmatic Excursion of the SS *Birma*', http://www.titanicology.com/Titanica/Inigmatic_Excursion_of_SS_Birma.pdf.)

128 The last wireless message from *Titanic* was probably the one recorded at 12.10 NYT. *Titanic* time would be 2.12a.m. As Bride noted, it was about 10 minutes before the ship sank.

129 United States Search and Rescue Task Force, 'Cold water Survival', Table of Expected Survival Time in Cold Water, http://www.ussartf.org/cold_water_survival.htm.

130 Rostron, BI 25401.

131 *Californian* had a total boat capacity for only 218 people, including crew, BI 6688.

11

THE CIRCUMSTANCES IN CONNECTION WITH THE SS *MOUNT TEMPLE*

Samuel Halpern

Mount Temple was one of the first ships to pick up and respond to *Titanic*'s call for assistance on the night of 14 April 1912. Like the rescue ship *Carpathia*, she too was turned around and headed for the distress coordinates that were sent out by *Titanic*. However, coming up from the south-west, she was forced to stop on the western side of that vast field of pack ice that lay between her and where *Titanic* had been. Over the years, questions stemming from the controversy over the *Californian* affair have arisen as to where she was and what her crew saw.

Mount Temple's Route of Travel

The Canadian Pacific's SS *Mount Temple* was an immigrant vessel of 8,790 gross tons, with a length of 485ft between perpendiculars and a beam of 59ft. She carried four masts and a single yellow funnel. At 1p.m. on Wednesday 3 April 1912, *Mount Temple* departed Antwerp on her sixty-second voyage westbound for St John, New Brunswick, and then on to Halifax, Nova Scotia, carrying 1,466 passengers, mostly steerage, and a crew of 143. She was equipped with twenty lifeboats with a total rated capacity of about 1,000.

Her planned route of travel would take her westward through the English Channel to a departure point just off Bishop Rock (49° 52'N, 6° 27'W) at the westernmost tip of the Isles of Scilly, then 1,734 nautical miles along the great circle path to the corner point for westbound steamers at 42°N, 47°W. From there she would go on a rhumb line course of 276° True for Cape Sable (43° 29'N, 65° 43.5'W) at the southernmost tip of Nova Scotia, a distance of about 830 nautical miles, and then into the Bay of Fundy and up to St John. Her speed was almost 11 knots.

At local apparent noon, Saturday 13 April 1912, *Mount Temple* was located about 200 nautical miles from the westbound corner point (42°N, 47°W), expecting to reach the corner in a little over 18 hours.

At 8.45p.m. New York Time (NYT), *Mount Temple* received a wireless call from the SS *Corinthian* saying that the SS *Corsican* had seen ice at 41° 25'N, 50° 30'W.[1] At the time this message was received, which was about 10.53p.m. ship's time,[2] *Mount Temple* was heading close to 245° True toward the westbound corner point.[3] After receiving the ice warning from *Corinthian*, *Mount Temple*'s captain, James Henry Moore, prudently decided not to turn his ship at the corner, but to continue on past the corner and head down to 41° 15'N, 50° 00'W, a decision that would take his ship about 10 miles south of the reported ice. From this new turning point he would then head for Cape Sable and then on up to St John. By doing so, he would only extend the total voyage distance by about 22 miles, or about 2 hours of steaming, and thereby avoid encountering ice along the way.

At about 6.23a.m. on 14 April, *Mount Temple* would have passed the longitude of the corner. She then continued steaming on the same course line until local apparent noon when her position was fixed by solar observation at 41° 38'N, 48° 20'W.[4] Some time in the forenoon that Sunday morning, *Mount Temple's* clocks were set back 22 minutes to account for the westward progress she was making. Apparent Time was now 3 hours 14 minutes behind GMT, or 1 hour 46 minutes ahead of NYT. The run time between noon 13 April to noon 14 April was 24 hours 22 minutes, and the ship would have covered a distance of about 265 nautical miles. With the ship's noontime position fixed, *Mount Temple* was put on a heading of 253° True to take her down to the new turning point at 41° 15'N, 50° 00'W. The distance was about 78½ miles. At about 7.12p.m. ATS, *Mount Temple's* course was changed to a heading of 281° True to make Cape Sable.

Side Note on Positions: In *Mount Temple's* logbook there was an entry for 13 April regarding a fireman (promoted from trimmer), George Luxon, who was put back on limited duty after suffering second-degree burns on 7 April. The position of the ship was recorded as 43° 02'N, 44° 13'W, but no time was entered. When compared to her noontime position for 14 April, this position shows that the ship was indeed on a course very close to 245° True as stated in testimony. There was another entry in the logbook for 3.50a.m. for 14 April concerning a three-month-old infant, Dozko Oziro, who died on board from bronchopneumonia. The ship's position written down in the logbook, 43° 56.5'N, 46° 43'W, was obviously an error because the ship was well south of 43°N latitude by that time. The dead reckoning position would have been about 42° 16.5'N, 46° 26'W based on the course she was on, the speed she was making, and the assumption that the time reported was accurate.[5] The ship's noontime position for 14 April as recorded in her logbook, 41° 38'N, 48° 20'W, agrees with *Mount Temple's* clocks being 1 hour 46 minutes ahead of NYT as presented in evidence.[6]

Intercept of *Titanic's* Distress Signals and Actions Taken

At 10.25p.m. NYT, 12.11a.m. *Mount Temple* ATS, *Mount Temple's* wireless operator John Durrant picked up a CQD message from *Titanic* that said she required assistance. The distress position given at that time, and reported to Captain Moore, was 41° 44'N, 50° 24'W, the same coordinates picked up by the land station at Cape Race, and by the steamships *La Provence* and *Ypiranga*. Despite responding to *Titanic's* call, it was difficult for *Titanic's* operator Jack Phillips to fully hear Durrant's response because of the loud noise caused by steam blowing off from the escape pipes on *Titanic's* funnels at that time. Durrant's message to Captain Moore read: '*Titanic* sends CQD. Requires assistance. Position 41° 44' north, longitude 50° 24' west. Come at once. Iceberg.' At the bottom of the message it said, 'Can't hear me.' At the time this message was received, Captain Moore was asleep. It was a steward who woke him up and handed him Durrant's message:[7]

> I immediately blew the whistle [on the speaking tube that goes up] on the bridge. I have a pipe leading down from the bridge, and I blew the whistle at once, and told the second officer to put the ship on north 45° east, sir, and to come down at once [to my cabin], and I informed him what was the matter, and told him to get the chart out.

At 10.35p.m. NYT (12.21 ATS), just ten minutes after receiving *Titanic's* initial distress call, Durrant picked up another CQD distress message from *Titanic*, the same that *Carpathia* picked up, which gave a 'corrected' position at 41° 46'N, 50° 14'W. This was immediately sent to Captain Moore:

> Before we had laid the course off I received another position, which read 41° 46' north, 50° 14' west; so that was 10 miles [*sic*] farther to the eastward, and it was that position that I laid my course for.

The new position was actually 10 minutes-of-arc, or about 7.5 miles, east of the first one he was given. He put down his own ship's position on the chart along with the corrected CQD position and then 'steered her by the compass north 65° east true [065°].'

The position of *Mount Temple* when she was turned onto this heading was given as 41° 25'N, 51° 14'W. That would put her 56.5 nautical miles from her previous 7.12p.m. turning point down at 41° 15'N, 50° 00'W. The time that *Mount Temple* was put on her course to the 'corrected' CQD position was marked as 10.40p.m. NYT in Durrant's wireless log. It would be 12.26a.m. *Mount Temple* ATS, or 12 hours 26 minutes since noon on 14 April. The distance travelled from her 14 April noon coordinates down to the turning point at longitude 50°W and then up to the turnaround point for 12.26a.m. is 135 nautical miles. Her average speed since noon was almost 10.9 knots, in full agreement with the information that was given.[8]

The chart below (Fig. 11-1) shows the path of *Mount Temple* for 14 April until the time she was turned around to head for *Titanic's* distress position in the early morning hours of 15 April. Also shown on the chart (for reference) are the locations of the two distress positions sent out from *Titanic* as well as the now known location of the wreck site.

The distance from the turnaround point to the CQD position is about 49½ nautical miles on a heading of 065° True, in agreement with what Captain Moore gave in evidence. If *Mount Temple* worked up to 11½ knots on her way to the rescue as reported, the time it would take to cover this distance would be about 4 hours 20 minutes for an expected time of arrival at the CQD location close to 4.45a.m. *Mount Temple* ATS.

At about 3.25a.m., Captain Moore rang down 'Stop' on his engine telegraph to let the way run off his ship because of loose ice that they started to encounter. He then proceeded ahead slowly until about 4.30a.m. when he reached 'a large ice pack right to the east of me, sir; right in my track – right in my course . . . it extended as far as the eye could reach, north and south.' Moore estimated that he was about 14 miles from the distress position at 3.25a.m. when he cut his engine the first time; a distance run of about 35 miles from the time he turned around. When he came to a stop a little over an hour later, he thought he was close to the CQD position, but he didn't quantify just how close. In the wireless log of John Durrant, there is an entry for 3.00a.m. NYT that read, 'All quiet; we're stopped amongst pack ice.' Ship's time would be 4.46a.m. *Mount Temple* ATS.

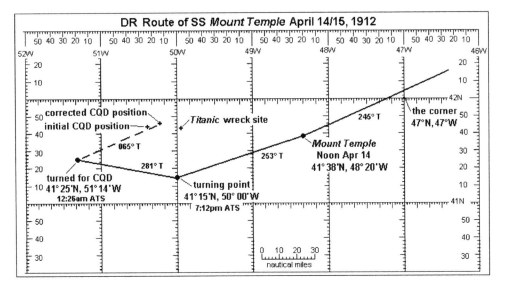

Fig. 11-1 The dead reckoning track of the SS *Mount Temple*, 14–15 April 1912.

Location of *Mount Temple* Relative to *Californian* and *Carpathia*

It must be emphasised that the positions given outside of the noontime position were deduced by dead reckoning, taking into account the ship's speed and course headings from a fixed starting position. That starting position was the one for noon 14 April. It does not include the effect of any current encountered along the way or any steering error. As was likely in the case of *Carpathia*, *Mount Temple* probably was set eastward somewhat by the North Atlantic Drift when she went down toward 41° 15'N latitude, and set southward somewhat as she approached the vicinity of where *Titanic* had been. What we do know is that she was stopped on the western side of the pack ice for at least 20 minutes if not a little more before she backed out of the ice at 5.06a.m. ATS (3.20a.m. NYT), about 20 minutes before sunrise,[9] to go SSE True trying to find an opening in the ice to pass through.

It appears that during the time that *Mount Temple* was stopped on the edge of the ice, she may have been sighted but not identified by both *Californian* and *Carpathia*.

As we have seen, Captain Lord said that there was a 'yellow-funnel steamer on the south-west of us, beyond where this man had left, about 8 miles away.' The time was a little before 5a.m. on *Californian* when he ordered his chief officer, George Stewart, to put the engine telegraph on 'Stand-by'. That was shortly before he sent Stewart down to wake up Evans, his wireless operator.[10]

About the same time on *Carpathia*, Captain Rostron saw two steamers to his northward:[11]

> At 5 o'clock it was light enough to see all round the horizon. We then saw two steamships to the northwards, perhaps seven or eight miles distant. Neither of them was the *Californian*. One of them was a four-masted steamer with one funnel, and the other a two-masted steamer with one funnel. I never saw the *Mount Temple* to identify her. The first time that I saw the *Californian* was at about eight o'clock on the morning of 15th April. She was then about five to six miles distant, bearing W.S.W. true, and steaming towards the *Carpathia*. The *Carpathia* was then in substantially the position of the *Titanic* at the time of the disaster as given to us by wireless. I consider the position of the *Titanic*, as given to us by her Officers, to be correct.

But what two steamers did Captain Rostron see at 5a.m. during the morning twilight before the sun came up? They apparently were not close enough to be identified. He didn't identify *Californian* until she came within 5 to 6 miles of him much later that morning, well after the sun was up.[12]

When *Mount Temple* was heading for *Titanic*'s distress coordinates she came up to a small tramp steamer, judged to be about 4,000 to 5,000 tons, that was heading eastward and showing a stern light to *Mount Temple*. This was 'between one and half-past one' in the morning.[13] This small steamer crossed *Mount Temple*'s bow going from port to starboard. From that time until about 9a.m. in the morning, this small tramp steamer was kept in sight. Later that morning it was seen to have two masts and one black funnel with a white band and some sort of device on it.[14] Captain Moore was not able to identify the vessel. This small tramp was also forced to stop by the same field of pack ice that caused *Mount Temple* to stop. She stopped a little to the southward from *Mount Temple*. Shortly before sunrise, both vessels backed out of the ice and went southward looking to find a way across:

> I searched for a passage to get through this pack, because I realised that the *Titanic* could not have been through that pack of ice, sir. I steered away to the south-south-east true, because I thought the ice appeared thinner down there, sir. When I got down, I got within about a mile or so of this other ship [the small tramp steamer], which had already stopped, finding the ice was too strong for it to go through.

We believe that it was both these two vessels, the small tramp steamer with two masts and one funnel, and *Mount Temple* with four masts and one funnel, that Captain Rostron saw at about

Fig. 11-2 The situation at 5 o'clock in the morning
on 15 April 1912.

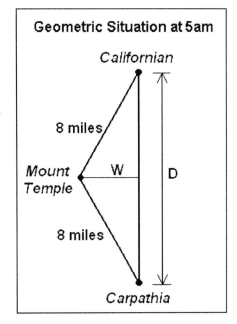

5a.m. in the morning before they both headed
southward looking for a passage through the ice.
Furthermore, we also believe the 'yellow-funnel
steamer' seen by Captain Lord and his chief
officer to their southward about 5a.m. was *Mount
Temple*.

If we take the 8-mile distance estimates
given by Captain Lord and Captain Rostron
to be approximately correct, then we find that
the three ships would have formed an isosceles
triangle as shown in Fig. 11-2.

The distance between *Californian* and
Carpathia, D, is easily derived if we know the
distance, W, from *Mount Temple* to the imaginary
line that formed the base of the isosceles triangle
connecting *Carpathia* to *Californian*. And since
Carpathia and *Californian* were both then on the
eastern side of the pack ice, and *Mount Temple* was on the western side, that distance, W, had
to be approximately the width of the pack which was estimated to be about 5 miles wide by
both Captain Moore and Captain Lord.[15] What that leads to is a distance between *Carpathia*
and *Californian* of about 12½ miles, assuming those 8-mile estimates by Lord and Rostron were
about right. This is more or less consistent with the estimated distance between *Titanic* and
Californian that we derived before.[16]

After going southward and failing to find an opening in the pack ice, *Mount Temple* was
turned around and headed back to the north:[17]

> After coming southward and trying to find some place I could get through, on the way back
> again – I suppose about 6 o'clock in the morning – that I sighted the *Carpathia* on the other
> side of this great ice pack, and there is where I understand he picked up the boats. So this
> great pack of ice was between us and the *Titanic's* position . . . This pack of ice between us and
> the *Carpathia*, it was between 5 and 6 miles. She [*Carpathia*] did not communicate with me
> at all. When we sighted her she must have sighted us . . . The *Californian* was to the north, sir.
> She was to the north of the *Carpathia* and steaming to the westward, because, after I had come
> away and after giving up my attempt to get through that pack, I came back again and steered
> back, thinking I might pick up some soft place to the north. As I was going to the north the
> *Californian* was passing from east to west . . . He was then north of the *Carpathia*, and he must
> have been, I suppose, about the same distance to the north of the *Carpathia* as I was to the
> westward of her.

The sighting of *Californian* to the northward slowly crossing the ice some time after 6a.m., and
Carpathia to the eastward about the same distance away is very revealing. Given that Captain
Moore's officers estimated the width of the pack ice as between 5 and 6 miles, and given that
Captain Rostron said that he was about 4 or 5 miles from the ice field when he first saw it,[18] we
find that the passing distance between *Carpathia* and *Mount Temple*, when the latter was heading
back northward, would be about 9 to 10 miles. If *Californian* was then about the same distance
from *Mount Temple* to the northward as *Carpathia* was to the eastward as Moore said, then we
find that *Californian* and *Carpathia* would be about 12½ to 14 miles apart as *Californian* was
cutting across the ice westward in an attempt to get to *Titanic's* reported distress position. The
situation as described by Captain Moore is shown in Fig. 11-3.

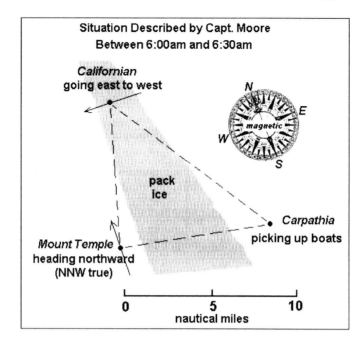

Fig. 11-3 Situation described by Captain Moore between 6 and 6.30a.m., 15 April 1912.

The times given by Captain Moore were, of course, approximate. But we do know that *Californian* was crossing 2 to 3 miles of pack ice up north shortly after 6a.m., and there was only a 4-minute difference between their clocks. We also know that at 6.52a.m. *Mount Temple* ATS [10.06a.m. GMT], a Prime Vertical sight of the sun was taken on *Mount Temple* which showed that she was on a line of longitude of 50° 09.5'W at that time.[19] What we do not know is the latitude at that time, which could only be surmised at best based on the drift of wreckage and known position of the wreck site.

Reported Sightings from *Mount Temple*

On 9 May 1912, an affidavit was submitted into evidence at the American inquiry from one Dr F.C. Quitzrau who was travelling as a second class passenger on *Mount Temple* at the time of the *Titanic* disaster. In that affidavit, Quitzrau said that he was awoken by the stopping of engines about midnight NYT, and was informed by stewards and passengers that word had been received by wireless that *Titanic* had struck an iceberg and was calling for help. He goes on to say:

> About 3 o'clock NewYork time, 2 o'clock ship's time, the *Titanic* was sighted by some of the officers and crew; that as soon as the *Titanic* was seen all lights on the *Mount Temple* were put out and the engines stopped and the boat lay dead for about two hours; that as soon as day broke the engines were started and the *Mount Temple* circled the *Titanic's* position, the officers insisting that this be done, although the captain had given orders that the boat proceed on its journey. While encircling the *Titanic's* position we sighted the *Frankfurt* to the north-west of us, the *Birma* to the south, speaking to both of these by wireless, the latter asking if we were in distress; that about 6 o'clock we saw the *Carpathia*, from which we had previously received a message that the *Titanic* had gone down; that about 8.30 the *Carpathia* wirelessed that it had picked up 20 lifeboats and about 720 passengers all told, and that there was no need for the *Mount Temple* to stand by, as the remainder of those on board were drowned.

This was the beginning of several hearsay stories that evolved in the wake of the *Titanic* disaster concerning the role *Mount Temple* played, or rather didn't play, in the rescue effort.

In the summer of 1912, W.H. Baker, *Mount Temple*'s new fourth officer that signed on before she departed from Halifax, wrote to Captain Lord saying that several officers and others told him about the events they had seen on the night *Titanic* went down.[20] He wrote:

> They were from ten to fourteen miles from her when they saw her signals. I gather from what was told me that the captain seemed afraid to go through the ice, although it was not so very thick. They told me that they not only saw her deck lights but several green lights between them and what they thought was the *Titanic*. There were two loud reports heard which they said must have been the 'finale' of the *Titanic*; this was some time after sighting her, I gathered ... I must tell you these men were fearfully indignant that they were not called up to give evidence at the time, for they were greatly incensed at the captain's behaviour in the matter.

In all instances, it is easy to show why these stories are not even close to being true. Many details, such as the green flares lit by Boxhall, were common knowledge by then. Based on simple navigational analysis, *Mount Temple* would have been more than 40 miles from *Titanic* at the time *Titanic* foundered. At that distance not even *Titanic*'s distress rockets would be seen. Even if we allow for an eastward current drift of as much as 6 miles, *Mount Temple* still would have been about 36 miles away from *Titanic* when she sank.[21]

Although *Mount Temple* could not have seen *Titanic* or her distress rockets, could she have seen *Carpathia*'s rockets at the time that Stone and Gibson saw them from *Californian*? And could Boxhall's green flares have been sighted from *Mount Temple* as she approached the western side of the ice field?

In terms of *Mount Temple* time, *Carpathia*'s rockets were going up at about 3.15a.m. She was then a good 10 miles from picking up the first boat, the one with Joseph Boxhall in it, which was seen about ½ point off their port bow when Boxhall lit one of those green flares. At about 3.25a.m. Captain Moore cut *Mount Temple*'s engine and then continued onward at slow speed for over an hour more. By about 4.00a.m., *Carpathia* was stopping to pick up the first boat. All during that time, Boxhall was showing these green flares to *Carpathia* as she approached. By about 4.45a.m. *Mount Temple* was stopped in the pack ice as noted from Durrant's wireless log. Taking into account Captain Rostron's estimate of 8 miles to the four-masted steamer at

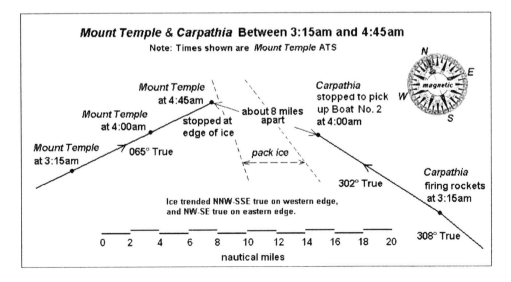

Fig. 11-4 *Mount Temple* and *Carpathia* from 3.15a.m. to 4.45a.m., Monday 15 April 1912.

5a.m., and that *Mount Temple* went ahead slowly between 3.25a.m. to when she stopped, we can work things backward in time to show the situation from 3.15a.m. to before *Mount Temple* backed out of the ice to head southward.[22] The picture that we get is shown in Fig. 11-4.

What we find with this method is that *Mount Temple* would have been about 26 miles from *Carpathia* about the time that Stone and Gibson saw *Carpathia's* rockets very low down on the horizon from the bridge of *Californian*. At 26 miles, those same rockets would have appeared very low on the horizon as seen from the bridge of *Mount Temple*. If seen by one of her officers, they easily could have been taken for distress rockets from *Titanic* except that they would be about 3 points off their starboard bow instead of toward the distress coordinates that they were headed for. If John Durrant reported to Captain Moore about what came over the wireless, Captain Moore would have known that *Carpathia* was firing rockets at that very time even if he did not see any himself. However, some of his officers and others may not have known about that.

Senator Smith:	Let me ask you right there, did you see the rockets from the *Carpathia*?
Mr Moore:	I never saw any rocket whatever, sir.
Senator Smith:	Is it possible that this passenger from Toronto [Quitzrau], who claims to have seen rockets, may have seen the rockets from the *Carpathia* at that time?
Mr Moore:	I do not think it possible, sir, because if the *Carpathia* was farther away it is not likely you would see her rockets. But you see, this ship says she is sending rockets up. So it is possible that other ships may have seen them. I do not know. I thought of sending rockets up, but I thought it far better to let it alone, because if other ships - they thought they saw them - might be coming to me, and I had not seen anything of the *Titanic* and did not know exactly where she was; because I think, after all, the *Titanic* was farther east than she gave her position, or, in fact, I am certain she was.

Of course Captain Moore did not know that *Titanic* sank to the east of her reported position until he took that Prime Vertical sight of the sun later that morning. But at the time that *Carpathia* was firing rockets he was headed toward the position that was given to him. He claims he did not see any rockets whatsoever, but it is possible that one or two of his officers had, and they may not have known that they came from *Carpathia*. We don't have any reliable information that says that Captain Moore was told that distress rockets were seen by anyone. At the time they were proceeding slowly because they were encountering loose ice along the way. For some, it may have seemed that Captain Moore was being overly cautious. Soon enough, a large field of pack ice was sighted in their path, and *Mount Temple* was forced to stop and remained there until it was light enough to look for a clear passage through the ice. Company instructions regarding going through field ice were very clear:

My instructions from my company are that I must not enter field ice, no matter if it seems only light. Those are my explicit instructions from my company. If I was to go through ice and my ship was damaged I would have pointed out to me that those were the instructions, that I was not to go into any ice, no matter how thin. As a matter of fact, I would not attempt to go through field ice if it was thick. The usual thing, on approaching ice, at night, is to stop and wait until daylight.

With over 1,600 passengers and crew on board, Captain Moore was not about to put their lives at risk. He had not heard anything from *Titanic* since 1.33a.m. ATS [11.47p.m. NYT], over 3 hours before he stopped.[23]

As far as the allegation that green lights were seen, by the time *Carpathia* stopped to pick up the boat Boxhall was in, it is estimated that *Mount Temple* would have been about 12 miles away. They still would have been too far for those green flares to be seen under normal conditions even if Boxhall lit one just as *Carpathia* came alongside, which itself seems unlikely.[24] But depending on how *Carpathia* was pointing, it is possible that her lights may or may not have been seen from *Mount Temple*.

When it became light enough to see all round, it was noted that there were about forty to fifty icebergs interspersed in the ice field ahead of them, with the largest estimated at about 200ft high.[25] Being stopped on the other side of that extensive ice field with so many large embedded icebergs, it is possible that what was on the other side could easily have been blocked from view. According to Moore, the only ship he saw at that time was the small tramp steamer with a black funnel and two masts that had also stopped on the western side of the ice just a little to the south of him.[26]

Despite the alleged 'greatly incensed' and 'fearfully indignant' officers and others that Baker alluded to, not a one came forward to testify as to what they saw that night. Is it any wonder that Sir Robert Ellis Cunliffe, the Board of Trade's solicitor, concluded, 'If there be anything in these allegations it is a matter for grave comment that those who make them have not hitherto communicated with the Board of Trade.'

Assessment of Actions Taken by Captain Moore

Like Captain Rostron of *Carpathia*, Captain Moore of *Mount Temple* turned his ship around soon after receiving *Titanic*'s initial call for assistance. He said his first order was to put his ship on a heading of N 45° E (045°) and then went to plot a course to the distress coordinates which were revised as soon as the so-called 'corrected' position was received by Durrant. According to Durrant's wireless log, *Mount Temple* was turned for the position at 10.40p.m. NYT, just 5 minutes after receiving the updated coordinates.

Like Captain Rostron had done, Captain Moore took decisive action to effect a rescue. He had all the officers called on deck and got all the crew out and swung out all his boats that were under davits. He had the gangway ready for lowering, had ladders ready to put over the side, and had ready ropes with riggings in the ends to lower.[27] Certainly not the actions of someone who would turn his ship away from another vessel in need.

But Captain Moore was not a reckless individual. He demonstrated his willingness to go to the aid of others, but he was not willing to put his own crew and 1,466 passengers at risk in the process. When ice was encountered at about 3.35a.m., he slowed his ship down and proceeded slowly. When he came up to the pack ice, he prudently stopped his vessel. As soon as it became light enough to see better, he proceeded to search for a safe passage through the ice. He knew by 8.30a.m. that it was hopeless when Durrant picked up a message from *Carpathia* [logged at 6.45a.m. NYT] saying that they had picked up twenty boats. He was assured of being released from his obligation when, at 7.40a.m. NYT [9.26a.m. ATS], he received a wireless message from *Carpathia* saying that there was no need for any vessel to stand by any longer as 'nothing more can be done.'

Captain Moore also recognised that the position sent out by *Titanic* was wrong. He confirmed that by getting his longitude from a Prime Vertical sight of the sun while *Carpathia* was seen to the east across the ice field where she was picking up boats. Yet, at the 1912 inquiries, it was *Carpathia*'s Captain Rostron and *Titanic*'s Joseph Boxhall who they believed when it came to *Titanic*'s foundering position and the given GMT time of her foundering. On both accounts, they were wrong.

We agree that Captain Moore did the best he could under the circumstances. We also agree with the statement he gave to Senator Smith at the American inquiry: 'I assure you that I did everything that was possible, sir, consistent with the safety of my own ship and its passengers.'[28]

Notes

[1]   Durrant, BI 9442.

[2]   It can be shown that on 13 April, *Mount Temple* ATS was 2 hours 8 minutes ahead of NYT. Some time in the forenoon of 14 April, her clocks were set back 22 minutes to account for her westward progress.

[3]   Moore, BI 9299.

[4]   Logbook of *Mount Temple*.

[5]   Clocks on *Mount Temple* were adjusted in the forenoon (AI p.759) each day. Care must be taken to take this adjustment into account when working navigational problems where ship times are given.

[6]   Durrant, BI 9436.

[7]   Moore, AI p.759–60. Moore said the time was about 12.30a.m. on Monday morning, 15 April. But that must have been on a clock that for some unknown reason had not been put back to reflect ATS carried from noon 14 April onward. The correct Apparent Time had to have been a little after 12.11a.m. when the CQD was first received.

[8]   Moore, BI 9266.

[9]   PV *Mount Temple*. Sunrise in the vicinity on 15 April was at 08.41 GMT.

[10] Lord, AI p.733; BI, 6963–71. We know that the first wireless message sent out by Evans was at 3.25a.m. NYT, or 5.15a.m. *Californian* time. Stewart, who also saw the yellow-funnelled steamer, was sent down to Evans several minutes before to wake him up. And from Durrant's wireless log, we know *Mount Temple* was stopped between 3.00a.m. NYT and 3.20a.m. NYT at the western edge of the pack ice when both Lord and Stewart were on the bridge discussing the events seen during the night and about resuming their voyage to Boston.

[11] From an affidavit written by Captain Rostron on 4 June 1912 in NY (see BI 25551.)

[12] In a reply letter he wrote to Captain Lord on 5 September 1912, Captain Rostron stated: 'I'm sorry I cannot give you any detailed description of the two steamers seen by me. All I know – one, a four-masted one-funnel steamer dodging about. I suppose amongst the ice to Nd. [northward]; the other, two masts and one funnel coming from W. to E. straight on his course. I did not see colour of funnels or notice anything which might distinguish either. You can imagine I was quite busy enough.'

[13] Moore, BI 9255.

[14] Moore, BI 9257. There were two steamship companies that appear to match the funnel description given by Captain Moore; one was the Hansa Line, and the other was the Deutsche Levante Line. (Ref: http://www.theshipslist.com/ships/lines/index.htm.) The Board of Trade embarked on a major search to identify this small tramp steamer as well as a small sailing vessel that *Mount Temple* sighted about 3a.m. on her way to the distress position. The primary method used by the BOT was to write to customs authorities in many major North American and Western European ports asking about ships that had cleared customs in the days before the disaster. Eventually the Board's files bulged with documents from both sides of the Atlantic, but neither ship was ever identified. (Ref: PRO MT9/920C, MT9/920D, MT9/920E, MT9/920F, MT9/920H, FO115/710, FO369/522.)

[15] Estimate from Captain Moore was 5–6 miles (AI p.765); estimate from Captain Lord was 5 miles (file No.62908–95. British SS *Californian*. Master, Lord. Received in Branch Hydrographic Office, Boston Mass., 22 April. Received in Hydrographic Office [Washington, DC] 23 April).

[16] According to James Bisset, who was second officer on *Carpathia* at the time, the smoke of a steamer was sighted on the fringe of the pack ice about 10 miles to the northwards after 4.30a.m. At the time, she was not making any signals, and they paid little attention to her because they were preoccupied with more urgent matters. He then goes on to say that they noticed that the steamer was under way about 6a.m. moving slowly in their direction. (James Bisset, *Tramps & Ladies*, Angus & Robertson, 1959, Ch.24.)

[17] Moore, AI p.778–9.

[18] Rostron, BI 25498–5504. *Carpathia* first came to within 2 or 3 miles of the pack ice at about 8a.m.

[19] The sun is on the Prime Vertical in the morning when it is exactly due east True.

[20] The letter, dated 6 August 1912, was written from *Empress of Britain* in Quebec.

[21] It seems that *Mount Temple* was set eastward by several miles, because if we account for when Moore stopped his engine at 3.25, we find that she would be about 14 miles from the CQD position by dead reckoning. Allowing 6 knots between 3.25 and 4.45, we find that *Mount Temple* would still have been about 7 miles short. However, later in the morning, about 6.52a.m., it was found that the

western side of the pack ice not far from where *Mount Temple* had previously stopped was 3 miles further east of the CQD longitude line. This suggests that *Mount Temple* was set more eastward than what her position by dead reckoning alone would show. The same effect appears to have happened to *Carpathia*, which fortunately allowed her to stumble upon *Titanic's* lifeboats while heading for an erroneous position.

[22] We assume that *Mount Temple* was making about 11.5 knots till 3.25a.m. and then slowed to an average of about 6 knots after that until she came to a stop by the edge of the heavy ice. For *Carpathia*, we assume she averaged about 13 knots between 3.15 to 4.00 to cover about 10 miles considering she had to manoeuvre around an iceberg as well as slow down before coming close to Boxhall's boat.

[23] PV *Mount Temple*.

[24] The height of eye on *Mount Temple's* bridge was about 50ft (AI, p.765). Taking the height of a hand-held flare from the boat to be 6½ft, we get a maximum range of 11.3 miles.

[25] Moore, AI p.765.

[26] As previously pointed out, the identity of that small tramp steamer was never found out, but it played no part in what was seen from *Titanic*. Later in the morning, it was seen from *Californian* coming up behind *Mount Temple* when *Californian* came down and passed *Mount Temple* on the western side of the pack ice. *Californian's* third officer, Charles Groves, testified that this tramp steamer had a black funnel (BI 8350), in agreement with what Captain Moore said. Captain Lord was to later claim that this small steamer was the Leyland Liner *Almerian* with two masts and a pink funnel. We suggest that on the morning of 15 April Captain Lord noticed a two-masted ship near *Mount Temple*, but took little notice of it, as he was searching for a way through the icefield that separated him from *Carpathia*. On his arrival in England, a sympathiser gave him this *Almerian* story, and Lord then decided that the two-masted ship he saw must have been that vessel. For a full account of the *Almerian* story, as well as other vessels reported near the scene on 15 April, see Dave Gittins' e-book, *Titanic: Monument and Warning*, 2005.

[27] Moore, AI p.768.

[28] Moore, AI. p 785.

This is widely believed to be the iceberg that *Titanic* struck. Three separate survivors described the fatal berg as 'something like the Rock of Gibraltar'. The photograph was taken on 20 April 1912 in the vicinity of floating wreckage and bodies by Stephan Rehorek, a seaman aboard the German liner *Bremen*, en route to New York. (Period Picture Card/Günter Bäbler)

Titanic's Commander Edward John Smith was born at Hanley, Stoke-on-Trent, on 27 January 1850. He joined the White Star Line in March 1880 as the Fourth Officer of the SS *Celtic*. He went on to become one of the WSL's most experienced and popular commanders. (*Illustrated London News*/Hall & Klistorner)

In this photograph of *Carpathia*'s forecastle deck can be seen three of *Titanic*'s recovered lifeboats. In the foreground is seen lifeboat No.9, immediately behind is an unidentified 30ft lifeboat and beyond that, emergency cutter No.1. (*Harper's Weekly*/Beveridge & Hall)

Here on the starboard side, the forecastle deck is crowded with male survivors; for most, a time of reflection. Many can be seen here staring vaguely out to sea. In the foreground is *Titanic*'s emergency cutter No.2. Two unidentified 30ft lifeboats can be seen behind. (*Harper's Weekly*/Beveridge & Hall)

The Cunard Line rescue ship *Carpathia*. This 13,600-ton vessel entered passenger service in 1903 and maintained a regular transatlantic service. On 17 July 1918, while serving as a troop transport ship, she was torpedoed and sunk by *U-55*. (Period Picture Card/George Behe Collection)

Captain Arthur Rostron with his officers aboard *Carpathia* while in New York. In 1928 Rostron was made Commodore of the Cunard fleet. He retired in 1931. To Rostron's right is Second Officer James Bisset who later went on to commanded both the *Queen Mary* and *Queen Elizabeth* during the Second World War. Years later, Bisset was appointed Commodore of the Cunard White Star Line. (Library of Congress Archive)

Carpathia recovered thirteen of *Titanic*'s twenty lifeboats. Numbers 1, 2. 3, 5, 6, 7, 8, 9, 10, 11, 12, 13 and 16. All boats' contents were later assessed by the C.M. Lane Lifeboat Company of Brooklyn, New York. On 13 May, the WSL *Oceanic* recovered collapsible A. (*The Sphere*/Beveridge & Hall)

Carpathia stopped outside the entrance to Pier 59 and dropped off *Titanic*'s thirteen lifeboats. They were then taken in tow by the Merritt & Chapman tug *Champion*. In the days proceeding, many of the lifeboats' TITANIC name plaques were removed by souvenir hunters. (Ioannis Georgiou Collection)

Twelve of *Titanic*'s lifeboats seen arranged in a row. Later, they were hoisted up to a second-floor loft between White Star Line Piers 58 and 59. It is believed they remained there until at least December 1912. No documented details remain of their eventual fate. (Hall & Klistorner)

United States Senate Investigating Committee questioning individuals at the Waldorf-Astoria in New York. The first two days of hearings took place in New York. Most of the remainder were held in Washington, with the exception of several further days in the Waldorf-Astoria and a visit to *Olympic* on 25 May. (Library of Congress Archive)

SS *Californian* was a 6,223-ton Leyland Line steamship. In November 1915 she was torpedoed and sunk by the German submarine *U-35*. Captain Stanley Lord was given command of the SS *Californian* in 1911. (Top left and right: Milner Maritime/Lower: Library of Congress Archive)

SS *Mount Temple* was a 8,790 GRT, twin-screw Canadian Pacific Railway Company steamship. In April 1912 she was under the command of Captain James Henry Moore. On 6 December 1916 she was captured and sunk by the German surface raider SMS *Moewe*. (Top and lower right: Charles Haas/lower left: Milner Maritime)

12

THE AFTERMATH OF THE DISASTER

Mark Chirnside and Dave Gittins

Effect of the Disaster on Modifications Made to *Olympic* and *Britannic* – *Mark Chirnside*

When the summer season came to an end in 1912, *Olympic* returned to the Belfast shipyard for her annual overhaul and an extensive refit. Although improvements were made to her passenger accommodation, the most important changes related to her watertight subdivision. These changes had been incorporated into the design of yard number 433, *Britannic*, which was still under construction. In May 1915, Harland & Wolff's naval architect, Edward Wilding, gave testimony at the limitation of liability hearings. He explained the purpose of these changes:

> After the accident to the *Titanic*, certain alterations were decided on, with a view to increasing the margin of safety. We had arranged prior to that, as I told the Court this morning, for any two compartments flooded. The owners desired, in view of the character of the accident, to see that she would float with a large number of compartments flooded; and to do that we carried up certain of the bulkheads to a greater height.

Olympic had experienced a number of poor passenger lists, which showed passenger numbers sharply down from prior to the disaster, although there were signs of recovery as the months wore on. The company would use the improvements to the two surviving ships' watertight subdivision in their advertising. When *Olympic* returned to service, the company described the improvements in detail and touted her safety features. In 1914 a descriptive pamphlet to mark *Britannic*'s launch dwelt heavily on her safety. It is difficult to assess what direct impact these advertisements had on the travelling public, however it is clear that *Olympic*'s popularity continued to recover in 1913 and 1914.

The changes involved:

• Raising five watertight bulkheads to the underside of B deck and increasing their stiffening so that it was commensurate with their greater height

• Several watertight bulkheads that originally extended watertight to the underside of D deck were effectively reduced in height and were now watertight only to E deck

• A new transverse watertight bulkhead was installed, dividing the electric engine room into two main compartments

• The cargo hatches and entrances at the fore and aft well decks saw their watertight integrity improved

• A watertight deck was fitted in the first forward hold

• An inner skin was fitted which extended the length of the boiler and machinery compartments, accounting for the majority of the ship's length

By raising the five watertight bulkheads, the ship could withstand the flooding of as many as six consecutive watertight compartments. 'She is divided into groups of six and she would float with any one of those groups flooded,' Edward Wilding testified:

> On looking at the plan, to the best of my recollection, the bulkheads which were extended to B deck were as follows: F bulkhead, which provided for the flotation of the ship with the six foremost compartments flooded; D and J, which provided for flotation with the six compartments containing the boilers, all flooded; bulkhead L to the bridge deck, which with bulkhead F provided for flotation with the four after boiler rooms, and two engine rooms, making six compartments, flooded; P bulkhead, which with J bulkhead and the new bulkhead extending to D deck provided for flotation with the two engine rooms and four compartments abaft it flooded.

In the first scenario, with the six foremost compartments flooded, over 300ft of the ship would have been open to the sea, accounting for about 35 per cent of her length between perpendiculars. The fact that the new arrangements allowed her to theoretically float with such a large proportion of her length flooded is perhaps ample proof of the lengths that Harland & Wolff went to in order to improve the margin of safety.[1]

The improvements to the watertight integrity of the fore and aft cargo hatches and entrances were important, in the sense that if the ship's first six compartments were completely flooded then it would cause the bow to sink so far that the fore well deck would be submerged.

When the subject of adding additional watertight decks was discussed, Wilding objected because of his well-founded fears that they could contribute to a loss of stability and the ship 'turning turtle'. He acquiesced to the additional watertight deck in a single hold, which was close to the bow. It was a small compartment that had little effect on the ship as a whole, but the watertight deck could prevent water rising in that particular compartment if the ship was damaged below the waterline only.

The inner skin's purpose was to protect the boiler and machinery spaces, as far as possible, from flooding if the ship's outer plating was damaged along the side. It was placed 30in from the ship's side, or the depth of the original web frames, and consisted of 'heavy plating, well stiffened . . . and being strongly connected by longitudinal plates and angles and specially strong connections at bulkheads and watertight divisions.' It was a considerable engineering achievement, as the description published by the *Marine Engineer and Naval Architect* in May 1913 made clear:

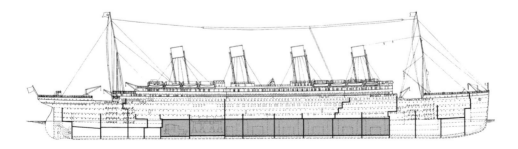

Fig. 12-1 Bulkhead arrangement for *Olympic* following her 1913 refit. The grey shaded area denotes the location of the inner skin. (Mark Chirnside Collection)

The wing boilers had to be removed to leave room for the riveters and platers to work at the inner shell, and to enable one of the boilers to be taken out of the ship the forward funnel and uptakes were temporarily removed. The auxiliary machine [*sic*] in the engine room and turbine room had also to be removed, and the ship's side valves and fittings, some of these valves weighing upwards of a ton. Consequently, the ship was entirely dismantled for the time being, which, of course, entailed a considerable amount of alteration to the pipes and fittings generally throughout the ship and the withdrawal of all the auxiliaries along the ship's sides, including their seats and fittings, whilst the placing of them further in involved additional labour. It may be mentioned also that as a further safeguard an extra line of piping of large diameter has been fitted, running right through the ship, enabling all the pumps to draw through this piping in case of emergency, so that any compartment can be pumped out by any of the bilge or ballast pumps, which are so arranged that in case of the valves being inaccessible through any contingency they can be operated from the upper deck.

There have been some suggestions that the purpose of the inner skin was to prevent panting of the ship's sides, and to strengthen the hull because of concerns that it was not already strong enough. One recent author, for example, wrote: 'The subsequent fitting of *Olympic* and *Britannic* with full double hulls was not for protection from puncture by icebergs but to stiffen the ship.'[2] These suggestions are baseless.

The structural design of the inner skin is, in fact, well documented. It is clear that its addition to the ship would have had very little or no effect whatsoever in preventing panting of the ship's sides or strengthening the hull. Although amply strong for its intended purpose of protecting the ship's interior from external flooding, there were few connections between the frames of the inner skin and the frames of the shell plating.[3]

It is also important to note that the shipbuilders 'made as few transverse connections as possible between the inner skin and outer shell' thereby 'effectively divorcing the inner skin from the shell for much of its length.' The reason was both logical and simple: if a raking collision forced shell plating and framing inwards, then a solid connection between them and the inner skin would simply result in the inner skin itself being pushed in and forced out of place: 'The net result would be sprung seams and sheared rivets on both the outer shell and inner skin, basically negating any protection the inner skin was supposed to provide to the ship in a raking collision.'[4]

The advantage of the inner skin was demonstrated by an incident that *Olympic* experienced in 1918.[5] While she was engaged as a troopship, a torpedo slammed into her port side amidships, between 10 and 20ft below the waterline. In this area, the hull plating was an inch thick and the seams quadruple riveted with steel rivets, but the unexploded torpedo's impact caused, in Captain Hayes' words: 'a dinge on her hull about eighteen inches or so in diameter, with a crack about six inches

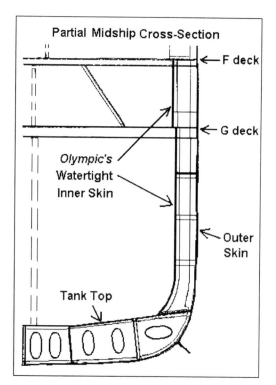

Fig. 12-2 *Olympic's* watertight inner skin.

long, in the centre of it.' The inner skin had never been intended to protect *Olympic* from enemy weapons in a war zone, but it protected the boiler rooms from flooding through the damage in the ship's side. In fact, the damage and subsequent flooding of this portion of the inner skin went undetected until she was dry-docked in February 1919. It would have been a different story had the torpedo exploded. Nonetheless, Edward Wilding had no doubt that if *Titanic* had been similarly equipped then she would not have gone down; such an inner skin would have prevented the complete flooding of the forward boiler rooms. It would not have protected them in the event of a much deeper wound, but then the transverse watertight bulkheads would have been the next line of defence.

Before the end of 1912, the shipbuilding firm of Harland & Wolff considered the possibility that *Olympic* and *Britannic*, as relatively new ships with over twenty years service ahead of them, would be converted to burn oil fuel later in their service lives, as did Cunard while their *Aquitania* was being built. They bore this in mind when designing the inner skin and, when *Olympic* was converted after the war, their foresight proved invaluable: the inner skin was utilised as oil fuel storage. One of Wilding's concerns, expressed after the *Titanic* disaster, was that the interior space between an inner skin and the outer hull might be hard to maintain and subject to corrosion. The storage of oil helped overcome that objection.

People intimately connected with the shipbuilding project, Edward Wilding of Harland & Wolff and Harold Sanderson of the White Star Line, stated publicly and, perhaps more importantly, in private that the intention with these modifications had been to increase the ship's powers of flotation. It is known that the cost of these changes to *Olympic* was some £156,000. While this may seem, to some, a large amount to spend, it is important to consider the context. In September 1908, the company's entire fleet was valued at £4,850,000 and they mortgaged it to help finance their ambitious construction of the *Olympic* class ships, including a bond issue of £1,250,000 in October 1908 and a further £1,500,000 in July 1914. In 1911, the company logged a profit of £1,073,752; in 1912, it fell to £885,332; and in 1913 it rose to a then record £1,080,918. It was important that they secured a worthwhile and continuing return on their investment. (By the time *Britannic* was completed, in cash terms the company had spent more on the three mammoth liners than their entire fleet had been worth when construction began.) *Olympic* had proved very popular in 1911, but the following year saw her average passenger lists lower than at any time until 1922, when the post-war immigration restrictions reduced third class travel to the United States.

Another change seen on *Olympic* and *Britannic* was the provision of an indicator on the bridge which showed whether the watertight doors were closed. It was a recommendation that had been made originally by *Olympic*'s chief engineer, Joseph Bell, following her maiden voyage, but it had not been fitted to *Titanic*. Provision was also made for the wireless operators to be able to communicate with the officers on the bridge without leaving their station, by means of another pneumatic tube. If all of these

Fig. 12-3 Advertisement for the 'New *Olympic*' in *Harper's Magazine*, 1913. (Mark Chirnside Collection)

modifications restored public confidence in *Olympic* and *Britannic*, the two largest ships in the company's fleet and the key to their prestigious express service, then it was surely a worthwhile investment.

The International Convention on the Safety of Life at Sea (SOLAS) – Dave Gittins

As a direct result of the *Titanic* disaster, the first International Convention on the Safety of Life at Sea (SOLAS) assembled in London on 12 November 1913. Its value was limited by the absence of many seagoing nations. It was essentially a gathering of the main users of the North Atlantic. The United States and Canada were the only nations of the western hemisphere present. Great Britain and the other major European liner-operating nations attended. Australia and New Zealand, both maritime minnows, were the only participants from more distant regions.[6]

Several men closely connected with the *Titanic* affair were present. From his place in the Chair, Lord Mersey saw before him the familiar faces of Sir Norman Hill, Sir John Biles, Captain Alfred Young and William Archer. Representative Joshua Alexander, Senator Theodore Burton and George Uhler were among the US delegates. The ghost of *Titanic* hovered near, and the convention felt her influence.

Opportunity was taken to make minor improvements to several international marine regulations. Article 14 of the convention strictly forbade the use of company night signals that might be confused with distress signals, reinforcing rules already enforced by individual nations. It also required all powered vessels more than 50 metres long to carry two steaming lights, thus reducing the chance of a large liner being taken for a small tramp steamer. A fixed stern light was made compulsory. Searchlights were recommended, not for detecting icebergs or other obstructions, but for use in rescue operations, as is still the practice.

Fig. 12-4 Remotely controlled searchlight on bridge of *Amsterdam*.
(Photo by Dave Gittins)

The introduction of uniform modernised steering orders was proposed. In a suggestion that would have dismayed Frederick Fleet, it was recommended that lookouts should *not* be provided with binoculars.

Article 10 was directly inspired by Lord Mersey's report on *Titanic*, and remains his most lasting legacy:

> When ice is reported on, or near, his course, the master of every ship is bound to proceed at a moderate speed, or to alter his course so as to go well clear of the danger zone.

Measures intended to increase the value of wireless communication at sea had already been taken by the International Radiotelegraphic Convention, held in London in 1912. Standards had been set for operators and penalties provided for those who breached operating regulations. The influence of the wireless manufacturers was reduced by divorcing the call signs used by ships from the make of wireless apparatus they carried. Henceforth the call signs would indicate the nations in which ships were registered. Operators were required to transmit all communications without discrimination. It was made clear that wireless operators were at all times under the control of their ship's master. Communication between the wireless room and the bridge by telephone or speaking tube became mandatory.

Because of the confusion created by amateur wireless operators on the morning of the *Titanic* disaster, strict regulations were imposed upon amateur wireless operators. With a few minor exemptions, amateur stations were restricted to outputs of less than 1-kW and wavelengths of less than 200 metres. Ironically, the frequencies thus imposed proved to be very suitable for long-distance communications and enthusiastic 'hams' were soon exchanging messages worldwide.[7]

The SOLAS convention sought to improve the likelihood of distress signals being heard, but it fell well short of requiring a continuous watch on the distress frequency by all ships. Its proposals were complex, but in broad terms all ocean-going ships engaged in international voyages, and having more than fifty persons on board, were required to maintain a continuous wireless service. Many freighters did not fall into this class, because of their small crews. These were required to maintain a continuous watch for at least 7 hours per day and to listen for signals for 10 minutes at the start of every second hour. To give concrete examples, *Carpathia* and *Mount Temple* were now required to employ at least two fully trained operators. As long as she continued to carry no passengers, *Californian* could meet the rules by carrying only one first class operator, plus an assistant capable of recognising important messages, such as distress signals. Exemptions granted to fishing vessels and ships operating inshore further limited the value of wireless, in spite of the fact that many emergencies occur inshore and in the fishing industry.

Article 34 provided that, in the event of an automatic signal detecting alarm being devised, ships carrying fewer than fifty persons could carry only one operator, while relying on the alarm outside normal working hours. In practice, this measure came into use, and continued until the last years of the twentieth century. Its value was shown in 1956, when the small freighter *Cape Ann* was summoned to the aid of the sinking *Andrea Doria* by an automatic alarm that woke her slumbering operator.

Articles 29 and 30 of the SOLAS convention required member nations to cooperate in developing improved methods of subdivision and attached regulations proposed details. None were as drastic as the changes made to *Titanic*'s sisters, which had more the air of panic measures than of practical shipbuilding. Among the proposals was a double bottom extending up the sides of the hull to a height above the top of the keel equal to one tenth of the ship's moulded beam. An extreme proposal required a ship of *Titanic*'s size to remain afloat with her bow flooded for a length equal to 28 per cent of her length (roughly to the after end of boiler room 6). Detailed standards were proposed for hatches, watertight doors and other fittings. Longitudinal bulkheads, so beloved by some theorists, were not specifically called for. Modern regulations permit them only under stringent conditions. The stability of a partly flooded ship must not be compromised by longitudinal bulkheads that restrict the transverse flow of water.[8]

To further ensure structural integrity, Articles XXIV and XXV prescribed periodic surveys of ships during construction, while in service and after accidents.

The organisation that became the International Ice Patrol had already begun operations. It owed its existence to neither of the *Titanic* inquiries but to motions introduced to the United States Congress by Joshua Alexander, chairman of the House Committee on the Merchant Marine and Fisheries, and Representative Jefferson Levy on 17 April 1912.[9] By 24 May, USS *Birmingham* was in the ice region and a continuous watch for ice was maintained until 6 July, with USS *Chester* providing relief.

The convention gave the Ice Patrol international support and defined its duties. Its tasks included the detection and destruction of derelicts, scientific studies of ice and the reporting of ice likely to endanger shipping. Article 7 required nations using the ice regions to pay for its operations according to the volume of their shipping. Consequently, 75 per cent of the cost fell on France, Germany, Great Britain and the United States.

Extraordinarily, the following regulation was much later added to Regulation 6 of SOLAS, with effect from 1 July 2002:

> Ships transiting the region of icebergs guarded by the Ice Patrol during the ice season are required to make use of the services provided by the Ice Patrol.

This rather belated rule is only partly concerned with increasing safety. Its main intention is to collect charges from ships carrying the flags of nations not contributing to the cost of the International Ice Patrol. On arrival in Canada or the United States, they are billed according to tonnage. The measure was necessitated by the huge increase in the number of ships flying flags of convenience.

The *Titanic* disaster is popularly reputed to have led to regulations requiring ships to carry lifeboats sufficient to hold all on board. However, this is more legend than fact. As Harold Sanderson and Sir Alfred Chalmers had pointed out, the provision of 'boats for all' was often impractical, given the technology of the period. The problem was particularly acute in the case of emigrant ships, which frequently carried more than 2,000 passengers in hulls less than

Fig. 12-5 Joshua Alexander (left) and Jefferson Levy. (Library of Congress Archive)

600ft long. Unless the number of passengers on such ships were to be greatly restricted, thus raising fares beyond the reach of many emigrants, a compromise would be necessary. This was recognised by Article 40 of the SOLAS Convention, which set out what it termed the 'Fundamental Principles':

> At no moment of its voyage may a ship have on board a total number of persons greater than that for whom accommodation is provided in the lifeboats and pontoon life rafts on board. The number and arrangement of the boats, and (where they are allowed) of the pontoon rafts, on a ship depends on the total number of persons which the ship is intended to carry; provided that there shall not be required on any voyage a total capacity in boats and (where they are allowed) pontoon-rafts, greater than that necessary to accommodate all the persons on board.

This principle was modified by Article XLII of the proposed regulations, and therein lies a tale.

ARTICLE XLII.
Additional boats and Pontoon Rafts.
If the lifeboats attached to davits do not provide sufficient accommodation for all the persons on board, additional lifeboats of one of the standard types shall be provided. This addition shall bring the total capacity of the boats on the ship at least up to the greater of the two following amounts:-
(*a*) The minimum capacity required by these regulations;
(*b*) A capacity sufficient to accommodate *seventy-five per cent* [author's emphasis] of the persons on board.
The remainder of the accommodation required shall be provided either in boats of Class 1 or Class 2, or in pontoon rafts of an approved type.

The proposed new lifeboat requirements were based on the length of the ship, measured between perpendiculars. This measurement provided a better idea of a ship's *boat*-carrying capacity than did Gross Registered Tonnage but, in the case of the crammed emigrant ships, it was still unrelated to *passenger*-carrying capacity. In many cases, 'boats for all' would prove quite impractical. Even on the largest ships, boat arrangements would remain subject to the old problem of lowering two or more boats from a single pair of davits.

If lifeboats and rafts were to be of use, there would have to be crews capable of using them. The convention recognised the need to train many members of ships' crews, whether seamen or not, in lifeboat work. Article 54 required the participating nations to issue certificates to persons qualified by training in lifeboat operation. Article 56 required crews to be informed of their emergency stations and duties before sailing. Article XLVII prescribed the number of certificated lifeboat crew to be carried. Interestingly, the scale envisaged lifeboats holding up to 210 persons, which exceeds the normal modern limit of 150. The number of motor lifeboats permitted was left to national authorities. Equipment for lifeboats was prescribed, and all such equipment was required to be stowed in the boats at all times.

The Convention included pledges of international cooperation on maritime safety, with the British Government providing a clearing-house for the exchange of new proposals and news of new safety devices. When the plenipotentiaries signed the Articles and Regulations on 20 January 1914, a new age of improved safety at sea appeared to be at hand. The first SOLAS Convention would come into force on 1 July 1915, and would be reviewed in 1920.

Among the lesser casualties of the First World War was the 1914 SOLAS Convention, which was never ratified by the governments of the participating nations. Ironically, the war removed some of the problems inherent in the Convention, for many of the most problematic emigrant ships were sunk, including *Carpathia*, *Mount Temple* and *President Lincoln*.

During the 1920s, elements of the 1914 Convention were implemented piecemeal by individual nations. Formal training in lifeboat operation was instituted and 'boats or rafts for all' became the norm, albeit with no real improvement in the boats or their launching equipment.

Fig. 12-6 Modern lifeboat test. *Rhapsody of the Seas.* (Photo by Dave Gittins)

In 1929, London was the scene of a new SOLAS convention, under the chairmanship of Butler Aspinall, an eminent maritime lawyer who had represented White Star at the British *Titanic* inquiry.[10] Eighteen nations participated. On 31 May 1929, they agreed to measures similar to those of 1914, with the addition of regulations to reduce the dangers of fires at sea. True to form, national governments took time to ratify the convention. The last to do so was the United States, in 1936. In the years before the Second World War, the search for marine safety paid much attention to fire prevention and control, particularly after the very public end of *Morro Castle*, which was destroyed by fire in full view of the New Jersey shore in 1934.

The 1948 convention, which came into force on 19 November 1952, formalised the new fire protection measures. To clarify the minds of future Herbert Stones, it introduced a new definition of pyrotechnic distress signals. Henceforth, they would consist of 'Rockets or shells, throwing *red* [author's emphasis] stars fired one at a time at short intervals.'

Conventions in 1960 and 1974 made further advances. Among their achievements was the abolition of the practice of carrying more than one boat under a set of davits. A factor in this decision was the loss of *Dara*, which burnt out and sank off Dubai in 1961. More than 200 lives were lost, party because of the failings of her doubled-up lifeboats.

By this time, shipping was changing very rapidly. Passenger liners were now only a minor part of the world's fleet. Attention turned towards the many kinds of specialised freighters, many of which were of unprecedented size, culminating in the monstrous 564,763 dwt *Seawise Giant*. Their cargoes were frequently potentially dangerous to life, property and the environment. Ferries, once humble small vessels plying sheltered water, were now large ships, carrying hundreds of passengers and vehicles, sometimes on the open ocean. SOLAS even covers nuclear-powered merchant ships, though these remain almost unknown. Because of the rapidity of change and the slowness of government reactions, the 1974 convention decided to introduce a process of 'tacit acceptance' of new regulations. The Intergovernmental Maritime Consultative Organisation (now the International Maritime Organisation), a United Nations agency, was authorised to make new regulations as new problems arose. The parties to SOLAS were deemed to have accepted them, if no objection was raised within a fixed time.

Under this regime, various improvements to marine safety have been made, most notably the introduction of the Global Maritime Distress and Safety System. This combines radio and satellite technology to enable distress signals to provide the precise position of the casualty and its identity. Another system provides bridge officers with the identity, position and course of every ship in their vicinity. The bridge of a large modern ship contains numerous colourful screens displaying information *Titanic's* officers could only wish for.

Fig. 12-7 Adapted from SOLAS
regulations.

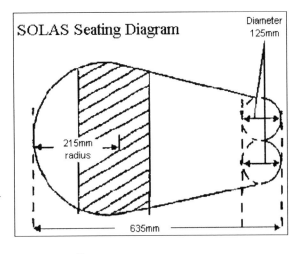

For all the innovations, some things remain little changed since the first SOLAS convention. Double hull shells, so beloved by armchair admirals, are used only on specialised freighters, notably modern oil tankers. For most ships, SOLAS requires only that the top plating of a double bottom 'shall be continued out to the ship's side in such a manner as to protect the turn of the bilge'. This applies to passenger ships and freighters.[11]

Lifeboats are now powered and enclosed, but 'grandfather' clauses in the regulations permit old boats to be used and some remarkably primitive lifeboats are still to be seen, generally on freighters.

The capacity of lifeboats is now determined by allocating seating according to a diagram (see Fig. 12-7) depicting an overhead view of a standardised passenger. This is more realistic than the methods of 1912, but a 150-seat lifeboat is still far from a comfortable pleasure boat.

The total capacity of lifeboats required has changed little since 1913. It is permissible for a passenger ship to carry lifeboats sufficient for only 75 per cent of those on board.[12] These must be supplemented by approved life rafts sufficient for 25 per cent of those on board, served by 'launching appliances' [small cranes], plus additional life rafts sufficient for 25 per cent, which are not required to have their own launching appliances. Because the number of lifeboats

Fig. 12-8 Life rafts under davits on *Amsterdam*. (Photo by Dave Gittins)

carried by modern cruise ships is limited by the ship's length, it is common for boats sufficient to hold only the ship's passengers, plus the necessary crew, to be carried. The bulk of the crew must trust in life rafts.[13]

As can be seen, the *Titanic* disaster definitely produced extensive changes to maritime safety regulations. However, their implementation was piecemeal. Dangerous practices, such as carrying more than one boat per pair of davits, continued well into the twentieth century. 'Grandfather' clauses in the regulations allow obsolete equipment to be used to the present day and open lifeboats, very similar to those used by *Titanic*, except for their GRP construction, may still be bought and used on older ships. As with other aspects of the *Titanic* story, there is a wide gap between the legend and the reality.[14]

Notes

[1] It is interesting to note that the original design, which would have enabled the ship to float with the first four watertight compartments flooded, accounted for nearly 200ft of the ship. The modifications therefore increased the ship's capacity to withstand such flooding from about 23 per cent of her length between perpendiculars to about 35 per cent.

[2] Brad Matsen, *Titanic's Last Secrets*, Twelve, 2008, p.304.

[3] The existing deep web frames, which were already connected to the shell frames and already very heavily stiffened by double-angle face bars and tied to the side keelsons (stringers) by full or half-diamond gussets, though also attached to the inner skin, would have received very little additional reinforcement from the 0.44 to 0.56in plates of the inner skin. In short, for most of its length, the inner skin was a free-standing structure inboard of the shell plates that was only rigidly connected to the fabric of the hull at the tank top, the underside of F deck, and at the side keelsons. There was only occasional vertical transverse connection to the shell plating in areas that were already more than sufficiently strong to resist panting, both due to the heavy nature of scantling of the frames and plates, and because of the heavy beams and knees connecting one side of the shell to the other.

[4] Information from Scott Andrews, October 2007.

[5] For further information about this incident, see the article by Mark Chirnside, 'Target *Olympic: Feuer!*' Titanic Historical Society journal *The Titanic Commutator*, No.184, 2008. It appears that the torpedo was fired at *Olympic* in September 1918.

[6] Records of the convention are in the House of Commons parliamentary papers 1914, volume LXX.

[7] US Dept of Commerce and Labor. Regulations Governing Radio Communication. September 1912. Regulations for Radio Apparatus and Operators on Steamers. July 1913.

[8] Unsymmetrical flooding is to be kept to a minimum consistent with efficient arrangements. Where it is necessary to correct large angles of heel, the means adopted shall, where practicable, be self-acting, but in any case, where controls to cross-flooding fittings are provided they shall be operable from above the bulkhead deck. These fittings together with their controls shall be acceptable to the Administration. The maximum angle of heel after flooding but before equalisation shall not exceed 15°. Where cross-flooding fittings are required the time for equalisation shall not exceed 15 min. Suitable information concerning the use of cross-flooding fittings shall be supplied to the master of the ship. SOLAS Regulations, Part B, Regulation 8, Section 5.

[9] *The New York Herald*, 18 April 1912.

[10] Information on SOLAS changes after 1914 provided by the National Ocean Service International Program Office and the United States Coast Guard via the internet.

[11] SOLAS Regulation 12, Part 2. Regulation 12-1, Part 2.

[12] The normal maximum capacity of a lifeboat is 150. A loophole in the regulations has permitted *Oasis of the Seas* and her sister to use boats with a capacity of 370.

[13] SOLAS Regulation 20.

[14] For more on the deficiencies of modern shipping, consult the detention lists put online by safety authorities in Britain, the United States, Australia and other advanced nations.

CHRONOLOGY OF EVENTS WITH REFERENCES AND NOTES

Samuel Halpern

This chronology reflects the order of events pertaining to the maiden voyage of *Titanic*. It is primarily based upon evidence that comes from survivor accounts as given in sworn testimony, affidavits, letters and other credible sources. The sources for the events included in this chronology are listed alongside each set grouped under a specified time. There is also a set of notes that explain how certain event times were derived, or offer additional pertinent information. In some cases, reference is made to specific articles and other publications where more details and in-depth explanations can be found. For most of the wireless messages shown, reliance was heavily placed on primary sources such as wireless logs or wireless station office forms that are available, rather than using some previously compiled list.

In all cases, we have tried to insure the relative accuracy of event sequences. However, the accuracy of event times themselves cannot be guaranteed. The reader must understand that actual clock times were only known for a relatively few events where someone took the time off of a clock or a watch. Even for the times associated with wireless messages, where messages were recorded using a standard time reference such as mean time for New York or Greenwich Mean Time (GMT), we find variances in the reported times put down by different operators describing the same communication. Some of this may have been caused by small inaccuracies in the clocks being used. In many cases, a time given was simply rounded to the nearest 5-minute interval. For example, if an event took place at precisely 11.43, you may find some people saying that it happened at 11.40 while others may say it happened at 11.45. And we find that this was true for times put down in many of the wireless logs where time was taken off of a nearby clock. In many situations, we have people guessing as to the time some event took place, or how long it was since the collision or some other event happened. And here we can only rely on what they said, or try and correlate their time estimate with the time of some other event or what others had to say.

The other difficulty arises from the fact that ships at sea did not carry the same time. They each carried what is called Apparent Time Ship (ATS) which was based on the ship's noontime longitude, or expected noontime longitude, for a given day. It was rare indeed for two ships to have been keeping the exact same time unless they happened to have crossed the same meridian when the sun reached its highest point in the sky. In this chronology, we use New York Time (NYT) as the standard time reference for all events because most of the wireless messages presented in evidence were recorded for ships that were west of the 40°W meridian, and the times put down in their wireless logs, called a *procès-verbal*, were recorded in NYT. To get to GMT, the reader simply has to add 5 hours.

We also show time as it would have appeared on *Titanic*'s wheelhouse clock. This was referred to in the IMM Co. rule book as 'bridge time' and was the time that was kept in the wheelhouse on the bridge, down in the engine rooms, and in crew spaces in the forecastle. It was the time that controlled when ship's bells were struck. For the most part, clocks in passenger places such as the main staircases, the lounges, reception rooms, saloons, libraries, and other public areas, would also show the same time as in the wheelhouse except between the hours of midnight and 4a.m. The reason for this is that the wheelhouse and engine room clocks served the needs of the deck and engine department crew who stood regular watches, and those watch sections had to share extra time imposed each night because of the nightly clock adjustments that were made as the ship travelled westward on her voyage. Those adjustments were made on a master clock in the chart room in two separate steps every night, one at midnight and the other at 4a.m., while clocks in passenger areas, controlled off of a second master clock in the chart room, were adjusted only once per night near midnight. It has been noted that a number of passengers happened to stay up late each night in the smoking rooms waiting for the midnight clock adjustment to take place so that they could set their personal timepieces accurately to the new time.

The level of detail presented in this chronology varies. The greatest level of detail is given beginning with 14 April through the morning hours of 15 April. More event details and additional references can be found in other sections of this book, or in the listed references and notes provided in this chronology.

In the interest of saving space, several abbreviations are used throughout this chronology such as: AB=Able-Bodied Seaman; ATS=Apparent Time Ship; BR=Boiler Room; C/E=Chief Engineer; 2/E=Second Engineer, etc.; C/O=Chief Officer, 1/O=First Officer, etc.; DR=Dead Reckoning; ETA=Expected Time of Arrival; MSG=Master Service Gram; OOW=Officer of the Watch; PV=*Procès-Verbal*; QM=Quartermaster; TR=Time Rush; WSL=White Star Line; WTB=Watertight Bulkhead; WTD=Watertight Door, etc. We also list the three-letter wireless call signs of the individual wireless stations, both ship and shore, that were involved.

Date & Time (NYT)	Titanic Bridge Time	Event	References	N
10 Apr 3.30a.m.	8.30a.m.	Deck crew mustered on the boat deck for a Board of Trade inspection. Two boats (nos 13 and 15) were manned and lowered on the starboard side, each with an officer, a QM, and 6 ABs. 5/O Lowe was in charge of one, and 6/O Moody was in charge of the other. This was the only boat drill that was conducted on *Titanic*.	Lowe, AI p.376; Scarrott, BI 503–505; Jewell, BI 248; Pitman, AI p.263.	1
10 Apr 7.15a.m.	12.15p.m.	12.15p.m. GMT. *Titanic* departs Southampton's Ocean Dock berth 44 to start her maiden voyage. She had 5,892 tons of coal on board, and 206,800 gallons of fresh water in seven tanks. Her first port of call was Cherbourg, but she was delayed about an hour because of a near mishap involving the steamer *New York* after she left the pier. Once under control, *Titanic* proceeded down Southampton Water to the Solent, and then to the Nab light vessel where she dropped off the pilot and took departure for the cross–Channel voyage to Cherbourg.	Pitman, AI p.261; BI App. Reports by BOT Officers; *The New York Times*, 'Titanic in Peril Upon Leaving Port', 11 Apr.	2
10 Apr 1.30p.m.	6.30p.m.	*Titanic* arrives at Cherbourg about 20 minutes before sunset. The 66-nautical-mile trip across the English Channel, from the Nab light vessel to the entrance to Cherbourg harbour, was made at 68rpm on her reciprocating engines; about 20.2 knots.	Eaton & Hass, *Titanic Triumph & Tragedy*, p.93; Ismay, AI p.3; http://www.titanicology.com/Titanica/SpeedAndRevolutions.htm.	
10 Apr 3.10p.m.	8.10p.m.	After taking on passengers and mails via the WSL steam tenders *Nomadic* and *Traffic*, *Titanic* departs Cherbourg for the overnight trip to Queenstown, her second port of call. Trip to Queenstown was made at 70rpm on her reciprocating engines; about 20.7 knots.	Eaton & Hass, *Titanic Triumph & Tragedy*, p.94; Ismay, AI p.3; http://www.titanicology.com/Titanica/SpeedAndRevolutions.htm.	
10 Apr 7.00p.m.	12.00a.m. 11.35p.m.	Clocks set back by 25 minutes from GMT to Dublin Mean Time.	See Chapter 5.	3
11 Apr 6.55a.m.	11.30a.m.	Time approximate. *Titanic* anchors 2 miles off Roche's Point outside Queenstown harbour to take on more passengers and mails. She was serviced by two WSL tenders, *Ireland* and *America*.	Behe, *On Board RMS Titanic*, letter by Margaretha Frolicher-Stehli (10a.m. 11 Apr), p.99, and letter by Edwina Troutt (11 Apr), p.109; Eaton & Hass, *Titanic Triumph & Tragedy*, p.102; Ismay, AI p.3.	
11 Apr 8.55a.m.	1.30p.m.	*Titanic* weighs her starboard anchor and turns a quarter circle and departs to the southward toward the Daunt's Rock light vessel (situated 4¾ miles due south of Roche's Point Light) to drop off the pilot and begin her maiden transatlantic crossing.	Beesley, *The Loss of the SS Titanic*, Ch. 2; Eaton & Hass, *Titanic Triumph & Tragedy*, p.101; British Islands Pilot Vol 3, 1917.	4
11 Apr 9.20a.m.	1.55p.m.	2.20p.m. GMT. *Titanic* takes departure off Daunt's Rock light vessel located at 51° 43'N, 8° 16'W outside Queenstown harbour. 'All ahead full' is ordered, and the ship works up to 70rpm on her reciprocating engines, 20.7 knots through the water, with twenty out of twenty-four double-ended boilers connected up. Her heading was about S45°W True to make a point south of the Old Head of Kinsale.	Halpern, 'Keeping Track of a Maiden Voyage', http://www.titanicology.com/WorkingThenUp.htm; http://www.titanicology.com/Titanica/SpeedAndRevolutions.htm.	
11 Apr 10.01a.m.	2.36p.m.	Alter-course point near 51° 33' N, 8° 32' W; about 3 miles off the Old Head of Kinsale. Course altered to about S76°W True for Fastnet light.	Halpern, 'Keeping Track of a Maiden Voyage'.	5

11 Apr 12.00p.m.	4.35p.m.	Off Fastnet light located at 51° 23' N, 9° 36' W. Course altered to about S80°W True. Proceeding on first rhumb line segment of great circle route to corner at 42° N, 47° W.	Halpern, 'Keeping Track of a Maiden Voyage'.	6
11 Apr 7.25p.m.	12.00a.m. / 11.31p.m.	Clocks keeping bridge time set back to 11.31p.m. extending the length of the first watch by 29 minutes. Clocks in public places set back to 11.01p.m.. Ship will now be keeping Apparent Time.	Pitman, AI p.294; http://www.titanicology.com/WatchTablesFile.htm.	7
11 Apr 11.54p.m.	4.00a.m. / 3.30a.m.	Clocks keeping bridge time set back to 3.30a.m. extending the length of the middle watch by 30 minutes. All clocks on board now back in sync.	http://www.titanicology.com/WatchTablesFile.htm.	8
12 Apr 4.24a.m.	8.00a.m.	Time estimated. Ship running at 72rpm on reciprocating engines making 21.2 knots through the water. Additional boiler lighted in boiler room No.2.	http://www.titanicology.com/WorkingThenUp.htm.	
12 Apr 8.24a.m.	12.00p.m.	Local Apparent Noon 12 Apr 1912 – Approx. location 50° 06' N, 20° 43' W. First day's run posted at 484 miles. Average speed for first day's run over 23h 4m was 20.98 knots. Proceeding on Great Circle route to the corner carrying about 72–3rpm on her reciprocating engines.	Halpern, 'Keeping Track of a Maiden Voyage'; http://www.titanicology.com/WorkingThenUp.htm.	
12 Apr 2.00p.m.	5.36p.m.	7.00p.m. GMT. Titanic's position 49° 45' N, 23° 38' W. Course heading about S69°W True.	See 2.45p.m. NYT message to La Touraine.	
12 Apr 2.10p.m.	5.46p.m.	Wireless message from La Touraine (MLT) to Titanic (MGY): 'To Capt. "Titanic". My position 7p.m. GMT lat. 49.28 long. 26.28 W. dense fog since this night crossed thick ice-field lat. 44.58 long. 50.40 "Paris" saw another ice-field and two icebergs lat. 45.20 long. 45.09 "Paris" saw a derelict lat. 40.56 long. 68.38 "Paris" please give me your position best regards and bon voyage. Caussin'	Turnbull, BI 16056–61.	
12 Apr 2.45p.m.	6.21p.m.	Wireless message sent from Titanic (MGY) to La Touraine (MLT): 'To Capt. "La Touraine", Thanks for your message and information my position. 7p.m. GMT Lat. 49.45; long. 23.38. W. Greenwich; had fine weather; compliments. – Smith'	Turnbull, BI 16065.	
12 Apr 3.24p.m.	7.00p.m.	Time approximate. Additional boiler connected up in boiler room No.2. Ship now running with twenty-one double-ended boilers on line.	http://www.titanicology.com/WorkingThenUp.htm.	
12 Apr 8.24p.m.	12.00a.m. / 11.36p.m.	Clocks keeping bridge time set back to 11.36p.m. extending length of the first watch by 24 minutes. Clocks in public places set back by 49 minutes to 11.11p.m..	http://www.titanicology.com/WatchTablesFile.htm.	
13 Apr 12.48a.m.	4.00a.m. / 3.35a.m.	Clocks keeping bridge time set back to 3.35a.m. extending length of the middle watch by 25 minutes. All clocks on board now back in sync.	http://www.titanicology.com/WatchTablesFile.htm.	
13 Apr 9.13a.m.	12.00p.m.	Local Apparent Noon 13 Apr 1912 – Approx. location 47° 22' N, 33° 10' W. Second day's run posted at 519 miles. Average speed over 24h 49m was 20.91 knots. Second day's run described by second class Purser Reginald Barker as somewhat of a disappointment. Titanic proceeding on great circle route to the corner. Heading changed to about S62°W True. Engineers call for 75 revolutions. Ship now running at 75 to 76rpm; about 22.0 to 22.2 knots through the water.	Halpern, 'Keeping Track of a Maiden Voyage'; Beesley, The Loss of the SS Titanic; http://www.titanicology.com/WorkingThenUp.htm.	

13 Apr 10.43a.m.	1.30p.m.	First class passenger Elisabeth Lines stops for coffee in the first class reception room. Soon Bruce Ismay and Capt. Smith arrive and sit down nearby to talk about the day's run. Mrs Lines overhears Ismay tell Smith 'We will beat the *Olympic* and get into New York on Tuesday.'	Chirnside and Halpern, 'Speed and More Speed'.	
13 Apr 5.13p.m.	8.00p.m.	Senior Marconi Operator Jack Phillips takes the first of a 6-hour night watch in the Marconi office. Junior Marconi Operator Harold Bride goes off duty to get some sleep.	Bride, BI 16333.	
13 Apr 8.13p.m.	11.00p.m.	*Titanic's* wireless transmitter starts to give trouble as a short develops in the secondary winding of a transformer. Bride called out of bed to help Phillips troubleshoot and repair the set.	Bride, BI 16790–1; Letter from Bride to W.R. Cross of Marconi Co. 27 Apr 1912.	9
13 Apr 9.13p.m.	12.00a.m.	Clocks keeping bridge time set back to 11.37p.m. extending length of the first watch by 23 minutes.	http://www.titanicology.com/WatchTablesFile.htm.	10
13 Apr 9.13p.m.	11.37p.m.	Clocks in public places set back by 45 minutes to 11.15p.m.		
13 Apr 9.36p.m.	12.00a.m.	**8-bells – Midnight change of watch.** 4/O Boxhall and 6/O Moody replace 3/O Pitman and 5/O Lowe. QMs Robert Hichens, Alfred Olliver and George Rowe replace QMs Arthur Bright, Walter Wynn and Walter Perkis. Lookouts Alfred Evans and George Hogg replace lookouts Frederick Fleet and Reginald Lee. Senior 2nd Engineer William Farquharson along with Senior Assistant 2nd Engineer Bertie Wilson take up watch in the engine and boiler rooms replacing Junior 2nd Engineer John Hesketh and Junior Assistant 2nd Engineer Jonathan Shepherd.	Halpern, 'Mystery of Time – Part 1'; http://www.titanicology.com/WatchTablesFile.htm.	
13 Apr 10.06p.m.	12.30a.m.	1-bell.	http://www.titanicology.com/WatchTablesFile.htm.	
13 Apr 10.36p.m.	1.00a.m.	2-bells.	http://www.titanicology.com/WatchTablesFile.htm.	
13 Apr 11.06p.m.	1.30a.m.	3-bells.	http://www.titanicology.com/WatchTablesFile.htm.	
13 Apr 11.36p.m.	2.00a.m.	**4-bells** – C/O Henry Wilde replaces 1/O William Murdoch as OOW. Lookouts Archie Jewell and George Symons replace lookouts Evans and Hogg. Normal time for Jack Phillips to go off duty, but because of repairs to the secondary winding of the transformer, Phillips stays on working with Bride. *Titanic* is now close to passing 40°W longitude near 45°N latitude. All wireless messages beyond this point would be logged in NY mean time in accordance with Marconi Company practice, but *Titanic's* transmitter is still under repair.	Halpern, 'Mystery of Time – Part 1'; Bride: BI 16334; Halpern, 'Keeping Track of a Maiden Voyage' (track chart); http://www.titanicology.com/WatchTablesFile.htm.	11
14 Apr 12.06a.m.	2.30a.m.	5-bells.	http://www.titanicology.com/WatchTablesFile.htm.	
14 Apr 12.36a.m.	3.00a.m.	6-bells.	http://www.titanicology.com/WatchTablesFile.htm.	
14 Apr 1.06a.m.	3.30a.m.	7-bells.	http://www.titanicology.com/WatchTablesFile.htm.	
14 Apr 1.36a.m.	4.00a.m.	Wheelhouse clock set back 22 minutes from 4.00 to 3.38 at this time extending length of middle watch	http://www.titanicology.com/WatchTablesFile.htm.	
	3.38a.m.	by 22 minutes. All clocks on board are now back in sync.		

Date	Time	Event	Reference	
14 Apr 1.58a.m.	4.00a.m.	**8-bells – Morning watch begins.** 3/O Herbert Pitman and 5/O Harold Lowe replace 4/O Joseph Boxhall and 6/O James Moody. QMs Bright, Wynn and Perkis replace QMs Hichens, Olliver and Rowe. Lookouts Frederick Fleet and Reginald Lee replace lookouts Archie Jewell and George Symons. Junior 2nd Engineer Norman Harrison along with Junior Assistant 2nd Engineer Herbert Harvey take up watch in the engine and boiler rooms replacing Farquharson and Wilson.	Halpern, 'Mystery of Time – Part 1'; http://www. titanicology.com/WatchTablesFile.htm.	
14 Apr 2.28a.m.	4.30a.m.	1-bell.	http://www.titanicology.com/WatchTablesFile.htm.	12
14 Apr 2.58a.m.	5.00a.m.	2-bells. Repair of the transformer in *Titanic*'s wireless transmitter completed by Phillips and Bride. All wireless messages will now be logged in NY mean time (NYT) instead of GMT.	Bride, BI 16790–1; Letter from Bride to W.R. Cross of Marconi Co. 27 Apr 1912; http://www. titanicology.com/WatchTablesFile.htm.	
14 Apr 3.28a.m.	5.30a.m.	3-bells.	http://www.titanicology.com/WatchTablesFile.htm.	
14 Apr 3.58a.m.	6.00a.m.	**4-bells.** 2/O Charles Lightoller replaces C/O Wilde as OOW. Lookouts Evans and Hogg replace lookouts Frederick Fleet and Reginald Lee. Ballast and fresh water tanks sounded by carpenter in accordance with IMM rules.	Halpern, 'Mystery of Time – Part 1'; http://www. titanicology.com/WatchTablesFile.htm; IMM Co. Rule 26.	
14 Apr 4.28a.m.	6.30a.m.	5-bells.	http://www.titanicology.com/WatchTablesFile.htm.	
14 Apr 4.58a.m.	7.00a.m.	6-bells.	http://www.titanicology.com/WatchTablesFile.htm.	
14 Apr 5.18a.m.	7.20a.m.	7-bells. Oncoming forenoon watch takes breakfast.	http://www.titanicology.com/WatchTablesFile.htm.	13
14 Apr 5.58a.m.	8.00a.m.	**8-bells – Forenoon watch begins.** 4/O Boxhall and 6/O Moody replace 3/O Pitman and 5/O Lowe. QMs Hichens, Olliver and Rowe replace QMs Bright, Wynn, and Perkis. Lookouts Jewell and Symons replace lookouts Evans and Hogg. Junior 2nd Engineer John Hesketh along with Junior Assistant 2nd Engineer Jonathan Shepherd take up watch in the engine and boiler rooms replacing Harrison and Harvey. Three remaining double-ended boilers lit up in BR No.2. Breakfast begins for passengers. Bars are opened.	Halpern, 'Mystery of Time – Part 1'; Barrett, BI 2224 & BI 2232; http://www.titanicology.com/ WatchTablesFile.htm; WSL Information for Passengers.	
14 Apr 6.28a.m.	8.30a.m.	1-bell.	http://www.titanicology.com/WatchTablesFile.htm.	
14 Apr 6.58a.m.	9.00a.m.	2-bells.	http://www.titanicology.com/WatchTablesFile.htm.	
14 Apr 7.10a.m.	9.12a.m.	*Caronia* (MRA) sends message to *Titanic* (MGY): 'Captain, "Titanic". West-bound steamers report bergs, growlers, and field ice in 42° N., from 49 to 51 W. April 12. Compliments. Barr.'	Turnbull, BI 16097–9.	
14 Apr 7.28a.m.	9.30a.m.	3-bells.	http://www.titanicology.com/WatchTablesFile.htm.	
14 Apr 7.50a.m.	9.52a.m.	9.40a.m. *Californian* ATS. ETA at the corner. Capt. Lord changes heading to N60°W by compass. *Californian*'s actual position at this time is approximately 42° 05' N, 47° 00' W.	http://www.titanicology.com/Californian/ Navigational_Incosistencies.pdf	
14 Apr 7.58a.m.	10.00a.m.	**4-bells -** 1/O William Murdoch replaces 2/O Charles Lightoller as OOW. Lookouts Fleet and Lee replace lookouts Jewell and Symons. Breakfast time ends for passengers.	Halpern, 'Mystery of Time – Part 1'; http://www. titanicology.com/WatchTablesFile.htm; WSL Information for Passengers.	

Date/Time	Time	Event	Reference	No.
14 Apr 8.05a.m.	10.07a.m.	*Californian* ATS. Ship's heading changed to N59°W by compass.	http://www.titanicology.com/Californian/Navigational_Incosistencies.pdf	
14 Apr 8.26a.m.	10.28a.m.	*Titanic* (MGY) sends message to *Caronia* (MRA): 'Thanks for message and information. Have had variable weather throughout – Smith.'	Booth and Coughlan, *Titanic - Signals of Disaster.*	14
14 Apr 8.28a.m.	10.30a.m.	5-bells. Divine Service conducted by Capt. Smith in first class saloon.	http://www.titanicology.com/WatchTablesFile.htm; WSL Information for Passengers.	
14 Apr 8.58a.m.	11.00a.m.	6-bells.	http://www.titanicology.com/WatchTablesFile.htm.	15
14 Apr 9.18a.m.	11.20a.m.	7-bells. Oncoming Afternoon Watch takes lunch.	http://www.titanicology.com/WatchTablesFile.htm.	
14 Apr 9.45a.m.	11.47a.m.	Message received from Capt. Krol of SS *Noordam* (MHA) to *Titanic* (MGY) by way of *Caronia* (MRA), 'Captain SS Titanic. Congratulations on new command. Had moderate westerly winds, fair weather, no fog. Much ice reported in lat. 42° 24' to 42° 45' [N] and long. 49° 50' to 50° 20' [W]. Compliments. Krol.'	Booth and Coughlan, *Titanic - Signals of Disaster.*	16
14 Apr 9.58a.m.	12.00p.m.	**Local Apparent Noon 14 Apr 1912** – Estimated noon position 43° 01.8' N, 44° 31.5' W. Third day's run 546 miles. Average speed for third day's run over 24h 45m was 22.06 knots. Revolutions kept at 75–6rpm on reciprocating engines. Course changed to S85°W on steering compass. Course to the corner S 60° 33.5' W True. ETA at corner set for 5.50p.m. **8-bells – Afternoon Watch begins.** 3/O Pitman and 5/O Lowe replace 4/O Boxhall and 6/O Moody. QMs Bright, Wynn and Perkis replace QMs Hichens, Olliver and Rowe. Lookouts Evans and Hogg replace lookouts Fleet and Lee. Senior 2/E William Farquharson alcng with Senior Assistant 2/E Bertie Wilson take up watch in the engine and boiler rooms replacing Hesketh and Shepherd.	Halpern: 'Keeping Track of a Maiden Voyage'; http://www.titanicology.com/WorkingThenUp.htm; Halpern: "'Mystery of Time – Part 1"; Halpern: "It's A CQD OM"	
14 Apr 10.10a.m.	12.12p.m.	12.00 *Californian* ATS. Her noon position recorded in her logbook showed 42° 05' N, 47° 25' W. Lord changes heading to N61°W by compass to head down for 42° N, 51° W to avoid reported ice. Based on a sustained speed of almost 11 knots all morning and afternoon, her true noontime longitude may really have been 47° 34' W, or 25 miles west of the corner longitude.	Lord. AI p.715, BI 6782 & 7115; Stewart, BI 8712–14; Lord's 1959 affidavit; http://www.titanicology.com/Californian/Navigational_Incosistencies.pdf.	17
14 Apr 10.14a.m.	12.16p.m.	12.00p.m. *Mount Temple* ATS. Her reported noon position is 41° 38' N, 48° 20' W. Ship heading down to 41° 15' N, 50° 00' W to avoid ice. She is averaging almost 11 knots.	Capt. Moore. AI p.783; PV *Mount Temple.*	
14 Apr 10.28a.m.	12.30p.m.	1-bell. 2/O Lightoller takes over as OOW temporarily allowing 1/O Murdoch to take lunch.	Lightoller, BI 13449.	
14 Apr 10.29a.m.	12.31p.m.	Captain Smith acknowledges receipt of ice warning from Capt. Krol of *Noordam* (MHA): "Captain *Noordam*. Many thanks. Had moderate variable weather throughout. Compliments. Smith.' Message received by *Caronia* (MRA) and forwarded to *Noordam.*	Booth and Coughlan, *Titanic – Signals of Disaster.*	
14 Apr 10.43a.m.	12.45p.m.	Capt. Smith shows *Caronia* ice message to 2/O Lightoller.	Lightoller, BI 13466.	
14 Apr 10.58a.m.	1.00p.m.	2-bells. 1/O Murdoch returns from lunch and assumes the OOW position. Luncheon for passengers begins.	Lightoller, BI 13449; WSL Information for Passengers.	

14 Apr 11.28a.m.	1.30p.m.	3-bells.	http://www.titanicology.com/WatchTablesFile.htm.
14 Apr 11.47a.m.	1.49p.m.	Message received from *Amerika* (DDR) to *Titanic* (MGY), 'To the steamer "Titanic" M.S.G. via Cape Race to the Hydrographic Office, Washington. D S "Amerika" passed two large icebergs 41 deg. 27 min. N., 50 deg. 8 min. W., on the 14th April.– Knuth.'	Turnbull, BI 16130.
14 Apr 11.52a.m.	1.54p.m.	*Baltic* (MBC) sends message to *Titanic* (MGY): 'Captain Smith, "Titanic". Have had moderate variable winds and clear fine weather since leaving. Greek steamer "Athenai" reports passing icebergs and large quantities of field ice today in lat. 41° 51' N., long. 49° 52' W. Last night we spoke German oil-tank steamer "Deutschland", Stettin to Philadelphia, not under control, short of coal. lat. 40° 42' N. long. 55° 11' W. Wishes to be reported to New York and other steamers. Wish you and "Titanic" all success. – Commander.' Capt. Smith would later give this message to Bruce Ismay, who in turn, would show it to several passengers before Capt. Smith asked for it back.	Turnbull, BI 16176; Chirnside and Halpern, 'Speed and More Speed'.
14 Apr 11.58a.m.	2.00p.m.	**4-bells.** C/O Wilde replaces 1/O Murdoch as OOW. Lookouts Jewell and Symons replace lookouts Evans and Hogg.	Halpern, 'Mystery of Time – Part 1'
14 Apr 12.28p.m.	2.30p.m.	5-bells.	http://www.titanicology.com/WatchTablesFile.htm.
14 Apr 12.55p.m.	2.57p.m.	*Titanic* (MGY) sends message to *Baltic* (MBC): 'Thanks for your message and good wishes; had fine weather since leaving. – Smith.'	Turnbull, BI 16178.
14 Apr 12.58p.m.	3.00p.m.	6-bells. Fireman John Thompson sees 2/E Farquharson chalk up 77 revolutions. If accurate, *Titanic* would be making about 22.3 knots through the water at this time.	Interview articles written in *New Haven Evening Register*, 22 April 1912, and the *New York American*, 22 April 1912.
14 Apr 1.28p.m.	3.30p.m.	7-bells.	http://www.titanicology.com/WatchTablesFile.htm.
14 Apr 1.58p.m.	4.00p.m.	**8-bells change of watch. First Dog Watch begins.** 4/O Boxhall and 6/O Moody replace 3/O Pitman and 5/O Lowe. QMs Hichens, Olliver and Rowe replace QMs Bright, Wynn and Perkis. QM Rowe takes the wheel. Lookouts Fleet and Lee replace lookouts Jewell and Symons. Junior 2/E Norman Harrison along with Junior Assistant 2/E Herbert Harvey take up watch in the engine and boiler rooms replacing Farquharson and Wilson.	Halpern, 'Mystery of Time – Part 1'
14 Apr 2.28p.m.	4.30p.m.	1-bell.	http://www.titanicology.com/WatchTablesFile.htm.
14 Apr 2.58p.m.	5.00p.m.	2-bells.	http://www.titanicology.com/WatchTablesFile.htm.
14 Apr 3.28p.m.	5.30p.m.	3-bells.	http://www.titanicology.com/WatchTablesFile.htm.
14 Apr 3.48p.m.	5.50p.m.	*Titanic*'s course altered from S85°W to N71°W by steering compass intending to make 265° True to the Nantucket Shoals light vessel. QM Rowe at the helm. *Titanic* would have been about 3 miles past the corner point if she continued to make the same speed made good as she had from noon 13 April to noon 14 April.	Halpern, 'It's a CQD OM'.

18

14 Apr 3.58p.m.	6.00p.m.	**4-bells change of watch. Second Dog Watch begins.** 3/O Pitman and 5/O Lowe replace 4/O Boxhall and 6/O Moody. QMs Bright, Wynn and Perkis replace QMs Hichens, Olliver and Rowe. QM Bright takes the wheel from Rowe. Lookouts Evans and Hogg replace lookouts Fleet and Lee. 2/O Lightoller replaces C/O Wilde as OOW. Ballast and fresh water tanks sounded by carpenter. Bruce Ismay shows the ice warning from *Baltic*, given to him earlier by Capt. Smith, to Mrs Emily Ryerson who was with Mrs Marian Thayer sitting near the companionway on A deck.	Halpern, 'Mystery of Time – Part 1': IMM Co. Rule 24; Chirnside and Halpern, 'Speed and More Speed'.	19
14 Apr 4.28p.m.	6.30p.m.	1-bell.	http://www.titanicology.com/WatchTablesFile.htm.	
14 Apr 4.40p.m.	6.42p.m.	6.30p.m. *Californian* ATS. Ship's DR position at 42° 03' N, 49° 09' W. Three large icebergs sighted 5 miles to their south.	See entry for 5.35p.m. NYT.	
14 Apr 4.58p.m.	7.00p.m.	2-bells. 1/O Murdoch takes over as OOW temporarily allowing 2/O Lightoller to have some dinner. The double-ended boilers that were lit in the morning in BR 2 are now put on line. Dinner for passengers begins.	Lightoller, BI 13587; Deposition of Alfred Shiers 1915 Limitation of Liability Hearings; WSL Information for Passengers.	20
14 Apr 5.10p.m.	7.12p.m.	*Carpathia* (MPA) exchanges TRs with *Titanic* (MGY) and receives one passenger message from *Titanic*.	PV *Carpathia*; Cottam, BI 17067.	21
14 Apr 5.13p.m.	7.15p.m.	1/O Murdoch tells lamp-trimmer Samuel Hemming: 'Hemming, when you go forward see the fore-scuttle hatch closed, as we are in the vicinity of ice, and there is a glow coming from that, and I want everything dark before the bridge.'	Hemming, BI 17705.	
14 Apr 5.20p.m.	7.22p.m.	*Titanic* (MGY) and *Californian* (MWL) exchange contact information. From the PV of the *Californian*: '5.20p.m. New York time, exchanged TRs M.G.Y. nil'.	Turnbull, BI 16192.	
14 Apr 5.26p.m.	7.28p.m.	7.12p.m. *Mount Temple* ATS. Capt. Moore changes his ship's course to 281° True for Cape Sable. Her DR location at this time is 41° 15' N, 50° 00' W.	Capt. Moore, AI p.783.	
14 Apr 5.28p.m.	7.30p.m.	3-bells. 2/O Lightoller returns from dinner and 1/O Murdoch tells him the temperature dropped another 4°. Lightoller goes out on bridge wing to take a set of star sights assisted by 3/O Pitman who will take the time of each sight.	Lightoller, BI 13578; Pitman, AI pp.272–3.	
14 Apr 5.30p.m.	7.32p.m.	Signal exchanged between *Carpathia* (MPA) and *Titanic* (MGY).	Cottam, BI 17067.	
14 Apr 5.35p.m.	7.37p.m.	*Titanic* (MGY) intercepts MSG message from *Californian* (MWL) to *Antillian* (MJL): 'To Captain "Antillian", 6.30p.m. Apparent Time, Ship: lat. 42° 3' N., long. 49° 9' W. Three large bergs five miles to southward of us. Regards. Lord'	Turnbull, BI 16197.	
14 Apr 5.38p.m.	7.40p.m.	Star sights completed. 3/O Pitman begins the sight reduction process.	Pitman, AI pp.272–3.	

Date/Time	Time	Event	Source	Page
14 Apr 5.58p.m.	8.00p.m.	**8-bells change of watch. First watch begins.** 4/O Boxhall and 6/O Moody replace 3/O Pitman and 5/O Lowe. Lookouts Jewell and Symons replace lookouts Evans and Hogg up in the nest. QM Rowe goes onto the after-bridge. QM Olliver takes the helm while QM Hichens takes the standby QM position. Junior 2/E John Hesketh along with Junior Assistant 2/E Jonathan Shepherd take up watch in the engine and boiler rooms replacing Harrison and Harvey. Upon seeing Boxhall enter the chart room, Pitman handed him the set of sights and said, 'Here is a bunch of sights for you, old man. Go ahead.' Ship's position for 8.00p.m. (worked up by 5/O Lowe) and entered in the Night Orders book.	Halpern, 'Mystery of Time – Part 1'; http://www.titanicology.com/WatchTablesFile.htm; Pitman, AI p.275; Lowe, AI p.383; IMM Co. Rule 114.	22
14 Apr 6.28p.m.	8.30p.m.	1-bell.	http://www.titanicology.com/WatchTablesFile.htm.	
14 Apr 6.53p.m.	8.55p.m.	Capt. Smith comes onto the bridge and starts a conversation with 2/O Lightoller concerning weather and seeing conditions.	Lightoller, BI 13615.	
14 Apr 6.58p.m.	9.00p.m.	2-bells.	http://www.titanicology.com/WatchTablesFile.htm.	
14 Apr 7.23p.m.	9.25p.m.	Capt. Smith to 2/O Lightoller: 'If it becomes at all doubtful let me know at once; I will be just inside.' Capt. Smith leaves the bridge to go inside to his quarters.	Lightoller, BI 13635-6.	23
14 Apr 7.28p.m.	9.30p.m.	3-bells. 2/O Lightoller tells 6/O Moody to ring up the crow's nest and tell the lookouts to keep a sharp look out for ice, particularly small ice and growlers. QM Hichens told to find the carpenter and tell him to look after the fresh water as it might freeze.	Lightoller, BI 13658 & BI 13671; Poingdestre, BI 2812–15; http://www.titanicology.com/WatchTablesFile.htm.	
14 Apr 7.30p.m.	9.32p.m.	Titanic (MGY) to Cape Race (MCE) from Amerika (DDR), 'Hydrographic Office, Washington. Amerika passed two large icebergs in 41.27N, 50.8W on the 14th of April. Knuth.'	Booth and Coughlan, Titanic - Signals of Disaster.	
14 Apr 7.43p.m.	9.45p.m.	QM Hichens calls upon 1/O Murdoch informing him it is 'one bell' (a quarter to 10) and he is due on deck in 15 minutes.	Hichens, AI p.450.	24
14 Apr 7.50p.m.	9.52p.m.	Wireless message transmitted from Mesaba (MMV) to Titanic (MGY) and all east-bound ships. 'Ice report in latitude 42 N. to 41° 25' N., longitude 49 W. to longitude 50° 30'W. Saw much heavy pack ice, and great number large icebergs. Also field ice. Weather good, clear.'	Solicitor-General, BI 15735.	
14 Apr 7.58p.m.	10.00p.m.	**4-bells.** 1/O Murdoch replaces 2/O Lightoller as OOW. Lookouts Fleet and Lee replace lookouts Jewell and Symons up in the nest. QM Hichens takes the wheel replacing QM Olliver having just taken the log reading by phone from QM Rowe on the afterbridge. Olliver takes the QM standby position. Ship travelled 45 nautical miles through the water since 8p.m., averaging 22.5 knots. Passenger Henry Stengel notices 'the engines were running faster than at any other time during the trip.'	Halpern, 'Mystery of Time – Part 1'; Hichens, BI 965; Stengel, AI p.971; http://www.titanicology.com/WatchTablesFile.htm.	
14 Apr 8.28p.m.	10.30p.m.	5-bells.	http://www.titanicology.com/WatchTablesFile.htm.	

Date	Time	Event	Source	No.
14 Apr 8.31p.m.	10.33p.m.	*Californian* ATS. Ship forced to stop because of a field of pack ice directly in her path. Derived DR position was 42° 02′ N, 50° 07′W, 17 miles from *Titanic's* corrected CQD position as later given.	Lord, BI 6702–4 and AI p.717; See also Chapter 10 of this Report.	
14 Apr 8.58p.m.	11.00p.m.	6-bells. Lights in the saloons are extinguished.	http://www.titanicology.com/WatchTablesFile.htm; WSL Information for Passengers.	
14 Apr 9.05p.m.	11.07p.m.	Wireless operator Evans on *Californian* sends wireless message to *Titanic*: 'MGY this is MWL. We are stopped and surrounded by ice.' Phillips on *Titanic* was busy working Cape Race (MCE) at the time, and told Evans to 'Keep out' [DDD].	Evans, BI 8990.	
14 Apr 9.13p.m.	11.15p.m.	Passenger Lawrence Beesley climbs into his top berth to read and where he 'noticed particularly the increased vibration of the ship.'	Beesley, *The Loss of the SS Titanic*.	
14 Apr 9.28p.m.	11.30p.m.	7-bells. Lights in the lounges are extinguished. Passenger Edith Rosenbaum, in the Reading & Writing room on A deck, is told 'Lights out, it is 11:30' by a steward. She takes two books and walks ahead to her cabin A-11 forward, turns on the light and prepares to turn in.	http://www.titanicology.com/WatchTablesFile.htm; WSL Information for Passengers; Edith Russell's 1934 account.	25
14 Apr 9.37p.m.	11.39p.m.	QM Hichens: 'All went along very well until [about] 20 minutes to 12, when three gongs came from the lookout, and immediately afterwards a report on the telephone, "Iceberg right ahead." … He [Mr Murdoch] rushed to the engines. I heard the telegraph bell ring; also give the order "Hard-a-starboard".' Upon hearing the lookout bells, QM Olliver leaves the compass platform for the bridge. Barrett in BR 6 hears the boiler room telegraph bell ring and sees the red light come on the illuminated telegraph indicating 'STOP' just moments before the collision. He and 2/E Hesketh call out to 'shut the dampers'. Ship's head starts to swing over to port as the tiller is now hard over to starboard.	Hichens, AI p.450; Fleet, BI 17280–1; Olliver, AI p.526; Barrett, BI 1860–6.	26
14 Apr 9.38p.m.	11.40p.m.	**Collision with iceberg.** Location approximately at 41° 45.5′ N, 49° 55′ W; Boxhall abreast captain's quarters walking toward bridge. QM Olliver steps onto bridge and sees 1/O Murdoch at the WTD switch. He also sees the peak of the iceberg pass the bridge and hears Murdoch call 'Hard-a-port'. 4/O Boxhall steps onto bridge in time to see Murdoch still about the WTD switch. Leading Fireman Barrett sees water pouring in 2ft above the stokehold plates in BR 6. No.10 stokehold, and jumps through the WTD into BR 5 with 2/E Hesketh just seconds before it closed. He then notices water coming into the empty starboard side forward bunker of BR 5. Coal falls all around trimmer George Cavell in the aft bunker of BR 4, and immediately he starts to dig himself out. QM Rowe reads the taffrail log out on the poop. It shows the ship travelled 260 nautical miles through the water since noon, averaging 22.29 knots.	Halpern, 'Collision Point'; Boxhall, AI p.228; QM Olliver, AI pp.526–37; Boxhall, AI pp.229–31; Barrett, BI 1868 & 1917; Cavell, BI 4201–3; Rowe, AI p.523.	27
14 Apr 9.39p.m.	11.41p.m.	Capt. Smith comes through the wheelhouse onto the bridge and asks Murdoch 'What have we struck?' Murdoch replies, 'An iceberg, Sir.' Smith tells him to close the WTDs. Murdoch says, 'They are already closed, Sir.' Boxhall, Murdoch and Smith step out briefly onto the starboard bridge wing to look for the berg as the ship's head is now swinging to starboard with the tiller hard over to port.	Boxhall, AI pp.229–31; Hichens, AI p.450; Olliver, AI p.531.	

				28			29

Date	Time	Description	Sources
14 Apr 9.40p.m.	11.42p.m.	4/O Boxhall drops down to inspect forward passenger spaces. 2/O Lightoller notices that the ship's engines have stopped and decides to get out of his cabin to investigate. Beesley notices engines have stopped and decides to go up the second class staircase to the boat deck to investigate. Greaser Thomas Ranger notices changeover valves in turbine room had come up indicating the turbine engine had stopped. AB Scarrott sees iceberg off starboard quarter as ship's stern is pulling away as ship is seen turning to port. Trimmer Dillon down in the engine room notices that the ship's engines had stopped and then soon started to reverse. Lamp Trimmer Hemming hears hissing sound as air escapes from forepeak tank. On *Californian*, 3/O Groves drops down to talk to Capt. Lord about an approaching 'passenger steamer coming up on us' from abaft their starboard beam.	Boxhall, BI 15573; Lightoller, BI 13743, AI. p.60; Beesley, *The Loss of the SS Titanic*; Ranger, BI 4002; Scarrott, BI 355–6; Dillon, BI 3716–29; Hemming, BI 17716; Groves, BI 8169–72.
14 Apr 9.41p.m.	11.43p.m.	After seeing Capt. Smith put the engine telegraphs to 'stop' and then what appeared to be 'half speed ahead', standby QM Olliver was told to go down and find the carpenter and tell him 'to go and take the draft of the water'. Trimmer Dillon sees the ship's engines start to go ahead slowly. Henry Stengel notices that the ship's engines appear to be moving again, but was not sure why.	QM Olliver, AI pp.526–37; Dillon, BI 3716–29; Stengel, AI p.975.
14 Apr 9.42p.m.	11.45p.m.	Fireman Shiers, having seen the iceberg off the starboard quarter disappearing into the night, now notices the ship was still moving but not by much. Sees ice on the well deck. Lightoller sees 1/O Murdoch looking out on port bridge wing, and also notices that the ship was moving only 4–6 knots through the water. He then decides to cross to the other side where he sees Smith looking out on the starboard bridge wing. Hemming discovers peak tank flooding fast from air hissing out of vent pipe, but soon finds out that the forepeak tank was dry. Boatswain's Mate Haines: 'Just as I got there the chief officer, Mr Wilde, had gotten there, and the lamp trimmer was there, Mr Hemming, We said the forepeak tank was filling; the air was coming out and the water was coming in.' Many of the crew see ice on the forward well deck after coming up from below including Leading Fireman Hendrickson who, like Shiers, said he got a glimpse of the iceberg. Lightoller meets Pitman after returning to his cabin.	Shiers, BI 4532–47; Lightoller, BI 13753–61 and AI. p.60; Hemming, BI 17716 & 17724; Haines, AI pp.655–7; Poingdestre, BI 2799–804 & BI 2821–5; Hendrickson, BI 4842–51.
14 Apr 9.44p.m.	11.46p.m.	Engines put on 'stop' for the last time after ship moved further away from the iceberg which had disappeared off the starboard quarter. Ismay finds Smith on bridge, asks him what happened, and is told that the ship struck ice and may be damaged seriously.	Dillon, BI 3716–29; Ismay, BI 18505–14.
14 Apr 9.45p.m.	11.47p.m.	*Virginian* (MGN) standing by as 'Cape Race (MCE) working continuously with *Titanic* (MGY).' Last signal exchanged between *Carpathia* (MPA) and *Titanic* (MGY) prior to distress message going out. Phillips did not know what happened to *Titanic* at this point in time other than some mishap took place. Bride was to later tell Senator Smith 'that he [Phillips] thought she had got damaged in some way and that he expected that we should have to go back to Harland & Wolff's.' Hendrickson decides the collision was nothing serious and goes back down to his quarters to turn in again. 2/E Hesketh tells everyone to return to their stations, and Barrett and Shepherd climb up the escape to go back to BR 6.	PV *Virginian*; Cottam, BI 17067; Bride, AI p.145; Hendrickson, BI 4852–3; Barrett, BI 1926 & 1935–7.

14 Apr 9.48p.m.	11.50p.m.	AB Buley hears water entering hold 1 and sees tarp ballooning over hatch. Boatswain's Mate Haines sees tarp ballooning over hatch in hold 1, and goes to inform C/O Wilde. Leading Fireman Hendrickson told about water coming in a: bottom of firemen's tunnel after returning to his quarters on G deck, sees water coming in from starboard side looking down from G deck, and decides to go to the engine room to tell the engineers. Barrett sees water about 8ft over the stokehold plates in BR 6, and returns to BR 5 with Shepherd. Poingdestre returns to the mess room where the carpenter tells him that there is 7ft of water in hold 1. Hichens notices an initial 5° list to starboard. 4/O Boxhall returns from his inspection forward, reports no damage seen, ordered to find the carpenter to sound the ship forward, and meets the carpenter coming up the ladder from A deck on his way down. After carpenter reported to Capt. Smith that holds 1, 2 and 3, were flooding, Smith decides to go below to find C/E Bell and/or meet up with Thomas Andrews. Andrews is seen coming through first class saloon, then down pantry stairs to E deck, and turn aft towards engine room by Saloon Watchman James Johnstone.	Buley, AI p.607; Haines, AI p.657; Barrett, BI 1926 & 1935–7; Hendrickson, BI 4853–6, 4865–70; Poingdestre, BI 2821–5; Hichens, AI p.451; Boxhall, BI 15576–83; Johnstone, BI 3367–72.	
14 Apr 9.50p.m.	11.52p.m.	Call comes in from engine room to send all the stokers up. Stokers coming out onto E deck seen by Olliver as he was heading down to the engine room with a note for C/E Bell. Harvey in BR 5 tells Barrett to stay behind. Suddenly the lights go out in the stokeholds. Barrett is told to get lamps for BR 5. Trimmer Cavell comes out of the bunker in the aft part of BR 4 just as the lights go out. 4/O Boxhall sees water within 2ft of G deck by mail room. Capt. Smith seen coming down working staircase onto E deck and going towards engine room. This was soon after Andrews was seen going in that direction. *Californian's* 3/O Groves notices steamer appeared to be stopped and most of her deck lights appeared to be shut out. Time noted at 11.40p.m. *Californian* ATS by the striking of 'one bell' to inform the watch below that they were due on deck in 20 minutes.	Barrett, BI 1957–61, 1970–93; Olliver, AI p.534; Cavell, BI 4215–18; Boxhall, BI 15374–9; Mackay, BI 10696; Johnstone, BI 3367–72; Groves, BI 8217; Stone, BI 7823.	30
14 Apr 9.53p.m.	11.55p.m.	Leading Fireman Threlfall woken up by a shout from someone. He has to wade through water in the passage from his quarters on G deck to get to a spiral staircase to go up to the mess deck. Saw water flowing down staircase into stokehold tunnel. Lookout Symons hears 'all hands standby, as you may be wanted at any moment' called by boatswain. Then goes and sees water coming onto G deck around coamings of hatch in hold 1. Hendrickson, on his way to the engine room, meets Hesketh coming along on E deck and is told to get lamps to bring down into the stokeholds. Cavell is told to get lamps to bring down to BR 4. James Johnstone, after following Andrews from the engine room to the mail room, sees flooding in baggage room down on G deck looking from F deck landing near squash court steps in hold 3. Assistant 2nd Steward Wheat sees water coming onto G deck in hold 3 just after meeting with James Johnstone.	Threlfall, Bridgewater Mercury, May 1912; Symons, BI 11354–6, BI 11402–13, 11418; Hendrickson, BI 4896–902; Cavell, BI 4240–3; James Johnstone, BI 3395–7; Wheat, BI 10901–18.	31
14 Apr 9.55p.m.	11.57p.m.	*Carpathia* (MPA) signals *Mount Temple* (MLQ) 'Good Night.' Makes note that his signals were very weak. This was at the time that Cottam was preparing to turn in. Capt. Smith seen going back up the working staircase by Saloon Steward Mackay. Olliver delivers Bell's response to C/O Wilde and then told to find the boatswain and tell him to get the boats ready for lowering.	PV *Mount Temple*; PV *Carpathia*; Mackay, BI 10697; Olliver, AI p.535–6.	32

14 Apr 9.58p.m.	12.00a.m.	Clocks did NOT go back as planned at this time because of the accident. Boxhall returns from mail room and informs Capt. Smith of flooding seen there. Smith said nothing to him and went off the bridge. Boxhall told (by Wilde?) to call out the off-duty officers. 'All hands up and about the boats' ordered by the boatswain in the forecastle. Olliver told by Moody to get muster list for the boats. Joseph Wheat starts closing WTDs on F deck at WTB-F.	Pitman, AI p.294; Boxhall, BI 15584–8 & BI 15378–85; Lightoller, BI 13785; Symons, BI 11418; Olliver, AI p.536; Wheat, BI 10937.	33
14 Apr 10.00p.m.	12.02a.m.	Lights come back on in stokeholds. Barrett returns to BR 5 and noticed the water gauges were low. Told to get some men down to draw fires. Hendrickson returns with lamps, attempts to go down into BR 6 first but finds the water too high there. He then goes down into BR 5 and is told to put his lamps up by the boiler gauges and start drawing fires. 2/E Harvey tells Hendrickson to get more men down. Norman Chambers sees three 'officers' inspect flooding in mail room and first class baggage room. Water is seen within 2ft of F deck there at this time but appeared not to be rising much according to a remark overheard from one of those officers.	Barrett: BI 2007–14; Hendrickson, BI 4903–11; Chambers, AI p.1042: Pitman, BI 14949–67.	34
14 Apr 10.03p.m.	12.05a.m.	Returning from calling upon the off-duty officers, Boxhall goes right along the line of boats on the port side and sees the men on deck (from his watch) already starting with the work. He goes to uncover boats on the port side. Pitman, already dressed, comes on deck, notices that boats on the port side are being uncovered, notices that steam is blowing off from the boilers, and goes aft and finds Moody who tells him about ice in the forward well deck. Pitman then goes forward to investigate. Captain Smith seen going toward mail room with Chief Purser McElroy and a mail clerk. Hendrickson goes forward to get more men and sees tarp over hatch 1 ballooning up, and heads back to engine room to report. Beesley notices an officer (Moody?) starting to uncover boat No.16 as he starts to go down the second class staircase from the boat deck for the second time.	Boxhall, BI 15384–5; Pitman, BI 14949–55; Robinson, BI 13277–83; Hendrickson, BI 4912–29; Beesley, The Loss of the SS Titanic.	
14 Apr 10.06p.m.	12.08a.m.	Pitman sees the ice in well deck and goes to investigate for structural damage under the forecastle head. He sees a group of firemen come up with their belongings, and sees water coming in from under and around hatch in hold 1 down on G deck.	Pitman, BI 14957–67.	35
14 Apr 10.08p.m.	12.10a.m.	Pitman returns to boat deck and sees boats being uncovered on the starboard side. Dillon and others ordered to open all the WTDs going forward from the engine room all the way into BR 4. Annie Robinson sees water within six steps (about 4ft) of coming onto E deck by stairs going down to the mail room. This was just after seeing Smith and Andrews come back from the mail room. She overhears Andrews tell Smith, 'Well, three have gone already, Captain,' a reference to three watertight compartments (holds 1, 2 and 3). Smith separates from Andrews to go back up to the bridge.	Pitman, BI 14968–9; Dillon, BI 3913 & 3916–17; Robinson, BI 13277–83; Bullock, Thomas Andrews Shipbuilder.	36
14 Apr 10.10p.m.	12.12a.m.	QM Hichens hears Capt. Smith give order to swing out the boats and have passengers called up with lifebelts on. Ismay hears Capt. Smith giving some order about getting the boats out.	Hichens, BI 1041–3; Ismay, AI p.3.	37

14 Apr 10.13p.m.	12.15a.m.	Capt. Smith gives notice to the two Marconi operators that they may need to send a CQD but not to send it until he tells them to. Wheat said this was about the time that stewards were ordered to rouse passengers and get them on deck with lifebelts. Chief Baker Joughin sends thirteen men up with four loaves of bread each to put into the boats.	Bride's exclusive *NY Times* interview; Wheat, BI 13229; Joughin, BI 5924.	
14 Apr 10.20p.m.	12.22a.m.	Thomas Andrews is seen by William Sloper and Anna Warren running up the staircase three steps at a time toward the bridge. He tells Capt. Smith that the ship cannot be saved and has only 1 to 1.5 hours left.	See Chapter 7.	38
14 Apr 10.23p.m.	12.25a.m.	After escaping from 3ft of water on E deck after the collapse of a wooden bulkhead separating the crew's quarters from third class space, AB Poingdestre goes back up to the boat deck in time to hear Capt. Smith order the boats be loaded with women and children. Smith then goes to the Marconi room and tells Phillips to send a call for assistance after giving him the ship's position.	Poingdestre, BI 2842–58; See Chapter 7.	39
14 Apr 10.25p.m.	12.27a.m.	First CQD transmitted by Phillips with distress coordinates 41° 44'N, 50° 24'W. This call is received by *La Provence* (MLP), *Mount Temple* (MLQ) and the land station at Cape Race (MCE). *Frankfurt* (DFT) also picks up a signal from *Titanic*, but possibly thinks it is a routine TR exchange through all the atmospherics. Phillips possibly hears *Frankfurt*'s call sign [DFT] despite the noise of steam blowing off. Boxhall comes on bridge to see a light that was reported off *Titanic*'s port bow. He asks Capt. Smith if it is serious and Smith tells him that Thomas Andrews thinks she has from 1 to 1.5 hours left. Boxhall asks Smith if distress message was sent, and Smith suggests that he check the position after Boxhall tells him that the ship was ahead of her DR. Andrews tells Stewardess Annie Robinson to put her lifebelt on so passengers can see her.	List of wireless messages in BI Report; Log of messages at Cape Race; Capt. Moore, AI p.759; PV *Frankfurt*; Boxhall, BI 15610; Halpern, 'It's a CQD OM'; Robinson, BI 13305.	40
14 Apr 10.28p.m.	12.30a.m.	*Ypiranga* (DYA) hears CQD call from *Titanic* (MGY): 'CQD here, position 41.44N, 50.24W. We require assistance.'	PV *Ypiranga*; List of wireless messages in BI Report.	
14 Apr 10.31p.m.	12.33a.m.	*Caronia* (MRA) picks up distress call from *Titanic* (MGY) saying 'I require assistance immediately.'	PV *Caronia*.	
14 Apr 10.33p.m.	12.35a.m.	Boxhall shows Smith his coordinates and is told to take it to the wireless cabin.	Boxhall, BI 15391.	
14 Apr 10.34p.m.	12.36a.m.	*Titanic* (MGY) communicates with *Asian* (MKL). Boxhall leaves 'corrected' position with Phillips who is busy at the transmitting key.	PV *Ypiranga*; Boxhall, AI p.233.	
14 Apr 10.35p.m.	12.37a.m.	CQD from *Titanic* (MGY) received by *Carpathia* (MPA): 'Come at once. We have struck a berg. It's a CQD OM. Position 41° 46'N, 50° 14'W.' Cape Race (MCE) hears corrected position 41° 46'N, 50° 14'W transmitted from *Titanic*. *Baltic* (MBC) hears about *Titanic* via *Caronia* (MRS). *Birma* (SBA) hears *Titanic* calling for assistance.	List of wireless messages in BI Report; Marconi Co. letter to Wreck Commission, 1 May 1912.; PV *Mount Temple*; Halpern, 'The Enigmatic Excursion of the SS *Birma*'.	
14 Apr 10.36p.m.	12.38a.m.	*Ypiranga* (DYA) hears CQD from *Titanic* (MGY) with corrected position: 'MGY sends CQD here is corrected position 41.46N, 50.14W. Require immediate assistance. We have collision with iceberg. Sinking. Can hear nothing for noise of steam.'	PV *Ypiranga*.	

14 Apr (p.m.)	(a.m.)	Event	Reference	
14 Apr 10.38p.m.	12.40a.m.	First lifeboat launched, No.7, starboard side forward. Lookout Hogg put in charge.	See Chapter 7 – lifeboat launch timetable.	
14 Apr 10.40p.m.	12.42a.m.	*Mount Temple* (MLQ) hears *Titanic* (MGY) calling CQD. Capt. Moore turns his ship for the corrected distress position. *Mount Temple* at DR location 41° 25' N, 51° 14'W, or 49.5 nautical miles heading 065° True for the Boxhall CQD position. *Mount Temple* ship's time was 12.26a.m. ATS. *Frankfurt* (DFT) communicates with *Titanic*. Receives *Titanic's* position and is asked to tell her captain 'to come to our help, we are on ice.' *Frankfurt* acknowledges with 'OK, stdbi.' Bride is sent to tell Capt. Smith that *Frankfurt* responded to their call. He finds Smith on the boat deck overseeing the loading and lowering of the boats. Smith tells Bride to find out *Frankfurt's* position.	PV *Mount Temple*; Capt. Moore, AI p.759; Durrant, BI 9436–7; PV *Frankfurt*; Bride, AI p.147.	
14 Apr 10.41p.m.	12.43a.m.	Boat No.5 launched. 3/O Pitman put in charge.	See Chapter 7 – lifeboat launch timetable; Pitman, AI p.289.	41
14 Apr 10.43p.m.	12.45a.m.	Assistant 2nd Steward Wheat sees water flowing down first class stairs from E deck down to F deck by Turkish baths. He estimates the time as 'about a quarter or ten minutes to 1.' Greaser Scott and others ordered to open all the WTDs aft of the engine room. The engineers want to get to a portable suction pipe to bring forward.	Wheat, BI 10956–72; Scott, BI 5600–4.	
14 Apr 10.45p.m.	12.47a.m.	12.35 *Californian* ATS, 2/O Stone goes to speaking tube to answer a call from Capt. Lord. First distress socket signal sent up by 4/O Boxhall on *Titanic*. *Baltic* (MBC) calling *Titanic* (MGY), but gets no response.	Stone's signed statement to Capt. Lord 18 Apr 1912; Wormstedt, Fitch, Behe, 'Lifeboat Launch Sequence Re-Examined' 2010; Halpern, 'Rockets, Lifeboats, and Time Changes'; PV *Baltic*.	42
14 Apr 10.46p.m.	12.48a.m.	*Frankfurt* (DFT) calls *Titanic* (MGY) and gives his position for 12a.m. at 39.47N, 52.10W. *Titanic* asks, 'Are you coming to our assistance?' *Frankfurt* asks, 'What is the matter with you?' *Titanic* replies, 'We have struck iceberg and sinking; please tell captain to come.' 'OK; will tell the bridge right away.' 'OK; yes; quick.' 4/O Boxhall answers a call on a phone in the wheelhouse from QM Rowe out on the afterbridge. Rowe reports that he sees a boat in the water, and Boxhall tells Rowe to bring extra distress socket signals to the bridge. Both Rowe and QM Bright go down to the QM locker to get them.	PV *Mount Temple*; PV *Ypiranga*; Wormstedt, Fitch, Behe, 'Lifeboat Launch Sequence Re-Examined' 2010.	
14 Apr 10.47p.m.	12.49a.m.	*Carpathia* (MPA) gives position to *Titanic* (MGY) after Cottam hears *Titanic* finish communicating with *Frankfurt*. Bride is sent to tell Capt. Smith that *Carpathia* is coming. He finds him in the wheelhouse, and Smith follows Bride back to the Marconi cabin.	Cottam, BI 17068, 17115, 17125–34; Bride, AI pp.148–9.	43
14 Apr 10.48p.m.	12.50a.m.	Steward Ray sees water on E deck up to second funnel casing by the main first class stairway port and starboard sides. This is after going down to his quarters on E deck to get an overcoat having first witnessed boat No.7 lowered to the sea.	Ray, AI pp.803–4.	44
14 Apr 10.50p.m.	12.52a.m.	*Olympic* (MKC) hears *Titanic* (MGY) signalling some ship about striking an iceberg. They are not sure it is *Titanic* which has struck an iceberg because of interference by atmospherics and many stations working.	PV *Olympic*.	

14 Apr 10.51p.m.	12.53a.m.	Carpathia (MPA) calls Titanic (MGY) to confirm both positions. Titanic replies, 'All right.' This is followed by a call from Frankfurt (DFT) to Titanic, according to Cottam on Carpathia.	Cottam, AI pp.104–5.	45
14 Apr 10.52p.m.	12.54a.m.	Olympic (MKC) tries calling Titanic (MGY).	PV Ypiranga.	46
14 Apr 10.53p.m.	12.55a.m.	Boat No.3 launched. AB Moore put in charge. Cottam on Carpathia is overhearing messages and contacts Titanic to tell them that Olympic is calling them. Titanic tells him that 'he could not read him because of the rush of air and the escape of steam.' This is but minutes after his position confirmation message.	See Chapter 7 – lifeboat launch timetable; Cottam, AI pp.105–6.	47
14 Apr 10.55p.m.	12.57a.m.	12.45a.m. Californian ATS, 2/O Stone sees the first of eight white rockets burst over steamer on his starboard beam. Mount Temple hears 'MGY calling SOS.' Celtic (MLC) overhears Titanic telling Olympic 'I require immediate assistance.'	Signed statement by 2/O Stone to Capt. Lord, 18 Apr; PV Mount Temple; Marconi Co. letter to Wreck Commission, 1 May 1912.	
14 Apr 10.57p.m.	12.59a.m.	Mount Temple hears Titanic (MGY) calling Olympic (MKC).	PV Mount Temple.	
14 Apr 10.58p.m.	1.00a.m.	Boat No.8 launched on port side forward. AB Jones put in charge. Caronia (MRA) gives Baltic (MBC) additional information about Titanic.	See Chapter 7 – lifeboat launch timetable; Marconi Co. letter to Wreck Commission, 1 May 1912.	
14 Apr 10.59p.m.	1.01a.m.	Mount Temple (MLQ) hears Titanic (MGY) working Caronia (MRA).	PV Mount Temple.	
14 Apr 11.00p.m.	1.02a.m.	Mount Temple (MLQ) hears Titanic (MGY) calling Virginian (MGN).	PV Mount Temple.	
14 Apr 11.02p.m.	1.04a.m.	Ypiranga (DYA) hears Titanic (MGY) calling SOS–CQD and giving out her position. Olympic hears Titanic sending out signals of distress and tries to answer.	PV Ypiranga; PV Olympic.	48
14 Apr 11.03p.m.	1.05a.m.	Boat No.1 launched. Lookout Symons in charge. Portable suction pipe seen carried through the engine room by four men coming from last shaft-tunnel compartment aft and taken to BR 4 forward.	See Chapter 7 – lifeboat launch timetable; Scott, BI 5601.	49
14 Apr 11.05p.m.	1.07a.m.	Cincinnati (DDC) calls Titanic (MGY) and gives position 37.36N, 54.44W.	PV Ypiranga; PV Frankfurt.	50
14 Apr 11.08p.m.	1.10a.m.	Boat No.6 launched. QM Hichens in charge. Barrett sees rush of water in BR 5 in pass between boilers. Goes up the escape and sees water on E deck coming from forward at location of escape from BR. 5.	See Chapter 7 – lifeboat launch time able; Barrett, BI 2348–9.	
14 Apr 11.10p.m.	1.12a.m.	Titanic (MGY) gives Olympic (MKC) his position, 41.46 N, 50.14 W, and says, 'We have struck an iceberg.' Information reported to Olympic's bridge immediately. Olympic's distance from Titanic's distress position is 505 miles. Titanic's CQD overheard by Virginian (MGN). Baltic (MBC) also hears Titanic but faintly and notes that jamming is very bad.	PV Olympic; PV Virginian; PV Baltic.	
14 Apr 11.12p.m.	1.14a.m.	Titanic (MGY) calls Asian (MKL) and says 'Want immediate assistance.' Virginian (MGN) calls Titanic but gets no response. Cape Race (MCE) calls Virginian (MGN) and asks to report to captain that Titanic struck iceberg and requires immediate assistance.	List of wireless messages in BI Report; PV Virginian.	
14 Apr 11.14p.m.	1.16a.m.	Olympic (MKC) calls Titanic (MGY).	PV Ypiranga.	

14 Apr 11.15p.m.	1.17a.m.	*Frankfurt* (DFT) signals *Titanic* (MGY), 'I want to take your course.' Lookout Symons sees water up to second row of ports under *Titanic*'s name at the bow. Trimmer Cavell comes up the escape from BR 4 after seeing water coming over the stokehold plates there.	PV *Frankfurt*; PV *Ypiranga*; Symons, BI 11490; Cavell, BI 4248–65.	51
14 Apr 11:18p.m.	1.20a.m.	Boat No.16 launched. Master-at-Arms Bailey in charge. Trimmer Dillon is told to get a lifebelt and go up on deck as he comes into the engine room minutes after seeing water coming up over the stokehold plates in BR 4. Greaser Scott also told to go on deck with a lifebelt at this time. Leading Fireman Threlfall, pulling fires in one of the stokeholds, hears 2/E Hesketh say 'We've done all we can men, get out now.' Most of the remaining firemen, trimmers and greasers are ordered out of the stokeholds and engine rooms, and told to get lifebelts on and go up on deck.	See Chapter 7 – lifeboat launch timetable; Dillon, BI 3816–27, 3913; Scott, BI 5838–9; Threlfall, *The Bridgewater Mercury*, May 1912.	52
14 Apr 11:20p.m.	1.22a.m.	*Titanic* (MGY) tells *Olympic* (MKC), 'Captain says get your boats ready. Going down fast at the head. What is your position?'	PV *Olympic*; PV *Mount Temple*; PV *Ypiranga*; PV *Caronia*.	53
14 Apr 11:23p.m.	1.25a.m.	Boat No.14 launched. 5/O Lowe takes charge. Trimmer Cavell starts to go back down to BR 4, but does not see anyone there. He then goes up to the boat deck and sees two boats, nos 13 and 15, on starboard side aft.	See Chapter 7 – lifeboat launch timetable; Cavell, BI 4282–94.	54
14 Apr 11:24p.m.	1.26a.m.	*Baltic* (MBC) to *Titanic* (MGY), 'We are making for you, keep in touch with us.' *Olympic*'s position is 40° 52'N, 61° 18'W.	*Baltic* (MBC); PV *Olympic*.	55
14 Apr 11:26p.m.	1.28a.m.	*Frankfurt* (DFT) heard working *Titanic* (MGY). *Frankfurt* says, 'Our captain will go for your course.' *Titanic* replies, 'OK, tks, tks.'	PV *Ypiranga*; PV *Mount Temple*.	56
14 Apr 11:28p.m.	1.30a.m.	Boat No.12 on port side launched with AB Poingdestre in charge. Boat No.9 starboard side launched with Boatswain's Mate Haines in charge. *Titanic* (MGY) calling *Baltic* (MBC).	See Chapter 7 – lifeboat launch timetable; PV *Mount Temple*; PV *Ypiranga*.	57
14 Apr 11:30p.m.	1.32a.m.	*Virginian* (MGN) sends MSG to Cape Race (MCE) to inform *Titanic* (MGY) that they are going to her assistance. *Virginian* is 170 miles north of *Titanic*'s CQD position.	PV *Virginian*.	
14 Apr 11:33p.m.	1.35a.m.	Boat No.11 launched from A deck starboard side aft with AB Humphreys in charge. Portable suction pipe connected up to bilge system in BR 4 by this time.	See Chapter 7 – lifeboat launch timetable; Wilding: BI 20682–6.	58
14 Apr 11:34p.m.	1.36a.m.	*Olympic* (MKC) to *Titanic* (MGY), 'Commander, *Titanic*, 4.24a.m. G.M.T. 40.52 N., 61.18 W. Are you steering southerly to meet us? Haddock.'	PV *Olympic*; PV *Ypiranga*; PV *Mount Temple*; PV *Frankfurt*.	59
14 Apr 11:35p.m.	1.37a.m.	Land station at Cape Race (MCE) no longer hears any messages from *Titanic* (MGY).	PV *Virginian*	
14 Apr 11:37p.m.	1.39a.m.	*Titanic* (MGY) tells *Olympic* (MKC), 'We are putting the women off in small boats.'	PV *Ypiranga*; PV *Mount Temple*; PV *Baltic*; PV *Virginian*.	60
14 Apr 11:38p.m.	1.40a.m.	Boat No.13 launched from A deck. Leading Fireman Barrett takes charge.	See Chapter 7 – lifeboat launch timetable.	

Date	Time	Event	Source	
14 Apr 11.39p.m.	1.41a.m.	Boat No.15 launched from A deck. Fireman Dymond takes charge. This boat was seen to be coming down within 1 minute of boat No.13, and nearly lands on top of No.13 as the latter is swept aft by the discharge from the starboard side condenser pump.	See Chapter 7 – lifeboat launch timetable.	
14 Apr 11.40p.m.	1.42a.m.	*Titanic* (MGY) tells *Olympic* (MKC), 'Tell captain we are putting the passengers off in small boats.'	PV *Olympic*; PV *Ypiranga*; PV *Birma*.	61
14 Apr 11.41p.m.	1.43a.m.	*Titanic* (MGY) sends CQD and says, 'Engine room getting flooded.' AB Evans notices a 2.5ft gap between lifeboat 10 and the side of the rail on the boat deck. This indicates that the ship is listing to port about 10° at this time.	PV *Mount Temple*; Evans, AI p.677.	
14 Apr 11.43p.m.	1.45a.m.	Boat No.2 launched. 4/O Boxhall put in charge. *Olympic* (MKC) asks *Titanic* (MGY) what weather she has had. *Titanic* says, 'clear and calm.' Barrett in boat No.13 notices forecastle head not yet under water. Assistant Steward Walter Nichols in boat 15 notices that *Titanic's* propellers are half out of the water.	See Chapter 7 – lifeboat launch timetable; PV Mount Temple; Barrett, BI 2140–2; Nichols, *NY Times* article 22 Apr.	62
14 Apr 11.44p.m.	1.46a.m.	*Baltic* (MBC) calling *Titanic* (MGY).	PV *Ypiranga*.	
14 Apr 11.45p.m.	1.47a.m.	*Baltic* hears message transmitted by Bride, 'Engine room getting flooded,' as Phillips is outside and sees the well deck awash and the ship having a very noticeable list to port. *Frankfurt* (DFT) asks *Titanic*: 'Are there any boats around you already?' No reply from *Titanic*.	PV *Baltic*; Bride, BI 16540–53; PV *Mount Temple*.	
14 Apr 11.47p.m.	1.49a.m.	*Baltic* (MBC) tells *Titanic* (MGY), 'We are rushing to you.' *Baltic* says she is 243 miles east. *Olympic* sends MSG to *Titanic*; 'Commander, Titanic. Am lighting up all possible boilers as fast as can. Haddock.' Acknowledged by *Titanic*. Last signals from *Titanic* heard by *Mount Temple* (MLQ).	PV *Ypiranga*; PV *Baltic*; PV *Olympic*; PV *Mount Temple*.	63
14 Apr 11.48p.m.	1.50a.m.	Last distress socket signal fired from *Titanic* by QM Rowe. He then goes to take charge of collapsible boat C which is loading. On *Californian*, 2/O Stone and Apprentice Gibson see the last white rocket go up from the steamer now about 1 point on their port bow. Stone thinks it is about 1.40a.m. *Californian* ATS (which would correspond to 1.52a.m. on *Titanic*). Boat No.10 port side aft launched from boat deck with AB Buley in charge. Boat No.4 launched from A deck on port side forward with QM Perkis in charge.	Stone, BI 7935; Gibson's signed report to Capt. Lord 18 Apr; Halpern, 'Rockets, Lifeboats, and Time Changes'; See Chapter 7 – lifeboat launch timetable.	
14 Apr 11.49p.m.	1.51a.m.	*Frankfurt* (DFT) tries calling *Titanic* (MGY).	PV *Ypiranga*.	
14 Apr 11.50p.m.	1.52a.m.	*Ypiranga* (DYA) hears *Titanic* (MGY) send message that she is getting 'flooded'. This is the last that *Ypiranga* hears directly from *Titanic*. Phillips returns to wireless cabin and informs Bride who is at the transmitting key that 'the forward well deck was awash,' and 'they are putting the women and children in the boats and clearing off.' The ship's list to port is very noticeable.	PV *Olympic*; PV *Ypiranga*; Bride, BI 16540–53.	64
14 Apr 11.53p.m.	1.55a.m.	*Birma* (SBA) hears *Titanic* (MGY) say, 'Women and children in boats, cannot last much longer. MGY.' This apparently is the last message heard by *Birma* from *Titanic*.	Marconi office form of SS *Birma*; Halpern, 'Enigmatic Excursion of the SS *Birma*.'	
14 Apr 11.55p.m.	1.57a.m.	Capt. Smith comes into the wireless cabin and tells Phillips and Bride, 'You can do nothing more; look out for yourselves.' Last wireless message from *Titanic* (MGY) heard by *Carpathia* (MPA) is: 'Engine room full up to boilers.' *Frankfurt* (DFT) and *Birma* (SBA) try calling *Titanic*.	Bride's report to Marconi Co. 27 Apr; List of wireless messages in BI Report; Cottam, BI 17193–201; PV *Mount Temple*; PV *Caronia*; Bride, BI 16540–53.	

14 Apr 11.58p.m.	2.00a.m.	Collapsible boat C launched with QM Rowe in charge. *Asian* (MKL) hears *Titanic* (MGY) call SOS. Answers *Titanic*, but receives no reply. *Frankfurt* (DFT) calling *Titanic*.	See Chapter 7 – lifeboat launch timetable; List of wireless messages in BI Report; PV *Ypiranga*.	
15 Apr 12.00a.m.	2.02a.m.	*Ypiranga* hears 'Stdbi-stdbi-stdbi'.	PV *Ypiranga*.	65
15 Apr 12.03a.m.	2.05a.m.	Collapsible boat D launched with QM Bright in charge. QM Bright sees forecastle head going under as boat D is lowered. Boat C reaches the water at this time and QM Rowe notices that the well deck is completely submerged.	See Chapter 7 – lifeboat launch timetable; Bright, AI p.837; Rowe, AI p.524.	66
15 Apr 12.10a.m.	2.12a.m.	*Virginian* (MGN) thinks he hears *Titanic* (MGY) calling very faintly, 'his power greatly reduced.' According to Harold Bride, last message sent by Phillips is a general 'CQD MGY' call that goes unanswered. Marconi cabin then abandoned, and Bride goes out and climbs to the top of the officers' quarters and helps to push collapsible B off onto the boat deck. *Mount Temple* (MLQ) hears *Olympic* (MKC), *Frankfurt* (DFT) and *Baltic* (MBC) calling *Titanic*, but no replies are heard.	PV *Virginian*; Bride, BI 16566; Bride's report to Marconi Co. 27 Apr; PV *Mount Temple*.	67
15 Apr 12.13a.m.	2.15a.m.	While down in the lounge pantry on A deck, just aft of the third funnel casing by the ship's aft expansion joint, Chief Baker Joughin hears 'a kind of a crash as if something had buckled . . . It was like as if the iron was parting' after the ship had taken a lurch. He then rushes up to the boat deck and transfers his watch from his front pocket to his back pocket as he is making his way aft following a crowd of people rushing to get onto the poop deck. He notices the time is 'a quarter past two then' and the lights on the ship are still on. 2/O Lightoller ses the water is up to the crow's nest and coming onto the forebridge just as the ship took 'a bit of a dive' and he goes into the water. Collapsible boats A and B are swept off.	Joughin, BI 6040–9 & 6359–64; Lightoller, AI pp.90–1, BI 14052; See Chapter 7 – lifeboat launch timetable.	68
15 Apr 12.15a.m.	2.17a.m.	Trimmer Dillon on *Titanic*'s poop deck sees the ship take 'one final plunge and righted herself again.' Lookout Symons in boat No.1 sees the stern 'come well out' as the ship pitches down suddenly as all the lights go out. At the same time, Symons sees the ship split in two 'abaft the after expansion plate' with the stern righting itself without the bow. Apprentice Gibson on the upper bridge of *Californian* sees the lights of the steamer disappear. He notes the time as 2.05a.m. by *Californian*'s wheelhouse clock as he is sent down by 2/O Stone to inform Capt. Lord that the ship they were watching has disappeared.	Dillon, BI 3858; Symons, BI 11510–25; Gibson, BI 7533, 7565.	69
15 Apr 12.18a.m.	2.20a.m.	**Stern section disappears below the surface. Location 41° 43.5' N, 49° 56.8' W.** Symons sees stern go straight up accompanied by 'a sound like steady thunder' and then disappear. Dillon sees fourth funnel fall aft toward him as the stern goes down pulling him under. He soon is picked up by boat No.4. 3/O Pitman [boat 5] sees the ship disappear at '2.20 exactly, ship's time. I took my watch out at the time she disappeared, and I said, "It is 2.20," and the passengers around me heard it . . . 2.20a.m., the 15th of April.'; Mrs Marian Thayer [boat 4]: 'It was 2.20a.m. when the *Titanic* disappeared, according to a wrist watch worn by one of the passengers in my boat.'; Miss Daisy Minahan [boat 15]: 'This was at 2.20a.m. by a man's watch who stood next to me.'	Ballard, *The Discovery of the Titanic*; Symons, BI 11512; Dillon, BI 3861–76; Pitman, AI p.294; Halpern, 'Mystery of Time – Part 2'.	70

Date	Time	Event	Reference	No.
15 Apr 12.20a.m.	2.22a.m.	*Virginian* (MGN) hears two 'V's signalled faintly in spark similar to *Titanic's*.	PV *Virginian*.	71
15 Apr 12.25a.m.	2.27a.m.	*Birma* (SBA) tells *Frankfurt* (DFT) he is 70 miles from *Titanic*.	PV *Mount Temple*.	
15 Apr 12.27a.m.	2.29a.m.	*Virginian* (MGN) hears the transmission of a 'CQ' Unable to make out signals which seemed to end abruptly. Spark sounded 'blurred or ragged'.	PV *Virginian*.	72
15 Apr 1.16a.m.	3.18a.m.	*Caronia* (MRA) hears some ship say 'We are firing rockets. Lookout for rockets.'	PV *Caronia*.	73
15 Apr 1.25a.m.	3.27a.m.	*Carpathia* (MPA) sends, 'If you are there, we are firing rockets.'	PV *Mount Temple*.	
15 Apr 1.39a.m.	3.41a.m.	At 3.25 ATS on *Mount Temple*, Capt. Moore orders 'Stop' on his engine telegraph to take the way off his ship because of ice getting a bit thick. He believes he is about 14 miles from the CQD position. He then proceeds slowly.	Capt. Moore, AI p.762–4; See Chapter 11.	
15 Apr 1.40a.m.	3.42a.m.	*Carpathia* (MPA) calling *Titanic* (MGY).	PV *Mount Temple*.	
15 Apr 1.58a.m.	4.00a.m.	*Birma* (SBA) tells *Frankfurt* (DFT) that she thinks she hears *Titanic* (MGY), and sends, 'Steaming full speed to you, shall arrive you 6 in the morning. Hope you are safe. We are only 50 miles now.'	PV *Mount Temple*; Durrant, BI 9571.	74
15 Apr 2.00a.m.	4.02a.m.	*Carpathia* (MPA) calling *Titanic* (MGY).	PV *Mount Temple*.	
15 Apr 2.13a.m.	4.15a.m.	4.10a.m. *Carpathia* ATS. Boat No.2 arrives with Joseph Boxhall in it.	See Chapter 7 – Lifeboat pickup sequence table; Halpern, '12.35a.m. Apparent Time *Carpathia'*.	75
15 Apr 2.15a.m.	4.17a.m.	*Virginian* (MGN) signals *Birma* (SBA) who tells *Virginian* that she is 55 miles from *Titanic* and has not heard anything from her.	PV *Virginian*.	76
15 Apr 2.48a.m.	4.50a.m.	Approx. 4.45a.m. *Carpathia* ATS. Boat No.1 arrives.	See Chapter 7 – Lifeboat pickup sequence table; Halpern, '12.35a.m. Apparent Time *Carpathia'*.	
15 Apr 3.00a.m.	5.02a.m.	4.46a.m. *Mount Temple* ATS. Durrant notes in his PV that 'All quiet. – We're stopped amongst pack ice.'	PV *Mount Temple*; See Chapter 11.	
15 Apr 3.05a.m.	5.07a.m.	*Birma* (SBA) and *Frankfurt* (DFT) working.	PV *Mount Temple*.	
15 Apr 3.20a.m.	5.22a.m.	*Birma* (SBA) and *Frankfurt* (DFT) working. It is 5.06a.m. *Mount Temple* ATS. Capt. Moore backs his ship out of ice and starts heading SSE True to find an opening across the pack ice.	PV *Mount Temple*; Capt. Moore, AI p.767.	
15 Apr 3.24a.m.	5.26a.m.	*Birma* (SBA) says that they are 30 miles off *Titanic's* distress position.	PV *Ypiranga*; See also: Halpern, 'The Enigmatic Excursion of the SS *Birma'*.	
15 Apr 3.25a.m.	5.27a.m.	*Californian* (MWL) calls CQ. *Mount Temple* (MLQ) answers and advises him of *Titanic* and gives him *Titanic's* distress position.	PV *Mount Temple*.	
15 Apr 3.40a.m.	5.42a.m.	*Californian* (MWL) working *Frankfurt* (DFT). *Frankfurt* sends him the same information as given to him by *Mount Temple*.	PV *Mount Temple*.	

15 Apr 3.48a.m.	5.50a.m.	Approx. 5.45a.m. *Carpathia* ATS. Collapsible boat C arrives. (This boat was set adrift afterwards.)	See Chapter 7 – Lifeboat pickup sequence table; Halpern, '12:35a.m. Apparent Time *Carpathia*'.	
15 Apr 4.00a.m.	6.02a.m.	*Californian* (MWL) working *Virginian* (MGN).	PV *Mount Temple*.	
15 Apr 4.03a.m.	6.05a.m.	Approx. 6.00a.m. *Carpathia* ATS. Boat No.5 arrives.	See Chapter 7 – Lifeboat pickup sequence table; Halpern, '12:35a.m. Apparent Time *Carpathia*'.	
15 Apr 4.15a.m.	6.17a.m.	*Virginian* (MGN) tells *Californian* (MWL), 'Captain: *Titanic* struck iceberg, wants assistance urgently, ship sinking, passengers in boats, his position lat. 41,46, long. 50.14. Gambell, Commander.'	Associated Press report interview with *Virginian's* Capt. Gambell 27 Apr. Also Lord, AI p.731.	77
15 Apr 4.18a.m.	6.20a.m.	Approx. 6.15a.m. *Carpathia* ATS. Boats nos 7 and 9 arrive.	See Chapter 7 – Lifeboat pickup sequence table; Halpern, '12:35a.m. Apparent Time *Carpathia*'.	
15 Apr 4.25a.m.	6.27a.m.	*Californian* (MWL) working *Birna* (SBA).	PV *Mount Temple*.	
15 Apr 4.33a.m.	6.35a.m.	Approx. 6.30a.m. *Carpathia* ATS. Boat No.13 arrives.	See Chapter 7 – Lifeboat pickup sequence table; Halpern, '12:35a.m. Apparent Time *Carpathia*'.	
15 Apr 4.48a.m.	6.50a.m.	Approx. 6.45a.m. *Carpathia* ATS. Boat No.16 arrives.	See Chapter 7 – Lifeboat pickup sequence table; Halpern, '12:35a.m. Apparent Time *Carpathia*'.	
15 Apr 5.03a.m.	7.05a.m.	Approx. 7.00a.m. *Carpathia* ATS. Boat No.11 arrives.	See Chapter 7 – Lifeboat pickup sequence table; Halpern, '12:35a.m. Apparent Time *Carpathia*'.	
15 Apr 5.05a.m.	7.07a.m.	After coming back up north, *Mount Temple* takes a Prime Vertical sight of the sun. They discover that they are at longitude 50° 9.5'W which is about 3 miles east of the CQD longitude. It becomes obvious to Capt. Moore that *Titanic* must have been further east because of a 5 to 6-mile-wide field of ice blocking their path eastward. Ship's time was 6.51a.m. ATS.	Capt. Moore, AI. p.777; SkyChart-III.	
15 Apr 5.18a.m.	7.20a.m.	Approx. 7.15a.m. *Carpathia* ATS. Boat No.14 and collapsible D arrive. (Both these boats were set adrift afterward.)	See Chapter 7 – Lifeboat pickup sequence table; Halpern, '12:35a.m. Apparent Time *Carpathia*'.	
15 Apr 5.20a.m.	7.22a.m.	*Mount Temple* (MLQ) signals *Californian* (MWL). Exchanges positions. *Mount Temple* says that the two ships are very close.	PV *Mount Temple*.	
15 Apr 5.33a.m.	7.35a.m.	Approx. 7.30a.m. *Carpathia* ATS. Boat nos 3, 8 and 15 arrive. (No.15 was set adrift afterward.)	See Chapter 7 – Lifeboat pickup sequence table; Halpern, '12:35a.m. Apparent Time *Carpathia*'.	
15 Apr 6.00a.m.	8.02a.m.	*Mount Temple* (MLQ) reports much jamming, and that *Carpathia* (MPA) and *Californian* (MWL) are in sight.	PV *Mount Temple*.	
15 Apr 6.03a.m.	8.05a.m.	Approx. 8.00a.m. *Carpathia* ATS. Boat nos 4, 6 and 10 arrive. (No.4 was set adrift afterward.)	See Chapter 7 – Lifeboat pickup sequence table; Halpern, '12:35a.m. Apparent Time *Carpathia*'.	
15 Apr 6.18a.m.	8.20a.m.	Approx. 8.15a.m. *Carpathia* ATS. The last boat, No.12, arrives with 2/O Lightoller at the helm.	See Chapter 7 – Lifeboat pickup sequence table; Halpern, '12:35a.m. Apparent Time *Carpathia*'.	78

15 Apr 6.33a.m.	8.35a.m.	Approx. 8.30a.m. *Carpathia* ATS. All survivors and last boat taken on board. Of the thirteen boats taken on board, six were put on the forward deck and seven are carried in davits.	Rostron's report to general manager of Cunard Co. 19 Apr.	
15 Apr 6.45a.m.	8.47a.m.	*Carpathia* (MPA) reports rescuing twenty boats.	PV *Mount Temple*.	
15 Apr 6.53a.m.	8.55a.m.	Approx. 8.50a.m. *Carpathia* ATS. Capt. Rostron orders full speed ahead while searching over the area.	Rostron's report to general manager of Cunard Co. 19 Apr.	
15 Apr 7.03a.m.	9.05a.m.	9.00a.m. *Carpathia* ATS. *Californian's* 3/O Groves hears *Carpathia's* bells strike as she is seen steaming away. *Californian* remains on the scene to search to leeward taking large circular sweeps before returning to where *Carpathia* abandoned five of *Titanic's* boats (C, D, 4, 14 and 15). Seen amongst the wreckage is overturned collapsible B.	Groves, BI 8367; Lord, AI p.723; Rostron, BI 25477.	
15 Apr 7.10a.m.	9.12a.m.	*Baltic* (MBC) receives MSG from *Carpathia* (MPA): From captain *Carpathia* to captain *Baltic*, 'Am proceeding for Halifax or New York full speed. You had better proceed to Liverpool. Have about 800 passengers aboard.'	PV *Baltic*.	
15 Apr 7.15a.m.	9.17a.m.	*Mount Temple* (MLQ) again reports much jamming, and that *Carpathia* (MPA) is working *Baltic* (MPA).	PV *Mount Temple*.	
15 Apr 7.30a.m.	9.32a.m.	*Baltic* (MBC) sends MSG to *Californian* (MWL): 'Stdbi immediately. You have been instructed to do so frequently. Balfour, inspector.'	PV *Mount Temple*.	
15 Apr 7.40a.m.	9.42a.m.	*Mount Temple* (MLQ) hears *Carpathia* (MPA) call CQ and says, 'No need to stand by him, nothing more can be done.' Operator Durrant then advises Capt. Moore, who reverses *Mount Temple's* course to leave the area.	PV *Mount Temple*.	
15 Apr 9.30a.m.	11.32a.m.	11.20 *Californian* ATS. *Californian* leaves scene of wreckage heading 271° True proceeding slowly across ice. DR position was 41° 33' N, 50° 01'W.	Lord, BI 7267–9; Stewart, BI 8830–1.	
15 Apr 10.20a.m.	12.22p.m.	*Frankfurt* reaches 41° 35'N, 50° 15'W. Sees *Californian* off port bow coming out of icefield.	Behe, '*Frankfurt* Incident'.	79
15 Apr 10.21a.m.	12.23p.m.	*Californian* takes a noon sight of the sun. Position is 41° 33' N, 50° 09'W. *Californian* just under 5 miles from *Frankfurt* at this time.	Lord, BI 7265.	80
15 Apr 10.26a.m.	12.28p.m.	Capt. Lord sees *Frankfurt* off to his north-west running down about SSE.	Lord, AI p.730.	81
15 Apr 2.00p.m.	4.02p.m.	*Olympic* (MKC) establishes communications with *Carpathia* (MPA).	PV *Olympic*.	
15 Apr 2.12p.m.	4.14p.m.	*Olympic* is at 41° 17'N, 53° 53'W, heading 090° True.	See entry for 2.35p.m. NYT.	
15 Apr 2.30p.m.	4.32p.m.	*Carpathia* is at 41° 15'N, 51° 45'W, heading 267° True for Nantucket Shoals light vessel.	See entry for 3.15p.m. NYT.	82
15 Apr 2.35p.m.	4.37p.m.	*Olympic* (MKC) sends message to *Carpathia* (MPA): 'Capt. *Carpathia*: 7.12p.m. GMT Our position 41.17 N, 53.53 W. Steering east, true; shall I meet you and where? Haddock.'	PV *Olympic*.	

Date	Time	Message	Source	
15 Apr 3.10p.m.	5.12p.m.	*Carpathia* (MPA) sends several messages to *Olympic* (MKC): 1. 'Capt. *Olympic*. 7.30 GMT Lat. 41.15 north, long. 51.45 west. Am steering south 87 west, true. Returning to New York with *Titanic's* passengers. Rostron.' 2. 'Capt. *Olympic*. Bruce Ismay is under opiate. Rostron.' 3. 'Capt. *Olympic*. Do you think it is advisable *Titanic's* passengers see *Olympic*? Personally I say not. Rostron.'	Booth and Coughlan, *Titanic – Signals of Disaster*.	83
15 Apr 3.15p.m.	5.17p.m.	*Olympic* (MKC) sends message to *Carpathia* (MKC): 'Capt. *Carpathia*: Kindly inform me if there is the slightest hope of searching *Titanic* position at daybreak. Agree with you on not meeting. Will stand on present course until you have passed and will then haul more to southward. Does this parallel of 41.17 N. lead clear of the ice? Have you communicated the disaster to our people at New York or Liverpool, or shall I do so, and what particulars can you give me to send? Sincere thanks for what you have done. Haddock.'	PV *Olympic*.	
15 Apr 3.25p.m.	5.27p.m.	*Carpathia* (MPA) sends to *Olympic* (MKC): 'Capt. *Olympic*. Mr Ismay orders *Olympic* not to be seen by *Carpathia*. No transfer to take place. Rostron.'	Booth and Coughlan, *Titanic – Signals of Disaster*.	84
15 Apr 4.10p.m.	6.12p.m.	*Carpathia* (MPA) sends message to *Olympic* (MKC): 'Capt. Haddock, *Olympic*. South point pack ice 41.16 north. Don't attempt to go north until 49.30 west. Many bergs. large and small, amongst pack. Also for many miles to eastward. Fear absolutely no hope searching *Titanic's* position. Left Leyland SS *Californian* searching around. All boats accounted for. About 675 souls saved, crew and passengers; latter nearly all women and children. *Titanic* foundered about 2.20am, 5.47 GMT, in 41.46 north. 50.14 west; not certain of having got through. Please forward to White Star, also to Cunard, Liverpool and New York, that I am returning to New York. Consider this most advisable for many considerations. Rostron.'	Booth and Coughlan, *Titanic – Signals of Disaster*.	
15 Apr 4.15p.m.	6.17p.m.	*Olympic* (MKC) informs *Carpathia* (MPA) that they will forward the information to White Star and Cunard immediately.	PV *Olympic*.	
15 Apr 4.35p.m.	6.37p.m.	*Olympic* (MKC) sends two messages to Cape Race (MCE) for forwarding. 1. *Olympic* to WSL office New York and Liverpool: '*Carpathia* reached *Titanic* position at daybreak. Found boats and wreckage only. *Titanic* had foundered about 2.20am in 41.16 N, 50.14 W. All her boats accounted for. About 675 souls saved, crew and passengers; latter nearly all women and children. Leyland Line SS *Californian* remaining and searching position of disaster. *Carpathia* returning to New York with survivors. Please inform Cunard. Haddock.' 2. *Olympic* to Franklin in WSL office NY: 'Inexpressible sorrow. Am proceeding straight on voyage. *Carpathia* informs me no hope in searching. Will send names survivors as obtainable. Yamsi on *Carpathia*. Haddock.'	PV *Olympic*.	85
15 Apr 5.20p.m.	7.22p.m.	*Californian* (MWL) transmits ice report to *Olympic* (MKC): 'Icebergs and field ice at 42.3 north 49.9 west; 41.33 north, 50.09 west.' He tells *Olympic* that he is 200 miles out of this course.	PV *Olympic*.	86
15 Apr 5.45p.m.	7.47p.m.	*Carpathia* (MPA) sends the following two messages to *Olympic* (MKC): 1. '(Private to Capt. Haddock, *Olympic*.) Captain: Chief, first, and sixth officers, and all engineers gone; also doctor; all pursers; one Marconi operator, and chief steward gone. We have second, third, fourth, and fifth officers and one Marconi operator on board. Rostron.' 2. 'Captain *Olympic*: Will send names immediately we can. You can understand we are working under considerable difficulty. Everything possible being done for comfort of survivors. Please maintain Stanbi. Rostron.'	PV *Olympic*.	

Notes

[1] The port side of the ship lay alongside the wharf, so the only boats that could be lowered were those on the starboard side. Lookout Jewell said the two forward boats were lowered, but it seems he must have been somewhat confused. We know that AB Scarrott was one of the seamen that manned boat No.13 during this drill, and that boat was one of four adjacent boats on the starboard side aft. We are also told that the two boats that were lowered were regular lifeboats, which excludes emergency boat No.1, the very first boat on the starboard side forward. Starting on the aft starboard side of the boat deck going forward, the first two boats that you come to would be nos 15 and 13, respectively.

[2] *New York* was moored alongside *Oceanic* at berth 38 down by the lower Test quays near the juncture of the Test and Itchen rivers. *New York* broke her moorings due to hydrodynamic interaction caused by the back-rush of water as *Titanic* was moving past the moored vessels, forcing *Titanic* to stop until several tugs were able to take control of *New York* and bring her back to the quay. Instead of the usual 5½ hours to get to Cherbourg, it took *Titanic* about 6½ hours because of this incident.

[3] The 25-minute clock adjustment on the night of 10 April would have been to change from GMT to Dublin Mean Time so they would show the local mean time when they arrived at Queenstown in the forenoon.

[4] The official departure point for transatlantic voyages leaving Queenstown was the Daunt's Rock light vessel just outside the harbour. (The Ambrose Channel light vessel at the entrance to lower NY harbour marked the end of the transatlantic crossing for vessels going to New York.) By IMM Co. Rule 116, all departures and arrivals in British and Irish waters were to be entered in the abstract logs in GMT. Arrival and departures from the United States and Canada were to entered in mean time for the 75th meridian (NYT).

[5] The 14.1 nautical miles from Daunt's Rock light vessel at 20.7 knots takes 41 minutes.

[6] The 55.2 nautical miles from Daunt's Rock light vessel to Fastnet light at 20.7 knots takes a total of 2 hours 40 minutes.

[7] Clocks on *Titanic* adjusted at midnight. Clocks in public places go back the full adjustment amount; clocks keeping bridge time used for watch keeping go back half the total adjustment amount at this time.

[8] Clocks keeping bridge time go back the remaining half of the total adjustment amount at 4a.m.

[9] Bride was clearly confused at the British inquiry. He said 11p.m. Friday to 5a.m. Saturday. However, this took place the night before the accident making the outage from Saturday night into early Sunday morning. That is why he planned to relieve Phillips earlier than usual Sunday night.

[10] From this point onward we will be showing greater detail.

[11] 45°N, 40°W on GC track is about 318 miles beyond noon position of 13 April. At 22.1 knots average over ground, time to cover that distance is 14h 23m. To get ATS: 12.00 + 14.23 − 0.23 = 26.00 = 2.00a.m.

[12] However, this took place the night before the accident making the outage from Saturday night into early Sunday morning as previously noted.

[13] There was 40 minutes between seven and eight bells during the morning watch to allow the oncoming watch enough time for breakfast. (Ref:WSL brochure given to passengers.)

[14] Time Turnbull gave as received was 1.26p.m. (Turnbull, BI 16110). The 1.26p.m. time was probably GMT, not NYT. If this was NY mean time it would suggest a 6 hour 16 minute delay in Smith's response back to Barr; far excessive compared to other responses Smith made that day. Based on navigational analysis, *Caronia* would have crossed 40°W about 7.32a.m. NYT, and her PV would then give GMT times after that. So it appears Barr's message was sent at 7.10a.m. NYT, and Smith's reply was received at 8.26a.m. NYT, consistent with other response times.

[15] There was 40 minutes between seven and eight bells during the forenoon watch to allow the oncoming watch enough time for lunch. (Ref:WSL brochure given to passengers.)

[16] *Noordam* sent this ice message to *Titanic* via *Caronia* at 2.30p.m. GMT. It was received by *Caronia* at 2.31p.m. GMT, and *Caronia* relayed the message to *Titanic* at 2.45p.m. GMT.

[17] It seems that an error may have been made when recording her noontime position in the scrap log where the departure distance from the corner longitude of 25 miles was accidentally put down for minutes-of-arc. When accounting for her speed and time between crossing 47°W and noon, the noontime longitude comes out to 47° 34'W. Her clocks would still be set for 1 hour 50 minutes

ahead of NYT. See: Samuel Halpern, 'Navigational Inconsistencies of the SS *Californian*', at: http://
www.titanicology.com/Californian/Navigational_Incosistencies.pdf.

18. The 266° True heading following the course change was discovered later by 4/O Boxhall after
getting compass deviation error following star sights. The intent was make 265° True from the corner
to the lightship.

19. In the second dog watch, the sequence of striking bells started with one bell at the first half hour.

20. In BI 13586 Lightoller said he thought he went to dinner at 7.05 and came back at 7.35. But he went
out to take star sights at 7.30 so he must have returned before that time.

21. The Marconi abbreviation 'TR' stands for 'Time Rush' messages. They are the messages that ships
exchanged with each other as soon as they entered into communications. They were used to inform each
other of any telegrams they may have for the other, and to check their clock times (BI 16215). Several
exchanges between *Carpathia* and *Titanic* followed into the evening. From PV *Carpathia* (BI 17067),
'5.30p.m. [NYT] signals exchanged with the "Titanic" at frequent intervals until 9.45p.m. [NYT].'

22. End of second dog watch marked with eight bells.

23. In an affidavit addressed to Senator Smith at the American inquiry, Miss Daisy Minahan wrote that
Captain Smith could not have been on the 'Bridge from 8.45 to 9.25' talking to an officer because
she saw him first leave a dinner party given by the Wideners in the restaurant between 9.25 and
9.45pm. She said she knew the time because her brother suggested at 9.25 that they should leave
and go to bed, which they did 20 minutes later. However, according to a newspaper account by Mrs
Lillian Minahan, Daisy's sister-in-law, she, her husband and Daisy retired early that evening, and that
'it was about 9.30 when I got into bed.' Obviously one cannot leave the restaurant at 9.45 and be
in bed by 9.30 the same night. One simple explanation is that Daisy's brother, Dr William Minahan,
either forgot to set his pocket watch back the night before (thus showing a time that was 45 minutes
ahead of ship's time for 14 April), or he simply suggested to his sister that it was later than it really was.

24. The reference here to 'one bell' must not be confused with the striking of the bell once after the
first half hour of a watch. It was also the practice to strike the bell once halfway between seven
bells and eight bells as a warning to those below that they were due on deck in 15 minutes. In this
case Hichens was simply implying that he went to tell Murdoch that he was due on deck in 15
minutes. The bell was not physically struck.

25. Lights in the smoking rooms were extinguished at midnight. (IMM Co. Rule 21; WSL passenger
brochure: 'Information for Passengers', shown on p.36 of Peter Thresh's book, *Titanic: The Truth Behind
the Disaster.*) The extinguishing of lights at midnight apparently included not only the smoking
rooms on *Titanic*, but also the Café Parisien, as some passengers were still up playing cards there
when the accident happened (e.g., Alfred Fernand Omont, Pierre Maréchal, Paul Chevré and Lucien
Smith). The clocks were expected to be put back at midnight, and a number of passengers stayed up
waiting for that to take place.

26. Time from when three bells were struck by Fleet to the moment of collision is estimated to be about
50–55 seconds. See Chapter 5.

27. Range of most accounts for the collision time was from 11.40 to 11.45. The American inquiry report
listed the collision at 11.46p.m.; the British inquiry report listed the collision at 11.40p.m. We have
taken the time of collision at 11.40p.m. *Titanic* ATS.

28. Shier's put this at 4–5 minutes after impact. Correlates well with Lightoller's observation.

29. Hendrickson's time. Our estimate based on his reported actions. From reconstructed PV *Carpathia*
(BI 17067), '5.30p.m. signals exchanged with the "Titanic" at frequent intervals until 9.45p.m.' If
Cottam's time was correct, this would have been just minutes after the accident.

30. Note given to Olliver apparently was written by Smith, but Olliver did not say who gave it to him to
take below. (Was Smith already going below to find Bell, or to meet up with Andrews if he knew that
Andrews was heading to see Bell?) There is no evidence that Andrews or Smith actually met up with
Bell. With lights out in the stokeholds Bell could have been almost anywhere trying to sort things
out. If Smith met up with Andrews at that time, Andrews may have told Smith he was going forward
to check on the reported flooding in forward holds that the carpenter reported. Boxhall said he saw
Andrews that night after the collision, but they didn't speak. Boxhall was uncovering boats between
about 12.00 and 12.25 and so it may have been after he came from the mail room.

31. It seems that the boatswain's mate gave the watch below a warning that they may be needed
topside before all hands were actually called out. Symons' observation about water around the hatch

coamings in hold 1 implies the ship was down at the head by almost 1° at this time. Lights were reported out in BR 5 (Barrett) and BR 4 (Cavell). Time of going to get lamps for the stokeholds estimated from Hendrickson's and Barrett's described actions. Johnstone estimated the time he saw the water was 25 minutes after collision; Wheat estimated the time he saw the water was 10–15 minutes after collision. Wheat had to be in the mail room shortly after Boxhall was, based on the water level seen. Mackay thought Smith had been aft for about 10 minutes before he saw him come back. Johnstone's and Wheat's observations were consistent with Boxhall seeing flooding coming within 2ft of G deck just a few minutes earlier.

32. Evans had his contact with *Mount Temple* at about 10.00p.m. NYT, while Durrant showed this contact with *Carpathia* was at 9.55p.m. NYT.

33. Boxhall said 20–30 minutes to call upon the officers. Lightoller thought it was about ½ hour, Pitman thought it was about 20 minutes. Wheat said it was about 5–6 minutes after seeing the water on G deck.

34. Lights coming back on estimated by the time taken for Barrett and Hendrickson to get lamps from the engine room to take to the stokeholds. From Chamber's observation of water level, the ship was down by the head about 1.3° at this time. The three officers he saw may have been engineers sent forward to inspect flooding. He did not recognise their department.

35. Pitman's time. Our estimate based on his stated actions.

36. Since it took Dillon 1 hour 40 minutes from time of collision to the time he left BR 4, and 1 hour 10 minutes from leaving engine room to leaving BR 4, that leaves 30 minutes after collision when he left the engine room to open the WTDs forward. From Robinson's water level account, the ship is down by the head by almost 2.0° at this time. At this point Smith knew things were very serious but he also knew the ship could stay afloat with the first four compartments flooded.

37. Ismay not sure when this was. Hichens not sure of specific time but said it was after 12.00. We put it before Wheat heard McElroy give order to have stewards get passengers up on deck with lifebelts on. Hichens left the bridge at 12.23.

38. Mrs Warren estimated this event took place about 45 minutes after the collision.

39. From Poingdestre's observation, the ship was down by the head by between 2½ to 3° at this time.

40. Boxhall was out on the boat deck uncovering boats when someone spotted a light off the port bow. Boxhall went to the bridge (presumably to get a pair of binoculars) to have a closer look at the reported light. He said he met Smith, who asked him how the work to clear the boats was going. It was then he asked Smith how serious was it, and Smith told him what Andrews had said. From context of the testimony, it was at this time he went to work on the ship's position, before he saw the light through a pair of glasses. Since we know the time that the CQD with his coordinates went out, this had to be about the time we show. It would take him about 5 minutes to work the position before he showed it to Smith who told him to take it to the Marconi cabin. It was after he left the position with Phillips that he went back on the bridge to look at the light of the stopped steamer off their port bow (BI 15391–2). Annie Robinson said it was about 45 minutes after the accident that Andrews told her to put her lifebelt on.

41. Scott said the order to open the watertight doors aft came at 'quarter to one'.

42. PV *Ypiranga* had 10.46p.m. NYT; PV *Mount Temple* had 10.48p.m. NYT. *Frankfurt*'s 12a.m. (midnight) for her position report was apparently ship's time. The question 'What is the matter with you?' probably came about because the 10.40p.m. NYT contact told *Frankfurt* that *Titanic* 'was on ice'. It may not have been clear to the German operator at first that *Titanic* was sinking.

43. From BI 17068 & 17115, it can be implied that Cottam returned close to 10 minutes after receiving the CQD with *Carpathia*'s position. Cottam overheard *Titanic* communicating with *Frankfurt* when he returned, so we put the time down at 10.47p.m. NYT.

44. Time based on Ray having seen boat No.7 being lowered (launched at 12.40) and then 5 minutes to reach the sea from 60ft. We assume Ray was by the emergency door from the working alley into the first class stairway within 5 minutes of seeing No.7 reach the water. Ray's observation is consistent with Wheat's observation which we put down for 12.45 except that water came up to that point in the working alley as well as the starboard side corridor by this time. Wheat said the working alley was still dry when he was there, but the water was coming from the starboard-side corridor to the staircase (BI 1104–5). *Titanic*'s starboard list may have started to straighten out by the time Ray arrived there which would explain why Ray saw water on both sides, while Wheat did not.

45. Cottam said this was about 4 minutes after he initially gave his position to *Titanic*.

46. *Ypiranga's* PV had 'MKC to MGN?????' Most probably it was a call to MGY. Note: an 'N' in Morse code is sent by a dash-dot while a 'Y' is a dash-dot-dash-dash.

47. We put this down as immediately after the contact attempt noted by *Ypiranga's* PV for 10.52 NYT. This implies that steam was still blowing off while *Olympic* was trying to contact *Titanic*. It probably stopped very soon after this.

48. PV *Olympic* listed this at 11.00 NYT.

49. Time estimated for bringing the pipe forward is based on getting four watertight doors opened aft assuming it took 5 minutes each.

50. PV *Frankfurt* shows *Cincinnati* and *Olympic* answering *Titanic* at this time.

51. PV *Ypiranga* only shows a contact between these two ships at this time. Symons' observation implies ship down at the head by about 4.0° at this time. Time based on boat No.1 launch time and allowing for boat being hung up by guy wire on the way down. Cavell said there were still men pulling the fires in BR when he went up the escape to E deck.

52. Dillon said it was 1 hour 40 minutes after collision [1.20a.m.]. Scott said he was ordered up at 1.20; Threlfall said this order came at 1.20.

53. PV *Ypiranga* has contact at 11.18 NYT. PV *Caronia* has these words at 4.15a.m. GMT [11.15 NYT]. PV *Mount Temple* and PV *Olympic* has this transmission with these words listed at 11.20 NYT.

54. We base this on the timing that the order came to abandon the stokeholds at 1.20a.m. ATS. Those two boats, 13 and 15, were lowered to A deck for loading.

55. See entry for 11.34p.m. NYT.

56. PV *Ypiranga* had 11.26p.m. NYT for this, while PV *Mount Temple* had 11.25p.m. NYT.

57. PV *Ypiranga* had this at 11.27p.m. NYT.

58. Wilding thought that it would take them at least a ½ hour to bring the pipe forward and get it connected up once all the watertight doors aft and forward were raised.

59. PV *Ypiranga* has 11.34 NYT, while PV *Olympic* had 11.35 NYT for this communication. PV *Frankfurt* only shows MGY and MKC working together at 11.35 NYT.

60. PV *Ypiranga* has this for 11.37 NYT. PV *Mount Temple* had this 'putting women off' message and the 11.34 message listed above for 11.35 NYT. PV *Baltic* lists the women in small boats message at 11.35 NYT. PV *Virginian* has this for 11.35 NYT.

61. Both have 'putting passengers off' message at same time 11.40 NY. PV *Birma* logged this at 1.30 ship's time which would correspond to 11.43p.m. NYT, but they rounded their times to the nearest 5 minutes.

62. PV *Olympic* had this at 11.45 NYT. Ship down at the head about 5° based on observations of Barrett and Nichols after these boats reached the water.

63. PV *Ypiranga* lists this at 11.47p.m. NYT. PV *Baltic* listed this at 11.50p.m. NYT. PV *Mount Temple* has the *Olympic* MSG sent at 11.47p.m. NYT. PV *Olympic* logs it at 11.50p.m. NYT. *Olympic* and *Baltic* PVs show messages in only 5-minute increments during these critical hours.

64. Based on observation reported by Phillips to Bride about the well deck being awash, *Titanic* was down by the head about 5.5° at this time.

65. This may have been the time that Bride heard Phillips tell *Frankfurt* to 'keep out of it, to stand by' as Phillips, according to Bride, was trying to communicate with *Carpathia*. But it seems that *Titanic's* power was now greatly reduced as steam pressure supplying the electric dynamo engines continued to drop. The last transmission from *Titanic* that *Carpathia* heard was about 5 minutes before. As Bride said, 'Mr Phillips called once or twice more, but the power was failing us and I do not think we were getting a spark, as there were no replies.' (BI 16561–66.)

66. Observation of well deck submerged and forecastle head under water implies ship was down by the head about 6.5° at this time.

67. This may have been the last transmission from *Titanic*, but strangely, it was not reported by any other vessels that were actually closer to *Titanic*. At this same time *Mount Temple* reported three other ships calling MGY and getting no response. These were *Olympic*, *Frankfurt* and *Baltic*. The PVs of those other vessels do not list these, nor do they say that they heard anything from *Titanic* at this time. But ship's PVs did not list every transmission that took place. If these vessels did try to call *Titanic* about this time, one or all of them should have been heard by Phillips since the ability to receive signals had nothing to do with *Titanic's* ability to transmit signals, or the electrical power supplied to the Marconi set. The receiver was a passive device that worked by a windup clockwork mechanism. The strength of received signals depended primarily on the strengths of the signals transmitted by the other vessels

and their distances away from the receiving vessel. Other wireless signals heard afterward were thought to have come from *Titanic*, even as late as 1.58a.m. NYT by *Birma*. It should be noted that Harold Bride estimated that he and Phillips abandoned the wireless cabin about 10 minutes before the ship went under (AI p.158) having heard no replies back to the last CQD message that Phillips sent out.

68 Lightoller's observation implies ship down at the head by about 10° at this time. Time is based on events just before breakup, and Joughin's observation of 2.15 on his watch.

69. Gibson said steamer had 'disappeared' and Stone said 'gone out of sight' in their respective reports to Capt. Lord on 18 April while *Californian* was still at sea. *Californian* ATS was 12 minutes behind *Titanic* ATS. Symons estimates lights went out 2–3 minutes before the stern disappeared.

70. Wreck site location taken at the centre of the boiler field. Numerous references to 2.20. Both the America and British inquiry reports listed the sinking at 2.20a.m. ATS. Several of the lifeboats had oil lamps that were lit enabling people to read their watches.

71. *Virginian's* operator assumed that this came from *Titanic*. Most likely this came from a far-off land station with a rotary spark gap transmitter that was being tuned before going on line.

72. *Virginian's* operator assumed that this came from *Titanic*. Most likely a far-off land station with a rotary spark gap trying to establish contact with another station. The transmission of the letters 'CQ' was used as a general call up signal by wireless stations worldwide. Harold Cottam on *Carpathia*, then perhaps only about 25 miles away, did not hear what *Virginia's* operator heard. Nor did John Durrant on *Mount Temple* report hearing these. Cottam later said that he did not believe that these faint signals came from *Titanic* when he found out about them at the British inquiry (BI 17147). And Durrant said that *Titanic's* signal did not appear to get weaker near the end (BI 9548) as his ship was getting closer. Both these vessels were much closer to *Titanic* than *Virginian* was. *Carpathia* reported being 58 miles from the CQD, *Mount Temple* reported being 49 miles from the CQD, and *Virginian* reported being 178 miles from the CQD, when they each picked up the first calls for assistance.

73 This most likely came from *Carpathia*. See message for 1.25a.m. NYT.

74. This was well after *Titanic* had foundered, close to the time that *Carpathia* was coming near to picking up the first boat.

75. *Carpathia* ATS was 1 hour 57 minutes ahead of NYT. (Ref: Halpern, '12:35a.m. Apparent Time *Carpathia*'.)

76 Notice that this came 17 minutes after *Birma* had told *Frankfurt* that she was only 50 miles away from the CQD location. This is likely an error in reception by *Virginian* who was plagued by atmospherics all night. *Birma* most likely transmitted that she was then 45 miles away. (Ref: Halpern, 'The Enigmatic Excursion of the SS *Birma*.')

77. Gambell said he sent this message at 5.45a.m. *Virginian* ATS. His ship was 1 hour 30 minutes ahead of NYT making the transmission time 4.15a.m. NYT. Log of *Californian* had this MSG message listed at 6.00a.m. *Californian* ATS (4.10a.m. NYT).

78 Lightoller was picked up from overturned collapsible boat B along with many others. He then assumed command of boat 12.

79. Time is 1 minute before local apparent noon for the longitude given on that date.

80. *Californian* ATS now 1 hour 39 minutes ahead of NYT at their local apparent noon for their given longitude on this date.

81. Lord said this was about 5 minutes past noon.

82. The longitude of *Carpathia* in the message, 51° 45'W, corresponds to a local mean time that is precisely 3 hours 27 minutes behind GMT. It was this time difference that later shows up in the message transmitted to *Olympic* at 4.00p.m. NYT which led to the erroneous foundering time of 5.47a.m. GMT.

83. These three messages were put down in *Olympic's* PV as being received with a number of messages from *Carpathia* at 3.15p.m. NYT. *Carpathia's* Marconi office form shows these three were sent at 3.10p.m. NYT.

84. This message was listed in *Olympic's* PV as being received with other *Carpathia* messages at 3.15p.m. NYT. *Carpathia's* Marconi office form shows it was first sent at 3.25p.m. NYT.

85. 'Yamsi' was the not so subtle way of saying 'Ismay' (spelled backward).

86 The first set of coordinates in this ice report, 42.3 north 49.9 west, were exactly the same as that sent to *Antillian* on 14 April at 5.35p.m. NYT. The second set of coordinates, 41.33 north, 50.09 west, corresponded to *Californian's* noontime location for 15 April when she departed the west side of the pack ice on her way to Boston.

14

SUMMARY OF THE FINDINGS OF THIS REPORT

Samuel Halpern

In this centennial report, we have attempted to address a number of questions about the loss of *Titanic* in light of the wealth of information now available to us today. The following is a summary of our findings:

About the Ship

1: How well was *Titanic* designed and how did she compare to other vessels of the period?

Titanic's design employed tried and tested materials and construction methods, combined with a number of technological improvements such as increased hydraulic riveting and strengthening measures commensurate with her greater size. The ship's structural design was similar to other large vessels of the 1907–14 period. Her strength was ample for her required service as demonstrated by the long and successful career of her sister ship *Olympic*. The calculated stress in tons per square inch on the uppermost structural deck shows that *Titanic* was built to the same standards as other contemporary vessels also built with mild steel of the period. The typical thickness of shell plating amidships on *Titanic* and her sister ship *Olympic* were very similar to other large vessels of the time. [Ref: Chapter 6.]

2: Could *Titanic* stand up to the most exacting conditions of the North Atlantic service?

The JMS marine engineering firm in early 2007 disproved the supposition that *Titanic* and her sister *Olympic* were weakly designed ships. Harland & Wolff designed *Olympic* and *Titanic* to handle a bending moment of 1,473,333ft-tons, or more than a factor of two times greater than the maximum bending moment in the JMS theoretical 'design' case for the North Atlantic service. The ship did not sink because she broke apart. She broke apart in the very last stages of sinking which imposed excessive stresses and bending moments on the hull as the stern was pulled further out of the water as the ship lost longitudinal stability. [Ref: Chapter 6.]

3: What provisions did *Titanic* have in her design for the safety of the vessel and those on board in the event of collisions and other casualties?

Titanic was divided into sixteen major watertight compartments by fifteen transverse watertight bulkheads. She was equipped with a cellular double bottom for protection against grounding accidents. She was labelled as a 'two compartment vessel' because she could remain afloat with any two adjacent watertight compartments completely open to the sea. In reality, she almost met a three-compartment standard except for three specific conditions that had nothing to do with the accident. In fact, she would remain afloat with all of the first four compartments flooded, all of the last four compartments flooded, flooding in adjacent boiler rooms nos 1 through to 4, or flooding in the reciprocating engine room and boiler rooms nos 1 through 3. *Titanic's* compartmentalisation would have met current SOLAS floodable length standards despite bulkheads that only extended as high as E and D decks forward. [Ref: Chapter 3.]

4: What lifesaving appliances were carried on board, and how did that compare to the requirements of the BOT and other ships of the time?

Titanic met or exceeded BOT requirements then in effect. She was equipped with forty-eight solid white lifebuoys, six 'Holmes Lights' for the lifebuoys, and 3,560 lifebelts. She had fourteen 30ft lifeboats, two 25ft emergency cutters and four 27ft collapsible lifeboats. She was equipped with sixteen sets of Welin davits on her boat deck for launching the boats. *Titanic* was also equipped with thirty-six socket distress signals in lieu of guns or rockets and was provided with twelve flare-up lights and two self-igniting deck flares. [Ref: Chapter 3.]

5: What means besides wireless telegraphy were provided to communicate with other vessels, and were those means utilised?

In addition to wireless telegraphy, *Titanic* was equipped with two Morse signalling lamps and a full complement of flags as required for company identification, signalling, dressing ship, etc. On the night of the accident, Morse signalling lamps were used in an attempt to gain the attention of a ship seen off her port bow. Socket distress signals were sent up at intervals in accordance with the rules of the road. WSL company signals, green handheld flares, were used by *Titanic's* Fourth Officer Joseph Boxhall in boat No.2 to attract the attention of the other lifeboats drifting on the sea. Those flares enabled *Carpathia* to find Boxhall's boat even though it was still too dark to be seen. [Ref: Chapters 3 and 7.]

6: What type of wireless installation was on board *Titanic* and what was its expected range?

Titanic's wireless installation consisted of a Marconi 5-kW rotary spark-gap generating set. The guaranteed working range of the equipment was 250 miles, but usually would work to about 400 miles or more. She also had an emergency 1½-kW backup set which, as it turned out, was not needed. [Ref: Chapter 3.]

7: What accommodation did the ship have for its passengers and crew, and how would they gain access to the boats in case of emergency?

There were various means for passengers and crew to gain access to the boat deck. This is covered in detail in Chapter 3 and in Appendix J.

8: Did *Titanic* comply with the requirements of the Rules and Regulations in effect at the time with regard to passenger steamers and emigrant ships when she departed on her maiden voyage?

Yes. [Ref: Chapters 3 and 8.]

About Passengers and Crew On Board

9: How many crewmembers were on board *Titanic* when she left Queenstown (distinguishing by department and positions held)?

There was a total of 891 crewmembers on board *Titanic* when she left Queenstown, 66 in the deck department, 325 in the engine department, and 500 in the victualling department. More specific details are provided in Chapter 4 and Appendices D, E and F.

10: How many passengers were on board *Titanic* when she left Queenstown (distinguishing by class, men, women and children)?

There was a total of 1,317 passengers on board *Titanic* when she left Queenstown, 324 in first class, 284 in second class, and 709 in third class. Specific details by gender and class are provided in Chapter 4 and Appendices A, B and C.

11: How many and who were lost and saved?

1,496 persons were lost; 712 persons were saved. Specific breakdowns are given in Chapter 4 and Appendices A through F.

About the Route Followed and Warnings Received

12: What instructions were given or known prior to the sailing as to the route to be followed and precautions taken for any dangers likely to be encountered during the voyage?

The normal route for steamers for that time of year was followed. There were no special sailing instructions. [Ref: Chapter 5.]

13: How far did the ship advance each day along the route she took? What were her noontime positions for each day, and what was her average speed of advance along the route for each day?

The total distance travelled from departure at Daunt's Rock light vessel outside Queenstown to where she collided with an iceberg was about 1,807 nautical miles. Her average speed made good over the three days, 12 hours and 18 minutes was 21.44 knots. Details for daily progress are given in Chapter 5.

14: What was the weather like along the route of travel?

Titanic experienced variable weather throughout. On the night of 14 April, she was in clear skies and flat-calm seas with temperatures dropping below freezing. Weather details for each day of her maiden voyage are given in Chapter 5.

15: Did *Titanic* have an adequate supply of coal on board? Was this a factor in limiting the speed of the vessel? Was *Titanic* out to break any records?

Titanic had enough coal on board to reach New York with enough reserve for two days extra steaming. Her speed was not limited by the supply of coal. But for the accident, *Titanic* would have bettered *Olympic*'s maiden voyage crossing time, arriving at New York's Ambrose light vessel late Tuesday night instead of the previously arranged time of 5a.m. Wednesday morning.

However, *Titanic* was not out to break, nor was she capable of breaking, the transatlantic crossing records held by the Cunard liners *Lusitania* and *Mauretania*. [Ref: Chapter 5.]

16: What warnings reached *Titanic* concerning the existence of ice along the route, when were they received, and what were the reported locations?

Details of ice warnings received, along with reported locations, are provided in Chapter 5.

17: Was *Titanic*'s course altered as a consequence of receiving such information, and if so, in what way?

Titanic's course was not altered in any way whatsoever from her intended track despite receiving numerous ice warnings along the way. Later claims that her turn at 'the corner' was delayed is not supported by the available navigational evidence. It seems that the story of a delayed turn came about in an attempt to explain how *Titanic* could have reached the longitude given in her distress position if her course was altered at 5.50p.m. ATS. We know now that her distress position was 13 miles too far west of where *Titanic* really sank, and when *Titanic* 'turned the corner', she was actually within 2 or 3 miles of the corner point at 42°N, 47°W. [Ref: Chapter 5.]

18: Were any directions given as to the speed of the vessel as a consequence of ice information received, and were they carried out?

There were no known orders given as a consequence of ice warnings received. *Titanic*'s speed was continually increased after she departed Queenstown, including connecting up additional boilers as late as 7p.m., 14 April. Her speed through the water was reported at 22.5 knots between 8 and 10p.m. that night. [Ref: Chapter 5.]

19: What precautions were taken by *Titanic* in anticipation of meeting ice? How did that compare to what was done on other vessels being navigated in waters where ice was expected?

There were no extra precautions taken while approaching the ice region except that the lookouts in the crow's nest were told 'to keep a sharp lookout for ice, particularly small ice and growlers.' Other vessels, such as *Mount Temple*, were deliberately taken well south of the region of known ice. [Ref: Chapter 5.]

20: Was a good and proper lookout for ice kept on board? Were binoculars provided for and used by the lookout men? Is the use of binoculars necessary or desirable in such circumstances?

There were only three men on the lookout at the time of the accident, two in the crow's nest, and the Officer of the Watch on the bridge. The lookouts were not provided with binoculars, which are mainly useful in identifying an object after it is sighted. Binoculars restrict the field of vision and can delay the spotting of an object if not properly used. [Ref: Chapter 5.]

21: Were searchlights provided for and used on *Titanic*? If not, should searchlights have been provided and used?

Searchlights were not provided. The topic was also raised and discussed at the British inquiry in 1912. At the first SOLAS convention in 1913, searchlights were recommended but for use in rescue operations, as is still the practice today. They were not recommended for detecting icebergs or other obstructions. [Ref: Chapter 12.]

About the Collision and Flooding

22: What time was carried on *Titanic* on the day of the accident, and how did it compare to time in New York?

Titanic carried Apparent Time Ship while at sea. Her clocks on Sunday 14 April 1912, were 2 hours and 2 minutes ahead of clocks in New York. [Ref: Chapter 5 and Appendix G.]

23: What was the time and location of *Titanic* when she collided with an iceberg?

Titanic struck an iceberg near 41° 46'N, 49° 56'W, at approximately 11.40p.m. ATS, 9.38p.m. New York Time (NYT), on Sunday 14 April 1912. [Ref: Chapter 5.]

24: How far ahead of the ship was the iceberg when it was first seen?

When the lookout bell sounded, the iceberg was about 2,000ft (⅓ of a nautical mile) ahead of *Titanic.* [Ref: Chapter 5.]

25: How fast was *Titanic* going before the moment of impact?

When the lookout bell sounded, *Titanic* was making about 22½ knots. At the moment of impact her speed would have been reduced to a little over 20½ knots, mainly due to hydrodynamic drag as the ship was entering a hard turn to port. [Ref: Chapter 6.]

26: What actions were taken to avoid collision or mitigate damage to the vessel once the ship came in contact with the iceberg? Was the collision unavoidable?

The first action taken was to turn the ship hard to port ('hard-a-starboard' helm order) in an attempt to avoid contact. This came after the lookouts up in the crow's nest reported an 'iceberg right ahead' by phone after the lookout bell was first struck three times signifying some object was sighted ahead. The engines were also ordered to stop, and possibly reverse, before contact in an attempt to mitigate damage, but the engines did not come to a stop or reverse until a minute or two after the collision had taken place. Once the ship's bow came into contact with the iceberg, the helm was shifted hard over to the opposite side as the berg passed aft of the bridge in an attempt to swing the stern away from the iceberg to mitigate any further damage along the starboard side. With hindsight, the collision may have been avoided if evasive action was taken as soon as the three-bell warning from the lookouts was sounded instead of after the phone call came down from the crow's nest. We do not know if the iceberg was spotted first from the crow's nest, or by the OOW out on the bridge wing. But the evidence shows that there was about as much as 30 seconds' delay between the three-bell warning and the order to put the helm hard-a-starboard. [Ref: Chapter 5.]

27: What was the extent of the damage caused by the collision?

Major damage to the ship took place in the first five watertight compartments. There was reported flooding in the forepeak tank, nos 1, 2 and 3 holds, and No.6 boiler room. There was also some slight damage in the forward bunker space of No.5 boiler room, and possibly some slight damage below the stokehold plate level in No.4 boiler room. [Ref: Chapter 6.]

28: What steps were taken, if any, to prevent the vessel from sinking?

The ship's pumps were started within minutes of the collision. However, the total capacity of all the ship's ballast and bilge pumps (1,700 tons per hour) was only 4 per cent of the initial flooding rate. [Ref: Chapter 6.]

29: How quickly was water entering the ship, and how did that affect the vessel's longitudinal and transverse stability?

The initial flooding rate would be a little over 11 tons of seawater entering the ship per second. By 45 minutes after impact, 12.25a.m. Apparent Time Ship (ATS), the ship had taken in about 13,500 tons of seawater. By 2.15a.m. ATS the ship had taken in about 33,000 tons of seawater. The ship remained essentially stable in both transverse and longitudinal directions until the very last minutes before she sank when she started to lose longitudinal stability causing stresses on her hull to exceed the design strength. Despite developing slight lists, first to starboard and then to port, the ship was never in danger of capsizing. [Ref: Chapter 6.]

30: Did a fire in one of the coal bunkers contribute to the loss of the ship?

No. See detailed discussion in Chapter 6.

31: When was it determined that the ship would not survive?

Our estimate is that by 45 minutes after the collision, it was realised that the flooding was uncontrollable in hold nos 1, 2 and 3, and No.6 boiler room (the second, third, fourth and fifth major watertight compartments from the bow). This meant that the ship could not be saved. At that time, Thomas Andrews estimated the ship had from 1 hour to 1½ hours left. The ship actually stayed afloat about 2 hours from that point in time. [Ref: Chapter 7.]

32: What was the affect of flooding on the stresses imposed on the hull of the vessel?

The calculated bending moment when the ship was down at the head by 10° was about 1,540,000 foot-tons in hog, which was slightly greater than the Harland & Wolff design point which was more that double the worst case service condition. As the vessel continued to trim down by the head, the bending moment continued to increase beyond this point until the break occurred. [Ref: Chapter 6.]

33: At what angle did the ship break in two? When did the break occur, and how long after did the ship sink?

The break started to occur somewhere after *Titanic* trimmed down more than 10° when two sharp cracks were heard as the bow took a sudden cant forward. This then pulled the stern higher out of the water to an angle of perhaps 30° before it started to settle back. This occurred about 2.17a.m. ATS, when all the electric lights suddenly went out as the ship was seen to break in two. After first returning to a near horizontal position, the forward part of the remaining stern section started to flood very rapidly causing the poop to rise up to a relatively steep angle before it started to slip forward. The stern section slipped under the surface of the water at 2.20a.m. ATS. There was not much suction reported when she finally disappeared. [Ref: Chapter 6.]

34: What was the time and location when *Titanic* foundered?

Titanic foundered on Monday 15 April 1912, at 2.20a.m. ATS, 12.18a.m. NYT, at 41° 43' 32"N, 49° 56' 49"W (the location of the centre of the boiler field). [Ref: Chapter 6.]

35: How deep is the wreck and what does the wreck site show?

The wreck lies at the bottom of the North Atlantic at a depth of 12,460ft (about 2½ miles down). She lies in two major pieces with the bow section about 750 yards north of the stern section. [Ref: Chapter 6.]

About Taking to the Boats and Calling for Assistance

36: What were the number, type and carrying capacity of the boats carried on board *Titanic*? Were there prior arrangements for manning and launching the boats should an emergency arise, and were any boat drills held?

Titanic carried a total of twenty lifeboats, fourteen of which were rated at sixty-five persons, two at forty persons, and four at forty-seven persons. [Ref: Chapters 3 and 8.] Boat assignment lists for the crew existed, but many of the crew did not know what boat they were assigned to. There were no lifeboat drills conducted which involved passengers or crewmembers other than the deck department crew. Before leaving Southampton, the deck department was mustered and two boats were lowered to the water and rowed about for a short time to satisfy the BOT officer. No further drills were conducted. [See Chronology in Chapter 13.]

37: How soon after the collision was the crew called out to uncover the boats?

The deck crew was called out to uncover the boats at about midnight, 20 minutes after the collision. [Ref: Chapter 7.]

38: How and when were passengers appraised of the situation?

The call to have passengers come up on deck with lifebelts on was apparently given 30 to 35 minutes after the collision (12.10–12.15a.m. ATS). Most were called out by stewards. There was no general alarm. [Ref: Chapter 7.]

39: When was the order given to actually load the boats with women and children and send them away?

The order to begin loading the boats with women and children came about 45 minutes after the collision (12.25a.m. ATS). [Ref: Chapter 7.]

40: Were passengers treated differently by class?

It does appear that different classes of passengers were in fact treated differently, particularly those in third class. This is borne out by survivor statistics as well as a number of survivor accounts that indicated that a number of steerage passengers were detained by closed or guarded gates. [Ref: Chapter 8 and Appendix J.]

41: In what order and at what times were the lifeboats launched? Who supervised the individual launchings? Who was put or took charge of each boat when it was sent away?

See Chapter 7 for list and other details.

42: How many people were in each boat as they arrived at *Carpathia*?

See Chapter 7 for list and other details.

43: In what sequence did the boats arrive at *Carpathia*?

See Chapter 7 for list and supporting details in Appendix I.

44: When did *Titanic* first call for help? When was the last call sent out?

The first wireless call for help was logged at 10.25a.m. NYT (12.27a.m. *Titanic* ATS). The last wireless call seems to have been sent out around 12.10a.m. NYT (2.12a.m. *Titanic* ATS). [Ref: Chapter 7.]

45: How many ships responded to *Titanic*'s call for assistance, and how far away were they from *Titanic*'s reported position?

See Chapter 7 for list and other details.

46: When did *Titanic* first fire distress rockets (socket signals)? When was the last one fired? Were they seen or heard by any other vessel, and did they respond?

The first distress rocket was sent up by Fourth Officer Joseph Boxhall at about 12.47a.m. *Titanic* ATS. The last distress rocket was sent up by Quartermaster George Rowe about 1.50a.m. *Titanic* ATS. [Ref: Chapter 7.] Eight of *Titanic*'s distress rockets were seen from *Californian* over a period of about an hour. *Californian* did not respond. [Ref: Chapter 10.]

About the Rescue and Actions of Other Vessels

47: What actions were taken by those on *Carpathia* when they first learned about *Titanic*? How long did it take for *Carpathia* to arrive on the scene, and what did they find?

Carpathia was turned at around 12.35a.m. *Carpathia* ATS, about 3 minutes after receiving a distress call from *Titanic*. It took *Carpathia* about 3½ hours to arrive on the scene coming up from the SE. The green flares fired by *Titanic*'s Fourth Officer Joseph Boxhall were spotted, and Boxhall's boat was alongside by 4.10a.m. *Carpathia* ATS. The other lifeboats from *Titanic* were seen as day began to break, and all the other survivors were picked up. Some wreckage from *Titanic* was also seen later in the morning, including overturned collapsible lifeboat B from *Titanic*. To the west was a vast field of pack ice that trended from NW to SE as far as the eye could see, and there were many icebergs all around. [Ref: Chapters 9 and 7.]

48: When did *Carpathia* leave the scene? When was the decision made to return to New York, and what path did *Carpathia* take when she departed the area of the wreckage?

Carpathia departed the scene about 9a.m. *Carpathia* ATS. She departed southward to go around a vast field of pack ice that extended down to latitude 41° 15'N. The decision to return to New York was made sometime after she left the scene of the accident. At the time she departed the area, she informed *Baltic* that she was 'proceeding for Halifax or New York full speed.' [Ref: Chapter 9 and Chronology in Chapter 13.]

49: Were *Titanic*'s distress rockets seen from *Californian*? How well do events seen from *Californian* correlate with events that took place on *Titanic*? Where was *Californian* relative to *Titanic* when *Titanic* foundered?

Eight of *Titanic*'s distress rockets were seen from *Californian*'s upper bridge by Second Officer Herbert Stone. While looking through a pair of glasses, *Californian*'s Apprentice James Gibson saw the flash on *Titanic*'s deck at the moment when one of the distress signals was fired. He then followed the streak of the burning fuse as the explosive shell went skyward, and then saw it burst into white stars. Three of *Carpathia*'s rockets were later seen from *Californian*'s bridge while *Carpathia* was coming up from the south-east and still a good 10 miles away from reaching the first lifeboat to be picked up.

50: What actions were taken by those on *Mount Temple* when they first learned about *Titanic*? When did *Mount Temple* arrive on the scene, and where was she relative to the location of *Carpathia* and *Californian*? What was reportedly seen by those on *Mount Temple*, and what actions were taken if any?

Mount Temple received a call for help from *Titanic* at 10.25p.m. NYT (12.11a.m. *Mount Temple* ATS). She was turned around within 5 minutes after receiving an updated set of coordinates from *Titanic* that were sent out at 10.35p.m. NYT (12.21a.m. *Mount Temple* ATS). By 4.46a.m. *Mount Temple* ATS, 4 hours 20 minutes after turning around and coming up from the SW, *Mount Temple* lay stopped on the west side of a vast field of pack ice with embedded icebergs that blocked her path further eastward. She was stopped about 8 nautical miles away from *Californian* which was to the northward, and about 8 nautical miles from *Carpathia* which was to the south-eastward. She was seen, but not identified, in the early morning twilight by both *Carpathia* and *Californian* about 30 minutes before sunrise. *Mount Temple* had a small tramp steamer with a single black funnel and two masts in sight a little to her southward. That steamer was also stopped on the western side of the pack ice. After stopping, *Mount Temple* took no further action until it became light enough to safely back out of the ice and head southward looking for a passage to get across to the other side. She eventually sighted *Carpathia* on the eastern side of ice field, and later saw *Californian* moving across the ice from east to west, about that same distance to the north as *Carpathia* was to the east. [Ref: Chapter 11.]

Appendix A

FIRST CLASS PASSENGERS

Lester J. Mitcham

When *Titanic* left Queenstown there were 324 first class passengers on board. Of those, 123 were lost and 201 were saved. Those lost are in **bold**.

Allen, Miss Elisabeth Walton
Allison, Mr Hudson Joshua Creighton
Allison, Mrs Bessie Waldo
Allison, Miss Helen Loraine [child]
Allison, Master Hudson Trevor [infant]
Anderson, Mr Harry
Andrews, Miss Kornelia Theodosia
Andrews, Mr Thomas Jr [H&W Guarantee Group – Shipbuilder]
Appleton, Mrs Charlotte Lane
Artagaveytia, Mr Ramon
Astor, Colonel John Jacob
Astor, Mrs Madeleine Talmage
Aubart, Mme Léontine Pauline
Barber, Miss Ellen Mary [maid to Mrs Cavendish]
Barkworth, Mr Algernon Henry Wilson
Baumann, Mr John D.
Baxter, Mrs Hélène
Baxter, Mr Quigg Edmond
Bazzani, Miss Albina [maid to Mrs Bucknell]
Beattie, Mr Thomson
Beckwith, Mr Richard Leonard
Beckwith, Mrs Sallie
Behr, Mr Karl Howell
Bessette, Miss Nellie Mayo [maid to Mrs White]
Bidois, Miss Rosalie [maid to Mrs Astor]
Bird, Miss Ellen [maid to Mrs Straus]
Birnbaum, Mr Jakob [WS List as Birnbaum Jakob]
Bishop, Mr Dickinson H.
Bishop, Mrs Helen Margaret
Björnström-Steffansson, Mr Mauritz Håkan [also on the WS List as H.B. Steffanson]
Blackwell, Mr Stephen Weart
Blank, Mr Henry
Bonnell, Miss Elizabeth
Bonnell, Miss Caroline T.
Borebank, Mr John James
Bowen, Miss Grace Scott [governess to Mr John Ryerson]
Bowerman, Miss Elsie Edith
Brady, Mr John Bertram

Brandeis, Mr Emil Franklin
Brereton, Mr George Andrew [booked as George Brayton]
Brewe, Dr Arthur Jackson
Brown, Mrs Caroline Lane
Brown, Mrs Margaret
Bucknell, Mrs Emma Eliza
Burns, Miss Elizabeth Margaret [nursemaid to Master Spedden]
Butt, Major Archibald Willingham
Cairns, Mr Alexander M. [manservant to Mr Carter]
Calderhead, Mr Edward Pennington
Candee, Mrs Helen Churchill
Cardeza, Mrs Charlotte Wardle
Cardeza, Mr Thomas Drake Martinez
Carlsson, Mr Frans Olof
Carrau Estévez, Mr José Pedro
Carrau y Rovira, Mr Francisco M.
Carter, Mr William Ernest
Carter, Mrs Lucile
Carter, Miss Lucile Polk
Carter, Master William Thornton 2nd [child]
Case, Mr Howard Brown
Cassebeer, Mrs Eleanor Genevieve
Cavendish, Mr Tyrell William
Cavendish, Mrs Julia Florence
Chaffee, Mr Herbert Fuller
Chaffee, Mrs Carrie Constance
Chambers, Mr Norman Campbell
Chambers, Mrs Bertha M.
Chaudanson, Miss Victorine [maid to Mrs Ryerson]
Cherry, Miss Gladys
Chevré, Mr Paul Romaine Marie Léonce
Chibnall, Mrs Edith Martha
Chisholm, Mr Roderick Robert Crispin [H&W Guarantee Group – Chief
 Draughtsman]
Clark, Mr Walter Miller
Clark, Mrs Virginia Estelle
Cleaver, Miss Alice Catherine [nursemaid to Master Allison]
Clifford, Mr George Quincy
Colley, Mr Edward Pomeroy
Compton, Mrs Mary Eliza
Compton, Miss Sara Rebecca
Compton, Mr Alexander Taylor Jr
Cornell, Mrs Malvina Helen
Crafton, Mr John Bertram
Crosby, Captain Edward Gifford
Crosby, Mrs Catherine Elizabeth
Crosby, Miss Harriette Rebecca
Cumings, Mr John Bradley
Cumings, Mrs Florence Briggs
Daly, Mr Peter Denis
Daniel, Mr Robert Williams
Daniels, Miss Sarah [maid to Mrs Allison]
Davidson, Mr Thornton

Davidson, Mrs Orian Scott
Dick, Mr Albert Adrian
Dick, Mrs Vera
Dodge, Dr Henry Washington
Dodge, Mrs Ruth
Dodge, Master Washington [child]
Douglas, Mrs Mary Hélène
Douglas, Mr Walter Donald
Douglas, Mrs Mahala
Duff Gordon, Sir Cosmo Edmund [booked as Mr Morgan]
Duff Gordon, Lady Lucy Christiana [booked as Mrs Morgan]
Dulles, Mr William Crothers
Earnshaw, Mrs Olive
Endres, Miss Caroline Louise [nurse to Mrs Astor]
Eustis, Miss Elizabeth Mussey
Evans, Miss Edith Corse
Farthing, Mr John [manservant to Mr Straus]
Flegenheim, Mrs Antoinette
Fleming, Miss Margaret [maid to Mrs Thayer]
Flynn, Mr John Irwin
Foreman, Mr Benjamin Laventall
Fortune, Mr Mark
Fortune, Mrs Mary
Fortune, Miss Ethel Flora
Fortune, Miss Alice Elizabeth
Fortune, Miss Mabel Helen
Fortune, Mr Charles Alexander
Francatelli, Miss Laura Mabel [secretary to, but listed as maid to Lady Duff Gordon]
Franklin, Mr Thomas Parnham
Frauenthal, Dr Henry William
Frauenthal, Mrs Clara
Frauenthal, Mr Isaac Gerald
Frölicher, Miss Hedwig Margaritha
Frölicher-Stehli, Mr Maximilian Josef [WS List as Stehli, Mr Max Frolicher]
Frölicher-Stehli, Mrs Margaretha Emerentia [WS List as Stehli, Mrs Max Frolicher]
Fry, Mr John Richard [valet to Mr Ismay]
Futrelle, Mr Jacques Heath
Futrelle, Mrs Lily May
Gee, Mr Arthur H.
Gibson, Mrs Pauline Caroline
Gibson, Miss Dorothy Winifred
Gieger, Miss Amalie Henriette [maid to Mrs Widener]
Giglio, Mr Victor Gaeton A. [secretary/valet to Mr Guggenheim]
Goldenberg, Mr Samuel Levi
Goldenberg, Mrs Nella
Goldschmidt, Mr George B. [WS List as Mrs George B. Goldschmidt]
Gracie, Colonel Archibald
Graham, Mr George Edward
Graham, Mrs Edith Ware
Graham, Miss Margaret Edith
Greenfield, Mrs Blanche
Greenfield, Mr William Bertram
Guggenheim, Mr Benjamin

Harder, Mr George Achilles
Harder, Mrs Dorothy
Harper, Mr Henry Sleeper
Harper, Mrs Myna R.
Harrington, Mr Charles Henry [manservant to Mr Moore]
Harris, Mr Henry Birkhardt
Harris, Mrs Irene Rachel
Harrison, Mr William Henry [secretary to Mr Ismay]
Hassab, Mr Hammad [manservant to Mr Harper]
Hawksford, Mr Walter James
Hays, Mr Charles Melville
Hays, Mrs Clara Jennings
Hays, Miss Margaret Bechstein
Head, Mr Christopher
Hilliard, Mr Herbert Henry
Hipkins, Mr William Edward
Hippach, Mrs Ida Sophia
Hippach, Miss Jean Gertrude
Hogeboom, Mrs Anna Louisa
Holverson, Mr Alexander Oskar
Holverson, Mrs Mary Aline
Homer, Mr Henry Haven [booked as H. Haven]
Hoyt, Mr Frederick Maxfield
Hoyt, Mrs Jane Anne
Hoyt, Mr William Fisher
Icard, Miss Rose Amelie [maid to Mrs Stone]
Isham, Miss Ann Elizabeth
Ismay, Mr Joseph Bruce
Jones, Mr Charles Cresson
Julian, Mr Henry Forbes
Keeping, Mr Edwin Herbert [manservant to Mr George Widener]
Kent, Mr Edward Austin
Kenyon, Mr Frederick R.
Kenyon, Mrs Marion Estelle
Kimball, Mr Edwin Nelson Jr
Kimball, Mrs Susan Gertrude
Klaber, Mr Herman
Kreuchen, Miss Emilie [maid to Mrs Robert]
Lambert-Williams, Mr Fletcher Fellows
Leader, Dr Alice
Leroy, Miss Berthe [maid to Mrs Mahala Douglas]
Lesueur, Mr Gustave J. [manservant to Mr Cardeza]
Lewy, Mr Ervin G.
Lindeberg-Lind, Mr Erik Gustaf [booked as Edward Lingrey]
Lindström, Mrs Sigrid
Lines, Mrs Elisabeth Lindsey
Lines, Miss Mary Conover
Long, Mr Milton Clyde
Longley, Miss Gretchen Fiske
Loring, Mr Joseph Holland
Lurette, Miss Eugenie Elise [maid to Mrs Spencer]
Madill, Miss Georgette Alexandra
Maguire, Mr John Edward

Maioni, Miss Roberta Elizabeth Mary [maid to the Countess of Rothes]

Maréchal, Mr Pierre

Marvin, Mr Daniel Warner

Marvin, Mrs Mary Graham Carmichael

Mayné, Mlle Berthe Antonine [booked as Mme De Villiers]

McCaffry, Mr Thomas Francis

McCarthy, Mr Timothy John

McGough, Mr James Robert

Meyer, Mr Edgar Joseph

Meyer, Mrs Leila G.

Millet, Mr Francis Davis

Minahan, Miss Daisy

Minahan, Dr William Edward

Minahan, Mrs Lillian E.

Mock, Mr Philipp Edmund

Molson, Mr Harry Markland

Moore, Mr Clarence

Natsch, Mr Charles H.

Newell, Mr Arthur Webster

Newell, Miss Madeleine

Newell, Miss Marjorie Anne [listed as (her sister) Alice]

Newsom, Miss Helen Monypeny

Nicholson, Mr Arthur Ernest

Nourney, Mr Alfred [booked to travel second class as the Baron von Drachstedt]

Oliva y Ocaña, Doña Fermina [maid to Mrs Peñasco y Castellana]

Omont, Mr Alfred Fernand

Ostby, Mr Engelhart Cornelius

Ostby, Miss Helen Ragnhild

Ovies y Rodriguez, Mr Servando Jose Florentino

Parr, Mr William Henry Marsh [H&W Guarantee Group – Electrician]

Partner, Mr Austin

Payne, Mr Vivian Ponsonby [secretary to Mr Hays]

Pears, Mr Thomas Clinton

Pears, Mrs Edith

Peñasco y Castellana, Mr Victor

Peñasco y Castellana, Mrs Maria Josefa

Perreault, Miss Mary Anne [maid to Mrs Hays]

Peuchen, Major Arthur Godfrey

Porter, Mr Walter Chamberlain

Potter, Mrs Lily Alexenia

Reghini, Mr Sante [manservant to Mrs White]

Reuchlin, Jonkheer Johan George Jr

Rheims, Mr George Alexander Lucien

Robbins, Mr Victor [manservant to Colonel Astor]

Robert, Mrs Elisabeth Walton

Roebling, Mr Washington Augustus 2nd

Romaine, Mr Charles Hallace [booked as Charles Rolmane]

Rood, Mr Hugh Roscoe

Rosenbaum, Miss Edith Louise

Rosenshine, Mr George [booked as George Thorne]

Ross, Mr John Hugo

Rothes, Lucy-Noël Martha, the Countess of

Rothschild, Mr Martin

Rothschild, Mrs Elizabeth Jane Anne
Rowe, Mr Alfred G.
Ryerson, Mr Arthur Larned
Ryerson, Mrs Emily Maria
Ryerson, Miss Emily Borie
Ryerson, Miss Suzette Parker
Ryerson, Mr John Borie
Saalfeld, Mr Adolphe
Sägesser, Mlle Emma Marie [maid to Mme Aubart]
Salomon, Mr Abraham Lincoln
Schabert, Mrs Emma
Serreplan, Miss Augustine [maid to Mrs Carter]
Seward, Mr Frederic Kimber
Shute, Miss Elizabeth Weed [governess to Miss Graham]
Silverthorne, Mr Spencer Victor
Silvey, Mr William Baird
Silvey, Mrs Alice Gray
Simonius-Blumer, Colonel Alfons
Sloper, Mr William Thompson
Smart, Mr John Montgomery
Smith, Mr James Clinch
Smith, Mr Lucian Philip
Smith, Mrs Mary Eloise
Smith, Mr Richard William
Snyder, Mr John Pillsbury
Snyder, Mrs Nelle
Spedden, Mr Frederic Oakley
Spedden, Mrs Margaretta Corning
Spedden, Master Robert Douglas [child]
Spencer, Mr William Augustus
Spencer, Mrs Marie Eugenie
Stähelin-Maeglin, Dr Max
Stead, Mr William Thomas
Stengel, Mr Charles Emil Henry
Stengel, Mrs Annie May
Stephenson, Mrs Martha
Stewart, Mr Albert A.
Stone, Mrs Martha Evelyn
Straus, Mr Isidor
Straus, Mrs Rosalie Ida
Sutton, Mr Frederick
Swift, Mrs Margaret Welles
Taussig, Mr Emil
Taussig, Mrs Tillie
Taussig, Miss Ruth
Taylor, Mr Elmer Zebley
Taylor, Mrs Juliet Cummins
Thayer, Mr John Borland
Thayer, Mrs Marian Longstreth
Thayer, Mr John Borland Jr
Thorne, Miss Gertrude Maybelle [booked as Mrs George Thorne]
Tucker, Mr Gilbert Milligan Jr
Uruchurtu, Don Manuel E.

Van der Hoef, Mr Wyckoff
Walker, Mr William Anderson
Ward, Miss Anna Moore [maid to Mrs Cardeza]
Warren, Mr Francis Manley
Warren, Mrs Anna Sophia Bates
Weir, Colonel John
White, Mrs Ella Bertha
White, Mr Percival Wayland
White, Mr Richard Frasar
Wick, Mr George Dennick
Wick, Mrs Mary J.
Wick, Miss Mary Natalie
Widener, Mr George Dunton
Widener, Mrs Eleanor A.
Widener, Mr Harry Elkins
Willard, Miss Constance Beatrice
Williams, Mr Charles Duane
Williams, Mr Richard Norris Jr
Wilson, Miss Helen Alice [maid to Mrs Spedden]
Woolner, Mr Hugh
Wright, Mr George Henry
Young, Miss Marie Grice

SECOND CLASS PASSENGERS

Lester J. Mitcham

When *Titanic* left Queenstown there were 284 second class passengers on board. Of those, 166 were lost and 118 were saved. Those lost are in **bold**. Names that were not on the White Star List are indicated with an asterisk (★).

Abelson, Mr Samuel
Abelson, Mrs
Aldworth, Mr Charles Augustus [chauffeur to the Carter family – see first class]
Andrew, Mr Edgardo Samuel
Andrew, Mr Frank Thomas
Angle, Mr William A.
Angle, Mrs Florence Agnes
Ashby, Mr John
Bailey, Mr Percy Andrew
Bainbrigge, Mr Charles Robert Reginald
Ball, Mrs Ada Elizabeth
Banfield, Mr Frederick James
Bateman, Rev Robert James
Beane, Mr Edward
Beane, Mrs Ethel
Beauchamp, Mr Henry William James
Becker, Mrs Nellie Elizabeth
Becker, Miss Ruth Elizabeth
Becker, Miss Marion Louise [child]
Becker, Master Richard F. [child]
Beesley, Mr Lawrence
Bentham, Miss Lillian W.
Berriman, Mr William John
Botsford, Mr William Hull
Bowenur, Mr Solomon
Bracken, Mr James H.
Brailey, Mr W. Theodore Ronald [Orchestra – Pianist] ★
Bricoux, Mr Roger Marie [Orchestra – Cellist] ★
De Brito, Mr José Joaquim
Brown, Miss Amelia Mary [cook to the Allison family – see first class]
Brown, Mr Thomas William Solomon
Brown, Mrs Elizabeth Catherine
Brown, Miss Edith Eileen
Bryhl, Mr Kurt Arnold Gottfrid
Bryhl, Miss Dagmar Jenny Ingeborg

Buss, Miss Kate
Butler, Mr Reginald Fenton
Byles, Fr Thomas Roussel Davids
Byström, Mrs Karolina
Caldwell, Mr Albert Francis
Caldwell, Mrs Sylvia Mae
Caldwell, Master Alden Gates [infant]
Cameron, Miss Clear Annie
Campbell, Mr William Henry [H&W Guarantee Group – Apprentice Joiner] ★
Carbines, Mr William
Carter, Rev Ernest Courtenay
Carter, Mrs Lilian
Chapman, Mr Charles Henry
Chapman, Mr John Henry
Chapman, Mrs Sarah Elizabeth
Christy, Mrs Alice Frances
Clarke, Mr Charles Valentine
Clarke, Mrs Ada Maria
Clarke, Mr John Frederick Preston [Orchestra – Bass Violinist] ★
Cohen, Miss Rachel Juli [booked as Miss Julie Christy]
Coleridge, Mr Reginald Charles
Collander, Mr Erik Gustaf
Collett, Mr Sidney Clarence Stuart
Collyer, Mr Harvey
Collyer, Mrs Charlotte Annie
Collyer, Miss Marjorie Charlotte [child]
Cook, Mrs Selena
Corbett, Mrs Irene
Corey, Mrs Mary Phyllis Elizabeth
Cotterill, Mr Henry
Cunningham, Mr Alfred Flemming [H&W Guarantee Group – Apprentice Fitter] ★
Davies, Mr Charles Henry
Davies, Mrs Elizabeth Agnes Mary
Davies, Master John Morgan Jr [child]
Davis, Miss Mary
Deacon, Mr Percy William
Del Carlo, Mr Sebastiano
Del Carlo, Mrs Argene
Denbuoy, Mr Albert Joseph
Dibden, Mr William
Doling, Mrs Ada Julia Elizabeth
Doling, Miss Elsie
Douton, Mr William Joseph
Drew, Mr James Vivian
Drew, Mrs Lulu Thorne
Drew, Master Marshall Brines [child]
Duran y Moré, Miss Asunción
Eitemiller, Mr George Floyd
Enander, Mr Ingvar
Fahlstrøm, Mr Arne Joma
Faunthorpe, Mr Harry Bartram
Fillbrook, Mr Joseph Charles
Fox, Mr Stanley Hubert

Frost, Mr Anthony Wood [H&W Guarantee Group – Foreman Fitter] ★
Funk, Miss Annie Clemmer
Fynney, Mr Joseph J.
Gale, Mr Harry
Gale, Mr Shadrach
Garside, Miss Ethel
Gaskell, Mr Alfred Edward
Gavey, Mr Laurence William
Gilbert, Mr William
Giles, Mr Edgar
Giles, Mr Frederick Edward
Giles, Mr Ralph
Gill, Mr John William
Gillespie, Mr William Henry
Givard, Mr Hans Christensen
Greenberg, Mr Samuel
Hale, Mr Reginald
Hämäläinen, Mrs Anna
Hämäläinen, Master Viljo Unto Johannes [infant]
Harbeck, Mr William H.
Harper, Revd John
Harper, Miss Annie Jessie Spiers [child]
Harris, Mr George
Harris, Mr Walter Jr
Hart, Mr Benjamin
Hart, Mrs Esther Ada
Hart, Miss Eva Miriam [child]
Hartley, Mr Wallace Henry [Orchestra – Bandmaster] ★
Herman, Mr Samuel
Herman, Mrs Jane
Herman, Miss Alice
Herman, Miss Kate
Hewlett, Mrs Mary Dunbar
Hickman, Mr Leonard Mark
Hickman, Mr Lewis
Hickman, Mr Stanley George
Hiltunen, Miss Marta Maria
Hocking, Mrs Elizabeth
Hocking, Mr Richard George
Hocking, Miss Ellen
Hocking, Mr Samuel James Metcalfe
Hodges, Mr Henry Price
Hold, Mr Stephen
Hold, Mrs Annie Margaret
Hood, Mr Ambrose Jr
Hosono, Mr Masabumi
Howard, Mr Benjamin
Howard, Mrs Ellen Truelove
Hume, Mr John Law [Orchestra –Violinist] ★
Hunt, Mr George Henry
Ilett, Miss Bertha
Jacobsohn, Mr Sidney Samuel
Jacobsohn, Mrs Amy Frances

Jarvis, Mr Denzil John
Jefferys, Mr Clifford Thomas
Jefferys, Mr Ernest Wilfred
Jenkin, Mr Stephen Curnow
Jerwan, Mrs Marie Marthe
Kantor, Mr Sinai
Kantor, Mrs Miriam
Karnes, Mrs Clare
Keane, Mr Daniel
Keane, Miss Hanora Agnes
Kelly, Mrs Fanny Maria
Kirkland, Revd Charles Leonard
Knight, Mr Robert J. [H&W Guarantee Group – Leading Hand Fitter] ★
Krins, Mr Georges Alexandre [Orchestra – Violinist] ★
Kvillner, Mr Johan Henrik Johannesson
Lahtinen, Revd William
Lahtinen, Mrs Anna Amelia
Lamb, Mr John James
Laroche, Mr Joseph Philippe Lemercier
Laroche, Mrs Juliette Marie Louise
Laroche, Miss Simonne Marie Anne Andrée [child]
Laroche, Miss Louise [child]
Lehmann, Miss Bertha
Leitch, Miss Jessie Wills
Lemore, Mrs Amelia
Lévy, Mr René Jacques
Leyson, Mr Robert William Norman
Lingane, Mr John
Louch, Mr Charles Alexander
Louch, Mrs Alice Adelaide
Mack, Mrs Mary
Malachard, Mr Jean-Noël
Mallet, Mr Albert Denis Pierre
Mallet, Mrs Antonine Marie
Mallet, Master André Gilbert Clement [child]
Mangiavacchi, Mr Serafino Emilio
Matthews, Mr William John
Maybery, Mr Frank Hubert
McCrae, Mr Arthur Gordon
McCrie, Mr James Matthew
McKane, Mr Peter David
Mellinger, Mrs Elizabeth Anne
Mellinger, Miss Madeleine Violet
Mellors, Mr William John
Meyer, Mr August
Milling, Mr Jacob Christian
Mitchell, Mr Henry Michael
Montvila, Fr Juozas
Moraweck, Dr Ernest
Morley, Mr Henry Samuel [booked as Henry Marshall]
Mudd, Mr Thomas Cupper
Myles, Mr Thomas Francis
Nasser, Mr Nicholas [anglicised from Niqula Khalil Nasr Allah]

Nasser, Mrs Adele
Navratil, Mr Michel [booked as Mr Hoffman]
Navratil, Master Michel Marcel [booked as Master Hoffman] [child]
Navratil, Master Edmond Roger [booked as Master Hoffman] [child]
Nesson, Mr Israel
Nicholls, Mr Joseph Charles
Norman, Mr Robert Douglas
Nye, Mrs Elizabeth
Otter, Mr Richard
Oxenham, Mr Percy Thomas
Padrón Manent, Mr Julian
Padrón Manent, Mrs Florentina [booked under her maiden name of Duran y Moré]
Pain, Dr Alfred
Pallás y Castelló, Mr Emilio
Parker, Mr Clifford Richard
Parkes, Mr Francis [H&W Guarantee Group – Apprentice Plumber] ★
Parrish, Mrs Lucinda Davis
Pengelly, Mr Frederick William
Pernot, Mr René [chauffeur to Mr Guggenheim – see first class]
Peruschitz, Fr Josef Maria
Phillips, Mr Escott Robert
Phillips, Miss Alice Frances Louisa
Phillips, Miss Kate Louise [booked as Mrs Marshall]
Pinsky, Mrs Rosa
Ponesell, Mr Martin
Portaluppi, Mr Emilio Ilario Giuseppe
Pulbaum, Mr Franz
Quick, Mrs Jane
Quick, Miss Winifred Vera [child]
Quick, Miss Phyllis May [child]
Reeves, Mr David
Renouf, Mr Peter Henry
Renouf, Mrs Lillian Elizabeth
Reynaldo, Mrs Encarnación
Richard, Mr Emile Phillippe
Richards, Mrs Emily
Richards, Master William Rowe [child]
Richards, Master Sibley George [infant]
Ridsdale, Miss Lucy
Rogers, Mr Reginald Harry
Rugg, Miss Emily
Sedgwick, Mr Charles Frederick Waddington
Sharp, Mr Percival James Richard
Shelley, Mrs Imanita
Silvén, Miss Lyyli Karoliina
Sincock, Miss Maude J.
Sinkkonen, Miss Anna
Sjöstedt, Mr Ernst Adolf
Slayter, Miss Hilda Mary
Slemen, Mr Richard James
Smith, Mr Augustus [anglicised from August Schmidt]
Smith, Miss Mary Ann [booked as Miss Marion Smith]
Sobey, Mr Samuel James Hayden

Stanton, Mr Samuel Ward
Stokes, Mr Philip Joseph
Swane, Mr George
Sweet, Mr George Frederick
Taylor, Mr Percy Cornelius [Orchestra – Cellist] ★
Toomey, Miss Ellen Mary
Troupiansky, Mr Moses Aaron V.
Trout, Mrs Jessie L.
Troutt, Miss Edwina Celia
Turpin, Mr William John Robert
Turpin, Mrs Dorothy Ann
Veal, Mr James
Wallcroft, Miss Ellen
Ware, Mr John James
Ware, Mr William Jeffery
Ware, Mrs Florence Louise
Watson, Mr Ennis Hastings [H&W Guarantee Group – Apprentice Electrician] ★
Watt, Mrs Elizabeth Inglis
Watt, Miss Robertha Josephine
Webber, Miss Susan
Weisz, Mr Leopold
Weisz, Mrs Mathilde Françoise
Wells, Mrs Adelaide Dart
Wells, Miss Joan [child]
Wells, Master Ralph Lester [child]
West, Mr Edwy Arthur
West, Mrs Ada Mary
West, Miss Constance Miriam [child]
West, Miss Barbara Joyce [infant]
Wheadon, Mr Edward Herbert
Wheeler, Mr Edwin Charles
Whilems, Mr Charles
Wilkinson, Mrs Elizabeth Anne [booked as Mrs Faunthorpe]
Williams, Mr Charles Eugene
Woodward, Mr John Wesley [Orchestra – Cellist] ★
Wright, Miss Marion
Yvois, Miss Henriette

THIRD CLASS PASSENGERS

Lester J. Mitcham

When *Titanic* left Queenstown there were 709 third class passengers on board. Of those, 528 were lost and 181 were saved. Those lost are in **bold**.

Abbing, Mr Anthony
Abbott, Mrs Rhoda Mary
Abbott, Mr Rossmore Edward
Abbott, Mr Eugene Joseph
Abd al-Khaliq, Mr Farid Qasim Husayn [WS List as Fared Kassem]
Abelseth, Miss Karen Marie
Abelseth, Mr Olaus Jørgensen
Abi-Al-Muna, Mr Nasif Qasim [WS List as Hassef Kassein]
Abu Sach, Mr Jirjis Yusif [WS List as Youssef Gerios]
Abrahamsson, Mr Abraham August Johannes
Adahl, Mr Mauritz Nils Martin [also on the WS List as Mauritz Dahl]
Ahlin, Mrs Johanna Persdotter
Ahmed, Mr Ali
Aks, Mrs Leah
Aks, Master Frank Philip [infant]
Alexander, Mr William
Alhomäki, Mr Ilmari Rudolff
Ali, Mr William
Allen, Mr William Henry
Allum, Mr Owen George
Al-Za inni, Mr Fahim Ruhanna [WS List as Lenni Fabini]
Andersen, Mr Albert Kaurin
Andersen, Miss Carla Christine Nielsine
Andersson, Mr Anders Johan
Andersson, Mrs Alfrida Konstantia Brogren
Andersson, Master Sigvard Harald Elias [child]
Andersson, Miss Ingeborg Constanzia [child]
Andersson, Miss Ebba Iris Alfrida [child]
Andersson, Miss Sigrid Elisabeth [child]
Andersson, Miss Ellis Anna Maria [child]
Andersson, Mr August Edvard [booked as August Wennerström]
Andersson, Miss Erna Alexandra
Andersson, Miss Ida Augusta Margareta
Andersson, Mr Johan Samuel
Andreasson, Mr Paul Edvin
Angheloff, Mr Minko

Arnold–Franchi, Mr Josef
Arnold–Franchi, Mrs Josefine
Aronsson, Mr Ernst Axel Algot
Asim, Mr Adola
Asplund, Mr Carl Oscar Vilhelm Gustafsson
Asplund, Mrs Selma Augusta Emilia
Asplund, Mr Filip Oscar
Asplund, Master Clarence Gustaf Hugo [child]
Asplund, Master Carl Edgar [child]
Asplund, Miss Lillian Gertrud [child]
Asplund, Master Edvin Rojj Felix [child]
Asplund, Mr Johan Charles
Assaf, Mr Gerios [WS List as Assaf Gerios]
Assaf, Mrs Mariyam
Assam, Mr Ali
Atta Allah, Miss Malakah
Augustsson, Mr Albert
Ayyub Dahir, Miss Bannurah [WS List as Ayoub Banoura]
Backström, Mr Karl Alfred
Backström, Mrs Maria Mathilda
Badman, Miss Emily Louisa
Badt, Mr Mohamed
Balkic, Mr Kerim
Banski, Mrs Marija [booked under her maiden name of Osman]
Ba qlini, Mrs Marijam Latif [WS List as Latifa Baclini]
Ba qlini, Miss Mariya Katarin [WS List as Maria Baclini] [child]
Ba qlini, Miss Eugenie [WS List as Eugene Baclini] [child]
Ba qlini, Miss Hileni Barbarah [WS List as Helene Baclini] [infant]
Barbarah, Mrs Katarin
Barbarah, Miss Saiide
Barry, Miss Julia
Barton, Mr David John
Beavan, Mr William Thomas
Bengtsson, Mr Johan Viktor
Berglund, Mr Karl Ivar Sven
Betros, Mr Tannous
Birkeland, Mr Hans Martin Monsen
Björklund, Mr Ernst Herbert
Bostandjusty, Mr Guentcho
Bourke, Mr John
Bourke, Mrs Catherine
Bourke, Miss Mary
Bowen, Mr David John
Bradley, Miss Bridget Delia
Braf, Miss Elin Ester Maria
Braund, Mr Lewis Richard
Braund, Mr Owen Harris
Brobeck, Mr Karl Rudolf
Brocklebank, Mr William Alfred
Buckley, Miss Catherine
Buckley, Mr Daniel
Bulus, Mrs Sultanah
Bulus, Master Akar [child]

Bulus, Miss Nur al-Ayn [child]
Burke, Mr Jeremiah
Burns, Miss Mary Delia
Cacic, Mr Jego Grga
Cacic, Mr Luka
Cacic, Miss Manda
Cacic, Miss Marija
Calic, Mr Jovo [booked as Jovo Uzelas]
Calic, Mr Petar
Canavan, Miss Mary
Canavan, Mr Patrick
Cann, Mr Ernest Charles
Caram, Mr Joseph
Caram, Mrs Maria
Carlsson, Mr August Sigfrid
Carlsson, Mr Carl Robert
Carr, Miss Jane
Carver, Mr Alfred John
Celotti, Mr Francesco
Chang, Mr Chip [WS List as Chang Chip]
Charters, Mr David
Cheong, Mr Foo [WS List as Cheong Foo]
Christmann, Mr Emil
Chronopoulos, Mr Apostolos M.
Chronopoulos, Mr Dimitrios M.
Coelho, Mr Domingos Fernandes
Cohen, Mr Gershon
Colbert, Mr Patrick
Coleff, Mr Fotio
Coltcheff, Mr Peju
Conlon, Mr Thomas Henry
Connaughton, Mr Michael
Connolly, Miss Catherine
Connolly, Miss Catherine
Connors, Mr Patrick John
Cook, Mr Jacob
Cor, Mr Bartol
Cor, Mr Ivan
Cor, Mr Liudevit
Corn, Mr Henry
Corr, Miss Ellen
Coutts, Mrs Mary
Coutts, Master William Loch [child]
Coutts, Master Neville Leslie [child]
Coxon, Mr Daniel
Crease, Mr Ernest James
Cribb, Mr John Hatfield
Cribb, Miss Laura Mae
Culumovic, Mr Jeso [booked as Joso Ecimovic]
Daher, Mr Tannous [WS List as Daler Tannous]
Dahl, Mr Charles [anglicised from Karl] Edwart
Dahlberg, Miss Gerda Ulrika
Dakic, Mr Branko

Daly, Mr Eugene Patrick
Daly, Miss Margaret [booked as (her sister) Marcella Daly]
Danbom, Mr Ernst Gilbert
Danbom, Mrs Anna Sigrid Maria
Danbom, Master Gilbert Sigvard Emanuel [infant]
Danoff, Mr Yoto
Dantcheff, Mr Ristju
Davies, Mr Evan
Davies, Mr Alfred James
Davies, Mr John Samuel
Davies, Mr Joseph
Davison, Mr Thomas Henry
Davison, Mrs Elizabeth Mary
De Messemaeker, Mr Guillaume Joseph
De Messemaeker, Mrs Anna
De Mulder, Mr Theodoor
De Pelsmaeker, Mr Alphonse
Dean, Mr Bertram Frank
Dean, Mrs Eva Georgetta
Dean, Master Bertram Vere [child]
Dean, Miss Elizabeth Gladys [infant]
Deeb, Mr Paul Elias [WS List as Elias Dibo]
Delalic, Mr Redjo
Denkoff, Mr Mitto
Dennis, Mr Samuel
Dennis, Mr William
Devaney, Miss Margaret Delia
Dika, Mr Mirko
Dimic, Mr Jovan
Dintcheff, Mr Valtcho
Donohue, Miss Bridget [incorrectly listed on the WS List as Bert
 O'Donaghue]
Dooley, Mr Patrick J.
Dorking, Mr Edward Arthur
Dowdell, Miss Elizabeth
Doyle, Miss Elizabeth
Drazenovic, Mr Jozef
Driscoll, Miss Bridget
Dropkin, Miss Jennie
Duquemin, Mr Joseph Pierre
Dwan, Mr Frank
Dyker, Mr Adolf Fredrik
Dyker, Mrs Anna Judith Elizabeth
Edvardsson, Mr Gustaf Hjalmar
Eklund, Mr Hans Linus
Ekström, Mr Johan
Elias, Mr Joseph
Elias, Mr Tannous [WS List as Elias Tanous]
Elias, Mr Joseph
Elsbury, Mr William James
Emanuel, Miss Virginia Ethel [child]
Estanislau, Mr Manoel Gonçalves [WS List as Manoel E. Goncalves]
Everett, Mr Thomas James

Fang, Mr Lang
Fardon, Mr Charles R. [booked as Charles Franklin]
Farrell, Mr James
Finoli, Mr Luigi
Fischer, Mr Eberhard Thelander
Fleming, Miss Honora
Flynn, Mr James
Flynn, Mr John
Foley, Mr Joseph
Foley, Mr William
Ford, Mr Arthur
Ford, Mrs Margaret Ann
Ford, Miss Dollina Margaret
Ford, Mr Edward Watson
Ford, Mr William Neal Thomas
Ford, Miss Robina Maggie [child]
Fox, Mr Patrick
Gallagher, Mr Martin
Garfirth, Mr John
Gheorgheff, Mr Stanio
Gilinsky, Mr Eliezer
Gilnagh, Miss Mary Katherine
Glynn, Miss Mary Agatha
Goldsmith, Mr Frank John
Goldsmith, Mrs Emily Alice
Goldsmith, Master Frank John William [child]
Goldsmith, Mr Nathan
Goodwin, Mr Frederick Joseph
Goodwin, Mrs Augusta
Goodwin, Miss Lilian Augusta
Goodwin, Mr Charles Edward
Goodwin, Mr William Frederick
Goodwin, Miss Jessie Allis Mary
Goodwin, Master Harold Victor [child]
Goodwin, Master Sidney Leslie [child]
Göransson, Mr Nils Johan [booked as John Olsson]
Green, Mr George Henry
Grønnestad, Mr Daniel Danielsen
Guest, Mr Robert
Gustafsson, Mr Alfred Ossian
Gustafsson, Mr Anders Vilhelm
Gustafsson, Mr Johan Birger
Gustafsson, Mr Karl Gideon
Haas, Miss Aloisia
Hagland, Mr Ingvald Olai Olsen
Hagland, Mr Konrad Mathias Reiersen
Hakkarainen, Mr Pekka Pietari
Hakkarainen, Mrs Elin Matilda
Hampe, Mr Léon Jérome [also on the WS List as Leon Mampe]
Hanna, Mr Mansour
Hanna Dib, Mr Boulos [WS List as Hanna Boulos]
Hannah, Mr Borak Suleiman Assi [WS List as Hanna Monbarek]
Hansen, Mr Claus Peter

Hansen, Mrs Jennie Louise
Hansen, Mr Henrik Juul
Hansen, Mr Henry Damsgaard
Hargadon, Miss Catherine
Harknett, Miss Alice Phoebe
Hart, Mr Henry John
Healy, Miss Honor
Hedman, Mr Oskar Arvid
Hegarty, Miss Hanora Kate
Heikkinen, Miss Laina
Heininen, Miss Wendla Maria
Hellström, Miss Hilda Maria
Hendekovic, Mr Ignjac
Henriksson, Miss Jenny Lovisa
Henry, Miss Bridget Delia
Hirvonen, Mrs Helga Elisabeth
Hirvonen, Miss Hildur Elisabeth [child]
Holm, Mr John Fredrik Alexander
Holten, Mr Johan Martin
Honkanen, Miss Eliina
Horgan, Mr John
Howard, Miss May Elizabeth
Humblen, Mr Adolf Mathias Nicolai Olsen [also on the WS List as Humblin Adolf]
Husayn, Master Husayn Mahmud [WS List as M. Housseing Kassan] [child]
Hyman, Mr Soloman Abraham
Ibrahim, Mrs Mariya Zahie Halaut [WS List as Mary Joseph]
Ibrahim, Mr Yusif [WS List as Brahim Youssef]
Ilmakangas, Miss Ida Livija
Ilmakangas, Miss Pieta Sofia
Ivanoff, Mr Kanio
Jabbour, Miss Hileni [WS List as Hileni Zabour]
Jabbour, Miss Thamini [WS List as Tamain Zabour]
Jalševac, Mr Ivan [WS List as Ivan Yalševae]
Jansson, Mr Carl Olof
Jardim, Mr José Neto
Jensen, Mr Hans Peder
Jensen, Mr Niels Peder
Jensen, Mr Svend Lauritz
Jermyn, Miss Annie Jane
Johannesen, Mr Bernt Johannes
Johansson, Mr Erik
Johansson, Mr Gustaf Joel
Johansson, Mr Jakob Alfred
Johansson, Mr Karl Johan
Johansson, Mr Nils
Johansson, Mr Oskar Larder
Johnson, Mr Alfred
Johnson, Mrs Elisabeth Vilhelmina
Johnson, Master Harold Theodor [child]
Johnson, Miss Eleanor Ileen [child]
Johnson, Mr Malkolm Joackim
Johnson, Mr William Cahoone Jr
Johnston, Mr Andrew Emslie

Johnston, Mrs Elizabeth
Johnston, Master William Andrew [child]
Johnston, Miss Catherine Nellie [child]
Jonkoff, Mr Lalju [WS List as Lazor Jonkoff]
Jonsson, Mr Carl
Jönsson, Mr Nils Hilding
Jussila, Mr Eiriik
Jussila, Miss Katriina
Jussila, Miss Mari Aina
Kalil, Mr Suleiman [WS List as Attalla Sleiman]
Kallio, Mr Nikolai Erland
Kalvik, Mr Johannes Halvorsen
Karajaic, Mr Milan
Karlsson, Mr Einar Gervasius
Karlsson, Mr Julius Konrad Eugen
Karlsson, Mr Nils August
Karun, Mr Franz
Karun, Miss Manca [WS List as Anna Karun] [child]
Keane, Mr Andrew
Katavelos, Mr Vassilios G. [WS List as Catavelos Vassilios]
Keefe, Mr Arthur
Kelly, Miss Annie Katherine
Kelly, Mr James
Kelly, Mr James
Kelly, Miss Mary
Kennedy, Mr John Joseph
Khalil-Khoury, Mr Betros
Khalil-Khoury, Mrs Zahie
Kiernan, Mr John Joseph
Kiernan, Mr Philip
Kilgannon, Mr Thomas
Kink, Mr Anton
Kink, Mrs Luise
Kink, Miss Luise Gretchen [child]
Kink, Miss Maria
Kink, Mr Vinzenz
Klasén, Mrs Hulda Kristina Eugenia
Klasén, Miss Gertrud Emilia [child]
Klasén, Mr Klas Albin
Kraeff, Mr Theodor
Krekorian, Mr Neshan [WS List as Krokorian Nichan]
Kutcher, Mr Simon [booked as Simon Lithman]
Lahoud-Ishaq-Mowad, Mr Sarkis [WS List as Lahoud Sarkis]
Laitinen, Miss Kristina Sofia
Laleff, Mr Kristo
Lam, Mr
Lam, Mr Len
Landergren, Miss Aurora Adelia
Lane, Mr Patrick
Larsson, Mr August Viktor
Larsson, Mr Bengt Edvard
Larsson-Rondberg, Mr Edvard A.
Lee, Mr Bing [WS List as Lee Bing]

Lee, Mr Ling [WS List as Lee Ling]
Lefebvre, Mrs Frances Marie
Lefebvre, Miss Mathilde
Lefebvre, Miss Jeanne [child]
Lefebvre, Master Henri [child]
Lefebvre, Miss Ida [child]
Leinonen, Mr Antti Gustaf
Lennon, Mr Denis
Leonard, Mr Lionel
Lester, Mr James
Lievens, Mr René Gustav Aimé
Lindahl, Miss Agda Thorilda Viktoria
Lindblom, Miss Augusta Charlotta
Lindell, Mr Edvard Bengtsson
Lindell, Mrs Elin Gerda
Lindqvist, Mr Eino William
Linehan, Mr Michael
Ling, Mr Hee
Linhart, Mr Wenzel H.
Livshin, Mr David [booked as Abraham Harmer]
Lobb, Mr William Arthur
Lobb, Mrs Cordelia K.
Lockyer, Mr Edward Thomas
Lovell, Mr John Hall
Lulic, Mr Nikola
Lundahl, Mr Johan Svensson
Lundin, Miss Olga Elida
Lundström, Mr Thure Edvin
Lymperopoulos, Mr Panagiotis K. [WS List as Peter Lemberopoulos]
Lyntakoff, Mr Stanio [WS List as Stanko Syntakoff]
MacKay, Mr George William
Madigan, Miss Margaret
Madsen, Mr Fridtjof Arne
Mäenpää, Mr Matti Alexanteri
Mahon, Miss Bridget Delia
Mäkinen, Mr Kalle Edvard
Mamee, Mr Hanna
Mangan, Miss Mary
Mannion, Miss Margaret
Mardirosian, Mr Sarkis [WS List as Mardirosian Sarkis]
Marinko, Mr Dmitri
Markoff, Mr Marin
Markun, Mr Johann [WS List as Markim Johann]
Matinoff, Mr Nicola
May, Mr Richard John [booked as J. Adams]
McCarthy, Miss Catherine
McCormack, Mr Thomas Joseph
McCoy, Miss Alice
McCoy, Mr Bernard
McCoy, Miss Catherine Agnes
McDermott, Miss Bridget Delia
McEvoy, Mr Michael
McGovern, Miss Mary

McGowan, Miss Annie
McGowan, Miss Catherine
McMahon, Mr Martin
McNamee, Mr Neal
McNamee, Mrs Eileen
McNeill, Miss Bridget
Meanwell, Mrs Mary Ann
Meehan, Mr John
Meek, Mrs Anna Louise
Meisner, Mr Simon
Meo-Martino, Mr Alfonzo
Mernagh, Mr John Robert
Mihoff, Mr Stoytcho [WS List as Mihoff Stoytcho]
Midtsjø, Mr Karl Albert
Miles, Mr Frank
Mineff, Mr Ivan
Minkoff, Mr Lazar
Mitkoff, Mr Mito
Mockler, Miss Ellen Mary
Moen, Mr Sigurd Hansen
Moor, Mrs Beila
Moor, Master Meier [child]
Moore, Mr Leonard Charles
Moran, Miss Bertha Bridget
Moran, Mr Daniel James
Morley, Mr William
Morrow, Mr Thomas Rowan
Moss, Mr Albert Johan
Moussa, Mrs Mantoura
Mubarik, Mrs Mefcosika Amenia
Mubarik, Master Gerios Youssef [child]
Mubarik, Master Halim Gonios [child]
Muslamani, Miss Fatimah [WS List as Mustmani Fat-ma]
Moutal, Mr Rahamin Haim
Mullen, Miss Katherine
Mullin, Miss Mary [booked as Mary Lennon]
Mulvihill, Miss Bertha Elizabeth [born Bridget Elizabeth Mulvihill]
Murdlin, Mr Joseph
Murphy, Miss Catherine
Murphy, Miss Margaret Jane
Murphy, Miss Norah
Myhrman, Mr Pehr Fabian Oliver Malkolm
Nackid, Mr Sahid
Nackid, Mrs Wadia
Nackid, Miss Maria [child]
Naidenoff, Mr Penko
Nakli Khoury, Mr Toufik [WS List as Nahli Tonfik]
Nancarrow, Mr William Henry
Nankoff, Mr Minko
Nasr Alma, Mr Mustafa
Nassr Rizq, Mr Saade Jean [WS List with the surname Jean Nassr]
Naughton, Miss Hannah
Nenkoff, Mr Christo

Nieminen, Miss Manta Josefina
Niklasson, Mr Samuel
Nilsson, Mr August Ferdinand
Nilsson, Miss Berta Olivia
Nilsson, Miss Helmina Josefina
Nirva, Mr Iisakki Antino Äijö
Niskänen, Mr Juha
Nofal, Mr Mansouer
Nosworthy, Mr Richard Cater
Nysten, Miss Anna Sofia
Nysveen, Mr Johan Hansen
O'Brien, Mr Denis
O'Brien, Mr Thomas
O'Brien, Mrs Johanna
O'Connell, Mr Patrick Denis
O'Connor, Mr Maurice
O'Connor, Mr Patrick
O'Doherty, Mr William John [travelled on a ticket in the name of James Moran]
O'Dwyer, Miss Ellen
O'Keefe, Mr Patrick
O'Leary, Miss Hanorah
O'Sullivan, Miss Bridget Mary
Ödahl, Mr Nils Martin
Öhman, Miss Velin
Olsen, Mr Carl Siegwart Andreas
Olsen, Master Arthur Carl [child]
Olsen, Mr Henry Margido
Olson, Mr Ole Martin
Olsson, Miss Elina
Olsson, Mr Oscar Wilhelm
Olsvigen, Mr Thor Andersen [WS List as Thor Anderson]
Oreskovic, Miss Jelka
Oreskovic, Mr Luka
Oreskovic, Miss Marija
Osén, Mr Olaf Elon
Pålsson, Mrs Alma Cornelia
Pålsson, Miss Torborg Danira [child]
Pålsson, Master Paul Folke [child]
Pålsson, Miss Stina Viola [child]
Pålsson, Master Gösta Leonard [child]
Panula, Mrs Maria Emelia Abrahamintytar
Panula, Mr Ernesti Arvid
Panula, Mr Jaako Arnold
Panula, Master Juha Niilo [child]
Panula, Master Urho Abraham [child]
Panula, Master Eino Viljami [child]
Pasic, Mr Jakov
Patchett, Mr George
Pavlovic, Mr Stefan
Peacock, Mrs Edith
Peacock, Miss Treasteall [child]
Peacock, Master Alfred Edward [infant]

Pearce, Mr Ernest
Pedersen, Mr Olaf
Peduzzi, Mr Joseph
Pekoniemi, Mr Edvard Johannes
Peltomäki, Mr Nikolai Johannes
Perkin, Mr John Henry
Persson, Mr Ernst Ulrik
Peters, Miss Catherine
Petersen, Mr Marius
Petranec, Mrs Matilda
Petroff, Mr Nedjalko [WS List as Petroff Nedeco]
Petroff, Mr Pastcho [WS List as Petroff Pentcho]
Pettersson, Miss Ellen Natalia
Pettersson, Mr Johan Emil
Plotcharsky, Mr Vasil
Pocruic, Mr Mate
Pocruic, Mr Tome
Pullnor, Mr Usher [WS List as Baulner Useher]
Qiyamah, Miss Adal Zajib [WS List as Adele Jane Vagil]
Radeff, Mr Alexander
Rafful, Mr Bahaus
Rasmussen, Mrs Lena Jakobsen [booked under her maiden name of Solvang]
Razi, Mr Rachid [WS List as Razi Raibid]
Reed, Mr James George
Rekic, Mr Tido [WS List as Tido Kekic]
Reynolds, Mr Harold J.
Rice, Mrs Margaret
Rice, Master Albert [child]
Rice, Master George Hugh [child]
Rice, Master Eric [child]
Rice, Master Arthur [child]
Rice, Master Eugene Francis [child]
Riihiivuori, Miss Susanna Juhantytär [WS List as Sanni Panula]
Rintamäki, Mr Matti
Riordan, Miss Hannah
Risien, Mr Samuel Beard
Risien, Mrs Emma Jane
Robins, Mr Alexander A.
Robins, Mrs Grace Charity
Rogers, Mr William John
Rommetvedt, Mr Knud Paust
Rosblom, Mrs Helena Wilhelmina
Rosblom, Mr Viktor Rickard
Rosblom, Miss Salli Helena [child]
Roth, Miss Sarah A.
Rouse, Mr Richard Henry
Rush, Mr Alfred George John
Ryan, Mr Edward
Ryan, Mr Patrick
Saad, Mr Amin
Saad, Mr Khalil
Sadlier, Mr Matthew
Sadowitz, Mr Harry

Sage, Mr John George
Sage, Mrs Annie Elizabeth
Sage, Miss Stella Anne
Sage, Mr George John
Sage, Mr Douglas Bullen
Sage, Mr Frederick
Sage, Miss Dorothy Florence
Sage, Mr Anthony William
Sage, Miss Elizabeth Ada [child]
Sage, Miss Constance Gladys [child]
Sage, Master Thomas Henry [child]
Salander, Mr Karl Johan
Salkjelsvik, Miss Anna Kristine
Salonen, Mr Johan Verner
Samaan, Mr Betros [WS List as Betros Seman (child)]
Samaan, Mr Hanna Elias
Samaan, Mr Elias
Samaan, Mr Youssef Omar
Sandström, Mrs Agnes Charlotta
Sandström, Miss Marguerite Rut [child]
Sandström, Miss Beatrice Irene [child]
Sap, Mr Julius
Sæther, Mr Simon Sivertsen
Saundercock, Mr William Henry
Sawyer, Mr Frederick Charles
Scanlan, Mr James
Scheerlinckx, Mr Jean Baptiste
Sdycoff, Mr Theodor
Serota, Mr Maurice
Shadid, Mr Dahir Abu
Shaughnessy, Mr Patrick
Shellard, Mr Frederick William Blainey
Shihab, Al-Amir Faris [WS List as Emir Farres Chehab]
Shine, Miss Ellen
Shorney, Mr Charles Joseph
Sihvola, Mr Antti Wilhelm
Simmons, Mr John
Sirkanian, Mr Arsun [WS List as Sirayanian Orsen]
Sivic, Mr Husein
Sjöblom, Miss Anna Sofia
Skoog, Mr Wilhelm Johansson
Skoog, Mrs Anna Bernhardina
Skoog, Master Karl Thorsten [child]
Skoog, Miss Mabel [child]
Skoog, Master Harald [child]
Skoog, Miss Margit Elizabeth [child]
Slabenoff, Mr Peko
Slocovski, Mr Selman Francis
Smiljanovic, Mr Jakob Mile
Smyth, Miss Julia
Smyth, Mr Thomas [incorrectly listed on the WS List as Thomas Emmett]
Søholt, Mr Peter Andreas Lauritz Andersen
Somerton, Mr Francis William

Spector, Mr Woolf
Spinner, Mr Henry John
Staneff, Mr Ivan
Stankovic, Mr Jovan
Stanley, Miss Amy Zillah Elsie
Stanley, Mr Edward Roland
Storey, Mr Thomas
Stoytcheff, Mr Ilia
Strandberg, Miss Ida Sofia
Strandén, Mr Juho Niilosson
Strilic, Mr Ivan
Ström, Mrs Elna Matilda [Not on the WS List]
Ström, Miss Selma Matilda [child]
Sunderland, Mr Victor Francis
Sundman, Mr Johan Julian
Sutehall, Mr Henry Jr
Svensson, Mr Johan
Svensson, Mr Johan Cervin
Svensson, Mr Olof
Tannous, Mr Charles R'ad [WS List as Charles Thomas]
Tannous, Mrs Thamine [WS List as Tamin Thomas]
Tannous, Master Essed Iskandar [WS List as Assad Thomas] [infant]
Tenglin, Mr Gunnar Isidor
Theobald, Mr Thomas Leonard
Thomas, Mr John
Thomas, Mr Tannous John [WS List as Thomas Tannous]
Thomson, Mr Alexander Morrison
Thorneycroft, Mr Percival Thomas
Thorneycroft, Mrs Florence Kate
Tikkanen, Mr Juho
Tobin, Mr Roger
Todoroff, Mr Lalio
Tomlin, Mr Ernest Portage
Törber, Mr Ernst Wilhelm
Torfa, Mr Assad
Törnqvist, Mr William Henry
Touma, Mrs Hannah [WS List as Hanne Youssef]
Touma, Miss Marianna [WS List as Maria Youssef] [child]
Touma, Master Gerios [WS List as Georges Youssef] [child]
Trembisky, Mr Berk [assumed the name Berk Pickard while in France]
Turcin, Mr Stjepan
Turja, Miss Anna Sofia
Turkula, Mrs Hedvig
Van Billiard, Mr Austin Blyler [WS List as Billiard, A. van]
Van Billiard, Master James William [WS List as Billiard, James] [child]
Van Billiard, Master Walter John [WS List as Billiard, Walter] [child]
Van de Velde, Mr Johannes Joseph
Van de Walle, Mr Nestor Cyriel
Van den Steen, Mr Leo Peter
Van Impe, Mr Jean Baptiste
Van Impe, Mrs Rosalie Paula
Van Impe, Miss Catharina [child]
Van Melkebeke, Mr Philemon Edmund

Vandercruyssen, Mr Victor
Vanderplancke, Miss Augusta Maria
Vanderplancke, Mr Julius
Vanderplancke, Mrs Emelie Maria
Vanderplancke, Mr Leo Edmondus
Vartanian, Mr Dawud
Vendel, Mr Olof Edvin
Veström, Miss Hulda Amanda Adolfina
Vovk, Mr Janko
Waelens, Mr Achille
Ware, Mr Frederick William
Warren, Mr Charles William
Wazni, Mr Yousif Ahmed
Webber, Mr James
Whabee, Mrs Shawneene [WS List as Georges Shabini]
Widegren, Mr Carl Peter
Wiklund, Mr Jakob Alfred
Wiklund, Mr Karl Johan
Wilkes, Mrs Ellen
Willer, Mr Aaron
Willey, Mr Edward
Williams, Mr Howard Hugh
Williams, Mr Leslie
Windeløv, Mr Einar
Wirz, Mr Albert
Wiseman, Mr Phillippe
Wittevrongel, Mr Camille Aloysius
Yarred, Miss Jamila [booked as Jamila Nicola]
Yarred, Master Elias [booked as Elias Nicola] [child]
Yazbak, Mr Antoni
Yazbak, Mrs Silanah
Ylieff, Mr Ylio [WS List as Ylio Ilieff]
Youssef, Mr Gerios [WS List as Youssef Gerios]
Youssef, Mrs Katarin [WS List as Catherine Joseph Peter]
Youssef, Master Makhkhul [WS List as Mike Peter] [child]
Youssef, Miss Marianna [WS List as Anna Peter] [child]
Zakarian, Mr Haroutyun Der [WS List as Zakarian Ortin]
Zakarian, Mr Mapri Der
Zimmermann, Mr Leo

Appendix D

DECK DEPARTMENT CREW

Lester J. Mitcham

When *Titanic* left Queenstown there were sixty-six deck department personnel on board. Of those, twenty-three were lost and forty-three were saved. Those lost are in **bold**. Names are arranged by capacity engaged.

OFFICERS	
Smith, Captain Edward John	Master
Wilde, Mr Henry Tingle	Chief Officer
Murdoch, Mr William McMaster	1st Officer
Lightoller, Mr Charles Herbert	2nd Officer
Pitman, Mr Herbert John	3rd Officer
Boxhall, Mr Joseph Groves	4th Officer
Lowe, Mr Harold Godfrey	5th Officer
Moody, Mr James Paul	6th Officer
SURGEONS	
O'Loughlin, Dr William Francis Norman	Surgeon
Simpson, Dr John Edward	Assistant Surgeon
BOATSWAINS, MASTERS-AT-ARMS, QUARTERMASTERS & LOOKOUTS	
Nichols, Mr Alfred	Boatswain
Haines, Mr Albert M.	Boatswain's Mate
Bailey, Mr Joseph Henry	Master-at-Arms
King, Mr Thomas W.	Master-at-Arms
Bright, Mr Arthur John	Quartermaster
Hichens, Mr Robert	Quartermaster
Olliver, Mr Alfred	Quartermaster
Perkis, Mr Walter John	Quartermaster
Rowe, Mr George Thomas	Quartermaster
Wynn, Mr Walter	Quartermaster
Evans, Mr Alfred Frank	Lookout
Fleet, Mr Frederick	Lookout
Hogg, Mr George Alfred	Lookout
Jewell, Mr Archie	Lookout
Lee, Mr Reginald Robinson	Lookout
Symons, Mr George Thomas Macdonald	Lookout

SEAMEN	
Anderson, Mr James	Able Seaman
Archer, Mr Ernest Edward	Able Seaman
Bradley, Mr T.	Able Seaman
Brice, Mr Walter T	Able Seaman
Buley, Mr Edward John	Able Seaman
Clench, Mr Frederick	Able Seaman
Clench, Mr George	Able Seaman
Couch, Mr Frank	Able Seaman
Davis, Mr Stephen James	Able Seaman
Evans, Mr Frank Oliver	Able Seaman
Forward, Mr James	Able Seaman
Holman, Mr Harry	Able Seaman
Hopkins, Mr Robert John	Able Seaman
Horswill, Mr Albert Edward James	Able Seaman
Humphreys, Mr Sidney James	Able Seaman [signed on as a Quartermaster]
Jones, Mr Thomas William	Able Seaman
Lucas, Mr William A.	Able Seaman
Lyons, Mr William Henry	Able Seaman
Matherson, Mr David	Able Seaman
McCarthy, Mr William	Able Seaman
McGough, Mr George Francis	Able Seaman
Moore, Mr George Alfred	Able Seaman
Osman, Mr Frank	Able Seaman
Pascoe, Mr Charles H.	Able Seaman
Peters, Mr William Chapman	Able Seaman
Poingdestre, Mr John Thomas	Able Seaman
Scarrott, Mr Joseph George	Able Seaman
Taylor, Mr C.	Able Seaman
Vigott, Mr Philip Francis	Able Seaman
Weller, Mr William Clifford	Able Seaman
Smith, Mr William	Seaman
Terrell, Mr Bertram	Seaman
OTHER DECK CREW	
Hemming, Mr Samuel Ernest	Lamp Trimmer
Foley, Mr John	Storekeeper
Maxwell, Mr John	Carpenter
Hutchinson, Mr John Hall	Joiner
Harder, Mr William	Window Cleaner
Sawyer, Mr Robert James	Window Cleaner
Mathias, Mr Montague Vincent	Mess Steward
Tamlyn, Mr Frederick	Mess Steward

Appendix E

ENGINE DEPARTMENT CREW

Lester J. Mitcham

When *Titanic* left Queenstown there were 325 engine department personnel on board. Of those, 253 were lost and 72 were saved. Those lost are in **bold**. Names are arranged by capacity engaged.

ENGINEERS	
Bell, Mr Joseph	Chief Engineer
Farquharson, Mr William Edward	Senior 2nd Engineer
Harrison, Mr Norman E.	Junior 2nd Engineer
Hesketh, Mr John Henry	Junior 2nd Engineer
Wilson, Mr Bertie	Senior Assistant 2nd Engineer
Harvey, Mr Herbert Gifford	Junior Assistant 2nd Engineer
Shepherd, Mr Jonathan	Junior Assistant 2nd Engineer
Hosking, Mr George Fox	Senior 3rd Engineer
Dodd, Mr Edward Charles	Junior 3rd Engineer
Hodge, Mr Charles	Senior Assistant 3rd Engineer
Coy, Mr Francis Ernest George	Junior Assistant 3rd Engineer
Fraser, Mr James	Junior Assistant 3rd Engineer
Hodgkinson, Mr Leonard	Senior 4th Engineer
Smith, Mr James M.	Junior 4th Engineer
Dyer, Mr Henry Ryland	Senior Assistant 4th Engineer
Dodds, Mr Henry Watson	Junior Assistant 4th Engineer
Ward, Mr Arthur	Junior Assistant 4th Engineer
Kemp, Mr Thomas Hulman	Extra Assistant 4th Engineer (Refrigeration)
Parsons, Mr Frank Alfred	Senior 5th Engineer
Mackie, Mr William Dickson	Junior 5th Engineer
Millar, Mr Robert	Extra 5th Engineer
Moyes, Mr William Young	Senior 6th Engineer
McReynolds, Mr William	Junior 6th Engineer

Creese, Mr Henry Philip	Deck Engineer
Millar, Mr Thomas	Assistant Deck Engineer

BOILERMAKERS, ELECTRICIANS & PLUMBER

Chisnall, Mr George Alexander	Boilermaker
Fitzpatrick, Mr Hugh J.	Junior Boilermaker
Sloan, Mr Peter	Chief Electrician
Allsop, Mr Alfred Samuel	2nd Electrician
Ervine, Mr Albert George	Assistant Electrician
Jupe, Mr Herbert	Assistant Electrician
Kelly, Mr William	Assistant Electrician
Middleton, Mr Alfred Pirrie	Assistant Electrician
Rous, Mr Arthur J.	Plumber

CLERK, STOREKEEPERS, MESSMEN & MESS STEWARDS

Duffy, Mr William Luke	Writer / Engineer's Clerk
Foster, Mr Albert Charles	Storekeeper
Kenzler, Mr Augustus	Storekeeper
Newman, Mr Charles Thomas	Assistant Storekeeper
Rudd, Mr Henry	Assistant Storekeeper
Knowles, Mr Thomas	Fireman's Messman
May, Mr Arthur William	Fireman's Messman
Blake, Mr Seaton	Mess Steward
Coleman, Mr John	Mess Steward
Fitzpatrick, Mr Cecil William Norman	Mess Steward
Gumery, Mr George	Mess Steward

GREASERS, FIREMEN & TRIMMERS ON THE 4 TO 8 SHIFT

Beattie, Mr Joseph	Greaser
Briant, Mr Albert [signed on as M. Stafford]	Greaser
Eastman, Mr Charles	Greaser
Godwin, Mr Frederick Walter	Greaser
Jukes, Mr James	Greaser
Kearl, Mr Charles Henry	Greaser
Kenchenten, Mr Frederick	Greaser
Morris, Mr Arthur	Greaser
Olive, Mr Charles	Greaser
Palles, Mr Thomas	Greaser
Phillips, Mr A. George	Greaser
Pitfield, Mr William James	Greaser
Prangnell, Mr George Alexander	Greaser
Ranger, Mr Thomas G.	Greaser

Self, Mr Alfred Henry	Greaser
Veal, Mr Arthur	Greaser
White, Mr Alfred Thomas	Greaser
Woodford, Mr Frederick	Greaser
Davies, Mr Thomas	Leading Fireman
Hendrickson, Mr Charles George	Leading Fireman
Mayo, Mr William Peter	Leading Fireman
Abrams, Mr William	Fireman
Barnes, Mr John	Fireman
Blaney, Mr James	Fireman
Bradley, Mr Patrick Joseph	Fireman
Butt, Mr William John	Fireman
Combes, Mr George	Fireman
Copperthwaite, Mr Albert	Fireman
Couper, Mr Robert	Fireman
Diaper, Mr John Joseph	Fireman
Dilley, Mr John	Fireman
Gradidge, Mr Ernest Edward	Fireman
Graham, Mr Thomas G.	Fireman
Haggan, Mr John	Fireman
Hannam, Mr George	Fireman
Harris, Mr Edward	Fireman
Head, Mr A.	Fireman
Hopgood, Mr Roland	Fireman
Jacobson, Mr John Henry	Fireman
James, Mr Thomas	Fireman
Jones, Mr Nicholas [signed on as N. Joas]	Fireman
Light, Mr William J.	Fireman
Lindsay, Mr William Charles	Fireman
Marsh, Mr Frederick Charles	Fireman
Mayzes, Mr Thomas A.	Fireman
McAndrews, Mr William	Fireman
McGaw, Mr Erroll Victor	Fireman
Moore, Mr John J.	Fireman
Nettleton, Mr George	Fireman
Norris, Mr James	Fireman
Nutbeam, Mr William	Fireman
Othen, Mr Charles Edward	Fireman
Paice, Mr Richard Charles John	Fireman

Painter, Mr Charles	Fireman
Podesta, Mr John Alexander	Fireman
Pusey, Mr Robert William	Fireman
Reeves, Mr F.	Fireman
Rickman, Mr George Albert	Fireman
Rutter, Mr Sidney Frank [signed on as S. Graves]	Fireman
Self, Mr Edward	Fireman
Senior, Mr Henry	Fireman
Shiers, Mr Alfred Charles	Fireman
Smither, Mr Harry James	Fireman
Sparkman, Mr James Henry J.	Fireman
Stanbrook, Mr Alfred Augustus	Fireman
Taylor, Mr T.	Fireman
Thomas, Mr Joseph	Fireman
Tizard, Mr Arthur	Fireman
Triggs, Mr Robert V.	Fireman
Van Der Brugge, Mr Wessel Adrianus	Fireman
Wateridge, Mr Edward Lewis	Fireman
Watson, Mr W.	Fireman
Worthman, Mr William Henry [signed on as W. Jarvis]	Fireman
Wyeth, Mr James Robert	Fireman
Young, Mr Francis James	Fireman
Billows, Mr Joseph	Trimmer
Binstead, Mr Walter	Trimmer
Calderwood, Mr Hugh	Trimmer
Eagle, Mr Alfred James	Trimmer
Ford, Mr H.	Trimmer
Harris, Mr Amos Fred	Trimmer
Hebb, Mr Albert	Trimmer
Hill, Mr James	Trimmer
Hunt, Mr Albert	Trimmer
Kearl, Mr G.	Trimmer
Long, Mr F.	Trimmer
Mitchell, Mr Lawrence	Trimmer
Moore, Mr Ralph William	Trimmer
Morris, Mr W.	Trimmer
Sheath, Mr Frederick	Trimmer
Shillabeer, Mr Charles Frederick	Trimmer
Skeates, Mr William Frederick	Trimmer

Snooks, Mr W.	Trimmer
Stocker, Mr Henry Dorey	Trimmer
Webb, Mr Sydney Augustus	Trimmer
Witts, Mr Francis Albert	Trimmer
Wood, Mr Henry	Trimmer
GREASERS, FIREMEN & TRIMMERS ON THE 8 TO 12 SHIFT	
Bannon, Mr John	Greaser
Castleman, Mr Edward	Greaser
Goree, Mr Frank	Greaser
Gregory, Mr David George	Greaser
Kelly, Mr James	Greaser
Moores, Mr Richard Henry	Greaser
Scott, Mr Frederick William	Greaser
Barrett, Mr Frederick	Leading Fireman
Ferris, Mr William	Leading Fireman
Mason, Mr J.	Leading Fireman
Pugh, Mr Percy	Leading Fireman
Ward, Mr James Allan	Leading Fireman
Adams, Mr R.	Fireman
Bailey, Mr George W.	Fireman
Barlow, Mr Charles	Fireman
Barrett, Mr Frederick William	Fireman
Beauchamp, Mr George William	Fireman
Biddlecombe, Mr Charles	Fireman
Biggs, Mr Edward Charles	Fireman
Black, Mr Alexander	Fireman
Blake, Mr Thomas Henry	Fireman
Blann, Mr Eustace Horatius	Fireman
Burroughs, Mr Arthur Peel	Fireman
Carter, Mr James [signed on as W. Ball]	Fireman
Cherrett, Mr William Victor	Fireman
Chorley, Mr John Henry	Fireman
Cooper, Mr Harry	Fireman
Corcoran, Mr Dennis	Fireman
Crimmins, Mr James	Fireman
Cunningham, Mr B.	Fireman
Fraser, Mr James	Fireman
Golder, Mr M. W.	Fireman
Hall, Mr J.	Fireman

Hands, Mr Bernard	Fireman
Harris, Mr Frederick	Fireman
Hart, Mr James [signed on as T. Hart]	Fireman
Hunt, Mr Thomas	Fireman
Hurst, Mr Charles John	Fireman
Instance, Mr Thomas	Fireman
Kemish, Mr George	Fireman
Lahy, Mr Thomas E.	Fireman
Marrett, Mr G.	Fireman
May, Mr Arthur	Fireman
McAndrew, Mr Thomas M.	Fireman
McCastlin, Mr Walter	Fireman
McQuillan, Mr William	Fireman
McRae, Mr William Alexander	Fireman
Milford, Mr George	Fireman
Niven, Mr John Brown [signed on as J. McGregor]	Fireman
Noon, Mr John	Fireman
Noss, Mr Bertram Arthur	Fireman
Rice, Mr Charles	Fireman
Roberts, Mr Robert George	Fireman
Saunders, Mr F.	Fireman
Saunders, Mr W.	Fireman
Scott, Mr Archibald	Fireman
Shea, Mr Thomas	Fireman
Street, Mr Thomas Albert	Fireman
Sullivan, Mr S.	Fireman
Turley, Mr Richard	Fireman
Williams, Mr Samuel S. [signed on as his brother Edward]	Fireman
Bevis, Mr Joseph Henry	Trimmer
Brewer, Mr Henry	Trimmer
Brooks, Mr James	Trimmer
Cavell, Mr George Henry	Trimmer
Coe, Mr Harry	Trimmer
Dillon, Mr Thomas Patrick	Trimmer
Dore, Mr A.	Trimmer
Ferrary, Mr Anton	Trimmer
Fryer, Mr Albert Ernest	Trimmer
Gosling, Mr Bertram James	Trimmer
Lee, Mr H.	Trimmer

Maskell, Mr Leopold Adolphus	Trimmer
Morgan, Mr Arthur Herbert	Trimmer
Perry, Mr Henry	Trimmer
Proudfoot, Mr Richard Royston	Trimmer
Read, Mr J.	Trimmer
Read, Mr Robert	Trimmer
Saunders, Mr W.	Trimmer
Smith, Mr Ernest George	Trimmer
White, Mr Albert [signed on as R. Morell]	Trimmer
White, Mr Frank Leonard	Trimmer
Wilton, Mr William	Trimmer
GREASERS, FIREMEN & TRIMMERS ON THE 12 TO 4 SHIFT	
Baines, Mr Richard	Greaser
Bott, Mr William T.	Greaser
Couch, Mr Joseph Henry	Greaser
Fay, Mr Thomas Joseph	Greaser
Jago, Mr Joseph	Greaser
Kirkham, Mr James	Greaser
McInerney, Mr Thomas	Greaser
Tozer, Mr James	Greaser
Ford, Mr Thomas	Leading Fireman
Keegan, Mr James	Leading Fireman
Small, Mr William	Leading Fireman
Threlfall, Mr Thomas	Leading Fireman
Webber, Mr Francis Albert	Leading Fireman
Allen, Mr Henry	Fireman
Barnes, Mr Charles	Fireman
Bendell, Mr F.	Fireman
Bennett, Mr George Alfred	Fireman
Benville, Mr Edward	Fireman
Bessant, Mr William Edward	Fireman
Blackman, Mr H.	Fireman
Brown, Mr John	Fireman
Burton, Mr Edward John	Fireman
Canner, Mr J.	Fireman
Clark, Mr William	Fireman
Collins, Mr Samuel A.	Fireman
Cross, Mr William	Fireman
Curtis, Mr Arthur	Fireman

Doel, Mr Frederick	Fireman
Doyle, Mr Laurence	Fireman
Dymond, Mr Frank	Fireman
Flarty, Mr Edward	Fireman
Godley, Mr George A.	Fireman
Hallett, Mr George	Fireman
Hodges, Mr W.	Fireman
Hurst, Mr Walter	Fireman
Judd, Mr Charles Edward	Fireman
Kasper, Mr Franz Wilhelm	Fireman
Kerr, Mr Thomas	Fireman
Light, Mr Christopher William	Fireman
Major, Mr William James	Fireman
Mason, Mr Frank Archibald Robert	Fireman
McGarvey, Mr Edward Joseph	Fireman
Mintram, Mr William	Fireman
Morgan, Mr Thomas A.	Fireman
Murdoch, Mr William John	Fireman
Noss, Mr Henry	Fireman
Oliver, Mr Henry	Fireman
Painter, Mr Frank Frederick	Fireman
Pearce, Mr John	Fireman
Pond, Mr George	Fireman
Priest, Mr Arthur John	Fireman
Richards, Mr Joseph James	Fireman
Sangster, Mr Charles	Fireman
Snellgrove, Mr George	Fireman
Stubbs, Mr James Henry	Fireman
Taylor, Mr James	Fireman
Taylor, Mr John	Fireman
Taylor, Mr William Henry	Fireman
Thompson, Mr John William	Fireman
Thresher, Mr George Terrill	Fireman
Vear, Mr Henry	Fireman
Vear, Mr William	Fireman
Wardner, Mr Frederick Albert	Fireman
Witcher, Mr Albert Ernest	Fireman
Allen, Mr Ernest Frederick G.	Trimmer
Avery, Mr James Frank	Trimmer

Blake, Mr Percival Albert	Trimmer
Carr, Mr Richard Stephen	Trimmer
Casey, Mr Thomas	Trimmer
Cooper, Mr James	Trimmer
Crabb, Mr Henry J.	Trimmer
Dawson, Mr Joseph	Trimmer
Elliott, Mr Everett Edward	Trimmer
Evans, Mr William	Trimmer
Fredericks, Mr Walter Francis	Trimmer
Gosling, Mr S.	Trimmer
Green, Mr George	Trimmer
Haslin, Mr James	Trimmer
Hinton, Mr Stephen William	Trimmer
Ingram, Mr Charles	Trimmer
Long, Mr William	Trimmer
McGann, Mr James	Trimmer
McIntyre, Mr William	Trimmer
Pelham, Mr George	Trimmer
Perry, Mr Edgar Lionel	Trimmer
Preston, Mr Thomas Charles Alfred	Trimmer
Snow, Mr Eustace Philip	Trimmer
White, Mr William George	Trimmer
SUBSTITUTE FIREMEN & TRIMMERS	
Black, Mr D.	Fireman
Brown, Mr Joseph James	Fireman
Geer, Mr Alfred Emest	Fireman
Hosgood, Mr Richard	Fireman
Kinsella, Mr Louis	Fireman
Lloyd, Mr William	Fireman
Witt, Mr Henry Dennis	Fireman
Cotton, Mr A.	Trimmer
Dickson, Mr William	Trimmer
Gordon, Mr J.	Trimmer
O'Connor, Mr John	Trimmer
Steel, Mr Robert Edward	Trimmer

Appendix F

VICTUALLING DEPARTMENT CREW

Lester J. Mitcham

When *Titanic* left Queenstown there were 500 victualling department personnel on board. Of those, 403 were lost and 97 were saved. Those lost are in **bold**. Names are arranged by capacity engaged.

PURSERS, CLERKS & MARCONI OPERATORS	
McElroy, Mr Hugh Walter	Chief Purser
Barker, Mr Reginald Lomond	Assistant / 2nd Class Purser
Ashcroft, Mr Austin Aloysius	Purser's Clerk
King, Mr Ernest Waldron	Purser's Clerk
Rice, Mr John Reginald	Purser's Clerk
Campbell, Mr Donald S.	Clerk
Taylor, Mr George Frederick [signed on as G.F. Turner]	Stenographer
Mishellany, Mr Abraham Mansoor	Chief Printer
Corben, Mr Ernest Theodore	Assistant Printer
Perkins, Mr Laurence Alexander	Telephone Operator
Phillips, Mr John George	Telegraphist / Marconi Co.
Bride, Mr Harold Sydney	Assistant Telegraphist / Marconi Co.
STOREKEEPERS	
Parsons, Mr Edward	Chief Storekeeper
Thompson, Mr Herbert Henry	Second Storekeeper
Bird, Mr Charles Frederick [signed on as W. Morgan]	Storekeeper
Kieran, Mr Michael	Storekeeper
Prentice, Mr Frank Winnold	Storekeeper
Ricks, Mr Cyril George	Storekeeper
Rogers, Mr Edward James William	Storekeeper
Williams, Mr Arthur John	Storekeeper

FIRST CLASS STEWARDS	
Latimer, Mr Andrew L.	Chief Steward
Dodd, Mr George Charles	Second Steward / Chief Dining Saloon Steward
Hughes, Mr William Thomas	Assistant Second Steward
Wheat, Mr Joseph Thomas	Assistant Second Steward
Burke, Mr Richard Edward	Lounge Steward
Back, Mr Charles Frederick	Assistant Lounge Steward
Abbott, Mr Ernest Owen	Lounge Pantry Steward
Webb, Mr Brooke Holding	Smoke Room Steward
Hamilton, Mr Ernest	Assistant Smoke Room Steward
Dolby, Mr Joseph	D-deck Reception Room Steward
Holland, Mr Thomas	Assistant Reception Room Steward
Stewart, Mr John	Verandah Cafe Steward
Broome, Mr Athol Frederick	Assistant Verandah Cafe Steward
Freeman, Mr Ernest Edward Samuel	Chief Deck Steward
Boston, Mr William John	Assistant Deck Steward
Hawkesworth, Mr William Walter	Assistant Deck Steward
Moss, Mr William Aaron	First Dining Saloon Steward
Burke, Mr William	Second Dining Saloon Steward
Goshawk, Mr Arthur James	Third Dining Saloon Steward
Ahier, Mr Percy Snowden	Saloon Steward
Allsop, Mr Frank Richard	Saloon Steward
Baggott, Mr Allen Marden	Saloon Steward
Bagley, Mr Edward Henry	Saloon Steward
Barker, Mr Ernest Frank	Saloon Steward
Barringer, Mr Arthur William	Saloon Steward
Barrows, Mr William	Saloon Steward
Best, Mr Edwin Alfred	Saloon Steward
Boughton, Mr Bernard John	Saloon Steward
Boyd, Mr John Charles Thomas Colliyons	Saloon Steward
Boyes, Mr John Henry	Saloon Steward
Bristow, Mr Harry	Saloon Steward
Brown, Mr Edward	Saloon Steward
Brown, Mr Walter James	Saloon Steward
Burr, Mr Ewart Sydenham	Saloon Steward
Butt, Mr Robert Henry	Saloon Steward
Butterworth, Mr John	Saloon Steward
Cartwright, Mr James Edward	Saloon Steward

Casswill, Mr Charles	Saloon Steward
Cave, Mr Herbert	Saloon Steward
Cheverton, Mr William Edward	Saloon Steward
Coleman, Mr Albert Edward	Saloon Steward
Cook, Mr George	Saloon Steward
Crafter, Mr Frederick	Saloon Steward
Crisp, Mr Albert Hector	Saloon Steward
Crowe, Mr George Frederick	Saloon Steward
Derrett, Mr Albert	Saloon Steward
Deslands, Mr Percival Stainer	Saloon Steward
Dinenage, Mr James Richard	Saloon Steward
Dyer, Mr William	Saloon Steward
Evans, Mr George Richard	Saloon Steward
Fairall, Mr Henry C.	Saloon Steward
Harrison, Mr Aragon Drummond	Saloon Steward
Hartnell, Mr Frederick	Saloon Steward
Hendy, Mr Edward Martin	Saloon Steward
Hoare, Mr Leonard James	Saloon Steward
House, Mr William H.	Saloon Steward
Howell, Mr Arthur Albert	Saloon Steward
Jones, Mr Reginald V.	Saloon Steward
Keen, Mr Percy Edward	Saloon Steward
Ketchley, Mr Henry	Saloon Steward
Kingscote, Mr William Ford	Saloon Steward
Kitching, Mr Arthur Alfred	Saloon Steward
Knight, Mr George Henry	Saloon Steward
Lake, Mr William	Saloon Steward
Lane, Mr Albert Edward	Saloon Steward
Lawrence, Mr Arthur	Saloon Steward
Lefebvre, Mr Paul Georges	Saloon Steward
Littlejohn, Mr Alexander James	Saloon Steward
Lloyd, Mr Humphrey I.	Saloon Steward
Lucas, Mr William	Saloon Steward
Lydiatt, Mr Charles	Saloon Steward
Mackay, Mr Charles Donald	Saloon Steward
McGrady, Mr James	Saloon Steward
McMicken, Mr Arthur David	Saloon Steward
McMullin, Mr John	Saloon Steward
Mellor, Mr Arthur	Saloon Steward

Nicholls, Mr Sidney	Saloon Steward
Orpet, Mr Walter Hayward	Saloon Steward
Perriton, Mr Hubert Prouse	Saloon Steward
Pryce, Mr Charles William	Saloon Steward
Pusey, Mr John E.	Saloon Steward
Ransom, Mr James	Saloon Steward
Ray, Mr Frederick Dent	Saloon Steward
Rimmer, Mr Gilbert	Saloon Steward
Robinson, Mr James William	Saloon Steward
Rowe, Mr Edward Matthew	Saloon Steward
Saunders, Mr D.E.	Saloon Steward
Shea, Mr John J.	Saloon Steward
Simmonds, Mr Frederick C.	Saloon Steward
Skinner, Mr Edward	Saloon Steward
Smith, Mr Reginald George	Saloon Steward
Stagg, Mr John Henry	Saloon Steward
Stroud, Mr Henry John	Saloon Steward
Symonds, Mr John	Saloon Steward
Taylor, Mr William John	Saloon Steward
Thomas, Mr Albert Charles	Saloon Steward
Thomas, Mr Benjamin James	Saloon Steward
Toms, Mr Francis A.	Saloon Steward
Toshack, Mr James Addison	Saloon Steward
Turner, Mr L.	Saloon Steward
Veal, Mr Thomas Henry Edom	Saloon Steward
Ward, Mr William	Saloon Steward
Warwick, Mr Tom	Saloon Steward
Weatherstone, Mr Thomas Herbert	Saloon Steward
Wheelton, Mr Edneser Edward	Saloon Steward
White, Mr Leonard Lisle Oliver	Saloon Steward
Whiteley, Mr Thomas Arthur	Saloon Steward
Wormald, Mr Frederick William	Saloon Steward
Yearsley, Mr Henry Frankes	Saloon Steward
Deeble, Mr Alfred Arnold	Saloon Watchman
Johnstone, Mr James	Saloon Watchman
Osborne, Mr William Edward	Saloon Watchman
Revell, Mr William James	Saloon Watchman
Smillie, Mr John	Saloon Watchman
Strugnell, Mr John Herbert	Saloon Watchman

Fletcher, Mr Peter W.	Bugler
Baxter, Mr Thomas Ferguson	Linen Keeper
Bessant, Mr Edward William	Baggage Master
Olive, Mr Ernest Roskelly	Clothes Presser
Holloway, Mr Sidney	Assistant Clothes Presser
Bennett, Mrs Mabel	Stewardess
Coghlan, Mrs Annie [signed on using her maiden name of Martin]	Stewardess
Gold, Mrs Katherine	Stewardess
Gregson, Miss Mary Josephine	Stewardess
Jessop, Miss Violet Constance	Stewardess
Leather, Mrs Elizabeth May	Stewardess
Marsden, Miss Evelyn	Stewardess
McLaren, Mrs Harriet	Stewardess
Prichard, Mrs Alice	Stewardess
Roberts, Mrs Mary Keziah	Stewardess
Robinson, Mrs Annie	Stewardess
Sloan, Miss Mary	Stewardess
Smith, Miss Katherine Elizabeth	Stewardess
Stap, Miss Sarah Agnes	Stewardess
Allan, Mr Robert Spencer	Bedroom Steward
Anderson, Mr Walter J.	Bedroom Steward
Bishop, Mr Walter Alexander	Bedroom Steward
Bond, Mr William John	Bedroom Steward
Brewster, Mr George Henry	Bedroom Steward
Crawford, Mr Alfred George	Bedroom Steward
Crumplin, Mr Charles George C.	Bedroom Steward
Cullen, Mr Charles	Bedroom Steward
Cunningham, Mr Andrew	Bedroom Steward
Davies, Mr Gordon Raleigh	Bedroom Steward
Donoghue, Mr Thomas	Bedroom Steward
Etches, Mr Henry Samuel	Bedroom Steward
Faulkner, Mr William Stephen	Bedroom Steward
Geddes, Mr Richard Charles	Bedroom Steward
Gill, Mr Joseph Stanley	Bedroom Steward
Hayter, Mr Arthur	Bedroom Steward
Hewett, Mr Thomas	Bedroom Steward
Hill, Mr James Colston	Bedroom Steward
Hogg, Mr Charles William	Bedroom Steward

Ide, Mr Harry John	Bedroom Steward
Janaway, Mr William Frank	Bedroom Steward
Kirkaldy, Mr Thomas [signed on as T. Clark]	Bedroom Steward
McCarthy, Mr Frederick James	Bedroom Steward
McMurray, Mr William Ernest	Bedroom Steward
O'Connor, Mr Thomas Peter	Bedroom Steward
Penrose, Mr John Poole	Bedroom Steward
Roberts, Mr Hugh H.	Bedroom Steward
Siebert, Mr Sidney Conrad	Bedroom Steward
Stone, Mr Edmond J.	Bedroom Steward
Swan, Mr William	Bedroom Steward
Theissinger, Mr Alfred	Bedroom Steward
Ward, Mr Edward	Bedroom Steward
Ward, Mr Percy Thomas	Bedroom Steward
Wareham, Mr Robert Arthur	Bedroom Steward
Wittman, Mr Henry	Bedroom Steward
Broom, Mr Herbert W.	Bathroom Steward
Major, Mr Thomas Edgar	Bathroom Steward
Morris, Mr Frank Herbert	Bathroom Steward
Pennal, Mr Thomas Francis	Bathroom Steward
Rule, Mr Samuel James	Bathroom Steward
Stebbings, Mr Sydney Frederick	Chief Boots Steward
Fellows, Mr James Alfred	Assistant Boots Steward
Guy, Mr Edward John	Assistant Boots Steward
Jackson, Mr Cecil John	Assistant Boots Steward
Rattenbury, Mr William Henry [signed on as W. Henry]	Assistant Boots Steward
Scott, Mr John	Assistant Boots Steward
Allen, Mr Frederick	Lift Attendant
Carney, Mr William John	Lift Attendant
King, Mr Alfred	Lift Attendant
Barratt, Mr Arthur	Bell Boy
Harris, Mr Clifford Henry	Bell Boy
Watson, Mr W. Albert	Bell Boy
Weikman, Mr August Henry [signed on as A. H. Whiteman]	Barber
White, Mr Arthur	Assistant Barber
McCawley, Mr Thomas W.	Gymnasium Instructor
Wright, Mr Frederick	Squash Racquet Court Instructor

Caton, Miss Annie	Turkish Bath Attendant
Crosby, Mr James Bertram	Turkish Bath Attendant
Ennis, Mr Walter	Turkish Bath Attendant
Slocombe, Mrs Maud Louise	Turkish Bath Attendant
Taylor, Mr Leonard	Turkish Bath Attendant
Walpole, Mr James	Chief Pantryman
McMicken, Mr Benjamin Tucker [signed on as B. Tucker]	Second Pantryman
Akerman, Mr Joseph Francis	Assistant Pantryman
Edwards, Mr Clement	Assistant Pantryman
Harris, Mr Edward	Assistant Pantryman
Levett, Mr George Alfred	Assistant Pantryman
Marks, Mr J.	Assistant Pantryman
Marriott, Mr J. W.	Assistant Pantryman
Smith, Mr F.	Assistant Pantryman
Wrapson, Mr Frederick Bernard	Assistant Pantryman
Ball, Mr Percy	Plate Steward
Bradshaw, Mr John A.	Plate Steward
Bunnell, Mr Wilfred James	Plate Steward
Hiscock, Mr Sidney George	Plate Steward
Hogue, Mr E.	Plate Steward
Hopkins, Mr Alfred	Plate Steward
Light, Mr C.	Plate Steward
SECOND CLASS STEWARDS	
Hardy, Mr John T.	Chief 2nd Class Steward
Jenner, Mr Harry	Second 2nd Class Steward
Kelland, Mr Thomas	Library Steward
Witter, Mr James William Cheetham	Smoke Room Steward
Edge, Mr Frederick William	Deck Steward
Bailey, Mr George Francis	Saloon Steward
Benham, Mr Frederick	Saloon Steward
Charman, Mr John	Saloon Steward
Conway, Mr P. W.	Saloon Steward
Dashwood, Mr William George	Saloon Steward
Davies, Mr Robert J.	Saloon Steward
Doughty, Mr W.	Saloon Steward
Franklin, Mr Alan Vincent	Saloon Steward
Gibbons, Mr Jacob William	Saloon Steward
Harris, Mr Charles William	Saloon Steward

Hawkesworth, Mr James	Saloon Steward
Heinen, Mr Joseph	Saloon Steward
Jensen, Mr Charles Valdemar	Saloon Steward
Jones, Mr Albert	Saloon Steward
Middleton, Mr M.V.	Saloon Steward
Moore, Mr Alfred Ernest	Saloon Steward
Parsons, Mr Richard	Saloon Steward
Pfropper, Mr Richard	Saloon Steward
Phillimore, Mr Harold Charles William	Saloon Steward
Randall, Mr Frank Henry	Saloon Steward
Ridout, Mr W.	Saloon Steward
Rogers, Mr Michael	Saloon Steward
Russell, Mr Boysie Richard	Saloon Steward
Ryerson, Mr William Edwy	Saloon Steward
Scovell, Mr Robert	Saloon Steward
Samuel, Mr Owen Wilmore	Saloon Steward
Stroud, Mr Edward Alfred Orlando	Saloon Steward
Teuton Mr Thomas Moore	Saloon Steward
Whitford, Mr Alfred Henry	Saloon Steward
Bliss, Mrs Emma	Stewardess
Lavington, Miss Elizabeth	Stewardess
Snape, Mrs Lucy Violet	Stewardess
Walsh, Miss Catherine	Stewardess
Barlow, Mr George	Bedroom Steward
Beedem, Mr George Arthur	Bedroom Steward
Bogie, Mr Norman Leslie	Bedroom Steward
Boothby, Mr W.	Bedroom Steward
Byrne, Mr J.E.	Bedroom Steward
Ford, Mr F.	Bedroom Steward
Hamblyn, Mr Ernest William	Bedroom Steward
Mackie, Mr George William	Bedroom Steward
Petty, Mr Edwin Henry	Bedroom Steward
Reed, Mr Charles S.	Bedroom Steward
Smith, Mr Charles Edwin	Bedroom Steward
Stone, Mr Edward Thomas	Bedroom Steward
Hinckley, Mr George	Bathroom Steward
Widgery, Mr James George	Bathroom Steward
Bulley, Mr Henry Ashburnham	Boots Steward
Chapman, Mr Joseph Charles	Boots Steward

Perrin, Mr William Charles	Boots Steward
Andrews, Mr Charles Edward	Assistant Steward
Christmas, Mr Herbert	Assistant Steward
Dean, Mr George H.	Assistant Steward
Gunn, Mr Joseph Alfred	Assistant Steward
Humphreys, Mr Thomas Humphrey	Assistant Steward
Kerley, Mr William Thomas	Assistant Steward
Lacey, Mr Bert W.	Assistant Steward
Nichols, Mr Walter Henry	Assistant Steward
Owen, Mr Lewis	Assistant Steward
Penny, Mr William Farr	Assistant Steward
Roberton, Mr George Edward	Assistant Steward
Terrell, Mr Frank Robert	Assistant Steward
Williams, Mr Walter John	Assistant Steward
Wood, Mr James Thomas	Assistant Steward
Pacey, Mr Reginald Lvan	Lift Attendant
Klein, Mr Herbert	Barber
Seward, Mr Wilfred Deable	Chief Pantry Steward
Pook, Mr P.	Assistant Pantry Steward
Longmuir, Mr John Dickson	Assistant Pantry Steward
Harding, Mr A.	Assistant Pantry Steward
Burrage, Mr Alfred	Plate Steward
Humby, Mr Frederick	Plate Steward
Jones, Mr Arthur Ernest	Plate Steward
THIRD CLASS STEWARDS	
Kieran, Mr James W.	Chief 3rd Class Steward
Sedunary, Mr Sidney Francis	Second 3rd Class Steward
Müller, Mr L.	Interpreter
Dunford, Mr William	Hospital Steward
Wallis, Mrs Catherine Jane	Matron
Akerman, Mr Albert Edward	Steward
Barton, Mr Sidney John	Steward
Baxter, Mr Harry Ross	Steward
Bristow, Mr Robert Charles	Steward
Brookman, Mr John	Steward
Cecil, Mr Charles	Steward
Chitty, Mr Archibald George	Steward
Cox, Mr William Denton	Steward
Daniels, Mr Sidney Edward	Steward

Edbroke, Mr Francis	Steward
Ede, Mr George B.	Steward
Egg, Mr William H.	Steward
Finch, Mr Harry	Steward
Foley, Mr William C.	Steward
Ford, Mr Ernest A.	Steward
Fox, Mr William Thomas	Steward
Halford, Mr Richard	Steward
Hart, Mr John Edward P.	Steward
Hill, Mr Henry Phillip	Steward
Hyland, Mr Leo James	Steward
Ingrouille, Mr Henry Peter	Steward
Knight, Mr Leonard George	Steward
Leonard, Mr Matthew	Steward
Lewis, Mr Arthur Ernest Read	Steward
Mabey, Mr J.	Steward
Mantle, Mr Roland Frederick	Steward
Mullin, Mr Thomas A.	Steward
Nichols, Mr A.D.	Steward
Pearce, Mr Alfred Emest	Steward
Port, Mr Frank	Steward
Prideaux, Mr John Arthur	Steward
Prior, Mr Harold John	Steward
Pugh, Mr Alfred	Steward
Rice, Mr Percy	Steward
Ryan, Mr Thomas	Steward
Savage, Mr Charles James	Steward
Sivier, Mr William	Steward
Slight, Mr Harry John	Steward
Talbot, Mr George Frederick Charles	Steward
Taylor, Mr Bernard Cuthbert	Steward
Thaler, Mr Montague Donald	Steward
Willis, Mr William	Steward
Winser, Mr Rowland [signed on as G. Evans]	Steward
Pearcey, Mr Albert Victor	Pantry Steward
CAPTAIN'S & GLORY HOLE STEWARDS	
Paintin, Mr James Arthur	Captain's Steward
Ashe, Mr Henry Wellesley	Glory Hole Steward
Crispin, Mr William	Glory Hole Steward

White, Mr J.W.	Glory Hole Steward
Wright, Mr William George	Glory Hole Steward

CHEFS, COOKS, BAKERS & BUTCHERS

Proctor, Mr Charles	Chef
Bochatay, Mr Alexis Joseph	Assistant Chef
Stubbings, Mr Harold Robert	2nd Class Cook
Simmonds, Mr William P.	Passenger Cook
Gollop, Mr Percival	Assistant Passenger Cook
Gill, Mr Patrick	Ship's Cook
Thorn, Mr Harry [signed on as H. Johnson]	Assistant Ship's Cook
Maynard, Mr Isaac Hiram	Entreé Cook
Caunt, Mr William Ewart	Grill Cook
Lovell, Mr John	Grill Cook
Kennell, Mr Charles	Hebrew Cook
Slight, Mr William Henry T.	Larder Cook
Jones, Mr H.	Roast Cook
Bedford, Mr William Barnet	Assistant Roast Cook
Windebank, Mr Alfred Edgar	Sauce Cook [substitute – signed on as an Assistant Cook]
Coombs, Mr Augustus Charles	Assistant Cook
Thorley, Mr William	Assistant Cook
Welch, Mr W.H.	Assistant Cook
Hutchinson, Mr James	Vegetable Cook
Ayling, Mr George Edwin	Assistant Vegetable Cook
Buckley, Mr Henry E.	Assistant Vegetable Cook
Ellis, Mr John Bertram	Assistant Vegetable Cook
Orr, Mr James	Assistant Vegetable Cook
Joughin, Mr Charles John	Chief Baker
Giles, Mr John Robert	2nd Baker
Davies, Mr John James	Extra 2nd Baker
Hine, Mr William Edward	3rd Baker
Burgess, Mr Charles	Extra 3rd Baker
Barker, Mr Albert Vale	Assistant Baker
Barnes, Mr Frederick	Assistant Baker
Chitty, Mr George Henry	Assistant Baker
Neal, Mr Henry	Assistant Baker
Smith, Mr James William	Assistant Baker
Wake, Mr Percy	Assistant Baker
Farrenden, Mr Ernest John	Confectioner

Leader, Mr Archie	Assistant Confectioner
Feltham, Mr G.	Vienna Baker
Maytum, Mr Alfred	Chief Butcher
Topp, Mr Thomas Frederick	2nd Butcher
Roberts, Mr Frank John	3rd Butcher
Barrow, Mr Charles Harry	Assistant Butcher
Hensford, Mr Herbert Ernest George	Assistant Butcher
Mills, Mr Christopher	Assistant Butcher
Porteus, Mr Thomas [signed on as T. Parker]	Assistant Butcher
Willsher, Mr William Audrey	Assistant Butcher
PORTERS & SCULLIONS	
Beere, Mr William	Kitchen Porter
Hardwick, Mr Reginald	Kitchen Porter
Shaw, Mr Henry	Kitchen Porter
Smith, Mr Charles	Kitchen Porter
Allen, Mr George	Scullion
Bull, Mr Walter	Scullion
Colgan, Mr E. Joseph	Scullion
Collins, Mr John	Scullion
Hall, Mr Frederick A. Jillard	Scullion
Hatch, Mr Hugh Vivian	Scullion
Ings, Mr William Ernest	Scullion
King, Mr G.	Scullion
Locke, Mr A.	Scullion [substitute]
Martin, Mr Frank	Scullion
Platt, Mr W.	Scullion
Ross, Mr Horace Leopold	Scullion
Simmons, Mr Alfred	Scullion
À LA CARTE **RESTAURANT STAFF**	
Gatti, Sig. Gaspare Antonio Pietro	Manager
Jeffery, Mr William Alfred	Controller
Vine, Mr H.	Assistant Controller
Phillips, Mr Walter John	Storekeeper
Nannini, Sig. Francesco Luigi Arcangelo	Head Waiter
Bochet, Sig. Pietro Giuseppe	2nd Head Waiter
Banfi, Sig. Ugo	Waiter
Basilico, Sig. Giovanni	Waiter
Bazzi, Sig. Narciso	Waiter
Casali, Sig. Guilio	Waiter

Gilardino, Sig. Vincenzo Pio	Waiter
Piazza, Sig. Pompeo	Waiter
Poggi, Sig. Emilio	Waiter
Ratti, Sig. Enrico Rinaldo	Waiter
Rotta, Sig. Angelo Mario	Waiter
Sesia, Sig. Giacomo	Waiter
Urbini, Sig. Roberto	Waiter
Valvassori, Sig. Ettore Luigi	Waiter
Vioni, Sig. Roberto	Waiter
Allaria, Sig. Battista Antonio	Assistant Waiter
Bernardi, Sig. Battista J.	Assistant Waiter
Beux, Mr David	Assistant Waiter
Crovella, Sig. Louis	Assistant Waiter
De Marsico, Sig. Giovanni	Assistant Waiter
Debreuq, Mr Maurice Emile Victor	Assistant Waiter
Donati, Sig. Italo Francesco	Assistant Waiter
Monoros, Sig. Javier [signed on as Jean Mouros]	Assistant Waiter
Pedrini, Sig. Alessandro	Assistant Waiter
Peracchio, Sig. Alberto	Assistant Waiter
Peracchio, Sig. Sebastiano	Assistant Waiter
Perotti, Sig. Alfonso	Assistant Waiter
Piatti, Sig. Louis	Assistant Waiter
Ricaldone, Sig. Rinaldo Renato	Assistant Waiter
Rigozzi, Sig. Abele	Assistant Waiter
Saccaggi, Sig. Giovanni Giuseppe Emilio	Assistant Waiter
Zanetti, Sig. Mario	Assistant Waiter
Zarracchi, Sig. L.	Wine Butler
Price, Mr Ernest	Barman
Scavino, Sig. Candido	Carver
Vögelin–Dubach, Mr Johannes Haus	Coffee Man
Grosclaude, Mr Gérald	Assistant Coffee Man
Turvey, Mr Charles	Page Boy
Bowker, Miss Ruth	1st Cashier
Martin, Miss Mabel Elvina	2nd Cashier
Rousseau, Mr Pierre	Chef
Coutin, Mr Auguste Louis	Entreé Cook
Monteverdi, Sig. Giovanni	Assistant Entreé Cook
Vicat, Sig. Alphonse Jean Eugene	Fish Cook
Dornier, Mr Louis Auguste	Assistant Fish Cook

Bolhuis, Mr Hendrik	Larder Cook
Pachera, Sig. Jean Baptiste Stanislas	Assistant Larder Cook
Jaillet, Mr Henri Marie	Pastry Cook
Desvernine, Mr Louis Gabriel	Assistant Pastry Cook
Chaboisson, Mr Adrien Firmin	Roast Cook
Cornaire, Mr Marcel Raymond André	Assistant Roast Cook
Bietrix, Mr George Baptiste	Sauce cook
Jouannault, Mr Georges Jules	Assistant Sauce Cook
Janin, Mr Claude Marie	Soup Cook
Villvarlange, Mr Pierre Léon Gabriel	Assistant Soup Cook
Salussolia, Sig. Govanni	Glass Man
Sartori, Sig. Lazar	Assistant Glass Man
Testoni, Sig. Ercole	Assistant Glass Man
Mattman, Mr Adolf	Ice Man
Blumet, Mr Jean Baptiste	Plateman
Aspeslagh, Mr Georges	Assistant Plateman
Mauge, Mr Paul Achille Maurice Germain	Kitchen Clerk
Tietz, Sig. Carlo	Kitchen Porter
Fey, Sig. Carlo	Scullion
Bertoldo, Sig. Fioravante Giuseppe	Assistant Scullion
MAIL CLERKS	
Smith, Mr John Richard Jago	British Mail Clerk
Williamson, Mr James Bertram	British Mail Clerk
Gwynn, Mr William H. Logan	U.S. Mail Clerk
March, Mr John Starr	U.S. Mail Clerk
Woody, Mr Oscar Scott	U.S. Mail Clerk

Appendix G

TIMES GONE WRONG

Samuel Halpern

There has never been agreement as to what was the true difference between time on *Titanic* and some external standard time reference such as GMT or mean time in New York. The American inquiry settled on a value of 1 hour 33 minutes between *Titanic* ATS and New York Time (NYT). The British inquiry settled on a difference of 1 hour 50 minutes. At the Limitation of Liability Hearings that were held in New York in 1915, a value of 1 hour and 39 minutes was given by the White Star Line. So let us take a look at how these three different, and incorrect, time differences came about.

Origin of the 1-Hour-and-33-Minute Time Difference

At 4.10p.m. NYT, Monday 15 April 1912, *Carpathia*'s Captain Rostron sent a wireless message to *Olympic*'s Captain Haddock that read:[1]

> Capt. Haddock, *Olympic*: South point pack ice 41.16 north. Don't attempt to go north until 49.30 west. Many bergs. large and small, amongst pack. Also for many miles to eastward. Fear absolutely no hope searching *Titanic*'s position. Left Leyland SS *Californian* searching around. All boats accounted for. About 675 souls saved, crew and passengers; latter nearly all women and children. *Titanic* foundered about 2.20a.m., 5.47 GMT, in 41.46 north 50.14 west; not certain of having got through. Please forward to White Star, also to Cunard, Liverpool and New York, that I am returning to New York. Consider this most advisable for many considerations. – Rostron.

The reported foundering time, 'about 2.20a.m., 5.47 GMT' implied that time carried on *Titanic* was 3 hours 27 minutes behind Greenwich Mean Time (GMT), or 1 hour 33 minutes ahead of mean time in New York, which was exactly 5 hours behind GMT.[2] In the official Senate report that came out of the American investigation into the loss of the SS *Titanic*, they wrote that *Titanic* struck an iceberg 'at 11.46p.m. ship's time, or 10.13p.m. New York time.' They listed the foundering time at '12.47a.m.' NY time. Their conclusion was based on the 1–hour–33–minute time difference that was implied in the content of that wireless message sent by Captain Rostron to Captain Haddock, and in the testimony given by *Titanic*'s surviving officers:

> Senator SMITH: Mr Boxhall, you seem to be the one upon whom we must rely to give the difference between ship's time and New York time; or, rather, to give ship's time and give the New York time when this accident occurred.
> Mr BOXHALL: At 11.46p.m., ship's time, it was 10.13 Washington time, or New York time.

So where did this 1–hour–33–minute time difference between *Titanic* time and New York Time (NYT) really come from? How did Captain Rostron get this information that was put in his message to Haddock?

Some people have suggested that the 1–hour–33–minute difference corresponded to the longitude where the collision took place. *Titanic's* Fourth Officer Joseph Boxhall's distress position longitude was 50° 14'W. That position works out to a time difference from GMT of 3 hours 21 minutes, or 1 hour 39 minutes ahead of NYT, not 1 hour 33 minutes ahead.[3] So how did this 1–hour–33–minute difference actually come about?

At 3.10p.m. NYT, Monday 15 April 1912, Captain Rostron sent a wireless message to Haddock that read:[4]

> Capt. Haddock, Olympic: 7.30 GMT Lat. 41.15 north, long. 51.45 west. Am steering south 87 west, true. Returning to New York with Titanic's passengers. – Rostron.

What is interesting about this particular message is that it was sent to *Olympic* just 1 hour before the one containing *Titanic's* foundering time, and it gave *Carpathia's* coordinates for 2.30p.m. NYT [7.30p.m. GMT]. In those coordinates we see a longitude of 51° 45'W, a longitude that has a Local Mean Time of precisely 3 hours 27 minutes 0 seconds behind GMT, or 1 hour 33 minutes 0 seconds ahead of mean time in New York.

Was this some sort of coincidence? Not likely. It seems that it was this time difference that was used in deriving the erroneous 5.47a.m. GMT foundering time for *Titanic* that was put in the message sent out at 4.10p.m. NYT by Captain Rostron. It was a direct response to a request from Captain Haddock that was received 35 minutes earlier, at 3.35p.m. NYT, asking for 'particulars' about *Titanic* so that *Olympic* could then send a report to Cape Race for forwarding to the Cunard offices in New York and Liverpool. Just like the erroneous distress coordinates contained in the 4.10p.m. NYT message, the 5.47a.m. GMT foundering time that was included in that message was an error that escaped recognition.

Origin of the 1-Hour-and-50-Minute Time Difference

The British Wreck Commission settled on a time difference of 1 hour and 50 minutes from NYT which appears to have come about by equating *Titanic* time to time on the SS *Californian*.

At the British inquiry, *Californian's* third officer, Charles Victor Groves, testified that he saw the deck lights of an approaching steamer shut out at exactly 11.40p.m. *Californian* time.[5] *Californian's* second officer, Herbert Stone, also testified that Groves told him that the stopped steamer seen on their starboard beam had been stopped since 11.40p.m.[6] Stone also told them that steamer's stern light disappeared at 2.20a.m.[7] The Commission also heard evidence from *Titanic* survivors that *Titanic* collided with an iceberg at 11.40p.m., and that she foundered at 2.20a.m. In addition, they heard that eight white rockets were seen to come from that steamer seen by *Californian* during the same period of time that *Titanic* was sending up distress rockets.[8] As a result, they seemed to conclude that time on *Titanic* must have been the same time as on *Californian*.

Time on *Californian* was set to 12.00 at noon that Sunday 14 April 1912. Time on *Californian* for her noontime longitude was 1 hour 50 minutes ahead of NYT. There is no reason whatsoever for *Titanic* to have carried the same time as *Californian*. The noontime positions of the two ships were far different. But it seems that the British Wreck Commission was not interested in such details. It was more convenient to equate the times that both ships carried to make a stronger case against *Californian*. The end result was that the British Commission decided on a time difference of 1 hour 50 minutes between *Titanic* ATS and NYT, the same as *Californian*.

Origin of the 1-Hour-and-39-Minute Time Difference

During the Limitation of Liability Hearings in New York in 1915 questions were raised as to the time of the collision and the time of the foundering. In the amended answers of the petitioner, the Oceanic Steam Navigation Company (also known as the White Star Line), the time of collision was given as 10.06p.m. NYT on 14 April 1912, and the time of foundering was given as 12.41a.m. NYT on 15 April 1912. The difference between these two events comes out to be exactly 2 hours 35 minutes.

On day ten of the American inquiry, *Titanic*'s Fourth Officer Joseph Boxhall told Senator Smith that he thought the ship collided with the iceberg about 11.45p.m. *Titanic* time:[9]

> There is a question about that. Some say 11.45, some say 11.43. I myself did not note it exactly, but that is as near as I can tell I reckoned it was about 11.45.

It appears that lawyers for the White Star Line had settled on Boxhall's 11.45p.m. for the collision time. The foundering time was accepted at 2.20a.m. This gave them the 2-hour-and-35-minute difference between collision and foundering times. Now equating their 11.45p.m. *Titanic* time to their 10.06p.m. NYT, and their 2.20a.m. *Titanic* time to their 12.41a.m. NYT, gives a difference between *Titanic* time and NYT of 1 hour and 39 minutes. This is the same as 3 hours 21 minutes behind GMT, and precisely corresponds to the famous Boxhall CQD longitude of 50° 14'W, the longitude of *Titanic*'s foundering that had been accepted up until the wreck was discovered in 1985.

So we see that there is very little mystery as to how the answers to those two questions asked of the petitioner were derived. The lawyers for the White Star Line simply took 11.45p.m. for the collision time, and 2.20a.m. for the foundering time, and were told to subtract 1 hour and 39 minutes from each, the time difference that corresponded to the longitude where everyone believed *Titanic* foundered. It was a simple thing for the White Star Line to do, and the interrogating lawyers did not bother to question how those times were derived.

Notes

[1] From copy of detailed wireless log made by *Olympic*'s operator E.J. Moore furnished to Senator William Alden Smith, 25 May 1912, AI p.1138.

[2] New York, and many other eastern cities in the United States, went onto Eastern Standard Time on 18 November 1883.

[3] The Boxhall CQD longitude was 50° 14'W. Expressing this in degrees, we get 50.23° west of Greenwich. If we divide this number by 15° per hour we get 3.35 hours, or 3:20:56. Rounding this to the nearest minute, we get a time that is 3 hours 21 minutes behind GMT, or 1 hour 39 minutes ahead of NYT.

[4] E.J. Moore, AI p.1138.

[5] Groves, BI 8217.

[6] Stone, BI 7823.

[7] Stone, BI 7971–4. Stone did not tell them that in his report to Capt. Lord, written on 18 April, he wrote that he told Gibson to report to Capt. Lord at 2a.m. that the 'steamer had gone out of sight.' In Gibson's report to Capt. Lord, he wrote: 'Just after two o'clock . . . she disappeared from sight and nothing was seen of her again.'

[8] The Commission also heard from Second Officer Lightoller who told them that he estimated that *Titanic* had sent up 'somewhere about eight' rockets at intervals of 5 or 6 minutes (BI 14160). Boxhall thought he sent up between half a dozen and a dozen (BI 15395), and Pitman told the American inquiry that it was about a dozen or more (AI p.293). The truth is that nobody counted how many were sent up, but they were sent up over a period of about an hour.

[9] Boxhall, AI p.918. He also told Senator Burton that he thought the collision was at 11.43 (AI p.932). He also told the British inquiry he used 11.46 in his calculation of the SOS position (BI 15639–40).

Appendix H

A FEW EYEWITNESS REPORTS

Captain Charles Weeks and Samuel Halpern

The following table provides a list of key eyewitness observations regarding the flooding or condition of the ship following the collision. The following abbreviations are used: AI=American Inquiry, ATS=Apparent Time Ship, BI=British Inquiry, BR=Boiler Room, NYT=New York Time, WTD=Watertight Door, WTB=Watertight Bulkhead. For lifeboat launch times, see table in Chapter 7.

Time Interval	*Titanic* ATS	Witness	Reference	Observation
0.00	11.40p.m.	multiple	AI p.450.	Collision with iceberg.
		Barrett	BI 1868, 1917.	Water pouring in 2ft above the stokehold plates in BR 6 at No.10 stokehold and in forward bunker in BR 5 starboard side.
0.05	11.45p.m.	Hemming	BI 17716, 17724.	Peak tank flooding fast but forepeak above tank was dry.
		Shiers	BI 4532–4.	Chunks of ice seen on well deck and iceberg disappearing off starboard quarter astern.
		Hendrickson	BI 4847–51.	
0.10	11.50p.m.	Buley	AI p.607.	Water heard entering hold 1 and tarp ballooning over hatch. Time is estimated.
		Hendrickson	BI 4847–54.	Water seen at bottom of firemen's tunnel coming from starboard side. Time is supported by Shier's observations on well deck.
		Poingdestre	BI 2821–25.	Told of 7ft of water in hold 1 by ship's carpenter.
		Hichens	AI p.451	A 5° list to starboard noted on inclinometer in the wheelhouse.
		Barrett	BI 1935–7.	Water seen 8ft over stokehold plates in BR 6.
0.12	11.52	Boxhall	BI 15374, 15379.	Water seen within 2ft of G deck in hold 3 on his second inspection forward. Time estimated between 11.50 and 11.55.
0.15	11.55p.m.	Johnstone	BI 3395–7.	Flooding in baggage room on G deck seen from F deck in hold 3.
		Wheat	BI 10901–18.	Water coming onto G deck in hold 3 just moments after meeting up with James Johnstone. Wheat estimated the time at 10–15 minutes after collision.
		Threlfall	*Bridgewater Mercury*, May 1912.	Water seen flowing down spiral staircase from leading firemen's quarters on G deck.
		Symons	BI 11356, 11402–13.	Water on G deck around coamings of hold 1 hatch; 'All hands stand-by' called by boatswain; Symons estimated this was '5 min to 12'.

0.22	12.02a.m.	Chambers	AI p.1042.	Saw three unidentified officers (engineers?) inspect flooding in post office/first class baggage rooms. Water was within 2ft of F deck in hold 3 at this time and appeared not to be rising very fast according to an overheard remark coming from one of the officers. Time 12.00–12.05 is estimate based on his actions and the rise of water seen in hold 3.
0.28	12.08a.m.	Pitman	BI 14958–66.	Water seen coming onto G deck from starboard side by hold 1 hatch.
0.30	12.10a.m.	Robinson	BI 13277–83.	Water seen within six steps of coming onto E deck (4ft below) in hold 3. She went to look just after seeing Capt. Smith and Thomas Andrews returning from the mail room about ½ hour after collision.
0.45	12.25a.m.	Poingdestre	BI 2842–58.	Water 3ft on E deck in crew's quarters. He estimated the time at 45 minutes after the collision.
1.05	12.45a.m.	Wheat	BI 10956–72.	Water seen flowing down first class stairs from E deck down to F deck just aft of WTB-F. Estimated time at 12.45–12.50.
1.10	12.50a.m.	Ray	AI pp.803–4.	Water on E deck up to second funnel casing seen on port and starboard sides of first class stairway.
1.30	1.10a.m.	Barrett	BI 2348–9.	Rush of water seen in BR 5 in pass between boilers. Water on E deck seen coming from forward at location of escape from BR 5. Depth not quantified. Time was Barrett's best guess.
1.37	1.17a.m.	Symons	BI 11490.	Water up to second row of ports under ship's name at bow. [Time based on lifeboat launch time of 1.05a.m. plus 10–15 minutes to reach water and pull away due to being caught up on guy wire at B deck while lowering.]
		Cavell	BI 4248–65.	Trimmer Cavell comes up the escape from BR 4 after seeing water coming over the stokehold plates there.
1.40	1.20a.m.	Dillon	BI 3811, 3913.	Water coming up over stokehold plates forward in BR 4. He estimated it was 1 hour 40 minutes after collision when ordered up from engine room.
		Scott	BI 5839.	All personnel ordered up from engine rooms. Said it was 20 minutes past 1.
		Threlfall	*Bridgewater Mercury*, May 1912.	Said that all personnel ordered up from stokeholds at 1.20a.m.
1.45	1.25a.m.	Cavell	BI 4282–94.	Went back down into BR 4 but came up again after seeing nobody there.
2.00	1.40a.m.	Evans	AI p.677.	List to port about 10° based on 2.5ft gap between lifeboat 10 and side of rail on boat deck.
2.05	1.45a.m.	Barrett	BI 2140–2.	Notices forecastle head was not under yet from boat No.13.
		Nichols	private letter.	Notices *Titanic*'s propellers were half out of the water from boat No.15.
2.12	1.52a.m.	Bride	AI p.1063; BI 16543–53.	*Baltic* responds to Bride's message at 11.50 NYT. Philips returns and Bride informs him of communications with *Baltic*. Philips reported seeing well deck awash, and a list to port was very noticeable.
2.25	2.05a.m.	Bright	AI p.837.	Forecastle head seen going under as boat D is lowered.
		Rowe	AI p.524.	Boat C reaches water and well deck was seen completely submerged.
2.35	2.15a.m.	Lightoller	AI p.90.	Water up to crow's nest and coming over the forebridge before he jumped in. Time is best estimated based on breakup events described below.
2.37	2.17a.m.	Gibson	BI 7565.	Lights of steamer that fired rockets disappeared at 2.05a.m. *Californian* ATS, 2.17a.m. *Titanic* ATS.
		Symons	BI 11510–11525.	*Titanic*'s stern came 'well out' as bow pitches down suddenly as all the lights go out. Ship appeared to split in two 'abaft the after expansion plate' with the stern righting itself without the bow. Time based on seeing remaining stern section go under 'two or three minutes' afterward.
2.40	2.20a.m.	multiple	AI p.294.	Remaining stern section disappears beneath the surface.

LIFEBOAT RECOVERY TIMES

George Behe

The assignment of specific times for the rescue of each of *Titanic*'s lifeboats would seem to be an uncomplicated task, since researchers might expect to make a list of the recovery times mentioned by survivors and then simply arrange those times in chronological order. Nothing could be further from the truth, since even the most cursory examination of the lifeboat recovery documentation reveals so many unexpected contradictions that any attempt to assign a specific recovery time to a specific lifeboat must necessarily be done tentatively as well as subjectively. Researchers can only assess the contradictory accounts to the best of their ability and then use their best judgement to create a chronological list of lifeboat recovery times – which is what the present author has done here.

Except for the recovery times of the first and last lifeboats (which were vouched for by *Carpathia*'s Captain Rostron), all of the recovery times offered here have been rounded off into 15-minute increments. One reason this was necessary is that, whereas some survivors might have been quoting the time they thought a particular lifeboat rowed up to *Carpathia*'s side, other survivors were apparently quoting the time they thought they actually set foot on *Carpathia*'s deck. We must also wonder how many survivors might have set their watches back the prescribed 47 minutes on the evening of 14 April, since the answer to that question would of course affect the perceived times that those survivors thought they reached *Carpathia*. No individual survivor account has been regarded as being completely authoritative, and the present author has been forced to use the existing accounts as a general guide in assigning approximate recovery times to specific lifeboats. I do not claim to have solved all of the timing problems connected with the lifeboat recovery chronology, but – even though my conclusions undoubtedly contain a number of errors – they are presented here as an attempt to make sense of a very complicated and confusing subject.

The often-muddled documentation that was used to compile the list of lifeboat recovery times is offered in this appendix as a jumping-off place for future researchers who are tempted to investigate the subject for themselves. The documentation has been subdivided into two separate categories of primary and secondary historical sources, and the accounts that were assigned extra 'weight' in compiling the present chronology are printed in **bold** type. A number of private passenger and crew letters appear in the list of sources as well, and the complete texts of these documents can be found in the author's two works, *On Board RMS Titanic: Memories of the Maiden Voyage* and *The Carpathia and the Titanic: Rescue at Sea*, both of which were published by Lulu Press in 2011.

The author has done his best to make sense of many contradictory passenger and crew accounts in compiling this lifeboat recovery chronology, and he hopes the reader will regard his efforts as being a reasonably successful attempt to separate the wheat from the chaff.

Boat No.2 – Approximate arrival time 4.10a.m.

Primary Sources

1. **Joseph Boxhall, AI p.911: 'A little after 4 o'clock.' Gracie p.174: 4.10a.m.**
2. **Mahala Douglas, AI p.1102: '4.10a.m.' First boat alongside.**
3. **Arthur Rostron (business letter that Captain Rostron wrote to Cunard's general manager in Liverpool), William Howard Taft papers, reel 440: First boat was recovered at 4.10a.m.**
4. **Elisabeth Allen letter to Archibald Gracie: First boat to be picked up.**
5. **Minnie Coutts letter to a friend: First boat picked up.**
6. **James Johnstone, BI 3541: First boat to board *Carpathia*. BI 3545: Picked up at dawn.**

Secondary Sources

1. Elizabeth Robert account, *St. Louis Times*, 19 April 1912: 'I was told that it was after 8 o'clock in the morning when we boarded the ship.'
2. Anton Kink, *Milwaukee Journal*, 24 April 1912: Was in the lifeboat by 1.30a.m. and reached *Carpathia* at 5a.m.

Boat No.1 – Approximate arrival time 4.45a.m.

Primary Sources

1. **Charles Stengel, AI p.973: It was the second boat alongside *Carpathia*.**
2. **Joseph Boxhall, AI pp.247–8: The second boat reached *Carpathia* half an hour after his own boat (boat No.2).**
3. **Frank Osman, AI p.538: The second boat was picked up 30 minutes after boat No.2.**
4. James Taylor BI 12264: Picked up at about 5.45a.m.
5. George Symons, BI 11695 & 11717: Picked up at least 5 hours after launch, 'a good time after daybreak.'
6. Laura Francatelli, letter, 28 April 1912: Picked up about 6.30a.m. Affidavit: Boat No.1 was of so little use that *Carpathia* didn't bother to haul it on board [an error].
7. Charles Hendrickson, BI 5090: Was picked up in broad daylight.

Collapsible C – Approximate arrival time 5.45a.m.

Note: Collapsible C was set adrift afterwards.

Primary Sources

1. **Bruce Ismay, AI p.951: 5.45 or 6.15a.m. ('I happened to see a clock somewhere on the ship when I got on her.')** 1914 Limitation of Liability testimony: Was picked up around daybreak.
2. George Rowe, AI p.520: '. . . daylight broke and the *Carpathia* was in sight . . . the ninth boat to be unloaded upon the *Carpathia*.'
3. Joseph Boxhall, AI p.248: '. . . and then [after boat No.1 arrived] I had passed up crews from either two or three boats from the same gangway before Mr Ismay came . . . it was quite daylight . . . it was daylight before I got my passengers on board the ship.' AI p.1247: 'It was one of the last boats that came.'

Secondary Sources

1. **William Carter**, *Philadelphia Inquirer*, 4 December 1921: 'We reached the side of the *Carpathia* before dawn.'
2. Emily Goldsmith, *Detroit News*, 24 April 1912: 'We rowed around for 6 hours until we were picked up by the *Carpathia*.'
3. Frank Goldsmith, *National Inquirer*, 23 September ? (modern–day interview): 'At 7.30, five hours after the *Titanic* sank, a ship called the *Carpathia* reached us.'

Boat No.5 – Approximate arrival time 6.00a.m.

Note: Boat nos 5 and 7 were tied together for most of the night and probably reached *Carpathia* within a short time of each other.

Primary Sources

1. **Karl Behr, unpublished memoir, 1944: 'Shortly after daybreak when we saw the *Carpathia* . . . [We] were alongside within perhaps half an hour. All around us other lifeboats were converging.'**
2. **Hedwig Frolicher, letter to brother, 18 April 1912: 'Ours was number two or three to arrive.'**
3. **Henry Frauenthal, 'My Experience in the Wreck of the *Titanic*': 'The Carpathia was in sight at about 4.30a.m., when all the small boats rowed toward her. We were taken on board at about six o'clock.'**
4. **Norman Chambers, *Lawrenceville Alumni Bulletin*, October 1912: Rowed for one hour to reach *Carpathia*. Several boats were already alongside, and one boat had been cast adrift [presumably collapsible C].**
5. **Washington Dodge, *The Loss of the Titanic*: Boat No.5 reached *Carpathia* before boat No.13.**
6. **Alfred Shiers, 1915 Limitation of Liability testimony: Rowed half a mile to *Carpathia* after daybreak.**
7. **Henry Etches, AI p.820: While boat No.5 was at *Carpathia*'s side, a baby was handed from boat No.7 to boat No.5.**
8. **Alfred Olliver, AI p.529: Boat No.5 was the fourth or fifth boat recovered.**

Secondary Sources

1. **Dorothy Gibson, unknown 1912 newspaper: 'It was shortly after 6 o'clock when we found ourselves alongside the *Carpathia*.'**
2. **Henry Stengel, *Newark Evening News*, 19 April 1912: 'After we [boat No.1] had been taken on board the *Carpathia*, we sailed about looking for other boats, and my wife [in No.5] was in the second one boat picked up after my own.'**
3. Richard Beckwith, *Waterbury American* 23 April 1912: '. . . picked up after daylight.'
4. Article about Bertha Chambers, *The New York Herald* 20 April 1912: 'Six hours elapsed before they were picked up by the *Carpathia*.'
5. Anna Warren, *Portland Oregonian* 27 April 1912: 'Our boat was picked up about 4.10 a.m . . . . I was in the second boat picked up.'
6. Helen Ostby, *Providence Journal* 21 April 1912. 'About daybreak the *Carpathia* came . . . We had to row a mile to the *Carpathia*.'
7. Spencer Silverthorne, *St. Louis Post-Dispatch*, 20 April 1912: Picked up around 6a.m. *St. Louis Republic* 21 April 1912: 'Myself and three or four other men were transferred into another boat, and we began to row towards the oncoming steamer. We reached it . . . about

6a.m.' [Note: Silverthorne said he was in Mrs Washington Dodge's boat, which Gracie says was No.5 while Mr Dodge believed it was No.3. (In Gracie's book, Mrs Spedden says that boat No.3 had the numeral 5 attached to one end, which might account for the confusion.) The single boat that Dodge saw launched before his wife's boat left the ship had to be No.7, and boat No.5 was launched shortly after boat No.7. Having said all of this, since Spencer Silverthorne claimed to have boarded the 'third boat' (No.5 was the third boat in line) but later transferred out of that boat (to No.7?), his estimated arrival time probably applies to boat No.7 instead of boat No.5.]

Boat No.7 – Approximate arrival time 6.15a.m.

Note: Boat nos 7 and 5 were tied together for most of the night and probably reached *Carpathia* within a short time of each other.

Primary Sources

1. **Herbert Pitman, AI p.299: 'It may have been 20 minutes' between the time boat No.5 arrived and boat No.7 arrived.**
2. **John Snyder letter to his father: Was picked up at about 5.30a.m.**
3. **William Sloper account of 18 April, *Hartford Times*, 19 April 1912: '. . . after waiting half an hour for our turn we were at last safely on board.'** [This was after dawn, and several other lifeboats were being unloaded ahead of boat No.7.]
4. **Archie Jewell, BI 197: '. . . there was nobody had any time [i.e. a watch].** BI 193–4: 7.00 or 8.00.
5. **Henry Etches, AI p.820: While boat No.5 was at *Carpathia*'s side, a baby was handed from boat No.7 to boat No.5.**
6. Helen Bishop AI p.1000: 5.05 or 5.10a.m.

Secondary Sources

1. **John Snyder, *Minneapolis Journal*, 19 April 1912: '*Carpathia* reached six of the lifeboats before we were reached.' *Minneapolis Tribune*, 19 April 1912: '. . . were picked up about 5.30. Our boat was the sixth to be picked up.'**
2. Helen Bishop, *Dowagiac Daily News*, 20 April 1912: 'We were afloat in the lifeboat from about 12.30 Sunday night until 5 o'clock Monday morning . . . We were about the fourth picked up by the *Carpathia*.'
3. James McGough, *Philadelphia Evening Bulletin*, 19 April 1912: 'It was after 8 o'clock in the morning when we saw the masts of a steamer coming over the horizon.'
4. Article about Alfred Omont, *Savannah Morning News*, 23 April 1912: 'It was 5 hours before they were picked up by the *Carpathia*.'
5. Article about Lily Potter, *Philadelphia Inquirer*, 20 April 1912: '. . . floated about for 8 hours before they were rescued by the Cunarder.'

Boat No.9 – Approximate arrival time 6.15a.m.

Primary Sources

1. **Robertha Watt, *The Spectrum*, April 1914: Picked up after sunrise.**
2. **William Ward, AI p.600: Boat No.9 was the fourth or fifth boat picked up.**
3. Kate Buss, 1932 memoir: They sighted *Carpathia* after dawn, 5 miles away.

Secondary Sources

1. **Sidney Collett, *Syracuse Post Standard*, 24 April 1912:'Our boat was the first taken up on our side of the ship.'**
2. **Marion Wright, *Cottage Grove Sentinel*, 9 May 1912:'We were in the water from 12.30 to 6.30 . . . 3. At 3.30 we saw the *Carpathia* approaching . . . Three hours later we were taken up her side.'**
3. Elisabeth Lines, *The New York Times*, 26 November 1975:'At about 5.30a.m. the *Carpathia* came into view.'

Boat No.13 – Approximate arrival time 6.30a.m.

Primary Sources

1. **Albert Caldwell, 17 April letter to Dr Walker: Picked up at daylight.**
2. Ruth Becker, *St. Nicholas magazine*, 1913: One of the first boats to reach *Carpathia*.
3. **Washington Dodge, 16 April account narrated to Dr Frank Blackmarr: Saw *Carpathia* at about daylight, reached her forty-five minutes later and saw three other boats unloading there. His wife and daughter (in No.5) were in the second of those three boats. *The Loss of the Titanic*: '. . . day began to dawn, and we could see this steamer come to rest, where we knew this lifeboat to be located [i.e. the first boat to be picked up] . . . We now began to pull towards the vessel, but although it was not more than two miles distant, we did not reach her until long after sunrise . . . We could now see numerous other lifeboats coming from all points and rowing towards the *Carpathia* . . . When our boat reached the ship's side we passed in front of her bow to reach the port side . . . An officer of the *Carpathia* called to us to come up on the starboard side. The vessel was then unloading lifeboats on each side . . . we were unable against the wind to make any progress. We finally had to disembark on the port side. As the *Carpathia* had taken aboard the occupants of four or five lifeboats before ours arrived, I was naturally consumed with anxiety to ascertain whether my wife and child were aboard. After a short search I found them.'** [Although Dodge says his wife was in No.3, it is apparent by his description of the launchings that she was actually in No.5. (Gracie concurs with this assessment, and in his book, Mrs Spedden said that boat No.3 had the numeral 5 at one end, which accounts for Mr Dodge's mistaken belief that his wife was in boat No.3.) This means that No.5 beat No.13 to *Carpathia*.]
4. Lawrence Beesley, 18 April account written on board *Carpathia*: Picked up about 4.30a.m. *The Loss of the SS* Titanic, p.142: About 4.30a.m.
5. Joseph Scarrott, BI 460: Picked up at 8a.m. Also, between 7.00 and 8.00.
6. George Beauchamp, BI 720:'It was 10 minutes past 10 when I was picked up by the *Carpathia*.'

Secondary Sources

1. Albert Caldwell, *Richmond Times-Dispatch*, 15 April 1962:'Our boat was one of the first to reach the *Carpathia*.'
2. Adelaide Wells, *Akron Beacon-Journal*, 23 [April?] 1953:'. . . *Carpathia* picked us up just as it was turning daylight.'

Boat No.16 – Approximate arrival time 6.45a.m.
Primary Sources

1. **Karen Abelseth, April letter to her father: Saw *Carpathia* at 6a.m. and reached her at 7a.m.**

2. **Edwina Troutt, 17 April diary entry: Reached *Carpathia* at 6.30a.m.**
3. **Charles Andrews, AI pp.624, 626: 'When daylight came we saw a light, which was the *Carpathia* . . . On the way to the *Carpathia* we saw some of our boats also proceeding. When we arrived there, there were one or two boats set adrift.'**
4. Ernest Archer, BI 18124: Was picked up at daybreak.

Boat No.11 – Approximate arrival time 7.00a.m.

Primary Sources

1. **Marie Jerwan, May 1912 letter to sister: Picked up at 7.30a.m.**
2. **Amelia Brown, 17 April letter to mother: Was on the water from 12a.m. until 6a.m.**
3. **Emma Schabert, 18 April letter to sister: Picked up 2 hours after sighting *Carpathia*.**
4. Charles Mackay, BI 10858: '. . . the last but three or four in.'
5. Elizabeth Nye, 16 April letter to parents: All but two lifeboats were already recovered before she reached *Carpathia*.

Secondary Sources

1. **Marion Becker, *Dowagiac Daily News*, 21 April 1912: 'We must have left the boat around 2 o'clock and were not picked up until 7 o'clock.'**
2. **Jennie Hansen, *Racine Daily Times*, 24 April 1912: [A rower rowed] 'from 12.30 until the boat was picked up by the *Carpathia* at 7.15.'**
3. Emma Schabert, *New York Evening World*, 19 April 1912: 'By my watch it was exactly 1.50a.m. Monday morning when the lights on the *Titanic* went out . . .' [and she sank shortly thereafter]. *New York Tribune*, 19 April 1912: 'We left the ship about 25 minutes before the ship sank. She sank at about 1.50 Monday morning. At 6 o'clock the same morning the *Carpathia* put in an appearance and we were picked up.'
4. Alice Silvey, *Washington Evening Star*, 25 April 1912: '. . . about 6 o'clock we reached the ship. Several boats had been picked up before ours and several more were picked up later.' *Duluth News Tribune*, 2 May 1912: 'It was about 6 o'clock . . . when we sighted the *Carpathia*.'

Boat No.14 – Approximate arrival time 7.15a.m.

Note: Boat No.14 towed collapsible D to *Carpathia*, and both boats were afterwards set adrift.

Primary Sources

1. **Edward Buley, AI p.605: Boat No.14 was the seventh or eighth boat alongside *Carpathia*.**
2. **Daisy Minahan, AI p.1109: After boat No.14 sighted *Carpathia*, it took 3 hours to row to her.**
3. George Rheims, 19 April letter to his wife: Boat No.14 rescued collapsible A at 8a.m. Limitation of Liability testimony: Was taken off of collapsible C at 6–6.30a.m. *Carpathia* stopped 2 miles away.
4. Joseph Scarrott, *Sphere*, 25 May: Boarded *Carpathia* at about 8.30a.m.
5. Harold Lowe, BI 15860: 6a.m.

Secondary Sources

1. **Charlotte Collyer, *The Washington Post Semi-Monthly Magazine*, 26 May 1912: '*Carpathia* arrived at dawn. She stopped maybe four miles away from us.'**

2. **Lillian Minahan, *Fond du Lac Daily Commonwealth*, 22 April 1912: '. . . at 7.30 the survivors . . . were hoisted in slings to the deck.'**
3. ***Fond du Lac Reporter*, 20 April 1912: Picked up by *Carpathia* at 7.30a.m.**
4. Eva Hart, 1962 newspaper interview: 'The *Carpathia* arrived at 8 o'clock in the morning and we were taken aboard.'
5. Elizabeth Brown, *Seattle Post-Intelligencer*, 27 April 1912: 'We were 9 hours in the lifeboat before the *Carpathia* came up to us.'
6. Edith Brown, *Seattle Daily Times*, 27 April 1912: 'We were in the boat for about 7 hours [before *Carpathia* was sighted].'

Collapsible D – Approximate arrival time 7.15a.m.

Note: Collapsible D was towed to *Carpathia* by boat No.14, and both boats were afterwards set adrift.

Primary Sources

1. **Rene Harris, *Liberty*, 23 April 1932: '. . . at 6.30 we were taken aboard the *Carpathia*.'**
2. **Arthur Bright, AI p.520: About the ninth boat picked up.**
3. **Hugh Woolner account, *New York Sun*, 19 April 1912: Boat No.14 towed collapsible D.**

Secondary Sources

1. **Mauritz Björnström-Steffanson, *St. Paul Pioneer Press*, 18 April 1912: 'We were picked up about 5 hours later [after *Titanic* sank at 2.20a.m.].'**
2. **Jane Hoyt, *Amsterdam* (NY) *Evening Recorder*, 22 April 1912: *Carpathia* came in sight at 4a.m., and 'it was 8 o'clock before we were on board the *Carpathia*.'**

Boat No.3 – Approximate arrival time 7.30a.m.

Primary Sources

1. **Henry Harper, *Harper's Weekly*, 27 April: '. . . it was a little before 4 o'clock in the morning when the *Carpathia* came in sight . . . within a short time after we sighted her she came up near us and stopped . . . within a few minutes the sun began to show its edge above the horizon and soon rose clear of the sea . . . The little lifeboats began rowing toward the *Carpathia* . . . Presently our boat came up to where they had a chair rigged.'**
2. Margaretta Spedden diary, *Commutator*, Vol.16, No.3: 'We were about the fifth to reach her [*Carpathia*].'

Secondary Sources

1. **Albert Dick, *Manitoba Free Press*, 29 April 1912: '. . . at 7.30 o'clock we were taken on board [*Carpathia*].'**
2. **Clara Hays, *St. Louis Post Dispatch*, 19 April 1912: 'It was 7 or 8 o'clock in the morning before we were taken aboard the *Carpathia*.'**
3. Edith Graham, *New York Evening World*, 19 April 1912. '. . . as day began to break we sighted the *Carpathia* . . . she steamed rapidly toward us and came to a stop. Other lifeboats from the *Titanic* were near us and we all pulled hard toward the *Carpathia*.'

Boat No.8 – Approximate arrival time 7.30a.m.

Primary Sources

1. **Entry in the diary of Mary Wick's sister: 'It was half past 7 when they were hauled up in a boatswain's chair.'**
2. Gladys Cherry letter to mother, *Memorials of Henry Forbes Julian*: Picked up at 8.30.

Secondary Sources

1. **Margaret Swift, *Brooklyn Daily Eagle*, 19 April 1912: 'It was somewhere after 7 o'clock in the morning when we reached the *Carpathia* . . . I think we got to the *Carpathia* about 8, for seven boatloads had been taken on board before we were able to reach the vessel . . . Others came after us.'**
2. Caroline Bonnell, *Decatur Review*, 19 April 1912: '. . . rowed hard for an hour' after seeing *Carpathia*'s searchlight. *Youngstown Telegram*, 19 April 1912: '. . . for an hour and a half after we first caught a glimpse of her we rowed furiously.'
3. Emma Bucknell, *Philadelphia Inquirer*, 20 April 1912: 'And then the sun came up . . . and off about ten miles we could make out the *Carpathia* . . . Then began the long row to the boat.'

Boat No.15 – Approximate arrival time 7.30a.m.

Note: Boat No.15 was set adrift after recovery.

Primary Sources

1. **William Taylor, AI p.550: About 7.30.**
2. Samuel Rule, BI 9655: Picked up just after daybreak.
3. Walter Nicholls, account written for the *Brooklyn Daily Eagle*, 19 April 1912: 'Started rowing toward the *Carpathia* after dawn.'

Secondary Sources

1. **Article about Frank Dymond, *Hampshire Telegraph*, 13 May 1912: 'They were rowing amongst the icebergs for 6 hours before the *Carpathia* picked them up.'**
2. Charles Dahl, *Manitoba Free Press*, 29 April 1912: Was in the lifeboat until about 6a.m.

Boat No.4 – Approximate arrival time 8.00a.m.

Note: Boat nos 4 and 12 both picked up survivors from collapsible B, so both boats probably reached *Carpathia* within a short time of each other. Boat No.4 was set adrift after recovery.

Primary Sources

1. **Andrew Cunningham, AI p.797: About 7.30a.m.**
2. **Emily Ryerson, AI p.1108: About 8a.m.**
3. Martha Stephenson, *The Titanic – Our Story*: After 6a.m.
4. Marian Thayer, Gracie p.192: 7a.m.

Secondary Sources

1. **Virginia Clark, *Helena Independent*, 28 April 1912: 'It was not until about 8.30 that we were rescued.'**

2. Ida Hippach, *Chicago Tribune*, 22 April 1912: '[*Carpathia*] stopped to pick up lifeboats about two miles from where we were and we rowed the distance over to the ship.'
3. Article about Eleanor Widener, *The Washington Post*, 19 April 1912: 'At 7 o'clock in the morning the boat in which she had found shelter was picked up by the *Carpathia*.'
4. Lucile Carter, *Baltimore Sun*, 19 April 1912: 'It was about 8.30 o'clock when the *Carpathia* came into sight.'
5. William Carter Jr, *Philadelphia Evening Bulletin*, 20 April 1912: 'Then in the daylight we saw the *Carpathia* coming and we were picked up.'

Boat No.6 – Approximate arrival time 8.00a.m.

Primary Sources

1. **Margaret Brown, account for the *Newport Herald*, 28 May 1912: Was the last boat to approach *Carpathia*.**
2. **Arthur Peuchen, AI p.350: 'It was after 8 o'clock that I looked at my watch; it was something after 8 o'clock that we got on.'**
3. Robert Hichens, BI 1140: About 7a.m. BI 1264: His lifeboat was cut adrift by *Carpathia* [a factual mistake].

Secondary Sources

1. **Arthur Peuchen, *Toronto World*, 20 April 1912: 'I rowed from 4 o'clock until 8, when we reached that steamer. We were about the last to get alongside.'**

Boat No.10 – Approximate arrival time 8.00 a m.

Primary Sources
1. **Kornelia Andrews, 17 April letter to a friend: Saw *Carpathia* at about dawn but didn't reach her until almost 9a.m.**
2. **William Burke, AI p.823: Boat nos 10 and 12 arrived at *Carpathia* tied together.**
3. Ellen Walcroft letter to *Maidenhead Advertiser*, 29 April 1912: It took 1 hour to row to *Carpathia*. Her boat was picked up at 6.45a.m.
4. Edward Buley, AI p.605: '...the seventh or eighth boat alongside.'

Secondary Sources

1. **Kornelia Andrews, *The New York Times*, 19 April 1912: '... saw the Carpathia approaching in the gray of the early morning. It was about 8 o'clock, I think.'**
2. **Anna Hogeboom, *New York World*, 20 April 1912: 'Shortly after 8 o'clock the *Carpathia* reached near enough for us to row to it, we having rowed about 9 miles and being the last lifeboat to reach the rescue ship.' *Daily Home News*, 20 April 1912: Ship struck at 11.45p.m., boilers exploded about 2a.m., reached *Carpathia* shortly after 8a.m. Last boat to reach *Carpathia*.**

Boat No.12 – Approximate arrival time 8.15a.m.

Note: Boat nos 12 and 4 both picked up survivors from collapsible B, so both boats probably reached *Carpathia* within a short time of each other.

Primary Sources

1. **Laura Cribb account, *New York Evening Journal*, 19 April 1912: Saw *Carpathia* a long time before they reached her.**
2. **Archibald Gracie, Gracie p.113: 8.30a.m. While standing on *Carpathia* he waved to friends in No.12, the last boat to reach *Carpathia*.**
3. **Arthur Rostron, BI 25499: 'It was only when we got to the last boat that we got close up to the wreckage. It was close up to the wreckage. It would be about a quarter to eight when we got there.' Business letter from Captain Rostron to Cunard's general manager in Liverpool, William Howard Taft papers, reel 440: Last boat was picked up at 8.30a.m. AI p.22: 'I manoeuvred the ship and we gradually got all the boats together. We got all the boats alongside and all the people up aboard by 8.30.'**
4. **James Bisset, *Tramps and Ladies*, pp.288–94: It was eight bells when he took the bridge as OOW from C/O Hankinson. He saw the last of *Titanic*'s lifeboats labouring toward *Carpathia* with Lightoller at the helm. He identified it as boat No.12 and said that 'the last castaways from the *Titanic* came on board the Carpathia at 8.30a.m.'**
5. **Frederick Clench, AI p.636: Boat No.12 picked up some of collapsible B's survivors.**
6. John Thayer Jr, *The Sinking of the SS* Titanic: Arrived at 'almost 7.30'.
7. John Poigndestre, BI 3072: No.12 tied up to two lifeboats until they saw *Carpathia*.

Secondary Sources

1. **Alice Phillips, *New York Sun*, 19 April 1912: 'About 8.30 in the morning we came across a life raft on which were 17 persons . . . Shortly after that we were picked up by the *Carpathia*.'**
2. **Madeleine Mellinger, *The Mail Star*, 16 June 1972: Lightoller was picked up from collapsible B by boat No.12, whose occupants boarded *Carpathia* around 8a.m.**
3. **Emily Rugg, *Wilmington Evening Journal*, 20 April 1912: They saw *Carpathia* reach the scene in the far distance, and they waited for several hours before she finally came up to them.** *Wilmington Every Evening & Commercial*, 20 April 1912: Her boat was picked up later than 5a.m. [deduced from her comments about a previous occurrence that happened at about 5a.m.].

Times of Astronomical Events that Bear on the Recovery Times

(Ref: United States Naval Observatory, Astronomical Applications, Data Services.)
Titanic sank at 5.18a.m. GMT (2.20a.m. *Titanic* ATS) at 41°43'57"N, 49°56'49"W on 15 April 1912. For that location:

Start of Astronomical Twilight: 7.00a.m. GMT (4.02a.m. *Titanic* ATS). At the start of Astronomical Twilight the sky starts to brighten a bit in the east, but it is still too dark to make out the horizon all around to take star sights.

Start of Nautical Twilight: 7.37a.m. GMT (4.39a.m. *Titanic* ATS). At the start of Nautical Twilight the horizon can be seen well enough all around to begin taking celestial sights for navigation, and the navigational stars are still visible.

Start of Civil Twilight: 8.11a.m. GMT (5.13a.m. *Titanic* ATS). At the start of Civil Twilight there is light enough to make out some distant objects, but too bright for a round of star sights to be taken. Only the brightest stars and planets remain visible.

Sunrise: 8.40a.m. GMT (5.42a.m. *Titanic* ATS).

THE QUESTION OF LOCKED GATES

Cathy Akers-Jordan and George Behe

Introduction

It is often claimed that, during the sinking, *Titanic's* steerage passengers were detained behind locked Bostwick gates (folding metal gates drawn across the entrances to stairways, etc.), but specific evidence to that effect has been sparse and poorly documented in the past. *Titanic* scholars have long believed that no such gates existed for the simple reason that none appear on the ship's deck plans, but the general public has long believed that being trapped behind such gates was a universal experience for *Titanic's* third class passengers. What evidence exists that would either document or refute the actual existence of such gates?

Immigration Laws

That at least some barriers existed on *Titanic* in order to keep the classes separate is undisputed, since immigration laws required such barriers on immigrant ships in order to prevent the spread of disease. Ships not in compliance with these regulations could be held in Quarantine for up to forty days until all passengers were medically examined, so passenger segregation was taken seriously by the shipping lines. Is it possible that these gates were responsible for the belief that *Titanic's* steerage passengers were deliberately detained behind locked gates below decks? Let us examine the evidence pertaining to the normal operation of these barriers during a routine crossing.

Steward John Hart stated that the gates separating third class from second class were normally kept unlocked but that a quartermaster or seaman was detailed at each barrier to make sure nobody passed through the gate.[1] Edward Wilding, a naval architect at Harland & Wolff, confirmed that there was nothing to prevent a steerage passenger from crossing these 'hinged gates' into second class 'except the watchfulness of the stewards and men'.[2]

Michael McKinney, a passenger on board *Olympic*, once described his own encounter with such a gated barrier that, in his case, separated first class from second class: 'Until one gets his bearings it is easy to get lost on this ship. You discover a cosy nook and then try to go there again and you can't find it. Last night I went down some stairs from the first class deck and found myself below in the second class quarters. A steward led me to the iron grating and passed me through.' (McKinney's use of the term 'iron grating' in the second class cabin area suggests that he was talking about a tall Bostwick gate instead of a low grating that could be easily stepped over by a man of average height.)[3]

Edward Wilding testified about the location of four individual 'emergency doors' on E deck that were ordinarily closed and separated steerage from second and first class. (See Fig. J-1 for the location of these doors.) According to Wilding, 'There is one [Door A] leading direct into the forward first class entrance [stairway] from Scotland Road up on to the top, and then you can go on there; one [Door D] from Scotland Road into the forward second class entrance [stairway], and one [Door E] from Scotland Road into the after second class entrance [stairway].' He added that a fourth emergency door [Door B] was located at the foot of the stewards' stairs accessing the first class pantry on D deck, and a *Titanic* deck plan held in the National Archives shows a fifth emergency door [Door C] accessing the stairs leading to the second class pantry.

Wilding testified that these emergency doors were shut with an 'ordinary handle' and that, although they were equipped with locks, he understood that they were 'not locked at sea. I have frequently passed through them at sea.' He added that Scotland Road was used by steerage passengers and crewmen 'extensively' and that the emergency doors were there in order to prevent the necessity of stationing crewmen at those locations as guards in order to prevent steerage people from crossing into second class. [See Fig. J-1.] 'That was the intention,' Wilding stated. 'If you do not put doors there, or barriers of some sort, you would have to have somebody continuously stationed there to prevent people going into the second class accommodation and losing their way, for example.'[4]

It is worth noting that the emergency doors leading from the steerage decks to the boat deck were indeed locked at certain times during *Titanic's* brief existence. Maurice Clarke, a Board of Trade immigration officer, testified that some of these doors were locked when he inspected *Titanic* at 8 a.m. on 10 April prior to the vessel's departure from Southampton. 'Well,' Clarke continued, 'the reason for having those doors locked is to keep the firemen and stewards and other people from passing through into the different places on sailing day. They are very congested. The ship is very congested from a lot of visitors – something like a thousand visitors.'[5]

As for specific routes for third class passengers to leave the steerage and reach the boat deck, Edward Wilding testified: 'They can go up the working passage, which has been referred to as Scotland Road, along this deck, and enter the forward first class entrance through an emergency door here; then go up this main stairway [see Door A, Fig. J-1], or they can continue still further on and go up this stewards' stairway. It is open to Scotland Road, as we call it, the big working alleyway [see Door B, Fig. J-1].'

Wilding went on and described what the steerage passengers must do after they ascended the main third class companionway: 'They come up on to an open deck. They can then go one of two ways, either up ladders at the after end of the bridge deck, or . . . B deck and along to the forward second class entrance, and then up to the boat deck, or they can go, as I understand, from some of the evidence they actually did go, through and past the second class library into the first class accommodation along the first class alleyway right to the first class entrance. I think one of the stewards gave evidence that he had taken two parties that way.'[6] [See Fig. J-8.]

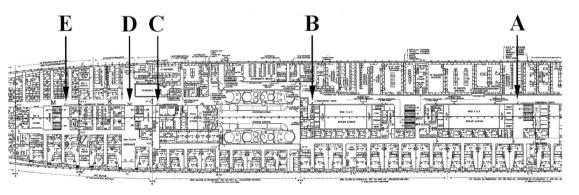

Fig. J-1 Emergency doors on *Titanic's* Scotland Road, E deck. Doors A, D and E were intended for passenger use, while doors B and C were for crew use. (Courtesy of Bruce Beveridge)

Fig. J-2 A 1924 view of *Olympic*'s second class purser's office on E
deck. A closed, panelled emergency door is visible behind the couple
facing the camera. (Courtesy of Bruce Beveridge)

After leaving E deck's Scotland Road and climbing the stairway to C deck, steerage passengers could then emerge into the open air on the aft well deck, which was designated as the third class promenade. In order to reach the boat deck from the aft well deck, it was necessary to climb a stairway at the top of which was 'a hinged gate which anyone can lift and walk through – port and starboard . . . That is the only thing preventing third class passengers in the ordinary course getting up to the boat deck.' Wilding added that the rail could be lifted up by hand 'quite readily' and that there was no means of locking it in order to prevent steerage passengers from passing through it.[7] Second class passenger Lawrence Beesley reported that a male third class passenger daily used to climb one of these two stairways and talk across the low gate with a female relative who was travelling in second class.[8] Likewise, second class passenger Edwina Troutt later said that her roommate Susan Webber talked across the same low gate with hometown friends who were travelling in steerage.[9] These gates can be seen in Figures J-3 and J-4, and the latter photo clearly shows a printed sign at the top of the stairs leading to B deck that warns: 'NOTICE: 3RD CLASS PASSENGERS ARE NOT ALLOWED ON THIS DECK.'

Low Gate at Top of Ladder

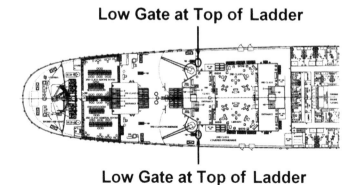

Low Gate at Top of Ladder

Fig. J-3 Plan showing *Titanic*'s aft well deck (C deck) and the locations
of the low gates at the tops of the two stairways leading up to B deck.
(Courtesy of Bruce Beveridge)

Fig. J-4 Low gate at the stairway leading from
Olympic's aft well deck up to B deck. (Courtesy of
Bruce Beveridge)

One final way for steerage passengers to reach the boat deck was to climb the interior stairways at the forward end of the ship and emerge into the open air on the forward well deck. Edward Wilding testified that, from the well deck, steerage passengers had to 'climb up by this ladder at the forward end of the bridge deck, round the corner of this house, either port or starboard, and then up by these ladders direct to the boat deck.'[10] Photographs indicate that, although it could be latched, the gate blocking the stairway leading from the forward well deck was not equipped with a mechanism that would allow it to be locked. [See Fig. J-5.]

As we have just seen in the case of *Olympic* passenger Michael McKinney, there were even barriers to keep first and second class passengers from straying into each others' territory. Archibald Gracie mentioned the existence of a low 'iron gate and fence that divide[d] the First and Second cabins' on the boat deck of *Titanic*, this gate being so low that Gracie was able to easily 'vault' over it. This same 'iron fence and railing' was later to stop a crowd of people (which Gracie called a 'mass of humanity') who were fleeing *Titanic's* flooding bridge area during the final moments of the sinking.[11] [See Figures J-6 & J-7.]

Conclusions

A number of gated barriers and closed doors equipped with locks did exist below decks, but it is unclear whether or not crewmen were routinely stationed at those barriers in order to

Fig. J-5 Low gate at top of stairway leading from *Olympic's* forward well deck up to B deck. (Courtesy of Bruce Beveridge)

Fig. J-6 Gracie's location and the low gates on the boat deck.

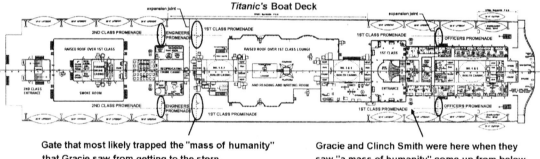

Gate that most likely trapped the "mass of humanity" **that Gracie saw from getting to the stern.**   **Gracie and Clinch Smith were here when they** **saw "a mass of humanity" come up from below.**

keep steerage passengers from wandering up into second class. (Steward Hart claimed that they were, but Edward Wilding said that the existing barriers were there as a *replacement* for such guards, which – if true – meant that a crewman was not routinely stationed there.) It appears that crewmen were not ordinarily stationed outside on the open deck as gate guards, but quartermasters and deck stewards nevertheless kept an eye on the steerage passengers in order to keep them from climbing the well deck stairways and crossing the low gates onto the second class decks.

Guarded Barriers Blocking Exits from the Aft Well Deck

Passenger accounts regarding events that took place at these guarded gates are seemingly contradictory, so we will present a brief summary of these accounts.

Whereas Edward Wilding claimed that gates barring the two stairways leading from the aft well deck to B deck had no hardware that would enable them to be locked, Daniel Buckley

Fig. J-7 The 'iron fence and railing' that divided *Olympic's* first and second class promenades. (Courtesy of Bruce Beveridge)

claimed that a steward pushed a passenger down one of these stairways and then locked the gate at the top in order to prevent anyone from getting through it. The fallen passenger broke through the locked gate, and 'all of the steerage passengers' then rushed through the opening and headed toward the boat deck.[12] However, it is likely that Buckley's gate was merely *latched* instead of locked, since no sign of a locking mechanism on these gates is visible on photographs taken at the *Titanic* wreck site.

On the other hand, Olaus Abelseth said that most steerage passengers waited patiently behind the closed gates even though many impatient ones bypassed the gates by climbing onto the well deck's cargo cranes, working their way up the booms and jumping onto B deck. Eventually an officer stepped up to the closed gate and called for all women to come up from the well deck, and after a time he returned and called for everyone else to come up.[13] Laura Cribb said that she easily got over the little closed gate at the top of the stairway,[14] whereas Frank Goldsmith and his mother were permitted to pass through the open gate without opposition.[15] A steward grabbed the hand of Annie Kelly and hurried her up the stairway and past the gate without any guards objecting, since crewmen were 'for letting all the people come up the stairs'.[16]

Elias Yarrad and his sister were initially prevented from passing through the guarded gate but were eventually permitted to pass and reached the ladder that led up to A deck.[17] A crewman prevented Helmina Nilsson from passing through the gate, but she eventually managed to slip past the barrier when he turned his back for a moment.[18] Sarah Roth was prevented from passing through the gate by a crewman who said, 'I have had orders not to let anybody come up this ladder or the steps on this deck,' adding, 'it is impossible for this ship to sink.'[19] Katherine Gilnagh and a number of other Irish girls were stopped at the gate by a crewman who would not let them pass until Jim Farrell shouted, 'Great God, man! Open the gate and let the girls through!' (The crewman allowed the girls to pass, and afterwards a man let Gilnagh stand on his shoulders in order to climb from B deck up to A deck.)[20]

Conclusions

Gates at the tops of the two stairways (Figures J-3 & J-4) apparently prevented most steerage passengers from leaving the aft well deck until officers gave them formal permission to do so. However, occasional passengers were permitted to pass through the gates without being detained, while others slipped past the gates unnoticed, forced their way past the guarded gates or else climbed up the cargo cranes and bypassed the gates altogether in order to reach the boat deck. (Some of the seeming contradictions in these stories might be explained by the fact that there were two different stairways leading from the aft well deck to B deck and that different crewmen might have periodically been stationed at these two gates during the sinking.)

Other Guarded Barriers Located Above Decks

Although no physical barriers seem to have existed on *Titanic*'s uppermost decks for the purpose of preventing unauthorised passengers or crewmen from stepping out onto the boat deck, occasional crewmen reportedly took it upon themselves to keep such people from accomplishing that goal. Arthur Peuchen testified that he saw an officer order a large number of crewmen to leave the boat deck and return to the lower decks from which they had come. 'When I came on deck first, on this upper deck,' Peuchen said:

> ...about 100 stokers came up with their dunnage bags, and they seemed to crowd this whole deck in front of the boats. One of the officers ... came along and drove these men right off that deck. It was a splendid act ... He drove them, every man, like a lot of sheep, right off the deck ... He drove them right ahead of him, and they disappeared. I do not know where they went, but it was a splendid act. They did not put up any resistance. I admired him for it.[21]

In a similar vein, Charlotte Collyer reached the boat deck and encountered an injured crewman who had come up from below. Mrs Collyer watched as the crewman 'staggered away and lay down, fainting, with his head on a coil of rope ... The officers now were running to and fro and shouting orders ... I saw First Officer Murdoch place guards by the gangways to prevent others like the wounded stoker from coming on deck. How many unhappy men were shut off in that way from their one chance of safety I do not know, but Mr Murdoch was probably right.'[22]

Conclusions

If such guards were indeed posted on the upper decks in order to keep fellow crewmen from reaching the boat deck, few *surviving* crewmen reported having encountered them.

Reports of Open Barriers Below Decks

A small body of testimony exists that has led past researchers to believe that *all* exits from the steerage decks were open during the sinking and that *all* steerage passengers had free and unimpeded access to the boat deck. Indeed, Stewardess Violet Jessop later stated that, to the best of her knowledge, steerage passengers were not detained behind locked gates as was depicted in the film version of *A Night to Remember*.[23]

It appears that certain exits from the steerage decks were indeed available to passengers who were either directed to those open barriers by stewards or else passed through certain unlocked doors that they ordinarily would not have opened. Passenger Berk Pickard testified that he found a door leading from steerage to second class wide open and that he went through it and proceeded up to the boat deck; Pickard added that afterwards, 'we could not get back again ... The steward would not allow us to go back. They made us all go forward on deck. There were no locked doors to prevent us from going back.' (The location of this open door is unknown, but it was most likely on E deck.)[24] Steward John Hart said that the unlocked gates in third class were definitely open when he led his passengers up to the boat deck,[25] and he added that the 'swing door' (emergency door) to second class was open when he saw it at 12.30a.m.[26] Hart didn't notice

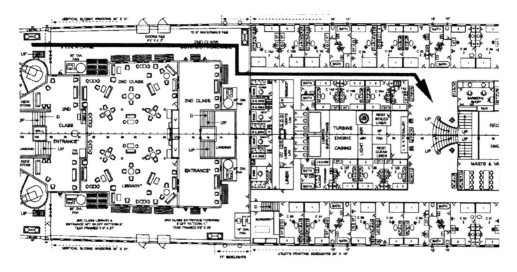

Fig. J-8 The route by which Steward Hart led steerage passengers from the aft well deck to a C deck stairway leading to the boat deck. (Courtesy of Bruce Beveridge)

any sailors preventing people from leaving the steerage decks, but he did see steerage passengers walking aft toward the aft well deck rather than climb the ladder that led up from the forward well deck towards the boat deck (perhaps because the forward stairway gate was guarded?).[27] From the aft well deck Steward Hart led a group of steerage passengers into the vessel and forward along C deck, past the second class library, through a (closed?) door leading to the first class area and then onward to the aft first class stairway next to the barber shop.[28] [See Fig. J-8.]

Conclusions

It appears that several exits from the steerage decks were open and gave steerage passengers unrestricted access to the second class decks after the collision. The door through which Steward Hart led passengers from steerage into first class seems to have been unlocked and freely accessible to all passengers, but it is possible that other passengers were deterred from using it and similar doors because of signs warning steerage passengers that they (ordinarily) were not permitted to open or pass through the doors in question.

Reports of Locked or Guarded Barriers Below Decks

Since the declaration that steerage passengers were detained behind locked or guarded gates during the sinking is one of the most disputed claims about the *Titanic* disaster, the present authors will quote the texts of these reports verbatim in order to present the substance of these claims as accurately as possible. Although we can speculate about the places on the ship where these gates were situated, it is not possible to pin down the exact locations of these barriers with any degree of certainty except to say that they seem to have been located somewhere on the lower decks. [Note: all passengers were third class unless otherwise stated.]

Mary Coutts

Personal account

Nearly everybody was on deck now, and we were just going when I saw the same officer. I said to him again that I had not got a life-preserver. He told me to follow him, and ordered the few people still in the corridors up on deck. He took us through quite a number of corridors and passages right into the first-class saloons to his own quarters. There he got his own life-belt and tied it on me… He then told us to go out a certain way, but when I got there neither Willie or I could open the door. We felt that we were trapped; but strange as it may appear, I was not a bit afraid . . . Presently we saw a sailor, and he showed us the way to the first-class deck. So you will see that it was only by great good luck we were saved.[29]

Eugene Daly

Personal account

After the accident, we were all held down in the steerage, which seemed to be a lifetime. All this time we knew that the water was coming up, and up rapidly. Finally some of the women and children were let up, but, as you know, we had quite a number of hot headed Italians and other people who got crazy and made for the stairs. These men tried to rush the stairway, pushing and crowding and pulling the women down. Some of them with weapons in their hands. I saw two dagos shot and some that took punishment from the officers. After a bit, I got up on one of the decks . . ."[30]

[Note: Daly specified elsewhere that the shootings actually took place on the upper decks and that they were connected with a subsequent officer suicide.][31]

Mary Davis (second class passenger)

Personal account

Oh, and I'm going to tell you about the steerage. Of course, we went down there to bring the cots down. And we went down to see what it was, oh – it was dreadful down there. And oh, it was just loaded, all the people, coming in the steerage, and they didn't even have a chance, they never ever had . . . There was an officer with a revolver standing at that gangway that we came up, keeping them from coming up. Oh, and I want to tell you that. I *don't* want to tell you that – I don't want to think of it more than I can help . . . I think it's a shame that they wasn't given a chance. It was a terrible thing.[32]

Elin Hakkarainen

Personal account as compiled by her son

The door at the end of the passageway was locked! I ran to the other end of the passageway and found the door locked also. After a bit of wandering I discovered another door which was unlocked and led to another passageway. I finally ran into my friend who had awakened me. A ship's steward appeared with a small group of women saying 'You better come with us.' He said, 'There is another way to get to the upper deck.' He directed us to a service ladder, which was used only by the crew to get around the ship. 'Follow me,' said the steward, 'We do not have much time.' We went up the ladder, through the second class dining room, up another flight of stairs to the second class promenade and finally up to the boat deck.[33]

Personal account as compiled by her son

Soon there was a hard and very fast knock at the door, and one of my friends from Finland dashed in to say the ship had struck something and was sinking. 'Where is Pekko?' she asked.

'He went to see why the ship had stopped. I don't know where he is now.'

'How did he get out of the passageway?' she continued. 'All the doors are locked!'

I was confused; I didn't know what to do next. After a few moments I grabbed my purse and life jacket and ran out to the passageway. The door was locked! Finally a ship's steward came and gathered a small group of us together and guided us. 'Come, there is another way to get to the upper deck.'[34]

Personal account as compiled by her son

I picked up my lifejacket and purse and left the cabin. I walked to the end of the passageway, but was stopped by a locked door! There were a number of other passengers in the passageway also looking for a way out. In a few moments a ship's officer appeared and directed us to a service ladder, which was used by the crew to get around the ship ... [This might have been the E deck emergency door to the second class pantry. At any rate, they climbed the stairway.] We ran through the second class dining area on D deck, up a flight of stairs to the second class promenade on B deck, and up another flight of stairs to the boat deck.[35]

Neshan Krekorian

Article about Krekorian

As it turned out, some of the European and Middle Eastern immigrants in the lower sections may not have had a chance. By law, the steerage passengers were separated from others, ostensibly to prevent the spread of infectious disease. Iron locks hindered their escape. Several locked doors had to be axed-open by Krekorian and others as they struggled to the outside decks. On deck, the scene was calm at first, but over the next two hours, things deteriorated. There weren't enough lifeboats to go around.[36]

Article about Krekorian

Krekorian told Hustak he remembered hearing the crash and feeling the ship 'scud back and tilt to one side' the night the ship hit the iceberg. Then confusion and panic set in. Affluent passengers on the higher decks were loaded into lifeboats, while steerage passengers were stuck on the lower levels. 'I think my father was above the engine room, but they automatically closed all the gates,' George [Krekorian] said. 'He told me there was an axe and he had to break the door down and get up three levels.' Once he was there, the story takes a horrific turn. He saw men watching from the deck as women and children were lowered in lifeboats to float in the icy Atlantic.[37]

Margaret Mannion

Account written by her grandson

Down below, the third class passengers began to get very panicky, especially as water started to rise above their feet. At last one brave Irishman jumped up and said, ''Tis do or die' and the rest of the men agreed. They stormed down the corridors followed by the ladies in their light clothes. Suddenly they were stopped by a large barrier at the foot of a stairway, but a few strong fellows managed to smash it down. They moved on with all their might. At one stage a sailor tried to stop them, but they took care of him. They soon reached the top where there were two more sailors standing with guns. They tried to threaten the passengers by firing shots in the air, but this did not frighten the men. They just threw the sailors out of the way and rushed to the lifeboats. Men from all three classes tried to get onto the boats, but some were shot down due to their actions.[38]

Bertha Mulvihill

Article about Mulvihill

After the disaster, Bertha complained bitterly to her family about the treatment that she had received from the White Star Line. Bertha told family members that all of them had been 'held below deck for the longest time.' She also said that 'every time we went up a stair they were locked,' and that Eugene Daly fought and pleaded with crewmembers to let the girls up on deck. Even after the crewmembers allowed them to go, it was not without incident. As they attempted to climb the stairs a fireman pushed his way up past Bertha, causing her to fall down several stairs.[39]

Margaret Murphy

Interview with Murphy

A crowd of men were trying to get up to a higher deck and were fighting the sailors; all striking and scuffling and swearing. Women and some children were there praying and crying. Then the sailors fastened down the hatchways leading to the third class section. They said they wanted to keep the air down there so the vessel would stay up longer. It meant all hope was gone for those still down there.[40]

Interview with Murphy

Before all the steerage passengers had even a chance of their lives, *Titanic's* sailors fastened the doors and companionways leading up from the third class section. That meant a certain death for all who remained below. And while the sailors were beating back the steerage passengers, lifeboats were putting away, some of them not half-filled.[41]

Hannah Touma

Article about Touma

She [Hannah Touma] was talking with friends. A lot were dancing in the hall and the dining area or playing their musical instruments. She was leaning against her cabin door when the iceberg hit the boat,' [Joseph] Thomas [Gerios Touma's son] said. The jolt made the cabin door slam shut, cutting Touma's index finger. 'While she was in the infirmary getting it treated, some passengers went on deck. They were told not to panic but to go to their rooms to pray,' Thomas said. Touma, who had gone upstairs with her son [Gerios], could not find her daughter. She went below, found Mary [Marianna] and grabbed her money and the note with her destination written on it. As she climbed the stairs, she said she saw ship hands close and lock the gates behind her. Trapped on the other side were some friends from her village. Confusion spread, but Touma managed to get the three onto a lifeboat.[42]

Article about Touma

Mrs [Hannah] Touma and her children George [Gerios Touma] and Maria [Marianna Touma] left their cabin below decks and 'raced, with Maria, down the passage way that led out of steerage. As they left the steerage area she heard a loud bang. Looking back she saw the steerage section's gate had been closed and was being locked. She thought it was for safety of some kind and did not bother to think about it much.'[43]

Anna Turja

Interview with her grandson

I wanted to mention that Grandma reported that as she and her companions went up from third class, a steward locked the gates behind them after failing to get them to return. So in at least one case, the gates were indeed locked. I don't think it was quite as widespread as Cameron depicts, though.[44]

[Note: It appears that the crewman tried to get Turja to return because he hadn't given her permission to pass through the gate. When she refused to comply with his wishes, he closed the gate to prevent other passengers from following her.]

Interview with her grandson

Late that Sunday night, she felt a shudder and a shake. Shortly thereafter, her roommate's brother knocked on the door and told them that 'something was wrong,' that they should wear warm clothing and put on their life jackets. Their little group started heading for the upper decks. A crew member tried to keep them down – ordered them back – but they refused to obey, and he didn't argue with them. She clearly remembers, however, that the doors were closed and chained shut behind them to prevent others from coming up. The others of the group continued up to a higher deck, 'where it will be safer,' they said, but out of pure curiosity and chance she remained on what turned out to be the boat deck. She thought it was too cold to go up further, and she was intrigued by the activity and by the music being played by the band, though she didn't know the names of the tunes. She remembers the band coming out of a room they had been playing in and the doors being locked after everyone had gotten out.'[45]

Adelaide Wells (second class passenger)
Personal account

I remember I dressed [my daughter] Joan because she was older and wouldn't cry,' Mrs. Wells said. 'What troubles we had getting up on deck! The wide stairway was blocked off and I had to take the children up a ladder – all by myself.'[46]

Article about Wells

Addie Wells and Emily Richards had strolled the deck of *Titanic* the night of the 14th, noticing how cold it was. She and her children were well asleep when *Titanic* struck the iceberg. She awoke to a tremendous jolt. She heard a commotion and a friend yelled 'Dress quickly: there's some trouble I believe, but I don't know what it is.' Having dressed the children she tried to get them to the boat deck but found many of the doors leading to the boat deck had been locked, she searched frantically until she found one that was unlocked. She would later admit that she did not realise the seriousness of the situation and thought it was some sort of drill.'[47]

Elizabeth Wilkinson (second class passenger)
Interview with Wilkinson

We had ample time to get up on deck and into the boats were it not that one of the officers assured us that there was no danger. I preferred to be outside, however, and as I was leaving I saw another officer going around and locking the cabin doors. Hundreds must have been locked in in that way, as only a few had gotten out before the officer went around. I don't know if they were ever freed again, but I feel certain that if it were only possible to make an examination of that boat, that hundreds would be found dead in their cabins with the doors locked.[48]

[The cabin doors were more than likely locked in order to prevent looting].

Conclusions

It is interesting to note that the seemingly contradictory experiences reported by these steerage passengers might be explained by the *timing* of their attempted departures from the steerage decks. Although Touma and Turja experienced no difficulty in walking past gated barriers, in both cases they noticed that the gates were then closed and locked *behind* them, which would of course have created serious problems for any passengers who attempted to cross those barriers afterwards. One such person might have been Margaret Devaney, who reported that the closed gate she encountered was about 5ft high. [See the following section for Devaney's account.] Passenger Addie Wells reported that she also encountered a stairway that was blocked off; this stairway must have been inside the ship, since Wells (a second class passenger) would not have encountered the outside gated stairway that prevented steerage passengers from leaving the aft well deck and ascending onto B deck.

It is important to note that, according to Able-Bodied Seaman John Poingdestre, there were no printed signs on *Titanic's* lower decks that would direct passengers from the steerage areas to the upper decks.[49] This might explain why many steerage passengers were unable to find alternate routes to the boat deck when they encountered closed, locked or guarded gates down on the steerage decks.

Reported Barriers in Unspecified Locations

A number of survivor accounts exist which describe the existence of gates in places on the ship that cannot be determined with certainty. Whereas some of these gates might have been the ones located on the aft well deck, it is likely that others were located somewhere inside the ship on the lower steerage decks.

Nasif Qasim Abi-Al-Muna

Article about Qasim

> 'There was a gate that kept the steerage passengers away from the first- and second-class decks at all times,' [Anthony] Belman [Nasif Qasim's grandson] explains. 'But when the trouble was first recognised, stewards opened the gate and called for all the women and children. Grandfather Belman sent his 12-year-old charge off with the stewards, to be put on a lifeboat. Eventually the stewards opened all the gates to the decks. But by the time Grandfather Belman and his third family member made their way to a deck, the last of the lifeboats had been lowered into the dark, icy Atlantic.'[50]

Margaret Devaney

Personal account

> Something had happened, but all our fears were for naught when the engines started up again, but that didn't last for long. Next thing an officer came to our cabin & ordered life belt on, said no more. We put on our life belts & taking our bags along went up on deck. There were very many people around, so we went up on the next deck, dropping our luggage before we went over the railing that was closed against us. One of my girl friends was very sea sick & she stopped on the way. The other girl stayed with her. I ran along & got to the side of the ship that was lowering the life boats.[51]

Taped interview

> Q: To continue with that question, if you can tell us about, what was it like, let's say, just before say the iceberg hit?

A: We were in bed. It was late and naturally when the engines stopped you realised there's something the matter because, after all, that you have with you all the time. And we had an older friend with three girls [unintelligible] and we had an older friend from home was kind of looking out for us. And we got up and got dressed and he came into our stateroom and he said to me 'Something has happened. We'll go up on deck.' So we went up on the deck, too cold so we came back to put more clothes on to see what has happening. So then was the only time they told us what to do. There was an officer there telling us to get our lifebelts on. And then we packed our tukas [laughing] and started up on deck and nobody stopped us. Nobody told us where to go or where to stay but we went up like that and we turned to the right and was where they were putting up the distress signal so we went up there for a while. So everybody seemed to be going away from there and we looked for our friends and we couldn't find them, so we three girls were alone. So then we came down the steps and across the thing with nobody there, across the boat, to get up, I guess, into the second class compartment. There we found there was a gate closed against us. That the railing around was about five feet high so then we had to climb up the ladder and climb over THAT. Then we got in, there was still nobody at all much around, and one of my friends was very seasick and she couldn't come any further, she had to stop, and the other girl stopped with her but something told me I should find a lifeboat or see where there was a lifeboat. So I went along with the intention of coming back and I got caught in the crowd and when I got out on the deck, straight ahead they were lowering a lifeboat and I got in the lifeboat.

Q: Was it true only women and children, for the most part, were allowed in the lifeboats?

A: No. That [they?] was always allowed in, you disguised yourself or you went in some way otherwise because the officers were there and they were shooting them if they disobeyed.

Q: They were shooting people who disobeyed?

A: [You couldn't of.][52]

Interview with Devaney

Taking our bags along, we went up on deck, [she said.] There were not many there, so the girls decided to go to another part of the stricken ship. They came to a railing where they had to put down their bags to climb it. Miss Hargarton became sick at this point and Miss Burns stayed to help her. Mrs O'Neill [Miss Devaney] went on until she came to a station where a lifeboat was being loaded.[53]

Interview with Devaney's daughter-in-law

I guess they realised at that point that the ship was going to go down and they wanted to save the lives of the rich people. So they locked the poor people in. My mother-in-law had to climb a gate and a lot of ladders to get to the upper deck and a lifeboat . . . When they realised they had to climb the deck and the ladders, Mary [Burns] refused to go. I guess she felt too sick.'[54]

Helga Hirvonen

Interview with Hirvonen

On the *Titanic* that evening steerage passengers were denied access to the lifeboats. They were told to wait and the passages to the upper decks were gated and guarded against them. Some time later – I don't know how long – it seemed that the big steamer was tilting. Then there was another rush from the promenade deck. The officers couldn't drive us back then. After some time there came a shouted order for the women to come up on another deck. Some of us understood and started.[55]

Annie Jermyn

Interview with Jermyn

We must have been in the third cabin for fully two hours before I was able to make my escape, which I did after climbing over the tall gate that held us prisoners, and which was surely twice as high as myself. This I accomplished after a dozen or more unsuccessful attempts by climbing ropes and any other piece of the ship that I could get hold of. In attempting to get over the gate, my efforts were cut off by men and other women, who would catch hold of me and pull me down again, that they might be able to get ahead of me. By the time I succeeded in getting over the gate, the water in the steerage had risen to quite a height, and it was easily understood that the ship had met its doom.[56]

Interview with Jermyn

[Jermyn said a heavy locked iron gate 10ft tall kept the steerage passengers in their steerage area.]

Miss Jermyn says it took her two hours to get over the gate, which barred the only exit. Nobody asked her to get into a boat, she asserts, although she stood on the deck near them in her night dress and bare feet. The last boat was about to start from the ship with only about fifteen aboard.

'Realising that it was my only chance, I sprang from the upper deck of the vessel into the boat, falling nearly thirty feet and landing on my chest and stomach. A second later a man fell beside me, but he had no sooner got up and taken a seat in the boat than an officer drew his revolver and shot him in the head. I fainted as they pitched the lifeless body of the poor fellow into the sea.'[57]

Bertha Lehmann (second class passenger)

Article about Lehmann

She said that she saw them lock 300 men in the steerage and did not know whether they later released them. The clamour they made, she said, was something too horrible to contemplate, and the band played, apparently, to drown the noise.[58]

Paul Mauge (kitchen clerk)

Personal account

After that we had been by the third class deck just at the back, and we have been trying to go on the second class passenger deck. Two or three stewards were there, and would not let us go. I was dressed and the chef was too. He was not in his working dress; he was just like me. I asked the stewards to pass. I said I was the secretary to the chef, and the stewards said, 'Pass along, get away.' So the other cooks were obliged to stay on the deck there; they could not go up. That is where they die ... They let me pass, me and the chef, because I was dressed like a passenger. I think that is why they let me pass.[59]

Interview with Mauge

The third class passengers were in terrible confusion almost immediately after the shock, comparatively mild as it then seemed to be. Everywhere there was a babble of many voices and a rush of men and women, some carrying bundles, some carrying children and others holding in their arms huge chunks of ice that had fallen upon the deck near the bow of the boat. Their panic was made the worse when, on reaching the gates that separated the steerage quarters from the rest of the ship, they found two stewards there who kept the gates locked against them, and the lifeboats were all on the far side of the gates. I had awakened the chef, M. Rousseau, and together, upon giving the stewards our names, we were permitted to pass the gates.[60]

Thomas McCormack

Article about McCormack

He was asleep when the ship struck the iceberg and awoke and dressed. He said he had to fight his way past members of the crew to the upper decks.[61]

Article about McCormack

McCormack was asleep in his berth when the collision occurred and did not wake until one of the Kiernans shook him. The three dressed and started for an upper deck. Officers, McCormack says, barred the way, pushing them back and striking them. McCormack, who is more than six feet tall, pushed his way past the officers on the deck. The Kiernans were lost.[62]

Ellen Shine

Interview with Shine

Those who were able to get out of bed went to the upper deck, where they were met by the members of the crew and first and second class passengers, who endeavored to keep them in the steerage quarters. However, the women rushed by the officers and crew, knocking them down, and finally reached the upper decks.[63]

Gunnar Tenglin

Interview with Tenglin's daughter-in-law

She'd heard him tell stories of how a steward slammed down the gates to keep third-class passengers below deck while the life boats were loaded, just like in the movie. But unlike anyone in the movie, Tenglin, a brave, outspoken man, protested.[64]

Shawneene Whabee

Interview with family member

When asked if Shawneene Whabee saw the crew lock gates to prevent the steerage passengers from coming up on deck, Sharon George replied: 'My Uncle told me that Shanini told him that they did, but she never mentions this in the article. In fact, in the article she states that the crew members "pulled" her out of steerage and brought her up onto the deck.'[65]

Conclusions

Although it is difficult to place the exact locations of these gates, it is striking to consider that several of the accounts (Hirvonen, McCormack, Shine) speak of passengers forcing their way past crewmen who were detaining them at the gates. These accounts are very reminiscent of those of Daly, Mannion and Murphy [see preceding section], who also described groups of steerage passengers who found it necessary to force their way past guarded barriers. Although Annie Jermyn's account of a male passenger being shot in her lifeboat is almost certainly false, the rest of her account is so low-key and believable that we can't help but be impressed by her description of her attempt to climb over a locked gate. In any case, it is notable that Jermyn – like Margaret Devaney – reported that the gate she encountered was a tall one instead of a low one that could easily be stepped over like the ones on the aft well deck.

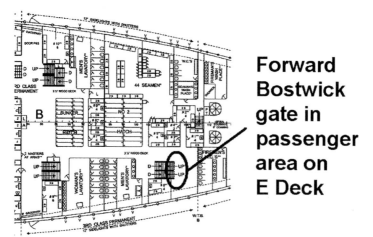

Fig. J-9 Forward Bostwick gate on *Titanic's* E deck. (Courtesy of Bruce Beveridge)

Forward Bostwick gate in passenger area on E Deck

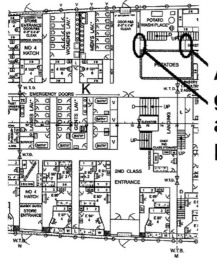

Fig. J-10 Close-up of the aft Bostwick gates on *Titanic's* E deck. (Courtesy of Bruce Beveridge)

Aft Bostwick gates in crew area on E Deck

Deck Plans

Several sets of *Titanic* deck plans exist, but only the National Archives' deck plans (used in the liability hearings) indicate the location of any Bostwick gates. Is this because no other Bostwick gates existed on *Titanic*, or is it because the existence of such gates was so expected and commonplace that they were not worth mentioning?

The Bostwick gates that are marked on *Titanic's* deck plans are located in two locations on E deck. The forward Bostwick gate on this plan [see Fig. J-9] was located in a third class passenger area and could have detained passengers had that area of the ship not flooded early. No passengers seem to have mentioned encountering this gate during the evacuation, probably because there was another stairway on the port side to use. (The forward Bostwick gate probably sealed off the stairs during cargo handling when the luggage was brought in through the D deck baggage door while at dockside.)

The second set of Bostwick gates on this deck plan [see Fig. J-10] was located in a crew area in the stern of the ship. No passenger accounts mention these gates, and it is unlikely that passengers were detained by them due to the fact that they secured the potato storage and a stores hoist.

A plan of *Titanic's* third class passenger accommodation is in the Smithsonian's Cropley Collection (National Museum of American History in the Division of Work and Industry) and is printed on the back of an *Olympic* deck plan issued in 1911. This plan is incomplete and depicts only two sections of F deck and one section of G deck, while missing is information on the G deck forward cabins and F deck forward cabins and how to get from the third class dining saloon to the forward cabins via Scotland Road.

The most notable information on this *Titanic* third class deck plan is that there is *no indication* of the forward Bostwick gate located on E deck that is clearly depicted on the National Archives' deck plan. The Smithsonian *Titanic* plan is also missing information about the E deck aft cabins and Scotland Road (amidship), D deck forward and aft cabins, C deck forward and aft cabins, the third class promenade and the B deck promenade. While some of this information could have been on the missing portions of the two sheets, the third class passenger accommodation plan does not seem like it would have been useful to passengers trying to find their way from one end of the ship to the other, or from lower to upper decks. One must assume that stewards helped passengers find their way around the ship on a regular basis.

Many third class passengers on *Titanic* mentioned gates or barriers of some sort below decks but didn't describe a specific location. To make educated estimates of these locations, the authors have examined evidence from *Titanic's* two sister ships. Descriptions of eight Bostwick gates were found in the specifications book for *Titanic's* younger sister *Britannic*, which was built after *Titanic* sank:

> Bostwick gate to be fitted in the doorways of No.4 hatch P & S on B deck. One to be fitted for access to the house on D deck just forward of 2nd class saloon; and one to be fitted to the Store house forward of the 2nd class forward entrance on E deck, and one at the after end of the passage to this house. One Bostwick gate was to be fitted to the stairs of the forward third-class entrance and two Bostwick gates to be between nos. 2 & 3 boiler casings, one forward and one aft of the stairs on the port side (for port use).[66]

None of these eight gates appear on *Britannic's* deck plans, although it seems probable that such fixtures wouldn't normally be shown on that type of general arrangement plan. There were enough differences between *Titanic* and *Britannic* that one cannot make parallel inferences from one to the other, especially since there is uncertainty as to where these gates on *Britannic* were actually located. What we know for certain is that Bostwick gates were specified for *Britannic* which were not shown on her deck plans, and that it is possible that there may have been more than the three fitted on *Titanic* which did show up on the plans presented at the liability hearings.

Similarly, little is known about the existence of Bostwick gates on board *Titanic's* older sister *Olympic*. Since the two ships were under construction at the same time, though, one could reasonably assume that arrangements for the installation of such gates were similar on both vessels at that time. *Olympic's* plans were greatly modified after the *Titanic* disaster, including adding and removing watertight bulkheads and doors on various decks. Although one such Bostwick gate is depicted on Scotland Road in a 1928 *Olympic* deck plan, the gate that is shown was almost certainly a 1920s addition for the purpose of securing a section of the main passageway, perhaps the result of the reclassification of cabin passengers.

Conclusions

The fact that some *Titanic* deck plans (e.g. the Smithsonian deck plan) do not depict the existence of any Bostwick gates cannot be regarded as proof that no such gates existed, since the National Archives' *Titanic* plan depicts two such gates that are missing from the Smithsonian plan. Likewise, existing *Britannic* deck plans do not depict *any* of the eight Bostwick gates that are clearly described in the vessel's specifications book. Once again, we must ask ourselves if the existence of such gates was so common and expected on board these three vessels that draftsmen did not bother to depict them when they were drawing up the deck plans. It is also possible that some of the barriers were not Bostwick gates at all but were some other form of decorative iron grating commonly seen in passenger compartments on ships of the era.

Expeditions

In 2001 and 2005 James Cameron returned to *Titanic* in an effort to film as much of the wreck as possible. The 2001 expedition was made into a documentary called *Ghosts of the Abyss*. The companion book of the same name shows a photo of the low gate on forward B deck.[67] It is closed but unlocked. (The present authors have not yet discovered any accounts in which steerage passengers described being detained at this low gate.)

The 2005 expedition was broadcast live on the Discovery Channel, and, at the authors' request, expedition participant Don Lynch kept an eye out for gates inside the ship and emailed the authors:

> Jim dove again after the show. It was nineteen hours, his longest ever. Ken [Marschall] and I just sat with him in the dining room for an hour talking about it. He did do Scotland Road, but it's a mess. I'm sure it became a water tunnel when the ship hit the bottom. There are pipes everywhere that have to be dodged, etc. There was no sign of a Bostwick gate on any of his dives.[68]

The Possible Location of *Titanic's* Locked Gates

The National Archives' *Titanic* deck plan shows not only the arrangement of *Titanic* as she left Southampton, but also the cabin classifications, cabin numbers and emergency escape routes. What it does not show are any gates that were located in the *crew* areas or gates that separated alternate passenger cabin blocks.

Titanic's maiden voyage was heavy on first and third class passengers. In fact, one section of E deck generally used by second class passengers was reserved for first class on this voyage. (This was one of the 'second class alternative first class' sections.) There was also a 'second class

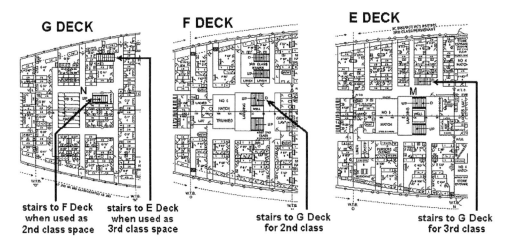

Fig. J-11   Plan showing Section N on G deck, which could be allocated for steerage or second class space. Stairway connecting G deck to F deck must have been gated for *Titanic's* maiden voyage to prevent third class passengers on G deck from straying into second class areas on F and E decks.
(Courtesy of Bruce Beveridge)

alternative third class' area that was utilised as third class accommodation on *Titanic*'s G deck – Section N. [See Fig. J-11.] Section N was small compared to the rest of third class as a whole, but there were plenty of berths there for women, children and families. This compartment had two staircases: one was the very bottom flight of the after second class staircase in the middle of the deck, and the other was a set of stairs rising from the port side of G deck, trunked through F deck, and exiting on E deck. The White Star Line booked G deck's Section N for third class, and – in order to keep third class passengers from going up and down the second class stairs – there would surely have been a gate. (Alternately, if Section N was booked as second class on any particular voyage there would have been a gate on the port side stairs somewhere along the flight from G to E deck, to keep third class from entering from Scotland Road. In a situation such as this, the gate for the staircase in the middle would be opened to allow free passage of the second class passengers to their compartments on the decks above.) These gates did not fall under the rules for emergency exits or third class escape routes, since they were class barriers. Gates *must* have been present in those locations, and they could easily have been locked for the simple reason that their purpose was not to detain third class passengers in case of an emergency. Even so, any crewman undertaking crowd control at the gated port side stairway on E deck would have prevented people from ascending the stairway from Section N up to E deck.

If *Titanic*'s second class stairs coming up from G to E deck were gated closed and were manned by a crewman stationed there, this might explain why some third class passengers saw no barriers and others did, why some crewmen let occasional passengers slip through a gate below decks, why Annie Jermyn found it necessary to climb over a 10ft gate, why second class passenger Mary Davis saw an armed crewman assigned to keep steerage passengers from ascending a stairway leading to second class, and why second class passenger Bertha Lehmann reported seeing crewmen lock an exit that prevented a clamouring crowd of third class passengers from ascending from the steerage decks to second class.

Other Obstacles to Steerage Survival on *Titanic*

Language Barriers

In addition to physical barriers, many of *Titanic*'s third class passengers were forced to contend with language barriers and social barriers. Using the table that sorts passengers by nationality, sex, and age in *Titanic Names: A Complete List of the Passengers and Crew* by Lee Merideth, it appears that about half the third class survivors were native English-speakers from the US, England, Canada or Ireland.[69] According to Merideth 'There were 140 third class passengers from Scandinavian countries (Finland, Sweden and Norway), and of those 104 or 74.2% did not survive. Worse odds yet were for the 63 third class passengers from south-eastern Europe (Bulgaria, Bosnia and Croatia). There were only two survivors, or a 96.8% loss.'[70]

John Poingdestre testified that there were no posted signs directing passengers from the steerage areas to the upper decks.[71] Although English-speaking passengers weren't necessarily literate, the absence of signs probably wasn't as much of an obstacle to them as were those faced by foreign passengers who couldn't speak English or understand instructions issued by the stewards. While language barriers could explain the loss of many third class passengers, especially whole families of non-English speakers like the Anderssons and Pålssons (from Sweden), that does not explain the loss of so many English-speaking families like the Goodwins and the Sages (from England). These families were either trapped below, were late in arriving on deck, or else chose to stay together rather than be parted at the lifeboats.

Social Barriers

Some third class passengers apparently waited for someone in authority to tell them what to do. When that didn't happen, some passengers took the initiative to save themselves, but others waited in vain or simply gave up. August Wennerstrom wrote about this subject in a detailed account which later came into the hands of Wyn Craig Wade, author of *The Titanic: End of a Dream*:

> One or our friends, a man by the name of John Lundahl who had been home to the old country on a visit and was going back to the United States said to us, 'Good-bye, friends; I'm too old to fight the Atlantic.' He went to the smoking room and there on a chair was awaiting his last call. So did an English lady. She sat down by the piano and, with her child on her knee, she played the piano until the Atlantic grave called to them both.[72]

According to Wade, Wennerstrom was appalled by those third class passengers who make no effort to help themselves, but instead prayed with Father Byles: 'Hundreds were in a circle with a preacher in the middle, praying, crying, asking God and Mary to help them. They lay there and yelled, never lifting a hand to help themselves. They had lost their own will power and expected God to do all the work for them.'[73] (Gus Cohen noticed the same thing.)[74] Despite the inertia exhibited by these passengers, however, survivor testimony makes it clear that many other third class passengers succeeded in saving themselves by their own initiative.

Rumour and the Perpetuation of 'Locked Gate Stories'

Although a number of routes were available for steerage passengers to gain unimpeded access to *Titanic*'s upper decks, at least some of *Titanic*'s third class passengers on the lower decks seem to have encountered closed or locked gates – many of which were guarded by crewmen whose duty was to prevent passengers from crossing those barriers before they received permission to do so. However, during the past century it has become 'common knowledge' among the general public that not just some, but *all* of *Titanic*'s steerage passengers were deliberately locked below decks and were abandoned there to meet their deaths inside the ship. How has this mistaken idea become ingrained in the public's mind?

The most likely answer to this question is that the general public of 1912 first learned about *Titanic*'s gated barriers when they read descriptions that surviving steerage passengers gave to newspaper reporters immediately after the sinking. The impact of these initial interviews was undoubtedly augmented by information that arose at the subsequent inquiries, where steerage survivors Olaus Abelseth and Daniel Buckley told of being detained behind the low gate located at the top of the stairway that separated the aft well deck from the second class area on B deck.

It is also possible that unintended emphasis was given to the subject on the first day of the American inquiry by Senator William Alden Smith, whose unfamiliarity with nautical matters caused him to ask Second Officer Charles Lightoller an inane question based on concerns expressed to him by families who feared that their loved ones were trapped in the ship's watertight compartments and were slowly suffocating on the bottom of the Atlantic.[75] Smith asked, 'Are you able to say whether any of the crew or passengers took to these upper watertight compartments as a final, last resort; I mean as a place to die?' Lightoller, who recognised the unreality of the question, replied that this was 'very unlikely', but one suspects that Smith's initial question might have planted this terrible idea in the public mind.

Ironically, the survivor who first wrote his own account about passengers being trapped behind iron gates was first class passenger Archibald Gracie, whose book about his experience on *Titanic* was published soon after the disaster. Gracie was running aft on the starboard side of the boat deck as the bow went under when:

> there arose before us from the decks below, a mass of humanity several lines deep covering the boat deck, facing us, and completely blocking our passage towards the stern . . . Instantly when they saw us and the water on the deck chasing us from behind, they turned in the opposite direction towards the stern. This brought them at that point plumb against the iron fence and railing that divide the first and second cabin passengers.[76] [See Fig. J-6.]

Although Gracie was describing low gates located on the boat deck, people who were unfamiliar with *Titanic's* physical layout might have assumed he was referring to tall, Bostwick-type gates. Colonel Gracie also mentioned seeing stewards locking cabins to prevent theft, which might have led some people to believe that passengers were being locked in their cabins.[77] (It is worth noting that Elizabeth Wilkinson feared that the cabin doors she saw being locked below decks might have inadvertently trapped hundreds of her fellow passengers in their rooms for eternity.)

In summary, it seems likely that survivor newspaper interviews, Senator Smith's questions, Abelseth's and Buckley's testimony about being detained behind the low gates on the aft well deck, Gracie's 'mass of humanity' trapped by a gate on the boat deck, and the locking of cabin doors by stewards were the basis of the mistaken notion that ALL of *Titanic's* third class passengers were purposefully detained/locked below decks. This belief was later perpetuated by folk songs such as 'It was Sad When That Great Ship Went Down', Walter Lord's writing style in his popular 1955 book *A Night to Remember*, and many *Titanic* films and TV features made since the 1958 film *A Night to Remember*.

Final Conclusions

Although there is little *physical* evidence of Bostwick gates on *Titanic*, and even though it would be rash for researchers to automatically accept the reliability of all 1912 newspaper interviews with survivors, the number of such interviews in which steerage passengers claimed to have been detained by closed or guarded gates is truly striking. Indeed, the number of steerage survivors who later *personally* wrote or spoke about the existence of such gates is significant enough that we are forced to conclude that *at least a few such gates did exist* somewhere inside the vessel – possibly preventing an exit from Section N on G deck. The present authors are also forced to wonder if Bostwick gates were so expected and commonplace that they were considered not worth depicting on deck plans. (It seems possible that when the plans were printed in 1911, the location of the Bostwick gates had not yet been determined and were therefore not included on the passenger accommodation plans for either *Olympic* or *Titanic*.) At any rate, the fact that *Britannic* deck plans fail to depict the eight Bostwick gates that are listed in her specifications book clearly demonstrates that the similar absence of gates on most *Titanic* deck plans cannot be regarded as proof that *Titanic* did not possess such gates.

As was mentioned earlier, one possible reason why some passengers had free access to the upper decks while others encountered locked or guarded gates might have depended on how early or late in the sinking their attempts to gain the upper decks were made. Whereas passengers who left the lower decks early in the sinking might have walked past open barriers without any hindrance, it seems possible that late-comers might have arrived at those same gates after stewards received orders to close them. (Touma and Turja both reported that the gates they encountered were closed right after they walked past the barriers, and a crewman told Sarah Roth that he had received specific orders not to allow any passengers to pass through the gate he was guarding.) Since Steward John Hart escorted two groups of steerage passengers to the boat deck without hindrance before he left the ship in boat No.15 at 1.40a.m., we are left to wonder if an order to close the gates might have been given sometime between 1.15 and 1.30a.m. Might such an order have been given because the upper decks were becoming so crowded with passengers that crewmen were having difficulty performing their duties efficiently?

Even though it is doubtful that most of the crewmen who were guarding gated barriers during the sinking were equipped with weapons, at least one second class passenger (Mary Davis) personally affirmed in recent years that she saw a crewman armed with a revolver who was stationed at a gangway in order to prevent steerage passengers from coming up the stairs. Even so, it is clear that *Titanic's* crewmen didn't always have the final say in their attempts to keep the steerage passengers below decks, since Margaret Mannion, Margaret Murphy, Helga Hirvonen, Thomas McCormack and Ellen Shine all described how groups of passengers successfully forced their way past guarded barriers in order to reach the upper decks.

There is also a hint in certain passenger accounts that the closing of several watertight doors at various places along E deck might have blocked passenger access to the usual exits from the lower decks [e.g., Hakkarainen's 'locked doors' at either end of the hallway, and Murphy's account of passengers being trapped when sailors fastened 'hatchways' in order to 'keep the air down there so the vessel would stay up longer']. Could a few passengers have been inadvertently trapped in a section of hallway when crewmen closed two consecutive watertight doors after it became clear that those doors would soon be needed to delay the rise of water inside the vessel?

At any rate, the present authors have concluded that a few closed gated barriers must have existed on *Titanic's* interior steerage decks and that one or two of those gates might have been locked. Even so, it appears that locked barriers were the *exception* rather than the rule and that it was actually the crewmen assigned to *guard* most of those gated barriers who were mainly responsible for preventing steerage passengers from leaving the lower decks and proceeding to the boat deck.

Notes

[1]   John Hart, BI 10151–75.
[2]   Edward Wilding, BI 19937–8.
[3]   McKinney letter to his wife describing a voyage on *Olympic*, *The Gimlet*, July 1912.
[4]   Edward Wilding, BI 19940–1.
[5]   Maurice Clarke, BI 24122–99.
[6]   Edward Wilding, BI 19915–18.
[7]   Edward Wilding, BI 19932–6.
[8]   Lawrence Beesley, *The Loss of the SS Titanic*, p.37
[9]   Judith Geller, *Titanic: Women and Children First,* p.104.
[10] Edward Wilding, BI 19914.
[11] Archibald Gracie, *The Truth About the Titanic*, pp.47–8.
[12] Daniel Buckley, AI p.1021.
[13] Olaus Abelseth, AI pp.1037–38.
[14] Laura Cribb, 'My Experience of the wreck of the R.M.S. *Titanic*'.
[15] Frank Goldsmith, 'Echoes in the Night', p.46.
[16] Annie Kelly, article about her in *Chicago Record-Herald*, April 1912.
[17] Elias Nicola-Yarrad, *Awake*, 22 October 1981.
[18] Helmina Nilsson, *Joliet News*, 25 April 1912.
[19] Sarah Roth, Sotheby auction of her 1912 *Titanic* account: http://www.shareholder.com/bid/news/20000405-15058.cfm.
[20] Notes regarding Walter Lord's interview with Katherine Gilnagh, 20 July 1955. Paul Lee's *Titanic Pages*, http://www.paullee.com/titanic/kgilnagh.html.
[21] Arthur Peuchen, AI p.335.
[22] Charlotte Collyer, *The Washington Post Semi-Monthly Magazine*, 26 May 1912.
[23] Violet Jessop, *Woman* magazine, 19 July 1958.
[24] Berk Pickard, AI p.1054–5.
[25] John Hart, BI 10151–75.
[26] John Hart, BI 10223–4.
[27] John Hart, BI 10230, 10244.
[28] John Hart, BI 9945-9949.
[29] Mary Coutts, letter to a friend, 18 April 1912. George Behe, *On Board RMS Titanic*, p.254.
[30] Eugene Daly account dictated to Dr Frank Blackmarr, 15 April 1912.
[31] Frank Blackmarr account of his interview with Eugene Daly, *Chicago Daily Tribune*, 20 April 1912.
[32] Mary Davis, transcription of taped interview by Josh Basar, 15 August 1977.
[33] Article about Elin Hakkarainen, 'Monessen and the Titanic', http://users.telerama.com/~cass/Finntitanic.html.
[34] Article about Elin Hakkarainen by her son Gerald Nummi (writing as his mother), *Yankee*, September 1987.

35 Gerald Nummi, *I'm Going To See What Has Happened* (written by Miss Hakkarainen's son, who was writing as his mother).

36 'Neshan Krekorian and the *Titanic*', an article based on interviews with Paul Solomonian (Krekorian's son-in-law) and with Krekorian's children, *St. Catharines (Ontario) Standard*, 10 April 2001.

37 'Remembering a *Titanic* survivor', interview with George and Angeline Krekorian (Neshan Krekorian's children), *St. Catharines Standard*, 13 April 2007.

38 Margaret Mannion account written by her grandson Michael Hopkins. Senan Molony, *The Irish Aboard Titanic*, p.124.

39 Tad Fitch, 'Coosan Coleen; Bertha Mulvihill, A *Titanic* Survivor Story', *The Titanic Commutator*, Vol.28, No.167, 2004.

40 Margaret Murphy, *Irish Independent*, 9 May 1912.

41 Margaret Murphy article, *New York American*, 29 April 1912.

42 Interview with Georges [Gerios] Touma's son Joseph L. Thomas, *Detroit News*, 17 April 2003.

43 Joseph Thomas, *Grandma Survived the Titanic*, AuthorHouse, 31 march 2006, p.7.

44 Interview with Anna Turga's grandson John Rudolph.

45 Article written by Anna Turga's grandson John Rudolph. Jim Sadur's *Titanic* website, http://www.keyflux.com/titanic/passdata.htm.

46 Adelaide Wells, *Akron Beacon-Journal*, 3 April 1953.

47 Encyclopedia Titanica, http://www.encyclopedia-titanica.org/titanic-survivor/addie-dart-wells.html.

48 Elizabeth Wilkinson, *Toronto Star*, 20 April 1912.

49 John Poingdestre, BI 3288.

50 Interview with his grandson Anthony Belman, *The Washington Post*, 18 March 1998.

51 Margaret Devaney personal letter to Ed Kamuda, 10 November 1966.

52 Margaret Devaney O'Neill taped interview, 'Titanic II', Titanic Historical Society recording, 1980.

53 Devaney interview, *Newark Evening News*, 2 April 1967.

54 Interview with Alice O'Neill (Margaret Devaney O'Neill's daughter-in-law), unknown newspaper *c.* 1982.

55 Article about Helga Hirvonen, 'Monessen and the *Titanic*', http://users.telerama.com/~cass/Finntitanic.html.

56 Annie Jermyn, Lynn (MA) *Daily Evening Item*, 26 April 1912.

57 Article about Annie Jermyn, *Baltimore Sun*, 27 April 1912.

58 Article about Bertha Lehmann in *The Courier* (Waterloo, Iowa), 26 April 1912.

59 Paul Mauge, BI 20128–32.

60 Paul Mauge, *The New York Times*, 23 April 1912.

61 Interview with Thomas McCormack's sister, Mrs Catherine Evers, *The New York Times*, 21 April 1912.

62 Article about McCormack, *New York Sun*, 21 April 1912.

63 Ellen Shine interview, *Newark Evening News*, 19 April 1912.

64 Interview with Gunnar Tenglin's daughter-in-law Mildred Tenglin, *Burlington (Iowa) Hawkeye*, 2 January 1998.

65 Email from Sharon George (Shawneen Whabee's granddaughter) to George Behe, 25 January 1998.

66 Email from Simon Mills to Cathy Akers-Jordan. 8 November 2005.

67 Don Lynch and Ken Marschall, *Ghosts of the Abyss: A Journey into the Heart of the Titanic*, Toronto: Madison Press Books, 2003, p.144.

68 Email from Don Lynch to the authors, 26 July 2005.

69 Lee Merideth, *Titanic Names: A Complete List of the Passengers and Crew*. Sunnyvale, CA: Historical Indexes Publishing Company, 2002, p.5.

70 Merideth, p.3.

71 John Poingdestre, BI 3288.

72 Wyn Craig Wade, *The Titanic: End of a Dream*. Rawson, Wade Publishers, 1979, p.256.

73 Wade, p.256.

74 Walter Lord, *A Night to Remember*. New York: Bantam, 1955, p.68.

75 Wade, p.100.

76 Quoted in *The Story of Titanic as Told by Its Survivors*. Jack Winocour, ed. New York: Dover, 1960, p.138.

77 Quoted in Winocour, p.129.

BIBLIOGRAPHY

Books and Booklets Referenced

Ballard, Dr Robert D., *The Discovery of the Titanic*, Madison Publishing Inc., 1987.

Beveridge, Bruce and Scott Andrews, Steve Hall & Daniel Klistorner, *Titanic: The Ship Magnificent* [*TTSM*], The History Press, Vol. I and II, 2008.

Beesley, Lawrence, *The Loss of the SS Titanic*, Houghton Mifflin Co., 1912.

Behe, George M., *On Board RMS Titanic: Memories of the Maiden Voyage*, Lulu.com Press, 2011.

Bisset, Commander J.G., *Ship Ahoy!! Nautical Notes for Ocean Travellers, with Charts and Diary*, 3rd Ed., Charles Birchall Ltd, Liverpool, 1924.

Bisset, James and P.R. Stephensen, *Tramps & Ladies*, Angus & Robertson, 1988.

Booth, John and Sean Coughlan, *Titanic – Signals of Disaster*, White Star Publications, 1993.

Bullock, Shan F., *Thomas Andrews, Shipbuilder*, Maunsel & Company, Ltd, 1912.

Eaton, John P. and Charles A. Haas, *Titanic Triumph and Tragedy*, 2nd Ed., W.W. Norton & Co., 1994.

Everett, Marshall, ed., *The Wreck and Sinking of the Titanic*, L.H. Walter, 1912.

Geller, Judith B., *Titanic: Women and Children First*, W.W. Norton & Co., 1998.

Gittins, Dave, *Titanic: Monument and Warning*, an e-book, 2005.

Goldsmith, Frank, *Echoes in the Night: Memories of a Titanic Survivor*, Titanic Historical Society, 1991.

Gracie, Colonel Archibald, *The Truth About the Titanic*, Mitchell Kennerley, 1913.

Howse, Derek, *Greenwich Time and the Longitude*, National Maritime Museum, Philip Wilson Publishers, 1997.

La Dage, John and Lee Van Gemert, *Stability and Trim for the Ship's Officer*, 3rd Ed., Cornell Maritime Press, 1983.

Lord, Walter, *A Night to Remember*, Bantam Books Inc., 1955.

Lynch, Don and Ken Marschall, *Ghosts of the Abyss: A Journey into the Heart of the Titanic*, Madison Press Books, 2003.

Matsen, Brad, *Titanic's Last Secrets*, Twelve, 2008.

McCarty, Jennifer and Tim Foecke, *What Really Sank The Titanic*, Citadel Press, 2008.

National Imagery and Mapping Agency, *The American Practical Navigator [Bowditch]*, Pub. 9, US Government Printing Office, 2002 Bicentennial issue.

Nicholls, Alfred E., *Nicholls's Seamanship and Viva Voce Guide*, 4th Ed., London, August 1910.

Padfield, Peter, *The Titanic and the Californian*, Hodder & Stoughton, 1965.

Reade, Leslie, *The Ship That Stood Still*, Patrick Stephens Ltd, 1993.

Rostron, Sir Arthur H., *Home From the Sea*, Cassell, 1931.

Shubow, Leo, *Iceberg Dead Ahead!* Bruce Humphries, Inc., 1959.

Smith, Sir Hubert Llewellyn, *The Board of Trade*, G.P. Putnam's Sons Ltd, 1928.

Söldner, Hermann, *RMS Titanic Passenger and Crew List*, Ruti, Switzerland, 2000.

Stringer, Craig, *Titanic People*, on CD, Family History Indexes, Northampton, England, 2003.

Thayer, John [Jack] B., *The Sinking of the S.S. Titanic*, 1940.

Wade, Wyn Craig, *The Titanic: End of a Dream*, Rawson Associates, 1979.

Printed Articles and Documents Referenced

Act of the Congress of the United States, 'To Regulate the Carriage of Passengers by Sea', 2 August 1882.

Board of Trade handbook, 'Regulations and Suggestions as to the Survey of the Hull, Equipments, and Machinery of Steam Ships Carrying Passengers', 1905.

Bride, Harold, 'Thrilling Tale by Titanic's Surviving Wireless Man', an unaltered, unabridged reprint from *The New York Times*, 28 April 1912, republished in Jack Winocour's *The Story of the Titanic as Told by its Survivors*, Dover Publications, 1960.

British Wreck Commission Report of the Court, 'Report on the Loss of the *Titanic*' [BI Report], 30 July 1912.

Chirnside, Mark, 'Mystery of *Titanic*'s Central Propeller', Titanic International Society [TIS] *Voyage 63*, spring 2008.

——, 'Target Olympic: *Feuer!*' Titanic Historical Society [THS] *The Titanic Commutator*, No.184, 2008.

—— and Samuel Halpern, '*Olympic* and *Titanic*: Maiden Voyage Mysteries', TIS *Voyage 59*, spring 2007.

——, 'Speed and More Speed', THS *The Titanic Commutator*, Vol.32, No.182 and 183.

Fitch, Tad, 'Coosan Coleen; Bertha Mulvihill, A *Titanic* Survivor Story', THS *The Titanic Commutator*, Vol.28, No.167, 2004.

Garzke, William *et al.*, '*Titanic*, The Anatomy of a Disaster', a report from the Marine Forensics Panel (SD-7), Proceedings of the 1997 Annual Meeting of the Society of Naval Architects and Marine Engineers [SNAME].

Garzke, William *et al.*, 'A Marine Forensics Analysis of the RMS *Titanic*', presented to the Chesapeake Section of SNAME, Norfolk, VA, June 2002.

Hackett, C. and J.G. Bedford, 'The Sinking of SS *Titanic* – Investigated by Modern Techniques', 1996 RINA Transactions.

Halpern, Samuel, 'A Minute of Time', THS *The Titanic Commutator*, Vol.29, Nos 171 and 172, 2005.

——, 'The Mystery of Time', THS *The Titanic Commutator*, Vol.31, Nos 178 and 180.

——, 'Time and Time Again', Irish Titanic Historical Society [ITHS] *White Star Journal*, Vol.19, Issues 1 and 2, 2011.

——, 'Rockets, Lifeboats, and Time Changes', TIS *Voyage* 70, winter 2009; and in British Titanic Society [BTS] *Atlantic Daily Bulletin*, December 2009.

——, 'Lights to Port – Lights to Starboard – An Objective Forensic Analysis of the Collision Between *Stockholm* and *Andrea Doria*', presented before a class on casualty analysis at the Maine Maritime Academy, Castine, Maine, November 2008. It is available for download at: http://www.titanicology.com/AndreaDoria/Stockholm-Andrea_Doria_Collision_Analysis.pdf.

——, 'It's a CQD Old Man', TIS *Voyage*, Issues 64 and 65; and in BTS *Atlantic Daily Bulletin*, September and December 2008.

——, 'Light on the Horizon', THS *The Titanic Commutator*, Vol.31–2, Issues 177, 178, 179 and 181.

——, 'We Could Not See One Body', THS *The Titanic Commutator*, Vol.32, No.181.

——, 'Keeping Track of a Maiden Voyage', ITHS *White Star Journal*, Vol.14, No.2, August 2006.

Harford, Kilian and Gerry Murphy, 'Titanic's Weather', ITHS *White Star Journal*, Vol.14, No.3, December 2006.

IMM Company, 'Ships' Rules and Uniform Regulations', Issued 1 July 1907.

JMS Naval Architects and Salvage Engineers, 'RMS *Titanic*: Alternative Theory: Complete Hull Failure Following Collision with Iceberg', Ship Structure Committee Project SR-1451, US Coast Guard (CG-5212/SSC).

Luke, W.J., 'On Some Points of Interest in Connection With the Design, Building, and Launching of the *Lusitania*', 48th Session of the Institute of Naval Architects, 21 March 1907.

Marine Accident Investigation Branch [MAIB], 'RMS *Titanic*: Reappraisal Of Evidence Relating To SS *Californian*,' Her Majesty's Stationery Office (*HMSO*), London, 12 March 1992.

Mengot, Roy and Richard Woytowich, 'The Breakup of *Titanic*', A Progress Report from the Marine Forensics Panel (SD-7), 16 April 2009.

Merritt, Diana and Randy Rahm, 'Managing Silo, Bunker, and Dust Collector Fires', Special Section: Asset Management, *POWER* magazine, November/December 2000.

Paola, Robert, 'Weather and the *Titanic*,' *Weatherwise*, April/May 1992.

Papoulias, Professor Fotis A., 'Ship Dynamics', TS4001 Lecture Series, Department of Mechanical Engineering, Naval Postgraduate School, Monterey, CA.

Rostron, Captain Arthur H., 'The Rescue of the "Titanic" Survivors', *Scribner's Magazine*, 1913.

Sims, Philip, 'Comparative Naval Architecture of Passenger Ships', *Transactions of the Society of Naval Architects and Marine Engineers (SNAME)*, Vol.111, 2003.

Stephenson, Parks, 'More Questions Than Answers – Another Point of View Re: *Titanic's* Final Moments – Missing Pieces', THS *The Titanic Commutator*, Vol.30, No.173, 2006.

US Dept of Commerce and Labor, 'Regulations Governing Radio Communication', September 1912.

US Dept of Commerce and Labor, 'Regulations for Radio Apparatus and Operators on Steamers', July 1913.

US Senate Documents (No.726, 62nd Congress, 2nd Session). Hearings into the loss of the SS *Titanic*, 19 April – 25 May 1912.

US Senate Report (No.806, 62 Congress, 2nd Session) of the Committee on Commerce, 'The *Titanic* Disaster' [AI Report], 28 May 1912.

Wreck Commissioner's Court, 'Proceedings on the Formal Investigation Ordered by the Board of Trade Into the Loss of the SS *Titanic*', 2 May – 3 July 1912.

Zhang, Shengming, 'The Mechanics of Ship Collisions', Department of Naval Architecture and Offshore Engineering, Technical University of Denmark, 1999.

Referenced Website Articles and Sources

American National Archives, 'Partial List of Titanic Survivors Taken to New York, April 18, 1912', http://www.archives.gov/research/immigration/titanic-survivors-to-ny.html.

Behe, George, 'The Man Who Dressed as a Woman', http://home.comcast.net/~georgebehe/titanic/page4.htm.

Capobianco, Michael, 'The Photometry of Starlight', http://mysite.verizon.net/michaelcapobianco/PhotometryStarlight.htm.

Dalbeattie Town History, 'The Life of William McMaster Murdoch', http://www.dalbeattie.com/titanic/wmmlifea.htm.

Elias, Leila Salloum, 'The impact of the sinking of the *Titanic* on the New York Syrian community of 1912: the Syrians respond.' http://findarticles.com/p/articles/mi_m2501/isv1-2_27/ai_n15694707/?tag=content;col1.

Encyclopedia Titanica, 'Titanic Crew Signing-On Particulars of Engagement', http://www.encyclopedia-titanica.org/pog/crew_pog.php.

Fitch, Tad and Sam Halpern, Bill Wormstedt, 'Setting the Record Straight', ET Comment, http://www.encyclopedia-titanica.org/setting-record-straight.html.

——, 'The Record Speaks', ET Comment, http://www.encyclopedia-titanica.org/the-record-speaks.html.

Halpern, Samuel, '*Titanic's* Masthead Light', *Great Lakes Titanic Society (GLTS)* website article, www.glts.org/articles/halpern/masthead_light.html, 2008.

——, 'They Were Gradually Working Her Up', http://www.titanicology.com/WorkingThenUp.htm.

——, 'Collision Point', *GLTS* website article, http://www.glts.org/articles/halpern/collision_point.html.

——, 'Changing Watch Schedules', http://www.titanicology.com/WatchSchedules.html.

——, 'She Turned Two Points in 37 Seconds', *Titanic Research & Modeling Association (TRMA)* research article, http://titanic-model.com/articles/Two_Points_in_Thirty_Seven_Seconds/Two%20Points%20in%20Thirty-Seven%20Seconds.pdf.

——, 'The Energy of Collision', http://www.titanicology.com/EnergyOfCollision.html.

——, 'Somewhere About 12 Square Feet', *TRMA* research article, http://titanic-model.com/articles/Somewhere_About_12_Square_Feet2/Somewhere_About_12_Square_Feet2.pdf.

——, 'Where Did That Water Come From?' http://www.titanicology.com/FloodingInBR4.html.

——, '12:35a.m. Apparent Time *Carpathia*', http://www.glts.org/articles/halpern/1235_ats_carpathia.html.

——, 'The Enigmatic Excursion of the SS *Birma*', http://www.titanicology.com/Titanica/ Inigmatic_Excursion_of_SS_Birma.pdf.

——, 'Navigational Inconsistencies of the SS *Californian*', http://www.titanicology.com/ Californian/Navigational_Incosistencies.pdf

Lee, Paul. 'Ismay's Escape', http://www.paullee.com/titanic/ismaysescape.html.

——, '*Titanic*: A Desperate Dialog', http://www.paullee.com/titanic/pv.html.

Mengot, Roy, 'The Wreck of RMS *Titanic*', http://home.flash.net/~rfm/.

National Oceanic & Atmospheric Administration (NOAA), National Weather Service, 'Estimating Wind Speed and Sea State', http://www.wrh.noaa.gov/pqr/info/beaufort.php.

Signed statement James Gibson to Captain Lord 18 April 1912, http://home.earthlink. net/~dnitzer/6Affidavits/Gibson.html.

Signed statement Herbert Stone to Captain Lord 18 April 1912, http://home.earthlink. net/~dnitzer/6Affidavits/Stone.html.

United States Naval Observatory, Astronomical Applications, 'Data Services', http://aa.usno.navy. mil/data.

Weeks, Capt. Charles B and Cathy Akers-Jordan, 'Joseph Groves Boxhall – Radio Interview, October 1962', http://www.encyclopedia-titanica.org/boxhall.html.

Wilkinson, Paul, '*Titanic's* Silent Distress Signals – A New Look at a Minor Mystery', 2004, http:// www.encyclopedia-titanica.org/articles/rockets_wilkinson.pdf.

Wormstedt, Bill, 'The Facts – What Did the Survivors See of the Breakup of the *Titanic*?' http:// wormstedt.com/Titanic/The_Facts.html.

—— and Tad Fitch, 'Shots in the Dark', http://wormstedt.com/Titanic/shots/shots.htm.

—— & George Behe & Tad Fitch, with contributions by Sam Halpern and J. Kent Layton, 'Titanic: The Lifeboat Launch Sequence Re-Examined' http://wormstedt.com/Titanic/lifeboats/ lifeboats.htm.

Other Suggested Reading

Behe, George M., *The Carpathia and the Titanic: Rescue at Sea*, Lulu.com Press, 2011.

——, '*Archie': The Life of Major Archibald Butt from Georgia to the Titanic*, Lulu.com Press, 2010.

Chirnside, Mark, *The Olympic Class Ships: Olympic, Titanic, Britannic*, The History Press, 2011.

Fitch, Tad and J. Kent Layton & Bill Wormstedt, *On a Sea of Glass: The Life & Loss of the R.M.S. Titanic*, Amberley Publishing, 2012.

Klistorner, Daniel and Steve Hall, Bruce Beveridge, Art Braunschweiger and Scott Andrews, *Titanic in Photographs*, The History Press, 2011.

Websites Worth Visiting

BBC's *Survivors of the Titanic Collection*: http://www.bbc.co.uk/archive/titanic/index.shtml.

George Behe's *Titanic Tidbits*: http://home.comcast.net/~georgebehe/titanic.

David Billnitzer's *The Titanic and the Mystery Ship*: http://home.earthlink.net/~dnitzer/Titanic.html.

Discovery Channel's *Titanic Explorer* (deck plans by Bruce Beveridge): http://dsc.discovery.com/ convergence/titanic/explorer/explorer.html.

Mark Chirnside's Reception Room – Olympic, Titanic, Britannic: http://www.markchirnside.co.uk.

Dave Gittins' *All at Sea With Dave Gittins*: http://www.titanicebook.com.

Samuel Halpern's *Titanicology*: http://www.titanicology.com.

Paul Lee's *Titanic Pages*: http://www.paullee.com/titanic/index.php.

Marconi Company's *MarconiCalling*: http://www.marconicalling.co.uk.

Robert Ottmers' *Titanic Inquiry Project*: http://www.titanicinquiry.org.

S. Swiggum's *TheShipsList*: http://www.theshipslist.com/ships/lines/index.htm.

Titanic Research and Modeling Association (TRMA): http://titanic-model.com.

Bill Wormstedt's Titanic: http://wormstedt.com/titanic.

J. Kent Layton's *Atlantic Liners*: http://www.atlanticliners.com.

INDEX

For the full Titanic experience visit The History Press website and follow the Titanic link. For stories and articles about Titanic, join us on Facebook.

www.thehistorypress.co.uk